COMPOSERS *of the* NAZI ERA

OTHER BOOKS BY MICHAEL H. KATER

Das "Ahnenerbe" der SS, 1935–1945: Ein Beitrag zur Kulturpolitik des Dritten Reiches (1974)

Studentenschaft und Rechtsradikalismus in Deutschland, 1918–1933: Eine sozialgeschichtliche Studie zur Bildungskrise in der Weimarer Republik (1975)

The Nazi Party: A Social Profile of Members and Leaders, 1919–1945 (1983)

Doctors Under Hitler (1989)

Different Drummers: Jazz in the Culture of Nazi Germany (1992)

The Twisted Muse: Musicians and Their Music in the Third Reich (1997)

COMPOSERS *of the* NAZI ERA

Eight Portraits

Michael H. Kater

New York   Oxford
OXFORD UNIVERSITY PRESS
2000

Oxford University Press

Oxford   New York
Athens   Auckland   Bangkok   Bogotá   Buenos Aires   Calcutta
Cape Town   Chennai   Dar es Salaam   Dehli   Florence   Hong Kong   Istanbul
Karachi   Kuala Lumpur   Madrid   Melbourne   Mexico City   Mumbai
Nairobi   Paris   São Paulo   Singapore   Taipei   Tokyo   Toronto   Warsaw

and associated companies in
Berlin   Ibadan

Published by Oxford University Press, Inc.
198 Madison Avenue, New York, New York 10016

Oxford is a registered trademark of Oxford University Press

Library of Congress Cataloging-in-Publication Data
Kater, Michael H., 1937–
Composers of the Nazi era: eight portraits / Michael H. Kater.
p. cm.
Includes bibliographical references and Index.
ISBN 0-19-509924-9
1. Composers—Germany Biography. 2. Music—Germany—20th century—
History and critism.
3. National socialism. I. Title.
ML390.K198   2000
780'.92'243—dc21   99-13272
[B]

9 8 7 6 5 4 3 2 1

Printed in the United States of America
on acid-free paper

Preface

This book is the last in a trilogy on music and musicians in the Third Reich. The first one was on jazz, the second on the general, mostly serious-music scene, and this one is about eight composers: Werner Egk, Paul Hindemith, Kurt Weill, Karl Amadeus Hartmann, Carl Orff, Hans Pfitzner, Arnold Schoenberg, and Richard Strauss. As in the first two volumes, I am trying to explore these musicians' relationship with the Nazi regime and examine the role their music played in it, if any. Of these composers, one or two are well-known, such as Strauss and Schoenberg (and much has been written on them already) whereas others are hardly known outside Germany, especially Hartmann and Egk. Why were they chosen? Each man's history was backed by a wealth of private papers to which I was fortunate enough to have access, and even in terms of raw and unsorted documents each history turned out to be sufficiently unique to tell me something new about the fate of music in the Third Reich in general and how the composers fitted into it in particular. Although the order of the composers treated in this book is random, certain cues during the writing of the biographies appeared to direct me from one name to the next. I sensed these cues intuitively and therefore cannot explain them. But I started with Werner Egk because I felt that in sketching his career in my previous book, *The Twisted Muse* (1997), I had left important questions unanswered. And I finished with Strauss because throughout the entire writing process he appeared as the greatest challenge, better attempted at the end. Strauss was of course the senior composer and to be largely recognized as such by his peers. But the order of the chapters indicates nothing about a ranking of these composers in music history (if that can at all be determined) or about my personal feelings about them or their music. Because each artist deserved a self-contained portrait and one should be able to read it independently of the other chapters, some phenomena are mentioned more than once in this book, with only a minimum of cross-reference. A good example is the Hindemith-Furtwängler affair of 1934–35, which affected both Hindemith and Strauss, or the "denazification" of Carl Orff, which also touched on the fate of his friend Werner Egk. From the point of view of institutional history, the struggle between Alfred Rosenberg and Joseph Goebbels for ultimate control of culture in the Third Reich is referred to repeatedly as well. I am asking the reader's indulgence if such repetition becomes too trying.

Many people helped me research and write this book, as they had helped me with the two previous ones. First, I have to thank the keepers of the records pertaining to each composer: notably Richard and Gabriele Strauss for complete permission to let me roam the family archive in Garmisch. Thereafter, Richard Strauss Jr. did not tire in answering any other nagging questions I had for him. My thanks also go to the archivists in charge of the papers of Hans Pfitzner at the Österreichische National-Bibliothek (Musiksammlung) in Vienna, the Hindemith papers at the Paul-Hindemith-Institut in Frankfurt am Main, the documents in the Carl-Orff-Zentrum in Munich, and the Egk and Hartmann *Nachlässe* at the Bayerische Staatsbibliothek (Handschriftenabteilung) in Munich. In the United States, I am indebted to archivists in charge of the Kurt Weill papers at the Weill-Lenya Research Center in New York and the Schoenberg papers, then still at the Arnold Schoenberg Institute on the campus of the University of Southern California in Los Angeles (and now in Vienna). I was able to cull other documents from national, regional and special archives in Germany, Austria, and Switzerland, such as the Berlin Document Center (now a part of the German Federal Archives system), the Koblenz Federal Archives, the Bayerisches Hauptstaatsarchiv in Munich, the Münchener Stadtbibliothek, the Stadtarchiv München, the Österreichisches Staatsarchiv in Vienna, the Lotte Lehmann Special Collection in Santa Barbara, the Zentralbibliothek Zürich, and other venues.

A number of witnesses granted me interviews, most of which I recorded and transcribed. They will eventually be made publicly available. These witnesses include Gertrud Orff in Munich, Liselotte Orff in Diessen/Ammersee, Elisabeth Hartmann in Munich, Newell Jenkins in Hillsdale, New York, and Gottfried von Einem in Vienna. Several witnesses corresponded with me, as did Richard Strauss Jr., Hans Hotter (Munich), Gertrud Orff, Clara Huber (Munich), Newell Jenkins, George J. Wittenstein (Santa Barbara), and Hans and Brigitte Bergese (Berlin).

Among many friends and colleagues who helped me with this project, I must single out Joan Evans of Wilfrid Laurier University in Waterloo, Canada, and Albrecht Riethmüller of the Free University of Berlin. With incredible patience, these two awesomely knowledgeable musicologists read every word I wrote in manuscript and suggested many significant changes (as they had already done in the case of my previous book). This help is all the more appreciated as I wrote my chapters from the point of view not of musicology but of sociopolitical and cultural history. Nonetheless, if I have strayed from the path of accuracy, especially in musicological terms, it still is not their responsibility but my own.

Further help, in various forms, was provided by Celia Applegate, Tamara Bernstein, David Farneth, Saul Friedländer, Bryan Gilliam, Alice Goldfarb, Hartmut Kaelble, Jürgen Kocka, Kim Kowalke, David Monod, Pamela Potter, Gerhard A. Ritter, Adelheid von Saldern, Reinhard Spree, Hans Vaget, Wedigo de Vivanco, Michael Walter, and Moshe Zimmermann.

Once again I have to thank the granting agencies. During the research and writing of this book I have been generously supported by the following institutions: York University Toronto as a Walter A. Gordon Fellow, the Canada Council (Ottawa) as a Senior Killiam Research Fellow for two years, and the Alexander von Humboldt-Stiftung in Bonn, which appointed me Konrad Adenauer-Preisträger. When for 1997–98 I was appointed Jason A. Hannah Visiting Professor of the History of Medicine at the University of Toronto (another research fellowship), I had sufficient time left over—apart from new medical–historical research I was beginning—to devote significant energies to the completion of this book. Besides the free time I gained through these fellowships, I received significant financial aid from the Social Sciences and Humanities Research Council of Canada in Ottawa, to enable me to travel to many foreign places, make contacts, and collect archival material. York University, too, provided funds on a more modest scale. All these institutions must be thanked.

I owe a great debt to the four librarians at York University's Scott Library who helped me procure the sources, as they have done so now for many years. They are Mary Lehane, Gladys Fung, Joan McConnell, and Linda Hurley. Without them, those library books or articles from Princeton, Berkeley, or Göttingen would never have arrived.

At Oxford University Press in New York, my gratitude goes out to Nancy Lane for signing on this book in the first place and to Thomas Lebien and Susan Ferber for giving me much-needed editorial advice thereafter. I especially appreciate the freedom they have provided me with as an author. Those presses must be praised which constrain their authors least.

Finally, my wife, Barbara, with whom I discussed musical and historical problems ad nauseam over the years, inspired many of the chapters in this book with her keen insights. As it turned out, she had her preferred composers and I had mine, as we reviewed them over dinner or on our many walks along the shores of Lake Ontario or the Loisach river in Garmisch. Although this ought not to be part of the academic exercise, I leave it to the reader to find out who my favorite composers are.

Contents

Abbreviations

ADMV	Allgemeiner Deutscher Musikverein (General German Music Society)
AI	Arnold Schoenberg Institute, Los Angeles, Archive
AM	Amtsgericht München, Registratur S, Schwurgerichtsakten
AMR	*Amtliche Mitteilungen der Reichsmusikkammer*
AMZ	*Allgemeine Musikzeitung*
APA	Author's Private Archive
BA	Bundesarchiv, Koblenz
BAB	Bundesarchiv, Aussenstelle Berlin (formely Berlin Document Center)
BBC	British Broadcasting Corporation
BH	Bayerisches Hauptstaatsarchiv, Munich
BS	Bayerische Staatsbibliothek, Munich, Handschriftenabteilung
CM	Carl-Orff-Zentrum, Munich
CSR	Czechoslovak Republic
DAF	Deutsche Arbeitsfront (German Labor Front)
DAZ	*Deutsche Allgemeine Zeitung*
DDR	Deutsche Demokratische Republik (German Democratic Republic)
DKW	*Deutsche Kultur-Wacht*
DM	*Die Musik*

DNVP	Deutschnationale Volkspartei (German National People's Party)
EB	Elly-Ney-Nachlass, Staatsarchiv, Bonn
ETA	Ernst Toch Archive, Special Collections, Music Library, UCLA
GDT	Genossenschaft Deutscher Tonsetzer (League of German Composers)
GEMA	Gesellschaft für musikalische Aufführungs– und mechanische Vervielfältigungsrechte
GLM	*Das Grosse Lexikon der Musik: In acht Bänden,* 8 vols., ed. Marc Honegger and Günther Massenkeil (Freiburg im Breisgau, 1978–82)
HJ	Hitler-Jugend (Hitler Youth)
IBD	*International Biographical Dictionary of Central European Emigrés, 1933–1945,* ed. Herbert A. Strauss and Werner Röder (Munich, 1983)
IfZ	Institut für Zeitgeschichte, Munich
ISCM	International Society for Contemporary Music
JdM	*Jahrbuch der deutschen Musik, 1943/1944,* ed. Hellmuth von Hase (Leipzig and Berlin, [1943/44])
KfdK	Kampfbund für deutsche Kultur (Combat League for German Culture)
LBI	Leo Baeck Institute, New York
LI	*Lexikon der Interpreten klassischer Musik im 20. Jahrhundert,* ed. Alain Paris (Munich and Kassel, 1992)
LP	Library of Washington State University, Pullman
MGG	*Die Musik in Geschichte und Gegenwart: Allgemeine Enzyklopädie der Musik unter Mitarbeit zahlreicher Musikforscher des In- und Auslandes,* 17 vols., ed. Friedrich Blume (Kassel, 1949–86)
MK	*Musik im Kriege*
MMP	Münchener Stadtbibliothek, Monacensia-Abteilung, Pfitzner-Briefe
NAW	National Archives, Washington
NG	*The New Grove Dictionary of Music and Musicians,* 20 vols., ed. Stanley Sadie (London, 1980)
NSDAP	Nationalsozialistische Deutsche Arbeiterpartei (National Socialist German Workers' Party—Nazi Party)
NSF	Nationalsozialistische Frauenschaft (National Socialist Women's Organization)
NSKG	NS-Kulturgemeinde (National Socialist Cultural Community)
NSV	Nationalsozialistische Volkswohlfahrt (National Socialist People's Charity)
NWH	Österreichische National-Bibliothek, Vienna, Handschriftenabteilung
NYA	New York Philharmonic Archives, Avery Fisher Hall, New York

OMGUS	Office of Military Government of the United States for Germany
OSW	Österreichisches Staatsarchiv, Vienna, Archiv der Republik
OW	Österreichische National-Bibliothek, Vienna, Musiksammlung, F68 Pfitzner
PA	Private Archive
PF	Paul-Hindemith-Institut, Frankfurt am Main
Promi	Reichsministerium für Volksaufklärung und Propaganda (Reich Propaganda Ministry)
RG	Richard Strauss-Archiv, Garmisch
RKK	Reichskulturkammer (Reich Culture Chamber)
RM	Reichsmark
RMK	Reichsmusikkammer (Reich Music Chamber)
SA	Sturmabteilungen (Brownshirts; Stormtroopers)
SM	Stadtarchiv, Munich
SMM	Städtische Musikbibliothek, Munich, Pfitzner-Briefe
SPD	Sozialdemokratische Partei Deutschlands (Social Democratic Party of Germany)
SS	Schutzstaffel (Security Squad)
Stagma	Staatlich genehmigte Gesellschaft zur Verwertung musikalischer Urheberrechte (State-approved Society for the Utilization of Musical Authorship Rights)
TG	*Die Tagebücher von Joseph Goebbels: Sämtliche Fragmente,* 5 vols., ed. Elke Fröhlich (Munich, 1987)
TGII	*Die Tagebücher von Joseph Goebbels, Teil II: Diktate, 1941–1945,* 16 vols., ed. Elke Fröhlich (Munich, 1993–96)
UCLA	University of California at Los Angeles
UCSB	University of California at Santa Barbara
UE	Universal Edition
Ufa	Universum Film-Aktiengesellschaft
USC	University of Southern California, Los Angeles
VB	*Völkischer Beobachter*
WC	Weill-Lenya Research Center, New York
ZM	*Zeitschrift für Musik*
ZNF	Zentralbibliothek, Zurich, Musikabteilung, Nachlass Furtwängler

COMPOSERS *of the* NAZI ERA

1

Werner Egk

The Enigmatic Opportunist

I

Werner Joseph Mayer was born in 1901 in the Swabian village of Auchses-heim, not far from Augsburg, the son of a Catholic and very musical pri-mary-school teacher of solid peasant stock. Whereas his father was strong and authoritarian, his mother was soft and inclined toward poetry. The family moved to Augsburg when Werner was six and already noticeably in-terested in music. His formal education there was that of a humanistic Catholic Gymnasium, led by Benedictine monks; Werner took in the Greek and Roman classics, but also Shakespeare, Goethe, Nietzsche, and Dos-toyevsky. He was fascinated by the new schools in art, Die Brücke of Dres-den and Der Blaue Reiter of Munich; the paintings of Franz Marc and Wassily Kandinsky became familiar to him. At age eighteen he entered the municipal conservatory; a few songs, music to poems by Rilke, Werfel, and Hofmannsthal, were the result. Visits to concert halls and the opera stage ensued; first he savored *Der Freischütz* and then *Tristan und Isolde*. Werner's father wanted him to enter the postal service, but the young man, almost equally gifted as a graphic artist and a writer, strove for a career in music. He moved to Frankfurt to perfect his piano skills and then, in the postwar turmoil of 1921, came to Munich. There he was introduced to a theater off the beaten track, began to write music for it, played in the or-chestra pit, and worked as a stage designer.

By 1923 Werner Mayer had met an accomplished violinist, who, after

3

giving him a few lessons, became his wife. His only son, Titus, was born in 1924. Perhaps because Mayer was such a common German name, he adopted a nom de plume: Werner EGK, an acronym based on his wife's name: "Elisabeth, geborene Karl."[1]

For a few years he moved with his family to Italy for health reasons, and new aesthetic influences overwhelmed the young musician: Italian opera, an enchanting landscape, and art. Composing chamber music, Egk stayed in the south till 1927; then again there followed artistically decisive, albeit economically insecure months in Munich. Egk eked out a living as a cinema musician, accompanying silent films. The year 1928 found Egk in Berlin, where he met the important representatives of the musical avant-garde: Arnold Schoenberg and Hanns Eisler. He learned to appreciate Alban Berg's opera *Wozzeck* under Erich Kleiber and *Die Dreigroschenoper* of Kurt Weill. By 1928 he had made Weill's personal acquaintance and through him met Hans Flesch, the Jewish brother-in-law of Hindemith's wife, Gertrud, and an important broadcast executive. This introduced him to the medium of radio. The Berlin station Funkstunde commissioned his first composition for broadcasting. Egk's sense for the dramatics of radio and stage was being sharpened. He returned to Munich in 1929 to work as a composer for the radio station there. In 1931, Lochham, on the outskirts of the Bavarian capital, became the permanent residence for the family. Egk joined like-minded musicians such as Fritz Büchtger, Karl Marx, and Carl Orff in a Vereinigung für Zeitgenössische Musik, or Association for Contemporary Music. He made friends with the avant-garde conductor Hermann Scherchen and the Strecker brothers of the music publishers firm of B. Schott's Söhne in Mainz.[2]

Egk's future career as a composer of opera was decisively launched with the composition of *Columbus,* not surprisingly initially written for radio. The work was premiered in its original broadcast version in July 1933 and in a subsequent stage version in April a year later, both in Munich. By this time it was clear that his predominant musical influence thus far had been Igor Stravinsky, whose sense of rhythm and colorful tone language put their stamp on Egk's music. Two other musical influences, but even more important in personal terms, were Hermann Scherchen and Carl Orff.

At the latest, by spring of 1931 Egk was collaborating with Scherchen during new-music festivals in Munich, at which some of his own works were premiered. In those last few years of the Weimar Republic, Scherchen was frequently in Munich, working with Egk, Orff, and their friends. The charismatic conductor evidently took great interest in Egk's plans for *Columbus,* which was just then being conceived. Egk in turn visited Scherchen in Winterthur, the provincial Swiss town where Scherchen had already been leading a local ensemble for several years. By 1933—the Nazis had taken over political power in Germany and the socialist Scherchen carefully avoided the Reich—the avant-garde conductor was keen to draw Egk into the modern-music workshops that he tried to organize in democratic countries such as France, and at which he sought to patronize the works of Egk's Munich colleague Karl Amadeus Hartmann. But because of the change in political climate and Scherchen's persistent absence from Germany, the contact between Egk and Scherchen soon lapsed.[3]

Werner Egk met Carl Orff as a teacher and mentor very early on, around 1921, when his Munich piano instructor Anna Hirzel-Langenhan sent him to Orff. They became more like friends; Orff remembers Egk, six years his junior, from those days as "dangerously gifted in several directions."[4] In the early 1920s, Egk did not stay long with Orff, but he returned to him as a friend and junior colleague toward the end of the decade when Egk got himself involved in various Munich musical functions. This included the exercises under Scherchen, but at the beginning of the Third Reich Orff appears to have presided over a group of young and progressive composers such as Büchtger, Marx, and including Egk, which was bent on experimenting with new things. In Egk's case this meant adapting his radio opera *Columbus* as a "scenic oratorio" to the live stage.[5] Orff was genuinely fond of Egk and was impressed by his music but also by the fact that he seemed to have been able successfully to interest the ruling Nazi Party in his work. Internationally, too, this group was being recognized, as correspondence from the antifascist "Permanent Commission for International Exchange Concerts" demonstrates, which included Edgar Varèse from the United States, Alexander Jemnitz from Hungary, and, still, the Jewish Ernst Toch from Germany. Egk gratefully acknowledged Orff's friendship. In February 1934, in the pages of a racist, regime-beholden publication, *Völkische Kultur,* he touted Orff's pedagogical *Schulwerk* project, a work which Orff at that time was bent on promoting in conjunction with the monopolistic Hitler Youth.[6]

Publications such as those for *Völkische Kultur* signify that Egk, despite being steeped in the modernist culture of Weimar, was early on trying to arrange himself with the new Nazi rulers. Somewhat later in 1934 Egk published another piece in that journal, at length citing Alfred Lorenz in a critical interpretation of Richard Wagner—Munich-based Wagner scholar Lorenz was known to be one of the most vicious anti-Semites of the music world, not just musicology.[7] All this contradicts the post-1945 judgment of one of Egk's biographers, that he was "hardly touched by the forces and tendencies of fascism and its coming to power."[8] Egk had, in fact, been touched as early as 1931 and 1932 when the *Völkischer Beobachter,* the Nazis' official broadsheet edited by party ideologue Alfred Rosenberg, had denigrated him for his modernist leanings.[9] Part of the reason for this was the proximity of Egk's music to that of his idol Stravinsky, who remained persona non grata in the circle surrounding Rosenberg from the end of the republic to well into the mid-1930s.[10]

Throughout 1933, as a matter of fact, some seesawing was going on between cultural administrators of the city of Munich with whom Egk had allied himself and the local representative of Rosenberg's Kampfbund für deutsche Kultur (KfdK), Paul Ehlers, who organized concerts for his "German Stage," whose emblem was the swastika. In a time of budgetary restraints at the tail end of the Great Depression, the plan was to manage a stage production of Egk's radio opera *Columbus* under the joint sponsorship of the city and the "German Stage." But despite repeated prodding by Egk himself, Ehlers wavered for the longest time, wondering whether the music, so reminiscent of Stravinsky, was really suitable for his genuinely Nazi audience. In the end, a concert performance planned for 30 November 1933 was canceled, but Egk persisted well into 1934. On 5 and 7 April of that year, the oratorio was finally performed, with the aid of three local choirs and the Munich Philharmonic; whether Ehlers had had his hand in it is not certain but may be assumed on the basis of a favorable review of the event in the *Völkischer Beobachter*.[11] If Ehlers had been assuaged, Egk was still being taken to task as late as February 1935 for his obvious allusions to Stravinsky, his professed love of Hindemith and Bartók, and his scarcely veiled disdain for Pfitzner. The man who criticized him then was Ludwig Schrott, another functionary in Rosenberg's entourage and a close friend of Pfitzner's.[12]

Egk hit upon the idea for a new opera, encouraged in this by Ludwig Strecker, the senior partner of Schott's publishers, who under the pseudonym of Ludwig Andersen (an obvious pun on Danish fairy-tale poet Christian Andersen), helped him write the libretto. It involved a fairy-tale opera *Die Zaubergeige,* or "The Magic Violin," which was premiered in Frankfurt on 20 May 1935. The libretto itself was seemingly unremarkable, for it presented the simple story of Kaspar, a naive and uncomplicated farmhand who, after some adventures, wins the love of Ninabella, the aristocratic young lady inhabiting the castle on the hill, before finally settling down to a harmonious and contented life with his peasant wife, Gretl. In this bittersweet comedy there is the character of Guldensack, or Money-Bags, an unsavory fellow who is eventually subdued and could easily be taken for a Jew.[13] The Swiss composer Heinrich Sutermeister in 1936 called this work an "opportunistic construction," and it may have been just that, not only because of the obviously suggestive villain Guldensack but for the entire plot, which was meant to remind German audiences of the tranquility of a simple life (preferably in the countryside, to service the official "Blood-and-Soil" mythology) that was not to call into question the order of things or the powers that be.[14] Egk himself pandered to the Nazis' penchant for anti-intellectualism when he wrote to Hamburg's Intendant Oscar Fritz Schuh that he wanted the work to be deft and emotional, "far removed from any playfully intellectualized ploys."[15] A recipe for acquiescence in the Nazi way of life, therefore, not a prescription for unrest—exactly in keeping with the aims of the Nazi government in Berlin. Hence the folksy side of the piece, its being close to the people, was generally lauded. "People's art," summed up one reviewer, and in this he was referring not merely to the plot but also to the music, which was melodious and tonal to a fault, if—for the cognoscenti—in stretches still betraying Egk's predilection for Stravinsky, especially rhythmically.[16] Of predictable consequence for Egk therefore were the favors showered on him by premier Nazi music critic Fritz Stege—an opponent of Alfred Rosenberg and his minions but a loyal adherent of

Goebbels—who henceforth treated the composer as a paradigm for music and musicians in Nazi Germany. Egk's danceable sequences from *Die Zaubergeige* were exemplary, wrote Stege in July 1936; after all, Egk was the man who had said that any piece of German music would have to be such that it could be performed at popular Nazi functions. Indeed, *Die Zaubergeige* was truly for the German people, was Stege's verdict as late as spring of 1940.[17] Small wonder, then, that the opera was quickly scheduled for performances in many German cities: Hanover, Kassel, Mannheim, Hamburg, Halle, Coburg, Krefeld, and Nuremberg.[18]

However, what most genuine Nazis may have regarded as obvious virtues was, in the manner of Heinrich Sutermeister, contemplated by more caustic listeners with guarded suspicion. Shortly after its premiere, Paul Hindemith was listening to excerpts from *Die Zaubergeige* in Frankfurt, demonstrated to him by conductor Bertil Wetzelsberger. He found them "repulsive to the highest degree. The silliest folk-dance melodies and harmonies with a few dissonances."[19] A follow-up concert piece based on the opera, featuring a solo violin with orchestra, was conducted by Egk at the music festival of Baden-Baden in April 1936, which at that time still benefited from its republican aura of serious music composed by the avant-garde. "Egk disappointed the expert with a magic violin concerto," reported Hindemith's (and Egk's own) publisher Willy Strecker, Ludwig's younger brother, to Hindemith, "while the layman thought it a riot." Hans Bergese, an assistant of Carl Orff in the process of doing some editing work for Egk, also felt that the Baden-Baden piece had been controversial at best.[20]

Nonetheless, Werner Egk had successfully begun to carve a niche for himself in the cultural establishment of the Third Reich. His next rung on the ladder of success was the Eleventh Olympic Games during the summer of 1936. According to his memoirs, Egk had been approached by German Olympic authorities to write orchestral ballet music for solo dancers Mary Wigman, Harald Kreutzberg, and choreographer Gret Palucca, as well as their massive corps de ballet. This Egk did, and after the performance the German functionaries asked him to permit his new composition to be entered into an international Olympic competition, because there were not enough applicants. Hence Egk, innocently enough, at the opening of the Games in mid-August won an Olympic Gold Medal in the section for sportive art, orchestral music.[21]

But the reality was much more political, for behind the scenes there were certain machinations that Egk may or may not have known about at the time but would have had plenty of opportunity to discover after 1945. The whole thing was an intrafascist scheme, because other music medals were also won solely by German composers, apart from one Italian. The final international jury had been made up of most of the German subjury, which already had chosen Egk, plus two German functionaries (including RMK general manager Heinz Ihlert), in addition to the reliably pro-Nazi Finnish composer Yrjö Kilpinen and the Italian-sponsored Gian Francesco

Malipiero. Already in June 1936, weeks before the Olympic event, Goebbels, the chief of the Reich Music Chamber (RMK), who most certainly had been pulling strings, had been told by Malipiero that Egk could be looked upon as the "future bearer of the Olympic Medal for Music."[22]

As could be expected, Egk's festive music, which he later marketed on Electrola records,[23] suited the Nazi Olympic organizers perfectly. Contrary to Egk's postwar statement, it had been one of more than 100 German entries.[24] The choral and instrumental work in four movements was rated as "original in melody and rhythm," with, propitiously, a "genuine folksiness."[25] It was defined as something that could be sincerely appreciated even by "naive, receptive listeners."[26] Alas, today's experts regard it skeptically. Berlin musicologist Rudolf Stephan has judged Egk's *Olympische Festmusik* a "model for National Socialist festive celebrations," fulfilling, through the use of clever devices, "the longing by the regime leaders for a monumental musical style."[27] Albrecht Riethmüller, also from Berlin, has said that Egk's hymn demonstrated an "extravagant use of techniques leading to an extreme paucity of musical substance."[28] Egk, already a skillful tunesmith in his own right, had begun to serve the political simplifiers through significant propagandistic channels.

After the Olympics, Werner Egk's star was to rise even further. Heinz Tietjen, the almighty Generalintendant of the Berlin Staatsoper under Minister-President Hermann Göring, had heard of the success of Egk's *Zaubergeige* in Frankfurt and had watched him conduct it at the Kassel stage, which also came under Göring, as part of the Preussische Staatstheater. At a time that the future of the new Generalmusikdirektor Clemens Krauss in Berlin, much disliked by Tietjen, was uncertain, but also because Furtwängler's position in Berlin then was in the balance, Tietjen was casting about for capable younger conductors whom he could easily control. Egk seemed like such a man; he was known to be dynamically gifted but still without direction, influence, or power, and Tietjen also knew that Egk had, more than passably, conducted his own and other works on a number of occasions.

Hence the Berlin Generalintendant invited Egk to have *Die Zaubergeige* performed in the capital, and later also to conduct it, in mid-February 1936. Tietjen was so moved by it all that he offered Egk a permanent post as Kapellmeister at the Staatsoper, at an annual salary of RM20,000. This was a position that actually preceded Herbert von Karajan's subsequent position by a couple of years.[29]

When in November 1994 I asked Egk's erstwhile friend, Viennese composer Gottfried von Einem, why the seasoned director of the Berlin opera would have appointed such a relative novice to one of the most important conducting posts in the Reich, he replied: "Egk was a first-class musician, but conducting is something else." According to von Einem, Tietjen completely suppressed legitimate doubts he may have had about Egk's conducting talent; all he wanted to see was "Egk's genius."[30]

This may be a subjective evaluation on von Einem's part, but Tietjen's official recognition of Egk certainly constitutes one of the first pieces in the strange series of puzzles that determine the biography of this idiosyncratic artist. There were more puzzles to come. The enigmatic Tietjen obviously liked what Egk was doing, so to show his appreciation and also to enrich the repertoire of his opera house, he commissioned Egk to compose a new opera based on Henrik Ibsen's drama *Peer Gynt*.[31]

Egk got to work, composing the music in his trademark angular style that stretched conventional tonality, again reminiscent of Stravinsky. Using Ibsen's story line, he wrote his own libretto, this time without the help of Ludwig Strecker. When the work was premiered under his direction at the Berlin Staatsoper on 24 November 1938, the reaction was two-sided, as it would remain after most subsequent performances throughout the Reich. On one hand, he had dealt with an obviously "Nordic" theme, which was to the credit of the myth-craving Third Reich. The music itself was generally well received, despite the fact that Stravinsky's influence was recognizable, but the expatriate Russian composer was still officially tolerated in Nazi Germany until the outbreak of World War II. Yet, on the other hand, some critics, especially those from the Rosenberg camp, rejected the figure of Peer Gynt, a proverbial loser, as unheroic, anything but in the mold of Nazi martial grandeur. The troll characters of the cavernous empire also were regarded as degenerate, like figures out of an expressionist creation by Ernst Barlach or George Grosz: They resembled the opposite of lean, blond Hitler youths. Egk's postwar remark that any of the head trolls could have been taken to be Hermann Göring, if a somewhat different costume had been imagined on them—a remark he claims to have made at a press conference before the dress rehearsal—is hardly credible. There was, after all, a reliable Nazi image one could draw on for the trolls, and that was—again after the model of "Guldensack" in *Die Zaubergeige*—the stereotype of the ugly, deformed Jew. It must remain open here whether Egk had actually intended one interpretation or the other; quite possibly, he had written the opera neither for nor against the Nazis. For the music, too, was not everybody's favorite: In a scene depicting a Latin American bar with an alluring redhead a tango was being played with hints of the hated jazz; there was the sound of muted trumpets usually used in jazz, and the often exotic rhythms went beyond the marching beat so loved by the Nazi rulers.[32]

A few weeks later, yet another, puzzling, stroke of luck would favor Werner Egk. On 31 January 1939, Hitler, along with Goebbels, decided to attend the opera, as they often did. The conventional wisdom that Goebbels personally disliked Egk's style[33] has never been proved and certainly is not documented in the minister's diaries; quite the contrary, what is documented there is Goebbels's delight at the prospect of Egk's winning the 1936 Olympic music medal. On the other hand, Egk's works had been attacked by Goebbels's Berlin Nazi Party tabloid *Der Angriff*, which, however, in those days was edited at arm's length from the propaganda ministry (Promi) without the tight control that Goebbels had exerted on it before 1933 and later exerted again over his wartime creation, the weekly *Das*

Reich. At any rate, it is true that at the time Goebbels admitted to a "strong suspicion" before entering the opera house, a sentiment he gratuitously extended to the personality of the Führer as well. And, indeed, Hitler had several reasons to be wary; Egk had something of an avant-garde reputation possibly reminiscent of Hindemith's *Neues vom Tage,* which had so disgusted Hitler in 1929, and his libretto was not based on the translation of Ibsen's *Peer Gynt* authored by Hitler's old Munich crony Dietrich Eckart, but on that by the much more respectable Christian Morgenstern. Moreover, Hitler had been warned by Göring not to see the opera, apparently because none of his own favorite opera singers were starring in it. But if the reports are correct, this was exactly what raised Hitler's ire: that one of his lieutenants should dictate to him when or when not to visit the opera! It is possible that once in his Führer box, Hitler decided to "like" the opera as a taunt to Göring; whether he genuinely did, we shall never know. According to his minister's chronicle, Hitler and Goebbels were ecstatic: "Egk is a huge, original talent. He moves in his own and very individualistic direction. Does not associate himself with anybody and anything. But he knows how to make music. I am totally delighted and so is the Führer. A new discovery for both of us; we have to remember this name." According to von Einem, who has his story from Egk himself, Hitler called the composer to his Führer box during the intermission in order to announce to him, in the presence of Minister Goebbels: "Egk, I am pleased to make the acquaintance of a worthy successor to Richard Wagner!"[34]

Immediately after the Berlin performance of *Peer Gynt,* Egk, according to his postwar memoirs, was asked by representatives of the propaganda ministry to present the opera at the Reich Music Festival to be held under Goebbels's auspices in Düsseldorf in May 1939, as it had been the year before.[35] Press reports at the time claimed that Egk's had been one of thirty-six works specifically submitted to the jury of the festival, whose aim it was to demonstrate the new, "Nordic" type of music Third Reich composers were now capable of writing.[36] Be this as it may, around the time that Egk conducted the work in Düsseldorf on 19 May, he was asked to make official pronouncements as a "leading personality of the German music establishment," in which capacity he said, among other things, that it was important for contemporary German composers to celebrate the Düsseldorf event and "eagerly to take in the richness of the new spiritual currents and the new opportunities for musical expression resulting therefrom."[37] Goebbels concluded the seven-day festival with a speech in which he excoriated the excrescences of elements "alien to one's race"—a clear reference to the "Jewish," atonal, and jazz music condemned in an exhibition of "degenerate music" at Düsseldorf the year before.[38] Egk was rewarded for his efforts; he received RM10,000 as an official commission to compose a new (Nazi-style) opera, which task, said the composer after 1945, he never fulfilled.[39] In analogy to performers who won similar prizes, Egk's commission was immediately referred to as the "national composition prize," a designation that was certainly correct according to the spirit of the venture

but technically false and protested loudly by Egk after World War II, in peculiar circumstances yet to be discussed.[40] It is certain that Egk got to use
the money to support himself while he was composing his next two works:
a ballet, *Joan von Zarissa,* actually yet another work commissioned by his
patron Tietjen and glowingly praised by Fritz Stege (premiered January
1940, Berlin), and a fuller version of the 1933 scenic oratorio *Columbus*
(January 1942, Frankfurt).[41]

In the 1940s *Joan von Zarissa* was sometimes paired with Carl Orff's
Carmina Burana, and hence the combination of these modern German
compositions seems to have symbolized the enduring friendship between
the two composers. Indeed, Egk and Orff were then beginning to be mentioned in the same breath.[42] However, in reality the relationship between
the two men at that particular time had become rather complex. At the
core of this was the fact that Egk, who nominally could be regarded as
Orff's pupil, had become fairly early on artistically and commercially more
successful than his older friend. In the winter of 1942–43, for instance, six
of Egk's compositions based on orchestra and choir were performed
throughout the Reich, but only one of Orff's—his *Carmina Burana.*[43] Orff
obviously had some difficulty coming to terms with this, although the
guarded language of most of his correspondence over those years hardly
betrays it.

Die Zaubergeige was premiered in Frankfurt in May 1935, more than
two full years before Orff's *Carmina Burana,* which had its opening day on
the same progressive stage only on 8 June 1937. Orff was eager to travel to
Frankfurt to witness his friend's first day of glory, but at the same time he
made it clear to the publisher they both shared, Schott's Söhne of Mainz,
that he also wished to demonstrate the score of *Burana,* by then completed,
to the "rather large number of conductors" expected to be at Egk's premiere. The publishers responded that there would not be too much of a
chance for that, because the Strecker brothers "will be more occupied with
Egk's *Zaubergeige* than with half of the *Burana* score." After the premiere,
although Orff admitted the huge success of *Zaubergeige* to a friend, he also
could not help complaining that the publishers had been so busy as to grant
him only "little time for consultations." Later Orff asked the firm, only half
in jest, what his own percentage "of Egk's great success" would come to.[44]

In 1935–36 Egk and Orff were both commissioned to write music for the
Olympic Games, with Orff's contribution designed for a somewhat different function. During this process Orff again did not fail to point out that in
his opinion, Egk was one of the strongest talents around, and he was not
just saying that because "many years ago" Egk had been his student. But in
the end it was Egk, not Orff, who was asked to submit his work to a prize
committee (with predictable results), so that Armin Knab, a distant composer friend of Orff's, wrote him cryptically: "Egk seems to have pulled
through."[45]

After 1937 Egk was hobnobbing with everybody who counted in the
music business, mostly in Berlin, and Orff could not help but hear about it.

This was the time that Orff was getting his first significant work, *Carmina Burana,* off to an initially rather shaky start in Frankfurt, whereas Egk was easily able to present his already established *Zaubergeige* in Orff's hometown of Munich.[46] And everything augured well for the premiere of *Peer Gynt* late in 1938; Orff himself had to concede that in comparison even with *Die Zaubergeige* it was "a giant step forward."[47] By 1939, Egk's work had already had good success in Berlin, and Orff's none.[48] Egk was making plenty of money; even apart from the Düsseldorf festival commission of RM10,000 in 1939, his net earnings were close to RM40,000 in 1937, nearly RM20,000 in 1938, and almost RM27,000 in 1939. Orff, however, was constantly begging his publisher for advances, for as a self-employed composer he could not make do with the meager royalties he earned.[49]

It is true that Werner Egk and his wife Elisabeth continued to see Orff socially, especially when in Munich, and after Orff had married, for the second time, in the summer of 1939.[50] It is also true that Egk and Orff did share like-minded friends, such as stage designer Caspar Neher, the director Oscar Fritz Schuh, and the critic Karl Heinz Ruppel—who were capable of criticizing the Third Reich. Later Orff was even said, by some of them, to have been a sort of elder statesman of this circle, small and ever so loosely organized.

But even here cabal was at work. One of Egk and Orff's friends was the Swiss composer Heinrich Sutermeister, born in 1910 and based in Berne, who, like Egk, considered Orff to be one of his more influential teachers. Judging by his correspondence of many years with Orff, Sutermeister, composer of an opera titled *Die Schwarze Spinne,* or "The Black Spider," tended to conspiracy and intrigue, and perhaps because he was jealous of Egk's early success and knew of their relationship, in the years from 1935 to 1941 he lost few opportunities to position Orff against Egk. If at one time he found Egk's work too superficial, at another he was warning Orff that Egk would steal from him. There were a lot of intrigues against Egk in Berlin, suggested Sutermeister in the summer of 1936, and Egk would have been shot down a long time ago but for Tietjen's protection.[51]

In this case Orff, who was a shrewd judge of character, undoubtedly could take those letters for what they were worth, but some of the carping may have left traces on him, and besides, Sutermeister was not the only acolyte with a sharp tongue. Yet another was Orff's onetime Munich assistant Hans Bergese, who in 1938 was working for the Berlin branch of the originally Munich-based Günther–Schule, Orff's cocreation which, at the end of the 1920s, had spawned the now universally famous *Schulwerk.* Bergese's criticism of Egk to Orff was not capricious like Sutermeister's but substantial and musically sound. Bergese, who knew Orff's early works as well as the current ones by Egk, for whom he was doing a piano reduction of *Peer Gynt,* wrote that this work was nothing but a "skillful improvisation." Because Egk mastered instrumentation with great virtuosity, he was able to mask "shortages of musical essence, as far as rhythm, melody, and especially form were concerned." Although momentarily successful with the public, Egk's music would never be pace setting because he stuffed too much into it. Egk was composing the sort of music Orff once started with, explained Bergese, but now was in the process of growing out of. Whereas Egk's music would be effective, Orff's was enchanting, divined Bergese. And, presciently, he was hinting that when Egk would long be forgotten, Orff's creations would still be around.[52]

II

Egk received his first big professional break, with possible political ramifications, at the level of the professional organization of musicians in the Reich Music Chamber. The connecting link here probably had been Professor Paul Graener, a nationally well-known composer of music in the post-Romantic style who as head of the composers' section (*Komponisten-Fachschaft*) of RMK was respected by his fellow Nazis. But he had not been particularly successful with his oeuvre even after 1933 and was thought to be lacking acumen at his job, where he was treated as little more than a figurehead by about 1937. He was born in 1872, and it had become obvious that Graener finally should retire from his duties by the time the war was on. Egk certainly knew him well from the Olympics in 1936, when Graener had been one of the German judges awarding him the prize, and their works had also appeared on double bills at concerts. By November 1940 Egk was assisting Graener in the defense of serious-music or *E-Musik* composers, whose share of royalties was threatened by representatives of light-entertainment music (*U-Musik*), led by Norbert Schultze and Marc Roland; they were demanding a larger share for their group. Goebbels, as head of the RMK, was backing Schultze and Roland because he thought light music to be more important than Beethoven and Mozart, to keep the fighting morale of ordinary soldiers at the fronts as high as possible.[53]

Serious composers, for decades led in this by Richard Strauss and the musicians' organizations he headed, in particular the Stagma (staatlich genehmigte Gesellschaft zur Verwertung musikalischer Urheberrechte), had since 1934 been guaranteed a so-called serious-music one third, amounting to one third of all the royalties centrally collected. By 1939–40, however, Goebbels was in the process of removing this, to the benefit of the *U-Musik* spokesmen. Although without any official function in the RMK any more, Strauss through his affiliation with Stagma was still bent on defending the serious-composers' privileges, with Graener pledged to assist him as best as he knew how. At a meeting called in the propaganda ministry for 28 February 1941, to settle this matter definitively, Egk was summoned to be present; his name had undoubtedly been forwarded by Graener, and Goebbels by this time of course knew very well who Werner Egk was. It is possible that Goebbels thought he could win a level-headed ally in the person of the dynamic Egk, but because he knew that Egk by this time was a solidly established *E-Musik* composer, he actually could not have been under any illusion as to what side Egk would take in the dispute. According to Egk's not always trustworthy memoirs, the meeting itself went terribly, with Goebbels insulting Strauss and also barking at Egk, but, claims the composer, he kept his thoughts to himself. The latter is questionable, however, for Egk's pocket calendar for the day records a "presentation for Dr. Goebbels." The minister himself confided to his diary that whereas Strauss had been senile and stubborn and Graener greedy, "Werner Egk is the most sensible." Today we may infer from these remarks that Egk tried to make the minister see the serious-music composers' point of view in discussion and that the intractable Goebbels in this case actually listened. Although nominally the "serious-music one third" was removed, something that was, technically, an equivalent, dictated by Goebbels, was put in place for composers of *E-Musik* until May 1945.[54]

Impressed with Egk's recent performance and at the same time disenchanted with Graener over the years, Goebbels decided in late May 1941 to replace the older with the younger man.[55] There were, in fact, several conferences among Egk, Graener, and other officials of the RMK and Promi before Egk was appointed on 7 June and formally introduced as the RMK's new composers' section head by the General-Secretary of the Reich Culture Chamber, Hans Hinkel, on 10 July. These scrupulously documented conversations belie Egk's postwar contention that his appointment came to him as a complete surprise; altogether, the chain of events regarding Egk's growing importance in the RMK adds yet another chunk to the larger puzzle of that composer's Nazi biography.[56]

Egk later claimed that he consulted with his musician friends before accepting the post, and indeed, at least one letter by Carl Orff suggests that such deliberations did take place and that Orff and his extended circle encouraged Egk to enter the lion's den, for the benefit of all of them.[57] But on the other hand, Egk must have known that from now on he might be called upon to do the egregious regime leaders' bidding in earnest, in a manner that was still quite inconceivable when he was working as a repertory conductor for culture czar Heinz Tietjen in Berlin. Even with just the official policy of anti-Semitism in mind, Egk must have been aware that in the most serious of cases those leaders' policies could be capricious, intolerant, and even lethal.

Hence Fred K. Prieberg's 1982 assessment of Egk's appointment is still valid. Tempering Egk's oft-stated contention that he accepted the job because he looked upon himself as a true representative of his colleagues who trusted him with their problems (which may or may not have been so), Prieberg has written that in actual fact Egk took this step because "Goebbels regarded him as the most dependable among all the available personalities who were known to have leadership qualifications, as defined by himself." This assessment corresponds to at least one officially published interpretation that in the case of Egk, Goebbels had appointed no one but "the man of his trust."[58]

Would there have been an alternative? Egk could have said no in the inter-est of political integrity with, in all probability, no harm to his musical career, or to his friends. There was a foil: Egk's new deputy was to be Franz Grothe, wisely a man from the *U-Musik* sector, who as a writer of popular film scores (*Watch out! The Enemy is Listening!*; *Roses from Tyrol*) not only knew Goebbels well but actually was considered a Nazi. But evidently he had not been the minister's or Graener's first choice. Originally, the honor was sup-posed to have gone to Grothe's film composer friend Theo Mackeben (*Ohm Krüger*), who, unlike Grothe, had a late-Weimar left-wing past, culminating in a collaboration with Brecht and Weill, which in that respect actually re-sembled Egk's own. After having been asked by Graener, Mackeben declined politely for reasons of "cultural egotism," and because he would probably not be found as active as the ministry rightfully expected.[59]

So, apart from possible political laurels on the one hand and the desire to work against the regime from within a Trojan Horse on the other, what tangible motives would Egk have had to accept such a tricky position? After scrutinizing his record as a composer of relatively modern works since 1933, his claim, stated even then, that he wanted to support novel trends in music, whatever that may have meant in the Third Reich, is plau-sible, and warrants further discussion.[60] But to stay with the sheer politics of the position for a moment, it is clear that through the composers' *Fach-schaft* of the Reich Music Chamber, Egk personally was unassailable and potentially in a position to exert a lot of power, in and of itself. He immedi-ately struck up a cordial relationship with Hans Hinkel, an SS general, which lasted to the very end of the regime, as a result of which agendas for composers' meetings were drawn up, albeit most of those not feasible be-cause of the exigencies of war.[61] He shared the responsibility for awarding prizes to composer colleagues, from 1942 to 1944, all of them naturally ac-ceptable to the Third Reich and with partial non-"Aryans" excluded.[62] He got into working relationships with leaders of the Hitler Youth and the SS, for whom he rendered artistic services of various sorts: speeches, musical arrangements, consultations.[63] Within the RMK, he represented the Third Reich at international composer functions organized in Germany or occu-pied countries by a Nazi-controlled commission.[64] He wrote a birthday laudation for Hugo Rasch, on his staff in the RMK, an old Nazi fighter, longtime member of the SA, and once a vicious enemy of jazz, the medium Egk himself had admired and utilized in several of his post-1933 composi-tions.[65] And last, but not least, he attempted to do justice to Goebbels's concern that *U-Musik* not be trampled under foot by serious-music com-posers in the Reich.[66]

But let us return to Egk and his new-music quest. For apart from political opportunism as a possible motive for entering the ranks of the RMK, Egk was truly convinced that through it he could advance the cause of a new style of music in the Third Reich that was neither based on the efforts by representatives of the German "Back-to-Bach" revival movement, such as Wolfgang Fortner or Ernst Pepping,[67] nor on the "atonality" of the Second

Viennese School of Arnold Schoenberg. At the same time, it was to be as sufficiently differentiated from the post-Romanticism of a Graener or Richard Strauss as had been Stravinsky's music in the 1920s, which had, of course, been a major inspiration for Egk's own oeuvre. Egk made public his aim of furthering "new music" when he was introduced as RMK *Fachschaft* leader in July 1941, and among everything else he said in his inaugural address and subsequently, this was the point on which today he appears to have been most credible.[68]

What exactly did that entail? First, Egk regarded as his foremost mission the support of new German stage works, as opposed to, for instance, new works from (Fascist) Italy or France. Egk mentioned opera, not accidentally, for it was the quintessential musical genre, not only of the Third Reich. Egk and the members of the loosely structured circle around Orff composed operas, Rudolf Wagner Régeny, for instance, and Heinrich Sutermeister (with pronounced pro-Nazi leanings), Boris Blacher, and Gottfried von Einem. Caspar Neher wrote libretti and designed stage sets for operas, and Oscar Fritz Schuh directed them. Egk personally continued to be lauded for his own innovative style, manifested in *Peer Gynt,* for instance, by Goebbels's foremost music critic, Fritz Stege. Most of the composers in this group at one time or another had been influenced, to varying degrees, by Stravinsky, some also by Kurt Weill.[69] This ultimately explains why these artists were in favor of Egk's appointment in the summer of 1941, and, consequently, Egk went ahead and in October of that year urged Goebbels that his own works and those of his friends—meaning specifically modern stage works—be supported. Surely he must have known that Goebbels wanted modern German compositions, thematically and musically acceptable ones of course, as part of the cultural Nazi Revolution.[70]

Second, under the constraints of totalitarian governance in the Third Reich, one had to play by the rules to advance or merely to survive; it simply would not do to define new goals for the future without recourse to official imagery, be it positive or negative: This was, after all, an ideologically determined polity, the cultural establishment not excepted. It is at this level that Egk was prepared to pay lip service or more to the regime, thereby either overriding his own convictions momentarily or, perhaps worse, demonstrating a genuine change of heart. As early as July 1940 Egk was quoted by Karl Holl in the *Frankfurter Zeitung* as saying that in rejecting late Romanticism with its "cult of the individual and ego-centricity," he preferred "an active weltanschauung," which later in the article was coupled with the "people's community and community culture" of the regime.[71] Egk, reported Holl, believed that "a strengthening effect on the community will take place, meaning an ethical as well as a political effect," after appropriate thematic treatments through the arts.[72] If this could easily be interpreted as a confession of Nazi ideology, Egk himself somewhat later did not shrink from denouncing formative musical impulses of the Weimar Republic. In Munich toward the end of 1941, now in his new official role, he delivered "an almost programmatic lecture"—within the context of a concert naturally also featuring his own works—in which he denounced the Schoenberg era, as "the time of atonality, as the last and lowest plateau of chaotic and decaying forces that had pushed themselves to the fore during the past decades."[73] In 1942, in a *Festschrift* for his boss the RMK president, unflagging Nazi Peter Raabe, he hailed the present age as one that had "positively distanced itself from the period of expressionism and atonality," and he managed to get in barbs against Strauss as well as against his former paragon Kurt Weill.[74] A year later still, in the Nazi Party's *Völkischer Beobachter,* Egk expanded on this theme by equating the "aesthetics of expressionism" with "nihilism"; indeed, current politics was trying, he claimed, "to eradicate this nihilism, not just in the graphic arts and sculpture, in architecture and literature, but also in music, which goes to show that art and politics are well connected."[75] Not only did these sentences echo the archetypal message of destruction by the Nazi rulers, but Egk had even seen fit to utilize the annihilative language of the SS and Auschwitz.[76]

As a composer in mid-career, Egk was to profit handsomely from his 1941 posting to the Reich Music Chamber. Already in September of that year he could afford to cancel the prestigious but nevertheless onerous contract with the Berlin Staatsoper in order to devote himself entirely to writing music, because he was offered an agreement with the Frankfurt stage director Hans Meissner, guaranteeing him premieres of new works for the next five years. Frankfurt suited Egk admirably, for Intendant Meissner and conductor Bertil Wetzelsberger were the sort of progressively inclined artists apt to perform works by the younger contemporary group who, according to the definition certainly of Egk and probably Goebbels as well, could be considered *acceptably* modern.[77]

Egk's ballet *Joan von Zarissa* and the reworked, more extensive version of *Columbus* (Frankfurt, 1942) now arrived at many of the Reich's stages and festivals, some of which were special Nazi functions. Even the moderately controversial *Peer Gynt* was still featured. The reviews were positive throughout, as if Egk could do no wrong.[78] In July 1942 one critic even wrote that Egk's music was typically manifest of the German "race."[79] Moreover, in 1942 Egk's music became the bedrock of modern-music events in Vienna, because Gauleiter Baldur von Schirach, in an attempt to acquire a distinctive profile for himself vis-à-vis Goebbels's centralist cultural administration in Berlin, thought him eminently presentable, notwithstanding the notoriously reactionary Viennese music establishment.[80] The Reich broadcast service network was also investing in Egk, scheduling interviews with him and portraying him as a composer ideally representative of his Bavarian home province. In 1944 Egk was placed into the most preferred category for a radio list of indispensable German composers.[81]

At the height of World War II, Egk scored what may have been his most spectacular coups outside the German Reich proper, namely, in Axis-ruled countries and, more frequently, in Wehrmacht-conquered and wholly Nazi-controlled territory. Already on 1 March 1941, before his appointment to the RMK post, his *Peer Gynt* had been performed, under his own direction, in Bratislava, capital of the Nazi puppet state of Slovakia. He again conducted the opera on 12 June 1941 in Prague, where SS Security Chief Reinhard Heydrich ruled as acting governor of the Czech "Protectorate." Somewhat later Egk profited from a staging of his new *Columbus* version in Zagreb, renamed Agram by the Nazis, and the capital of the newly established fascist puppet state of Croatia. Egk's work was billed there as a "representative example of the new German opera scene"—perhaps just what the composer had had in mind in his October 1941 letter to Joseph Goebbels.[82] And during March 1943 in Rome, Egk enthusiastically conducted three stagings of his *Joan von Zarissa* ballet, which, as far as Fascist Italy was concerned, had as its object "the multiplication of his personal fame," in the malicious words of Promi functionary and potential rival Dr. Heinz Drewes.[83]

Egk's repeated visits to occupied Paris, where, by his own admission, between 1942 and 1944 *Joan von Zarissa* was mounted approximately thirty times at the Paris Opéra, proved most spectacular, for the first time in the summer of 1942.[84] In addition, *Peer Gynt* was highlighted on 4 October 1943, in a French translation by André Coeuroy. The critiques by French reviewers such as Henri Sauget, Marcel Delannoy, Emile Vuillermoz, Guy Ferchault, Adolphe Borchard, and Robert Bernard were positive throughout; today one wonders what would have happened to any of the critics had they dared to be negative![85] As in the case of *Joan von Zarissa*, Egk not only conducted the work himself but was also provided ample opportunity to appear on French radio and to produce recordings.

Egk may have played down the official importance of such events in Occupied France in post-1945 statements, but there is no denying that activities such as his were important to the German war effort, for which reason the propaganda ministry fully sponsored them as a function of psychological warfare. According to German strategic planning, a military occupation would be easier to accept by the enemy if the Germans wooed a section of the cultural and politically influential elite of the subdued people, especially in the case of the sophisticated French. "For the French," decided Goebbels in February 1942, "cultural propaganda is still the best kind of propaganda. I shall therefore strengthen it even more than before."[86] Clearly, Egk was supposed to be part of this scheme; in fact, he had met with Goebbels in the middle of June 1942, when he was just beginning his sojourns in France.[87] Egk's onetime senior colleague in Berlin and now in Munich, Generalmusikdirektor Clemens Krauss, was about the same time being scheduled for a similar mission to Paris at the head of his Bayerische Staatsoper orchestra, "which is very strongly desired by the propaganda ministry," as Krauss informed Richard Strauss.[88] Such cultural junkets, and Egk's in particular, were logistically supported by a special Promi detachment in Paris headed by one Dr. Fritz Piersig, but also by former *Melos* editor Dr. Heinrich Strobel. This modernist-inclined music critic, married to a Jewish woman, in the face of Nazi threats had been described as a coward

by Kurt Weill as early as February 1933.[89] Now, during the war, he was stationed in the French capital, nominally as a German newspaper correspondent (while in reality trying to salvage his professional future and save the life of his wife), but for the sake of his regime credibility he compromised himself by doing the Promi's handiwork and helping such Nazi cultural ambassadors as Werner Egk, who, not insignificantly, was financed in all of this by Goebbels's ministry out of Berlin.[90]

Egk's role in wartime Germany stands out in contrast with that of other German musicians, who scrupulously avoided taking on a politicocultural stance on behalf of the Nazi regime in territory conquered by Hitler's army and being especially sensitive with regard to France, which had such an overwhelming cultural tradition of its own. As conductor Karl Böhm—who himself violated this ethical precept—put it ruefully in his postwar memoirs: "It is not hard to imagine that the French had anything but a fond opinion of us in those years."[91] After the war, Furtwängler prided himself on always having rejected the offer of a concert tour to France (which, alas, did not prevent him from accepting work in occupied Denmark and other Nazi satellite states).[92] The singer Heinrich Schlusnus by and large withheld his services as well.[93] And Erna Berger, the famous coloratura soprano and a close friend of Egk, admitted after World War II that she had greatly enjoyed performing at the Paris Opéra without thinking for a moment that in reality her concert constituted "a demonstration of enemy might before a prostrate opponent."[94]

Not surprisingly, various financial bonuses and official honors came his way in good time, to mark Werner Egk's success. His annual earnings rose well above the generous level he had been used to even by 1941.[95] At the height of the war, he was placed on an exemption list with respect to any sort of war service, including military conscription—a privilege only few of his colleagues shared.[96] As if to crown his career under the Nazi rulers, and coterminously with his triumphs in France, he was awarded the Martial Merit Order in 1943, in a group with staunchly National Socialist fellow musicians Michael Raucheisen, Hans Knappertsbusch, and Elly Ney.[97]

Still, even the most incriminating evidence we have so far does not point to the conclusion that Egk was a believing Nazi. In his writings, he may have betrayed earlier-held aesthetic principles (once symbolized by his admiration for Weill and Scherchen), and he certainly accepted high office under questionable masters. But he did this, calculatingly, for three reasons. First, he wanted to become professionally as successful and materially as secure as possible. Second, he was serious about championing a new, modern type of German music beyond Pfitzner and Strauss—toward this he thought he had found an ally in Goebbels. And third, seemingly paradoxical and yet another segment in the larger biographical puzzle, temperament, intelligence, and sensitivity informed his fundamental dislike of the Nazis, a dislike he shared with Carl Orff and his friends, and which he himself, systematically, imparted to his only son, Titus. As RMK *Fachschaft* chief, he may have fooled himself into believing that he could keep himself,

his immediate family, and his friends immune from the more dangerous reverberations of Nazism.

Egk's friendship with Orff had slowly strengthened again after Orff had had his own spate of success with the arrival of *Carmina Burana* on the Frankfurt stage in June 1937, a work that continued to augment his prominence as the war progressed.[98] This meant that the motivation, on Orff's part, for jealousy toward Egk began to evaporate somewhat. From 1941 on, Orff's and Egk's compositions, usually *Burana* and *Joan von Zarissa,* received frequent simultaneous exposure at opera theaters throughout the Reich.[99] In the spring of 1942, both composers' works were prominently featured at the Schirach-sponsored modern-music festival in Vienna.[100] They were also equally sought after by the national radio network.[101] Among the insiders, then, it became common to refer to Orff and Egk as a natural pair; both men were given to understand, by their critics, publishers, and even representatives of the regime, that they ranked among the most prominent composers of the era and that neither was the lesser artist.[102] As their publisher told Orff in January 1943: "You constitute an indivisible whole even on our account ledgers."[103] Although at the height of the war Egk was the one who had more works to go around for national performances, Orff could match him quantitatively with repeated productions of his singular *Carmina Burana,* which remained eminently popular with German opera producers.[104]

Egk's close link to Orff provided him with convenient, albeit looser ties to the artists revolving around Orff, but here it is important once again to qualify that circle. Its single unifying element was aesthetic, namely the promodernist tendency among its members, much of which was traceable to Stravinsky and Weill. The act of admiring Stravinsky, Orff, and modernism went hand in hand in with a fundamental dislike of the Nazi dictatorship but, as in the case of Orff and Egk themselves, did not necessarily preclude opportune arrangements with the regime. Hence Wagner-Régeny, who had a half-Jewish wife, early in the dictatorship tried to curry favor with Rosenberg's Kampfbund für deutsche Kultur, and the young Gottfried von Einem, who was held by the Gestapo in 1938 on suspicion of subversion, for a while admired the Führer and was a welcome guest at the Nazi shrine of Bayreuth.[105] As it turned out, occasional efforts to use the good offices of Werner Egk in the RMK for the sake of a composer's fortune (usually involving suspension from military service and invariably implicating Orff as intercessor) were few and far between and never, ever successful.[106] Artists such as Neher, Blacher, and Schuh, from the bosom of Weimar culture, cherished a spiritual relationship with Orff and, perhaps vicariously, with Werner Egk, who may have represented some sort of insurance for them should they run afoul of a regime that for the longest time showed few signs of cracking. Conversely, Egk and perhaps Orff, both of whose formal commitment to the rulers was already quite strong by 1943, might have been able to put to good use working relationships with a quarter-Jewish

Blacher or his pupil von Einem, who had ties with the anti-Hitler resistance, in case the regime did bounce and they might need an antifascist alibi.[107]

Egk may have wanted to be able, early in his career as RMK *Fachschaft* leader, to extricate colleagues from service with the armed forces.[108] But that such a thing was not possible he was to experience in his very own family, where his only child, Titus, ultimately became the victim. If, on the one hand, the figure of Titus serves well, for the biographer of Egk, to demonstrate the composer's relative impotence within the overall Nazi administrative machinery, it might also serve as proof that Egk, like Orff, was no friend of the Nazis—hence all the more despicable was his decision to collaborate with them in matters of music policy.

By the time Hitler took power in January 1933, Titus was ten years old. As was already pointed out, there is circumstantial yet not altogether incredible evidence to suggest that Titus was educated by his parents in a spirit of defiance against the Third Reich, and that Egk tried to influence even Titus's boyhood friends.[109] According to Egk after the war, he refused to send his son to religious instruction in school because the parish priest had declined to denounce National Socialism as a creed irreconcilable with Christianity. Egk also affirmed that Titus, having been inducted into the Hitler Youth, acted in such a fashion as to be ceremoniously demoted in front of his comrades from the modest rank he had attained.[110] Be this as it may, in June 1942 Titus Egk, now eighteen, was inducted into the German Labor Service, usually the prestage to full military conscription. He was posted to Wartenberg camp, in the Czech Protectorate. By November of that year, Titus had been released and sent home to Lochham, ill with jaundice. But already in December he was ordered back, to present himself to an artillery company stationed in Munich. Promptly, Titus developed angina, and, while he continued to be held in Wehrmacht camps, he later fell sick again with pneumonia. Clearly, the young Egk reacted with various forms of illness to forced service for a cause he had come to hate.[111] In the spring of 1943 his father was trying, through his good friend Hans Hinkel, to save the son from military headquarters altogether. Hinkel's entreaties to military officials in Berlin, however, remained without consequence.[112] Titus Egk seems to have been stationed in the vicinity of Munich as late as January 1944.[113] He was then sent to fight on the Italian front— on a suicide mission; during the Battle of Monte Cassino only he and one other from his company survived. He then was tried for mutiny by a military tribunal near Florence, as a result of which he was pressed into a punitive battalion and dispatched to the Eastern front, probably on a mine-sweeping mission, from which he never returned. His last letter dates from January 1945. Werner Egk recorded its arrival in Lochham as his penultimate entry in his wartime diaries. Egk's last entry, for the eleventh and twelfth of that month, reads ominously: "Beginning of the Russian Offensive."[114]

III

Until the present day, more than a decade after the death of the composer, three different interpretations of Werner Egk's career in the Third Reich have prevailed. The most benign holds that Egk was never a Nazi, that he was never interested in unfair advantage for himself, and that he was barely tolerated by the regime. Significantly enough, these versions of his Third Reich past have been circulated by two composers fairly close to him at the time: Gottfried von Einem and Boris Blacher.[115]

At the other end of the spectrum some critics have averred that Egk was "an official musician" of the Third Reich, who had identified himself with the ideas of the Nazis. In 1969 one young German composer and music critic went so far as to risk litigation from Egk after accusing him of having been "one of the most loathsome representatives of National Socialist music policy."[116] The truth is somewhere in the middle. Prieberg qualified Egk's alleged innocence in 1969 by saying, unequivocally, that "in the Third Reich, no one forged a career for himself whom the National Socialists did not want."[117] In 1980 a biographer of Richard Strauss charged Egk with having adapted his artistic and public behavior to a Nazi style and, contrary to the facts, with insisting later that he had been persecuted.[118] Five years hence, Egk, along with some of his composer friends such as Orff, was aptly described as a "reinsurer."[119] And as late as 1995 the U.S. author Frederic Spotts has written that Egk "tried to conceal the past and claimed he had in fact been persecuted."[120]

When Egk was faced with the end of the war in May 1945, he knew that difficult times would lie ahead for him. The first reality with which he was confronted was that the Office of Military Government of the United States for Germany (OMGUS), in this case its cultural branch based in Munich, had placed him on its so-called black list, ostensibly because of his prominent role in the RMK. This meant that although some U.S. personnel were privately partial to his music, he was put into professional limbo, the most immediate consequence of which was that his works were banned and his financial independence was curtailed until clarification.[121] At the end of 1945 and beginning with 1946 and even beyond, Egk was placed into the vortex of events and personalities that were as much the immediate results of the current legal precariousness contingent upon Germany's vanquished state as the ramifications of long-standing, and more recent, personal relationships. The players in this scenario, besides Egk himself, were his friend Carl Orff; Orff's wife, Gertrud; Orff's longtime student and current U.S. culture officer Newell Jenkins; and Brigitte Bergese, the wife of Orff's former assistant, Hans Bergese.

Perhaps the following forms yet another, if not the final, component in Egk's complex biographical puzzle. By the end of 1945 Egk, publicly unemployed since V–E Day, was living with his wife Elisabeth in their house in Lochham, not at all far from the Orff house in adjacent Gräfelfing. The Orffs at that time were sheltering Brigitte Fuchs-Bergese, her baby son, and her mother, all refugees from Germany's Eastern provinces, while Hans Bergese was in a U.S. prisoner-of-war camp. Brigitte Fuchs, who had gotten to know Orff in 1937 as a student at the Berlin branch of the Munich Günther-Schule, then managed by Gunild Keetmann and Hans Bergese, had married Hans in 1942, and by 1943, when her husband was stationed at the eastern front, had developed a great devotion for Orff, whom she once referred to as "our young father." She claims, quite plausibly, that Orff became romantically interested in her after she had moved to Gräfelfing in January 1945 but that she rebuffed him and that he was already openly involved with yet another woman. In any event, Brigitte Bergese developed a liaison with Werner Egk, whom throughout 1945 she saw on a regular basis. Gertrud Orff's personal diary gives the impression that the relationship between the Egks and Orffs in 1945 socially was a friendly one—with both men evidently facing a high degree of professional uncertainty.[122]

On 24 December 1945, Captain Jenkins, driving in from Stuttgart, made his first personal visit at the Orff home to join them in the celebration of Christmas. Brigitte Bergese today remembers Orff and Jenkins, both in a jolly good mood, arriving at the house in the afternoon together, where they met Elisabeth and Werner Egk. Orff and Jenkins obviously had had a lot to talk about already—presumably with respect to Orff's own political clearance at the hand of the Americans. Knowing that this also was a chance for himself, Egk asked the whole party over to his house in Lochham later, so that he might be able to impress Jenkins with piano renditions from his work *Columbus*. However, according to Brigitte Bergese, who by that time was back at the Egks' house, Orff and Jenkins arrived there in too animated a state and much too late in the evening for Egk to win over Jenkins with his piano playing.[123] The next day Frau Bergese risked a personal falling out with a furious Orff over this delay, when she accused him of having set this situation up on purpose because "you wanted to cut Egk out." The probable motives on Orff's part were, first, that his old professional envy of Egk was welling up again and, second, that, after all, he was jealous of Egk's current relationship with an attractive young woman he had desired for himself.[124]

In the next few days after the holidays, Jenkins ascertained for himself that "the suspicion was that Egk had been far more involved with the Nazis than Orff ever was. From conversations with my Munich colleagues—and I was not down there that often—I got the impression that Egk was having serious problems." When on 6 January 1946 Jenkins offered to his old friend Orff a possible way out of his personal dilemma, he added laconically at the end of his conciliatory letter that "for the present, I see no possibility of helping Egk."[125]

On 5 March 1946, ordinances were promulgated providing the German authorities with the means to clear their own nationals under the watchful eyes of the Americans. Musician suspects now placed in a new Category II—as Nazi fellow travelers corresponding to the former "black" category of OMGUS—were prohibited from performing or having their works performed and were subject to a freeze of their financial assets.[126] In order to end the uncertainty for himself and receive quick clearance (which then would enable him to have his five-year Frankfurt contract of 1941 honored to the end), Egk on 10 March initiated a charge against himself for a trial by the German judiciary.[127] Although a long-winded Munich trial eventually acquitted him on 2 May 1947, the German public prosecutor decided to resume proceedings on the state's own terms on 7 July 1947, using as its main argument that Egk had been a "profiteer" from the Hitler regime. With difficulty, Egk managed to vindicate himself through a final legal verdict on 17 October of that year.[128]

During this process, the behavior of the Orff couple was quite remarkable. Whereas Gertrud tried to help Egk by making a statement in his favor, her husband, Carl, said, slanderously, that the reason why Egk's operas had been successful and their composer had benefited from them financially during the Nazi reign was because of "many good reviews in the Nazi press."[129] In fact, as both composers were poised to have new works performed on European stages, the old rivalry between the two men—of which Gottfried von Einem spoke to me again in Vienna in November 1994, that "each was jealous of the other"—had received new fuel.[130] Orff's opera *Die Bernauerin* was performed in Stuttgart on 15 June 1947, to negative reviews in *Melos,* now once again edited by Egk's old friend Heinrich Strobel. Egk himself had completed a new ballet, *Abraxas,* which, so he was afraid, Orff might try to suppress with the aid of his own compositions.[131] All this should help to explain several critical comments Orff made with respect to Egk throughout 1947, such as the one in December, when he wrote to Oscar Fritz Schuh that lately Egk "had committed many mistakes, and I told him so, for which reason he is mad at me."[132] Egk, on the other hand, was more guarded but left no doubt as to whom he was referring when he summed things up for Viennese choreographer Erika Hanka, who was not an intimate of Orff: "In order to get this entire crap started, many colleagues and friends did their part. It would have been just too convenient to make Egk, the competition, disappear so cheaply. However, the competition has decided to stay around."[133] At the end of 1947, after Egk had finally been cleared, the two couples once again met socially. Gertrud Orff's diary entry reflects the circumstances aptly: "After a long hiatus, Egks have been here. But the mood was cool."[134]

The proceedings of the German *Spruchkammer* in Munich, whose task it was to denazify Egk so that he could be productively integrated into postwar democratic society, were cumbersome and fraught with mistakes because of ignorance and carelessness on the part of the jurists. Several of these mistakes Egk was able to exploit, in addition to maneuvers he orchestrated or oversaw, maneuvers designed for obstruction and obfuscation, in the hope that the web of lies and distortions would color his questionable career in Nazi Germany as positively as possible.

For instance, although the court early on maintained that Egk had been an "artist rooted in Nazi soil," it was never able to differentiate which of

Egk's musical compositions had actually been tarnished, in the sense of being obviously tailored for Nazi usage. But certain of Egk's oeuvre had been so designed—one piece for a nationalist mystery play entitled *Job der Deutsche* (1933), another for a similar play called *Die hohen Zeichen* (1939), to hail Germany's new imperialistic course, and yet a third as background for a Hitler Youth film, *Jungens* (1941), which was classified as outright Nazi propaganda by international film historians after 1945. The compromising quality was later indirectly unmasked by Egk himself, when he chose to omit those pieces from his Federal Republican catalog of works, officially published by the Schott firm in 1976.[135] Neither was the Munich court informed about key stages of Egk's official progress in the Third Reich, for example, his being awarded that high Nazi medal in the company of the odious anti-Semites Hans Knappertsbusch and Elly Ney (although the court did note that Ney, like Egk, had been a cocontributor to the *Festschrift* for Nazi Peter Raabe).[136] By getting insignificant but nonetheless easily traceable dates in Egk's curriculum vitae wrong, the court further showed its ineptitude. As a small but telling example, Egk did not cancel his Prussian opera contract in 1940, as the minutes of the court proceedings consistently recorded, but in 1941.[137]

Moreover, the court proved itself remiss in leaving the Nazi past of some of Egk's key witnesses unchecked.[138] Hence it committed an embarrassing blunder by calling to the stand Erich Kloss, the certifiably Nazi deputy conductor of Hitler's National Socialist Symphony Orchestra, as well as Karl Holl, the critic at the *Frankfurter Zeitung* who back in July 1940 in so many words had praised Egk as an epitome of Nazi cultural policy. In September 1947 Holl wanted the court to believe, in contradistinction to Egk's real function as a purveyor of new-German and Goebbels-sanctioned musical idioms, that recurrent presentations of the composer's works after 1933 really had been "foolhardy from a National Socialist perspective."[139]

As the court did not know where to turn for appropriate witnesses for the prosecution, Egk was in a unique position throughout the trial, because with his great *Fachschaft* experience behind him, he had recourse to many people. Not only could he marshal a lot of names for his defense, but he also instructed some of his witnesses as to the manner in which they were to represent his interests. Hans Schüler, who had survived as the Generalintendant of the Leipzig opera, he unabashedly asked to send in "a few words regarding my political and cultural-political attitude." Schüler was to make a deposition under oath using his "most magnificent letterhead stationery." And just to drive his main point home, Egk reminded Schüler that "my success is *exclusively* based on performance."[140] That some of his friends saw through this manipulation is proved not only by Orff's brusque reaction but also by the elegant response of the wily Tietjen, who politely refused to travel from Berlin to Munich, saying that he was too unwell to do so.[141]

The basis for Egk's defense, on which all other testimony was cleverly predicated, was the legend that his modern style had been diametrically opposed to the official aims of Nazi cultural policy, Goebbels's in particular.

Not knowing the intricacies of Third Reich policymaking and planning, but also ignorant of the prevalent intraparty divisions that characterized political governance in the Reich at all levels, the members of the court failed to grasp that Egk's aesthetic efforts had been completely at the behest of and in conformity with the propapaganda ministry, the divisions in this ministry (Egk versus Drewes versus Raabe) notwithstanding.[142]

From this followed several nontruths or half-truths which, monotonously repeated by Egk's defenders, were assiduously put on record and ultimately formed the basis for his acquittal. To these belonged the assertion that Egk's own works had constantly placed his personal safety at risk, that an overly powerful tide springing from the Rosenberg camp had consistently been on the verge of enveloping him, and that the vast majority of the press reviews in the Reich had been menacingly hostile. (A variation on this theme was that Egk had had to seek Baldur von Schirach's protection because Goebbels himself had been against him—a particularly hilarious distortion. For related reasons Egk also never mentioned his presence in the Führer box during the January 1939 *Peer Gynt* performance.) Conversely, whatever Egk himself had written in Nazi publications had been done either with tongue in cheek or with a view to deceiving the rulers, his hidden antiregime agenda clearly having been legible between the lines for the secretly initiated. The definition of Egk's *Fachschaft* office in the RMK was construed along the same lines: a factually nonexistent division between this *Fachschaft* on the one hand and the RMK and/or the Promi on the other was postulated and hence the hierarchical relationship between these three echelons of cultural power flatly denied. In essence, the court was told, Egk's *Fachschaft* of composers had possessed absolutely no power (a version Egk himself proliferated in his partially apocryphal memoirs)—as if the priority ranking of modern operas or the assignment of coveted money prizes during the war had never been official tasks.[143]

If in 1946–47 all this conjured up the image of active resistance to the Third Reich on the part of Egk, it was, indeed, intended. Other objectively questionable activities by the composer were conveniently subsumed under this opposition rubric. For instance, Egk's work in occupied Paris was certified to have occurred in the spirit of true culture and freedom-loving Frenchmen, although no one, not even Strobel, dared mention the French Resistance in this context for lack of any evidence. Egk spun the court a yarn (destined again to invade his memoirs) about his repudiation first of military conscription, and later still of the Volkssturm, that last-ditch, no holds-barred defense effort organized by the Nazi Party among boys and old men in each town and village. Of course, he knew as well as the court was unaware that he had been favored by a position on the *Gottbegnadeten-Liste,* or "Important Artists Exempt List," a privilege he expressly invoked with Hinkel in 1944 when finally the Volkssturm threatened. It fell into this groove when he and his friends repeatedly dwelt on the saga that he had helped many colleagues by virtue of his high office in the RMK—for this particular purpose that office was suddenly acknowledged as having had some weight![144]

Today, of course, we know that Egk helped only himself; the *Fachschaft* was a vehicle for getting through the tides. That it could be used in no other way, whether he wanted to or not, Egk demonstrated when composer Wagner-Régeny, the friend of Blacher, von Einem, and Orff, was in a psychotic state because of unbearable service in the Wehrmacht. Egk could do nothing to get him released from it, and there is no record that he even tried. After all, there could have been correspondence with Hinkel, as there was in the case of his son.[145] The person who accomplished the feat, uncannily, was Baroness Gerta Louise von Einem, Gottfried von Einem's mother and a Mata Hari-like woman with mysterious connections to the very top.[146]

Nonetheless, possibly using Orff as his model, Egk stated repeatedly during his Munich trial that he had been an active member of a German resistance movement, knowing full well that if he were believed, this would be his best alibi.[147] As it turns out, composer von Einem provides an important piece to this latest puzzle. Egk seized upon his recurrent war sojourns in Paris and contacts there with known anti-Nazi Frenchmen and German men such as Strobel, who had been, for the most part, clean, to invent the myth of a courier role he had played between dissidents in Germany and France. Expecting the worst for himself as early as the summer of 1945, Egk, after consultations with von Einem, who had just been installed by the Americans as the reliably antifascist mayor of the village of Ramsau, received from him a letter, in German, with a translation into Einem's somewhat unpolished English. It certified that Egk had been working, "since July 42 with the Austrian resistance movement. During his frequent voyages to Paris he conveyed very confidential news. It is a well established fact that the Gestapo in Paris had started very intensive investigations on his behalf." When I asked about the veracity of this in Vienna in November 1994, von Einem admitted that the whole thing had been cooked up, for neither had such an "Austrian resistance movement" ever existed, nor had Egk been a secret courier. Einem averred, however, that it had been necessary to manufacture such a document in order to help out his friend.[148] Einem, so it has now been ascertained, liked supplying compromised colleagues close to him with denazification affidavits, whether they were fireproof or not.[149]

Indeed, right after the war, with so many ends untied, von Einem needed Egk just as much as Egk needed von Einem. Although Einem was politically in the clear, his friend Herbert von Karajan was not, and Einem, who knew the conductor from his Berlin days, had decided to hitch his star to the wagon of the unquestionably mercuric but momentarily blackballed fellow Austrian. Einem was in close contact with former Nazi Party member Karajan, who was often in his native Salzburg at the time and waiting in the wings to restart his career, possibly with the help of some of the younger, more promising German artists he had worked with of late and who presumably had a cleaner slate than he did. This would include Einem himself and the other artists revolving around Orff. Werner Egk's new work, the opera *Circe*, was just completed and Karajan already had shown great interest in premiering it. There was talk about this happening throughout 1946 and 1947, while Egk was still on trial and Karajan suspended by the Allies, until both men were cleared in October 1947.[150] It was here that the old-boy network, vicariously spawned and presided over by Carl Orff, was to be stretched beyond the caesura of May 1945 and put to use for its free-floating members, some of whom, for a while, were in more dire straits than others. "Our circle," wrote von Einem clannishly to Egk in November 1947, "consists of you, Orff, Blacher, Wagner-Régeny, Neher, Schuh and Karajan." It was consistent with this networking that Einem, too, wanted from Egk a favor similar to the one he had rendered unto him in 1945. Hoping to make a visit to the United States in the autumn of 1947, Einem asked Egk for a political reference, ironically at a time in which Egk's fate was still in the balance; but, as the optimistic Einem must have thought, a resolution surely was just around the corner.[151]

Apart from any Austrian connection, other friends of Egk made up a story about a resistance cell reputed to have existed in Berlin, again with mysterious ties to Paris. But there was no consistency in the delivery of this tale, nor can any of the details be verified in the post-1945 literature. Some said that the Berlin Staatsoper under Tietjen that had employed Egk was "a resistance cell," which was of course balderdash.[152] Others maintained that Egk collaborated with a resistance group that ran a printing shop in the basement of Berlin choreographer Tatjana Gsovsky, and that for this group he acted as a messenger to Paris. Even if such a group ever existed, there is no proof that Egk performed any courier services, transmitting details about concentration camps and "crimes against humanity," as he himself claimed. Nor is there proof that the Gestapo was ever looking into his Paris activities.[153]

This is not to say that Egk never had the chance to assume such responsibilities on behalf of musicians who were less politically shielded than he was. One such colleague was Karl Amadeus Hartmann, who, financially supported in this by his father-in-law, practiced a passive form of resistance against the National Socialist regime from his base in Munich by not releasing any of his works to the German public. In his widow's recollection, Hartmann and Egk had shared similar goals during the late Weimar Republic (they both worked with Scherchen in Munich) but grew apart during the Third Reich precisely because their political and public styles had become different. Least of all musically, remembers Frau Hartmann, could her husband concur with Egk. Hartmann found *Die Zaubergeige,* whose Munich premiere he was sufficiently interested in to attend, "too angular," and he did not like the fact that Egk "always introduced notes into his compositions that were supposed to sound modern."[154] Although they hardly talked to each other any more, according to Frau Hartmann, Egk respected her husband's views and never gave him away to the authorities. (This was not difficult, because the RMK already knew all there was to know about Hartmann.) Once Hartmann mustered enough courage to ask Egk to courier some mail to his refugee brother in Switzerland, who in late-republican

Munich had been a card-carrying Communist, but Egk refused. At the beginning of 1946, as Egk was preparing himself for trial, he visited Hartmann and asked for his help. There was "great tension," remembers Frau Hartmann, and in the end Egk got a sheet of paper out of him, on which Hartmann attested to Egk's decency toward him during the regime—hardly more than cliches, really, and there was nothing at all about resistance in any way or form. It was telling that Hartmann, like Tietjen, carefully avoided making a personal appearance in Egk's courtroom.[155]

Egk's final bid to convince the denazification court of his opposition status consisted of a story that once again involved the Orffs, but this time only Gertrud, as her husband would have none of it. Allegedly Frau Orff and a few other residents of Lochham and Gräfelfing had been persuaded by Egk to sign a standard statement, carbon-copied for distribution to as many neighbors as possible, to the effect that Egk had created an information network of monitors, who would await the arrival of the Americans late in April 1945, then to inform the victors about the political persuasion of known citizens, especially Nazis. Apart from the conspicuous absence of Carl Orff from this scheme, for which he had more than one good reason, when asked about this in 1992 Frau Orff was sufficiently vague about it to justify the assumption that the whole thing had just been another concoction by Werner Egk, designed to help him out of a spot in a hurry. "It would be impossible to describe Egk as a resister," was Gertrud Orff's final word to me in this matter.[156]

Nevertheless, the Munich jurors accepted the resistance version, and henceforth Werner Egk was able to go his own way after his acquittal of 17 October 1947, all the more so because in April 1948 the prosecution decided to forswear an appeal it had planned to launch in November.[157] Egk almost benefited from a stroke of good luck as early as May 1947, when, after two years spent merely as a composer, his first acquittal occurred. By that time he had in hand a declaration of intent by the Frankfurt opera management to premiere his *Circe*, completed in the autumn of 1945, provided he were to win his case; the balance of the original Frankfurt contract was worth 18,000 marks to him. That particular venture came to naught because the new Frankfurt opera bosses allowed themselves to be guided by the resumption of the legal proceedings against Egk in July 1947, which they now used as a pretext to ignore the original agreement. Not until June 1966 was *Circe* performed, and then under a changed title, in Stuttgart.[158]

The Frankfurt intendants would have been interested in a letter sent to the Munich court in September 1947, by Otte, an incensed detractor of Egk, who was asking how it could happen that one of the greatest beneficiaries of the Nazi regime was enabled "to appear publicly before his completed denazification, while he is virtually masquerading as a political victim." Otte continued to complain that "if in 1933 the Communists instead of Hitler had assumed power, then Egk would certainly have become a functionary all the same." And he could not help questioning the court whether its members knew that Egk's "clique of friends were using the press to drum up publicity" on his behalf.[159]

Trenchantly, this letter writer was exposing cardinal faults of the German denazification process that allowed so many Nazi travelers either to go completely unchallenged or to receive a much lighter sentence than was due to them.[160] It is true that Egk's "clique of friends" was advancing the composer's interests on the assumption that he would soon be cleared, which of course was part of Egk's overall strategy. Not coincidentally, the person who most aided Egk in this regard was his old comrade Heinrich Strobel (who also was in cahouts with him at court), particularly in the pages of his just resurrected journal *Melos*. Even before the tentative acquittal of May 1947, when Egk could not yet go public, Strobel made sure to print flattering notices about Egk in *Melos*.[161] After that first acquittal of 2 May, and because of advance networking by Strobel and other friends, Egk was immediately able to take advantage of contract offers for old and new works from stages in Berlin, Hamburg, Vienna, Milan, Wiesbaden, Cologne, Leipzig, and Düsseldorf.[162] It was thus possible for him to resume his old public career as conductor, mostly of his own works, months before he was legally denazified. Strobel's *Melos* alone secured him a good press, and much of the subsequent concertizing was done at the new *Südwestfunk* radio station in Baden-Baden, where Strobel now occupied the key position of music section chief.[163]

Beginning with early 1948, Egk's renewed rise to prominence and professional power constituted one of the many personal success stories in the cultural establishment of postwar Germany, former Nazi implications and the workings of denazification courts notwithstanding. Already in 1949 Egk was able to accept high office in the professional GEMA (Gesellschaft für musikalische Aufführungs- und mechanische Vervielfältigungsrechte), an offspring of the Reich Music Chamber's Stagma, being elected its president only a year later. Also in 1950 he became rector and a professor of composition at the Hochschule für Musik in Berlin for a few years, until he permanently moved back to his native Bavaria. The year 1951 saw him as a fellow of the Bayerische Akademie der Schönen Künste. In 1954 he founded and presided over the Deutscher Komponistenverband—a reincarnation of the Nazi composers' *Fachschaft*. In 1976 he was accorded an international honor when he became president of Confédération Internationale des Sociétés d'Auteurs et Compositeurs, with its seat in Paris, Egk's old stomping ground.[164] And he resumed his prodigious production as a composer.[165] Similar such biographies, of course, were those of Herbert von Karajan, Elisabeth Schwarzkopf, and Karl Böhm, among others.[166] By 1969 one music critic felt called upon to write that Egk had become "a powerful man," and Egk himself was beginning to be challenged because of suspected dark spots in his personal and professional record. These actions were functions of his cumulative prominence no less than reactions to the composer's failure ever to come totally clean with the public, and even with himself.[167]

2
Paul Hindemith
The Reluctant Emigré

In the Weimar Republic, Paul Hindemith's most important traits, both personally and musically, were his unpredictability and adaptability. On the one side, Hindemith became known early in the republic as a composer of avant-garde stage works such as *Mörder, Hoffnung der Frauen* (1919), *Nusch-Nuschi* (1920), and *Sancta Susanna* (1921). The music of these creations was as experimentalist as their texts were irreverent. His late-republican cantata, the *Badener Lehrstück vom Einverständnis,* with a text by Bertolt Brecht, and the scandalous *Neues vom Tage,* both from 1929, connected to the output of this beginning phase but also marked the definitive end of Hindemith's most pronouncedly avant-garde efforts. On the other side, roughly between the halfway point and the end of the republic, Hindemith resorted to a respectable neo-Baroque style with compositions for chamber groups such as his String Quartet No. 4 (1923) and his opera *Cardillac* (1926). Still, his musical interpretation of the *New Objectivity,* his idea of *Gebrauchsmusik* or utility and applied music, and his regular appearances at the new-music festivals of Donaueschingen and Baden-Baden in most contemporary minds placed him firmly in the modernist camp. This impression was supported by other factors: his pedigree as a student of the progressive teacher (if not composer) Bernhard Sekles at the Hoch'sche Konservatorium in Frankfurt; his early interest in jazz, film, and radio; his close association with modernist and politically left-wing conductor Hermann Scherchen; and his patronage of other outstanding new-music organizations such as Munich's Vereinigung für Zeitgenössische Musik.[1]

But his political awareness as a contemporary of the November Revolution was less than developed; Hindemith's sense of anarchism and revolt at the beginning of the republican era, indeed his sense of politics, was fuzzy and naive rather than serious and well-founded.[2] It seemed that politically he could be typecast as little as he could be artistically. As a musician, he left himself open to many influences. This showed in the chamber music programs he performed with the highly regarded Amar Quartet: works by J. S. Bach, Handel, Stamitz, Dvořak, Reger, and Pfitzner were given hardly less attention than those of the moderns such as Stravinsky, Webern, Bartók, and Schoenberg.[3] The Amar Quartet performed Pfitzner's Quartet in C–sharp minor (1925) with enthusiasm as much as fourteen times until the period ending in December 1931, and Pfitzner's Piano Trio (1896) at least once. In fact, there is the record of a touching correspondence between the young Hindemith and the much older Pfitzner in 1925–26, marked by mutual respect, according to which the violist felt humility and gratitude toward the older master to be allowed to premiere the string piece in Berlin.[4] Hindemith had a similarly healthy respect for the traditionally oriented conductor Wilhelm Furtwängler, ever since he had met him in 1919 as a twenty-four-year-old, even though Furtwängler had warned him, characteristically, not to waste time with "compositional experiments."[5]

By the same token, Hindemith's relationships with fellow modernists do not always appear to have been the most amiable, and he reserved many a caustic remark for them, as they did for him. Possibly because of jealousy after having composed alternate scores for a radio cantata, *Der Lindbergh-flug*, also with a text by Brecht, Hindemith collided with Brecht's friend Kurt Weill. In the summer of 1929 Weill complained that Hindemith was causing a mess at the new-music festival in Baden–Baden, where the piece was premiered, and that he was getting ready to tackle him. Later Weill minced no words when he wrote that Hindemith's role in Baden-Baden that summer had been "very shitty." Hindemith's music for Brecht had been "of an unsurpassable superficiality. It has been conclusively proved that his music is much too shallow for any text by Brecht."[6] In 1931 Hindemith released a damning musical verdict about Wolfgang Fortner to their common publisher Willy Strecker of B. Schott's Söhne in Mainz; at that time Fortner was in a neo-Classicist phase inspired by Hindemith.[7] Nor was there much love lost between Hindemith and Carl Orff, with whom he was associated at the Munich contemporary-music festival; on the subject of Hindemith, Orff stated in January 1932: "Clever, but without any character, non-pedagogical worm-like music."[8] And for Hermann Scherchen, who directed the Munich events, Hindemith by then had nothing but scorn: Reportedly, Scherchen "functioned badly as a conductor . . . I am decidedly against him . . . his time has more or less passed."[9] Hindemith even waxed sarcastic about his progressive friend, Jewish conductor Otto Klemperer, who, he said in

July 1932, wanted him to be present at a concert performance in Vienna, "apparently as a token goy."[10]

After 1930 Hindemith was composing works that were putting his once controversial avant-garde reputation well behind. Ineluctably, he now was again committed to what was regarded as an extension of traditional tonality. Musicologist James E. Paulding has written that Hindemith enlarged on the "Austro–German symphonic tradition" by achieving "a balance between strong, linear writing and a new expansion of the traditional tonal system."[11] Emblematic for all his works at the time of the outgoing republic were his Concert Music for Piano, Brass and Two Harps, opus 49, and his Concert Music for Strings and Brass, opus 50, both composed in 1930. In both of these the melodic lines are characterized by "strong plasticity, the form remains manageable, the rhythm becomes stronger and the harmony more controlled." In opus 49 Hindemith quoted a *Volkslied*.[12] Hence what David Stanley Smith, dean of the Yale School of Music, said about Hindemith in January 1940, was true even at the watershed between the Weimar Republic and the Third Reich: "At one time, he was an extreme modernist but lately he has softened his style so that it is accessible to the average listener."[13]

By about 1932 or so Hindemith was thinking once more about an opera, a work he pored over in earnest by 1933 and which was fated to be premiered much later, in May 1938, in Zurich.[14] This was *Mathis der Maler*. Excerpts from the then still unfinished opera, fashioned into three movements, were premiered as a symphony, the so-called *Mathis-Symphonie*, under Furtwängler's baton in Berlin on 12 March 1934. Hindemith's excerpts, "revealing great richness of orchestral sound, are based on tonal and often triadic harmony. The underlying forms are constructed on classical models and, in contrast with much of his earlier music, true development occurs here."[15]

The work was greeted with enthusiasm nationwide, even by that considerable number of Nazi critics fond of polemicizing against Hindemith at the time.[16] It underlined Hindemith's implicit claim—one that was shared by his close circle of friends and certain key figures in government and party alike—to act as a reformer of opera specifically, and German music generally, even in a National Socialist–governed Reich.[17] On the occasion of the premiere, critic Heinrich Strobel spoke of a "totally new simplicity and plasticity of the musical language."[18] In the more recent judgment of Claudia Maurer Zenck, the Mathis project "conformed very precisely to the official expectations for modern German music in the Third Reich."[19] The libretto for the actual opera too, having been written by Hindemith himself and harking back to the Reformation era, historic halcyon years for the Nazis, closely accommodated the *Zeitgeist,* especially as the hero was Matthis Nithart, popularly known as Matthias Grünewald. Nithart was considered to be arch-Gothic, a painter much beloved by Nazi art historians such as Wilhelm Pinder and expressionist artists such as Emil Nolde, who empathized with the National Socialists (even though, as in the case of Gottfried Benn, a fellow expressionist and writer friend of Paul Hindemith, a lasting positive relationship with the regime never developed—a delicious irony that eventually could not have escaped the future émigré composer).[20] If Nithart ever served as an autobiographical paradigm for Hindemith (and advocates for this exist),[21] he was not a symbol of "inner emigration," recoiling from tyranny, as some Hindemith admirers have insisted, for at the end of the plot he arranged himself with his alter ego, Cardinal Albrecht; elements of the play such as the Peasants' War fitted with the Nazi ideal of the "Struggle for the Reich"; Hindemith's Mathis exhibited typically German attitudes, not the least of which turned out to be acquiescence to the powers that be, as, repeatedly, the cardinal extended to him favors and understanding, ultimately causing the introspective Mathis to resign himself to temporal authority.[22]

But because of Hindemith's obviously strong and early association with what was known as the modernism of Weimar culture, he was attacked by right-wing forces in the same way that the Bauhaus was attacked, and clearly for ideological reasons. These assaults intensified after January 1929, when Alfred Rosenberg founded his Kampfbund für deutsche Kultur. Hindemith, who was married to Gertrud née Rottenberg, whose father was the Jewish director of the Frankfurt opera but whose mother was not Jewish, and who knew as his best friend (and brother-in-law once removed) Hans Flesch, a Jewish executive with the Berlin radio Funkstunde, was accused of "Jewish protection" in the Völkischer Beobachter, also edited by Rosenberg.[23] Among other things, the Kampfbund berated his educational work for an elite state school in Plön, Holstein, in the spring of 1932.[24] In these last months before the National Socialist takeover, Hindemith himself made no secret of his opposition to fascism, expressing his point of view openly in the classes he taught at Berlin's Hochschule für Musik, and continuing this practice even after January 1933.[25]

And while the Nazis intensified their attacks in the months after Hitler's installation as chancellor, Hindemith carried on his musical liaisons with Jewish artists such as cellist Emanuel Feuermann and violinist Simon Goldberg. He had to be careful, for every town in Germany was ruled by a different local Kampfbund dictator, with some of them, for example Lübeck's, more unrelenting than others. In April 1933, Hindemith's publisher, Willy Strecker, had reason to believe that half the composer's works were blacklisted by the Kampfbund nationwide as those of a "cultural bolshevist," and well-known Nazi authors such as Karl Grunsky polemicized against him.[26] Franz von Hoesslin, a conservative conductor of Bayreuth Festival fame, to ingratiate himself with the new rulers, wrote them a letter making the point that he had always been a "champion of German music, above all our great Classical and Romantic composers," and that it had been out of the question for him to conduct something so odious as Hindemith's opera Neues vom Tage.[27] Throughout 1933, Hindemith had plenty of Nazi enemies who claimed that he had never been "a representative of German music," or that stylistically, he was "at home everywhere but in the German people's soul."[28] It was potentially damaging when Hans Hinkel, one of the up-and-coming architects of Nazi culture, advised inquirers officially that Hindemith's compositions were "hardly in accordance with what we mean by art in our present National Socialist state."[29]

But Rosenberg and like-minded Nazis notwithstanding, there were currents that actually favored some sort of an accommodation between the composer and the regime. One of these was the musical stream Hindemith himself was creating in terms of his nonoffensive music for *Mathis der Maler,* significantly in a time span from 1932 to 1934. To many, Hindemith appeared as the herald of a Nazi-conformist, modern music that revolutionaries in the cultural arena, certainly Goebbels and, principally, also Hitler were seeking. He is "the leader of the younger, contemporary generation of modernists," wrote Munich critic Claus Neumann in June 1933, expressing these sympathizers' views.[30]

Another theme of continuity between the republican era and the Third Reich that Hindemith himself did a lot to hone was youth (*Gebrauchs-*) music. His compositions for the students at Plön (*Morgenmusik, Tafelmusik, Kantate, Abendkonzert*) had impressed many, not least among them Nazi educators affiliated with the Hitler Youth, who took an active interest in the composer well into 1934.[31] Indeed, the entire idea of music education in Germany on a wider plane seems to have intrigued Hindemith, who was already a music professor in Berlin and was slated for guest lectures in composition at his old stomping grounds, the Frankfurt Hoch'sche Konservatorium early in 1934.[32] Throughout 1933 and into the spring of 1934 Hindemith talked about larger music-pedagogical plans not only with representatives of the Hitler Youth, the Reich education ministry, the Reich Labor Service, and the German Labor Front but even with functionaries of Rosenberg's Kampfbund. These were grandiose visions expressed in heady rhetoric: In one letter, Hindemith spoke not merely of youth but of "the most wide-spread musical education for the people," eventually to result in "the musical shaping of millions."[33]

Such language once more raises the question whether Hindemith, in the first two years of Nazi rule, was merely content with sitting still and waiting things out, as some letters of the period suggest, and which is the leading theme of traditional Hindemith biography.[34] There was, after all, that surprising and ego-flattering interest shown in him and his talents by prominent regime agencies, as well as the unequivocal backing he received from his Berlin conservatory colleagues, a number of whom were exposed Nazis and one of whom, well-intentioned, even recommended him to Deputy Führer Rudolf Hess.[35] All those factors combined motivated Hindemith initially toward acceptance of the powers that be: an attempt to play a constructive role in Hitler's Germany for as long as was humanly feasible. In late summer and early fall of 1933, a suitable time for assessing Hitler's first few months of rule, when his friend and potential librettist Gottfried Benn admonished him to take heart and recognize "this final effort at regenerating a whole people" against the backdrop of "such admirable willpower," Hindemith was adamant in refuting rumors that he planned to emigrate, assuring friends and colleagues that he "had been asked to cooperate and had not declined," and, specifically, that he thought it his responsibility "to export German culture, beginning with music."[36] Such a fundamentally positive attitude on his part explains why he accepted a leading position in the newly instituted Reich Music Chamber under Strauss and Furtwängler in February 1934, why his music figured prominently during a "festive concert" organized under the auspices of that Chamber in the very same month of his appointment, and why he still met with no significant resistance—having various of his works performed all over Germany at that time: in Lübeck, in Wiesbaden, at the Königsberg radio station, and, of course, his *Mathis der Maler* symphony under Furtwängler in Berlin.[37]

II

The short-term consequences of the Mathis symphony premiere for Hindemith were twofold and mutually exclusive: On the one hand, he had affirmed the prerogative "to be counted among the leaders of German music also in the new Germany, because of his ability, and in spite of his ideological baggage." But on the other hand, it was these very ideological infractions against Nazi weltanschauung which his enemies, primarily the followers of Rosenberg who had become enraged by his success under Furtwängler, now were to use in a renewed campaign to remove him from the scene.[38] Until the early summer of 1934, both elements seemed to balance each other, raising Hindemith's hopes that the torrid winds would soon subside. The composer's acolytes too were certain that the Furtwängler performance in itself augured well for the future of modern music in the Reich. Still in March, the painter Conrad Hommel, a friend of Willy Strecker from Mainz who just then was working on a portrait of Joseph Goebbels, had been in touch with the minister in regard to a Matthias Grünewald exhibition. There were more performances of the *Mathis* symphony scheduled all over Germany, as well as in Switzerland, Holland, Czechoslovakia, Britain, the United States, and even Brazil. Hindemith was striving to complete the score for the fuller opera version, the premiere of which Strecker clearly envisioned later in the year, perhaps not in Berlin, to avoid more scandal, but in Frankfurt, known for its progressive tendencies under Generalintendant Hans Meissner.[39]

But Hindemith also had to contend with much ill will, and not all of it from within the Rosenberg camp. Early in April Richard Strauss, who approved of him in principle but just could not countenance his earlier modernist, nor his later neo-Classic, style, was enraged that Hans Heinz Stuckenschmidt had dared to call the younger man "the German master who is basing himself on Bach and Handel." In May, Hindemith, while in Switzerland, reportedly denounced Hitler, who was relentlessly opposed to him in any case; the result was a selective broadcast ban of his works, at the discretion of central Berlin authorities. And sure enough, when Hans Rosbaud, Hindemith's old friend from conservatory days, wished to conduct the *Mathis* symphony at Radio Frankfurt, permission was denied. By June it was publicly and categorically stated that all of Hindemith's operas had fallen victim to a cleansing of the national opera repertoire since Hitler's coming to power—a cleansing initiated more by self-censorship on the part of insecure, local opera administrators rather than decreed by Berlin.[40]

After the 1934 summer break, Hindemith's enemies redoubled their efforts. "Again, people are talking about a new wave against Hindemith," wrote teacher and critic Eberhard Preussner from Berlin. In September 1934, the music journal *Die Musik* fell under the influence of Rosenberg's Nazi Party office and thus could henceforth be used as a weapon against the composer.[41] Rosenberg's Kampfbund für deutsche Kultur, having changed into a larger organization called NS-Kulturgemeinde (NSKG), or Nazi Cultural Community, watched over Hindemith's every move like a hawk and especially took note of the musician's foreign concert tours, on which he was likely to perform in the company of émigré Jewish colleagues, such as violinist Simon Goldberg in Holland and conductor Paul Breisach in Austria, both formerly of Berlin.[42] At a time during which Hindemith himself, with his case being increasingly publicized abroad, was becoming aware of his success on foreign stages and through the international sale of his recordings, he was tempted to think again, and this time more seriously, about emigration. The *threat* of emigration at least became a tool with which to impress not so much his enemies, who would surely have welcomed such a move, but his influential friends who might be impelled to toil on behalf of an official acceptance of his oeuvre in the Third Reich—his publisher Strecker, the colleagues at the Hochschule für Musik, and, above all, the personally sympathetic Wilhelm Furtwängler.[43]

Between the beginning of October and the end of November 1934 Furtwängler took up the cue and did what he thought to be best to assuage the authorities and keep Hindemith in the country, with the composer placing total trust in the conductor's efforts. Furtwängler's strategy centered on a personal approach to Hitler, with the aim of explaining to him the significance of someone like Hindemith for the Third Reich and trying to remove the Führer's deep-seated resentment. An important part of the objective was to receive Hitler's blessing for a staging of the completed *Mathis* opera, perhaps early in 1935 in a city less exposed than Berlin, for example, Leipzig. At one time Hindemith volunteered to perform for Hitler the 1932 cantata he had written for the school in Plön. But although various meetings did take place, involving Furtwängler, Goebbels's highest ministerial officials, and even Hess and Göring, the conductor never met with the Führer. In the background, Rosenberg was sitting tight and rubbing his hands, waiting for the final kill.[44]

It was Furtwängler himself who, through a terribly ill-considered maneuver, precipitated the end of Hindemith's formal career in Germany and, ironically, almost his very own. On 25 November, and with Hindemith's knowledge, Furtwängler published a programmatic article, polemically titled "The Hindemith Case," in Berlin's widely read daily *Deutsche Allgemeine Zeitung.* In it, he explained Hindemith's modernist "sins of his youth" without excusing them and defended the composer as "racially of pure Germanic stock," as a "pronouncedly German type," of which his recent *Mathis* symphony was the most telling manifestation. And, alluding to Hindemith's frequently uttered emigration threat, he concluded by saying that the Third Reich could ill afford to do without such a "truly productive musician" as Paul Hindemith.[45] With the wrath of Hitler and Rosenberg upon him, and having dared the authority of his two superiors, Joseph Goebbels for the Berlin Philharmonic and Hermann Göring for the Berlin Staatsoper, Furtwängler was compelled to resign most of his official positions in early December.[46] It remained for Hindemith to ask for a temporary leave from his teaching duties at the Berlin Hochschule für Musik. At the end of that eventful year, at his voluntary exile in Switzerland, Thomas Mann witnessed frenetic applause for the composer when Hindemith's Viola Concerto, opus 48 of 1930, was performed in the Zurich Tonhalle.[47]

Furtwängler's action had not been motivated by any special love of Hindemith's music; quite the contrary, as it was to Strauss, Hindemith's style was alien to Furtwängler's own, he who was always trying to compose like and preferred to conduct the works of nineteenth-century Romantic masters. As did Hitler, Furtwängler even thought *Neues vom Tage,* a work he appeared to advocate in his notorious article, to be "assuredly bad." That much is clear from the conductor's own musings in the diaries he kept throughout the Third Reich and beyond.[48] What then was the reason for his action? Like Strauss, Furtwängler believed that Hindemith was a genuine talent that deserved not to be quashed. Moreover, he knew of Hindemith's value as a cultural symbol for the Third Reich abroad, as much as he knew about his own. Third, Furtwängler, whatever his own sympathies with the Third Reich may have been, had an almost pathological tendency to identify with and protect its victims, Jews, non-Jews, and sometimes even National Socialists. Finally, since January 1933 the conductor had propelled himself into a power vortex where a show of strength, and the need to win, particularly against Göring and Goebbels, had become part of his *raison d'être.*[49]

At the start of 1935, Hindemith's wish to be accepted by the National Socialist regime had been flatly denied. Never before in his career had the cards been so stacked against him. He had had to bear strong attacks from Rosenberg and Goebbels, with Hitler and Göring on the side of his enemies.[50] Richard Strauss, who as head of the Reich Music Chamber had been less than enthusiastic in his support in the past, now appeared to applaud Goebbels's general guidelines for the conduct of artists in the Third Reich—which was bound to offend Hindemith, although Strauss patronizingly divined that his younger colleague "could stay on" as a member of the Chamber's leadership council.[51] Hindemith's erstwhile ally Furtwängler ostensively made a qualified peace with the regime in late February, publishing a statement of reconciliation with Goebbels, which actually embarrassed Hindemith.[52] The chances of the composer's full opera version of *Mathis der Maler* being performed in Germany now were slimmer than ever, and the entire future of his oeuvre as well as his professorship was in doubt.

Against this background, the evidence for 1935 and 1936 points to a surprising determination on the part of Hindemith to stay the course in Germany and, through the collection of as many bonus points as possible, effect his rehabilitation, although he was clearly hurt by the attacks.[53] Such evidence contradicts the interpretation of previous biographers that the composer withdrew "to a state of internalization, which bore the signs of 'inner emigration.'"[54] The "inner emigration" did not yet occur (nor would it later), and although Hindemith had threatened physical leave taking in the months before, that had only been a pressure tactic. He was to take a long time to make up his mind until he finally left Germany, and Europe, at least physically.

Although for Hindemith a German premiere of his *Mathis* opera remained the key to his overall repatriation, such an opportunity, when it briefly presented itself early in 1935 at the progressive Frankfurt stage, was quickly and predictably stifled.[55] Then in late January Hindemith was offered a chance to travel to Turkey—whose government, headed by a dictator, was positively disposed toward the Third Reich—to help reform the music higher-education system there. Hindemith saw this as an occasion to remain out of sight for a while and allow the grass of goodwill to grow again; his employers, the Berlin Hochschule für Musik and the Reich ministry of education, concurred, in their own and in the interests of their valued colleagues.[56] But contrary to others who left Nazi Germany for Turkey at that time, with racial and political motives driving them, emigration was out of the question for both Hindemiths. He would go and have a look, he wrote in mid-February: "I do not wish to go for good . . . but wish to stay living in Germany."[57]

Before he entrained for Ankara early in April, Hindemith had reason to believe that a mission to Turkey, sanctioned officially by Reich authorities, would help him in combination with efforts being made on his behalf at that time by President Strauss in the uppermost echelons of the Reich Music Chamber. A solution of the Hindemith problem was carefully planned, in conjunction with Hindemith's supporter and RMK functionary Gustav Havemann, at the leadership council meeting of 26 February for the meeting on 16 March. On that day it was decided that Strauss should personally discuss the matter with Goebbels, with the object of permanently reinstating Hindemith as professor at the Hochschule and to guarantee the abeyance of a ban on the composer's works, "so long as the number of performances cannot be seen to be serving as an advertisement for atonal music." Reportedly, Strauss did speak to Goebbels, and although

Hindemith's teaching post still remained uncertain, the music ban, for the moment at least, was successfully avoided.[58]

Paul and Gertrud Hindemith remained in Turkey from 6 April to the end of May 1935, at which time they returned to Berlin via Paris. During this period Hindemith embarked on a constructive course toward a reform of the Turkish public music system, which entailed proposals for the training of indigenous pedagogues and performers and the use of German-tried methodologies and materials, and during which he collaborated with Turkish politicians, musicians, and German exiles.[59] What is remarkable during this and ensuing sojourns is Hindemith's endeavor not only to satisfy his Turkish hosts but also to play up to the German authorities lest they consider him a traitor (or, in fact, a potential émigré). Before he left in the spring of 1935 he wrote to Hochschule rector Fritz Stein, still his nominal superior, a convinced Nazi, but also a staunch Hindemith supporter, that his upcoming journey should not be interpreted as "an action against the Hochschule or even against Germany." Turkey, which, Hindemith said, was in the potential sphere of influence of nations other than the Reich, should be secured for a "cultural influence" by the Germans, and the composer expressed relief that the German Foreign Office was sponsoring the venture.[60] While in Turkey and after his return, Hindemith mentioned the rivaling efforts by Soviet and French experts but that it remained his goal to safeguard for "the German musical culture a future field of influence of the greatest possible extent, and hence work for German prestige abroad."[61] Hindemith obviously wanted to buy the Nazi regime's benevolence, and already by May 1935 Willy Strecker thought he had reason to speak of Hindemith's "rehabilitation."[62] Regardless of whether Hindemith meant these sentences in all innocence or had constructed them in a spirit of cold-blooded calculation, they sounded like collusion with the Nazis. For was it not clear to the composer that by propagandizing "German musical culture" and "German prestige abroad," he was essentially advertising the Nazi values of 1935?

In the following months, any signs of hope were canceled out by those of despair. After his return from Ankara, Hindemith witnessed the performance of his *Mathis* symphony in Paris on 29 May, in the presence of a confident Furtwängler.[63] But two weeks later his friend and relative Hans Flesch was sentenced to one year's imprisonment by the Nazis for alleged graft and corruption while with the German broadcast network of the republic, although Flesch was immediately set free because of previous incarceration.[64] After Havemann's intercession—having distributed Hindemith's official Turkish work report to many authorities—Goebbels, for one, seemed to have dropped his objection to a Frankfurt premiere of the *Mathis* opera. Hitler too, for a change, seemed more favorably disposed.[65] But in early July, Hindemith's interveners Strauss and Havemann both were forced out of the Reich Music Chamber on matters unrelated to Hindemith's, thus losing all positions of power. A few days later an irate Walther Funk, state secretary in Goebbels's propaganda ministry, cast aspersions on Hindemith's carefully worked-out rehabilitation proposal, sending scathing remarks to his underling Hans Hinkel.[66] Still, at the end of August Hinkel, encouraged in this by Hochschule Rektor Stein, again tried to move Goebbels with respect to Frankfurt, offering, in the bargain, to appease the chronically hostile Rosenberg. Goebbels appeared to acquiesce, but Rosenberg remained adamant.[67] At that time several stage directors interested in premiering Hindemith's new opera did not dare to take the risk, although no formal ban had as yet been issued.[68]

The period between September and December 1935 was marked by renewed attempts to stage the opera, through Meissner in Frankfurt or Furtwängler in Vienna, and by renewed failures in this regard. At the same time it was becoming clear that both Hinkel and Goebbels were on the verge of abandoning Hindemith. By the end of the year it was a fact that none of Hindemith's works had been publicly performed anywhere in Germany.[69]

As if to reassure the authorities but also to reinforce his permanent appointment with the Berlin Hochschule für Musik, Hindemith swore a formal oath of allegiance to his upper-most employer, Reich Chancellor Adolf Hitler, on 17 January 1936. By itself this act was nothing unusual for any publicly employed person, but special significance derived from it, of course, in Hindemith's very peculiar circumstances.[70] About a week later there was hope that Hindemith's reputation in the Reich might indeed profit from expeditious action in London, when, upon the death of King George V, he was able to compose, on quick demand, a suitable elegy, which was duly performed to great acclaim. Immediately, probably thinking of Germany's attempted rapprochement with England, Hindemith seized the opportunity when he wrote to Strecker: "Should we not exploit this situation? Should this not hit the daily press? After all, it is not an everyday occurrence when the BBC commissions a foreigner to compose a piece on the death of its King and has it broadcast by all its stations."[71] Havemann again drove this point home with Hinkel, and indeed, there seemed to come a few breaks for Hindemith. On 14 February he once again played a viola concerto in Berlin, and his newly written Sonata in E major for Violin and Piano was presented at the Baden-Baden music festival in April. Also in that month, one of his viola sonatas was featured by virtuosos of the Nazi student organization in Hamburg. The composer himself was allowed to travel on a second mission to Turkey. In June, Göring's Luftwaffe commissioned a work from him. At this juncture, there was renewed talk about Hindemith's opera premiere either in Frankfurt or in Hamburg. It was now getting difficult to tell whether Hindemith was in for a carrot treatment or a stick.[72]

The stick, of course, was closer at that time than Hindemith himself dared to realize. A combination of events finally spelled the composer's doom. First, a new violin sonata and a piano sonata, begun in 1935 in Turkey and completed in Berlin, were scheduled for public performances by the renowned soloists Georg Kulenkampff and Walter Gieseking in summer. Violinist Kulenkampff gave his concert in Berlin but was immediately reprimanded by Funk. Contemporaneously, pianist Gieseking was ordered to remove his new piece from the program of a forthcoming event. At a time at which Hindemith's fate officially still hung very much in the balance, the authorities had been irked by the loud applause Kulenkampff had reaped after his recital. A few weeks later Hitler, who simply could not forget the tartness of *Neues vom Tage,* in his 1936 Nuremberg party rally speech on 9 September railed against "Bolshevism in politics and culture, art and politics." In October this was the cue for Goebbels finally, through the convenient channels of the Reich Music Chamber, to prohibit any and all of Hindemith's works from performances anywhere in the Reich.[73] From now until May 1945, Hindemith's music vanished from the Nazi state, with certain significant exceptions, which were in keeping with some of the loose code governing cultural affairs in the country.[74]

As for Hindemith and his "half-Jewish" wife Gertrud, already declared an unwanted non-"Aryan" more than a year earlier, they now could have known that the hour had struck and that they should leave Germany at once. But still the composer persevered. Hoping against hope, he had Furtwängler intervene with Goebbels, who just shrugged the conductor off, and put his faith in Gieseking, who, at any rate, did not even dare play Hindemith's piano sonata outside the Reich. Yet for early 1937, Hindemith again had set his sights on Turkey, and, for later that year, a tour to the United States represented a different sort of silver lining on the horizon. Still, in March 1937, when he finally decided to resign from the Hochschule effective 1 October, he did not fail to reflect favorably on his contributions on behalf of the Third Reich in Asia Minor.[75] Against his better knowledge (or perhaps because the Hindemiths, Strecker, and Stein kept insisting), Furtwängler was repeatedly still trying for an audience with Hitler, which ultimately happened, much too late, in August of that year. "It is the Führer's opinion," reported Furtwängler, "that H. is backed by merely a small circle of followers, about the size and significance of which we are all dead wrong, and that it would not make any sense to alter the general direction of his cultural policy because of such a small clique."[76]

Since April 1937 and while her husband was again abroad, Gertrud Hindemith was gradually dissolving the couple's household in Berlin, and she professed ignorance as to their possible whereabouts for the fall of that year. Under the circumstances, it is quite astonishing that Paul and Gertrud Hindemith formally kept residing in Berlin throughout the remainder of 1937 and into late summer of the following year. In January 1938, Hindemith again reported to authorities on his recent activities in Turkey. Then, with Goebbels's indifferent acquiescence, the opera *Mathis der Maler* was finally premiered in Zurich on 28 May. As expected, it was a huge international success. As a final insult, the Nazis had had samples of Hindemith's oeuvre included in their exhibition of "degenerate music" in Düsseldorf, also during May. Then, on 16 August, the Berlin residence was finally abandoned. Paul and Gertrud Hindemith moved to Bluche, a small village in the Swiss Alps, on 29 September. "Decent music and a clean conscience," these are the things that currently matter, wrote Hindemith to his publisher Willy Strecker, the man who, more than anybody, had tried for the longest time to keep him in the country.[77]

III

It is difficult to shake off the impression that Hindemith chose Switzerland because it was close enough to Germany to facilitate an easy and quick return should the occasion present itself. At the same time, the small country might provide a neutral platform from which to escape to safer grounds should a continued stay in central Europe become unbearable. On the basis of the evidence so far, one must disabuse oneself of the notion that from 1933 on Hindemith was either an "internal emigrant" while in Germany or "in exile" at Bluche or later, while he was continuing his sojourns in the United States, begun in 1937. As can be shown next, he was a somewhat reluctant newcomer to America even after he had been forced, by external circumstances, to settle there permanently, and after World War II had made it clear that a return to Germany would be impossible.[78]

Hindemith's first ties with the United States may be traced to the start of his career, subsequently providing him with many opportunities to settle there long before he actually did so in 1940. The American premiere of his String Quartet in F minor, opus 10, was sponsored by the noted patron of music, Elizabeth Sprague Coolidge, at her South Mountain Festival (later to become the Tanglewood Festival near Boston) as early as 1923. In January 1930, Sprague Coolidge invited the composer to Chicago, to participate in a contemporary-music event she was planning for the fall. But Hindemith, explaining that he was too busy in Germany, declined, holding out the prospect of a visit in 1931 instead. Still, his *Konzertmusik* for piano, brass, and two harps, opus 49, was written for this patron and performed in Chicago as planned. In 1931, Leopold Stokowski was interested in performing Hindemith's works in the United States, with a possibility of his opera *Cardillac* being staged in Philadelphia, but the economic depression appears to have prevented that. As if to compensate the composer, Serge Koussevitzky performed a new work by Hindemith in Boston on the occasion of that city's symphony orchestra's fiftieth anniversary. Eclectic music circles in America were aware of Hindemith's works in the early 1930s as far away as Los Angeles, certainly well before Hitler came to power—a distinction not every modern German composer then enjoyed.[79]

After January 1933 Hindemith's name became even better known in the American music scene because of prominent German and Austrian Jewish émigrés being forced to make their home there. Hindemith's old friend Otto Klemperer, for one, conducted the *Mathis* symphony in New York in the fall of 1934.[80] As early as the beginning of 1935, Americans expressed interest in a musical tour by Hindemith, both as conductor, presumably of his own works, and as the superb violist that he was. This was after the

Furtwängler debacle in Berlin, when the Turkish officials were also approaching Hindemith, and at the time the composer's feelings were in favor of such sojourns, "for a few months in the year," without having to give up residence in Germany.[81] But in the end Hindemith did not make a decision for the Americans in 1935, although he was given a chance to do so until the beginning of June.[82] In early winter of 1936—Hindemith's works had just been banned in the Nazi Reich—the Americans released a news item to the effect that the composer would be traveling on a tour to the United States early in the following year, again under the partial auspices of Sprague Coolidge.[83] Events surrounding Hindemith were now beginning to assume a hue of dark foreboding, with the composer still careful not to put off the German authorities completely. Gertrud Hindemith was weighing the options carefully when she wrote to Strecker in mid-March of 1937 that her husband had decided to give notice to the Berlin Hochschule für Musik on the day of his departure for New York; at the same time, he did not wish to assume a permanent post in Basel lest he be definitively blacklisted in the Reich. In any event, the planned American tour was not thought to constitute an affront to the Germans. Frau Hindemith wrote resignedly: "I know exactly what it means for him not to be able to work for and in Germany any more."[84]

Paul Hindemith sailed for his first tour of the United States at the end of March 1937; he stayed until the end of April. Two subsequent tours followed, in February–April 1938 and in January–May 1939. His activities there as a lecturer, performer, and even composer have been well documented elsewhere and need not be repeated.[85] What is of interest here, however, is Hindemith's attitude to the New World as a victim of Nazi cultural policy and putative émigré, if not exile, and, linked to this question, his residual sentiment as a German patriot and, farther removed, as a new Swiss resident with the potential for acquiring that country's citizenship.

On his first two tours in 1937 and 1938, Hindemith liked many things very much, as some of them accorded with his particular sense of humor and humanity and his openness for novel cultural phenomena. Thus he greatly enjoyed the music of Duke Ellington's celebrated band at the Harlem Cotton Club; he was touched by his East Coast family relatives' friendly concern for his personal well-being; he was feted at dinners, and the prospect of influential teaching positions was held out to him. Except for a fairly severe review by influential New York critic Olin Downes, his music too was very much appreciated. He lunched with Koussevitzky and, as a musician who had always had a penchant for the movies, was inspired by Walt Disney's new animated cartoon feature, *Snow White and the Seven Dwarfs*.[86]

But although, consumed by the new impressions of the first journey, he already mentioned the possibility of permanently settling in America, the second trip initially found him disappointed, lonely, and depressed. Promised teaching opportunities at the Juilliard School in New York and Northwestern University near Chicago had obviously not materialized, and in a letter to Willy Strecker on 21 February 1938 he woefully called America the "land of limited impossibilities." Hindemith was left with the chores of making his own travel arrangements, he remained largely un-escorted on his various trips, and his fees were never sufficient, certainly not enough to take his companionate wife along. Some of the concert arrangements (notably one at Harvard) went awry, and in performances musicians tended to play the wrong notes. Of a *Mathis* symphony concert in Buffalo during 1937 he remarked: "*Mathis* went well, with the exception of the principal flutist, who was so drunk he blew everything wrong insofar as he played at all, and he kept looking at me the whole time with a friendly smile. . . . In the rehearsal I had bawled out one of the brass players for coming in too soon before the final chord." There was interest in a staging of his opera *Mathis der Maler* expressed by Metropolitan Opera Company executives, but nothing came of this in the end.[87]

Hindemith undertook his third tour to the United States, from 28 Janu-ary to 5 May 1939, as a man who, technically at least, was in a position to say that he had now been liberated from the Nazi yoke. But no such senti-ment shines through his preserved private correspondence, not even to his wife Gertrud, by Nazi standards a half Jew, who currently was safe in Bluche. On the contrary, rather than showing sympathy with Jews from all walks of life forced to flee to America from Germany and Austria, and with whom he could have identified quite closely, Hindemith made tasteless, supposedly funny remarks about few "non-Hebrew" passengers and a cer-tain "Herr David" in a letter to his wife on board the steamer taking him to New York. And later in October, back in Switzerland, he wrote to Strecker about American Jewish violinist Louis Krasner that his was not a very en-lightening presence, "in consideration of which it would be understandable if one were to be caught up in anti-Semitism."[88]

Hindemith's activities on this third trip resembled those of the two pre-vious ones, but they were more intense and took him across the entire continent. Again they were marked by frenzy and an astringent need for money.[89] On the minus side were mediocre or bad musicians, unnecessarily annoying personal meetings with Walt Disney, Salvadore Dalí, the former reactionary if powerful Viennese music critic Julius Korngold, and the er-ratic Russian choreographer Léonide Massine, not to forget disenchanting encounters in the film factory of Hollywood. But on the plus side Hin-demith could chalk up satisfying professional experiences with first-rate or-chestras such as the Boston Symphony, and personal get-togethers with co-musicians Pierre Monteux, Ernst Toch, and Otto Klemperer. In the Western hemisphere, there truly was a renewed interest in his overall oeuvre, indeed in a permanent American residence.[90]

But to this Hindemith still could not commit himself, as he continued to favor instead the relative safety of Bluche and the potentiality of a come-back in Germany. It was as an unreconstructed European, if not a national-istic German, that he wrote, in March 1939, to Gertrud that "despite all swimming pools, the most fantastic subtropically blooming trees and Balinese bar or rare-book libraries, I would prefer Bluche a thousand times over." As he had written to his wife already in February, he would not be averse to earning the expenses for a year's residence in Bluche with a few months of guaranteed and lucrative work in America.[91]

Indeed, for the balance of the summer of 1939 and even on the edge of war, there was a final, desperate, effort under way in Germany to restore Hindemith's fortunes. Based on the 1938 success of the Zurich world premiere, a scheme was engineered by Schott's Söhne and Generalintendant Heinz Tietjen of Göring's Preussische Staatstheater to interest the Prussian minister-president once more in a Berlin performance of the *Mathis* opera. Yet by July it had become obvious that the Nazi authorities wanted none of this, for German artists bent on performing Hindemith works abroad had had to suffer official reprimands.[92]

Hence when Hindemith finally had to make the decision in favor of permanent settlement in the United States, he was driven not by an inner voice of conscience but by those disheartening circumstances, the need for money, and, of course, the outbreak of World War II itself. Still, at this crucial juncture in late summer and early fall, it took a good deal of persuasion on the part of well-meaning friends (in contrast to the Germanocentric Willy Strecker) to get Hindemith to agree to a more finite relocation on the American continent, not least because they feared an early invasion of Switzerland by the Wehrmacht. Yet deep down, Paul and Gertrud Hindemith thought that Bluche was just too nice a place to leave, what with its possibilities for growing and canning vegetables, bottling wine, writing music, and participating in local theater productions. Berlin, with all its complications, so it still seemed to them, was very far away.[93] Even while on the *S.S. Rex* from Genova to New York in early February 1940, Hindemith wrote to his wife: "I am not in the least impressed by the achievements of 'God's Country.' If I could return with good grace and with the prospect of a somewhat secure existence I would have the ship turned around right away."[94]

As is well-known, upon his arrival in the United States, Hindemith taught for a term at the University of Buffalo, with side trips to Cornell, Wells College, and later Yale. After this difficult and not particularly lucrative regimen, in which the bleak landscape in and surrounding Buffalo especially depressed him, he was offered the position of a visiting professor in the Yale School of Music in September, after Gertrud had arrived earlier in the month. Still, the fact that as late as the spring of 1941 Hindemith had signed only a limited three-year contract with Yale shows how difficult he found the new adjustment, although he had asked for his so-called First Papers, designed for permanent residency, already at the end of 1940. As Luther Noss, then a junior colleague of Hindemith's at Yale, has observed, in 1944 Hindemith accepted another three-year appointment, "still preferring not to commit himself to a longer term," until in 1947 he took the Battell Chair in Theory of Music, which conveniently had become vacant. This then was Hindemith's first tenured position in America, after he had become a U.S. citizen in 1946.[95]

Apart from the materialistic accoutrements of success—a comfortable house, a nice car, sufficient means to travel—Hindemith produced a significant number of compositions[96] as a sign to himself and the world that he was gradually finding fulfillment and satisfaction as a faculty member of Yale University and a resident of New Haven. But two sets of circumstances still showed him to be the Central European, the German, evidently reluctant to accept full integration into an American style of life as expressed, in this case, by its individual system of higher education. One scenario demonstrated Hindemith's strong personality as a teacher, the other his hard-driven vision as a reformer of the Yale music school. In both situations Hindemith came across as characteristically autocratic.

As a teacher, both at Yale and at the Tanglewood summer school and festival to which Koussevitzky had summoned him, Hindemith was stern to the point of being callous. At Yale he treated even the most gifted and advanced of his students as if they were mere beginners, frustrating them with the most basic of chores. Instead of encouraging student compositions and music productions, for example, he did the opposite, preventing young and ambitious talents from coming forward early. The only student he seems to have believed in consistently was the young German Jew Lukas Fuchs, who now called himself Lukas Foss. Newell Jenkins, an advanced New Haven–born student, who had already studied conducting with Carl Orff in Munich before the war and was looking forward to graduation in 1941, was discouraged by Hindemith in his attempt to stage *The Apothecary* by Joseph Haydn. "Absolutely not," decreed Hindemith during consultation, "this is not a German conservatory." At Tanglewood, too, Hindemith found himself in opposition to coinstructor Aaron Copland, who encouraged the public performance of student compositions, whereas Hindemith found that "not a single student had created music worthy of production." Sometimes it seemed as if Hindemith's autocratic temperament rendered him inhuman: After one of the Tanglewood courses in 1940 Charles Naginski, a young Jew originally from Egypt, drowned himself in the Housatonic River, apparently because Hindemith had found him wanting in contrapuntal technique. The German composer simply could not share the optimism inherent in the American educational system but instead had to play the role of the harsh Teutonic taskmaster.[97] On the other hand, one has to consider what Joan Evans has aptly termed "the bigger picture, including the fact that émigré composers discovered to their dismay that American composition students were less well prepared than their German counterparts."[98]

The matter of the Yale music reform was closely tied to Hindemith's regular appointment to the faculty in early 1941. Characteristically, the composer had made this appointment contingent upon certain changes he viewed as necessary for the future of the school, and his own part in it. Initially delighted, university president and provost asked him to present a written proposal. But after they had digested Hindemith's detailed plans for change, they realized that these amounted to nothing less than a complete revamping of the music school according to strictly hierarchical principles, much like the Berlin conservatory Hindemith had taught at for ten years. As Noss recalls, upon hearing about it, "there was panic in the ranks." Even though Hindemith lectured the faculty and administration intelligently on his proposed alterations, people were aghast and no immediate action was taken. After a heated confrontation between the composer and a few key music-school members, a compromise of sorts was reached, with many of the changes Hindemith had envisaged being implemented, such as not to elicit contradictions. Hindemith, for one, was sufficiently happy to report to Strecker that "the school has been totally reformed, essentially according to my plans."[99] When all was said and done, had a former Weimar left-wing democrat, who, for whatever reason, had failed to fit into the German dictatorship, succeeded in effecting a measure of autocratic change in an American university?

IV

In the fall of 1949, Hindemith received an offer from the University of Zurich to join its faculty as a full professor. Having declined several similar offers since May 1945 from Germany, the composer accepted. But because he still wanted to maintain his association with Yale, he worked out a scheme by the terms of which he would teach at both universities in alternate years. Hindemith lectured at Zurich in 1951–52, then returned to New Haven for a full complement of courses in 1952–53. Thereafter, deeming such commuting from one continent to another too arduous for himself and his wife, he resigned from the Yale faculty to relocate to Zurich on a permanent basis in 1953, leaving his American colleagues to wonder whether Hindemith had ever liked being in the United States in the first place.[100]

It may be surmised that although the suspicions of his Yale colleagues were largely unfounded, Hindemith, who had been so hesitant in leaving Germany and even neutral, neighboring countries earlier, saw the Swiss invitation of 1949 as a chance to come back to a spot close to the source of his personal and professional life, without having to commit himself further. In no way was he "prepared to return and declare himself for his homeland as an exile," as some scholars have alleged.[101] Others have spoken, more correctly, of his "conflicting emotions concerning Germany."[102] Indeed, the fact that until 1949 and beyond he would not move back outright to his country of birth may be explained in terms of a number of complex circumstances: the desolate condition Germany was in after May 1945 (for instance, with the houses of his publisher Strecker in Mainz and Wiesbaden reduced to rubble); Hindemith's own hurt pride, after what Germans had done to him from 1933 to 1938; and, not least, uncertainty over how he and his music would be treated, specifically, how his formidable international prestige would be regarded in a country now totally devoid of any of its own.

In this context, it is important to note that Hindemith's status in Nazi Germany after he had left for Bluche in the fall of 1938 had not been that of an unqualified symbol of degenerate art but remained ambivalent. Of course, there were many Nazis for whom he continued to be the product of a "Jewish-Marxist environment."[103] In a book about opera published in 1940 Nazi musicologist Ludwig Schiedermair did not mention the composer at all.[104] In the same year Walter Trienes, in an article titled "Music in Danger," castigated Hindemith for obscenity, jazz, and banality and used, as his prime example, the old Nazi shocker *Neues vom Tage*.[105]

On the other hand, Hindemith had been the most prominent composer of the younger generation in Germany at the beginning of Nazi rule, and his work was universally famous and secretly admired by many in the Reich. Also, his modest efforts on behalf of German culture in Turkey until 1937 in a strange and roundabout way may have started to pay him dividends, so that even his publisher benefited. Strecker's firm of Schott's Söhne continued to carry the name of Hindemith and the *Mathis* title in the masthead of its official stationery and in fact published some of his newer works, such as his *Ludus tonalis* in 1943.[106] In particular, music educators continued to concern themselves and their students with Hindemith's compositions, with the students sometimes taking the initiative, for Hindemith's legacy as a composer and pedagogue persisted tenaciously underground.[107] Throughout the war, a number of party, government, and cultural agencies in Germany were interested, despite the official ban, in performing or holding instructive lectures about Hindemith's music—and a few actually got away with it.[108]

From one important vantage point, that of education broadly speaking, there was a tremendous need for a return of Hindemith and his music to a German landscape physically devastated, in the spring of 1945, but also one that was culturally barren. During the Third Reich, Germany's cultural elite had been chased out, killed off, or compromised, with few writers, artists, and musicians left to participate in a process of reeducation. And this process was very necessary: whereas older Germans had to be reintroduced to pre-Hitlerian democratic values, younger ones had to be taught from the ground up.[109] Peter Heyworth relates a telling episode about Otto Klemperer, back in Frankfurt for the first time after the war in March 1947. In a hotel lobby the conductor was playing several themes on the piano, with blank faces staring at him. "What were they?" asked Klemperer. It was Mendelssohn, whom nobody had recognized.[110]

Schott's Söhne was therefore correct when Hindemith's publishers wrote to Munich's Generalmusikdirektor Karl Amadeus Hartmann, partially responsible for the introduction of quality contemporary music in the local music scene, that a composer such as Hindemith was owed a quintessential place on a list of musicians whose works would have to be especially performed. However, the publishers also remarked that "a large part of the audience will have to make an initial effort in finding the path to the new music and the art of Hindemith." Toward this, the publishers recommended Hindemith's *Mathis* symphony, *Nobilissima Visione* (his ballet suite of 1938), and his Symphonic Dances (1937), the last two to be played by a string quintet.[111] Hartmann's colleague in Stuttgart, Bertil Wetzelsberger, who appeared as one of the least corrupted of musicians in the Third Reich, agreed that Hindemith, next to Stravinsky and Bartók, would be ideal to impart the new musical standards to a curious young German generation.[112] Music academies such as the Salzburg Mozarteum, in Austria but directly adjacent to Bavaria, and music faculties such as the one of the newly founded University of Mainz in the French occupation zone, were planning to make Hindemith's music an integral part of their educational and recital curricula. Hindemith's compositions were accorded special importance at the Darmstadt music courses held at Kranichstein Castle in the summers of the late 1940s, with piano teachers such as Berlin's Helmut Roloff—one of the few genuine resisters among musicians against Nazism—singling out Hindemith sonatas for pianistic instruction. The composer's *Craft of Musical Composition* (Parts I and II), published originally in Germany in 1937 and 1939, was said to constitute one of the fundamental texts.[113]

Not surprisingly, the difficulties of adjustment were immense. Germans who had been socialized in the phony culture of the National Socialists often could not understand the bold, new forms that Hindemith's music represented. Sometimes, of course, it was a matter of degree. One music student in Leipzig in 1947 found some of Hindemith's music tolerable only because he thought pieces by Schoenberg much worse. At the University of Mainz, on the other hand, Hindemith ranked third, behind Carl Orff and Schoenberg, in a poll of recently performed contemporary works. Many prejudices from the Nazi era endured. One eager piano student complained that he was set upon by his teacher not to practice the moderns, such as Boris Blacher and Hindemith. The teacher was young—obviously still an enthusiastic graduate of peculiarly Nazi education. Upon hearing of this, the editors of the resurrected journal *Melos* commented: "Our current music pedagogy is in such dire straits that even our young ones cannot fail to take notice."[114]

Consequently, starting in 1945, Hindemith's music was performed often on the concert and opera stages of Germany's four military-occupied zones. Hindemith received reports about those musical events from the very beginning, and already until the end of 1945 they were numerous.[115] It benefited Hindemith that the Schott firm had kept his music in its catalog throughout the war, ban or no ban.[116] There was a great receptivity among the cognoscenti for some of his earlier works, such as excerpts from *Neues vom Tage,* but the commercially minded Schott house favored his later, more tonal compositions, as being more accessible to a general public largely alienated from the Weimar avant-garde style. This oeuvre included *Nobilissima Visione,* which purist critics predictably thought too closely to resemble the line of composition pursued in the *Mathis* symphony—not the brand of modernism they, for their part, would have preferred. As one samples Hindemith performances for 1946, 1947, and well into 1948, it is indeed clear that it was his newer, post-1932 compositions—the Symphony in E-flat major (1940), the revised *Marienleben* songs of 1936–38 (originally written in 1923) and the Sonata for Two Pianos (1942)—that characterized the concert repertoire. The *Mathis-Symphonie* no less than *Nobilissima Visione* seems to have been a particular favorite.[117] National highlights undoubtedly were German stagings of the opera *Mathis der Maler,* with the German premiere in Stuttgart in December 1946, which impressed fellow composers such as Carl Orff (who had also attended the 1938 Zurich premiere), and subsequent performances during the following year in Düsseldorf and Frankfurt.[118]

Hindemith himself remained reluctant to return to Germany, and the commotion surrounding his music, whether performed on stage or on radio, had much to do with that. From the very first time that he was urged to come back in 1945 he felt irritated, thinking that his famous name would be exploited by unconscionable careerists—particularly those in the music business who once again needed firm ground under their feet, not least because of a too obviously compromised past. He asked Strecker not to divulge his New Haven address on Alden Avenue, "for beggars' and schmooze letters are already pouring in alarmingly." Neither did the potential roles of inquisitor or purifier appeal to him. He was especially wary of old friends, real or imagined, who might use personal knowledge of aspects of his private life to further their own ends.[119] Hindemith kept himself at a distance even from colleagues who wished him well and did not think at all of using him. One of these was Hartmann of Munich, whom the Nazis had treated hardly more kindly than Hindemith and who would gladly have arranged the German premiere of the *Mathis* opera for him, ideally under Hindemith's old Frankfurt friend Hans Rosbaud. Hindemith warmed to the idea of a Munich *Mathis* staging but was cool toward Hartmann's proposal of chairing the new German chapter of the International Society for Contemporary Music (ISCM).[120]

Hindemith was even more leery of Heinrich Strobel, who, never shrinking from hyperbole, used the refounded *Melos* journal to orchestrate a veritable pro-Hindemith campaign. "What does he know about me anyway?" was the composer's reaction, "little more than nothing." For a genuine representative, said Hindemith, he would pick a man "who stands on higher spiritual ground than a mere journalist (albeit a very good one)."[121] As Evans has pointed out, these were strange comments from Hindemith about a man who had been a longtime supporter of his from the Weimar era, publishing the very first book on his music with Schott in 1928.[122]

Hindemith also must have sensed that if he returned to Germany permanently in those early postwar years, he would have to contend with downright hostile people. One of those most certainly would have been his old colleague from the days of the 1920s Amar Quartet, violinist Licco Amar, born into a Turkish Jewish family in Hungary and one of the musicians resettling as exiles to Ankara during Hindemith's Turkish reorganization phase. Perhaps because Hindemith had taken so long in severing his ties with Nazi Germany,[123] Amar bore a grudge against the composer, which manifested itself through less than amicable cooperation in musical politics during both musicians' Turkish period. "The 'reforms' that Hindemith started at that time have borne no fruit at all," crabbed Amar in a letter to Rosbaud in May 1946, "and the persons that he sent there have done more harm than good." Amar, who was considering a move back to Germany, preferably Berlin, was convinced that if Hindemith returned there as well, his own professional chances would be reduced to zero. Whether Hindemith found out about Amar's particular feelings is not known. At any rate, in an aura of foreboding the composer wrote, at the beginning of 1947, that he neither wanted to be "a victim of this entire horde of 'friends' nor become officially active in Germany in any way, musically or otherwise."[124]

Perhaps, despite all the trappings of official welcomes and special festivities, Hindemith picked up some of these bad vibrations during the three tours he undertook with his wife to Germany, between 1947 and 1951. On the first one, from April to September 1947, he conducted a few of his own works in Italy, Austria, Holland, Belgium, and England, but significantly not in Germany, where he visited only for a few days for the purpose of seeing his old mother and the Streckers. Nonetheless, he did attend a Frankfurt performance of his *Mathis* opera and, once recognized, was fervently celebrated. In 1948, Hindemith was reluctant to go to Germany on a second tour, in part for financial reasons. Again, he was distrustful of the people he might meet. "I am constantly being plagued by old friends," he complained to Strecker, "by those who want to become so and others who claim they once were, and I have no taste for any of them, being overworked and not anxious always to be the sucker for others." However, this time, between July 1948 and March 1949, he conducted not only in Italy, Switzerland, and Austria but also in Germany. In January and February 1949 he also gave lectures for the U.S. Military Government—in the spirit of the much-needed cultural and political reeducation. As Geoffrey Skelton has observed, this suited him much better than returning as an emigrant "ostensibly seeking re-acceptance." After his mother had died in Butzbach in November 1949, Hindemith did not even travel to Germany for her funeral. But a third visit to the country of his birth occurred in 1950, on which occasion he appeared as violist, conductor, and lecturer in Berlin, Baden-Baden, and Hamburg. By this time the Zurich offer had come through, and the Hindemith couple spent several days in that Swiss city. But although the Free University of Berlin awarded him an honorary doctorate in 1950 and the City of Hamburg the Bach Prize in 1951, this third tour of 1950 would remain his last one before finally resettling in Zurich in 1953.[125]

Hindemith's fractured relationship with Germany—the reluctant émigré till 1938, the reluctant remigrant after 1945—was not helped by his complicated relationship with Arnold Schoenberg, whose popularity in the country of his greatest influence was also on the rise after 1945. In the modernist camp of the Weimar Republic, perhaps the majority of experts had judged the older Schoenberg to be the more important of the two composers, but then there were some modernists who, say by 1932 or even earlier, were stridently opposed to the serialism of the Second Viennese School led by Schoenberg, and they would favor a by that time much more conventional Hindemith, especially as he was moving into the Third Reich. After 1945, Schoenberg was to compound the difficulties Hindemith would have with a renewed presence in Germany.

Their mutual relations were never smooth. During the 1920s, at his experimental stage, some of Hindemith's music had exhibited a certain "affinity" with Schoenberg's atonal expressionist but preserial compositions; clearly, Hindemith liked Schoenberg's music.[126] In 1923 Schoenberg passed a cynical comment on Richard Strauss's famous remark to Hindemith that with a talent as great as his there was no need for him to compose in an atonal manner—unmistakingly, Schoenberg was taking Hindemith's side.[127] A year later Schoenberg commended the younger composer and Scherchen for their intention to honor him on his fiftieth birthday, as Hindemith was making "a splendid sign of a proper attitude to his elders"—a condescending comment which Scherchen probably passed right on to Hindemith.[128] Characteristically, as a professor at the Berlin Hochschule für Musik from 1927, Hindemith made it clear to his students that he did not like "twelve-note composition."[129] In the early 1930s Schoenberg still thought Hindemith in his camp, next to Bartók, Hauer, and Krenek.[130] In January 1935, from Los Angeles, Schoenberg was wondering in a letter to Alban Berg what would become of Hindemith after the Furtwängler scandal of late 1934; should Hindemith and European members of the Second Viennese School not take steps to form a "defensive alliance"?[131] For his part and for transparent reasons, Hindemith in March 1935 allowed Willy Strecker to denounce the famous exile, as he commented that once he, Hindemith, had also been accused of the "decadent intellectual musical efforts of a Schönberg."[132]

By this time, Schoenberg seems to have caught on, for when Hindemith was on his first visit to California in March 1939, neither of the two made an effort to see the other, Hindemith maliciously writing to his wife that "it serves him right" if at UCLA Schoenberg was now forced to give harmony lessons to beginners.[133] In turn, whereas in his classes Schoenberg could not afford to ignore Hindemith, he was not overly charitable toward him either. "He concedes Hindemith's talent and facility," recorded one of Schoenberg's UCLA students in her diary, "but thinks that many of his experiments—for example, the complete divorcement of theatre music from what is happening on the stage—are simply *pour épater le bourgeois*. And besides, it seems, he has too much self-confidence."[134] Still, Otto Klemperer, who knew both composers sufficiently well to warrant such an assessment, thought that

Schoenberg had respect for Hindemith, and this verdict may have held true until the end of the war, at least.[135] For the years from 1945 until his death, Schoenberg definitely thought that Hindemith was in a camp opposite to his, believing him to be an arch-conspirator.[136] This judgment probably was clouded by events as they were unfolding in the contemporary German music scene, and over which Hindemith himself had little or no control. In March 1951, four months before his death, Schoenberg made a bitter reference to the "clique of intriguers" surrounding Schott and Hindemith who were, allegedly, conducting war against the Second Viennese School, notwithstanding the fact this was a "war" Schoenberg appeared to be actually winning at the time. Schoenberg spoke of Hindemith's "scientific, beer-inspired drivel" and hailed all those younger Central European composers who had not yet been affected by the "Hindemith frenzy."[137]

Those events in the contemporary-music scene (as exemplified in new-music festivals such as Darmstadt's and specialist journals) entailed nothing more or less than the quick ascendance in postwar Germany of Hindemith as a modernist, his peak, and then his gradual decline, which was caused by the advance of the Second Viennese School, in particular Schoenberg. To a certain degree they were masked by Hindemith's continuing success, described earlier, as an instrumentalist, a lecturer and educator, and, above all, a beloved conveyor of tonal music.

During 1945 and 1946, when the German interest in Hindemith was steadily growing, Schoenberg's work still met with relative indifference. "He commands the interest of a small circle," observed the Schott-published journal *Melos,* which notoriously championed Hindemith. Hindemith's neo-Classic works, the oeuvre of his maturer years, were in the center of musical events at the Darmstadt new-music courses of 1946; atonal music was peripheral.[138] The year 1947 marked the apex of Hindemith's popularity, caused to a large extent by the Stuttgart premiere of *Mathis der Maler,* in December 1946. But 1947 also marked the beginning of a German Schoenberg renaissance: Hindemith and Schoenberg's works were both performed in a chamber-music concert organized by the Frankfurt-based Studio für neue Musik. Later in the year in Wuppertal, the pianist Else C. Kraus again played works by both composers. Although Hindemith once more made his mark at the Darmstadt summer festival, not least because of an emphasis on his ballet *Nobilissima Visione,* the presence of Schoenberg champion Hermann Scherchen there cast a shadow over Hindemith followers. Some specialist journals were now chancing some criticism of Hindemith's concept of modernity in the *Mathis* opera, and there was slightly more attention being paid to twelve-tone music. For the balance of the year, there were more joint Schoenberg and Hindemith programs as well as more single billings of Schoenberg works. This trend continued in the years ahead.[139]

In 1948, as Hindemith's neo-Classicism remained dominant (along with that of Stravinsky and Bartók) and the composer was honored at a Hindemith festival in Aachen, Schoenberg's music spoke to larger and larger audiences. And to the extent that the admiration for Hindemith was becoming more qualified (epigonal elements were detected in his oeuvre for the first time), Schoenberg now became the rage for declared modernists, as signally demonstrated at that summer's program at Darmstadt, a stone's throw from Hindemith's birthplace Hanau. Slowly, Hindemith's music was being compartmentalized: His were said to be the creations of an *Altmeister,* a time-honored, proven master, whose music was in the process of becoming part of history. Rightly or wrongly, his post-1930 works were viewed in proximity to the late Romantics; by dyed-in-the-wool avant-gardists, criticism was implied. Hindemith, no more the pioneer that he once was, called twelve-tone music the failed outcome of an attempt to subject "tones to an extra-musical set of laws."[140]

The years from 1949 to 1951, the period of Hindemith's protracted leave taking from the United States, were marked by an accentuation of the very same trends: a revaluation of Schoenberg's music by the connoisseurs and a discounting of Hindemith's as that of a onetime pioneering but now dated modernist. Hindemith was forced to realize, writes Albrecht Riethmüller, that he would not be able once again "to place himself in the vanguard of a composers' movement," as he had done in the 1920s. And so his musical image slowly seemed to mutate from that of a composer to that of a conductor, or pedagogue, or scholar. After the 1949 Darmstadt events, Hindemith was informed by Strecker that searching young musicians were confused, throwing his latest works onto the scrap heap. Defiantly, Hindemith replied that "a place on the scrap heap is a place of honor." He felt strangely vindicated, for much earlier had he not warned of a false sense of enthusiasm in postwar Germany? In 1950 Hindemith's music and that of the Second Viennese School had become antithetical, with the searing avant-gardists, helped in this by Berg acolyte Theodor Wiesengrund Adorno and René Leibowitz, siding with the latter. This was in spite of Hindemith's continued spate of public and media success, during a year in which his fifty-fifth birthday was celebrated in several cities. At the annual Darmstadt festival Bartók now had replaced Hindemith as the token representative of (modern) nonserial music. Compositions of the Second Viennese School predominated.[141]

The same was the case in 1951, coincidentally the year of Schoenberg's passing and Hindemith's uncertain return to Europe from America. In Germany, Schoenberg's music even appears to have gained in importance because of the death of its creator. Hindemith's currency, on the other hand, does not seem to have risen as a consequence of his tentative comeback to a German-speaking country, adjacent to Germany itself. Serial music for the moment had overshadowed his own compositions, which he himself still considered not to be out of date.[142]

In conclusion, it is moot to speculate in what direction Hindemith would have moved by the early 1950s, had he chosen any one of the other options available to him at various stops on his winding career path: to remain in Germany beyond 1938, to stay in Switzerland after 1940, never to return from the United States at all, or to come back to a post-Hitlerian Germany with a desire wholly to reintegrate himself. Clearly, none of these possibilities appealed to him. Hindemith's was an artistic fate quite unique: He was the reluctant émigré who, once having left his country after much procrastination, was just as reluctant to go back to it forever, even though he did so vicariously, by choosing to resettle nearby.

3

Kurt Weill

A Survivor on Two Continents

I

Kurt Julian Weill, the son of a Jewish cantor from Dessau and descendant of a long line of rabbis, had begun to compose seriously by 1916 as a callow youth of sixteen and still without the benefit of formal conservatory schooling: *Sehnsucht (Yearning)*, a song for voice and piano; *Ofrahs Lieder*, a song cycle based on poems by the eleventh-century Jewish poet Judah Halevi; an opera entitled *Zriny*; and, increasingly, chamber music. His early predilection for vocal music was remarkable, and it led him to the genre of musical theater for which he was to become famous while still in his twenties.[1] In Berlin by 1920, Weill studied first with Engelbert Humperdinck and then with Ferruccio Busoni; in 1922 he joined the Novembergruppe, that unique collective of leftist Berlin artists whose music section was to include Wladimir Vogel, Hanns Eisler, Stefan Wolpe, and the critic Hans Heinz Stuckenschmidt. After the group's fleeting association with Socialist conductor Hermann Scherchen, works by mostly modernist composers were performed: Berg, Webern, Schoenberg, Hindemith, Stravinsky, and, the same age as Weill, Ernst Krenek.[2] Weill experienced an early spate of successes. After he had begun to work with Germany's leading expressionist playwright, Georg Kaiser, on his opera *Der Protagonist* in 1923, he wrote to his parents in August 1924 that only Richard Strauss would be asked to commit himself to the premiere of an opera that was still in its infancy.[3]

Weill's three other important operas up to 1928 were *Royal Palace, Na und?,* and *Der Zar lässt sich photographieren,* the last one again with Kaiser as librettist. What characterized these early but already mature pre-Brechtian works, in the words of Kim H. Kowalke, was Weill's "adoption of popular dance idioms and jazz-influenced instrumentation," which complemented his "quest for clarity and simpliticy."[4] The premiere of *Der Protagonist* under Fritz Busch in Dresden on 27 March 1926 quickly made Weill well-known all over Germany, so that barely a week later he wrote home, enthusiastically overstating his case: "It is actually very exciting to become a world celebrity overnight . . . my telephone never shuts up."[5]

Kurt Weill did become world famous after the production of his first collaborative efforts with Bertolt Brecht, first *Mahagonny Songspiel* in Baden-Baden, 1927, and especially *Die Dreigroschenoper,* based on John Gay's *The Beggars' Opera,* in an off-beat Berlin theater on 31 August 1928, and starring his wife Lotte Lenya as Jenny. He was now "the most successful composer for the stage to have emerged in Germany since the foundation of the Weimar Republic." This work immediately swept major German cities such as Frankfurt and Munich, but also Vienna and Budapest; within one year, it had been performed 4,200 times.[6] The mixture of cynicism and social criticism that characterized it, and for which librettist Brecht was chiefly responsible, was even stronger in Weill and Brecht's next coproduction, *Aufstieg und Fall der Stadt Mahagonny,* again featuring Lenya, which premiered in Leipzig on 9 March 1930, then already facing the organized opposition of Nazi Brownshirts. At a subsequent performance in Frankfurt, local SA men threw stinkbombs onto the stage.[7] This was the beginning of a hypernationalist, even fascist, trend in the outgoing years of the republic, to suppress outright or sabotage any of Weill's works, especially if they were associated with Brecht. Weill himself, who had tried to interest Prussian Staatstheater Generalintendant Heinz Tietjen in a Berlin performance (after Tietjen had seen and liked the opera in Kassel), was forced to realize that more and more stage directors were shunning politically risky productions—at a time at which mounting economic difficulties were compounding the precarious political situation. After the crafty Tietjen had backed off and Max Reinhardt too had declined, the opera was finally staged in December 1931 by Ernst Aufricht, who had already been in charge of the Berlin premiere of *Die Dreigroschenoper,* at the less conspicuous Theater am Kurfürstendamm.[8]

Between 1930 and Hitler's ascension to power in January 1933 Weill oscillated between pessimism and optimism. After the Reichstag elections of 14 September 1930, which had given the Nazis an unexpectedly large number of seats, he wondered "what kind of people (butchers and train robbers) from now on will decide on the fate of art works in Germany."[9] But he was also aware of the fact that democratic checks and balances in Germany were becoming increasingly attenuated and that, quite apart from the destruction wrought by radical Nazis, the bourgeois right dominated by men such as media czar Alfred Hugenberg showed an alarming tendency toward censorship and proved stifling for artistic endeavors of any kind. Weill knew that the ongoing economic depression could always provide additional justification for those politicians who would curb the Bauhaus (just then relocated in Weill's hometown) or close the Berlin Kroll-Oper.[10]

Weill was incensed over the fact that even in such dire circumstances, theater and opera directors would give in so easily and capitulate, which in his own situation always came down to a refusal to accept one of his works for a season's run. Hence in January 1931 he agreed with theater critic Alfred Kerr's sarcastic verdict that currently, many stages were closed because of "an overflowing of directors' pants."[11] Later in the year, his new coproduction with Brecht, the "school opera" *Der Jasager,* had already been featured for some months and had even received some good regional reviews, which inspired momentary optimism. But that was dampened again by the continued deterioration of the political scene, with right-wingers generally gaining ground under Chancellor Heinrich Brüning and signs of extreme violence on the radical right. So in July, Weill cautiously asked his Viennese publishers for a transfer of future royalties to his bank in Zurich.[12]

During 1931 Weill was completing his opera *Die Bürgschaft,* with a libretto not by the abrasively uncompromising Brecht but by their stage designer, the more accommodating Caspar Neher. In the last months of the republic, this work, albeit lacking the pungent social criticism a Brecht would have imputed, nonetheless became emblematic of the erratic state of Weill himself. Already in the fall of 1931 the Stuttgart stage refused to present it because of a "panic fear of political difficulties." When it opened at the Städtische Oper in Berlin under Fritz Stiedry in March 1932, it became the object of scathing attacks by Nazi critics, led in this by the stooges of Alfred Rosenberg's Kampfbund für deutsche Kultur, although some bourgeois papers actually liked it. However, it lasted through merely three stagings in Berlin, and of eight houses which had initially shown an interest, only Düsseldorf and Wiesbaden remained committed.[13] And although Weill was uplifted by the impression that *Die Bürgschaft* in Berlin, Düsseldorf, and Wiesbaden had proved more of a box-office attraction than Pfitzner's maudlin new opera *Das Herz,* he wrote resignedly to Tietjen: "I am convinced that these months will be decisive for the future of a theater culture in Germany in the years to come."[14]

To the extent that Weill misjudged the political fortunes of the Nazis after the elections of July 1932, which had made them the largest party in the Reichstag, his spirits rose intermittently. In the middle of August he told his Viennese publishers that currently, one should not hold too pessimistic a view of music and theater in Germany. In September—weeks before the November elections so daunting for the Nazis—he opined that because the Hitlerites had suffered severely in the past few weeks, this would be good for German culture and, in particular, for the commercial future of *Die Bürgschaft.*[15] At the turn of the era—from republic to dictatorship—Weill was reasonably confident on a number of counts: He saw at least a fighting chance to produce his latest work, *Der Silbersee,* in Germany, if only in the provinces; *Die Dreigroschenoper* had been sold to an American company on Broadway; and there were prospects for a "Saison Kurt Weill" in Paris (French productions of *Bürgschaft* at the Opéra; *Mahagonny*), after a successful run of the film version of *L'opéra de quat' sous* there since October 1931.[16]

Even after Hitler's power takeover on 30 January 1933, Weill might have had reason to believe that he could stay in Germany, perhaps because at the beginning he thought that the Third Reich was but a fleeting phenomenon. "I believe that what is going on right now is so sick," he wrote to his publisher on 6 February, "that I don't know how this can last longer than a few months." Such naiveté explains why he would have gone ahead with the production of his new musical play *Der Silbersee,* simultaneously in Leipzig, Magdeburg, and Erfurt.[17] To be sure, there was plenty the Nazis did to disturb the performances at the end of February, the most auspicious of which was again in Leipzig, under Gustav Brecher. For not only did the composer represent a risk (if anybody, was it not he who had stood for the "gutter culture" of Weimar?), but also some of the cast. In Leipzig, one of the lads in the plot was played by Joachim Gottschalk, who, married to a Jew, would commit suicide as a protest to the Nazi regime in November 1941. Detlef Sierck, soon to emigrate to Hollywood to continue directing films as Douglas Sirk, was the stage director. In Magdeburg, the lead part of Severin was played by Ernst Busch, the intrepid interpreter of workers' songs who had a long association with the Weimar political left. Kaiser's text was more socially critical and ideologically sensitive than Neher's had been for *Die Bürgschaft*; Weill's music, like that for *Die Bürgschaft,* represented a further extension of *Mahagonny,* although the jazz band of *Dreigroschenoper* fame had now been replaced by a "medium-sized opera orchestra, and the song style . . . branched out towards both opera and cantata." Having run against scathing criticism by Nazi reviewers in all three cities, this winter fairy tale, in which Frau von Luber, the wicked witch, obviously personified a fascist, was taken off the repertories under Nazi pressure in early March.[18]

No sooner had *Der Silbersee* been reviled by the Nazi press than Weill was quick to point out that almost all the non-Nazi papers, not yet censured, praised his new work, and that even Nazi critics had restrained themselves. He thought that by the fall Hitler's government would have disappeared, for no one believed in its staying power. Hence his hopes for future German productions of *Der Silbersee* were very high, at least according to the correspondence with his publisher.[19] On the other hand, he already had his feelers out in Paris: There was potential for a French film with the firm of Pathé-Nathan, collaboration with the film director Jean Renoir, and a French *Bürgschaft* premiere. Weill had influential friends in Paris, such as the Vicomtesse Marie-Laure de Noailles, the patron of the arts; Darius Milhaud, the composer; and Le Corbusier, the architect.[20]

The decision was made for Weill in early March when friends intimated to him that he and his wife Lotte Lenya were on a Nazi blacklist and their arrest was imminent. Weill's friend, the Jewish conductor Hans Curjel, who himself would soon resettle in Zurich, recalls how Weill and Lenya asked him to store a suitcase full of precious books for them. Discovering that this was incriminating leftist literature, Curjel dumped them, one by one, at the side of Berlin's municipal Avus freeway. As Lenya made her way to Vienna to join her present lover, Weill himself, assisted by Caspar and Erika Neher, crossed the border into France on 22 March.[21]

During his first few months in Paris the composer had to contend with claims by his Austrian publishers, Universal Edition, to the effect that his former contract with them had become null and void because of Weill's sudden loss of German royalties. On these his generous advances from the Viennese firm had chiefly been based. The dispute ended relatively amiably with Weill being released from the contract for the period of one year (and then indefinitely); in the short run it meant the loss of past reliable income but ultimately a chance for new contractual arrangements, into which he entered forthwith.[22]

Although, as an exile in Paris, Weill generally kept his spirits high, he was artistically less successful than his former good fortune in France might have led him to expect, and he disappointed several of his contemporaries. Whereas the film plans with Renoir evaporated quickly, he was able to write music for a ballet, *Die sieben Todsünden,* for the plot and dialogue of which Brecht once again had been engaged, though having traveled up from Carona (Switzerland) for the purpose, he showed little enthusiasm. The work, financed by an eccentric Englishman whose wife, Tilly Losch, was the lead dancer, was premiered by "Les Ballets 1933" on the Champs Elysées in June and was a commercial failure. German exile Harry Graf Kessler found the music—whose high quality is still beyond dispute today—little different from that of *Die Dreigroschenoper.* When it opened in London in July, Weill showed himself to be content with its overall success there.[23]

But there were other setbacks. Certain of the French, nationalist and even fascist-inclined, were suspicious of Weill either because he was a Jew or because he was a man of leftist persuasion, or both.[24] Two new musical plays he completed by 1935, *Marie Galante* and *A Kingdom for a Cow,* became box-office failures in Paris and in London, where critics held his *Dreigroschenoper* in low regard. Hopes for a possible refuge in England, despite several visits there, were eventually dashed. An epic biblical play, *Der Weg der Verheissung,* which he started to work on in conjunction with stage director Max Reinhardt and poet Franz Werfel, caused him a never-ending string of frustrations. And although in early 1934 he had moved into a spacious house in Louveciennes near St. Germain and was not wanting for money, he was mostly without Lotte Lenya, from whom he had been divorced in September 1933. Realistically, the only things Weill could console himself with were a successful premiere of his Second Symphony (the last of his "Classical" works, composed in Europe), under the baton of Bruno Walter in Amsterdam in October 1934, and prospects for a successful professional career in the United States.[25]

II

Weill had fled to France in March 1933 because he was quite well-known there and had connections to people who would help him out. Paris was, in fact, a logical destination for other artists like him, for instance, Schoenberg, who also arrived there in May.[26] Other musicians emigrated to England, which was considered to be similarly safe from Nazi influence at that time, and so was Austria, although it was beginning to have indigenous fascist problems and Hitler was occasionally demonstrating an appetite for annexation.[27] But the number of countries in which one could hide from the Nazis was always limited by language barriers, the nature of one's art, and the relative unwillingness of strangers to extend a welcome. Prague, which became the home of many exiled German Social Democrats, briefly also received Brecht and later Stuckenschmidt, whereas hard-line Communists might try the Soviet Union. In view of possible Nazi aggression, which was, however thinly, already written on the wall, no one knew for how long a safe haven could be provided. Some artists, in fact, were later caught up with by the invading Nazis, as happened to the violinist Alma Maria Rosé, originally from Vienna, who was seized in France and sent to her death in Auschwitz, and to Kurt Gerron, the original Tiger Brown of *Die Dreigroschenoper,* who was captured in Holland, likewise to die in Auschwitz.[28]

Although Weill could probably have stayed in Paris profitably for a while longer, it had always been his dream to go to America, whose characteristic musical idiom, jazz, figured so prominently in his 1920s stage works. He was not lacking connections. Leopold Stokowski had conducted *Der Lindberghflug* with the Philadelphia Orchestra in April 1931, and although American critics had been less than kind, Weill, at that point optimistic, was hoping that later in the year Stokowski would also perform *Die Bürgschaft* in the city of brotherly love—a hope that did not materialize. But when Weill learned that American Broadway producers were becoming serious about acquiring the U.S. rights to *Die Dreigroschenoper* in 1932, he himself wanted to travel to New York to oversee its production. He still clung to this plan in early April 1933 in Paris, when the musical play was about to begin its Broadway run, which, however, turned out to be a disaster.[29] A year later he was again ready to move from Paris to Hollywood on short notice to join Josef von Sternberg and Marlene Dietrich in the production of a musical film for Paramount, a scheme that appears to have foundered on the untrustworthiness of Sternberg.[30]

When Kurt Weill and Lotte Lenya, who had finally rejoined him after her peripatetic life in southern Europe, arrived in New York in September 1935, they were greeted by a few proponents of avant-garde music who knew about their art and introduced to a wider circle of cognoscenti. Knowing his closest relatives to be safe, Weill immediately took to this land of his dreams, attempting to adjust to it as best he could and in defiance of all difficulties. His was a mentality that had helped him as an adolescent and was to see him through now. "Don't get too serious," he had written to his sister Ruth when but twenty years old, "don't set yourself too many goals and be too introspective. Rather, allow this beautiful, heavenly life to envelop you and, at all times, thank your Maker that you may be alive and derive joy from every little sun-ray. Joy is everything." Echoing this early belief, he remarked in May 1949: "Lenja and I came here in 1935 and fell immediately in love with this country, and my success here (which people usually ascribe to 'luck') is mostly due to the fact that I took a very positive and constructive attitude towards the American way of life and the cultural possibilities in this country."[31]

Weill and Lenya had to struggle against several odds in the first few years of their U.S. residency. Having lost their savings in Europe and being forced almost immediately to make a new living, the composer at first tried to rely on what reputation he had been able to build for himself in his protean European years. Yet in spite of that small if reliable group of modern-music admirers, he was soon to find out that his distinction as a "serious" composer would not carry him very far. When in December the sympathetic, New York-based League of Composers organized an all-Weill recital of operatic and theater music, in which Lenya sang parts from *Mahagonny* and other works, the reception was cold and no helpful contacts resulted.[32]

Weill experienced inordinate frustration with the one work he had put so much stock in while still in France, despite the annoying friction with coauthors Reinhardt and Werfel. With Lenya cast merely in two minor roles, *Der Weg der Verheissung* had been renamed *The Eternal Road* for Broadway and planned as a huge production. Then, although the U.S. production company was declared insolvent and Werfel returned to Europe already during 1936, Weill himself kept his hopes high for an artistically and commercially successful staging. Ultimately his musical score—already reduced by Reinhardt and Werfel—was prerecorded, to be broadcast each night through loudspeakers. The Old Testament musical opened in January 1937 at the Manhattan Opera House, far removed from Manhattan's theatrical mainstream. Initially it played to full houses, with music, including synagogue melodies, "harmonically much milder and more traditional than any of the German works." But it soon became obvious that financially it was not viable. In February, Weill complained to Lenya that "last week the box office went down from 29,000 to 22,000, which to me is a true sign that there is no real interest in this kind of show on the part of the public." And although many critics had reacted positively, the show closed on 15 May, leaving a tab of unrecoverable debts, and Weill himself had not earned a single cent.[33]

In May 1936 Weill and Lenya had been in Chapel Hill, North Carolina, to work with noted playwright Paul Green. Later in the year, through Green and others' help they had joined the innovative Group Theater in Connecticut, and Weill started composing a Broadway musical, *Johnny Johnson,* to Green's libretto. It opened at the 44th Street Theater in November and saw sixty-eight performances. And although this was on no account a bad record for a newcomer from Europe and Weill's sophisticated score is still remembered in music textbooks, on the whole the show was judged only moderately successful, and Weill's earnings were modest. Thereafter in January 1937, as poverty was still troubling the couple, Weill journeyed to Hollywood to try to earn money through work on a film score. After all, had Dietrich and Sternberg not wanted him to do this earlier, from France? But here Weill found the adjustment more difficult. "My first impression of this place is rather awful," he reported back to Lenya, "the scenery is magnificent, with mountains in the background, like Salzburg. But what they've built into it! It looks exactly like Bridgeport."[34]

His labor on the film lasted until June 1937, paying some essential bills, but halfway through his compositions Weill was informed that production of the movie was halted. When under the title *Blockade* it finally found its way into the cinemas, Weill's score had not been used. This meant that he had not been allowed to make himself an instant name, as he needed to do to duplicate his stellar European record quickly. While in Tinseltown, Weill refused to sell himself short, however, to other movie producers who might have offered him cheap and easy work, because "it's obvious I'm more expensive than all the others." Thinking himself supported in this by the remarkably musical Charlie Chaplin, who allegedly told him how much he admired his craft, Weill took solace in the fact that the quality of his music was too high to be used in commercial films, although financially, of course, this hurt him. This may have been precisely the problem: As a film composer, Weill was deceiving himself. Realistically, someone soon convinced him that he would really be happier, not to say richer, on Broadway. Reinvigorated, Weill returned to the East Coast and applied for his American citizenship from New York by late summer, via a short trip to Canada.[35]

In May 1938 Lenya wrote to Weill, who was just then again in Hollywood, that there was hardly anything left in their bank account.[36] But in October of that year, Weill's next musical, *Knickerbocker Holiday*, which he had written in cooperation with the renowned playwright Maxwell Anderson, opened on Broadway and ushered in a wave of spectacular successes. It featured the popular actor Walter Huston in 168 performances, and then went on a U.S. tour. Financially secure from 1939 on, Weill was allowed to savor his next achievement, *Lady in the Dark*, with lyrics by Ira Gershwin and book by Moss Hart, which opened on Broadway in January 1941. It utilized typically American themes such as indulgence in fashion magazines and the fashionableness of regularly visiting a Freudian psychoanalyst. Apart from pushing Weill into the "mainstream of Broadway musical theater," *Lady in the Dark* made the composer truly wealthy, netting him many times the average American income. In April of that year and as a symbol of their good fortune, Weill and Lenya bought Brook House, a home refurbished in an agreeably modern style on a fourteen-acre lot north of Manhattan, next to the Andersons, who had become close personal friends.[37] Was Weill's astonishing ascent due to his ability to fill the void Ira's brother George Gershwin had created after his death in July 1937?[38]

Lady in the Dark was important not least because it was the first of Weill's American ventures to generate incidental rewards of the kind he had already enjoyed in Europe. Songs from the musical were quickly popularized in recorded renditions by Benny Goodman, Danny Kaye, Eddie Duchin, Sammy Kaye, and Mildred Bailey, among others; notable among them was "My Ship," which entered the repertoire of all-time jazz standards. And although Weill, newly attuned to success, was on the verge of impatience with his agent Arthur Lyons in June 1941, the film rights of *Lady in the Dark* had already been sold to Paramount in May, for the highest price fetched by any Broadway play thus far.[39]

Indeed, this once again brought Weill back to the steamy studios of Hollywood, but also to some of their denizens who, like himself, originally hailed from Europe. In this case it was Marlene Dietrich, with whom, harking back to Paris and Berlin, he had almost worked several times before, and in whom he was now interested for the leading role in *One Touch of Venus*. This time, the story was coauthored with Ogden Nash and Sid Perelman—a fairy tale about an average young man who is pursued by a statue turned human, Venus, as she leads him to a tryst in a hotel room until she realizes that the vagaries of earthly life are not for her. There were several meetings and letter exchanges between Dietrich, Weill, and his producer, Cheryl Crawford, on both sides of the continent, from the summer of 1942 to that of 1943, with Dietrich acting the precious star and playing the Brecht–Weill song "Surabaya Johnny" on her musical saw. In the end she declined Weill's offer, most likely because she also wanted an option for the movie rights and was afraid to sing, if not to act, on a live Broadway stage.[40] The role then fell to Mary Martin (the mother of television classic *Dallas*'s Larry Hagman), who helped make this stage work another hit, after a Broadway opening on 7 October 1943 and, eventually, 567 performances. At the time, it was rivaled only by Rodgers and Hammerstein's *Oklahoma!* and eagerly accepted for film adaptation by United Artists. For 1943 alone, Weill earned $ 100,000.[41]

From now on it was summits and valleys, but Weill was philosophical enough to take adversity in stride. In 1943, a motion picture was made of his earlier musical, *Knickerbocker Holiday*, but even more important was the fact that one of its main melodies, "September Song," soon became an artistic and commercial triumph, with Bing Crosby recording it at the end of December. Meanwhile "Speak Low," from *One Touch of Venus*, had been featured by many different bands and singers, among them Frank Sinatra, Benny Goodman, Count Basie, and Guy Lombardo and His Royal Canadians, over fifty times in the month of December alone, and by January 1944 it had reached the "hit parade." At that time, Weill reported to his parents that *One Touch of Venus* was "the most successful musical of the season," although, in fairness, it was still being strongly rivaled by *Oklahoma!* and also *Carmen Jones*. The downturn came in March 1945, when his latest musical, *The Firebrand of Florence*, based on the life of the roguish sculptor Benvenuto Cellini, disappointed audiences, so that it had to close in April. Nonetheless, Weill himself thought it musically to be "the best thing I have written in years, a real opera, with large choirs and ensemble skits, full of melodic invention."[42]

The postwar years, from May 1945 to his death in April 1950, found Weill in a situation of ever-changing fortunes, the highlight of which was a continual stream of wealth and the low point his failing health. What he said to his parents at the time of the *Firebrand of Florence* fiasco today reads like an omen for the alternation of extremes ahead: "I have long ago become used to this up-and-down curve of success, and I have felt for some time now that after the giant successes of the last years a reversal was in order."[43] As a U.S. citizen, Weill's works were again being played in a haphazardly reconstructed Germany, albeit only his older ones, and selectively at that.[44] Although he went on a trip to Europe in the spring of 1947, he pointedly left Germany off his itinerary—one can only imagine his grief over the moral entanglements of his homeland and the destruction of his beloved Berlin. Back in the United States, his favorite younger brother Hans died in March 1947 of what essentially was high blood pressure. Weill was fated to succumb to the same disease on 3 April 1950, after significant honors that should have been his had been denied to him. One was membership in the American Academy of Arts and Letters, to which, unlike Hindemith, he was not elected.[45]

III

If individuals define themselves socially in terms of their relations with contemporaries, then such definitions, for artists in exile from Nazi Germany, took on a special significance.[46] For it was not only their private persona that was affected and shaped by the new environment but also their creativity. The cover of a recent book on German musicians in exile significantly shows Kurt Weill sitting at a piano in New York, during rehearsals for *One Touch of Venus* in 1943, surrounded by happy men and women, coartists as much as acolytes.[47] Whereas this picture conveys the image of the immigrant Weill, the optimist who admirably accommodates himself to new circumstances and makes the best of them—an image this study also subscribes to in large measure—matters were never as easy as they appeared after the conclusion of a successful Broadway show or the signing of a lucrative contract with a Hollywood film producer. In the book's photograph, while most people around Weill are smiling, the composer himself plays the piano with a somber expression on his face, as if wanting to say: For the rest of you, it is all right to enjoy yourselves, but if you only knew how hard I have to struggle.

As we already know, struggle he did, to complete and have his works performed, to compete with the others, to make a home for himself and Lenya near New York, to guarantee a sufficient income for them both. What may have been somewhat overlooked in a characterization of this outwardly contented man are the more complex aspects of the dealings he had with his colleagues, impresarios, and patrons, European émigrés, many of them Jewish, and, not least, with his wife Lotte Lenya and other women, and how these may have interacted with his psyche. Particularly regarding his relationship with women, the timely publication of a rich exchange of letters between himself and Lenya, spanning more than two decades, now affords us new insights.[48]

Although, after his emigration to the United States, Kurt Weill was generally perceived as congenial in relations with native-born Americans, he tended to be reserved and sometimes downright hostile in the company of other émigrés, not only because of the potential element of rivalry in a struggle for survival but also because of their often brash and brazen attitudes, and because they reminded him too much of a past he was strenuously trying to forget.[49] Especially after he had become well-known by the time World War II broke out, Weill was frequently seen amid other exiled personages of standing, as in April 1943, when the tenth anniversary of the Nazi book burning was marked at Hunter College in New York. The author Fritz von Unruh was there, as was Bertolt Brecht, and the actress Elisabeth Bergner and other stage celebrities, and manuscripts by Thomas Mann and Albert Einstein were auctioned.[50] One does not know how Weill was feeling at that time, but it has now come to light that on several occasions he expressed his repugnance over having had to share the company of fellow émigrés, especially successful ones, such as film composer Erich Wolfgang Korngold. For example, after attending a concert by his old acquaintance Otto Klemperer and thereafter a casino in Los Angeles in February 1937, he wrote home to Lenya: "Marlene [Dietrich] was there, but I didn't talk to her. . . . In the greenroom with Klemperer was the wunderkind Korngold grown old. I put on my haughtiest face and stayed for only two minutes. All of them are abundantly disgusting."[51]

Weill could be intemperate to his professional associates and risk putting himself in the wrong, as his exchange with agent Arthur Lyons, over the alleged delay in signing a film deal for *Lady in the Dark* of June 1941, shows.[52] He may also have accused Meyer Weisgal unjustly, the producer of *The Eternal Road* who had been returning to the United States on the same boat with him, when preparations of the musical score were going badly in August 1936, which Weill took to be "the most terrible humiliation."[53] Other collaborators on projects of his fared little better. Although his relationship with librettist Ira Gershwin is generally portrayed as productive and amiable, Weill frequently complained to Lenya about his laziness and apparently confronted Gershwin with it, risking something of a showdown.[54] Weill called Dietrich "a stupid cow, conceited like all Germans," because she was vacillating too long with regard to *One Touch of Venus*.[55] Franz Werfel was to him a "beast" because of the cuts earmarked for his score of *The Eternal Road*, but he reserved even worse epithets for the main architect of the biblical play, Max Reinhardt.[56] Whereas before his flight to Paris Weill admitted to not having had "much of a contact" with the famous theater director (which may have irked him even then), after a workshop meeting in Salzburg in August 1935, also attended by Werfel and Weisgal, he described him as "lazy," evidently not smelling "enough money," and added gratuitously that "for quite a while now his veneration of money has made me feel like puking." Having battled him, like Werfel, because of the inordinate reductions in his music, he held him as responsible as he did Weisgal for the demise of the stage work when it was finally running on Broadway early in 1937: "Reinhardt keeps behaving like a big flaming asshole. He's furious because he isn't getting any money, but of course he won't lift a finger."[57]

Nor were other musicians spared, especially if they were in danger of up-staging him. Klemperer, who had taken a qualified interest in Weill in the outgoing Weimar period and in late 1933 even performed Weill's *Kleine Dreigroschenmusik* with the Los Angeles Philharmonic Orchestra, was denigrated as a conductor in 1937 and at the height of World War II was remembered to Lenya merely as of "fake voice" and "stupid chicken eyes." Moreover, at that time Weill made disparaging remarks about Stravinsky's ballet music, concluding that the self-exiled Russian had "lost his talent."[58] Also notable is the uncharitable sentiment Weill reserved for composer, critic, and scholar Theodor Wiesengrund Adorno, because Adorno wanted him to resume his historic collaboration with Brecht in April 1942. Adorno to him was another "flaming asshole"—evidently a favorite metaphor of Weill's.[59]

Weill's relationship with the vastly successful George Gershwin was especially problematic, because here was a composer at least as gifted as himself, and one with a similar penchant both for "serious" and Broadway music. Gershwin, hardly two years older than Weill, had had a luncheon meeting with him in April 1928 after traveling from Paris to Berlin. Until that time, already safely ensconced as one of the chief proponents of "Weimar Culture,"[60] Weill himself had found nothing but good things to say about his American counterpart.[61] But after *Die Dreigroschenoper* had flopped on Broadway in the spring of 1933, Weill became suspicious that Gershwin, who was then dominating Broadway and living in New York quite ostentatiously, had had something to do with it. A year later in Paris, perhaps to defeat that nagging suspicion, Weill clung to the version told to him by a new American acquaintance that in reality *Die Dreigroschenoper* had been "a tremendous success in New York," that everyone thought that it represented "a new path," because they were "tired of all that jazz music, including Gershwin, and that my music would be the only sort that could take its place."[62] This self-delusion may still have had a hold on him when Weill actually met the composer of *An American in Paris* at a party in his opulent apartment on 72nd Street. Gershwin remembered Weill, of course, and told him that he had enjoyed the recent recording of *Die Dreigroschenoper* songs, except for the "squitchadicka" voice of the leading lady. Unbeknownst to Gershwin, that lady of course was Lenya, who was standing at Weill's side.[63]

But although Gershwin facilitated for Weill and Lenya important contacts and his *Porgy and Bess,* just premiered, did not fail to make a great impression on Weill, the émigré from Europe rightly felt that in the United States, Gershwin would always be his senior. Hence Weill continued his malicious remarks about Gershwin to Lenya, even though the entire Gershwin clan was taking an increasing interest in him, and George's older brother, the lyricist Ira Gershwin, would soon enter into a working relationship with Weill. As a malignant brain tumor was slowly affecting George in the early summer of 1937, this was more often manifested in the composer's erratic behavior. Not knowing the cause of this, Kurt Weill was not amused. "Gershwin behaved obnoxiously," he wrote to Lenya a few weeks before George's death in Hollywood, "but this bumpkin is just too dumb even to bother with."[64]

One of the colleagues with whom Weill could have socialized, but did not, was Arnold Schoenberg. At least one historian has maintained that Weill was a former student of Schoenberg.[65] But Weill never did study with the older master. This does not mean that Schoenberg did not influence him. There was a time in Weill's early development when he felt himself strongly drawn to Schoenberg. This important juncture seems to have been in June 1919. At the beginning of that month Weill had written to his brother Hans that Strauss, Pfitzner, and the conductor Arthur Nikisch were "our most significant musicians," although he already found Strauss somewhat "artificially modern."[66] But less than two weeks later Weill told of a meeting with Hermann Scherchen, who had advised him to study in Vienna with Schoenberg, "the recognized champion of a new music."[67] At the end of the month Weill, according to another letter to his brother, felt that Strauss paled in comparison with Schoenberg, who offered him such new insights that he was rendered speechless. Sooner or later, he would have to travel to Vienna.[68]

Although this never came to pass, it has been alleged that Schoenberg directly influenced Weill's earliest, serious compositions, such as his long unperformed First Symphony (1921). By 1925—Schoenberg was now known as the inventor of the twelve-tone system—Weill, in essays for *Der deutsche Rundfunk,* described Schoenberg as "the most hotly controversial personality of the modern-music scene," nonetheless acknowledging him as the true successor of his own teacher, Busoni, just deceased.[69] Two years later, Schoenberg too seems to have found something to appreciate in Weill's approach to composing, so that he recommended him, albeit unsuccessfully, for membership in the Preussische Akademie der Künste.[70] Schoenberg's attitude changed, however, after Weill had begun his association with Bertolt Brecht, which to him symbolized opening up to a mass audience, whereas Schoenberg was becoming more elitist. In the last years of the republic, writes Alan Chapman, Weill and Schoenberg were "on a collision course." In fact, according to one former student, Schoenberg was using examples from *Die Dreigroschenoper* to demonstrate to his Berlin master class what was "craftsmanlike trash."[71]

In September 1934—Weill was now in Paris, and Schoenberg in the United States—Weill promised to honor an earlier pledge to Universal Edition in Vienna, their mutual publisher, to assist Schoenberg's son Georg. No one knows if this ever came about.[72] Later, on his several sojourns in Los Angeles, Weill never once bothered to visit Schoenberg, who was of course teaching at the University of California and living in Brentwood, between Hollywood and Santa Monica, where Weill usually worked. Weill was quite aware of Schoenberg's presence, for in 1940 he reemphasized his own, anti-elitist, approach to composing music, in contrast to that of Schoenberg, who, he said, was writing "for a time fifty years after his death."[73] Ultimately, Weill must have felt slighted when in April 1947 Schoenberg was awarded the Distinguished Achievement Prize of the National Institute of Arts and Letters.[74]

If after 1933 Weill's relationship with Schoenberg was virtually nonexistent, the one with Brecht was highly problematic. From the beginning of their cooperation in 1927, there were always three points of contention. One was that Weill was never as radically leftist as the dramatist. The second was that Weill always held the music of their stage works to be more important than the ideologically freighted texts. And third, Brecht habitually managed to outsmart Weill in money matters, a tactic the composer always tended to be slow to catch on to. In pre-Hitlerian Germany, tensions came to a head when, during the Berlin rehearsals for *Aufstieg und Fall der Stadt Mahagonny* in December 1931, Brecht hit the camera of a press photographer, who took a picture of the two, from his hands, screaming in a fit against Weill: "I'll throw the fake Richard Strauss in full war paint down the stairs." Brecht disapproved of Caspar Neher as his successor in the role of librettist for Weill's operas; he was less dismissive of Georg Kaiser. In any event, Weill and Brecht's subsequent cooperation on *Die sieben Todsünden* in Paris during the spring of 1933 turned out to be a limp affair; allegedly Brecht did it only because of an acute lack of money.[75]

Before Brecht retreated for some years to Scandinavia, he and Weill met again briefly in New York in late 1935. The occasion was the premiere of *Die Mutter,* which Brecht had cowritten with Hanns Eisler, the unrelentingly Marxist student of Schoenberg. Although a renewed cooperation between Brecht and Weill at that time was not beyond the realm of possibilities, it was cut short after Weill had observed Brecht's autocratic treatment of members of the New York Theater Union, which had produced *Die Mutter.*[76]

In the years to follow, as Weill was becoming well-known in the United States and Brecht was doing less well in his European exile, the original production rights for *Die Dreigroschenoper* had been put in doubt because of changing conditions on the European continent. In a letter to Brecht dated February 1939 Weill claimed that the musical had been performed a number of times in non-Hitlerian Europe, without him, Weill, having received a cent. Thereafter, Brecht kept hinting at a possible renewal of artistic cooperation, perhaps in the shape of a Hollywood film version of *Auf-*

stieg und Fall der Stadt Mahagonny. Reportedly, Weill had come to the conclusion that however little he himself was earning from any European productions of their earlier joint works, Brecht was making not a penny more—a situation that was far from the truth.[77]

In March 1941, as Brecht was getting ready to move to the United States, along with wife Helene Weigel, two children, and his Danish mistress Ruth Berlau, Weill was successfully solicited to contribute money to the task of relocating Brecht. The extended Brecht family arrived "half-starved" in Santa Monica, via Siberia, in July, helped along by artists and intellectuals such as Dorothy Thompson, Fritz Lang, Fritz Kortner, Ernst Lubitsch, Lion Feuchtwanger, Brecht's former lover Elisabeth Hauptmann—and, of course, Kurt Weill.[78]

And in early 1942, Brecht was ready to collaborate with Weill again, if solely on his very own terms—for he had already begun independent negotiations with the African-American producer Clarence Muse late in 1941.[79] Brecht was interested in staging a black American version of *Die Dreigroschenoper*, with Paul Robeson in the leading role. But Weill was skeptical, because he disliked Brecht's proposal of a simple translation of the German original libretto into English, preferring, instead, a total American adaptation, and even that he thought to be much too sophisticated for black American audiences to appreciate.[80] Specifically, on 31 March Weill wrote to Muse that he would have to retain "complete control of the musical changes, the arrangements, the orchestrations and all questions of the musical interpretation." He also wanted to make sure "that you choose a cast which will do justice to my score."[81] This was timely advice, for a few days later Weill received a letter, ironically from Wiesengrund Adorno, the former student of Alban Berg who had habitually polemicized against jazz and would continue to do so in his lifetime. Not only did Adorno urge Weill to go ahead with a black production of *Die Dreigroschenoper* for the sake of Brecht's own material well-being, but he also insisted that the music be rearranged in true American jazz fashion, restyled and reimprovised by a thoroughly Negro band, affecting, in equal parts "text as well as music."[82] Such changes would have benefited Brecht, as they would have amounted to an abandonment of Weill's original artistic autonomy for the sake of Brecht's text. Meanwhile, Weill suspected with good reason that Brecht had already conspired with Muse in a translation of whatever German libretto he selected into the American vernacular, to the detriment of the music.[83]

By the beginning of April Weill was waxing sarcastic about the whole affair to Lenya, denouncing "the good old swinish Brecht method."[84] However, Brecht then wrote to Weill: "I would like to propose to you that we resume our cooperation and liquidate the misunderstandings and tiresome semi-separations, precipitated so easily in such unfortunate times as ours, and because of the distance."[85] Weill was again feeling sorry for Brecht and was inclined to hand him a monthly stipend for some time; Lenya solidly opposed this.[86] When the draft for a contract arrived from Brecht's agent, George Marton, Weill found it in complete disregard of his own concerns, "as crooked and exploitative as only contracts with Communists can be." Telling Brecht that people were free to do with *Die Dreigroschenoper* whatever they liked, he refused to sign.[87] All Marton could do to save face was to tell Weill that it was Brecht "who needs the royalties, as you realize, very badly."[88] Indeed, as Weill later explained somewhat apologetically to Paul Robeson's wife Eslanda, if the Marton contract had become legal, it would have been for Brecht, not Weill, to reap any financial rewards.[89]

Thereafter, Brecht continued with his customary rudeness in his dealings with other people on the West Coast, including his old mentor Erwin Piscator and actresses Elisabeth Bergner and Luise Rainer. Predictably, relations between him and Weill remained cool, although the composer visited him in California in October 1942, and Brecht, Weill, Lenya, and other German émigré artists collaborated in programs of the U.S. Office of War Information for the sake of the war effort in April 1943.[90] Two other schemes of Brecht's had floundered by late 1944. One was to have Weill write music for his old play *Der gute Mensch von Sezuan* and have it staged on Broadway. The other was a planned collaboration on *Der gute Soldat Schweik*. By this time, Weill had had enough of Brecht's cheating ways.[91] "I am afraid that Brecht's insistence on preserving certain rights for himself would make any moving-picture backing or any eventual movie-sale impossible," remarked the Hollywood-experienced composer already in January.[92] In May 1945, after Brecht had unsuccessfully tried his hand at a Hollywood script about the French Resistance, the two men met again in Los Angeles, when Weill found him "nice, but awfully dull. The same old doubletalk."[93] The relationship remained stalled at this negative level until Weill's death. "I almost never see Brecht," Weill reported to Caspar Neher's wife Erika in July 1946, "he is the same old megalomaniacal egotist and still obsessed with his old stupid theories, without a trace of character development."[94] In September 1947 the dramatist returned to Europe as a consequence of his disastrous hearing before the Committee on Un-American Activities.[95] From 1948 to 1949, Brecht successfully acquired for himself Weill's old rights and share of the royalties for *Die Dreigroschenoper* in Germany, a case of fraud Weill had to entrust to the expertise of his lawyers.[96] No doubt to discuss this matter, Weill evidently tried to meet with Brecht on a European journey planned for 1950, but the composer's death in April 1950 put an appropriate end to one of the most bizarre relationships in the modern history of culture.[97]

IV

From the time he first met her in 1924, Kurt Weill's most critical interpersonal relationship was always with his wife, Lotte Lenya. She moved him as a person more than did anybody else, and to a large extent she directed his artistic energy, influencing, in particular, his musical sensitivity, also with regard to her own creative talents. She did this both by virtue of her strong erotic power and her own irrepressible artistic autonomy. The complexity of their relationship may have served as a catalyst in these processes. As if under the dictates of a shared Karma, they were simultaneously at extreme opposites and ineluctably drawn to each other. "Their union was symbiotic," observed John Simon, and they came to lead "a marriage of sometimes untrue bodies, but always true minds."[98]

Karoline Wilhelmine Charlotte Blamauer was born in 1898 in a shabby suburb of Vienna as the daughter of a poverty-stricken working-class couple; her father, a coachman who often came home drunk, appears to have abused her sexually as a child. To escape from the drab family surroundings, she joined a small neighborhood circus in which she danced and stood on her head and did a low-wire act. Thus she was drawn to the world of theater and what later would be called show business and her life. In her early teens she became a child prostitute, although the extent of that activity has never been ascertained. After being taken to Zurich by an aunt at the age of fifteen, the slight, nimble girl managed to receive ballet lessons, was accepted by the corps de ballet of the municipal theater, and soon was dancing minor parts. Richard Révy, the theater director, noticed her and assigned her small acting roles for the stage. Eventually, he ended up teaching her; he also became her lover. At the time this was happening, during World War I, Karoline nicknamed him "Vanja" (after the character in Chekhov's play they were studying); he in turn named her "Lenja." Inspired by her mentor, who had preceded her there, Lotte Lenja, as she now was calling herself, sought out more promising prospects in Berlin during 1921. The German capital was then at the beginning of its famous jazz, cabaret, and theater culture. Soon Karoline was dancing and playing small parts on several of the less prominent stages, until Révy introduced her to Georg Kaiser, one of Germany's foremost dramatists. Kaiser took a liking to her and soon invited her to move in with his family at their house in Grünheide, outside Berlin. It was here on one summer day in 1924 that she met Kurt Weill, who came for a working weekend with Kaiser. "People have sometimes asked me," she said later, "was it love at first sight. I don't think so. . . . If you talk about love, that takes a little time." Kurt and Karoline were married in Berlin on 28 January 1926.[99]

Lotte Lenya (as she would later be called in the United States) was sexy but not beautiful, endowed with charm and wit and spunk; her lasciviousness to many was an additional attraction. With her early sexual experience and her ever-apparent need to express her sexuality openly, she, even at the time of her marriage to Weill, who was two years younger, had the makings of a femme fatale. By contrast, Kurt's sheltered upbringing in a respected Jewish middle-class family in smalltown Dessau had imbued him, by the time he was an adolescent, with an awe for innocent girls, but not without some of the customary antifeminine prejudices of the German *Bürgertum*. Probably not initiated to active sex until he met Lenya, he idolized girls and constructed the image of a dream woman who, he might have known, rarely existed in real life. He preferred girls who would not think too hard, he romanticized to his brother Hans in May 1919. "Intelligent girls" who knew how to converse well were merely blue stockings; what an artist like him needed was a girl who embodied a combination of sensuality and spirituality, that which fascinated Goethe as the "eternally feminine" and was missing from the merely intelligent ones. A year later he joked in a letter to his sister Ruth when he drew up a caricature: He might well marry one of her girlfriends, as long as she was "very pretty, very stupid, not musical, and with a dowry of one million."[100]

Had Kurt found a dream girl in Lenya? From the beginning, their marriage was unconventional, for to the same extent that Weill withdrew to his inner-directed creativity, she sought compensation through unbridled promiscuity, while they were both working in Berlin. The conflict is encapsulated in the following exchange, which, according to Lenya, occurred in their dwelling as the 1920s were drawing to a close. Often having left her to her own devices and being habitually late for dinner, Weill was asked by Lenya whether her presence around him meant anything to him and whether he actually loved her. Weill's oft-quoted incredulous answer was: "But darling, you come right after my music!"[101] Although this kind of reply may be typical of any fanatically creative spirit and indeed may be of timeless validity (it was stated publicly in 1993 by jazz saxophonist Sonny Rollins),[102] it made Lenya feel second best and encouraged her numerous extramarital affairs, apparently with Weill's knowledge. Reproached about this by a mutual friend, she said: "I don't cheat on Kurt. He knows exactly what's going on."[103] At this point it is difficult to determine who did more harm to whom, for harm there surely was—notwithstanding the many assurances, not least by the couple's biographers, that everything was always all right because it was based on candidness and mutual understanding.[104] "There was a lot of hurt in his eyes," another common friend recalled when dwelling on how, back in those Berlin days, he had asked Weill about his marriage and the conversation had inevitably drifted to the subject of Lenya's chronic philandering.[105]

Kurt's reaction to years of Lenya's nymphomania, while he was having raucous success with stage works that were themselves defying convention, was that he fell in love with Erika Neher, stage designer Caspar Neher's wife, in the fall of 1931, as they were working on *Die Bürgschaft*.[106] Lenya had just been in Russia, and Erika Neher had her own need for succor, as her husband was showing signs of infidelity.[107]

In his recent biography of Weill, Ronald Taylor maintains that the affair was virtually one-sided in that Erika Neher needed a shoulder to cry on whereas Weill himself did his best to console her without maximum commitment.[108] But letters by Weill to Frau Neher in the Weill-Lenya Research Center well beyond Weill's and Lenya's arrival in New York in September 1935 prove differently: Notwithstanding his sworn and necessary companionship with Lenya, Weill appears to have been passionately in love with Erika, who was three years younger. Thus one day before Hitler's political takeover—Weill being despondent for professional but even more so personal reasons, for Lenya was with her current lover—the composer confided to Erika: "Because I'm always alone and can't often talk to you about it, what I'm experiencing now is something like taking lessons in human degradation. . . . But you protect me from that, my good angel. . . . This honest and great passion, this certainty that there is still such a thing as beauty, truth, and love . . . I am always filled with gratitude toward you, my dearest, sweetest, most tender, richest little angel."[109] From Paris in May, he wrote to her (who had just driven him to the French border with her husband Caspar): "Little angel, dearest, most beloved, sweetest angel . . . the thought of you makes me quiet and happy, and my thoughts of you are sad but very beautiful."[110] And from New York, where she was then sending him her most passionate letters, he let her know in May 1936 that if he had his way, he would return to her at once, "to help you with my deep, strong love."[111] After she had told him that it would be best if she stopped the correspondence, he protested: "This would be quite terrible for me. . . . The other day, when I met L., I had to think how utterly inconceivable it would be right now to live with anybody else but you."[112] He expressed a strong sexuality of his own: "Every fiber in my body is waiting for you, for the reunion with you, this wonderful, singular experience, which such a union with you means for me."[113]

To be fair to Lenya, she was, for some of this time (from April 1932 to October 1934) involved in one of the more meaningful love affairs of her life, deep enough, at least, formally to undo her marriage with Weill, which occurrence, until she and Kurt emigrated to New York, was sufficiently traumatic for Weill to cause him to cling to Erika. It must not be underestimated that from January 1926 on, Kurt and Lenya's marriage had been corroded to a point where, in June 1933, they filed for divorce in Berlin and legally had their union dissolved in September.[114]

Lenya met Otto von Pasetti, the son of an Austrian colonel, during a Vienna production of *Aufstieg und Fall der Stadt Mahagonny* in April 1932, in which he, a handsome tenor of twenty-nine, was cast as Jim, with herself playing Jenny. "That's a nice looking boy," she whispered to an acquaintance in the wings, and immediately he knew there was trouble.[115] Apart from show business, Pasetti and Lenya shared a love of gambling, something that was anathema to the strictly brought-up composer. For months before and after Hitler's assumption of power, which was such a critical juncture for Weill, Lenya and Pasetti spent time together, most of it outside Germany and in gambling casinos and, even while he was in Paris, out of Weill's own sight, but with some of his money. Perhaps because of their former "agreement," and because Pasetti promised to help in the liquidation of his and Lenya's Berlin property, Weill magnanimously invited both lovers to star in the Paris staging of *Mahagonny Songspiel* (also known as *Das kleine Mahagonny,* first performed in 1927) in June 1933. At this time she proceeded to disappoint even Pasetti by entering into a passionate lesbian relationship with fellow Austrian Tilly Losch, with whom she had performed in *Die sieben Todsünden* just a few weeks earlier. There is a tragic irony in the fact that although Lenya seems to have been almost willing to have a child with Pasetti, a thought that devastated Weill, he wanted her (and, if unavoidable, Pasetti) to be near him while in Paris. On the other hand, Lenya seems to have regretted her divorce from Weill soon after it had become legal, the more so as Pasetti was turning increasingly into a rogue, one who would eventually defraud the Weills with the money they had entrusted to him. In the fall of 1934 Lenya, by herself, went to a Paris pension, where she cut her wrists. For a short period, the affair with Pasetti being over, she once again belonged to Weill alone.[116]

But then she met the expatriate German painter Max Ernst, and her newest relationship was under way, until the spring of 1935. "Sexual energy she knew something about," writes her biographer Donald Spoto, "and apparently she allayed any fears about impotence—so successfully, in fact, that his erotic obsession for her even eclipsed his work for several weeks that winter." Ernst being seven years her senior, Spoto likens him to the classic father figure that she had sought in Révy and perhaps even Weill, who again looked upon the new situation, half bemused, half sad, and also needing her in his own special way, very much despite himself.[117]

Once in the United States, Lenya went on a binge of mostly superficial affairs, which she usually initiated and terminated at will, and with no regard for Weill. Taylor speaks of Lenya's "restless craving for other men"—indeed only few of the probably countless names of these are known—from 1936 to 1950.[118] The first was Paul Green, the North Carolina playwright, whom she favored around the end of summer 1936 while staying with new friends in Connecticut; Weill of course knew about it (while his relationship with Erika Neher was just ending), but Green's wife evidently did not.[119] There was a Billy Jones, whom she referred to as "wild animal Bill," and with whom she impulsively drove off to Texas in 1937.[120] In 1942, twenty-year-old Howard Schwartz was attracted to her presence (he could have been her son); when he was killed as a member of the U.S. Air Force in 1943 she seemed heartbroken.[121] Also during 1942, while on a theater tour through the U.S. heartland, she dallied with one of the actors playing a Nazi villain; in the summer of 1944, more seriously, she conquered Quentin Anderson, the just-separated son of their great friend Maxwell Anderson. Even as the Duchess in the *The Firebrand of Florence,* a role Weill had custom-designed for her early in 1945, she could not resist carrying on with one of the chorus singers backstage.[122]

It has been said that part of the reason for Lenya's carnal romps in the United States lay with her new professional unhappiness.[123] Although there is some truth in this, she would scarcely have behaved differently had she been extremely successful in show business since coming to the United States in the autumn of 1935, for she had exhibited a similar pattern while in the limelight in Europe. On the other hand, her new state of relative obscurity vis-à-vis Weill's incremental successes contributed to a feeling of insecurity that may have been compounded by an already bad conscience over her habitual adultery, yet also by occasional signs of infidelity on the part of Weill. It was a vicious cycle, with the inevitable consequence of more adultery and an ever lower self-esteem.

Whereas Weill's music was universal, needing no refinement in foreign-language classes, Lenya, as an actress, was severely limited by her German accent, even though, as a singer—as with Marlene Dietrich—this could be said to be charming. But even that concession by Americans amounted to little more than condescension. "It is too difficult for actors with her originality," remarked Weill realistically in 1949, but he added, dubiously, that she had made "a perfect adjustment" and was "contented taking part in my work as she always did."[124]

It was not until January 1937 that Lenya was engaged on stage in the two minor roles of *The Eternal Road,* which had a medium-term and economically disastrous run. Then, employed as a soubrette at the New York club Le Ruban Bleu, she was featuring standards from *Die Dreigroschenoper, Aufstieg und Fall der Stadt Mahagonny,* and Marc Blitzstein's *I've Got the Tune,* and she also premiered Weill's new song, "The Right Guy for Me," from his recent film work in Hollywood. She was thus once again utterly dependent on Kurt Weill, whom she had actually remarried in a simple ceremony on 19 January. For her nightclub work, she received good notices in the local papers, but this particular job was over after only four weeks.[125]

There were more nightclub dates to come her way, and during the war she took on a small role as a European maid (which allowed for a German accent) in the play *Candle in the Wind,* starring Helen Hayes; it was written by Maxwell Anderson, who charitably had kept her special talents in mind. The play opened in Boston in mid-September 1941 and then ran in New York for a respectable ninety-five performances. In 1942 came Lenya's months-long tour with that show through mostly midwestern and southern states.[126] If any of this work did not bestow national acclaim on the actress, the negative reactions to her in *The Firebrand of Florence* in 1945 mortified her, a role to which both she and Weill had looked forward with great anticipation (after he had had to labor to get that concession from lyricist Ira Gershwin).[127] Close to the end of Weill's career, Lenya had profited artistically through singing songs or playing parts from her husband's European and newer American scores, apart from having influenced and inspired him. However, unlike back in the Old Country, she had not once succeeded in starring as one of the leading ladies in any of his post-1935 plays—instead, those roles had all fallen to such Anglo-American actresses as Mary Martin, Gertrude Lawrence, and Helen Hayes.

Lenya's companionship agreement with Weill theoretically entitled him to the same sexual liberties that she was arrogating to herself, with the decisive difference, of course, that the composer's greatest need was to compose and be emotionally secure rather than to wear himself out in steamy amours. However, vexed by Lenya's continuous adventures, whether serious or not, and having had to leave the other great love of his life, Erika Neher, behind, Weill too succumbed to temptation whenever he was away from Lenya for a significant length of time. Usually this was during his extended stays in Hollywood, where ambitious young starlets easily were his, who thought him to be an up-and-coming film composer with some influence. How many young beauties he bedded there is not known, but in accordance with their principle of mutual honesty, Lenya knew about it and does not appear to have minded, as long as it did not get serious.[128]

But serious it did get, if not with a starlet. Toward the end of Kurt Weill's life, the affair—another irony in that couple's joint biography—came to involve an old acquaintance of Lenya. When after her romance with Max Ernst, Lenya had become restless in Weill's house in Louveciennes in March 1935 and Weill himself was briefly in London, he had urged her to visit the Révy couple in Berlin, to recuperate after a minor operation.[129] Lenya's old mentor and paramour, Richard Révy, had by then wed a second wife, Alma ("Jo") Staub-Terlinden, daughter of a Swiss art patron who was born in 1911 and, like Lenya, had taken ballet lessons. Because of rheumatic fever she had had to abandon a dancing career and had gone into costume designing before marrying Révy. They had had a son, Thomas, before immigrating to Los Angeles as a protest against Nazism; neither of them was Jewish.[130]

When Weill was again in Hollywood in June 1944 he looked the couple up, encouraged in this by Lenya. She asked Kurt to tell them that she would write, "eventually."[131] In several letters from then on, Weill reported to Lenya, innocently enough, on occasional lunches and dinners with the Révys, but also on drives to the beach in Santa Monica with Alma "Jo" and her son Thomas, now entering his teens. Lenya kept promising to write but never actually did.[132] Undoubtedly she was finding writing impossible as she was coming to realize that the relationship with Jo was in the process of becoming more to Kurt than one of the typically superficial Hollywood flings. One first sign of alarm to Kurt must have been Lenya's letter to him of 7 July in which she wished him "fun" with Jo at the ocean, "as long as it stays in the limit of not forgetting . . . you know what I mean."[133] Some two weeks later Lenya wrote to Weill that she was "jealous" of Thomas, giving him the cryptic message that she hoped he did not love the boy more than he loved her. Weill replied that it was "sweet of you to say that you are jealous of Thomas." And as if to assuage her fears, he added: "Sometimes, on my way to Ira, I am having lunch with Joe and about once a week we go to the beach. She is nice and quiet and doesn't bother me when I want to be alone."[134]

Weill continued his visits and excursions in the company of members of the Révy family, evidently seeing a good deal of Richard as well, while Lenya continued to promise to write.[135] It was becoming apparent that what drew the composer to the former ballet dancer were exactly those qualities Lenya lacked: finer, more delicate features, fairer hair, a quiet, perhaps for him ideally soothing, disposition, and greater depth—in any case, not the nerve-grating dynamo that Lenya could be.[136] Above all, it seems that Jo was totally dedicated to Kurt and to him alone, rather than spreading her favors all over the landscape as did Lenya. Although Weill, during his years in the

United States, was usually hesitant to use the word "European" in a positive sense, this attribute described for him the obviously still very withdrawn Révy couple, as opposed to loud "Broadway-Americans."[137] Perhaps Jo Révy did not challenge Weill's creativity as did Lenya, but neither did she insult his pride and violate his sensibilities. During a visit to California in the fall of 1944 Lenya had become fully aware of the changed situation, even though Weill kept trying to tell her later that there was "nothing for you to be worried about."[138]

As long as Weill remained on the West Coast, he went on seeing Jo Révy, and after he had moved back home to New City, the lovers maintained a correspondence, thus far unavailable to scholarship. Early in 1950, when Weill was in fact planning a vacation in California, Lenya became genuinely afraid of what by that time had clearly become a long-term relationship and an acute threat to their marriage. So she warned him that should he travel, she would not be there on his return. He duly canceled his visit.[139]

Did the frustration elevate his blood pressure? For merely a few months later Kurt Weill lay dying. In the New York hospital on 3 April, Lenya was at his bedside when he asked her: "Do you really love me?" "Only you," she replied.[140] After a few days, at the funeral, a black-veiled woman emerged from a limousine. Characteristically, Lenya had had the decency to notify her rival of long standing. Having taken a long look at the woman, Lenya asked an old friend: "What did he see in her?" And the friend replied: "Lenya, it's very simple. He found in her the qualities you don't have: the loyalty, the faithfulness, and so on."[141] This must have been the most devastating moment in Karoline Blamauer's life.

V

Two additional factors governed Kurt Weill's personal and professional life: one was his relationship to Judaism and Jews and the other was the quality of his music as either specifically European or American. Inasmuch as they can be ascertained, they, too, defined Weill as a person.

No matter what the Nazis said, Weill was no more a composer of "Jewish music" than Felix Mendelssohn or Gustav Mahler had been,[142] but his Jewish religion and cultural background exerted an influence on the sort of music he wrote and where he wrote it. For one thing, as a young man he seems to have been more fully conscious of his Jewish roots than recent biographers are willing to concede, and even as a successful artist who was part of the culture of Weimar, there is no evidence that he ever "suppressed" the Jewish side of his persona, to a point where it had to be "reasserted" by the time he was beginning work on *The Eternal Road* in 1934.[143] After all, much of Weimar culture was the result of efforts by German, Austrian, Hungarian, Polish, and even Russian Jews—assimilated or not, baptized or not, and even though a content analysis in terms of "Jewish" elements is next to impossible, protagonists as well as detractors of this culture knew about the phenomenon, without themselves being able to give a meticulous accounting of it.[144]

Most of Weill's Jewish artist friends did not try, and neither did Weill himself. Nonetheless, there can be no question that even in 1932 he had not forgotten where he was coming from. He was born in the small town of Dessau, the original home of the great Jewish philosopher Moses Mendelssohn, Felix's grandfather. Whereas Felix's father had already been baptized, Weill never was; indeed in his youth he purposely moved in the religious and cultural circle of the Jews his father was serving as a distinguished synagogue cantor. As a music student Weill took the Jewish tradition seriously; *Ofrahs Lieder,* his song cycle written when he was only sixteen, was based on the work of a Jewish poet who had lived during the Crusades, a time of ferocious anti-Jewish pogroms.[145] As an eighteen-year-old, already in Berlin, he signed on as choir director for the Jewish congregation of Friedenau, at least for the High Holidays. But he had his problems with this female choir, whose members did not respect him much, and he found it difficult to adapt his work to the rites of the Jewish service of an obviously reform temple.[146] The rites themselves became suspect to him some five years later, as they seemed to obscure what he himself wished to embrace as a simple faith, the "innocent belief of children," but which thus far had proved too elusive. And he despised other Jews who followed the trend of the day, either as outwardly pious Philistines or as Zionists, or even as ostentatiously assimilated Germans.[147] The "belief of children" was something he may have wished to realize for himself as late as 1932, when he entertained plans for a "school opera" to be entitled *Naboths Weinberg,* and which was meant "to treat a social theme within a biblical framework."[148]

Weill's drift from "traditional religion to a secularized one," as it has aptly been described by Guy Stern, was paralleled in those formative years by an unrelenting criticism of the Jewish diaspora in Central and East Central Europe in general and Germany in particular, a criticism from which, often in ironic tones, he did not exempt himself.[149] This criticism tended to reflect many of the stereotypes of modern anti-Semitism, which some Jews had also internalized—certainly in relation to their Eastern brethren—and which Weill played on with a subjectively endearing sense of humor, developed and honed in Jewish tradition and argot, which stopped just short of sarcasm.[150] Hence in 1918 he thought that a proclivity for criticism was a Jewish trait, possessed by him as well, of course.[151] Eastern Jews were reported to present compositions with Yiddish lyrics and to do so in a dilettantish and inferior manner, while their Eastern Jewish audience was observed to display "a typically 'east-Jewish' restlessness."[152] Whereas Jews were often turned into scapegoats by the Gentiles, Weill said, the Zionists did not make things better, because they always presented themselves as such obvious targets.[153] His verdict that Jews were "simply not productive" unless they impressed outsiders as corrosive and destructionist, besides being an oxymoron, was sadly premonitory of Third Reich ideology—yet this metaphor of Weill's, coined in 1919, demonstrates better than any other his wry sense of humor as well as his pronounced aptitude for self-effacement.[154]

Of course, Weill was made acutely aware of his Jewish roots when he was forced to flee to Paris in March 1933; this awareness did not occasion a return to Judaism as a religion as in the case of Schoenberg slightly later but, rather, intensified already existing pro-Jewish sympathies and redirected his inner self to purely religious issues. As we know, these issues were used to highlight the present plight of German Jews "in the context of racial persecution," that of incremental ostracism and banishment, by way of stark biblical precedents (the captivity of Zion; the destruction of the Second Temple).[155] When Weill met with Reinhardt, Werfel, and the American impresario Meyer Weisgal in Salzburg in May 1934 to discuss the project further, he, like his fellow Jews, fully subscribed to the religious part of the legal contract then drawn up, "to devise, write and compose a musical biblical morality play to express the spiritual origin, the earliest mythical history and the eternal destiny of the Jewish people to whom they belong."[156] During the drawn-out process of composing the music, Weill was at pains to use, if sparingly, original Jewish liturgical motifs, especially as the basis for the rabbi's voice parts, and psalmodic recitatives for the rabbi and Jehovah. The scene of Abraham's attempted sacrifice of Isaac was concluded with a "jubilant fugue"; Rachel and Jacob communed via a duet with *Volkslied* characteristics; Gypsy melodies, perhaps not so Jewish, accompanied the dance around the golden calf. To be sure, not all this music harked back to pure biblical traditions (as Weill had never been a "Jewish composer" per se), but much of it turned out to be music with a Hebrew theme.[157]

When it opened on 7 January 1937 in New York, *The Eternal Road* was understood to be some sort of sequel to *The Romance of a People*, composed and conducted by Isaac Grove, which had been performed in 1933 on the occasion of the Chicago World Exhibition, commissioned by Jewish organizations, and likewise based on episodes from the Old Testament.[158] It did not fail to impress other prominent émigré Jews, victims of the Nazis, as the religious pageant it was meant to be. Reportedly, Albert Einstein, who came over from Princeton to see the show, felt that Weill had "bridged the most difficult gap, of creating original music, and yet avoiding modern nuances which would have made it non-biblical and thus inappropriate."[159] At the end of the day, Weill's strengthened commitment to Judaism had been persuasively documented, notwithstanding the fact that aesthetically the "show" was closer to Hollywood than to the historic Temple in Jerusalem, and the music was sometimes "thin," as critic Paul Bekker charged, and that altogether, in the professional judgment of Max Reinhardt's son Gottfried—himself a stage producer—the score did not number "among Kurt Weill's inventive and enduring compositions."[160]

In 1936, Weill's transfer to the United States, the home of generations of Jews since the nineteenth century and latterly a haven for many European

Jews, may have heightened his awareness of current Jewish issues in general and his own situation in particular.[161] But it also amplified his past dislike of what the Nazis often pictured as a caricature of the figure of the unassimilated Jew, a caricature he frequently experienced as real, if perhaps unfairly so, especially among Eastern European Jews in Hollywood. Hence his earlier prejudices against Russian and Galician Jews were perpetuated, and in particular he came to express a dislike of fairly recent Jewish immigrants from the Austro-Hungarian realm (of the type that now controlled the movie world). "It was one of the worst gatherings of refugees I've ever gone through," he lamented to Lenya in August 1944, "a German language evening of the worst kind—because it wasn't even German but that awful mixture of Hungarian and Viennese. The main topic of conversation was gossip about the other refugees, and a long discussion about 'g'stürzte' (a kind of Potato pancakes, it seems)."[162] Weill made fun of friends who had "their Jewish noses fixed," of Jewish men who liked to surround themselves in public with Gentile "'alien girls,' the very essence of whores," of "mechuggene brazilianische Jiddenne" (crazy Brazilian Jewesses), and after having visited his parents in Palestine during 1947 he deemed Tel Aviv "a very ugly city with a jewish-fascist population that makes you vomit."[163] Yet he also enjoyed the "wonderful Jewish comedian Willy Howard" and said about himself and Lenya, after having once again been confronted with her adultery, that "in the Jewish tradition, the husband always forgives his wife."[164]

Toward the end of his life and being profoundly disturbed by the genocide Hitler perpetrated on the Jews of Europe, Weill contributed, with a singular fervor, to commemorations of the Holocaust. This he did signally as early as 1943, at a time at which news of the full extent of the catastrophe was only just beginning to penetrate the protective wall the Allies had built around themselves, American Jews not excluded.[165] The American-Jewish producer Ben Hecht tells the touching story of his attempt to stage a grand memorial for Hitler's Jewish victims in New York, in the spring of 1943. After having assembled thirty of the city's most prolific intellectuals to discuss his ideas with them, all but two left Hecht's meeting in disgust. These Jews, interprets Hecht in retrospect, did not want their cushioning American identity destroyed by being reminded of their Jewish origins. Only two of the thirty stood by his side: the playwright Moss Hart and Weill. As Hecht remembers it, "Kurt Weill, the lone composer present, looked at me with misty eyes. A radiance was in his strong face. 'Please count on me for everything,' Kurt said."[166] The pageant We Will Never Die, written by Hecht, with music by Weill and directed by Hart, was staged in Madison Square Gardens in March of that year. Narrators and actors included Paul Muni, Edward G. Robinson, and Frank Sinatra. A climax was the recitation of the Mourner's Kaddish, in veneration of the departed; beyond that, Weill had employed other melodic devices from Mosaic liturgy. Some 40,000 people attended, and Weill deemed it all "a giant success."[167] He created other such genuinely Judaic pieces, albeit on a smaller scale, for subsequent occasions.[168]

As much as may have been said about Weill's ethnocultural and religious identity, more has been pronounced on his musical one, before and after 1933. For many years until fairly recently, it has been dogmatically maintained that there were two Weills—one the serious composer of European fame; the other a musician with a "commitment to the mass public in the USA during the 1940s"—and that their personalities never blended.[169] The distinction came down not only to a question of periodization but also to one of quality, because it was inferred that Weill's Broadway success amounted to a "sacrifice of artistic integrity on the altar of American commercialism."[170]

Such criticism commenced as soon as Weill had turned his back on Nazi Germany and was, for the time being, attempting a new career for himself in Paris. After Bruno Walter had premiered Weill's Second Symphony in Amsterdam in October 1934, American critics dismissed it, the informed Olin Downes from *The New York Times* calling it "dreary, dull, and witless."[171] The split-personality theory about Weill seriously took hold after his death in 1950, when the Third Reich that had driven him out was over and critics and musicologists alike sat down to consider his musical legacy. In that year, whereas the Americans tended to discount his earlier European works, the Europeans elected to repudiate his American creative phase. These asynchronous motions came to light when during a League of Composers tribute in July 1950 the New York Philharmonic neither performed nor mentioned Weill's European oeuvre, and Heinrich Strobel wrote, in what was intended as a German homily, about Weill's American period as one that did not count, because he had succumbed to the "demands of Broadway with its stage works and films." While the New York-based League ignored the question of musical quality altogether, Strobel conjured it up with malicious relish.[172] One by one, noted fellow musicians and critics such as Adorno, Stuckenschmidt, Philipp Jarnach, Klemperer, and Weill's old Berlin friend, Hans Curjel, all subscribed to Strobel's view (Jarnach perhaps because of his falling out with Weill dating from the late republican period).[173]

Subsequently, the European critics continued the biographical line of the "Americanized" Weill, who had surrendered maturity and quality for the sake of an easily earned dollar.[174] For example, there was talk about "kitsch" in Weill's musical *Johnny Johnson* (1936), and "sentimentality" in *Knickerbocker Holiday* (1938).[175] The East German writer Jürgen Schebera excelled at this art and, political turncoat after the fall of the Berlin Wall in 1989 that he was, made no serious attempt to reverse his long-held prejudice in a new biography of Weill published in 1995 by Yale University Press.[176] The Briton Ronald Taylor, another of Weill's more recent biographers, harped on the same contentious issue, and even an American, John Simon, suggested opportunism when he wrote in June 1996 that Weill, "with his remarkable adaptability, managed to write 'American' music as effectively as he had written 'European.'"[177]

However, is the distinction between "European" and "American" music not just as specious as the one between so-called serious music and jazz, translatable, in the words of Stephen Hinton, into the equally false-ringing argument regarding "the critical versus the commercial, the highbrow versus the middlebrow"?[178]

Weill's post-World War II indictment had to originate in Germany for two reasons. First, after the end of the war and unlike Hindemith, Weill refused to return to the country of his birth even for a visit, for which he was not forgiven. Second, it was in Germany, the home of the haughty *Bildungsbürgertum,* that the distinction between "serious" and "popular" music was upheld as an immutable doctrine like nowhere else in Europe, as a criterion of breeding, social class, and moral character. By being seen as defending the "popular," Weill was logically condemned for having betrayed the "serious."

To place this into perspective, more sober critics have recently pointed out that Weill himself had been aware of these issues, as problems of post-World War I modernity and reaching into his "American" phase, from the 1920s on. As two of his protagonists have commented, the questions for him were large ones, in a universal sense: "How can the polarities of 'popular' and 'serious,' 'high' and 'low' be reconciled within art and society? Without a wider audience, how can new music justify its continued existence and subsidy? Can art again entertain? How can music function within contemporary theater?"[179] Indeed, key in Weill's overall aesthetic concept, and able to harmonize the seeming extremes of low- and highbrow art, was his conception of musical theater, which, as Strobel himself had to concede in 1950, had already gone a long way in replacing conventional opera *before* the composer's exile, and the ideal realization of which, as Weill confessed to Ernst Krenek, he had found—after the Weimar stagings—on American Broadway.[180] According to this interpretation, there was no stylistic break at all. Some of Weill's friends became aware of this after the production of the musical *Johnny Johnson* by the avant-garde Group Theater in New York in 1936; there were equally positive verdicts regarding the—admittedly different—*Eternal Road* (1937) and *Knickerbocker Holiday* (1938).[181]

Weill's own pronouncements document that he himself never saw a stylistic break. At the base of his thoughts, by the middle of the 1920s, was his reflection on the masses as a broader audience for works of art than any cultured German Philistine would allow. Conversely, he repudiated the elitism of his contemporary composer colleagues, who entertained an unbefitting "feeling of superiority toward their audiences."[182] In 1929, around the time of *Die Dreigroschenoper* and *Aufstieg und Fall der Stadt Mahagonny,* he proclaimed: "The boundaries between 'art music' and 'music for use' must be brought closer together and gradually eliminated. That's why we've attempted to compose music that's capable of meeting the musical needs of the broad population without giving up artistic substance."[183] Despite the stringency of Brecht's text and the sophisticated combination of banality and seriousness that characterized his own music in *Die Dreigroschenoper*—qualities a progressive conventionalist such as Klemperer could still admire, whereas he condemned the "smut" of the later work—Weill was intent, in 1934, on finding someone who would "convert the ballads into hit-songs without changing the essence of my music."[184]

Such an adapter, he knew even then, could only come from the United States.[185] Upon beginning his work there, Weill announced that "The Broadway legitimate stage is to the American public what the opera houses and concert halls are to the European. I have always believed that opera should be a part of the living theater of our time. Broadway is today one of the great theater centers of the world. It has all the technical and intellectual equipment for a serious musical theater." In 1936 Weill decried the Philistine custom of condemning every form of light music as inferior, maintaining that rather than differentiating between serious and light music, the division should be between good and bad music.[186] Until his death in 1950, Weill never strayed from the path of that conviction, of which his appreciation of a broader audience formed a large part. His parallel view, that because of his European background and training and his special abilities he was writing better musicals than the denizens of Broadway had hitherto been used to, was in no way meant as a denial of that American potential.[187] As Weill informed his former publisher in Vienna in 1937, he increasingly looked upon his work in the United States as an extension of what he had been doing in Europe; this would refer, in equal measure, to the "serious musical plays" of his American beginnings and the "more distinguished" musical comedies of the early 1940s.[188] Although, toward the end of his life, Weill tended, once again, to call them "opera," they were in the genre of musical theater he had envisaged as one of the most creative artists of the Weimar Republic, and of which *Die Dreigroschenoper* had merely been the first of many prominent examples.[189]

4

Karl Amadeus Hartmann

The Composer as Dissident

I

Even in Germany today, Karl Amadeus Hartmann is the least known of the eight composers whose portraits are presented here. The reason for this, ironically, lies in the fact that during the Third Reich he was the least exposed artistically, and this by his own choice, but also because of his local insularity, as he left Munich only occasionally and without fanfare. He was born in Munich on 2 August 1905, the youngest of four sons, to an artist father, Friedrich Richard Hartmann, whose specialties were still lives with flowers as well as landscapes, and his mother Gertrud, interested in Richard Wagner, Zola, and Balzac. His parents being solidly lower middle class and always on the verge of indigence, Karl Amadeus entered a primary-school teachers' seminar in 1919 and then, short of graduation, settled for the inauspicious job of an office clerk, until he followed his calling to become a musician by enrolling in Munich's renowned but stodgy Akademie der Tonkunst in 1924, where he studied with Joseph Haas, for three years. Concentrating on composition, Hartmann also specialized as an instrumentalist on trombone and piano. He made good if unenthusiastic use of those skills when he earned part of his living as a freelance trombonist for the Munich opera toward the end of the republic.[1]

Hartmann was intellectually and artistically so curious that he came to enjoy the support not only of his father but especially of his brother Adolf, himself a painter and destined to end up as an art professor in Berlin. As in the case of the equally lower-middle-class and ten-years-older Paul Hindemith, two influences worked on him that were to shape his early productive life quite decisively: Social Democracy with its promise of greater equality and well-being for a larger number of people and progressive impulses in contemporary art. The father was pointedly Socialist, insists Hartmann's widow, Elisabeth, today, and when he died in 1925, the composer's mother, although a good Catholic, continued bringing up her sons in a left-wing mold. Karl Amadeus himself never joined either the Communist or the Social Democratic Party, but his brother Richard became a card-carrying Communist, distributing anti-Nazi leaflets around Munich at the time of the presidential election in July 1932 and then again upon Hitler's coming to power, and hence he quickly had to flee to Switzerland to escape marauding Stormtroopers who missed him by a hair's breadth at his mother's house.[2]

Hartmann's initial musical influence was that of Weber, whose opera *Der Freischütz* fascinated him as a young boy, but later also Schubert (*The Unfinished*) and Strauss's *Salome* and *Elektra*. These works guided his earliest efforts in composition, and undoubtedly they eased his entrance to the academy, whose staunch insistence on the late-Romantic tradition soon grated on him. Hartmann's early sojourn in modernism was fostered by impulses from the art world of his father and the revered brother, Adolf, five years his elder; both were part of a group of prolific forward-looking artists calling themselves Die Juryfreien, those independent of outside judgment or censure, which had originated in 1910 and two years later inspired the famous exhibition of the Blaue Reiter.[3] Adolf was a leading member of the Juryfreien in 1928 when Karl Amadeus persuaded these artists to allow him to organize a series of concerts, to enhance their exhibitions, which were to feature the new music of younger composers, in the artistically otherwise reactionary Bavarian capital. Indeed, this was done through 1932, and compositions by Bartók, Casella, Hába, Hauer, Hindemith, Krenek, Milhaud, Schulhoff, Stravinsky, Büchtger, Orff, and Egk were heard. Among these composers, the three last mentioned were of course Munich residents, and Hartmann seems to have seen a good deal of them, especially Egk, through whom he got to know the Socialist conductor Hermann Scherchen. Büchtger and Scherchen, who frequently came visiting, soon initiated a parallel modern-music series of their own.[4]

Hartmann's modest musical oeuvre by that time had been decidedly touched by jazz, the art form of choice but also something of a fad among young European composers. His earliest known compositions were the *Kleine Suite für Klavier,* only recently discovered, and his Suite No. 2, both composed for piano between 1924 and 1926, when he was a student. Cakewalk syncopes in the first work and a movement entitled "Jazz" in the second reveal this influence. It was again predominant in *Jazztoccata und Fuge für Klavier,* composed in 1928, at the commencement of the Juryfreien concerts. Significantly, its percussive piano passages are reminiscent of Bartók. In September 1932, in the same series, Hartmann's sonata for piano and *Burleske Musik* (for horns, piano, and percussion) were performed, along with chamber works by Poulenc, Satie, Bartók, and Hindemith. In those years Hartmann blended "Futurism, Dada, jazz, and other currents in a carefree manner, in a number of compositions," as he later recalled—all of them characterized by polymetric rhythm and a pronounced percussive texture. At the same time, Hartmann's engagement as a Socialist manifested itself through music he composed for texts by Karl Marx and the young Communist lyricist Johannes R. Becher.[5] "Hartmann's creativity as a composer," writes his biographer Andrew McCredie, "from the beginning was characterized by its purpose, to destroy the barriers erected by race, religion, and social status."[6]

Hence Hartmann was already programmed for a collision course with the National Socialist regime even before it came into being in January 1933. And when it did, he realized, as he said later, "that it was necessary to give testimony, not out of despair and fear of that regime, but as a counter-measure. I said to myself that freedom will eventually prevail, even if we ourselves are obliterated."[7] To be sure, his decision to internalize his opposition to the Nazi regime and to express it through music may have been aided by his failure, in the first few months of the dictatorship, to carry on, as a publicly exposed artist, in a normal fashion. For unknown reasons, Bavarian Radio advised him in March 1933 that although his *Burleske Musik* had been received in February (two weeks after Hitler's political takeover), no commitment could be made regarding its acceptance for broadcasting. Obviously, it fell through.[8] The leading publisher B. Schott's Söhne in Mainz, too, informed him in August that his newly composed concertino for trumpet could not be marketed, for the volume of its projected circulation would be negligible.[9] And the premiere for a didactic piece for children, planned for the fall under the auspices of the Juryfreien in Munich, never came to pass, for that collective of free spirits was naturally disbanded.[10]

Hartmann's various musings on the irreconcilability of ethos, art, and bad politics are all post-World War II, and hence in retrospect they might ring hollow as the confessions of an anti-Nazi artist.[11] But such a view ignores a combination of important circumstances, chief among them that the special dedications or libretti for his compositions at the time left no doubt as to where he stood vis-à-vis the Nazi regime, that after 1933 he avoided going public inside the Third Reich and instead sought exposure abroad, and that he associated himself, in various manners, with known antifascists and their internationally staged events.

As has to be the case with music, the core of Hartmann's anti-Nazi confessionalism were the texts. "My husband searched out all the texts that were automatically oppositional," remembers Frau Hartmann.[12] But there were musical elements as well, which were unquestionably anathema to Nazi ideology, such as his open ear for jazz motifs (Hartmann never surrendered his treasured jazz record collection) or allusions to well-known Communist musical themes and to Jewish melodies.[13]

Hartmann's first String Quartet of 1933 (*Carillon*) made "extensive use of a Hebrew song."[14] The composer then began crafting a major confessional work in the form of a chamber opera, *Des Simplicius Simplicissimus Jugend*, in late 1934, when his despondency over the Third Reich was already palpable. It harked back to a story written by the seventeenth-century German poet Hans Jakob Christoph von Grimmelshausen, in which the hero, a country boy, lives through the ordeals of the Thirty Years' War (1618–48). As the name implies, Simplicius is a simpleton who among other disturbing oddities witnesses a hermit digging his own grave in order to die in it, joins up with a band of ravaging mercenaries, moves to the court of a despot in the role of court jester, and finally survives the slaughter of the despot and his hired guns at the hands of rebellious peasants. His concluding words are: "Praised be the judge of truth!" In this stage work, Hartmann, who had conceived the scenario and libretto with the help of Scherchen and Munich theater director Wolfgang Petzet, clearly was cultivating an antihero image to serve as a foil for the ideal of tough and heroic Hitler youths that the Führer and his party espoused.[15] Whether by happenstance or design, the contrariness of Hartmann was validated when the Nazi composer Ludwig Achilles Maurick (originally Dutch) had a piece of his own premiered at the official Düsseldorf Reich Music Festival in May 1938. In contradistinction to Hartmann, in this opera, *Simplizius Simplizissimus: Ein Spiel für Soli, Sprecher, Chor und Orchester*, based on the same character of Grimmelshausen's gruesome narrative, the hero is shaped according to Nazi criteria: After all the tribulations, Maurick's Simplizius turns out to be a valiant soldier who at the end of the day has done his duty for the fatherland.[16] Hartmann's opus—impossible to produce in Germany—eventually was scheduled for a Brussels Radio performance in May 1940 after translation of the libretto into Flemish, but the invasion and occupation of Belgium by the Wehrmacht prevented this.[17]

Yet already in 1935 Hartmann was able to have his music heard, albeit abroad, in Prague, which at that time was filled with anti-Hitler émigrés. Hartmann made a political statement by having a symphonic poem, *Miserae*, performed under Scherchen's baton at that year's International Society for Contemporary Music festival, in early September. The work was dedicated to "my friends, who had to die in the hundreds and who are sleeping in eternity, we shall not forget you." It was dated "Dachau 1933/34." The symphonic poem, whose orchestration called for "jazz cymbals" along with more conventional instruments, impressed fellow musicians and critics alike. The Italian composer Luigi Dallapiccola, earlier a follower of Mussolini until his marriage to a Jewish woman cured him of the Fascist illness, judged it as "painful, solemn, and sometimes depressing"; from then on, the two composers were friends. The Jewish critic Max Brod wrote in the *Prager Tageblatt* about the "disturbing symphonic poem 'Miserae' (wretchedness)," about the "infinite sing-song of the brass, reminiscent, from a distance, of nocturnal music by Mahler." Even the *Frankfurter Zeitung*, still one of the more permissive dailies in the Reich, lauded the work as "technically excellent" and superior to other compositions of the period, by virtue of its "power of expression and spiritual potency."[18] Hartmann's newfound Belgian friends had the work performed once more in Brussels, in October 1938.[19]

In May 1936 Hartmann wrote to his Hungarian colleague Alexander Jemnitz: "Presently I am working on a cantata (for contralto and large orchestra) (with a text based on Walt Whitman), in which I describe our life. The poems, which I have considerably altered, embrace the entire difficult, hopeless life, and yet no idea is being stifled by death. I think I have made some progress with this work in the direction of a kind of music that concerns all humankind."[20]

With the onset of World War II in the fall of 1939 Hartmann's already hopeless life threatened to become even more difficult. He expressed his anxiety about the impending global conflagration in his *Concerto funèbre* for solo violin and strings, and it was premiered in St. Gall, Switzerland, in 1940 by his friend, the conductor Ernst Klug, with whom brother Richard had found temporary refuge. Hartmann visited both on that occasion. He called this a "music of sorrow," in contrast to the official mood of jubilation over the brutal German conquest of Poland. The piece was framed by two chorales; the adagio as the second movement was meant as a lamentation, whereas the eighth notes of the allegro—the third movement—manifested the guns of war in dynamic rhythm. The work was dedicated to his four-year-old son, Richard.[21] Hartmann's *Sinfonia tragica* followed in 1940. He wrote it for his Belgian friend, the antifascist musicologist and conductor Paul Collaer, but once again, because of the tribulations of war, it could not be performed in Brussels, although this had been planned for 1941. Collaer had already withdrawn to a country home outside the Belgian capital, after resigning from his post as director of the music department of the Belgian broadcasting system. The *Sinfonia*'s first and second movements were incorporated into what was to become Hartmann's Third Symphony after 1945.[22]

A period of inertia followed, caused by extreme desperation and fear. Hartmann became paranoiac in expectation of the worst for his manuscripts. In December 1942 he inquired of Viennese publisher Universal Edition whether the seven autographs of scores, among them *Simplicius* and a string quartet, which he had entrusted to the firm without retaining copies in Munich, were safe beneath the hail of enemy bombs. Even if the seven autographs were at risk in Vienna, the work would have been safe, according to the composer's statement after the war, that at the height of the conflict he had buried all his scores in a zinc container, two meters deep in the mountains.[23] At any rate, he did not compose again until late in 1944, after having learned that the Gestapo had arrested a dissident sympathizer, the Communist chemist Robert Havemann. In 1946 he let Havemann know that this symphony had been named *Song of Woe* (*Klagegesang*) and that despite many attempts he somehow had not been able to find a proper ending for it. Now, after the war, he was able to finish it in "brilliant D-flat major."[24]

Hartmann's last wartime composition was the Second Piano Sonata, a piece once more dedicated to the victims of the Nazi terror system. It was inscribed: "Endless was the queue—endless was the misery—endless was the suffering." Hartmann had conceived it after watching 20,000 Dachau camp inmates shuffle by the house of his in-laws on Lake Starnberg on their death march at the end of April 1945, just before the Americans liberated the camp. Reportedly, Hartmann had been deeply moved by the sight of a high-ranking Nazi living across the street (probably Interior Minister Wilhelm Frick), who allowed bread to be passed to the wretched men, with the result of utter pandemonium.[25] Beginning with *Miserae,* Hartmann had come full circle.

As someone who practiced "inner resistance," how did Hartmann function in view of the authorities, within his immediate family, and in the social environs of his residential base? On all three questions, the evidence so far is less full-bodied and reliable than one might wish, and hence the final picture is somewhat hazy.

Regarding the authorities, Hartmann mainly had to deal with the Reich Music Chamber, the agency most immediately responsible for his professional and political conduct, on several occasions. At the most bureaucratic level he did receive in 1941 what must be regarded as a negligible honorarium from work of his performed in France, through the staatlich genehmigte Gesellschaft zur Verwertung musikalischer Urheberrechte (Stagma), the income distribution agency controlled by the RMK.[26] After all, in the fall of 1933, Hartmann, by default, had become a member of the composer's section of the music chamber, pending the observance of a minimum requirement for most, namely his providing proof of full "Aryan" lineage for himself and his wife. Now, despite repeated calls to do so since 1935, he never answered this query as he should have. Still, the assessment of this omission as a clear-cut case of "opposition" by McCredie amounts to an overinterpretation.[27] It is true that by 22 January 1936, Hartmann appears to have received his final notice from the RMK, threatening the implementation of paragraph 10 of the law of 1 November 1933 governing membership in this and other culture chambers; this paragraph was meant to exclude all unreliable musicians (after an initial blanket inclusion), especially Jews and hardcore Marxists.[28] But Hartmann must have known that by ignoring the RMK letters he did not take too high a risk, because several of his colleagues acted much as he did, especially if they were not Jewish, without any serious consequences for their life or professional future.[29] Because he was not active in the German music scene and, as Frau Hartmann emphasizes, always "remained very quiet," he really did not much need the RMK professionally, although in a formal sense he remained its member, without paragraph 10 having been used against him. "He still has not supplied full proof of his racial pedigree, either for himself or his wife," noted RMK officials in July of 1941, and simply left it at that.[30] Whether or not he knew it, Hartmann was the beneficiary of gray zones of policy and executive sloth governing much of the workings of the music chamber since its inception in November 1933. Besides, the 1941 wording suggests that he seems to have made at least a token effort to satisfy the Berlin functionaries, in spite of his widow's recent assertion that "my husband never reacted, since he did not wish to furnish the documentation, even though he would have been able to."[31] Hence the conclusion is valid that Hartmann was a member of the RMK from the beginning, without ever being evicted, no matter what he did or did not do.[32]

Arguably more tension between Hartmann and the RMK was caused after the composer's attendance at the ISCM festival in Prague, where Hermann Scherchen, who in Nazi eyes was extremely dubious, conducted his ideologically inspired symphonic poem *Miserae* on 1 September 1935. In the first instance, the ISCM was an international institution deemed to be hostile to fascist intentions and not recognized by the RMK. Early in 1934 Germany seceded from the ISCM, because its government suspected the "progressive experiments of immature hotheads," who were said to speak an international musical language "even when they were not Jewish."[33] Since June 1934, the ISCM's German-led counterpart was the Counseil Permanent pour la Coopération Internationale des Compositeurs, headed at this time by RMK president Richard Strauss and including, as its international members, composers thought to be partial to the Nazi cause.[34] Hence by traveling to Prague, Hartmann probably was aware that he was doing something the Nazi authorities would not approve of, especially as he had not asked the RMK for express permission, which, he might have known, would have been denied. In the second instance, Hartmann's work was performed not only under the baton of Scherchen but also with this treacherous inscription on the score: "To My Friends . . . Dachau 1933/34." And the fact that he communed with so many antifascist-minded colleagues at the festival could not have helped Hartmann much either.

Nevertheless, Hartmann's defenders have overestimated the dangers associated with this visit. McCredie emphasizes the direct link between the Prague event and the subsequent letters from the RMK, placing the composer "under pressure" to furnish his family documents.[35] He and others, including Frau Hartmann, have stressed the displeasure of the German authorities both with his unauthorized attendance and the Dachau dedication, which allegedly resulted in censorial inquiries from the RMK as to the nature of the Prague celebrations, coupled with a stern injunction that henceforth the RMK's permission to attend any musical activities abroad was mandatory.[36]

Again, one has to qualify. The facts are that Heinz Ihlert, the general manager of the RMK, wrote to Hartmann on 21 September stating that he knew of the composer's recent sojourn. Then he continued politely: "I would be grateful if you could sketch for me, very briefly, your impressions of this event." Hartmann immediately obliged, receiving, on 9 October, a thank-you note from Ihlert, with a reminder that professional trips abroad required the RMK's blessing.[37] Although from then on Hartmann showed himself concerned in letters to his friends, warning, sometimes in veiled language, that regarding foreign trips abroad he would have to proceed with caution, he still felt safe enough to undertake such trips without even bothering to declare them officially to the RMK.[38] Instead he traveled—as he did to the ISCM festival in London in 1938 and several times to Swiss Winterthur—as a private citizen on the strength of his personal passport.[39]

As for the Dachau dedication, Fred K. Prieberg has already pointed out that the telltale inscription was visible, on the original score, only for conductor Scherchen on the podium in Prague, and that Hartmann would have committed virtual suicide had he made this—as yet unpublished—text more public.[40] Not least because there is no mention in his personal file, it may be safely assumed that the RMK never learned of it. Nor did the chamber or any other Nazi authorities henceforth brand his music "atonal" or "degenerate," as some of Hartmann's interpreters have averred.[41] Such a verdict, too, surely would have shown up in his detailed political evaluation, generated by his Munich party chapter office and kept on file in the Berlin RMK headquarters. If anything, this evaluation was positive for Hartmann. It stated, on his RMK master file card of July 1941, that the matter of his unauthorized trip to Prague was considered "closed, in agreement with the ministry"—the propaganda ministry of course, to which the music chamber reported.[42]

Why was it "closed," and in agreement with the ministry? Had Hartmann done such a good job of "reporting" as to get himself off the hook once and for all? Was it the prospect of other reports at future international meetings that made it possible for him simply to slip out of Germany without any cumbersome formalities? The question has to be asked, for subsequent political evaluations of the composer by his Munich-Schwabing NSDAP chapter "Siegestor" dating from late 1941 are so positive as to be downright puzzling. After the RMK had asked the Siegestor chapter to comment on Hartmann's political reliability, it was reported that "he wishes to be received into the party," and that, as a member of NSV, the National Socialist People's Charity, he "contributes well, if judged according to his income." Apologetically, it was stated that the reason why his wife was not a member of the NSF, the Nazi Women's League, was that she was not always well, and that because of his youth, son Richard had not yet joined the Hitler Youth.[43] The surprisingly favorable summary, however, read as follows: "Some years ago the person in question was not yet nationally minded, but he is so now. He always salutes with the Hitler greeting. As has been ascertained, his reading consists of National Socialist literature. The cell leader responsible for his residence knows him by 'his ever generous handouts.'"[44]

What was going on here? Did Hartmann lead a double life, known to the outside world as a resister to the Third Reich, and useful to the Nazi authorities as a spy? Is that how he bought for himself peace and noninterference in his artistic endeavors from the Reich Music Chamber, the agency whose member he actually was, notwithstanding post-1945 attempts by his protagonists to befuddle that issue? Moreover, did he lie when in 1946 he wrote to Hindemith that his "political attitude prevented [him] from making any concessions," or to the Danish composer Knudåge Riisager, that as an "antifascist" he had been "in no party organisation, nor in the military, Volkssturm, labor service—nowhere did I participate"?[45]

If there is no easy answer, it may be partially inferred from repeated assurances Elisabeth Hartmann made to me in conversation, that her husband always had to act with extraordinary circumspection, so that, for instance, when he reported to the authorities on Prague in 1935, he mentioned nothing about the Communist Hanns Eisler's presence there.[46] Furthermore, Hartmann himself has said that he survived the war only "through much cunning and shrewdness."[47] Such craftiness may have included visits to the Schwabing party office, during which hearty Hitler salutes were given and explicit mention was made of an impending decision to join. Many anti-Nazi Germans were known to have behaved in the same vein, especially during the war, contributing generously to Nazi collections when party canvassers knocked on people's doors and name lists were checked off, precisely because this act alone could serve as a precaution against further party inroads. Still, only a highly placed Nazi could have influenced the Siegestor party chapter to the point of manufacturing such a positive character assessment on behalf of Hartmann, and as far as we know today, the couple had merely casual contacts with the obligatory block wardens—nominally superior to the category of "cell leader" mentioned in the report and responsible for their Wilhelmstrasse flat.[48] Although it is doubtful, the couple may have known, on somewhat more personal terms, Interior Minister Wilhelm Frick, whose country home was close to that of Karl Amadeus's in-laws in Kempfenhausen on Lake Starnberg. With a little girl of Frick's family, most likely his granddaughter, Richard frequently went to school when the Hartmann family resided there.[49] But, on the other hand, neither the composer nor his widow has mentioned anything about the nature of that neighborly relationship (if it was one in the true sense of the word), nor that Frick ever interceded on their behalf—and such patronage surely would have been recorded in the personal files.

Nonetheless, although traces of doubt cannot be entirely removed, we must continue to accept the hitherto reported version that Hartmann was opposed to the Hitler regime and, together with his family, made it through the Third Reich without having to sell his soul. If his compositions and personal connections outside Germany provide one set of evidence for this, his lifestyle and the nature of his intra-German social intercourse provide another. We may deduce this from Hartmann's relationship with his former Munich colleagues, his dealings with Anton Webern in Vienna, and his private circle of friends, reputed to have consisted exclusively of anti-Nazis.

Hartmann's change, after January 1933, in his relationship to Carl Orff, Werner Egk, and their musical friends is telling. Orff, who eventually was to become the leader of a loose, progressively inclined group of younger composers who all revered Stravinsky as their patron saint, hung on to his own professional existence precariously, until the success of *Carmina*

Burana after 1937, at which time he became established in the Reich. His main adversaries in Nazi Germany were Alfred Rosenberg and his local Munich deputies. Hence Orff, for musical as well as ideological reasons, might have had occasion to draw close to Hartmann, his sometime compatriot of the time of the Juryfreien and similar Munich groups. But after 1935, at which time, for Orff, the worst possible harassment was over, the two men drifted apart, even though Orff appears to have been aware of Hartmann's score for *Simplicius*. Hartmann's relationship with Egk took a similar course; he did go to hear the Munich performance of *Die Zaubergeige* but thought it musically contrived. Orff's cohorts, the composers Karl Marx (no relation to the social critic) and Fritz Büchtger, both of whom aligned themselves with the Nazi regime, also became strangers. Elisabeth Hartmann's verdict today is that none of those musicians could communicate with Hartmann in any way, because they all were, more or less, opportunists bent on preserving or improving whatever acceptable status they already enjoyed in the Third Reich—a status they had to regard as threatened through an association with her husband.[50]

Hartmann visited Anton Webern for a few weeks in late fall of 1942.[51] He took informal lessons from this famous member of the Second Viennese School and also accompanied him to the Wiener Staatsoper, where he was astounded that nobody would even notice the master. Although they got along very well musically, politics did become an issue toward the end of Hartmann's stay in Vienna. As for himself, Webern, the student and friend of the persecuted serialist Arnold Schoenberg, had reached the conclusion that Hitler was a great man.[52] "The conversation kept returning to politics," Hartmann wrote home to his wife. "I should not have steered it there, for I learned things that, in my strong leaning towards anarchism, I would rather not have heard. This is because he seriously defended the viewpoint that, for dear order's sake, *any kind* of authority should be respected and that the State under which one lives would have to be recognized at any price."[53] In November 1942, just before he left again for Munich, Hartmann cabled to Elisabeth: "Alien to me. No contact with Webern."[54] She later recorded that "Hartmann could not understand the world any more," especially since Webern must have suffered from the oppressive cultural policy to the same extent that he himself did.[55]

In Munich Hartmann evidently was tied into a circle of friends whose highly educated, upper-middle-class members were staunchly anti-Nazi and sometimes on the verge of active resistance. The full extent of these activities is still obscured, nor does the circle appear to have had a name or ties to other local resistance groups such as the "White Rose," although it is assured that its nominal head was a Dr. Robert Steidle. He and Hartmann, Elisabeth Hartmann, and like-minded souls such as a certain theater director Schöpf are said to have congregated for musical soirées, where Hartmann directed a small orchestra, "which covered for our antifascist activities." There were clandestine listenings to the BBC as well as discussions about the political situation. Through these friends, Hartmann appears to have met a cultured military physician of some influence who helped him obtain dispensation from the Wehrmacht on faked medical grounds. Possibly, this doctor also played a role in freeing from the draft Hartmann's pianist friend, Martin Piper, even though another musician friend, Michael Peter, whose entire family was reputedly anti-Nazi, did have to serve the colors and was captured by the French at war's end. To effect Peter's release from POW camp in April 1946, Hartmann wrote to authorities in Paris that he had aided three French soldiers interned by the Nazis during the war, Edmund Lavallée, who was in a camp near Vienna, Martial Auzanneau, near Hartmann's summer home in Kempfenhausen, and Lavallée's brother-in-law Jean Vigué, a pianist who was actually a friend of the composer. In 1946 Hartmann insisted that he had helped these Frenchmen out with food, clothes, and books, and that he even managed to have a "concert grand" shipped to Vigué's prisoner-of-war camp at Moosburg (Stalag VII/A no. 78887), such that the pianist was able to provide his coprisoners "with many a beautiful and spiritually valuable hour."[56] The veracity of this last claim has still to be determined.

Could Hartmann afford such an expensive shipment? His means to sustain a livelihood for himself, his wife, and his son were meager at best. He depended almost exclusively on the generosity of his father-in-law, Alfred Reussmann, the well-to-do manager of a Bavarian ball-bearing factory. Karl Amadeus had met Reussmann's daughter Elisabeth in 1929, when she was but sixteen and still in Gymnasium, and they got married, against her parents' wishes, in late 1934, as soon as she was of age. But instead of disinheriting their daughter, Alfred and Antoinette Reussmann magnanimously decided to support the intrepid couple, along with grandson, Richard, born in 1935, by providing them with a flat in Schwabing's Wilhelmstrasse (they themselves lived nearby in fashionable Königinstrasse, adjacent to the luxuriant English Gardens) and letting them have the use of their summer home in Kempfenhausen near Starnberg. Here the Hartmanns stayed permanently after 1942, not least on account of the bombs now hitting the Bavarian capital.

The entire arrangement was painful to the composer for a number of reasons. First, Hartmann was a kept man. As such, he had to swallow his pride in accepting money and all manner of aid from another man who initially had even been against him—not a small feat for a Central European male of Hartmann's generation! Second, even with this assistance, and having no earnings of his own to speak of, money for basic subsistence was never enough, and hence Hartmann was continually pining for opportunities to earn it abroad, either through the publication of his music or by way of prizes international juries might award him. These prizes almost always eluded him, and in early 1937 Hartmann had a nervous breakdown. Third, raising a son, as an "antifascist" at that, in those circumstances was the most trying feat of all. Young Richard was a liability not only when he went to school with the little Frick girl, to whom in his innocence he could have divulged something dangerous, but also in acutely treacherous situations, as when the parents were listening to the BBC, even if it was declared to be a German station. One episode, told by Frau Hartmann in 1994, is significant. An uncle of hers, from her mother's side which tended to favor the Nazi regime, made Richard a Christmas gift of a toy gun when he was just short of age ten. This was in 1944, perhaps the most critical year of the Nazi regime, when the war itself had been decided. His father broke it into pieces without giving the astonished boy a good reason. As it turned out, Richard Hartmann grieved long and hard over his broken gun.[57]

II

Because during the Nazi period Hartmann's music could neither be published nor performed in Germany, he became excessively dependent on foreign or German émigré musicians, both for his social contacts and for his professional reputation. Moreover, because this dependency was such an exclusive one, apart from his private relationship with his immediate family and a few trusted Munich friends, it tended toward the compulsive, and Hartmann's role in it increasingly became one of self-centeredness, sometimes to the point of narcissism. One almost receives the impression that he had to exaggerate his suffering to others to compensate for his self-adduced lack of recognition and loneliness in the country of his birth. In any event, he sometimes flaunted his misfortune, almost turning this into an obsession, and in that process ran the danger of deforming his personality. In this sense, then, his act of "inner emigration" was not, or not entirely, an expression of quiet withdrawal but closer to exhibitionism. Nonetheless, because rare historical examples exist that bear this out, we have only a thin yardstick by which to judge Karl Amadeus Hartmann.[58]

Even in May 1933, when it was not yet entirely clear what sort of role Hartmann was going to play in the Third Reich and several doors signifying a neutral, dignified compromise might still have been open to him (he also was not yet married and was entirely self-supporting), he seems to have complained to the Danish composer Riisager about conditions in the Third Reich. Riisager, although sympathetic, did not think Hartmann's situation unique: "I understand what you have to go through, and I am convinced that the worst is yet to come. The entire world is crazy, and for us artists, this is an entirely bad time. Here in Denmark, things are also not going very well, and new music is being performed only sporadically." Several months later Riisager, in his safe Kingdom of Denmark, tried to help Hartmann by scheduling his concertino for a performance.[59]

To begin with, Hartmann's relationship with foreign colleagues was complicated by his unbending insistence on the immutability of certain passages in his music that were technically so demanding as to be impossible to play, and also by a measure of sloppiness and sloth that manifested arrogance. This attitude cost him performance chances. Thus, in December 1934, Felix Galimir, of the Viennese Galimir Quartet, had to inform him that in what later was to become Hartmann's *Carillon* string quartet, there were a lot of harmonies "which one cannot play (actually getting them to sound)," assuring him at the same time that in the notation nothing had been changed from his original intentions. However, on the whole the piece was so difficult that the Galimir Quartet had been able to master merely the first movement, not enough to take it on a tour to Spain, where a quartet by Wladimir Vogel had been substituted.[60] The Hungarian String Quartet repeated this complaint in the spring of 1936 and in addition griped about Hartmann's careless pencil notation, "which looks very pretty on paper, but in practice wreaks nothing but havoc."[61] One reason why *Des Simplicius Simplicissimus Jugend* could not be premiered at the Brussels World Fair in 1935 was that the composer was incapable of completing the elaborate score on time.[62] Four years later he had to forego a chance of having his concertino for trumpet played by the Italian-Swiss broadcasting system in Lugano because the trumpet soloist was not given enough time to learn the technically tricky part.[63] The selection committee for the International Music Festival of the ISCM in Paris in December 1936 passed over Hartmann's cantata for contralto and orchestra (known as *Symphonisches Fragment* by 1938) on the grounds that it was too long.[64] Dante Fiorillo, a minor New York composer and a plagiarist, who for years remained interested in Hartmann's works, presumably because he wanted to exploit them, characteristically informed him that the cantata, though a "masterpiece," did not attract instrumental groups because "they object to the Work being so large and for voice."[65] Potentially a more serious matter for Hartmann was the Basel conductor Paul Sacher's charge—whether or not it was justified—of undue "technical difficulty" as one of the reasons for declining to perform the composer's oeuvre.[66]

Because he craved recognition abroad, Hartmann more often than not adopted an obsequious tone in his correspondence with chamber group principals, conductors, and impresarios, who were in a position either to perform his work or to bring it to the attention of international juries or broadcast stations. And when he did not appear to be mercenary, Hartmann could sound offended and even angry.

A case in point is Hartmann's relationship with the Slovenian avant-garde composer Slavko Osterc, whom he had met at the ISCM festival in Prague in the fall of 1935. Evidently, the two men got along very well, on musical as well as on ideological grounds; Hartmann's mentor Scherchen, too, liked Osterc, speculating about a guest performance of his own in Ljubljana. In 1936, as Hartmann was getting his cantata ready for the ISCM Paris competition, he wrote Osterc unabashedly that he had learned from Jemnitz of his seat on the Paris jury. Announcing that he would send him his composition directly to Ljubljana, he expressed his hope that Osterc would take his side during the judging. After having seen the cantata beforehand in Ljubljana, suggested Hartmann, Osterc might travel to Paris without wasting time in searching out other quality work among the many entries to be expected there. He later thanked Osterc for his apparent willingness to represent his interests on the jury and in so many words said he was confident that Osterc would be able to influence other jurors. Hartmann tried to excuse what today could be interpreted as an attempt at influence peddling with "the especially difficult conditions" in Germany. The fact that Scherchen put additional pressure on Osterc on Hartmann's behalf, and Hartmann was aware of this, could have motivated the composer to suppress further whatever scruples he might originally have harbored. As it turned out, of course, Scherchen and Hartmann's joint interference ended in failure.[67]

In another case Hartmann maneuvered himself into a strained relationship with Paul Sacher. The noted conductor and impresario, already a champion of Stravinsky, had written Hartmann in June 1938 that he was interested in performing works of Hartmann during the upcoming season, warning him, however, that he did not yet know the composer's "style of music," and that at first reading he found it, "if anything, unfamiliar."[68] Hartmann replied by asking Sacher to return to him the score of the symphony for strings (later his Fourth Symphony), which he had sent him earlier, because he wanted to make additional changes.[69] After the composer visited Sacher in Basel, the conductor informed him in May 1939 that he saw no possibility of performing any of his works, including the string symphony, because he was already overcommitted, especially to Swiss composers, and found it, as well as the chamber opera *Simplicius,* a touch too modern for local audiences.[70] Hartmann rebuked Sacher, arguing that, after all, the conductor had "promised" to perform him, whereupon Sacher spoke of a "misunderstanding," insisting, whether it was true or not, that he had never given any such promises.[71]

Despite these difficult professional relationships, Hartmann actually still did resonably well on the non-German musical circuit. In early 1936 he was awarded first prize from the Gesellschaft für Zeitgenössische Kammermusik "Carillon" in Geneva for his string quartet (the one with the Hebrew melody, which other musicians had found so difficult to play), later appropriately named *Carillon.* Serving on the jury were the Italian composer Gian Francesco Malipiero and the Swiss conductor Ernest Ansermet.[72] In May 1937 the Viennese Emil Hertzka Memorial Foundation awarded Hartmann's *Anno '48/Friede,* a work for soprano, mixed choir, and piano, an honorable mention, behind compositions by Austrians Hans Erich Apostel and Ludwig Zenk; Hartmann's piece was dedicated to the memory of Alban Berg, and Berg's old friend Anton Webern was one of the judges.[73] At the annual ISCM festivals across Europe Hartmann was a fairly regular guest, with the ones in Prague (1935) and London (1938) singling him out for special recognition and honors.[74] And in 1938 he enjoyed a number of successes with premieres, broadcasts, and acceptances in Belgium, which were cut short only by the outbreak of the war.[75]

Some of this success abroad was due to Hermann Scherchen. For the left-wing conductor was by far the greatest influence on Hartmann as a professional musician; he also proved to be the most problematic human factor in the composer's life. Scherchen was a musical genius with diversified artistic and scholarly interests, in particular a pioneering champion of Weimar modernist culture, but at the same time he was an egomaniac and a consummate womanizer, who ruthlessly exploited the many talented people flocking around him for the sake of his own prominence.[76] In this sense, he was similar to fellow Marxist crusader Bertolt Brecht, with whom he worked closely during the end of the republic and shared, as mistress, the idealistic and beautiful actress and singer Carola Neher, destined by 1942, unlike her two circumspect lovers, to perish in Stalin's Gulag.[77] In many ways, Scherchen discovered Hartmann's real talents and helped bring them to full bloom. But in others, he impeded him and made his days miserable. From a safe exile in Switzerland, Scherchen tried to monopolize Hartmann, knowing full well that in National Socialist Munich the composer had little room to breathe. Always in awe of his mentor, who was fourteen years his senior, Hartmann has politely spoken, toward the end of his life, about vacillations in Scherchen's "character and intellect," but in 1994, Elisabeth Hartmann was much more forthright.[78] Although she acknowledged to me that her deceased husband had learned a lot from him, she also remarked that it was terrifying to know "how mean Scherchen could often be."[79]

In 1929, when Hartmann was already in touch with Die Juryfreien, Scherchen had started to collaborate with Fritz Büchtger in the Munich Vereinigung für Zeitgenössische Musik. During its four extended festival weeks from 1929 to 1931 the Vereinigung featured the works of mostly younger, modern composers; and on one such occasion, in 1930, Scherchen conducted Hindemith's Brechtian *Lehrstück* and Stravinsky's *Histoire du soldat,* which Hartmann probably listened to. As already mentioned, Hartmann appears to have met Scherchen in person through Werner Egk, who together with his friend Carl Orff was active in the Vereinigung; in Munich's confined avant-garde circles, their paths naturally crossed.[80] The first decisive meeting between Scherchen and Hartmann probably occurred in 1931, when the composer began to learn the craft from the maestro, and as he emphasized later, nothing of musical import had happened to him "until Hermann Scherchen showed the way for me and my compositions." Hartmann became totally beholden to Scherchen's personality and cosmos.[81]

Why this early dependence on the charismatic conductor should not have encouraged Hartmann to leave Germany, as Scherchen himself had already done, as soon as the Nazis came to power in January 1933 remains somewhat of a mystery. His wife maintains that he would have emigrated given a chance (and had he had an internationally viable reputation to smooth his path abroad), but in greater likelihood this explanation applies to the period after 1934, when Hartmann was already married, a child was on the way, and, quite possibly, his socially and economically influential in-laws were opposed to seeing their daughter leave home.[82] Others have suggested that for the sake of his art alone, he was too deeply rooted in Bavarian soil to leave Germany.[83] As was suggested previously, it is probable that in the first eighteen months or so of the regime Hartmann seriously attempted to salvage his professional integrity while remaining a denizen of the Third Reich, he had a few publicity and commercial leads, his mother and fiancée were living in Munich, and many democratic-minded Germans at that time were hoping for a quick end to what they at first regarded as only a loosely secured dictatorship, until the brutal Röhm Purge of June 1934 taught them about Hitler's true totalitarian intentions.[84]

For Hartmann's compositions, Scherchen's inspiration was immediate, starting in 1932. One of the first such works was the concertino for trumpet, which Scherchen premiered at his avant-garde workshop-festival in Strasbourg in July–August 1933.[85] Another work seems to have been that for solo cello and orchestra, dedicated to Hartmann's friend, the Hungarian cellist Vilmos Palotai, but it is reportedly lost. Yet another was the first string quartet, now expressly dedicated to Scherchen (composed in 1933 and later known as *Carillon*).[86]

From 1933 on, when Scherchen could not risk going to Germany any more, Hartmann was in the habit of traveling to Winterthur to study with him, sometimes for up to three months. Hartmann would copy parts, correct and edit other people's scores, and compose under the maestro's supervision.[87] When Scherchen invited Egk to his international summer workshop in Strasbourg in 1933, which was jointly sponsored by the city's Conservatoire and town hall, he expected him to conduct new scores by Hartmann, besides some by Egk's friend Orff and other, younger representatives of the European avant-garde, like Egk himself.[88] Through Scherchen Hartmann met influential personalities such as Joachim Röntgen, who was in a position to schedule performances in the regular concert series of the Musikkollegium Winterthur, which of course was a bedrock of support for Scherchen himself. These chances increased after Röntgen had learned of Hartmann's great *Miserae* success under Scherchen at the ISCM festival in Prague in September 1935.[89] As 1935 was drawing to a close, Hartmann's gratitude for Scherchen knew no bounds; he felt deeply indebted to him and went out of his way to show it: "You know full well that I have no one besides yourself who would stand up for me and share his wonderful skills in such a magnanimous manner with me."[90]

A photograph taken of the thirty-year-old composer together with his mentor Scherchen at Prague shows him at the pinnacle of early international acclaim, but at the same time it symbolizes his subjection to the conductor. On the picture, the physically tall and powerful-looking Scherchen towers over the much smaller, though already somewhat portly Hartmann, who appears pumped up with pride. Scherchen has an arm condescendingly around Hartmann's shoulder, but he eyes the younger man through his rimless spectacles as a snake would eye its unsuspecting prey, calculatingly, his thin lips pressed tightly together. The photo calls to mind the poet Elias Canetti's succinct observation about Scherchen, that he was difficult to the point of being capriciously offensive to his friends, although at the same time he could be extremely engaging.[91]

A year earlier, in the fall of 1934, the seeds had already been planted for conflict. While on his honeymoon in Switzerland, Hartmann had visited Scherchen and discussed with him the scenario for what was to become Hartmann's chamber opera *Des Simplicius Simplicissimus Jugend*. Typically, Scherchen later published the first version of the libretto in his Brussels firm Ars Viva (the second, final version did not become official until Schott's Söhne issued it in 1957), giving all the credit for the text to himself and ceding none to the cocreators, the dramaturge Wolfgang Petzet and the composer Hartmann.[92] Between 1934 and 1945, despite what Hartmann took to be a mutual understanding and constant reassurances by Scherchen, the conductor not once deigned to stage the opera, taunting Hartmann in November 1938 that he could not care less who would end up premiering the work, which, after all, had originated entirely with him. Hurt to the core, Hartmann replied that he could not have been happier had Scherchen included *Simplicius* at any one time in the many series of concerts he was constantly organizing, but "unfortunately, you have conducted something by myself only twice thus far." These were bittersweet allusions to Strasbourg and to Prague.[93]

In fact, the years from 1934 to 1939 were marked by occasional highlights, but on the whole by setbacks in the relationship between the conductor and his composer acolyte, with Scherchen clearly exploiting Hartmann's isolation, keeping him on call just in case he might need him. As far as Hartmann was concerned, he found it difficult to rid himself of his debt of gratitude to Scherchen, always exaggerating the potential of the mentor's benefaction on his behalf and underestimating his self-reliance. This naiveté would cost Hartmann dearly in the long run and probably contributed to the acute depression he suffered during the war years.

Exploiting the momentum of Hartmann's recent success, Scherchen in December 1935 picked the composer's brains about his impression of the ISCM festival in Prague, wanting to know how one could improve on the content and format of such international events—undoubtedly with a view to organizing his own, as he had done in Strasbourg, involving his Brussels music-publishing firm Ars Viva. Hartmann dutifully agreed to meet the deadline of 20 December, which in the end had to be extended.[94] In April 1936 the composer's success at Geneva, when the string quartet (*Carillon*) won first prize, reflected well on Scherchen, who then asked the flattered composer to introduce the Italian festival participant Dallapiccola and his newest scores to him.[95] When later in the year Hartmann's colleague Jemnitz published in the Budapest paper *Népszava* a positive review of the libretto for *Simplicius* (which coauthor Scherchen himself had sent from Brussels to the Hungarian capital), Hartmann, overjoyed, immediately requested Jemnitz's permission to make this review available to Scherchen's Brussels firm.[96] Next Scherchen obliged his composer friend by interceding on his behalf with Osterc in the matter of the Paris ISCM jury.[97] That having failed, Hartmann in January 1937 asked Scherchen to put in a good word for him with Zurich jurors, who were about to judge the cantata *Anno '48/Friede* in a recently announced competition. Chances there, too, were slim, because Krenek, one of the jurors, had written a cantata utilizing verses by the poet Andreas Gryphius, as did Hartmann's. Predictably, he failed (this time because of a conflict of interests which Krenek could have neutralized by remaining neutral), as Hartmann grieved in a letter to Scherchen dated 9 February 1937. And once again he had left himself wide open to attack or ridicule by his chosen mentor.[98]

And those were not long in coming when, in May 1937, Scherchen complained to Hartmann that so far not a single German student had applied to study with him at a new workshop planned by him in Switzerland, allegedly because Hartmann had not done his duty of printing German prospectuses to advertise the event. In the margins of a letter by Scherchen that today still breathes the émigré's suspicion and contempt, Hartmann noted meekly in pencil: "Scherchen does not take into account how difficult life and work are in Germany!"[99] Then, in a letter dated 22 May, he tried to allay Scherchen's fear of personal disloyalty.[100] But the conductor's revenge, for something that Hartmann had not been responsible for in the first place, was already taking its course. Hartmann learned that when Scherchen had recently been visiting a Budapest publishing firm, he had barely mentioned the composer's name, causing not even a ripple of interest among the publishers for Hartmann's works.[101] Scherchen held out an invitation to Hartmann to the upcoming ISCM festival in London in the summer of 1938, and the composer accepted gladly, most certainly in the hope that Scherchen would finally produce his *Simplicius* or at least find him an international publisher for the score.[102] But the reunion in London took quite a different turn. Scherchen, who by this time had developed an inexplicable hatred of *any* German musician who had not emigrated like himself, interpreted Hartmann's presence in England as a sign that he had sufficiently ingratiated himself with Nazi authorities to be able to travel abroad, and Scherchen immediately held it against him. (Was it possible that Scherchen suspected Hartmann of an unsavory collaboration with the Reich Music Chamber in Berlin?) Scherchen hurled invective at the composer and acted rudely toward his wife.[103] On a subsequent journey to Winterthur, Hartmann pointedly avoided Scherchen, who continued to be suspicious.[104] Meanwhile, their mutual friend Jemnitz attributed Scherchen's agonizing behavior to a megalomaniacal streak, when he wrote toward the end of 1938: "He, who earlier on worked only for the cause and through it became great, now uses the cause just for himself and thereby becomes smaller."[105]

Hartmann remained dependent on Scherchen, not least emotionally, well into the war, with the conductor playing his old tricks on the composer, who was left more in a state of paralysis rather than anger conducive to rebellion. As before, Scherchen's special treatment for Hartmann consisted of promises, which kept Hartmann busy in an effort to fulfill various formalities and chores, not the least of which was the careful mailing of valuable manuscripts, with nothing coming of the action in the end. Scherchen, on the other hand, was trying to ensure that he had a contact person in the Third Reich even during wartime, should he ever need him.

A few months before the outbreak of hostilities, Scherchen raised Hartmann's hopes by asking that the score of his newly completed work for string orchestra (later to become his Fourth Symphony) be sent to the Winterthur Musikkollegium, adding later that he had also proposed it to the BBC in London and was himself interested in performing it in the near future. Despite Hartmann's reminders, however, nothing happened with it; the Musikkollegium returned the score to Munich without further ado.[106] In 1940 Scherchen offered to Hartmann the prospect of Furtwängler conducting one of Hartmann's more recent compositions, as both men had reportedly spoken about this during one of the Berlin maestro's occasional visits to Switzerland. But Scherchen added, as a safety measure, that this could occur only if Furtwängler were indeed able "to come to grips with your music." Whether Furtwängler ever tried to do so is not known; in any event, Hartmann's music never resonated from a Berlin concert stage.[107] Scherchen also told Hartmann that he had brokered performances of his works at Radio Beromünster in Zurich, but Hartmann's repeated inquiries in Switzerland fell on deaf ears.[108]

There were more hollow-sounding requests by Scherchen for Hartmann's works, some new and some older ones, including of course *Simplicius*.[109] The other side of the coin was that whenever Scherchen really thought he needed Hartmann, he was not shy to ask. In December 1940 Scherchen once again wanted more students to attend his new conductor master classes at the Berne conservatory; Hartmann himself was supposed to make the trip. Several months later Scherchen needed Hartmann's services in the procurement of the photocopy of a rare manuscript extant only in a Schwerin library; the composer was called upon to look after it.[110] It could have been little consolation to Karl Amadeus Hartmann that, at the climax of the war, Anton Webern thought highly of the relationship between the two musicians, and that toward war's end Jemnitz told him that Scherchen seemed to have changed for the better, for "his basic disposition fortunately appears to have improved once more." When in early 1945 Hartmann tallied everything up, he could not but realize that he had seen himself through World War II alone, with the dependable help of his loyal family, but in isolation from most fellow composers at home and abroad and without the assistance of the still admired erstwhile mentor.[111]

III

After World War II Hartmann emerged as one of the few artists who had remained in Germany yet had not been tainted by National Socialism or the Third Reich, either personally or professionally. Logically, the U.S. authorities responsible for occupied Bavaria were seeking his cooperation in rebuilding the culture of the German nation and through it, reintroducing democracy.[112] Hence in the summer of 1945 they asked Hartmann to become the Generalintendant of the Bayerische Staatsoper in Munich, a post

Hartmann refused for lack of experience. Instead, in September he accepted the position of dramaturge, and as such was commissioned by OMGUS to help restore the musical culture by way of matinee performances.[113]

Conditions were daunting at first. "Everything had to be built up from scratch," remembers Frau Hartmann, "there were no singers, no props, and no streetcar ran." Venues were hard to come by, because almost every structure had been bombed, but performances finally started on 7 October 1945, in the still extant but small Prinzregententheater. Hartmann had organized a concert consisting of the *Lustspielouvertüre* by Ferruccio Busoni, the Fourth Symphony by Gustav Mahler, and the orchestral suite *Iberia* by Claude Debussy.[114]

In the time ahead, a mixture of classical traditionalism and avant-garde music was to become the hallmark of the concerts, with the latter weighing heavier in the balance.[115] But if the music of the nineteenth century played any role at all, it was mostly because Hartmann found it difficult, certainly at first, to attract audiences exclusively interested in the modern works he himself so much favored. Because there was a didactic motive behind the venture, it was necessary to reintroduce music lovers to an entire epoch of modern music of which they had become disabused from the start of the Nazi period—a problem Hindemith faced on his post-1945 tours to Germany as well. He had to proceed with extreme caution, wrote Hartmann to Scherchen as late as January 1947, "since the audience has totally lost its understanding of modern music and even the musicians are helpless in coping with the strange sounds." Apparently, for every concert 200 seats were to be reserved for students at lower prices, a measure that hardly seemed necessary, as most of their elders regarded the series with so much ill will.[116]

Hartmann, long an admirer of Schoenberg, Berg, and Webern, was particularly keen to have the works of the Second Viennese School performed, but Bartók, Stravinsky, Prokofiev, Milhaud, Honegger, Toch, and Hindemith were also among his chosen masters. In the first season, up to the autumn of 1946, he managed no fewer than ten concerts.[117] Well into 1947 Hartmann patronized young, promising German composers, such as Hans Werner Henze, who at twenty-one was then still a student of the (Nazi-compromised) Wolfgang Fortner, and younger French composers, such as Pierre Petit, Pierre Barbaud, Roger Albin, and Michel Ciry. He used his old connections, asking Riisager for a new score of his, or begging Sacher for works by contemporary Swiss or French composers.[118] In early February 1946 Hartmann was bold enough to approach Hindemith regarding a German premiere of *Mathis der Maler,* reminding the U.S. resident that he had traveled from Munich to Zurich in May 1938 to witness the opera's world premiere there. "At the time, in the early morning after the late-night banquet," reminisced Hartmann, "the two of us were sitting in a house in Zurich, and we spoke about Munich and Germany. Meanwhile, what we thought would happen did in fact happen, yet to what extent!" Hindemith thanked him politely, and with interest in the opera staging. But as it turned out, the German premiere of *Mathis* occurred at the end of the year, at the Stuttgart opera, a few hundred hundred miles from Munich.[119]

It could not have been for lack of artistic talent that such an ambitious plan was not realized in Munich itself. As Hartmann had been quick to remind Hindemith, he enjoyed as overall organizer the loyal assistance of Hans Rosbaud, a first-class conductor and Hindemith's old friend from Frankfurt conservatory days. Another conductor then working in Munich, Bertil Wetzelsberger, was not as stellar, Hartmann had to admit, but, as a modernist, still had his merits. Nevertheless, the number of cooperating artists at first was small because of a possible Nazi past which, politically incriminating, was not conducive to the democratic process.[120] Hartmann's concerts were not confined to opera but included everything from chamber music to large symphonic works, requiring a variety of artists; he frequently found himself in a quandary, whenever, against all expectations, a colleague turned out to be politically compromised. Two days before a scheduled concert, remembers Elisabeth Hartmann, the Americans might intervene and announce a sudden ruling: This singer is prohibited! The concert was then unceremoniously canceled.[121]

Was it because Hartmann knew his old mentor Hermann Scherchen to be beyond reproach in this regard that he asked him to rejoin him? For in May 1946 he invited Scherchen to consider conducting a symphonic program in August. Scherchen's answer, however, was still suffused with suspicion. Replied Hartmann: "There really is no point in constantly mistrusting each other. You started doing this in London in 1938, and whenever I met you in the years to follow, dear Doctor, you never stopped doubting me."[122]

To be sure, whatever personal doubts Hartmann himself may still have harbored about Scherchen in the first few months after the war, he knew for certain that the conductor was not an active fascist. Nor a slumbering one, of the kind that he had reason to believe plenty existed in the land, just waiting to topple the good ship democracy at the earliest possible opportunity. "Unfortunately it is obvious that the spirit of Nazism is still buoyant everywhere," Hartmann lamented to Scherchen early in 1947, "and anti-Semitism is alive and well."[123] More than a year later he informed Krenek that "gradually they are all returning to the scene, those who were the bosses for twelve years, and they are trying to push us against the wall, for even today we are in a small minority."[124] Indubitably there were ex-Nazis who, under one cover or another, tried to encumber the OMGUS-sponsored concert series; they were the very same ones who had learned to hate Mendelssohn and Mahler for the sake of some mediocre, regime-sponsored post-Romanticist such as Paul Graener or Max Trapp.[125] For that reason Hartmann early on sought to introduce composers who were the very opposite of Nazi artists, such as the Schoenberg student (and Communist) Hanns Eisler, and as late as 1962—two years after Jewish cemeteries had been desecrated all over Germany—he exhorted his contemporaries to be "watchful" and to speak up "whenever we detect the stirrings of totalitarianism."[126]

Indeed, the skeptics and detractors persisted when toward the end of 1947 Hartmann proceeded to convert his initial OMGUS concerts into a series of his own, which, in unabated recognition of his mentor, he christened Musica Viva.[127] As it happened, one phenomenon sprang from the other, Hartmann keeping his title (and nominal position) of Generalmusikdirektor at the Bavarian State Opera till his death in 1963.[128] Hartmann continued to champion younger German composers, who, if anything, had been out of favor with the Nazis, such as Boris Blacher, whose theories of variable meter intrigued him, as well as the important non-Germans, such as the Frenchman (and Nazi-banned Jew) Darius Milhaud, the Jewish-American Aaron Copland, and his old Italian friend Luigi Dallapiccola. In addition to the opera, he could now also use the newly constituted Bavarian broadcast system as a tool; from February 1948, the concerts were performed by the orchestra of Radio Munich. Up until 1963 Musica Viva came to mirror whatever was the newest musical development in Germany, to the point where even some of Hartmann's older favorites, such as Bartók, were considered outdated by some of his younger followers, who wanted the boldest avant-garde. Various modernist musicians conducted; in October 1957 it was Stravinsky. Ironically, this was slowly changing Munich's time-honored reputation of a stuffy guardian of convention to one of daring progressivism (even though after Rosbaud's departure in 1948 the Philharmonic, for a while at least, reverted to the kind of traditionalism that had long been its hallmark).[129] Of ever-increasing importance to Hartmann was Henze, who became a close friend and today acknowledges the older composer as one of his main influences. Hartmann premiered Henze's madrigal *Das grosse Testament,* along with works by Wladimir Vogel and himself, in early 1949. And a decade before his death Hartmann took under his wing one of the most revolutionary Germans ever to compose music: the twenty-five-year-old Karlheinz Stockhausen.[130]

For a few years Hartmann's relationship with Scherchen remained problematic, but in mature age they came to terms, as the conductor had to recognize that his former student had, possibly, attained a position more important than his own. Frau Hartmann today recalls that his manner being, as always, unbearable (what with Scherchen notoriously insulting other visiting musicians, especially women), he was invited to Munich only sparingly, conducting his first Musica Viva concert as late as February 1953. But Hartmann continued to acknowledge him, until a few years before his death the two men finally became personal friends. Nonetheless, Scherchen went on humiliating Hartmann posthumously, even in the presence of his widow. This was, after all, one of the stranger human relationships in Germany's modern musical history.[131]

Another tenuous affiliation was that between Hartmann on the one side and Carl Orff and Werner Egk on the other. Orff, who after the war claimed to have been on the side of the enemies of the Third Reich, yet had no contacts with Hartmann to speak of, especially not as a member of Hartmann's sworn circle, seems to have regarded the new Generalmusikdirektor with suspicion at first. But eventually the Hartmann and Orff couples saw each other socially on a more regular basis; Orff entertained the Hartmanns with his famous piano antics, giving renditions of all his works and those of others, and is reported particularly to have liked Hartmann's Sixth Symphony (1953). He frequented concerts of Musica Viva, during some of which his own compositions were performed. Orff, being the easy manipulator of people that he was, saw no particular difficulty in arranging himself, on a month-to-month basis, with a potential rival who now was in an obvious situation of prominence.[132]

Eventually, Egk's works also were heard under the auspices of Musica Viva. Hartmann's personal liaison with the composer, however, was more complex. On the one hand, Egk had denied Hartmann special favors during the Nazi regime, such as acting as a courier to Switzerland for Karl Amadeus's brother Richard, and, like Orff, he too had made certain never to be seen in Hartmann's company. On the other, Egk spent years after May 1945 trying to clear his name with the American and Bavarian authorities because of his collusion with the Nazis as a RMK official after July 1941. Early in 1946, no less opportunistic than Orff, Egk came to see Hartmann at his flat in an attempt to solicit his support of Egk's resistance legend. In the recollection of Frau Hartmann, the atmosphere was "very tense." Hartmann evidently did not speak out against Egk, but he also could do nothing truly convincing for him. Hartmann's affidavit, written under oath and dated 11 March 1946 contains obvious nontruths, which could easily have been uncovered by the denazification judges had they tried. For instance, Frau Hartmann does not recall, as Hartmann then claimed existed, special documents signed by Egk on behalf of Hartmann, after July 1941, to protect the dissident against National Socialist recriminations—and, surely, Egk being Egk, he would not have had the will or the power to sign such papers. Nor are such documents presently preserved in Egk's surviving papers. Similarly, there is no written proof that Egk saved Hartmann from a "total work detail" by vouching for the "artistic value and significance of my oeuvre." Egk also never helped Hartmann to travel to Switzerland to meet his exiled brother, for after July 1941 Hartmann had stopped making such trips. Small wonder then if, in order not to be cross-examined on these points, Hartmann on 5 September 1947 pretended to have been too unwell to make a personal appearance in denazification court three days earlier, a claim that was never backed by a medical certificate. On 5 September Hartmann merely repeated that Egk had been sympathetic toward him before 1945, adding, implausibly, that "personally, I know nothing about his political associations."[133]

Hartmann slowly began to reconstruct his own oeuvre and also to compose new works; for the first few years after 1945, these processes went hand in hand and were not without complications. There had been at least two important caesuras in Hartmann's productive life: the first around 1931, when he had met Scherchen, who then changed his artistic course (so that, claims Hartmann, he destroyed all his earlier works, a claim only partially substantiated), and the second in May 1945, when the phase of secretiveness and a nominally illegal professional existence were over. In the summer of that year, Hartmann was faced with several awesome tasks: Because most of his music had so far not been properly published, he had to consolidate and issue it. Some of it was lost, had been disowned by the composer, or was in holdings thought to be unsafe or inaccessible. Much of it was unfinished and needed to be amalgamated with other half-completed works or with new music yet to be written. Moreover, Hartmann now felt motivated to make new artistic and ideological statements, over and beyond the ones he had already rendered, but how to integrate the old with the new, or with works still in gestation?

Thus of the five symphonies Hartmann wrote between 1945 and 1953—a phase of high productivity for him—only one, the Second Symphony, was a new and self-contained opus, composed in 1945–46, which Rosbaud premiered in 1950 in Donaueschingen. What went under the label of First Symphony in 1950 embodied the cantata of 1936, known by 1938 as *Symphonisches Fragment* and premiered in Frankfurt in 1948. The Third Symphony of 1948–49 incorporated the *Sinfonia tragica* of 1940 and the *Klagegesang* of 1944. The Fifth Symphony of 1950 contained the concertino (sometimes also referred to as concerto) for trumpet written in 1932, which itself had been modified in 1948–49. Overall, Hartmann's *Werkverzeichnis* at the time of his death in 1963 constituted a confusing list, more like a patchwork quilt, reflecting the composer's manifold uncertainties over time. Indeed, it was not until 1955 that Hartmann was able to say with equanimity that "today I am contented with my music."[134]

Despite such fragmentation in his oeuvre, supported by his newfound personal freedom as well as his posts within OMGUS and his own Musica Viva, Hartmann came to prosper as an original composer of the post–World War II era. He honed his own oeuvre, which remained strictly tonally based, in spite of his veneration of the Schoenberg circle and occasional experimentation with serialism. One by one, those earlier signal works were performed: his opera, now renamed *Simplicius Simplicissimus,* in a concert version under Rosbaud in Munich in March 1948, and a full stage version in Cologne in October 1949. His First Symphony was premiered, still as *Symphonisches Fragment,* under fellow composer Winfried Zillig in Frankfurt in the spring of 1948, and the *Concerto funèbre,* in a new version, in 1959 in Brunswick.[135]

Predictably, Hartmann collected his share of prizes and honors: the music prize of the City of Munich in 1949, the art prize of the Bayerische Akademie der Künste in 1950. Three years later, he became a fellow of that academy. He was awarded the Schoenberg Medal of the resurrected ISCM in 1954 and made a member of the West Berlin Akademie der Künste in 1955. The music prize of Brunswick was his in 1959—by that time Hartmann was collecting approximately one prize per year.[136]

Altogether, then, this is the biography of a successful artist conscious of the ethical demands made on him, privately and professionally, right to the end of his life, or almost so. A questionable episode almost sullied his integrity at the peak of success in the postwar period. This was when the ministry of culture of the German Democratic Republic (DDR) offered him the chance to defect to that Communist state so that he might duplicate his Musica Viva series there. On the part of the East Berlin regime, this move was a calculated one, for of course it knew about his leftist leanings and his once exiled Communist brother Richard, and that in his youth Hartmann had composed music to the texts of Johannes R. Becher, now a high DDR administrator of culture and soon to head the culture ministry himself. More significantly, Hartmann had been in touch with the Communist Robert Havemann, signaling his willingness to discuss "politics" with the prolific chemist. For his part, Havemann after the war had become president of the Kaiser-Wilhelm-Gesellschaft for the Advancement of Science. In March 1946 Havemann wrote back to Hartmann to say: "I dare say that Berlin and our zone of occupation are considerably more advanced than you would be in Bavaria, and I could imagine that you yourself might be very interested in coming to Berlin. People would certainly be very interested in your music here." It was an open invitation for Hartmann to leave the West for the sake of some important career in the East. In 1946 Hartmann resisted this temptation, and then again in 1950, but at that time not without having to endure Havemann's visit in Munich and his strident attempts to convert him. Easily accepting the Communist image of the DDR as an antifascist state, Hartmann is said to have been almost ready to go until he reconsidered the discriminatory treatment of Schoenberg and the Second Viennese School as reprehensible "formalists" at the hands of the Communist regime. To his credit, Hartmann made his decision in favor of creative freedom and democracy and stayed in Munich.[137] Had he not done so, he would have moved, once again and this time willingly, within the confines of a totalitarian regime, similar in its oppressive nature and censorial intent to the one from which he had just barely escaped.

5

Carl Orff

Man of Legend

I

Who was Carl Orff? Who was Carl Orff in the Third Reich? There is probably no modern German composer whose life and career, especially after the Nazi takeover, have been as shrouded in mystery or confusion as his. And this, although an early post-World War II judgment had held that no one could properly evaluate Orff's oeuvre by paying heed merely to his musical persona.[1] Despite this timely warning, the Munich historian of culture Jens Malte Fischer has lamented as recently as March 1995 that Orff's career, especially during the Third Reich, has so far never been examined in depth.[2] Why then did another Munich historian of culture insist just a few months later that a dissertation on Orff and National Socialism would yield little original knowledge and nothing sensational whatsoever?[3]

There are, indeed, two schools of thought on the theme of Carl Orff in the Third Reich, one claiming that he was if not a direct victim of the Nazis seriously wronged by them and at best tolerated. The other maintains that not only was Orff a collaborator of the Nazis and himself a bona fide National Socialist but his music too was symptomatic, particularly of Nazi ideology.

Orff himself consistently said that his work, especially the scenic cantata *Carmina Burana,* was proscribed by the Nazi regime and that he was suspect as a composer and a citizen because he had felt beholden to the idea of a "European commonality" rather than one of narrow-minded German nationalism. His use of Latin in *Carmina Burana,* so he asserted, manifested this conviction and hence constituted an act of opposition.[4] Orff's second wife, Gertrud, has taken this further by contending that Orff always was "a conscious anti-Nazi" and his compositions were "officially not wanted."[5] To a greater or lesser degree, colleagues, critics, and scholars alike have reinforced this interpretation over the years, Hans Heinz Stuckenschmidt being the first to emphasize, as early as 1946, that Orff, along with Hindemith, Boris Blacher, and Richard Mohaupt, was barely abided by the Hitler regime.[6] Biographer Ernst Krause supported this in 1971, and as respected a musicologist as Carl Dahlhaus in 1982 forbade anyone ever to doubt Orff's political or moral integrity.[7] Orff's composer friend Rudolf Wagner-Régeny, too, echoed Stuckenschmidt when in his memoirs he wrote that for such artists as himself and Werner Egk and Orff, any creative work had been in spite of circumstances, by way of "laboriously hanging on."[8] Orff or Egk, reemphasized musicologist Ludwig F. Schiedermair in 1990, had nothing to do with the political or musical *Zeitgeist* of the Nazi era, as they had both been neither members nor sympathizers nor fellow travelers of Hitler's movement.[9] As recently as 1995 Orff's chief apologist, Franz Willnauer, demanded that the composer's oeuvre finally be "set free from the odium of 'National Socialist music,'" while German historian Reiner Pommerin rejoiced that after May 1945 Orff's music could be performed again.[10]

But how well documented are such acts of anti-Nazi defiance? There is evidence, or, rather, the suspicious lack of it, to suggest that the composer's anti-Nazi record may not have been as sterling as his protagonists have maintained. Thus why would Karl Laux, who had been a music critic in the Third Reich and after 1945 continued to ply his trade as an ostensibly democratic professional in Communist East Germany, avoid in 1949 any mention of the Third Reich in a short biographical sketch of Orff?[11] And what about other omissions by zealous Orff backers? In 1995, an internationally touring centenary exhibition showed a slate of quotations by or about the master, from 1895, the year of his birth, to 1982, that of his death. Of the twelve dates mentioned, only two were from the era of the Third Reich, and both referred, positively, to *Carmina Burana.* Tamara Bernstein, a Toronto music critic, jested that she wanted to award to the Orff Foundation headed by Willnauer, which was responsible for the exhibition, the Kurt Waldheim Award for Selective Memory Loss, "for blanking out those 10 pesky years, 1937–1947."[12] A year later, three full pages detailing Orff's life and work from 1895 to 1995—appended to the catalog of an Orff exhibition sponsored by the Munich Carl-Orff-Zentrum—devoted barely seven entries to the Third Reich period, missing, in the process, a reference to one of Orff's more controversial works, the incidental music for Shakespeare's *A Midsummer Night's Dream* of 1939, as did the catalog text itself.[13]

Harsh judgments rendered by interpreters of the other side of Orff's life bear careful scrutiny. Andrea Seebohm's verdict in 1985 that Orff, like Egk and Wagner-Régeny, had been a "reinsurer," was comparatively kind, at about the same level as Harvey Sachs's opinion that Orff had been "Nazi-sanctioned."[14] At the end of 1988 some critics experienced a production of Orff's *Carmina Burana* by the Amsterdam Concertgebouw Orchestra under Riccardo Chailly as "a Christmas greeting from Nazi Germany."[15] Thereafter, the closer the Orff centenary of 1995 got, the harsher became the accusations. In 1992 came a reminder from the venerable daily *Frankfurter Allgemeine Zeitung* that Orff had been "a genuine sympathiser of the Third Reich," and in 1995, in the equally venerable weekly *Die Zeit,* Eleanore Büning declared the composer a member of the Nazi Party.[16] The American reviewer Matthew Gurewitsch found it difficult, at first sight, to associate the name of Carl Orff, in the manner of the "thought police," with Nazism. Possibly he had, however, committed a grave omission. For "the most haunting clue may be a photograph of Carl, age three, holding a tin drum."[17] Was this irony or malice? Not enough; a New York psychiatrist and Holocaust survivor, on the eve of a double staging of the Jewish Kurt Weill's *Die sieben Todsünden* and Orff's *Carmina Burana* by the New York City Opera in early 1997, protested with the exclamation, "After all, Carl Orff was a Nazi!"[18]

Was it Carl Orff's attitude toward the Third Reich or the nature of his compositions that became important in determining whether this composer had been a Nazi? As far as the latter is concerned, attention has centered on his signature piece, *Carmina Burana,* as well as on the music for Shakespeare's charming comedy, because Orff's new creation has been seen as supplanting the time-honored composition of Felix Mendelssohn-Bartholdy. Thus, in a New York exhibition on culture and politics in Nazi Germany in 1993, it was noted that Orff had received a substantial amount of money for his music to *A Midsummer Night's Dream,* as a substitute "for the classic version by the vilified Jewish composer Felix Mendelssohn."[19] In August 1995 Alex Ross wrote in *The New York Times* that "the completely unscrupulous Orff accepted a commission to write a replacement score for Mendelssohn's verboten 'Midsummer Night's Dream,' one of the shabbiest acts in musical history."[20]

And what about *Carmina Burana* itself, through which Orff was to establish his world fame? Was there something intrinsically fascist in the music, as the Geneva professor of English and Comparative Literature, George Steiner, suggested in 1998: "Orff's 'Carmina Burana' is fascist trash, and can be shown to be so in musical terms"? Or, as music apart from ideology, was the scenic cantata badly crafted? The latter was suggested by Nicolas Slonimsky's contemporary judgment, when he characterized the piece, tongue in cheek, as an "amalgam of heterogeneous neo-medieval, ecclesiastical, ethnic and popular melodic and rhythmic elements, accoutred in bland modalities and marked by a hypnotically repetitive asymmetrical cantillation alternating with monometrical ululation and syncopated hockets."[21] Sydney musicologist Richard Toop has recently taken this caricature of a critique one step further by arguing that it is "almost impossible to debase an overblown, crude piece of music from a Nazi sympathiser with a taste for smutty lyrics."[22] Various critics have found *Carmina Burana* "ideologically questionable" or "prototypical of culture under National Socialism"; one said the composition was successful because Hitler himself had seen and liked it.[23] The negative association between Nazism, the music, and the lyrics was graphically conjured up by Toronto musician and writer Elissa Poole, who described the initial chorus of Orff's main composition as "terrifying when the singers spit out their Latin fricatives like powerful jack-booted automatons."[24] But how does all this accord with the fact that a Communist, who had been incarcerated by the Nazis, declared in 1946 that "once in the concentration camp, I heard *Carmina Burana*. After that, I actually felt better for several days"?[25]

As a final consideration, Carl Orff's name to many has become synonymous with fascist art and culture, frequently by way of a rather cavalier prejudgment. In this manner the British musicologist Gerald Abraham has generalized that "the only kind of modernism acceptable in the Third Reich was the rhythmically hypnotic, totally diatonic neo-primitivism of Orff's scenic cantatas."[26] Other cognoscenti have insinuated that Orff's music exemplifies "the inhuman face and perverse 'appeal' of National Socialism."[27] Most dismissive in recent times has been composer Berthold Goldschmidt's 1994 reference to "this terrible supermarket music of the third-rate Carl Orff."[28] Who, then, was Carl Orff?

II

Orff was born in Munich in 1895 into a family of high military officers and scholars. One or two of his immediate ancestors appear to have been very musical; his mother is said to have been an accomplished pianist even as a teenager. It was she who taught preschooler Carl the fundamentals of harmony and how to make the piano sound. But the father, too, played piano, and often there were duets and quartets performed in the home. As a schoolboy, Carl would prefer to walk to the Gymnasium, using his streetcar fare to buy scores. His first musical influences were Bavarian military marches, but in 1909 he came to relish *Der Fliegende Holländer,* and more operas after that. Richard Strauss and especially Debussy impressed him.[29]

In 1911 Orff, who had already written a few Lieder to texts by Heinrich Heine and Theodor Storm, published his first song cycle, ten poems by Karl Stieler: *Eliland: Ein Song vom Chiemsee,* opus 12. Still heavily under the influence of Debussy he entered the Bayerische Akademie der Tonkunst in 1912 but found its approach to composition uninspiring and aloof, and so he left. After a stint as a Munich theater Kapellmeister he was serving on the eastern front by 1917 but was sent home after having suffered near-lethal shock in a collapsed dugout. In 1918–19, he was Kapellmeister in Mannheim and Darmstadt. After his return to Munich, he composed his first song cycle based on lyrics by Franz Werfel (1920). Renewed studies in

1921 with Heinrich Kaminski near Benediktbeuern at the foot of the Bavarian Alps were just as fruitless as his brief acquaintance with Hans Pfitzner in Munich, whose opera *Palestrina* he actually admired, but Kaminski introduced him to late-Renaissance composers such as Orlando Lasso, Giovanni Gabrieli, and Claudio Monteverdi. It was the latter who triggered a lifelong artistic love affair between Orff and the old masters.[30]

After 1923, Orff's somewhat narrow Bavarian horizon was widened, as in 1924 he briefly made the personal acquaintance of Bertolt Brecht, whose lyrics offered fresh potential for the composition of songs. The Brecht Cantatas and additional songs based on Werfel's stanzas were to result in 1929–32. These Brecht works already showed the seminal influence of percussion, as Orff had begun to conceptualize this medium in the institutional framework of the Munich Günther-Schule, founded in 1924 by the multi-talented artist Dorothee Günther from Hamburg, whose partner and collaborator in the school Orff became. Other associates who had joined Orff and Günther as instructors by 1932 were Gunild Keetmann and Hans Bergese, instrumentalists equally adept at composition. The students were young girls, to be trained in the use of simple, sometimes exotic instruments (with great emphasis on percussion *and* melody), musical improvisation, rhythm, singing, and dance.[31]

Orff owed additional artistic impulses to two typically Weimar cultural institutions. One was the previously mentioned Vereinigung für Zeitgenössische Musik, founded in 1927, as an island of modernism in reactionary Munich, by local chamber musician Fritz Büchtger. Before long, other forward-looking musicians joined this experimental circle: Udo Dammert, the pianist; Werner Egk, the composer (and already a sometime student of Orff); Karl Marx, the composer and choir director and also Orff's student; and Orff himself. From 1929 to 1931 this association organized four separate festivals featuring mostly modern composers but, significantly and no doubt due to Orff himself, the performance also of old masters such as William Byrd and Hans Leo Hassler, sometimes in modern arrangements or stage settings. Among the contemporary works presented were those of Bartók, Hába, Hindemith, Milhaud, Egk, Marx, Schoenberg, and Stravinsky. Orff contributed "music as an element of dance," from the *Schulwerk* just being created in the Günther-Schule, and he himself conducted his own arrangement of Monteverdi's opera *Orfeo*. On a few occasions, Hindemith and his Amar Quartet joined in, and so did the trail-blazing modernist conductor Hermann Scherchen.[32]

The handmaiden of these series was the Munich Bach–Verein e.V., which was founded in 1909 by Ludwig Landshoff for the purpose of stilistically faithful reproductions of Bach's works and those of his contemporaries. After Landshoff resigned in 1928, the Bach–Verein was taken over by Edwin Fischer, the famous pianist, while Karl Marx assumed the direction of a refashioned choir. In 1931 Fischer himself gave up the Bach–Verein for the sake of his pianistic career, and in 1932 Orff took over as conductor in the Bach–Verein, with Marx continuing to direct the choir. Apart from its regular cooperation with the Vereinigung, one of the milestone stand-alone performances of the Bach–Verein was a new rustic-Bavarian arrangement of the *St. Luke Passion* (after a manuscript thought to be in Bach's hand), in which Orff took a major part: first in Munich in April 1932, then in November of that year in Berlin.[33]

Both St. Luke events were progressive enough to act as thorns in the flesh of the purists among Baroque-music lovers, in Munich as well as in the capital, and hence they played an important part in identifying Carl Orff as an avant-garde composer.[34] Those purists included conservatives of all stripes but also National Socialists, who laid their own cultural-political claim to Bach and the Baroque era.[35]

By 30 January 1933, then, the grand day of National Socialist reckoning, Carl Orff at age thirty-eight had defined himself as a person, a musician, and, not least, a political being. Orff had proven to be a somewhat shy man with a high intelligence and caustic wit, careful when entering into human relationships, particularly close or permanent ones, including those with the opposite sex. In 1920, he had married the gifted opera singer Alice Solscher, but by 1925, when daughter Godela was three years old they were divorced. Throughout the republican phase, he appears to have had many fleeting unions, particularly with the young women from the Günther-Schule, who all were dependent on and reportedly worshipped him, but among them there was no steady companion who might have become his wife or the much-needed new mother for his daughter, as the Australia-bound Solscher did not raise the child.[36] Beyond early childhood, hardly anything today is known about Orff's ties with his three-years-younger sister Maria.[37] And whereas he seems to have enjoyed many professional acquaintances, he really had no close personal friends. His correspondence, even during the Weimar years, when, unlike later, nothing had to remain hidden from state censorship or party scrutiny, betrays a guardedness rarely observed in the surviving papers of other artists of that era. What it does reveal is the portrait of a man who, possibly through the autosuggestion of *sacro egoismo,* thought mainly of himself.[38]

As a musician until 1933, Orff was a modernist, but an idiosyncratic one, even given the criteria of latitude provided by the Weimar cultural establishment. While consciously accepting as his model of modernity the music of Igor Stravinsky, whose percussive approaches he incorporated into his own creations after 1924, he would have no truck with other expressions of Weimar modernism, in particular atonality or anything remotely akin to the Second Viennese School, or the new jazz. Schoenberg to him was anathema. He remained staunchly diatonic, although, perhaps under the continuing influence of the old masters such as his favorite composer Monteverdi, he was developing a certain predilection for monody.[39]

Orff's peculiar position as a Weimar modernist is thrown into stark relief by an examination of his dislike of Mahler, Hindemith, and the avant-garde periodical *Melos,* edited at this time by Heinrich Strobel. Mahler, one of the historic pioneers of German musical modernism, was berated by Orff as

the creator of "unqualified crap." One of Mahler's compositions he characterized as "tense and twisted music, as in the totally amateur opening lines.
It represents the nadir of musical misunderstanding to have such insincere
non-music published."[40] In 1932 he vilified Hindemith for music written
for German youth in Plön. Orff accused him of "obscuring the fundamentals from the beginning with his subjective artistry," leaving "interesting
end results" only for the initiated, not those who were supposedly being
schooled. Ultimately, Orff thought Hindemith's didactic examples "clever,
but without any character, non-pedagogical worm-like music."[41]

In 1932, Orff's relationship with Strobel may have suffered from his pronounced vanity and his attendant unwillingness to accept even constructive
criticism. In October the composer had responded positively to Strobel's
suggestion that he send him something about his *Schulwerk* for *Melos*. But
then a not entirely favorable critique appeared in the journal about Orff's
choir music—presumably his new arrangement of *St. Luke Passion* as performed in Berlin, indicting, especially, one of Orff's trademarks already at
this time: the "dangerous monotony." Wrote Orff, offended, to a friend: "I
just read in Melos a not very fortunate report about my efforts in Berlin.
. . . Although it means well, too much has been misrepresented. Only he
who knows my work from the ground up will understand what I am trying
to do."[42] Orff's contribution for the journal never materialized.

Orff's essays at other levels of the modernist music culture toward the
end of the Weimar period were promising but might again have been
wrecked by a combination of bad luck and the composer's venal stubborn-
ness. When the renowned International Society for Contemporary Music
became interested in featuring Orff's Brecht Cantatas, using the Kittel
Choir in Berlin, Orff declined, in distrust of Kittel and thinking of conceptual frameworks for a staging of his own—sometime in 1933. The matter
came to naught.[43] Shortly before Hitler's takeover he considered producing
Weill's *Die Bürgschaft* in Munich, most certainly with the Bach–Verein, but
neither Weill's music nor his personality had really been close to his own,
and the end of the republic fittingly doomed this enterprise.[44] Scherchen,
whom he knew from mutual tasks within the Vereinigung für Zeitgenössische Musik, performed Orff's new composition *Entrata* at Radio Königsberg, where the conductor was Generalmusikdirektor, in 1930, but Orff always had mixed feelings about this maestro with an equally large ego, who
nonetheless considered featuring the Brecht Cantatas as late as January
1933.[45]

Brecht Cantatas, Hermann Scherchen, and Kurt Weill: Were these not
props for a politically leftist scenario? In March 1931 Orff strongly
protested the impression he had made with some that he was a Communist.[46] In fact, like many artists, Orff was never moved by politics, although
in the republic, where he had his freedom, he tended to the left in the bohemian sense of the word, as was in keeping with his antitraditionalist
craftsmanship and several of the left-leaning modernists surrounding him
on a daily basis. Brecht personally may have impressed him, for sometimes

he was sporting one of those typically Brechtian leather jackets and caps—hence the misleading epithet.[47] Scherchen of course was a left-wing Social Democrat. Also left of center were Scherchen's collaborators in Prussia, cultural administrator Leo Kestenberg and youth-music pioneer Fritz Jöde, who supported Orff's novel approaches, although Orff sometimes found both less than reliable.[48]

There is no ideological or political discourse between Orff and those left-leaning people to be gleaned from the records; to the composer, only music, music theater, or musical education mattered. But the same holds true for persons in his orbit who were of conservative persuasion or, worse, obvious early backers of the growing Nazi Party and detractors of Weimar democracy. Chief among those were Fritz Reusch, Georg Goetsch, and Ludwig Kelbetz, potential or actual Nazis who after January 1933 filled important posts in the educational system of the nation, particularly through the Hitler Youth.[49]

Significantly, Carl Orff did not reply to a derogatory comment made in a letter by Reusch to him, in June 1932, in which Reusch characterized two mutual acquaintances as synonymous with "overbreeding, decadence, brains, and commotion," against whom, Reusch wrote, he had "a racist aversion, even if they are not Jews."[50] Of the men in question, the music pedagogue Erich Katz was Jewish, and Erich Doflein, his colleague at the Freiburg municipal music school, was married to a partially Jewish woman.[51] Clearly, Orff did not connive in racial slurs against his Jewish colleagues and friends, yet neither does he seem to have opposed those, as he kept himself out of any controversy involving anything but his personal life and music. But Jewish friends he had: apart from Katz, the Heidelberg singer Karl Salomon, the Mannheim composer Max Sinzheimer, and the Frankfurt composer, cellist, and teacher Matyas Seiber, who had founded a jazz class at the Hoch'sche Konservatorium.[52]

III

After January 1933 the National Socialist regime began coordinating cultural institutions in Germany and nazifying them, a process that was at first haphazard because several agencies at once thought themselves primarily responsible for this. The most visible of these was the Kampfbund für deutsche Kultur (KfdK) (Combat League for German Culture) of party ideologue Alfred Rosenberg, which had polemicized against manifestations of Weimar's so-called gutter culture since its inception in early 1929. Because its national headquarters was at the Nazi Party seat in Munich, Orff had already been one of its targets, what with his obvious idolization of the Jewish poet Werfel as well as the Marxist dramatist Brecht and his irreverent modernism as expressed in suspect rearrangements of Monteverdi's music, the St. Luke Passion, and his central role in the Zeitgenössische Vereinigung and the Bach–Verein.[53]

Whereas it is clear that in the Weimar Republic Orff was never a dyed-in-the-wool leftist, it is equally clear from all the evidence available that he thoroughly disliked most of the things that National Socialism and the Third Reich came to stand for, before and after Hitler's takeover, and that he never joined the Nazi Party. The crudities and banalities of the Nazis, expressed, not least, through their cultural ambitions, were anathema to Orff's arcane sense of aesthetics and his perception of an artist's role. Whatever he may have understood about National Socialist politics, he found it more convenient, in what later became recognizable as typical Orffian style, to look the other way, so as not to be affected personally. When a Nazi friend, an actor from Brunswick, wrote him months after the caesura of January that it would be in his best interests, including professional ones, to adopt "the great Hitler principles," Orff ignored him. His friend's conviction that Orff's kind of music would be especially suited for the adumbration of "volkish communal celebrations" at that time left the composer unmoved. In private, he was making fun of the Nazis, as in a letter to an archivist friend in Bamberg, whom he once greeted sarcastically "with several heils."[54]

The local Munich Kampfbund chieftain was Paul Ehlers, an old Nazi Party member and pronounced anti-Semite, who in later years was fond of looking back on "the decades of our fight against the increasing Jewification of the German music establishment," a fight during which he had prayed for the coming of the savior who would throw the defilers out of the temple.[55] Although Ehlers regarded Orff with as much suspicion as Orff regarded him, he seems to have thought, for a while, that it might be possible to win this exotic but promising composer over to the Nazi side. Moreover, Orff held a prominent position in the Bach-Verein, the control of which was on Ehlers's agenda, and hence Orff's connivance was considered as within the realm of possibilities. Orff, on the other hand, had heard—which was undoubtedly true—that not all Kampfbund chapters were equally militant and that individual arrangements with local leaders could be made. Hence, by the middle of 1933 Orff decided to meet with the Munich chapter members to acquaint them with his work, a step which could not, however, stop Ehlers from increasing his pressure on the Bach-Verein.[56] Here Ehlers had a more reliable mole in the person of Fritz Büchtger (the founder of the Zeitgenössische Vereinigung), who quickly joined the party, the Stormtroopers, and the Kampfbund itself. By the fall, the entire leadership of the Bach-Verein, including Orff, had been impelled to resign, with Ehlers holding all the strings. Orff agreed to honor conducting commitments until the fall of 1934, but thereafter cut his association with the Bach-Verein, the Zeitgenössische Vereinigung having long been dissolved.[57]

Yet one other reason why Orff had been eager to talk to Ehlers and his circle was his determination to preserve the pedagogical opportunities that so far had resulted in important work toward the *Schulwerk* project in the Günther-Schule. While the school's day-to-day director, Dorothee Günther, herself had opened the door of this institution to Nazi influence by joining the party and the Combat League, Orff remained interested in retaining control over the various *Schulwerk* publications to be produced and marketed.[58] In the coming years, he lost interest in Günther, Keetmann, and the instructional activities of the school as such (which was finding ever more ways of catering to the Nazi regime),[59] but held on to two associates who continued to be involved in the emerging *Schulwerk,* the young musicologists Wilhelm Twittenhoff and Hans Bergese.

And so, after the start of the Nazi regime, as Orff's regular activities as conductor and composer were somewhat in limbo, pending a clarification of his relationship to the new powers that be, Orff turned increasingly to the *Schulwerk* both as a source of income and as a means to adapt to the new rulers. Income was important, because until he became nationally famous in the early 1940s, Orff was notoriously short of money.[60] The *Schulwerk* seemed salable because of the Nazi pedagogues' military-inspired emphasis on rhythm and the novelty of the product per se, for the new Nazi culture wardens wanted new German works.[61] Since before 1931, when the first brochure in a broader-conceived *Schulwerk* series had been published, the project was in fluid gestation: written instructions based on Orff's core ideas regarding rhythmic-melodic exercises, improvisation, and the use of a simple, even primitive orchestra, such as gongs, recorders, rattles, and metallophones, dictated by Orff's earlier interest in old and exotic musical instruments.[62]

Orff gradually came to use his irregular contacts with Ehlers and other members of the Munich Kampfbund to interest Nazi authorities in the *Schulwerk,* attaching great importance to Günther's new party connections. Not only did he wish the *Schulwerk* to appear as "not suspect" to the Kampfbund, but, as he advised his publisher Willy Strecker of B. Schott's Söhne in Mainz, the present circumstances were "very conducive to its aims," and it would simply be a matter of letting oneself be discovered by the trend-setting school of pedagogy.[63] After unreconstructed Kampfbund scribes had attacked Orff's didactic mission, especially his use of exotic instruments, in their home journal *Kultur-Wacht,* Orff wrote a spirited reply to justify himself. He likened *Schulwerk* exercises to the brand of *Hausmusik* currently in vogue among the Nazis and protested any positive comparison with "atonal music" or jazz—two genres fundamentally condemned by the regime. He then referred the author of the hostile article to Ehlers, with whom he had consulted in the matter, and who had, in fact, a copy of his protest letter on file.[64]

From 1933 to 1937 Orff took care, in conjunction with his publisher, to tailor his *Schulwerk* series as much as possible to the goals of the Nazis, as they then appeared, without, it may be assumed, wanting to falsify any facet of its originally conceived character. Fortuitously, both Orff's and the Nazis' intentions were compatible in several respects. Apart from an appreciation of *Hausmusik* and a shared aversion to atonality and jazz, there was the mutual appreciation of *Volksmusik,* or folk songs thought to resonate within the bosom of the people, and to which the Nazis had imputed *Blut und Boden* qualities to which neither Orff nor his publisher appeared to object.[65] On the contrary: In March 1934, Orff informed Schott that he was just so glad his objectives were "concurrent, to the highest degree, with what is being required today."[66] As for his publishers, they desired nothing less than that "every Hitler girl and every Hitler boy should end up contented" with Orff's *Schulwerk* manuals.[67] Orff's music-pedagogical system, declared spokesmen of Schott a few years later, had become the bedrock of instruction courses everywhere, from conservatories and music schools to educational institutions of the Hitler Youth. After all, Orff had successfully eclipsed the "exaggerated artistry" of the past decades, as he had striven for a "genuine basis, rooted in race and Volk."[68] However, that last statement was considerably overblown. Although, contrary to Orff's postwar utterings, the *Schulwerk* series continued to be published in several issues until 1939, the Hitler Youth, his most hoped-for client, had occasionally mentioned it in its literature but not officially adopted it because of its relative complexity, which was unsuited to the coarse music culture of future Wehrmacht soldiers and SS killers to be trained by it.[69] But neither had other projected uses materialized: within the NS-Kulturgemeinde (NSKG), the successor organization of Rosenberg's Kampfbund für deutsche Kultur, for special performances in the giant, open-air, Nazi *Thing* stage (to which Günther, too, wished to direct her energies), the new Dietrich-Eckart Stage in Berlin, or within the specifically Nazi primary-school teacher seminars.[70] Although the highest Nazi censorship office certified that the *Schulwerk* series was going to be instrumental "especially in this time of political change," it was simply not true, as Orff asserted in December 1935, that "more and more official places" were becoming interested in the project.[71]

Nonetheless, through his efforts for the *Schulwerk* Orff came into contact with several regime-connected persons, some of whom he had actually known before 1933, who now tried to smooth his path to success and would remain his friends for years to come. Chief among them was Wilhelm Twittenhoff, with a recent Ph.D. in musicology, who, after studying with Orff and writing some articles about the *Schulwerk,* joined the Günther-Schule in 1934, thereupon working mostly with the master. In his post-1945 memoirs, Orff characterized Twittenhoff as a pedagogue who had evolved from the German music youth movement (formerly led by Jöde), but he neglected to mention that Twittenhoff was closely tied to the Stormtroopers and the Hitler Youth.[72] That this Nazi aspect was strategically important to the composer at the time was explained in a letter to Schott in April 1934: Apart from his being favorably disposed toward the *Schulwerk,* Orff appreciated the fact that the young doctor was "in touch with today's requirements through his current work, and possibly well-suited to our plans."[73] Judging from his writings, Twittenhoff had a clear idea of how music could assume an important role in the shaping of the "communal life of National Socialist youth," particularly because he was active in several Nazi youth training centers.[74] Thus it was he who actually tried out *Schulwerk* ideas in regular Hitler Youth camps, such as those in

Annaberg and Brunswick.[75] When in 1937 the *Schulwerk,* including Twittenhoff's own publication in the series, was once again assaulted by members of the Rosenberg clique, Orff and Schott's editors could rest secure, knowing that Twittenhoff was able to counterattack effectively as an influential leader of the Hitler Youth.[76] This turned out to be just another case of Nazi infighting.

Besides Twittenhoff, Orff could rely on acquaintances who, in one way or another, were all in a position to galvanize their sympathy for him and his *Schulwerk* into tangible support of one sort or another, from within the new Nazi educational institutions in which they were now functioning. In the teacher-college administration there was Fritz Reusch, Orff's friend from the republic, who also collaborated closely with Twittenhoff.[77] Other allies in the pre–World War II phase included Ludwig Kelbetz, originally a fanatical (and at times illegal) Nazi from the Republic of Austria who rose to high rank in the Third Reich's Hitler Youth and with whom Orff had touched base in preregime days. There was the composer Cesar Bresgen, a Hitler Youth music instructor eventually working out of Salzburg and, last but not least, Orff's old colleague from the Bach-Verein Karl Marx, who after the Anschluss of Austria in March 1938 landed himself a tenured lectureship in the exclusively Hitler Youth conservatory in Graz.[78]

In April 1937 Twittenhoff, who was about to embark on a regular teaching career at the Hitler Youth conservatory in Weimar, informed Orff that he had had a long talk with his boss, Wolfgang Stumme, formerly a student of Jöde and now the chief of all music activities in the Hitler Youth under Baldur von Schirach, regarding the composer's newest work, the scenic cantata *Carmina Burana.* Although Stumme thought he could do little or nothing for the work in the pages of Hitler Youth pedagogical literature, part of which he controlled, he personally expressed great interest in it and signaled his intention to attend its world premiere in Frankfurt in June.[79]

Why the need for this? At that time, Orff could still use all the official help he could get. For a few years now, Orff had been busy composing a vocal work with sparse instrumental, percussive accompaniment, which was obviously influenced by Stravinsky's *Les noces* (1923) as well as by Orff's own, earlier exercises for the *Schulwerk.* Melodically, it harked back to the Werfel songs of 1930; Orff himself described its music as one of "static architecture." Instead of a full-blown plot, the mixed choir and three soloists merely suggested the interwoven themes of springtime, joyful brawling and drinking, and sexual pleasure. Experts then and later detected in the piece many of Orff's favorite structural elements: monody, allusions to the *Volkslied,* modal influence, a bareness in phrasing which, combined with repetitive techniques, bordered on the primitive but conveyed at the same time the impression of archetypal, elementary dynamics.[80]

Those qualities of the work were not necessarily non-German, nor could they automatically invoke the wrath of dogmatic National Socialists. But neither were they immediately appealing to non-Germans: The Jewish refugee music critic and musician Abraham Skulsky, for one, found the cantata harmonically "too light . . . either not primitive enough or not sufficiently modern: somewhere between the two," as he wrote from Brussels.[81] In the main, the problem was threefold. First, although not even bordering on atonality, the piece was not in the safe tradition of post-Romanticism the Nazis had so far preferred but sounded strangely out of place with its exotic harmonies and rhythms; although his status was improving, Stravinsky in Germany was still suspect to many Nazis, especially Rosenberg followers.[82] Second, the text of *Carmina Burana* was a mixture of Latin, middle-high-German, and medieval French, anything but the argot of the new regime. Both Orff and Schott knew about this as a potential problem before June 1937. Orff had joked to his Bamberg-based text coauthor, Michel Hofmann, about a year before, that "no one will publish and perform the Burana. 'Un-German.'"[83] Willy Strecker of Schott warned that the music was too provocative and the text too Latin; the whole thing was hardly conducive to Robert Ley's "Strength-through-Joy" program. And third, because the plot conjured up Eros, the hybrid language was explicitly sexual, even pornographic. Whereas this might not have presented a problem for some singers, in order to understand what they were singing about most of them were given subtexts with German translations, which embarrassed especially the young girls in the choir. This, in turn, was reason enough for the Nazis, with their bigoted sense of sexuality (and several stage directors fearing them), to object to the work.[84]

Carmina Burana for a time had difficulty being accepted at other German stages after its controversial Frankfurt premiere, particularly because there now was more than just one Nazi agency that could indict it: Rosenberg's chief music critic, Herbert Gerigk, was influential as chief reviewer of *Die Musik* as well as the Nazis' own *Völkischer Beobachter,* both of which immediately published two identical, rather stinging reviews.[85] There was no telling for the moment how far Gerigk might still be able to go, especially as insiders knew that he and in particular his colleague Friedrich Herzog had played an odious role in bringing down Hindemith at the turn of 1934.[86] And as that had happened in collusion with the just-established music-control agencies of Reich Propaganda Minister Joseph Goebbels, Orff, the editors at Schott, and several sympathetic stage directors and conductors—for example, Karl Böhm in Dresden—were also uncertain about the reactions of President Peter Raabe of the RMK and Heinz Drewes in the Promi's own music supervision department.[87] Hence, there was apprehension in the years before *Carmina Burana*'s premiere and even for a couple of years thereafter, most of it informed by the knowledge of what had happened to Hindemith and *could* happen to Orff, for whatever reason, irrespective of actual music censorship policies in the Reich, which were seldom overt and clear-cut, and irrespective also of the perceivable diminishing influence of Rosenberg's henchmen.[88]

On the other hand, several factors immediately worked in Orff's favor and augured well for the continued success of *Carmina Burana.* One was tied to the nature of the performance itself, officially produced, as it was, by the annual Tonkünstlerfest series of the Allgemeiner Deutscher Musikverein (ADMV) (albeit the last such event under Nazism). None other than Raabe of the RMK was its champion.[89] Opera director Hans Meissner of Frankfurt and the city's culturally ambitious mayor Fritz Krebs represented a second factor. In the republic, Meissner had been an able avant-garde artist on the political left. After the watershed, like so many, he had opportunistically exchanged membership in the Social Democratic Party (SPD) for that of the Nazi Party (NSDAP) and, as turncoats are apt to do, from 1933 in Frankfurt ostentatiously sought to ingratiate himself with the Nazis, at the same time trying to remain true to his former aesthetic principles: Even contemporaries saw this as an attempt to square the circle.[90] Thus anything that Meissner sponsored at his (from Weimar days) comparatively progressive Frankfurt opera was really fairly safe from outside interference. This was all the more so because Meissner had the full backing of his employer, Frankfurt's lord mayor and Nazi Kreisleiter Krebs, a high SS officer, who had been a Hitler follower since 1922 and as such a virulent anti-Semite but now also a member of the presidial council of the RMK under Goebbels and Raabe, thus affording Orff double protection.[91]

In fact it was Krebs who only two weeks after the premiere presented Orff with a money prize of RM500, which, although financially modest, politically was of enormous significance to the composer.[92] Indeed, the small number of negative critiques was easily and quickly outbalanced by raving reviews, in Frankfurt and elsewhere, so that still in June Orff could proudly write to Strecker: "Meanwhile you will have read the Burana reports, ninety percent of which are excellent."[93] As Orff was easily able to dismiss the vitriol by Gerigk in the *Völkischer Beobachter,* friends of his were assuring him that "the hoped for, *really great* success has finally materialized."[94] In Berlin, influential music critic Edwin von der Nüll, who as an intimate of Göring a few months later would finagle Herbert von Karajan's phenomenal and long-lasting success at the Berlin Staatsoper, assured Orff that he was in touch with Wilhelm Rode, Goebbels's bumbling chief at the propaganda minister's own Deutsches Opernhaus, as well as with the Promi itself.[95] Also in the capital, Wilhelm Matthes, one of the most vicious anti-Semites among Nazi critics from the Weimar era and an old intimate of Hans Pfitzner, offered to conduct *Carmina Burana* himself, quoting Goebbels's latest speech, according to which "experiments are desirable and critics, apart from being critical, should show their own mettle or whether they can improve upon the things which they are always so fond of criticizing."[96] Orff was now instantly intent on getting Fritz Stege, the uppermost music critic in the country and squarely in Goebbels's camp, interested in his oeuvre.[97]

Late in 1937, notwithstanding any of the fears the composer or his publishers might still have entertained, *Carmina Burana* really took off. "All things considered," rejoiced Orff in October, "I see a silver lining. Berlin especially has made very promising and important offers. And things are moving very well in general."[98] Early in 1938 the secular cantata was again on the program of the Frankfurt opera, and it stayed there into 1939. "It is a constant drawing card."[99] A disciple of Pfitzner complained to his master that he simply could not understand why *Carmina Burana* was so popular in the city on the Main River, while Pfitzner's *Das Herz* was being so neglected.[100] At the end of 1938, Orff's work played to enthusiastic reviews in Bielefeld; the composer himself was ecstatic.[101]

After World War II Orff, who through some of his stage plays had found a way with fairy tales, constructed two interrelated legends about the premiere and subsequent fate of *Carmina Burana*. The first, based on the sparse evidence of Nazi disagreement he did have but lacking any basis in fact, was that the work had been banned outright from 1936 to 1940 and had generally been declared "undesirable" for the entire Third Reich. Without closer examination, this version of events was thereafter propagated by his hagiographic followers and ultimately helped in spreading Orff's German reputation as an anti-Nazi.[102] To this was tied the second legend that at the time of the scenic oratorio he had informed his publisher Strecker henceforth to forget everything he had composed before 1937.[103] That the veracity of this story has already been questioned in connection with other music-historical legends of the Third Reich is significant in itself[104]; as for verification, I have not been able to receive it either from Schott in Mainz or the Orff-Zentrum in Munich. In any event, the real reason for Orff's manipulation is not immediately obvious. Now why would Orff, in retrospect, have wished to place such emphasis on the originality and singularity of *Carmina Burana*? The answer is this: because, as the alleged victim of Nazi blacklisting, it would establish him as a creator of anti-Nazi art and hence as an anti-Nazi himself. As post-1937 events were to show, after the catastrophe of 1945 Orff was in dire need of such an alibi.

Because the premiere of *Carmina Burana* had very much pleased Frankfurt's Lord Mayor Krebs, he delegated Meissner, in March 1938, to ask Orff whether he would write music for *A Midsummer Night's Dream,* hence "replacing earlier compositions for Shakespeare's work."[105] This has to be put into more then one context. In the first place, there had been a national competition going on in this area for some time, in which numerous Reich agencies and composers were involved; one of those successfully asked was Rudolf Wagner-Régeny, who had contracted with the Kampfbund as early as 1934 and whose ersatz piece had been performed publicly a year later.[106] Moreover, as far as Frankfurt was concerned, it lay in the very personal interests of Krebs the anti-Semite to have such a replacement for the Jewish Mendelssohn's music commissioned, for, as he published for everyone to read, he was already of the opinion that through the elimination of Jewry from the cultural life of the German people, "the feats of our cultural institutions not only have not deteriorated, but have markedly improved." This he wanted to see happening on his own turf.[107]

Orff consented immediately, presumably because he badly needed the generous advance of RM5,000 that was offered but also because he had himself tried his hand at stage music for Shakespeare's play as early as 1917. Now he wished to write something truly suited to the theater, and not as schmaltzy and sugar-sweet as, allegedly, Mendelssohn's famous original.[108] But there was a third, more politic reason. Because in 1938 Orff was still not certain about his place in the regime's cultural establishment, he seized on this opportunity to secure his position via the good offices of Lord Mayor Krebs, who not only had been Frankfurt's local Kampfbund leader,[109] but now also seemed to back entirely the modern and therefore possibly still suspect endeavors of opera director Meissner, with which Orff could identify.[110]

At the time, the commission did not sit too well with Schott's principals because they, who continued to support Stravinsky and in their heart of hearts recognized the foolishness of anti-Semitism in the music business, were aware of the potential explosiveness of this issue. He had placed himself in a "nasty wasp's nest" with this music, they cautioned Orff, for would he ever be able to "dispatch Mendelssohn"?[111] Strecker himself warned Orff that in the past few years several *Midsummer Night's Dream* compositions had been commissioned, with the aim of "putting the non-Aryan Mendelssohn out of business." Currently, three quarters of all the German stages were performing these works and hence the saturation point was near; besides, it was relatively costly to produce them.[112] Offended, Orff replied that he was in a different class than those other *Midsummer Night's Dream* composers, who on the whole had done a less than perfect job.[113] In reality, Orff himself had qualms about the whole thing, for several times he was very close to suffering writer's block.[114] Nevertheless, in mid-August 1939 he had mastered the chore, and no sooner was the work finished than he asked Krebs's permission to dedicate it to the city of Frankfurt.[115] After its Frankfurt premiere on 14 October Strecker was enchanted, agreeing with Orff's earlier prediction that this incidental music would represent an iteration "from the sugar-sweet to a dry Old English" subject.[116] Although Orff was not entirely happy with the artistic direction of the play, he was satisfied that the music itself had been "very successful," and he was hoping for many more acceptances outside Frankfurt.[117] As for Krebs, he also was content. As a consequence of his long-term political goals, within which the "Aryan" *Midsummer Night's Dream* music had prominently figured, an Institute for Research into the Jewish Question at Frankfurt was realized in 1941, under the auspices of his old mentor, Alfred Rosenberg.[118] In March 1943 Krebs thanked Orff once again, expressing his hope that many more compositions would flow from his pen, which, too, would benefit "the new Germany."[119]

The Frankfurt performance had represented Orff's third version of the piece so far, and he was at work on a fourth one by 1941.[120] Ideally, he wanted that version to be performed in Berlin, but, reportedly, Gustaf Gründgens, who was becoming increasingly disenchanted with the Nazi regime, as Generalintendant of the Berlin Staatstheater was against it, because he did not wish to compromise his traditionally cordial relationship with the Mendelssohn family.[121] A final possibility to have the newest version staged in Leipzig during 1944 foundered in the war's turmoil.[122]

As Hans Maier, once Bavaria's minister of culture under Franz Josef Strauss and presently a member of the Orff Foundation, observed during Carl Orff Year in 1995, Orff should have known not to rewrite Mendelssohn's classic Shakespearean music for Nazi use, even though his main motive may have been a long-standing aesthetic one. Orff should have known that, as Maier put it, "for the Nazis, there was nothing in music that was not, at the same time, also political."[123] Other composers, more prominent than Orff, had known this well, among them Pfitzner, who waxed sarcastic about the whole scheme, and Richard Strauss, who grumbled as early as 1935 that "the Midsummer Night's Dream has to suffer a terrible, Aryan ersatz music, to the derision of the whole world."[124]

Indications that Orff knew full well that he was doing something distasteful, even morally wrong, can be found less in his regime statements than in his postwar attempts to hone the various legends he had already begun constructing. In so doing, he was using two separate approaches. One was to put the Frankfurt composition, and equally so the newer version intended for Leipzig and still awaiting a premiere, out of people's minds, at least for the time being. This is shown by a strenuous correspondence he had with Gottfried von Einem, who in 1946–47, without a Nazi record and on the new Salzburg Festival board, had a say in whether the as yet unperformed Leipzig-bound version could be premiered in the Austrian city. Orff counseled "the greatest restraint," so that Einem, several months later, asked the composer whether the work was "a Nazi commission or something like that."[125] Orff's tortuous explanation, once again employing the aesthetic argument, gave away his bad conscience, when he wrote that the piece "naturally is in no way 'tainted,' nor has this particular version ever been produced. In spite of this, certain circles have held it against me that I confronted the Romantic masterpiece by Mendelssohn with an unromantic counterpart."[126]

The other post-1945 approach, several years later, was simply to stress the continuity between his first *Midsummer Night's Dream* composition attempts from 1917 to beyond 1945 in order to make the 1938–44 episodes seem insignificant, or part of an ongoing, unstoppable creative process that had nothing to do with the Third Reich and its anti-Semitism. This is suggested by his postwar memoirs. Significantly, what Orff has listed there beyond the cataclysmic year of 1945 are several renewed and successful attempts at bringing his music for Shakespeare's *Midsummer Night's Dream* to full stage fulfillment, the logical successors to the 1917 archetype, as if the Nazi interlude had never occurred.[127]

IV

Notwithstanding any legends Orff constructed around the origins and development of *Carmina Burana* in the Third Reich from June 1937, the work became a roaring success after the beginning of World War II. Its spate of celebrated performances was touched off on 4 October 1940 by a sensational staging under the baton of Dresden's Karl Böhm, who had earlier declined it because of its then still controversial nature.[128] Strecker and Orff agreed that press reviews on the whole were excellent, even those in regime papers—additional proof that Orff's old party foes were increasingly being pushed against the wall.[129] In the years to follow, there were providential performances in Essen, Cologne, Mainz, Görlitz, Frankfurt, Göttingen, Hamburg, Aachen, and Münster, the last two under Herbert von Karajan and Hans Rosbaud, respectively.[130] Even Munich's musical circles, always more on the conservative side, received the oratorio warmly—once in 1942 and then for another long season early in 1944.[131] Particularly memorable were the Berlin stagings under Karajan, after that meteoric conductor had moved from Aachen to the capital, from January 1942 on, at times in conjunction with Egk's *Joan von Zarissa*. Goebbels's uppermost critic Fritz Stege exulted with praise over the often-sold-out performances, and Orff remarked proudly that the *Burana* had become "the great successful hit."[132]

The *Carmina Burana* success story in the last years of the Third Reich raises again the problem of the National Socialist quality of Orff's music, as it was composed and performed under Hitler, apart from the issue of Orff's personal status as a Nazi, on which the evidence is unequivocal. Although just as easily posed, the musical question is not easily answered. Apart from the origin of Orff's music in the culture of Weimar and his own preference for Stravinsky (who, coincidentally, more than flirted with fascism and was an anti-Semite as well), the use of ostinato rhythms, melodic economy, rudimentary diatonicism, repetition and monophony, and thematic allusions to *Volksmusik* and *Hausmusik* all were generically akin to a peculiarly Nazi aesthetic in German music between 1933 and 1945.[133] Yet even if pressed, musicologists today show themselves reluctant to identify, in Orff's music and especially that of *Carmina Burana*, a distinctive "fascist" quality. On the other hand, a few respected scholars, for instance those as widely apart as Albrecht Riethmüller (Berlin) and Richard Taruskin (Berkeley), have admitted that they find the cantata of 1937 quintessentially Nazi.[134] Orff's third wife, Luise Rinser, not too long ago wrote of the attacks by post–World War II music critics, who had called his works anti-spiritual, capable of numbing the listener, of delivering him to irrational powers, thus betraying fascistoid traits. And she added that she could not defend him.[135]

In a recent analysis of music in the Third Reich, works by Orff, Egk, Gottfried von Einem, Rudolf Wagner-Régeny, and Boris Blacher have been subsumed under a special rubric of modernism—of a type the Nazis, and especially Goebbels, actually desired, in order to lend credence and legitimacy to their overall revolutionary intentions in the cultural field and which by its very structure, and not to offend known Nazi aesthetic norms, were sometimes more and sometimes less removed from the criteria that had determined modern music in Weimar. To those criteria belonged, to mention only two, a predilection for jazz and a polyrhythmic architecture, neither of them a quality Orff happened to espouse but which younger composers close to him, such as von Einem and Blacher, even Egk, empathized with to variable degrees.[136]

Contemporaries of Orff would have agreed with the sentiments of Rieth-müller and Taruskin, without having put their fingers on any textbook rules or being able precisely to define the *Zeitgeist*. The convinced Nazi educator Reusch wrote to Orff in February 1942—after the composer's picture had been featured in Goebbels's intellectually high-brow tabloid *Das Reich*—that "time has worked in favor of *your* spiritual and musical ideas, and what *you* (and Egk) are presently experiencing must represent the climax of your life's work." In 1944, Carl Niessen, an expert on modern opera, thought the choreography for Orff's *Carmina Burana* a new beginning for the German operatic stage, evoking "centuries-old dreams" for a "visible cantata" in a "scenic space," in contrast to what Kurt Weill had once done with the choir, having created a mere "show-business joke" in *Der Zar lässt sich photographieren*: "long-bearded, dotty old men in black coats"—a scarcely veiled reference to Jews.[137] Oscar Fritz Schuh, the stage director of the Vienna opera and not a Nazi, also thought Orff had created something archetypally new with a music that picked up where the pre-Romantic phase had left off and now was aiming for a style "which could symbolize *the* salvation of music in general."[138] At a different level Willy Strecker, sales figures in his head, thought *Carmina Burana* trend setting, thinking it commercially viable to the point at which watered-down, popularized versions of the kind played in hotel lobbies could create a sort of public demand that would make Orff's new genre a commonplace commodity (and him, presumably, rich).[139]

The carnal cantata was also performed in Vienna, yet if it did not find the same enthusiastic echo there, it was not for lack of trying or official support. Since August 1940 the Gauleiter of Vienna was former Hitler Youth chief Baldur von Schirach, son of a theater intendant and brother of an opera singer, and something of a poet himself. The Schirach family had been ennobled by Empress Maria Theresa two centuries ago, and so one of Schirach's ambitions in culture-saturated Vienna was to outdo Reich Propaganda Minister Goebbels as a patron of the arts, featuring what he considered to be truly outstanding German music, traditional but also avant-garde, and always commensurate with Nazi ideology, of course. The traditionalist he chose to champion was Strauss, and the two progressives were Rudolf Wagner-Régeny and Orff. Walter Thomas, by inclination a progressive theater expert but a man who politically sympathized "with the wrong side," acted as the authorized spokesman of the Gauleiter. No sooner had Schirach and Thomas got to work than they felt the wrath of Minister Goebbels upon them.[140]

Orff's institutional ties with Vienna were firmed up after he had attended the premiere of Wagner-Régeny's *Johanna Balk* on 2 April 1941, under the protection of the Vienna Gauleiter. Its progressive stage director, Schuh, was

a guest in the Orffs' Munich home in early July. Three months later a propo-
sition was made, presumably by Schuh and Thomas and with the full backing of Schirach, that Orff conclude a working contract with the Viennese; he
was asked to reveal his plans. Orff was in Vienna in the middle of October to
finalize the blueprint for a contract, with the "best possible" conditions. The
new working agreement was to take effect by 1 April of 1942.[141]

And this is precisely what happened. According to a letter by Orff to
Berlin Generalintendant Heinz Tietjen, Schirach, probably through Schuh,
granted the composer a commission for a full-feature work to be premiered
by the Wiener Staatsoper; Orff then offered *Antigonae,* about which he had
already done some serious thinking.[142] This commission became the foundation for a three-year contract, according to which Orff was to be paid
RM1,000 per month. The signatories were Orff on the one hand and
Thomas on the other, he on behalf of Schirach's Gau administration in Vienna. The Reich beneficiary was to be the Wiener Staatsoper, which received the right of first refusal. According to the contract of 17 March
1942, Schirach was ceded the privilege of accepting or rejecting an original
work proposed by Orff within three months; he also had the prerogative to
choose the venue, the orchestra, and the conductor, but only in consultation with the composer. The overriding principle accorded perfectly well
with Schirach's new cultural ambitions, "that the support of certain composers is in the interest of, particularly, the Wiener Staatsoper."[143]

True to contract, Orff got to work on *Antigonae* and received his
monthly RM1,000, starting April 1942; until April 1945 he was to collect
RM36,000 exactly.[144] This sum helped him in several ways. He could continue to shore up his monthly income, which had been sagging until the
recent good fortune with *Carmina Burana.*[145] It facilitated the Vienna premiere of the scenic cantata which, little cared for by tradition-minded critics and the Viennese public, did become a favorite of Schirach and his wife,
who personally got to like the Orff couple, and with whom Orff himself
"got along very well." To show her personal sympathies, Frau Henriette
von Schirach, the daughter of Hitler's personal photographer, made Frau
Orff a gift of Austrian sunflower seeds. In addition, the work quite impressed Richard Strauss, who was then spending time in his Viennese villa
in the Jacquingasse, and whose condescendingly benign judgment Orff
came to treasure.[146]

The continuous triumph of *Carmina Burana* and the propitious relationship with Vienna ran parallel to and sometimes interrelated with other
compositional achievements. Orff's penchant for fairy tales and legend that
had already attracted him to *A Midsummer Night's Dream* produced the
fairy opera *Der Mond,* in Munich under Clemens Krauss in February 1939,
and the parable *Die Kluge,* premiered four years later, once again in Frankfurt. There also was *Catulli Carmina,* from a workmanship perspective an
inferior sequel to *Carmina Burana,* but with similarly sexual content,
which saw its first performance in Leipzig on 6 November 1943. Commercially, it could not ride on the coattails of its by then famous predecessor.[147]

Der Mond was modeled on a plot by the Brothers Grimm, in which four foolhardy boys steal the moon, come to their death, and then keep the moon's company in their second life in the underworld. This play may have been intended for children more than adults, yet it brought grief to its creator, for not only did Orff dislike the production by Krauss, but subsequent stagings were also difficult because of an alleged pagan, anti-Catholic animus in the plot (which would antagonize Catholic communities) and psychological problems caused by the appearance of dead people and dark underworld scenes—untimely reminders of lethal bombings and terrifying anti-airraid blackouts.[148]

In *Die Kluge,* a clever girl solves three riddles, thereby deceiving the king who has imprisoned her father until, with the last riddle, she reconfirms his love and is kept on as his wife. The piece contained passages decrying the erosion of justice, which could be, and locally were, interpreted by the audience as criticism of the dictatorship. Whether Orff actually intended them as such still must be left open to question; it would have been somewhat out of character for a generally accommodating composer. Besides, Nazi Kreisleiter Krebs once again was glad to have received the work for Frankfurt. After Göttingen's staging during 1944, when university students in the audience clapped, hollered, and booed in obvious approval with the renegade lines, Orff himself remained unmolested by regime charges. Most critics interpreted the plot as not being very serious, more along the lines of a raucously funny comedy. It was a "curious mixture of fairy tale and burlesque," wrote music critic Oskar Kaul from Würzburg, controversial but ably exposing the problems of modern opera direction, and thereby pointing to "entirely new ways of music-dramatical configuration."[149]

By 1944 Orff found himself at the pinnacle of a career that had miraculously turned itself around, from one of an impecunious political near victim at the start of the Nazi regime to that of an artistically acclaimed and officially recognized composer. If the Third Reich had had a Stalin Prize, Carl Orff would have received it. In fact, the Reich Music Chamber awarded him a veritable equivalent in the summer of 1942: RM2,000 reserved for composers in prize category 3 of a "state subsidy" (category 1 being designed for Strauss, Pfitzner and Graener), which he shared with genuine Nazi composers such as Armin Knab and Wolfgang Fortner.[150] Although there is no proof whatsoever that Orff believed in the ideology of Nazism or approved of the day-to-day politics of the Third Reich, party representatives thought, in June 1942, that politically he was without blemish.[151] Indeed, there is incremental evidence that after the success of *Carmina Burana* had converted him to something of an icon in the cultural establishment, Orff profited from various perquisites and privileges the regime had to offer and came close to allowing his name to be used for its devious purposes.

As the money prize demonstrates, this became especially apparent in Orff's relations with the propaganda ministry or its subordinate agencies. In 1941, a directive went out from its press section specifying that henceforth, any of his compositions to be performed should be treated favorably by the critics.[152] Around that time, Schott publishers and Orff both were recognizing the publicity value of a Promi seal of approval; Schott was indeed delighted to report in May that by this time, the ministry had showed itself "very interested" in the scenic cantata.[153] RMK President Raabe decreed in February 1942 that Orff not be stripped of his telephone service because of "his significance to the German music establishment."[154] In May 1943 Orff was invited to the ministry to demonstrate his new composition, *Catulli Carmina*; reportedly, this caused "great enthusiasm," and "in other respects, too, my talks were extremely successful."[155] A few weeks later Goebbels's broadcasting system was scheduling a special feature, "A Selection of Compositions by Carl Orff"; more of his music was to be broadcast in the series "The Great Concert—Eternal Music of Europe." In 1944, Orff belonged among those few German composers "whom the broadcast network cannot do without."[156]

The year 1944 represents one of ultimate distinction for Carl Orff, as far as the regime was concerned, as Goebbels himself was being made more aware of his compositions and general importance. Reportedly, after Wolfgang Liebeneiner, production chief of Goebbels's pet film company Ufa, had played the minister a tape with Orff's music in a Neu babelsberg studio, Goebbels was beside himself that this composer had so far been withheld from him.[157] Rainer Schlösser, chief of theater in the propaganda ministry, and Gauleiter Karl Hanke of Silesia also talked to Goebbels about Orff, and one of the results of these representations was an offer by the minister to Orff to compose special "combat music" for his newsreel service—a service Goebbels was personally watching over like a hawk.[158]

In the summer of 1944 Orff's name was added to that of specially selected German artists who were to be exempt from war service requirements of any kind.[159] By this time Goebbels was eager to meet Orff in person. For on 12 September he recorded in his diary, after having listened to *Carmina Burana* on the radio, that "in the case of Carl Orff we are not at all dealing with an atonal talent. On the contrary, his 'Carmina Burana' exhibits exquisite beauty, and if we could get him to do something about his lyrics, his music would certainly be very promising. I shall send for him on the next possible occasion."[160] Orff was now in the process of riding out the Third Reich in style. In good Orffian fashion, he elegantly avoided one final pitfall when Hans Hinkel, of Goebbels's Reich Culture Chamber, asked him to contribute, along with other artists, a homily to be published in honor of the Führer, as the patron of German culture, in those final hours of his struggle for the Reich. Orff typically obliged by sending a noncommittal verse, not by himself but by the Romantic poet Friedrich Hölderlin, "on the threshold of the year of decision, December 1944."[161] He dedicated it to "Adolf Hitler, the patron of German Art."[162] Whether he wrote this line with tongue in cheek is not certain, but it is possible; in any event, Orff knew that he had paid his final premium for insurance. Gustaf Gründgens, the great theater director with whom Orff gladly would have cooperated in the years gone by and who, disillusioned with the regime leaders, had left for the front long ago, had ignored the request. Whereas Hitler placed his contempt for Gründgens on record, he would have found no fault with Orff.[163]

V

In November 1945, six months after the capitulation of the Nazi government, Carl Orff received a letter from an old Berlin acquaintance asking him how things were in Munich. How was the theater scene, was everybody taking up arms against the former rulers?[164] Orff had reason to be worried. At the end of the regime, he had come out on top as one of its major composers. His efforts to sell his educational work to Nazi institutions surely was documented somewhere, perhaps in the Schott firm's archive or in the Hitler Youth files. He had accepted an official commission to replace Mendelssohn's *A Midsummer Night's Dream* music. What had become his most personal work, *Carmina Burana,* ultimately turned into a calling card for the Third Reich.

Although at the end of 1945 the criteria for political and social survival were not yet quite clear to most Germans, OMGUS, to which Bavaria now had surrendered, had already made it sufficiently evident that persons who had compromised themselves under the Nazis had to expect retribution and that those Germans who were to be employed by the Allies in the democratic reconstruction of the country had to be virtually spotless. It was becoming manifest that anyone who desired service with the newly formed bureaucracy had to have a clean slate; persons who were self-employed and continued to be so, as Orff had been, had less to fear. But short of a total and explicit exoneration by the Allies, everyone's career was virtually on hold, and Orff's was no exception.[165]

Toward the end of 1945, this posed itself as a crucial question for him personally, for—not for the first time in his life—Orff was considering employment either in a teaching situation at a conservatory or, more likely, as intendant at a municipal opera. One opportunity was the post of artistic director of opera and theater in Stuttgart, but he also wanted to have his new opera, *Die Bernauerin,* which he had begun to work on while on the Vienna Gauleitung payroll, premiered in a properly exposed setting, perhaps in Hamburg or in Munich, under democratic auspices.[166]

By a stroke of luck, the newly appointed German bureaucrats, under Württemberg's Minister of Culture Theodor Heuss in Stuttgart, came to be in touch with a U.S. supervisory officer who had once been Orff's student in Munich, in 1938–39. Newell Jenkins, with a bachelor's degree in music from Yale, had a colorful background. His grandfather, of an established New England family, had taken up residence in Dresden in the nineteenth century and become court dentist to the King of Saxony. Keenly interested in music, he had become a friend of Wagner. His son, Newell's father, had retained his German ties, so that at the age of seventeen Newell himself, who was born in 1915 in New Haven, went to Dresden to learn German and study music in 1932. In 1938 he settled in Munich to study conducting under Orff, after some time in Freiburg, where his teacher Erich Doflein had suggested Orff as an ideal mentor. Generously supported by his well-off family back in the United States, Jenkins stayed in Munich until the outbreak of war in September 1939. He had obviously become attached to Orff's personality and valued his musical skills, for while still on his return voyage he wrote to the master from Lucerne that now he would have "in America a student, and I also hope a friend, who will pass on the modest bits and pieces that have been stuffed into his small brain, as faithfully as possible." And he concluded that sooner rather than later he would come back.[167]

Come back he did, but not without having graduated and after an arduous war path through North Africa and Italy, where he served in the ambulance corps. Eventually, because of his cultural background and his fluent knowledge of German, he ended up as the OMGUS Information Control Division theater and music control officer for U.S.-controlled Baden-Württemberg in Stuttgart, there since the formation of that territory in September 1945, and officially to begin his mission on 1 January 1946. Already in December 1945 he became interested in the fate of his old German friends, Doflein in Freiburg and, aware of the pending Stuttgart stage appointment, Carl Orff in Munich. As for the latter, he had managed to find out through his Munich counterparts that Orff was, provisionally, on an index, until his record had been cleared beyond a doubt.[168]

Because Jenkins had a constructive interest in the Stuttgart theater matter but also because he wanted to help his friend Orff clear his name, if at all possible, he obtained permission from his Munich OMGUS colleagues to look him up and discuss the situation. The music and theater officer, with the honorary rank of a Captain of the U.S. Army, arrived with jeep and driver at the Orff house in Munich-Gräfelfing on 24 December; they all celebrated Christmas Eve in high spirits, and later the two men moved over to Werner Egk's nearby house. The fact that they reached it unexpectedly late—too late for Egk to produce details of his own compromised situation—suggests that some strategy had meanwhile been discussed between the master and his former student as to how Orff could benefit personally and professionally from the Americans' new presence and how the occupiers, on the whole ignorant of German cultural affairs, in return might make use of Orff's considerable expertise.[169]

The problem was how to get Orff's name removed from its provisional place in category 3 of four possible categories: 1, White; 2, Gray-Acceptable; 3, Gray-Unacceptable; 4, Black. Persons in categories 3 and 4 were banned, but if Orff could be moved from 3 to 2, his future was secured. Jenkins therefore tried to search Orff's soul as to some possible anti-Nazi activity; today it may be assumed that he did this honestly and without knowing any details of Orff's involvement, however tenuous, with the Nazi regime. Hence, on 7 January 1946, after consulting with his superiors in Bad Homburg, Jenkins sent a letter to the composer outlining the conditions: "If you have truly been active in an antifascist manner and can prove it, you would be of tremendous use not only to us, the American occupation authorities, but also to the future German reconstruction." This would apply especially if Orff, as he had not yet decided, were to accept a teaching position. Jenkins drove home his most important point once more: "To examine your own conscience and furnish proof of *active* resistance against the previous government. For those people are scarce, and, as I said, they are of the greatest value to everyone."[170]

When I arrived in Munich to commence research on Orff's Nazi past, I was told both by his fourth widow, Liselotte Orff, and one of his most learned acolytes, Werner Thomas, the officially designated biographer of Orff by the Orff Foundation, that Orff's name had been cleared immediately after the war by a U.S. intelligence officer named Jenkins.[171] Curious to learn more, after great difficulty I finally located the American, who after a distinguished conducting and teaching career had retired to Hillsdale in western New York State. Jenkins and I talked for a whole day about Orff, and he remembered him mostly sympathetically. When I asked the crucial question of how Orff had satisfied him in early 1946, with details of an opposition to the Nazis, Jenkins said to me the following: "His proof was that he had worked together with Kurt Huber, they had founded some kind of a youth group. . . . The danger came when he and some kids or maybe Huber himself were discovered passing out leaflets. Huber was arrested and killed." Orff, Jenkins continued, had received some help through friends and fled into the mountains, where he stayed until it was safe for him to return.[172]

Since I first presented the results of my interview with Jenkins, the veracity of his statements regarding Orff and Orff's involvement in the "White Rose" resistance movement of Kurt Huber and the Scholl siblings has been questioned.[173] But circumstantial evidence supports that Orff actually told Jenkins what Jenkins claimed he did. One is a letter penned by Orff's Swiss friend Heinrich Sutermeister in December 1946, repeating essential details of Orff's alleged involvement with Huber's group, details Sutermeister had received from Jenkins during an automobile trip to Wiesbaden. Wrote Sutermeister to Orff: "Finally I heard something more concrete about you. I did not have a clue, about Prof. Huber, of the difficult times you had to endure, persecuted as you were. Your music and your work must have been your only consolation. I remembered very well from that period, when you told me of Gestapo torture methods and then was not aware that you yourself and your best friends had been in the greatest danger."[174] The other testimony is a letter to the editor of *Frankfurter Allgemeine Zeitung* in July 1995, in which a man from Hamburg, apparently a former private student, certifies that in 1946 Orff had told him in his house in Gräfelfing that a certain U.S. officer named Newell Jenkins was trying to play him up as a former resistance fighter, to the extent that he,

Orff, was having trouble calming the man down. The letter writer's conclusion that Orff could not have been the one to invent the "White Rose" legend but that, because of his insistence, it must have been Jenkins, makes no sense in light of the fact that in early 1946, Jenkins could not possibly have known about that resistance group unless informed of it by Orff.[175]

After another meeting between Orff and Jenkins in Stuttgart early in March 1946, the composer was sent to OMGUS headquarters in Bad Homburg a few weeks later, to be examined on political and psychological grounds. The resultant report of the American experts, dated 1 April 1946, speaks of Carl Orff as an "applicant for licence as composer and orchestra conductor."[176] Orff, described by the examining psychiatrist Major Bertram Schaffner as "retiring and unobtrusive," but also as "egocentric" and "diplomatic," presented a mixed bill of goods. He tried to play down his importance in the Nazi regime by insisting that his music had not been appreciated by it and that "he never got a favorable review by a Nazi critic," thus squarely lying about Stege and other officially sanctioned journalists. In line with that was his blanket claim that "he was not well thought of at the Propaganda Ministry," conveniently ignoring the final Nazi years. As the commencement of his great success with *Carmina Burana* he identified its performance at La Scala in Milan in 1942, suppressing the truth about the path-breaking Dresden premiere under Böhm two years earlier and moving himself, his oeuvre, and his civic and artistic responsibilities out of the jurisdiction of the Third Reich. He said that he had received no *order* from the Nazis to reinvent the incidental music to Shakespeare's *Midsummer Night's Dream,* when he knew that he had received an *offer* and a commission through the offices of Kreisleiter Krebs in Frankfurt and had accepted both. He also testified that he had never collected "a prize or title," making no mention of the RM2,000 from the RMK and RM500 from Krebs.

On Kurt Huber and the "White Rose," Orff was conspicuously silent. Whereas he volunteered the information that the professor was killed in Munich in 1943 after he had published music with him and that, indeed, Huber had been "one of his best friends," Orff mentioned nothing about his own role as cofounder of Huber's resistance group. At first glance, this appears to contradict Jenkins's postwar testimony and exposes the American conductor as mendacious. Yet the matter was more complicated. While there is no reason to doubt Orff's "White Rose" story in early conversations with Jenkins—accounts that Jenkins, for his part, welcomed because they would help his old friend and, in addition, fulfill American and democratic German cultural needs in Stuttgart—Orff himself had decided, till the end of March 1946, to abandon this version of events for two reasons. One was that he did not need it any more, since by that time he had made up his mind, apparently much against Jenkins's own intentions,[177] to decline the Stuttgart position, which would have made him a public servant and hence would have exposed him closely to political scrutiny for an indefinite length of time. Rather, he wanted to compose and occasionally guest-conduct.

This explains why he figured in Bad Homburg as "composer and orchestra conductor." Second, regardless of whether Jenkins had believed the initial "White Rose" story, Orff must have known that any official version of it, as recorded by his Bad Homburg interrogators, was easily verifiable, for instance through an interview with Clara Huber and surviving members of the group, and that in that case it would have to stand up to reality.

For the time being, Orff's sojourn in Bad Homburg had been successful. He was glad he had duped, first, Jenkins, and then the Captain's colleagues at U.S. military headquarters. So he returned home and told Jenkins that psychiatrist Schaffner had been "a very stupid man" and that he, Carl Orff, was "so much brighter than all the other people about him."[178] The Americans' recommendation was that he should be classified as "Gray C, acceptable" and that he ought to be licenced as "composer and orchestra conductor."[179] Although he had expected a "White classification,"[180] it still meant that from now on, nothing could stand in the path of his postwar social, political, and professional progress. Eschewing not only the directorship in Stuttgart but also any kind of teaching position (which again might have subjected him to harsher scrutiny), Orff was immediately free to look for a German stage to produce his *Die Bernauerin* (which had been completed in January 1946), and free, of course, to compose music for further German productions. *Die Bernauerin,* starring his daughter, actress Godela Orff, in the leading role, was duly staged in Stuttgart on 15 June 1947, exactly one month before Jenkins was set to leave Germany. Plans from the summer of 1946 to produce *Die Bernauerin* in Munich were also approved by local OMGUS authorities. That a special American friend had helped him was in the air: Orff received forthwith requests from other suspect colleagues to have Jenkins intercede on their behalf, requests Orff met with stony silence.[181]

What, then, about the question of Orff's "White Rose" involvement, had he told the truth? Whereas the composer had known the Munich scholar for years, his tale to Jenkins about participation in Kurt Huber's Nazi resistance was more than a "satyr's game after the end of tragedy," as Hans Maier has trivialized: It was a blatant lie.[182] Orff and Huber, an associate professor of psychology with an interest in musical folklore, including the Bavarian species, had known each other since the outgoing years of the Weimar Republic.[183] Toward the end of the 1930s Orff even considered Huber's close cooperation in the *Schulwerk* project, but his friend was occupied with too many other things.[184] After Huber, who had first lived in Munich-Schwabing, moved to Gräfelfing, meetings between the two men became more frequent. Orff tried out *Carmina Burana* on Huber, and later also *Der Mond* and *Die Kluge*. "Carl Orff and my husband enjoyed a really good friendship," remembers Huber's widow Clara, "which expressed itself especially in musical terms. As far as I can recall, they hardly ever talked about politics."[185]

Indeed, politics would not have interested Orff, and especially not the kind to which Huber subscribed. By inclination, Huber, like Reusch, was *völkisch* and ideologically akin to the Nazis, although with the passage of time his relations with the Nazi hierarchy soured, mostly for personal reasons. He assigned similar values to the *Volkslied* as did the Nazis, and hence he fitted in with National Socialist cultural planning. In 1935–36 he was to help found a "German School of *Volksmusik* and Dance" in Munich, as a counterweight against "the champions of Marxist tendencies and Jewish products." In this, the Hitler Youth was to play an important part.[186] Huber believed in musicianship that was "rooted in the soil," for the purpose of retaining the "purity of genuine German folk art," in the song of the fathers, "whose *völkisch* race was congenitally tied to our own."[187]

Although after the beginning of the war the two men continued to meet, sometimes with their wives, their professional contacts were weakening.[188] By the time that Huber actively joined the White Rose student resistance cell in January 1943, the Huber and Orff couples had not been seeing each other for about three months.[189] Orff's name has never surfaced in conjunction with the White Rose in the critical literature or in memoirs, and Gertrud Orff and Clara Huber have supplied additional assurances in writing that Orff had not been a part of it.[190] In a television documentary of 1995, Frau Huber further insisted that Orff "had not been a member."[191] Although Orff, after the war, claimed that he had known the Scholls and warned them about driving out the demons, this is highly unlikely and merely another attempt at fabricating legends. It is even doubtful that he was aware of the existence of the group, though his friend, the musicologist Thrasybulos Georgiades, was privy to their meetings. George J. Wittenstein, a retired professor of surgery at the University of California in Santa Barbara, informed me in 1997 that he was one of two surviving members of the White Rose inner circle, the editor of the third and fourth anti-Hitler leaflets, who miraculously escaped death. In his recollection, Orff "was never a member of the White Rose, nor did he and Huber co-found it." In any event, the student resisters' sudden arrest and Huber's own on 27 March 1943 caught Orff by surprise, as Clara Huber noticed one day later, when he came to visit.[192] Huber's condemnation to death on 8 April and his execution on 13 July certainly frightened Orff, for in the Third Reich everyone could become guilty by association, and hence he vanished for a while in the clinic of an acquaintance in nearby Ebenhausen.[193]

Orff's post-1945 legend regarding oppositional activity against the Third Reich must be interpreted in the context of the two other previously-mentioned legends he was constructing at that time: that *Carmina Burana* was blacklisted by the regime and hence the work of a resister and that (to emphasize the singularity of this) all previous works of his did not matter and were to be shredded by his publisher. All three legends were intertwined and served only one purpose: to establish a pedestal for a spotless Carl Orff in the postwar era.

The matter of the Nazi ban on *Carmina Burana* (at which Orff hinted again during the Bad Homburg interrogation) has already been dealt with in detail. But it is important to take a second look at Orff's claim regarding the caesura of 1937, a story that was publicly repeated by Wieland Wagner in 1965 on the occasion of Orff's seventieth birthday.[194] The fact that there are several variants of this tale alone makes one suspicious. Ulrich Dibelius, for instance, wrote in 1966 that Orff *told* publisher Strecker to withdraw his earlier works at the time of the Frankfurt *premiere* on 7 June 1937. Five years later, another biographer maintained that Orff had *written* this to Strecker. Yet another version has it that Orff *told* Strecker so after the successful *dress rehearsal*.[195] The origin of the legend is actually traceable to Orff himself, who held, in his so-called *Dokumentation* (a multivolumed memoir interspersed with documents and comments by his acolytes also designed to spread various truths, half-truths, and falsehoods), that he *did tell Strecker after the dress rehearsal* in Frankfurt: "Everything I have written so far and which unfortunately you have printed, you may now destroy. With *Carmina Burana* begin my collected works."[196] What Orff added to these monstrous, self-important sentences in 1979 was that they had, meanwhile, been "much cited."[197] As far as can be made out, however, those sentences had never been cited before 8 May 1945, either by word of mouth or in writing. In fact, they could not have been, because Orff continued, after 1937, to be interested in, to labor on and complete, and to offer for performance at least five works he had conceived or begun to craft before 1937: apart from the *Midsummer Night's Dream* music they were *Orpheus* or *Orfeo* (Monteverdi-Orff), *Tanz der Spröden* (Monteverdi-Orff), *Entrata* (Byrd-Orff), and *Die Klage der Ariadne* (Monteverdi-Orff).[198] Some of these he continued to own up to even after May 1945.[199]

Orff's manipulation of his own past corresponded uncannily with his ability to manipulate people, to suit his very own ends. Both his daughter, Godela, and his third wife, Luise Rinser, have testified that Orff had no qualms about using people for as long as he needed them and then casting them aside, as has his assistant Hans Bergese, who knew him as well as anybody for the entire period of the Third Reich, in May 1946. And in 1958, composer Karl Amadeus Hartmann warned his friend Rinser that Orff "walked all over people."[200] It appears that this tactic complemented Orff's extreme egocentricity, observed by Bad Homburg psychiatrist Schaffner; both Bergese and Godela Orff have spoken of his obsessive quest to become famous since youth. All this manifested itself especially painfully when the composer talked to Clara Huber the day after her husband had been arrested. Instead of comforting her, he started pacing the room, shouting "I am ruined! I am ruined!"[201]

After the war, one of the first persons to be manipulated in this way was Newell Jenkins himself. Jenkins knew far too much about Orff, for instance, his refusal to emigrate during the Sudeten crisis in the fall of 1938, when Jenkins had offered him connections in New York and the chance to start afresh in the United States.[202] The fact that Orff could not go then because he was too much rooted in Bavarian soil, as several of his works evinced, was, among others, a legitimate excuse to stay, but Orff was suspicious of Jenkins, in case Jenkins used this reluctance against him, and it was embarrassing at any rate.[203] Jenkins also knew of Orff's initial attempt to rehabilitate himself through the White Rose canard and obviously had not been pleased by Orff's decision not to oblige him in Stuttgart. But on the other hand, Orff was well aware that Jenkins's days in Germany were numbered. So in May 1947, with the culture officer having merely a few weeks left, Orff tried to squeeze him once more, on matters he did not wish to specify in a personal letter to him.[204] Yet the meeting does not seem to have materialized, or whatever favors Orff had had in mind from Jenkins were not granted. Already in June therefore, a month before Jenkins left the country, Orff had the bad grace to write to a friend that the officer had adopted "a highly unfriendly attitude" toward him, and by September 1948 his official line had become that although Jenkins had represented "connections," he had been gone "for a long time" and he, Orff, had "never been compelled to use his help."[205] Putting Jenkins out of his mind and that of other people as well was the best guarantee that nobody would ever learn of the ruse Orff had once used with that officer, to start his reinvention process.

Jenkins was not Orff's first sacrificial lamb, nor would he be his last. As a rule, whenever something went wrong in his life, it was not Orff's but the other person's fault. "He was extremely sensitive to criticism," remembers Rinser.[206] Sometimes the victims did not know they were being blamed. One such artist was Clemens Krauss, who directed and conducted the premiere of *Der Mond* in Munich in early 1939. The consensus then as now is that Krauss, an avant-gardist no more, tackled something modern in his day and for his own taste with great integrity, as best he could, and, all things considered, was successful.[207] Although after the war Orff conceded as much and at the time he wrote Krauss an obsequious letter of gratitude, he showed duplicity by attributing everything that he thought had gone wrong in Munich to the conductor, behind his back.[208] After the end of the war, it was Hans Meissner who was being dropped. He, who had often annoyed the composer because of his dithering and dallying regarding premieres and other performances while he was still powerful in Frankfurt but had also vigorously championed Orff, by 1945 was interned by the Allies as a formerly instrumental Nazi. He himself and his wife begged Orff to intercede on his behalf, without receiving as much as a polite reply.[209] Bertil Wetzelsberger, long Meissner's progressive conductor, to whom Orff owed the premiere of his epochal *Carmina Burana* in June 1937, became the target of Orff's rage after the composer had reason to believe that the less than successful June 1947 premiere of *Die Bernauerin* in Stuttgart was exclusively Wetzelsberger's fault. Then Orff exonerated Wetzelsberger, for his reading public's benefit, in the partially apocryphal *Dokumentation*.[210] Orff also abused Bergese, who had collaborated with Orff and Huber on a *Volkslied* series, "Music of the Landscape," eventually published by Schott in the 1940s. Whereas Bergese claims he had actually cocreated the concept for the project and alongside Huber and Orff arranged the songs for piano,

Orff had seen fit to list him on the cover not as coauthor or originator but merely as the arranger.[211]

Orff even exploited his daughter, Godela, who as a child was entirely dependent on him, because she was deprived of love and sustenance by her mostly absent mother. She tells of the many fairy tales and fantasies her father tried on her as a child, and which delighted her.[212] But when she became a young adult and interested in men, Orff would have none of it; he wanted her only to himself. By 1943, the year of Godela's marriage, their relationship had become acrimonious, although Orff wrote to a physician who had treated her in his sanatorium that there existed a "particular harmony between father and daughter," when in fact, according to Godela, he was intent on nothing else but disturbing that marriage.[213] Godela Orff, too, maintains that her father discarded her when she did not fit into his plans any longer, most likely after his marriage to Gertrud Willers, and that she felt hurt. The exception was her acting career, which flattered him and his works and hence he supported it; it is significant that she starred in his first postwar production, *Die Bernauerin,* in June 1947, even though Orff himself did not find it in his heart to attend the premiere, to lend her emotional support, because he wanted to show the disagreeable conductor Wetzelsberger a cold shoulder.[214] By the 1950s, Orff and his daughter were no longer on speaking terms.[215]

Godela admits that as a child she was jealous of the many young women Orff would bring home for trysts, mostly nubile students from the Günther-Schule, who adored the composer without qualification.[216] Psychologists could properly analyze what appears to have been an obsession with sex, which expressed itself in *Carmina Burana* and *Catulli Carmina*; Jenkins reports that Orff "always talked about exciting sexual things," and there are indications that he liked to read about them, too.[217] Not surprisingly, Orff's relationship with women was always complicated; he had no fewer than four wives. According to Luise Rinser, he was in the habit of trying out a new partner while still with the old one, as if for some kind of insurance. When he started courting Gertrud Willers, an attractive and well-off pupil from the Günther-Schule who was young enough to be his daughter, he was still tied to Maja Lex, an exotic dancer of Italian-Japanese extraction. He married Willers in July 1939 because she promised this restless, narcissistic man emotional and especially financial stability. That marriage failed for good in 1954, because Orff had become interested in Rinser, a war widow of a student of Hindemith and an author, who had once been jailed by the Nazis for the sort of political crime Orff then wished he had committed, but he held on to Willers almost until the day of his wedding with Rinser. Before that, in 1945, Orff had attempted a relationship with Brigitte Bergese, Hans Bergese's wife and also originally from the Günther-Schule, who was living with the Orffs in Gräfelfing, while Hans himself was still in a prisoner-of-war camp. Brigitte Bergese withstood his advances and turned instead to Egk, not knowing then that Orff was at the same time carrying on an affair with his secretary, who also stayed under what used to be the Willers' roof. By the time Orff's marriage with Rinser was falling apart in 1958–59, Orff was already intimate with her secretary, Liselotte Schmitz, who lived with them in the farmlike house in Diessen on the Ammersee and who then became Orff's last wife.[218]

Consider egocentricity, disregard for other people's interests, unwillingness to become personally committed or emotional, tremendous charm and charisma, and bursts of creativity alternating with bouts of disease or lethargy during which work was sluggish (as in the creation of the Midsummer Night's Dream music). Moreover, consider extreme moodiness and a talent for making up fantasy, legends, or lies which, as Rinser thinks, Orff himself often came to believe. What emerges here is the profile of a man who was mentally ill. Several more clues in his behavioral pattern lead us to conclude that Orff, at least since young adulthood, must have been suffering from manic depression, which strikes so many creative people and, until more recent times, has often gone entirely untreated.[219] In Orff's case, the cause for what, in medical terms, may have been bipolar II is not known, nor is its severity, yet one of the clues could be the young soldier's near-suffocation experience in the war trench, which evidently caused him to have crying fits and nightmares as a mature adult, led to at least one terribly embarrassing experience with Rinser in public, and produced an overall sentiment of fear. This fear may have been responsible for Orff's often asocial behavior (with his preference for shabby exercise clothes to formal dress), his avoidance of human contact with members of the establishment, in the Third Reich as much as after, and the manner in which he treated former friends in correspondence when he thought they were dispensable or, worse, could embarrass him.[220]

This is especially apparent from his relationship with his former Jewish friends from before 1933, whose letters after the regime change he answered either lackadaisically or not at all. Jenkins tells of how Orff wished to keep from being associated with his old friend Erich Katz when that musician, a former assistant to Freiburg musicologist Wilibald Gurlitt, had been spotted leaving Orff's Munich apartment after a visit with Orff in 1938—around the time of Kristallnacht, which then resulted in Katz's months-long incarceration.[221] Granted, the Nazi regime had placed taboos on such social intercourse, but was Orff especially afraid to associate with Jews because he was himself a "quarter Jew" by Nazi standards, having told no one about it, including regime authorities?[222]

One final clue bolsters the hypothesis of Carl Orff as a psychically sick man: his overriding sense of guilt. Psychiatrist Peter Whybrow writes that guilt feelings are typical signs of depression: "Memories recalled are predominantly sad or associated with guilt."[223] Luise Rinser remembers how Orff used to be tortured by guilt feelings.[224] Guilt about what? One can only conjecture: during the Weimar Republic, because he had survived the trench cave-in and his comrades had not? during the Third Reich, because his grandmother had been Jewish and he saw himself escaping the horrible fate of former Jewish friends? in the new democracy of Germany, because he had lied about the White Rose to Jenkins?

Orff has left testimony of his guilt feelings in the case of three men whose expectations he could not have lived up to by the time they died. To come to grips with this guilt, he wrote letters to each one, as if he were still alive. These letters, in their highly emotional quality, which is rather untypically Orffian, read as if Orff and the men had always been soul brothers. One letter was to Erich Katz, who died in Santa Barbara in 1973, after Orff had made no attempt to resume the relationship. Katz, on the other hand, always acknowledged the friendship and, as Orff was informed by Katz's companion, spoke of him warmly just before his death.[225] Another was to Karl Amadeus Hartmann, the fellow Munich composer who had struggled through the Third Reich as a bona fide opponent of the Hitler regime, and whom Orff had been careful to avoid during that period, yet whose company, as a culture administrator authorized by the Americans, Orff eagerly sought after 1945.[226] "Dear, dear Amadeus," wrote Orff disingenuously in December 1963, "we had quite a different agreement. Since I am so much older than you I thought that I would precede you. . . . This once was our Bavarian consensus, and as usual we were of one mind."

The third and most significant letter was to Kurt Huber. Already in January 1946, by the time Orff was using the friend's resistance as his alibi, Orff wrote: "Dear and revered friend! Never in my life did I write you a letter. You were there and always close, and to experience your existence was delightful. . . . Seldom, really seldom did you speak of your *own* plans . . . you were, almost exclusively, listening to my concerns." Orff composed these lines at his wife's Gräfelfing house on Ritter-von-Epp-Strasse, which had now been renamed Kurt-Huber-Strasse. The letter was published, in 1947, as the last contribution to an official, commemorative volume honoring Kurt Huber, edited by his widow, Clara.[227] Until his death in 1982, it would serve as Carl Orff's certified proof that he had made amends.

6

Hans Pfitzner

Magister Teutonicus Miser

In July 1997, there was much commotion at New York's Lincoln Center Festival. The critics' attention was centered on *Palestrina,* an opera by Hans Pfitzner, a hardly known German composer of the twentieth century, which had, during the previous season, been staged by the Royal Opera in London. Upon examining the score and sampling the music, one critic called one of the scenes "heartbreaking and sublimely silly."[1] Another commented on the existence of a mysterious quote from the pessimistic German philosopher Arthur Schopenhauer at the top of the score.[2] A third noticed "little revelation, no moment of musical epiphany, no shock of surprise, only Pfitzner's unrelenting and passionate sincerity."[3] A fourth observed about Pfitzner that he "grumbled yet coped through the Third Reich as through the rest of his career," whereas yet another noted that "he lent his name, his music and his actions to the Nazi cause."[4]

What was the flurry all about? It seems that for better or worse, Pfitzner had been rediscovered. Until *Palestrina*'s earlier staging in London and now New York, in his lifetime and after his death in 1949, only few judgments had been passed on Pfitzner, one of the least-well-known composers of the Nazi era, to whom Gerald Abraham, for example, had devoted a mere two pages in his *Concise Oxford History of Music.*[5] One of the most charming men he had ever known, remembered fellow composer Gottfried von Einem, and the famous baritone Hans Hotter concurred, adding that starring in the role of Borromeo, a leading character of Pfitzner's opera *Palestrina* (written 1912–15), had been one of his fondest professional experiences.[6] Although he had the reputation of being cantankerous, wrote pianist Elly Ney in July 1933, the members of the orchestra saw nothing of it. "They loved him dearly, as did the audience."[7] People would usually portray him as someone who abides no opinion other than the one with which he can fully agree, as if he were nothing but a know-it-all, averred a sycophant of Pfitzner, the Nazi critic Walter Abendroth in 1940.[8] Walter Thomas, Baldur von Schirach's governor of cultural affairs in Vienna during the war, detected some austere qualities: Pfitzner's music represented the stern ethos of conquest rather than merely beautiful sound. "Life does not mean enjoyment! Life means suffering, solitude, a thorn-crowned search for God. To find Him means to deny the world. Music is the path to this goal."[9]

These sentences, if they truly apply to Pfitzner, suggest a thinker as much as a composer. Indeed, one of his post-World-War II biographers has written, rightly or wrongly, that Pfitzner was the only composer of the Nazi era who attempted to come to grips with National Socialism intellectually and spiritually, after the catastrophe of 1945.[10]

Originally of Saxon stock, Hans Erich Pfitzner was born on 5 May 1869, in Moscow, where his father worked as a modest orchestra violinist. When he was two, his family moved to Frankfurt, which henceforth he always regarded as his hometown, his father becoming the concert master of the municipal theater orchestra. Not having finished the Abitur at Gymnasium, Pfitzner attended the Hoch'sche Konservatorium from 1886 to 1890. From then on he held low-paying jobs as teacher of piano and theory in Koblenz and Berlin, for a few months also as Kapellmeister of the theater in Mainz. He was Erster Kapellmeister at the Berlin Theater des Westens when, in 1908, he was appointed to the moderately prestigious post of opera director and head of the conservatory in Strasbourg, then in Imperial German Alsace. From there he was driven by Germany's defeat in World War I and the resultant annexation of the province by the French. Reduced to utter poverty, he retired to a small house in Schondorf on Ammersee southwest of Munich, which devoted friends had bought for him and his family. For his livelihood, he agreed to teach a master class at the Preussische Akademie der Künste in Berlin, which position he largely treated as an absentee professorship but retained until 1929, when the Bavarian state engaged him as conductor at the Bayerische Staatsoper and in the broadcast system, in addition to professor of composition at the Bayerische Akademie der Tonkunst in Munich.[11]

Until 1908, then, when he was almost forty, Pfitzner found himself professionally and economically at sea; attempts to receive notice as a musician, from famous composers such as Brahms and Max Bruch, had ended in failure.[12] Partially as a consequence of this, three factors attained significance in his life after 1918. One was the tendency of reverent friends to form a cult around an underrecognized master and to make him benefit from their support, spiritually, morally, and materially, a support Pfitzner learned to exploit to the utmost for the rest of his life. A second was the formation of a belief within himself, and a tacit understanding among the knowing few that because of artistic, if not actually national, greatness hidden to the masses, he was entitled to sinecures, such as appointments to institutions where he put in much less than the required hours of work. The third was a heightened sense of having been personally slighted by Germany's enemies, symbolized by his expulsion from Strasbourg, which turned him into a rabid German chauvinist and enemy of the Weimar Republic.

As a composer, Pfitzner's music was an extension of late Romanticism. Until the premiere of his opera *Palestrina* in Munich in 1917 under Bruno Walter—always his most important work—his oeuvre was either little or not at all acknowledged. At first influenced by Wagner and Schumann, he later developed a taste for Weber, Heinrich Marschner, and Schubert; near the top of his list stood Brahms. Bayreuth in those formative years meant little to Pfitzner (and never very much thereafter), mainly because of Cosima Wagner's dismissive attitude toward Brahms and Schumann. His first significant work was the opera *Der arme Heinrich* (1891–93), staged in 1895 and featuring the gaunt Heldentenor Bruno Heydrich, who actually saved the Mainz premiere (in contrast to his son, Reinhard, who later would threaten the composer). What followed were *Die Rose vom Liebesgarten* (1897–1900), after motifs by the Romantic painter Hans Thoma and, like its predecessor, Wagnerian yet weak in dramatic construction, stylistically heavy and bombastic, and melodically dated but containing "a wealth of musical ideas." In the self-referential *Palestrina,* the hero was a brooding church-music composer in defiance summoned to the regnant Council of Trent; this caused the admiring Thomas Mann, at the time of the premiere a friend of both Walter and Pfitzner, to comment that the work, "a piece of dying Romanticism," was "absolutely enchanting." It was clear, as Pfitzner communicated in August 1932 to tenor Wilhelm Rode, that he despised French and Italian operas, wishing to replace them entirely with "truly national German opera." Pfitzner himself composed even more, albeit lesser, German operas, next to a plethora of chamber works, choral pieces and Lieder, and concertos for violin, cello, and piano. For such a conservative repertoire, he was able to attract merely a string of unremarkable soloists, the exceptions being Alma Moodie, the violinist, Walter Gieseking, the pianist, and, toward the end of the republic, the prominent trio led by Elly Ney, who, fiercely conservative in her own right, always felt a particular affinity for this composer. Such music remained limited to Germany and a few European countries in the best of times—only once, in 1923, was one of Pfitzner's cantatas performed in New York, by the competent, though not stellar, Artur Bodansky.[13] By the end of the republic, Pfitzner had reason to complain to his publisher that not a single opera of his had found its way to a foreign stage.[14]

If Mann's judgment appeared to encapsulate the strong reactionary, epigonal qualities of Pfitzner's creations, things were not always what they seemed. For underneath the cover of convention, there lurked interesting progressive impulses, if not of the proverbial avant-garde. Pfitzner sometimes seemed split: Whereas in 1935 he grimly recalled Donaueschingen as the place "where those *atonal* music festivals wrought havoc," anathema to his professed conservativism, he himself had not been averse to musical experiments.[15] "The music of the 1920s shows quite clearly that Pfitzner kept abreast with the more radical vein of twentieth-century music in harmony and counterpoint, if not in rhythm," writes John Williamson, as he points to Pfitzner's "choral fantasy" *Das dunkle Reich* (1929), whose chromaticism in part approaches complete tonal disruption.[16] Schoenberg's pupil Winfried Zillig detected tonal boldness even in Pfitzner's other important choral work, *Von deutscher Seele* (1921), also in his Piano Concerto (1922) and in the second act of *Palestrina,* but particularly in his String Quartet in C-sharp minor, opus 36, of 1925, which was expanded into the Symphony opus 36a in 1932.[17] And with that, even the modernist journal *Melos* was impressed, at the end of the republic. In its pages, Karl Wörner commended the predominating fourth and fifth intervals of the new symphony and a "linear and tonal abstraction" that paralleled the recent works of Schoenberg and veritably identified Pfitzner as an exponent of New Music.[18]

Now Pfitzner would not have been flattered by the analogy with the head of the Second Viennese School, whom, as a symbol of Cultural Bolshevism and un-German Weimar republican decay, he had early, and firmly, lodged in his contemporary matrix of negative values and whose opera *Die glückliche Hand* (1908–13) he had managed to remove from the program of the Tonkünstlerfest in Duisburg in 1929.[19] This was so, notwithstanding the fact that in 1920 he had asked conductor Hermann Scherchen to discuss with him some of Schoenberg's newer music.[20] But in the mid-1920s Pfitzner did have a brief working relationship with another modernist, who was then still young enough to defer to him and whom the master evidently was to hold in high regard until the end of his life: Paul Hindemith.[21] That composer and violist was eager to premiere the Quartet in C-sharp minor with his Amar Quartet in December 1925 in Berlin and hence kept up a correspondence about this with Pfitzner in the preceding months, as well as after. At the end of 1925 he was letting Pfitzner know that the Amar Quartet would henceforth perform the work "in every halfway decent town." Characteristically, as far as Pfitzner was concerned, Hindemith thereafter played his quartet not nearly as often as he had first expected (Hindemith actually performed it no fewer than fourteen times up to the end of 1931), but the older composer was gracious enough to accede to the younger's request for a critical review of his own oeuvre.[22]

As a more commonplace phenomenon, Pfitzner's ostensive rejection of artistic representations of modernism in the Weimar Republic, especially music, interacted strongly with his political convictions at the time. At its premise was the subjective and widely shared awareness of Germany's hurt national pride after the shameful defeat of Versailles. This resulted in the equation of Pfitzner's music and personality with what were axiomatically perceived as intrinsically German values, so that the composer styled himself, and was styled by his multiplying congregations of acolytes, as "Hans Pfitzner the German." The ascription of what were identified as German virtues to Pfitzner and his conventionally constructed music was as arbitrary as it was potentially demagogic: By being labeled quintessentially German there was imputed to Pfitzner the man, intellectual, and composer a morally regenerative and didactic function that could be utilized in the political control of certain segments of society for the sake of state and nation.[23]

This was especially so as Pfitzner himself strongly espoused what were then seen as national values, not the least of which were the historically grounded tradition of German Romanticism and a positive reflection on the Middle Ages and the German Reformation. In all German provinces, this national value system was avidly embraced by reactionary political formations such as the recurrently active and ultimately defeated civil defense corps (*Einwohnerwehren*) (the local Schondorf unit of which Pfitzner himself joined), conservative parties and their leaders such as Gustav von Kahr, and nationalist icons such as the generals and admirals Erich Ludendorff, Paul von Hindenburg, Alfred von Tirpitz, and Adolf von Trotha, as well as writers and publishers on the right such as Moeller van den Bruck, Hugo Bruckmann, and Oswald Spengler, another Schopenhauer follower, with whom he personally did not get along too well.[24] Grounded in this position, Pfitzner proceeded to take up arms against the already stereotyped, putative enemies of the republic, as the Allied-sanctioned antipode to the once powerful Second Reich that had ensconced him in Strasbourg: Social Democrats, parliament, Bolshevists, foreigners such as the French and Americans, and, of course, Jews. Artistically specified, from their ranks were recruited the purveyors of popular culture such as newfangled cinema and operetta, cheap-effects composers such as Ernst Krenek, who had flaunted his Negrophile *Jonny spielt auf,* and the Jewish Kurt Weill, who had manufactured the sterile *Die Bürgschaft,* to say nothing of composers with sub–rosa, even half-serious pretensions, such as Emmerich Kálmán, Paul Abraham, Giacomo Puccini, and Eric Satie.[25] At the very beginning of the republic, as chauvinistic a writer as Mann summed up Pfitzner's qualities, lauding his "high conservatism," his "genuine-born Germanness," and his fight against "that Italian silliness."[26]

Pfitzner's prefascist polemics against what German conservatives regarded as the gutter culture of the Weimar Republic culminated in his protracted invective against Jews. To him, they were the perpetrators of the postwar disaster. Pfitzner totally bought into the right-extremist notion that Weimar was the artifical creation of an international Jewish conspiracy—a Jewish Republic. Hence he equated Jewry with internationalism, Bolshevism, disorder, and revolution, including in this scheme the arts. Programmatically he wrote: "During the shame and crime of revolution we experienced with grief that German workers, German people allowed themselves to be seduced by Russian-Jewish criminals and showered them with an enthusiasm that they denied their German heroes and benefactors." Because Jews to him were the instigators of revolutionary modernism, he rejected them in music and the other arts as well. Pfitzner's anti-Semitism was therefore not predominantly biological; instead he tended to treat Jews as a collective cultural phenomenon, and his wrath was directed against individuals only insofar as they were clearly recognizable as personifications of that phenomenon.[27]

Only too often, this formula proved him right, from his twisted perspective. One of his most celebrated anti-Semitic tracts was a book of 1920, dealing with what he termed the new aesthetics of musical impotence, which he immediately identified as a sign of decay. Indeed, "decay" became one of the overused words in his intellectual lexicon. That book was directed against the prominent Frankfurt music critic Paul Bekker, a Jew, who had authored a biography of Beethoven. Pfitzner charged him with having denied the power of musical impulse, of genius per se, and having put in its place artificial construction and the mechanics of rationalization. For Pfitzner, music was a product of the soul not the brain; Jews intellectualized everything instead of being able to feel with their hearts. Pfitzner hurled similar accusations at the music scholar Alfred Einstein and, from a different angle, his former pupil and Strasbourg assistant, Otto Klemperer, who had allegedly been involved in an intrigue to unseat him. In all this he was strongly supported by the members of the various Pfitzner societies springing up in major centers, the one in Munich including anti-Semites in the mold of the publishers Hugo and Elsa Bruckmann; the philosopher Professor Hugo Dingler; Eugenie Göring a relative of Hitler's vassal; the conductor Hans Knappertsbusch; the historian Professor Karl Alexander von Müller; and the composer Siegmund von Hausegger. By the same token, the Bayreuth circle surrounding Hans von Wolzogen applauded his efforts, even though he did not court it.[28]

Pfitzner's mode of thinking about Jews had two important consequences. The relative deemphasis on the biological meant that he could include as his targets composers or other men of culture who were not ethnic Jews but met his criteria of internationalism, disorder, decay, and revolution. One of these was Ferruccio Busoni, who was half-German, half-Italian, and whom he attacked, for revolutionary utterances in music, even in 1917, three years before the massive polemic against Bekker. Had Pfitzner only known that Busoni would soon become the teacher of the Jew Kurt Weill! The other consequence was that Pfitzner, by claiming not to direct his attacks ad hominem (which was hardly true), could make exceptions among Jews for his choice of friends. There were two notable examples. The most prominent was Paul Nikolaus Cossmann, a wealthy Jew from Frankfurt who had been his childhood pal and then moved on to Munich to found the reactionary journal *Süddeutsche Monatshefte*. The other was Bruno Walter, whose gradual rise to prominence Pfitzner witnessed and indeed profited from, as evidenced during the premiere of *Palestrina* in 1917. (A third one may be said to have been his first wife, Mimi Kwast, daughter of his Frankfurt conservatory teacher James Kwast, who had a Jewish grandfather, but then love is known to be blind, even, and especially, in the case of one Hans Erich Pfitzner, as shall be seen later.) Still, two important caveats applied to both Cossmann and Walter to make them acceptable to Pfitzner even as Jews. Cossmann was not only ultra-nationalistic, as was the composer, but he was also, like several of his contemporaries (for instance, Foreign Minister Walther Rathenau), dominated by Jewish self-hatred. Although Walter did not suffer from that particular malady, he was sufficiently conservative to hold parliamentary democracy in contempt and admire strong, authoritarian governments, as events in Austria and Italy after 1933 were to prove. And whereas Walter, born Schlesinger, was not baptized, Cossmann could claim conversion to Catholicism as an additional token of his Germanness.[29]

All this suggests that during the republican period, Hans Pfitzner must have been a convinced Nazi. However, he was not; mainly for two reasons. First, he was above mere party politics, as were so many rightist intellectuals in the Weimar era—beyond supporting bourgeois right-wing parties such as the German National People's Party (DNVP), which represented most of his causes.[30] Second, as an elitist, Pfitzner had difficulties accepting rough-and-ready street-brawl methods by what he regarded as troglodytes, who would be incapable of showing any appreciation for his music. This was quite obvious from his haughty correspondence of that period. Besides, he wanted followers to flock to him; he himself was a follower only of high ideals and personalities long dead: demi-gods such as Wagner, the Romantic poet Joseph Freiherr von Eichendorff (1788–1857), and especially Schopenhauer, the pre-Spenglerian philosopher of pessimism, who held that the world was ruled by pain, which could only, temporarily, be removed by the arts, particularly music.[31]

However, he did meet Adolf Hitler in early 1923, if not quite of his own doing. The occasion was Pfitzner's hospital stay in Munich-Schwabing after a gall bladder operation from 22 January to 12 February, when his friend Cossmann, who fiercely admired Hitler, arranged a meeting through one of the historic founders of the Nazi Party, Anton Drexler, already a former visitor of Pfitzner in Schondorf. Hitler and his seedy mentor, the erstwhile Wagnerian critic and playwright Dietrich Eckart, arrived in the composer's hospital room, Hitler planting himself at the foot of the bed and, in typical fashion, doing most of the talking. Also present were Mimi Pfitzner and Drexler. The topic was the scourge of Jewry and, in particular, its responsibility for the beginning and loss of World War I, about whose terrors Hitler related first-hand accounts in vivid color. Soon the conversation drifted on to the—like Cossmann—scurrilously anti-Semitic thinker Otto Weininger. Born in 1880 in Vienna, he had converted to Protestantism and developed a theory of women being inferior to men and Jews inferior to "Aryans." A homosexual and fearing himself to be more feminine than he wanted to be, he had shot himself in 1903 in the house where Beethoven had died. Hitler expressed his satisfaction over that fact, remarking, in Pfitzner's recollection, that "this was the only Jew whom he was willing to tolerate, since he had removed himself from this world." But then Hitler got angry, possibly after Pfitzner had averred that one could not possibly expect all the Jews on this earth to dispatch themselves in this way. Yet even Pfitzner's argument that by killing himself, Weininger had eliminated not only a Jew but also an anti-Semite, did not placate the Führer of the Nazi Party. "Could one imagine that a Frenchman would kill himself only because he is a Frenchman?," pondered Pfitzner decades later. In any event, Hitler left in a huff, remarking to Eckart that he wanted to have nothing further to do with this Jewish rabbi.[32]

Undaunted, and still thinking Hitler a great man, perhaps on the model of his main character Palestrina, Pfitzner attempted to resume contact with the Führer, trying to see him in Munich after leaving the hospital, but Hitler was not available.[33] He tried again after the aborted Beer Hall Putsch of November 1923, learning of Hitler's imprisonment in Landsberg and going out to buy him a morale-boosting book, a shabbily bound edition of Conrad Ferdinand Meyer's *Huttens letzte Tage,* published in 1922, which had as its lead theme struggles of liberation and national unification. I saw this in the Bavarian State Library. Pfitzner dedicated it thus: "To Adolf Hitler the great German. Hans Pfitzner, 1 April 1924."[34] He affixed a note, written in Schondorf on that date: "Dear Herr Hitler, the unspeakable which everyone must feel today, who is still a part of *our* Germany, now, shortly before Germany totally ceases to exist or rejuvenates itself—this I wanted to express to you somehow, as the embodiment of our greatest hope." These sentences and the rest of the short text were clumsy rather than eloquent; Pfitzner asked Hitler whether he remembered the Schwabing hospital meeting and reminded him—a characteristic Pfitznerian twist—that Germans would always be betrayed most vulnerably by Germans. The awkwardness of the text and the fact that Hitler did not want to be reminded of the Schwabing meeting, not to mention obvious signs of obsequiousness on Pfitzner's part, probably would have caused the Führer simply to disregard the composer from then on. As it turned out, Pfitzner never mailed either the book or the letter.[35]

All things considered, the composer was not faring very well in the Weimar Republic, especially, as the hated modernists were in ascendance until about 1930, and his cultural and political pessimism did not help.[36] In particular, Pfitzner was suffering from many problems in interpersonal relations, with his tendency to lecture to friend and foe on matters concerning his music and other things as well. One had to be Pfitzner to be liked by Pfitzner. As a person, he became further embittered because of the death of his wife in 1926 and the meningitis of his oldest son, Paul, who had to be committed to institutionalized medical care. Politically, he remained on the right, to the point of alienating old and more flexible supporters. And economically, he was more insecure than he should have been, with additional, unnecessary, complications arising from his notorious tactlessness. At the end of the republic, his relations with colleagues in the music establishment of Berlin and Munich served as sad and poignant commentaries on what had been an extraordinarily strenuous, even frustrating, career since World War I.

Pfitzner cultivated a patronizing style with his publishers, always giving them the impression that it was an honor for them to serve him. Flaunting his alleged reputation as a polymath, he was quick to insult colleagues behind their backs, as when he said about conductor Erich Kleiber, who in 1923 stood to conduct his opera *Die Rose vom Liebesgarten* in Berlin, that he, Kleiber, was not his friend but would be one as soon as it was of service to him to play host to a genius. Pfitzner openly called Hans Knappertsbusch a liar because he thought the Munich conductor had insulted him in the Eastern provinces. And he chastised lesser conductors for oversights ordinary mortals would have found too trivial to mention. Thomas Mann broke with him in 1925 when it was clear that under no circumstances would Pfitzner, unlike Mann, give the Weimar Republic even the slightest chance of political survival.[37]

Pfitzner's gratuitously offensive manner and his self-serving attitude compounded already complex financial matters even further. In November 1923, the final phase of Germany's disastrous inflation, he had refused to be remunerated with paper money from his publisher, which was understandable. But then when the currency had stabilized early in 1924, he demanded the preposterous amount of 50,000 new rentenmarks for rights to *Die Rose vom Liebesgarten,* which his publisher refused to pay because that exceeded the figure in the original contract, and many performances of the opera on German stages simply were not in the offing. Two years later, in the case of *Palestrina,* Pfitzner was torn between exercising his author's right regarding the shape and direction of that opera on a Duisburg stage and the possibility of making more money by leaving it more commercialized for public consumption. In 1927, Pfitzner seems to have been behind his publisher in demanding that the opera *Das Christelflein* (1906) be performed, by mere students of the Cologne conservatory, in a regular opera house costing much money, and charging a performance fee far too high for the conservatory to afford. In the same year conductor Peter Raabe of Aachen added insult to injury by scheduling Pfitzner's violin concerto for public concert and broadcast transmission without expending funds for the sheet music for the orchestra musicians beforehand. Just before the event, Pfitzner's work was substituted with a repertory piece by Brahms, already well rehearsed, thus leaving the composer with lost income and very angry.[38] In January 1933, Pfitzner thought he was so badly off financially that he did not shrink from asking Werner Reinhart, a wealthy Swiss patron known for his magnanimity toward composers, to buy three museum artifacts from him for the not inconsiderable sum of RM1,500, which an acquaintance of the composer happened to owe him.[39] Reinhart did not respond.

Palestrina made for tension with Generalintendant Heinz Tietjen at the

Berlin Staatsoper by early 1929, after Pfitzner thought he had reason to believe that the opera would be staged at a commercially viable time and with
Leo Blech as conductor—including the possibility of guest conductor appearances by the composer himself. As it turned out, *Palestrina* was to be
scheduled for July of that year, which Pfitzner thought to be disastrous for
ticket sales. To make matters worse, Blech eventually declined to conduct
the opera, causing Pfitzner to accuse him: "Never have you in all your life
conducted even a single note of mine, whenever you could help it." Blam-
ing the Berlin opera administration for wanting to turn *Palestrina* into a
"fifth-rate matter," he withdrew his permission for the work to be performed. Tietjen then told him this was a mistake, for even in July the staging would have made him some money because of all the foreigners there.
(Tietjen probably knew better, as did Pfitzner: In those years foreigners in
Berlin were interested in other things than a Pfitzner opera!) A compromise
was then reached when Max von Schillings was contracted to conduct the
opera in January 1930, with Pfitzner in charge of direction.⁴⁰

The tribulations in Berlin continued because of differences over Pfitzner's
latest opera, *Das Herz*. It was composed in 1930–31, to a script by Hans
Mahner-Mons, a debonair student and friend of Pfitzner and popular author of detective fiction; Pfitzner himself had turned the text into verse.
Such poetry was approaching kitsch, but the plot, too, was maudlin: a medieval physician with magical powers, invoking his young, dead wife,
whose heart was claimed by the devil. "The personal significance is too obvious to need much labouring," writes one recent critic, "the figure of the
wife, renunciation, and the hostility of the world" suggesting Pfitzner's own
career and resonances from *Palestrina*.⁴¹

Das Herz was to be the composer's last opera; it crystalized his problems
with money as well as personal and professional relationships, as in his
dealings with such friends as Mahner-Mons, conductors, and publishers. At
a time of renewed economic depression, Pfitzner notoriously was asking his
publisher, Otto Fürstner, for royalties that could not be justified, especially
as the prospects for a commercial success with *Das Herz* were once again
dim. Although Pfitzner won the occasional sum of money, for example, a
Beethoven Prize (in Berlin in 1931), and also entered into stable employment with the Bavarian government in May 1929, he felt the need to sup-
plement his income by continuing his constant guest conducting. After the
opera had been premiered under Tietjen and Furtwängler in Berlin on 12
November 1931, Pfitzner was dissatisfied because the Generalintendant, in
collusion with Mahner-Mons, had messed about with the stage direction on
which he, Pfitzner, thought himself an authority ever since his comprehen-
sive duties in Strasbourg. He accused Furtwängler of having dragged the
tempi. In addition, Pfitzner was irked, as he should have been, by more
than the usual share of bad reviews. Fürstner wanted to withhold money
from the composer, and they reached a compromise only after considerable
wrangling.⁴²

Das Herz was simultaneously premiered in Berlin and Munich, there under the baton of Knappertsbusch, the resident Generalmusikdirektor, with whom Pfitzner had previously experienced friction. Principally at issue between the two musicians, apart from temperament, were Knappertsbusch's tendency to neglect rehearsals, whereas the composer could never get enough of those, especially for his own works, and Pfitzner's propensity for interference with the direction of his operas, which, as their creator, he looked on as a sacred right. Pfitzner's overbearing attitude as an expert in composing, conducting, and directing had alienated him from most notable conductors by the end of the republic, including Fritz Busch, Furtwängler, and, of course, his Munich colleague Knappertsbusch. As Fürstner had projected, to be commercially viable *Das Herz* brought in far less revenue in Munich (as in other venues) than it should have, and for that reason Munich's Intendant Baron Clemens von Franckenstein, in agreement with Knappertsbusch, scheduled it less frequently than Pfitzner would have liked. This held true, in Munich at least, in the case of other Pfitzner operas as well, such as *Der arme Heinrich* and *Die Rose vom Liebesgarten*. In one of his charactistic theatrical poses, Pfitzner announced in April 1932 that he would henceforth refrain from setting foot on the Munich stage. This despite a contract that required him to conduct one of his operas at least six times per year. To many colleagues it appeared that Pfitzner had succeeded, at the end of the republic, in estranging himself from his environment as an "eternal malcontent," as he himself had admitted as early as 1929.[43]

II

Hans Pfitzner's journey through the Third Reich also became twisted and ultimately tragic. It turned out to be that of a frustrated believer, who, denied intimate communion with his idols the supreme political leaders, was forced to make do with their underlings in day-to-day mundane dealings. At the beginning in January 1933, despite the unpleasant and fleeting personal encounter with Hitler in 1923, Pfitzner harbored high hopes for himself as the Bard Laureate of the Thousand-Year Reich, whose precise function in that polity was yet to be circumscribed.[44] Realizing that this would take time, he began his Nazi career by accepting the support of Alfred Rosenberg and the men of his Kampfbund für deutsche Kultur (KfdK), among whom the composer's authorized biographer, Berlin music critic Walter Abendroth, was a recognized authority. KfdK colleagues of Abendroth scheduled Pfitzner, who was a bad public speaker, in a lecture series on German culture, alongside Nazi ideologues Herman Wirth, Hans F. K. Günther, Walther Darré, and Hanns Johst, where, fittingly, he was to speak on "Music as the Expression of the German Soul."[45] However, commensurate with Rosenberg's standing at the time, their help was often ill coordinated and they lacked power. When in the spring of 1933 Pfitzner was given to understand that through Rosenberg's good offices he might be appointed opera director of Düsseldorf, he pursued this issue seriously, only to learn that the party philosopher and his men had acted over the heads of Düsseldorf municipal politicians.[46] Presumably also, because he was seen as the candidate of Rosenberg for the post of Generalintendant of the municipal opera in Berlin, vacant after the death of Max von Schillings, not he, but Kammersänger Rode, a favorite of Hitler and well enough acquainted with Joseph Goebbels, signed the contract later in the summer. Vis-à-vis the Berlin Staatsoper of Minister-President Hermann Göring, Berlin Gauleiter Goebbels soon turned the municipal opera into his very own Deutsches Opernhaus, where Pfitzner's influence henceforth was nonexistent.[47]

Pfitzner suffered additional setbacks in the first year of Hitler's rule, including demeaning treatment at the hands of Munich opera conductor Hans Knappertsbusch and Generalintendant Franckenstein, an extension of relations from the end of the republic, and an injunction, issued to him by Bavarian Justice Minister Hans Frank and Reich Interior Minister Wilhelm Frick, against traveling to the Salzburg Festival in July. In the Munich case, complaints on both sides ranged anywhere from petty technicalities to major differences over interpretation, the value of the composer's own operas on the program, or Pfitzner's notorious absences as guest conductor-on-contract, with Pfitzner and Knappertsbusch, politically in full agreement, acting out the worst of personal animosities.[48] In the Salzburg affair, Pfitzner, who was to conduct his own Violin Concerto, opus 34 (1923), the new Symphony in C-sharp minor, and Schumann at the July festival, was prevailed upon by the authorities to publish an open letter in the press condemning the current attitude of the Dollfuss regime in Vienna, then much at odds with Hitler's foreign policy, as an affront against "the awakening forces of Germandom," to which the composer himself was committed. Pfitzner later claimed, especially in a letter of justification to his friend, Austrian citizen Bruno Walter, that force had been used, namely, by Frank, to make him write this letter. That, however, may be discounted in light of the fact that Strauss, too, having been warned, had shrugged off any consequences and put in a Salzburg appearance. Characteristically, Pfitzner, so intent on scoring points with the new rulers, decided not to travel, doubtless after being pressured, but ultimately of his own volition, thinking that an embarrassment with the Austrians would be easier to bear than the wrath of the new German rulers.[49]

Because Pfitzner was eager to have the correct connections in the Third Reich and not to miss out on his moment of official glory when it would finally arrive, he cast about for relationships other than the one with the Rosenberg stooges. In search of better long-term insurance, he instinctively sought out representatives of Propaganda Minister Goebbels. First in line here was Hans Hinkel, whom Pfitzner had already approached with an eye on the Berlin municipal opera job and who would soon play an instrumental role in establishing and maintaining Goebbels's various culture subchambers. Hence, in September 1933 Pfitzner followed up on his summer action by complaining to Goebbels's lieutenant, as he had done already before, that "in the new Germany" he was still not receiving his due; why, Hinkel himself had not even found time to attend any of his operas, nor had he read Pfitzner's books, which the composer had so considerately sent to him. Pfitzner was, however, grateful that Hinkel had recommended him to various opera intendants in the Reich.[50] Moreover, after November 1933 Goebbels and his advisers took the well-considered step of appointing Pfitzner to the presidial council of the newly formed Reich Music Chamber, which provided the composer with yet another avenue of official approach, should he need it. But Pfitzner was piqued when, in February 1934, during a "composers' festival" organized by the RMK, neither he nor his works were as strongly showcased as he had been led to believe.[51] Worse, Hinkel had not made good on his promise to recommend Pfitzner to German opera houses, as stage director, conductor, or composer, as befitted a polymath, at least not effectively enough to show results.[52]

In May 1934, on the occasion of Pfitzner's sixty-fifth birthday, his reliable supporters sang his praises everywhere in Germany; he received congratulatory telegrams from Rosenberg and Goebbels, among others.[53] Then at a time at which there was renewed tension between the composer and the Munich opera directors, a bombshell exploded. Effective 1 July, Bavarian Minister of Culture Hans Schemm sent Pfitzner into retirement, and he lost his position as opera conductor, stage director, and academy professor. To add insult to injury, his pension was calculated at such a low level that it amounted to only a few hundred marks per month. Pfitzner was furious, but his protests, within Bavaria at first, that he had been wrongfully dismissed—if not legally, then certainly morally—met with little sympathy. It was duly noted that he had been remiss as opera conductor by working less than his 1929 contract had stipulated and that he had taught hardly any students at the Akademie der Tonkunst, where others had had many more, especially his venerable colleague Joseph Haas. Salaciously, Knappertsbusch mentioned the "quite understandable aversion on the part of most opera members against working with him artistically."[54]

Beginning with the summer of 1934, the regulation of Pfitzner's pension status, which eventually involved the bureaucracies of both Bavaria and the Reich, took many years and sometimes assumed ludicrous proportions, until Goebbels himself, with Hitler's tacit approval, in early 1937 settled for an amount acceptable to the composer, though in his view not enough for him to dispense with concertizing. (Pfitzner's argument assuredly was specious, for in 1936, as an example, he was earning more than RM27,000 after taxes from freelance work—more than the wages of an expert surgeon.) The tiring details of this settlement process have already been published elsewhere, yet some of them cast additional light on a composer who was increasingly finding himself persona non grata at the highest regime levels.[55] "I denounce this Germany from the bottom of my heart," cried out Hans Pfitzner, the German, at one of the low points of this debacle.[56]

An interesting aspect of the affair is that Pfitzner sought out, and was granted, an opportunity to spar with Prussian Minister-President Göring not just over the question of the pension but also the more principal issue of why his operas were neglected at Göring's Staatsoper. Pfitzner probably knew, as he had been informed about the Munich scene, that the reason was money—as always, Pfitzner's operas simply did not draw an audience. Nonetheless, wanting to make a case out of this and knowing that he was prominent enough to receive a hearing, he asked Göring in late 1934 for a meeting. Apart from the money matter, the immediate occasion was that Staatsoper conductor Clemens Krauss, the noted Strauss devotee, had just removed *Der arme Heinrich* from the program. Göring, who had been briefed about the pension problem by his fiancée, the onetime Stuttgart actress Emmy Sonnemann, an acquaintance of Pfitzner's Stuttgart friend Generalintendant Otto Kraus, ordered Pfitzner to appear in person, after the two men had exchanged insulting letters. At the meeting in Göring's sumptuous office on 5 February 1935, the minister-president charged the composer with having misrepresented his economic situation, only to be accused in turn of neglecting Pfitzner's operas. According to Pfitzner's halfway credible memorandum, Göring posed in the role of the mighty statesman: "We have saved Germany, and whether you write a couple of operas more or less is irrelevant." The composer then played on his national reputation as Pfitzner the German, when he countered: "I did not just compose music, but I also worked on behalf of Germany wherever and whenever I was able to. Please open this volume of my collected works!" Then Pfitzner took on the charge that *Der arme Heinrich* was not bringing in the cash by pointing to the fact that it had not been been offered at the Staatsoper for thirty-four years. Göring: "If I thought *Der arme Heinrich* was a good work, I would have it performed, even if it did not make a penny. But not one Pfitzner opera ever earns any money." Pfitzner: "Not even *Palestrina?*" Göring: "I liked *Das Herz.* But not *Palestrina,* no no. At the end of the first act there is a wonderful spot. But in the second act, the voices go (sings): ta ta ta, tuu tuu tuu." After further ado, Pfitzner by his own report dared Göring to dispatch him to a concentration camp, with Göring replying that had Pfitzner not come by himself, he would have fetched him by force. This tragicomical encounter did little to change Pfitzner's artistic fortune in Berlin; *Der arme Heinrich* remained in abeyance, *Palestrina* was not yet ruled out. Göring and Pfitzner reconciled each other in subsequent correspondence; the hedonistic politician probably did not envy the composer his Munich villa and car with chauffeur for a second, so that he may even have done his part in the pension settlement of early 1937. In any event, Pfitzner was flattered by all the attention, especially as henceforth he was on the social mailing list of the just married Göring couple.[57]

The documents suggest that Hitler had initially authorized Schemm's June 1934 measure, leading to Pfitzner's unexpected pension dilemma.[58] At the same time, it was he who stood behind the composer's financial rehabilitation in 1937, because the matter, in party circles at least, was simply becoming too embarrassing.[59] Indeed, the pension episode symbolizes the ambiguous relationship between the Führer and the composer like nothing else. Behind it lay the admiration by a musician for a man who to him embodied all the values of the Supreme German—what Pfitzner himself tried to express more mystically, and not unlike Richard Wagner, through art. On the other hand, the consummate politician, while flattered early by the attention of a man then nationally much better known than himself, could sense in Pfitzner the ability to analyze critically whatever passed before his eyes and through his mind, sometimes perhaps at the expense of self-damage, for Pfitzner knew no taboos. Such criticism, Hitler knew, might strike him too, once he bared his soul too much or kept the composer around. Besides, in the arts, Hitler was never the man to keep a court composer, court poet, or court sculptor, even court architect; there were always several: Josef Thorak and Arno Breker, the sculptors; Paul Ludwig Troost, Albert Speer, and Hermann Giesler, the architects; and really no composers. Hitler monopolized people, but he would never allow people to monopolize him. Pfitzner's music, too, was not necessarily pleasing to a layman like himself who adored Wagner and music much more common.[60] Ultimately, Pfitzner's early-expressed megalomaniacal obsession with a Leader spooked Hitler; because he looked a tad like the stereotype of a Jew and may have taken Weininger's side in the Schwabing argument, Hitler took it for granted that Pfitzner was at least partially Jewish. It was in 1934, when Pfitzner was rejected as conductor at the September Nazi Party rally, that he first found out that Hitler thought he was half-Jewish. In that particularly devastating year, this devastated Pfitzner even more.[61] Until the end of the war, Hitler believed in Pfitzner's sullied pedigree, even though Goebbels, who knew better, could have told him, and perhaps even did tell him, the truth.[62]

The advances and retreats in their relationship throw light on both the artist and his politician. In March 1933, Pfitzner, sure his star had risen, asked Hitler by letter to remember the Schwabing meeting and to consider saving from dismissal his onetime pupil, the Jewish conductor Felix Wolfes of Cologne. Obviously advice on racial policy was the last thing Hitler needed from this composer, and his suspicions regarding the Jewishness of Pfitzner were reinforced. A few months later Pfitzner committed his second tactical mistake by trying to meet Hitler in the Munich Brown House and talk to him about the incarceration of his Jewish friend Cossmann, but as he had done in the republic, Hitler let Pfitzner know that he was not available. At the end of the year, Pfitzner persisted in inviting the Führer personally to performances of *Palestrina* in Berlin, predictably to no avail.[63]

The cataclysmic year of 1934, besides the party rally rejection, brought pressure on Pfitzner to furnish proof of his racial purity, an imposition he found detestable and was eventually able to trace to the Führer.[64] All the same, Pfitzner lauded the Wagner disciple publicly in mid-August, writing that "today there is no one beside him with the strength of body, spirit or soul, him whom we have known as our German Führer for the past ten years."[65] Was this because he already knew that Hitler had expressed his wish to have the composer's sixty-fifth birthday celebrated by getting as many German orchestras as possible to perform his music?[66] Then again, at the end of that year, when Pfitzner did conduct Beethoven's Ninth Symphony for the Schiller Festival in Weimar, Hitler and Goebbels both attended the performance, but Hitler later prevented Pfitzner from attending his inner circle, when they, with other musicians, were drinking and chatting deep into the night at Hitler's favorite hotel Elefant, as was the Führer's custom.[67]

Hitler continued to keep Pfitzner at arm's length. In the summer of 1937, the new German National Prize, the Third Reich substitute for the Nobel Prize, was awarded to Rosenberg, with Ferdinand Sauerbruch, the surgeon; Furtwängler; and Thorak having made the short list. Pfitzner's name briefly came up but was immediately dropped.[68] Nevertheless, the self-styled genius continued to hope for a face-to-face meeting with the Führer, as between two great men. Perhaps at a private soirée in November 1937, where at Minister Wilhelm Frick's house the master was invited to play the piano?[69] In late 1938 Pfitzner continued to honor Hitler, citing, not without irony, the Führer's party rally maxim ten weeks before *Kristallnacht* that as a National Socialist he was used to "striking back immediately, after every attack."[70] In the spring of 1939 Pfitzner had reason to believe that Hitler had forestalled official celebrations on the occasion of his seventieth birthday in Munich—a city whose cultural developments, especially under Clemens Krauss, the Führer was watching like a hawk.[71] To the Jewish Wolfes in exile (that sounded convincing) he wrote that Hitler had taken such action—today it is documented nowhere, but blown out of all proportion by Pfitzner's post-1945 apologists. The fact is that even if Hitler interceded in Munich (Krauss's own hand in this is more likely), special Pfitzner festivities went on all over the Reich, for instance, in nearby Salzburg and in Frankfurt under Hans Meissner.[72] At the same time, Pfitzner acolyte Abendroth advised the master not to forget to telegraph Hitler for his birthday on 20 April, for, failing this, "who knows how such omission will be regarded."[73] In the summer Pfitzner considered traveling to Switzerland, after he had spoken derisively of "Fidi," Winifred Wagner's deceased composer husband Siegfried, who had the respect of the Führer. Pfitzner's crony Abendroth feared that Hitler might have found out about this; now he was afraid the sarcastic Pfitzner would spread unsavory, damaging stories about Hitler and his mistress, Eva Braun, in Switzerland. "A great deal can still be taken from you, and us in the bargain," warned Abendroth, "your entire life's work may be boycotted. So please listen and conduct yourself in Switzerland as if you were already in a concentration camp."[74]

Just before World War II, Pfitzner's disenchantment with Hitler seems to have reached its apex, although he never entirely gave up hope for that meeting of two great minds. In June 1939 he bitterly complained to an acquaintance—typically not heeding the postal censors—of Hitler's "general, great antipathy, which this man has against me as a composer and which hardly surprises in the case of an admirer of the *Badenweiler Marsch,* of *Arabella* and *Die lustige Witwe.* My attitude as a German also does not impress him; if I were an ex-Communist, things would be different."[75] During the war, attempts by Fritz Todt, Speer's predecessor as Reich Minister of Armaments and a great admirer of Pfitzner's music, to effect a change of mind in Hitler never came to fruition, for only days after Todt had secured Martin Bormann's cooperation in the scheme his plane crashed fatally in East Prussia on 8 February 1942.[76] Indifferently, Hitler allowed Pfitzner commemorations to take place in Germany in 1944—within limits. As if by rote, the German Master contributed his voice of support to a paean to the Führer one last time, to the man who "had taken the fate of the German people into his hands."[77] In 1944: some fate, some hands! Pfitzner would, incredibly, qualify his relationship with Hitler and the Third Reich in the postwar era.

The ambiguities of Pfitzner's association with Hitler paralleled that with Jews, and his intellectual discourse with "The Jewish Question," both of which were often contradictory and illogical. Already in the Weimar Republic Pfitzner had exasperated staunch anti-Semites with his published declaration of 1930 that although Jewry might pose "dangers to German spiritual life and German Kultur," many Jews had done a lot for Germany, and hence anti-Semitism per se and as an expression of hatred was to be condemned—such words were in keeping with his partial abstraction of this particular form of xenophobia.[78] During the Third Reich some construed this statement as a blanket defense of Jews, thus contributing to his malaise in the pension affair.[79] However, in the mold of true racists Pfitzner personalized Jew hatred after 1933 as well, as he had done inconsistently before, for instance, when he continued to call the music critic Einstein a "repulsive Jew boy." To Göring he complained, stereotypically, about "international Jewry and intellectual bolshevism of the arts."[80] In a public gathering of Rosenberg's NS-Kulturgemeinde (NSKG), the successor organization of the KfdK, he referred, derogatorily in May 1936, to the Jewish teacher of one of his critics, and he thought nothing of recommending to his daughter, a young physician, that she acquire a job after the many vacancies created by "the expulsion of the Jews."[81] What is more, Pfitzner's closest associates at the time, the music critics Walter Abendroth of Berlin and Victor Junk of Vienna, were egregious anti-Semites, who expressed their sentiments frequently, in public as in private.[82]

On the other hand, Pfitzner being Pfitzner, he reserved for himself the right to make exceptions, on artistic grounds and regarding real people in the anti-Semitic world of the National Socialists. Against the protestations of the simple-minded Bavarian Minister of Culture Schemm, a cobbler's son, he sought to perform Marschner's opera *Der Templer und die Jüdin,* because the Jewish heroine was, after all, a very attractive character.[83] Apart from trying to protect his Jewish pupil Wolfes, he also sought to help Hans Schwieger, a young conductor from Mainz with a Jewish wife, who desired a post in Münster. He could not oblige Schwieger, even though Furtwängler, too, was backing him.[84] Pfitzner, unlike fellow composers Carl Orff and Rudolf Wagner-Régeny and a host of lesser ones, refused to participate in a scheme to replace the Jewish Felix Mendelssohn-Bartholdy's incidental music for *A Midsummer Night's Dream,* because this German Master still thought Mendelssohn to be "a master of the first order."[85] Pfitzner's mockery of Nazi-dictated anti-Semitism might have come from an unreconstructed regime critic when he quipped, in 1938, that he was afraid to consult a certain ophthalmologist, the best specialist in Munich, because reputedly "his great-grandmother had once observed a quarter Jew crossing the street."[86]

In his friendship to the companions of his youth and early professional life Pfitzner became equivocal: Relations with Bruno Walter were disturbed shortly after January 1933, and those with Paul Cossmann had started to sour even before. Walter, himself kept out of Germany, where he had been a fixture of the musical scene for decades, from his safe base in Salzburg could not understand why Pfitzner had ostentatiously refused to travel there in the summer of 1933 and was not easily persuaded that extreme political pressure had been applied. In Vienna during 1936, Walter was attempting to perform *Palestrina,* not *Das Herz* as Pfitzner would have liked, but found the general atmosphere not congenial, and his friends, the Austrofascist politicians, opposed. Finally, because of connections in high quarters, he was able to conduct the opera in October 1937, without Pfitzner being present, who then blamed Walter for having kept him misinformed. Matters were not helped by the fact that the composer's new Cello Concerto in G major, opus 42 and completed in 1935, was said to feel "foreign" by Walter, whom Pfitzner had wanted to premiere it. In 1938, when Walter had to leave Austria, Pfitzner was afraid that the fate of *Palestrina* in Austria was henceforth sealed. The two men never met again.[87]

Pfitzner's friendship with Cossmann had begun to weaken in the final half of the republic. One reason had been Cossmann's sympathy with the composer's two rebellious children after the death of their mother in 1926. Another was Pfitzner's objection to what he regarded as unconscionable meddling in musical affairs on Cossmann's part, as the publicist was seen to be siding with the problematic Furtwängler.[88] In 1933, Cossmann's arrest and incarceration, first in Stadelheim prison and then in Dachau, moved Pfitzner to compassionate action in which he risked his own safety. In addition to trying to see Hitler, he personally wrote to Reich President Hindenburg and Hitler's deputy Rudolf Hess; the music-loving Bavarian Justice Minister Frank interceded with Munich Gauleiter Adolf Wagner and even with Himmler.[89] It is *possible* that in this connection Pfitzner had his much-cited interview with Gestapo chief Reinhard Heydrich, although uncharacteristically he has left no account of it (as he did in the case of his rendezvous with Hitler and Göring), so that the probability remains that Heydrich summoned him, on account of anti-Nazi utterances only.[90] In January 1934 Pfitzner admitted to a mutual acquaintance that he had tried everything possible but now knew "no further approach to pursue."[91] Cossmann was released in the spring of 1934, for reasons yet unknown; whether Pfitzner's interference had been instrumental is likely but by no means certain. Pfitzner could not prevent the journalist's renewed arrest and captivity in Theresienstadt in the summer of 1942; in the fall of that year Cossmann died, long ailing, of dysentery.[92]

Because Pfitzner never became the Third Reich's Court Composer, in the way that Furtwängler became its Court Conductor, he had to make do with the support of lesser party greats. These could range anywhere from local officials of Rosenberg's KfdK or, later, NSKG, to bureaucrats in the Reich Music Chamber, Gauleiter, and governors of newly occupied territories. To his chagrin, Göring, in whom he once had set store after what had seemed a decent compromise in 1935, Goebbels, the head of the RMK, and especially Hitler eluded him. But at the end of the day, as all the records are tallied up, Pfitzner turns out to have been the most highly nazified of the prominent composers in the sense that he actively sought the Nazis' help, authorization, and blessing, and was rewarded with the personal friendship of many, if not all, important leaders. Hence the statement that "Pfitzner regards National Socialism with approval" was, in February 1940, a credible party assessment.[93] In that situation, he never had to bother with formally joining any Nazi organization, but in addition to his RMK presidial post, he was appointed a Reichskultursenator by the propaganda ministry in 1936, an honorific title but adding some more prestige.[94]

Pfitzner's contract activities for regime agencies logically grew out of the organization that had supported him loyally at the beginning and at local levels, especially Munich. And although he tried to branch out, it would see him through to the end: the NSKG, which had merged with the "Strength-through-Joy" agency in Robert Ley's German Labor Front (DAF) by 1935. Pfitzner became active, as a musician and speaker, for Nazi students who were organizationally linked to the NSKG in the mid-1930s; this led to full-fledged Nazi-student Pfitzner programs as late as 1944.[95] Pfitzner's birthday on 5 May usually was the ideal occasion to stage extended festivities for a man who otherwise complained chronically that the official Germany was neglecting him. These birthdays also served the local Munich NSKG chapter well, as it organized "Pfitzner Weeks" from 1935 on. Not least, in 1937 the Munich NSKG reconstituted the Pfitzner Society (after the original one had been disbanded because of President Cossmann's arrest), with Furtwängler obliged to chair the Berlin branch.[96]

Typical of several such events was the Pfitzner Week staged by DAF for the Gau of South Hanover-Brunswick in late 1941, whose program content Pfitzner was allowed to influence to the point not only of conducting the lion's share, music of his own choosing (Beethoven's, Schumann's, and his own), but also of picking the soloists.[97] As in the case of Hanover, if Pfitzner could not have his way immediately, he would sulk or play the tyrant until he was successful. Naturally, he always made his self-serving gestures appear to coincide with the good of the new Germany, a formula easily subscribed to by most of the hare-brained middling party organizers.

In a few cases, however, Pfitzner met with the opposition of party men whose ego was at least as large as his own. That was the case in Saxony, where the stubborn, uncultured Gauleiter Martin Mutschmann ruled, who in his younger years had been peddling self-manufactured lingerie, dragging a paddy wagon from door to door. He also had the dubious distinction of having driven the noted conductor Fritz Busch from Dresden, against Hitler's own wishes, in early 1933.[98] In 1941 Pfitzner had good reason to believe that Mutschmann was putting up resistance to the performance of his Christmas opera *Christelflein* at the Saxon State Opera, ostensibly because of its Christian symbolism, but in reality because the composer had once briskly dismissed homemade and tasteless publications by Mutschmann himself, which dealt parochially with Saxony. Although Pfitzner liked to say so, there never was an official boycott of his music in Dresden; truth has it, though, that Dresden's resident conductor Karl Böhm was not a follower of Pfitzner (nor was his successor Karl Elmendorff), abhorring, in particular, the mawkish opera *Das Herz* and successfully avoiding the performance of *any* Pfitzner work.[99]

Tension with Mutschmann certainly contributed to the reluctance with which the Saxon town of Zwickau enlisted Pfitzner's help toward the organization of a Schumann Festival and the founding of a Robert Schumann Society planned for 1943 under the Gauleiter's aegis. Pfitzner's presence there was virtually obligatory, for Schumann was one of his heroes and he was always touting the Romantic composer's alleged nationalism, love of Richard Wagner, and suspicion of Jews. In the end, all went well: The Schumann Festival of June 1943 was placed under the motto "Pfitzner-Schumann," Pfitzner was appointed musical director and participating musician, and next to Schumann's own, his works were highlighted in Zwickau, while the new Schumann Society, with its president Hanns Johst the Nazi poet, welcomed the composer as one of the members of the board. This thoroughly politicized festival was repeated in June of the following year, with Pfitzner being assisted by the highly opportunistic soprano and Nazi Party member Elisabeth Schwarzkopf.[100]

Meanwhile, Pfitzner's relations with Goebbels's RMK remained friendly but were never especially strong. Pfitzner possessed a loyal ally there in the person of Alfred Morgenroth, who tried to solve day-to-day problems in his interest and even edited a *Festschrift*; President Peter Raabe was devoted, inviting him to prestigious meetings, where the master's music might be played; chief of the composers' section (until 1941) Paul Graener, too, was not lacking in respect. In the summer of 1942, Graener's successor, Werner Egk, helped see to it that Pfitzner, along with Strauss and Graener, received the highest money prize then awarded to a German composer, the sizable amount of RM6,000. When Pfitzner turned seventy-five in 1944, the RMK under Morgenroth in Berlin arranged yet another Pfitzner Celebration.[101]

In contrast, Pfitzner's association with Goebbels as the chief of the RMK, and with Heinz Drewes, a friend of Strauss who headed a separate music department in the propaganda ministry, was markedly cooler. Apart from Strauss, there were a number of reasons for this, the main one being that

Goebbels's sentiments were influenced by Hitler's prejudice and by his own distasteful involvement in Pfitzner's pension affair. Second, as far as Pfitzner was concerned, he could never forgive the propaganda minister for having appointed Rode as intendant of his newly constituted German Opera. Third, Pfitzner, no practicing Christian, had reason to believe that Goebbels and Drewes conspired in what he thought were occasional campaigns against the outwardly Christian content of his operas—as symbols of the churches that had to be subdued. In December 1942, at any rate, Pfitzner was full of spite against the way in which, he said, the ministry was trying to suppress him, ignore his works, and discredit them. But he was conveniently forgetting that Goebbels had featured him at the Düsseldorf Reich Music Festival in May 1938, had appointed him a culture senator, for what it was worth, and in 1941 had even accorded him the extremely generous amount of RM50,000 as a sign of special recognition. On the other hand, Goebbels never cared to receive Pfitzner in person as he did other artists, and he was suspicious of the composer's later affiliation with Gauleiter von Schirach in Vienna (as he was of Strauss's) and with General-Governor Hans Frank in Cracow, who was ineluctably falling into disrepute with the supreme leaders as the war dragged on.[102]

This war afforded Pfitzner rare opportunities to improve his national profile, if he was unconscionable enough to take advantage. And, at most times, he was. First, he was able to present himself and his music, with great fanfare for old times' sake, in newly conquered Strasbourg, the capital of Alsace where he had once worked. The occasion was the Upper Rhenish Culture Days of November 1940, to inspire "new German cultural life." According to a newspaper report, the event became a personal triumph for Hans Pfitzner; of the six works he conducted on 15 November with the help of German, not French, soloists and the Munich Philharmonic, five were his own and only one was by Beethoven.[103]

A year later, there was a similar, politically charged act in The Hague, in occupied Holland under Nazi Commissar Arthur Seyss-Inquart, which was dubbed "Pfitzner Commemoration" and paired with a "Pfitzner Festival" at the Nazi-controlled Dutch Broadcasting System.[104] After a few months this was followed by festivities in Posen and Cracow, in annexed and occupied Poland, respectively. In Posen, Maria Greiser, a concert pianist who was married to Gauleiter Arthur Greiser, performed Pfitzner's Piano Concerto in E-flat in November 1941; several months hence Pfitzner was asked to be the principal at "Posen Music Week" in September 1942.[105] The special purpose of that week was to instill German cultural values into the educational system of the newly conquered lands, to counterbalance what were considered to be inferior Polish traditions. Pfitzner the German was to be the role model, and he played it well. By way of preparation, Pfitzner was promised preferred treatment in Posen at the hands of the Gauleiter and his cultured wife; Greiser even topped Pfitzner's own demands for an honorarium. The music week itself, where Pfitzner got to work with singer Schwarzkopf for the first time, turned into an unabashed mixture of Pfitzner cult and Nazi propaganda. Pfitzner received yet another money prize and lent his name to a newly founded music scholarship. In addition, a street in Posen was named after him. At the end, the composer overflowed with thanks to the Gauleiter.[106]

Hans Frank, the lover of musical and other arts, and General-Governor of the Generalgouvernement of Occupied Poland with headquarters in Cracow, merely a short ride from Auschwitz, contacted Pfitzner in September 1941. He had heard that the composer was going to give a concert for the Germans in Cracow and thanked him for this "tremendous cultural-political favor, in the service of the fight for Germandom in the East."[107] Frank, with his particular interest in music, had taken great care to groom a symphony orchestra in Cracow, which in early 1942 was just coming under its third conductor, Paul Hindemith's younger brother and cellist of Amar Quartet fame, Rudolf Hindemith. Musicians such as Wilhelm Kempff, Elly Ney, Ludwig Hoelscher, and Tiana Lemnitz had already concertized there.[108] From early 1942 on, Frank repeatedly obliged himself not only to have Pfitzner's works performed in Cracow but also to have the master present as conductor. He offered his own limousine for transport, or a separate coach on a scheduled train. Pfitzner came, for an initial visit, in November 1942, when he conducted a predictable program of Schumann, Wagner, and his own works.[109] In June 1943, when the chimneys of nearby Auschwitz were going full blast, Pfitzner was planning to have his neglected opera *Das Herz,* dealing with love and redemption, staged in Cracow. Because this fell through, Pfitzner and the Cracow intendant Friedrichfranz Stampe were working on *Das Christelflein* for Christmas. This, too, did not materialize because in the fall 1943 the composer's Munich villa was bombed. Pfitzner himself regretted this, but all the same thanked the General-Governor for the "large Christmas bird and the sausage" he had received at his provisional quarters. He would gladly come in the spring, wrote Pfitzner, and could he, again, travel in the governmental coach?[110] Pfitzner was especially honored in absentia after a concert by the Cracow Symphony in May 1944, but he did not arrive again until July, when he stayed for several days, leading the symphony and performing song cycles.[111] Two months later Frank's star in Berlin had fallen so low that Goebbels called him "a political criminal of the first order."[112] The governor corresponded with Pfitzner until March 1945, when the end was almost there. The composer reciprocated after the catastrophe, as the politician was waiting for his date with the hangman at Nuremberg. "Take this heartfelt greeting as a token of sympathy in difficult times," telegraphed Pfitzner the German. On Wednesday, 16 October 1946, he fastidiously recorded Frank's execution in his pocket calendar. Greiser had already been hanged by the Poles.[113]

III

Pfitzner's nagging sense of disappointment with the Third Reich, springing from his never-changing misanthropic nature, disposed him to ill relations with fellow conductors, musicians, intendants, opera directors, and even members of his immediate family. His was the life of the great but neglected Palestrina, the history of a man fated to be jilted by all but a small circle of believers, chief among whom were his biographers Walter Abendroth, Erich Valentin, and Joseph Maria Müller-Blattau and the Munich Nazi Party hack Ludwig Schrott. Especially after January 1933, Pfitzner gave the impression of someone who sought out human relationships only for the purpose of impressing people with his historic greatness and, predictably failing in this, taking pleasure in condemning them. The intrinsic value of his music in all this was secondary; power for power's sake was everything. Befitting a cult leader, he was just as prepared to throw at people his dissertations on various subjects, mostly art and aesthetics, in particular his personal manual for musicians, *Werk und Wiedergabe* (1929), which he deemed infallible and mentioned at every possible opportunity.[114] With his increasingly pompous demeanor and brooding mien, he made himself disliked by most and frequently became the target of sarcasm and scorn. One intendant reacted this way: Wherever Pfitzner goes, he wants to "conduct, direct, and play all the parts; that would be his ideal."[115] At the height of the war, Hans Meissner of Frankfurt was less charitable when he observed that Pfitzner was now becoming critical to the point of "objecting to the results of his own stage direction."[116] Pfitzner himself complained toward the end of the Third Reich that it was "not easy to produce one's work almost for an entire life more or less incognito and at the same time to suffer from virtually ineradicable prejudices and misjudgments."[117]

But how much truth lay in this statement? Although the list of Pfitzner's grievances from 1933 to 1945 is a long one, that of his public achievements is even longer.[118] No other composer except for Strauss was celebrated as impressively on birthdays, as was Pfitzner in 1934, 1939, and 1944, when he turned from sixty-five to seventy-five.[119] Several Pfitzner festivals were organized, among them those in Dessau (December 1935), Salzburg (April 1940), and Brunswick (January–February 1942).[120] The maestro was constantly invited to conduct his own works, and often those of Schumann, Brahms, Beethoven, and Wagner; in the short span of 102 days, from October 1934 to January 1935, he led orchestras, all over Germany, no less than twenty-one times. This was nothing unusual for conductors, but Pfitzner was not one of the youngest. Until the end of the regime, certain evenings were dedicated solely to his compositions, and he collected numerous special honors. All his stage works were in the repertory nationwide, with Leipzig alone staging four of them from 1933 to 1941.[121]

In his dealings with the music establishment of major German centers, Pfitzner was fond of singling out Leipzig—despite its obvious patronage— Berlin, and Dresden for punishment, because, no matter what, he thought they were neglecting his oeuvre. However, as the detailed records show, the opposite was often true (not only in the case of Leipzig), although Pfitzner could turn the working relationship even with the most well-intentioned of musicians into a veritable trial. The problems with Berlin harked back to the pre-1933 Tietjen era and were then compounded by the presence in the city of Rode, Krauss, and, not least, Furtwängler. About Leipzig and Dresden the composer remarked bitingly in March 1941 that they had conspired "totally to ignore" his operatic works.[122] But it was in Munich, Frankfurt, and Vienna where Pfitzner experienced his greatest difficulties, if not his greatest defeats.

In February and March 1933 the composer conducted the Munich Philharmonic, and then again a year later, when his own *"Kätchen"-Ouvertüre* (1905) was featured. In May of that year Munich's elders presented him with the Goethe Medal for Science and Art. Less than ten months after that, Pfitzner's Staatsoper conducting contract having been canceled, the maestro performed Schumann's opera *Genoveva* at Radio Munich.[123] Still he found occasion to reproach Oskar Walleck, the new Generalintendant of the Staatsoper, in December of that year because his own opera, *Der arme Heinrich,* had only been offered once and was not scheduled for a replay. Pfitzner accused Walleck of having broken an earlier promise to honor all of his works at the opera.[124] In March 1938 the master should have been mollified by the fact that once again an entire evening was dedicated to his works, among them his Duo for Violin and Cello with Small Orchestra, opus 43 (1937), which was premiered in the Bavarian capital—all conducted by him. In May 1939, on his seventieth birthday, the Richard Wagner League of German Women under Minister-President Ludwig Siebert's chairmanship held a celebration by reading from his works, but of course the Führer's boycott for Munich was in place and no music was heard. Wrote an embittered Pfitzner to a colleague: "I am sitting there in Munich, isolated. I don't think I will need Munich and shall retreat, instead, to Salzburg."[125] The master should have been reconciled by the Munich Philharmonic's offer to perform his new work, *Kleine Symphonie,* opus 44 (1939), in November 1940, but a few months before the event he remembered that he had promised the premiere somewhere else and asked to retract it. Rather than accepting any blame, Pfitzner wrote accusingly: "I for my part fail to understand this hunt for premieres," adding gratuitously that like Mahler, he was always interested in the "best performance" rather than the first. In this case, Munich's Generalmusikdirektor Oswald Kabasta could not oblige.[126] Nonetheless, Pfitzner's Munich career ended reasonably peacefully with performances of his Piano Concerto (1922) and his new String Quartet in C minor, opus 50 (1942), by the respected Strub Quartet, in 1942, so that in 1944 Nazi Lord Mayor Karl Fiehler could still write that Munich, Pfitzner's present domicile, truly was "Pfitzner Town."[127]

If Munich was "Pfitzner Town," Frankfurt was where he had grown up since the age of two, and therefore he was entitled to special privileges. Here Paul Hindemith's father-in-law, the Jewish Ludwig Rottenberg, had conducted *Palestrina* in 1923, a performance Pfitzner disliked intensely. Early in 1933 the Frankfurt directors staged a new production of the work, also not entirely to the satisfaction of the composer who, nevertheless, accepted Frankfurt's Goethe Prize a year later.[128] Again in 1934, Radio

Frankfurt's music director Hans Rosbaud invited Pfitzner to perform some of his Lieder with the singer Gisela Derpsch, for an honorarium the master considered offensive. Obviously, stronger shows of protest were called for. Hence, when an even newer production of *Palestrina* in July was not to Pfitzner's satisfaction, he demonstratively stayed away from the opening. His official excuse was that he had not been invited to key rehearsals and his suggestions in *Werk und Wiedergabe* had been ignored.[129] Frankfurt tried again with *Das Herz,* the last and least successful of Pfitzner's operas, in November 1937. This time the composer acted as director and conductor, yet Walter Dirks's local review was only lukewarm. Pfitzner once more blamed the city's artists for what obviously had been a mediocre effort and swore up and down that he had "finally had it with Frankfurt."[130]

Suitably impressed, Meissner tried to placate the master by promising to perform *Das Herz* again, along with the remaining Pfitzner operas, starting with *Der arme Heinrich,* in October 1938.[131] This performance, conducted by Bertil Wetzelsberger after close consultation with Pfitzner, took place without incident and was positively, if not enthusiastically, reviewed by Dirks.[132] But the use of a revolving stage in a fourth refashioning of *Palestrina* six months later affected the composer so negatively that he shouted to the audience: "I am now leaving this performance with a sense of loathing."[133] Pfitzner received yet another Goethe Prize, and then followed his *Der arme Heinrich, Das Herz,* and the inevitable *Palestrina,* all in May 1939, and all more or less ignored by Frankfurt's cultural elite.[134] *Die Rose vom Liebesgarten* and *Das Christelflein* were next. This entire spectacle—all five of Pfitzner's operas—was repeated in May 1940 as well as in 1941, to less than full acclaim and on financially questionable terms, perfunctory Goethe awards for the master being always near at hand.[135] Obviously, Frankfurt took the cultivation of Pfitzner seriously, wrote Abendroth, contented for his hero.[136] Yet in 1942, only three Pfitzner operas were staged, and in 1943 none at all, because the bombs had taken their toll.[137] And so, for the record, Pfitzner the German, by temper and tantrum, had enforced his home rights.

Finally, Vienna—the Austrian metropolis, the base of one of the largest throngs of Pfitzner cultists, was problematic for the composer, for he had seriously insulted his Austrian devotees after the 1933 Salzburg Festival incident, and until the Anschluss in the spring of 1938 Walter had done little to reverse that situation. Because of the customarily good receptions there (but also because he remembered well the staging of *Die Rose vom Liebesgarten* by Mahler in 1905) Pfitzner always liked to be in Vienna.[138] After the Anschluss his friend Victor Junk, the old and formerly illegal Austrian Nazi, was briefly put in charge of musical affairs; his aim now was to schedule all of the master's operas.[139] But already in 1939 Pfitzner had reason to believe that he was being sabotaged in Vienna, possibly by the circle surrounding the new Gauleiter Josef Bürckel. This condition had not been altered by 1940, Pfitzner's works being absent from opera as well as from concert stages. Matters were complicated by the fact that Pfitzner believed he was in line for a professorship, which somehow never materialized.[140] With the regime transition from Bürckel to Schirach in August 1940 nothing much changed, although the new Gauleiter was known to have said that he was "particularly fond" of Pfitzner's music.[141]

In June 1941 Junk was able, as the Vienna reviewer for *Zeitschrift für Musik,* to call national attention to Pfitzner's treatment in the former Austrian capital, and somewhat later musicians were performing some of his Lieder and chamber works, but his operas remained unstaged.[142] In the main, Pfitzner himself stayed persona incognita in Vienna because Walter Thomas, Schirach's new plenipotentiary for musical affairs, was a follower of Strauss and, to a lesser extent, Carl Orff and other Nazi-tolerated moderns, and Pfitzner's long-standing rivalry with Strauss precluded pride of place in Vienna. Whereas Schirach, whose sister Rosalind worked for the master, seems to have had no particular views on Pfitzner the person, he did admire Strauss tremendously and showed considerable interest in the moderns as well.[143] Finally, in April 1942, *Palestrina* was mounted at the Wiener Staatsoper, conducted by Pfitzner's old antagonist, the crusty Knappertsbusch, and, unlike the Frankfurt events, this performance played to a full house of fans. Somewhat later Knappertsbusch also conducted the cantata *Von deutscher Seele,* and Friedrich Wührer even premiered the composer's new *Sechs Studien für das Pianoforte,* opus 51 (1943).[144] But although Pfitzner received Vienna's Beethoven Prize in 1943 from Schirach's own hands, he found sufficient cause to complain to Thomas that despite *Palestrina,* his treatment by the cultural establishment in the city still was unacceptable.[145] Finally, in May 1944, the Viennese celebrated the master's seventy-fifth birthday in proper form, as he received the city's golden honor ring.[146] It is interesting that virtually on the last day of 1944 the Viennese planned the performance of a "Pfitzner Cantata" for January 1945; indubitably, it never came to pass.[147] In any event, the Viennese had made their peace with Pfitzner, and he with them—after his death in Salzburg in May 1949, he was buried in Vienna.

Pfitzner, who never was the number one composer in the Third Reich and never the official one, was also not the chief conductor, as here he had Furtwängler, Krauss, von Karajan, Böhm, and others to contend with. Even as a composer-conductor, Strauss was more esteemed. In conductor series— although he was sometimes paired with Strauss—Pfitzner was more typically billed with lesser names on a program, such as Georg Schneevoigt, Leopold Reichwein, or Peter Raabe.[148] This was bad enough, but what really grated on him was that he usually had to make do with second-rate musicians, both instrumentalists and singers, on his concertizing tours, as the premier performers were too expensive. There were a few notable exceptions: the pianists Walter Gieseking and Elly Ney, the cellist Ludwig Hoelscher, and the violinists Wilhelm Stross and Max Strub. To Gieseking Pfitzner admitted that he was the only "big shot" that would ever play his Piano Concerto, and it was always a given that the vaunted coloratura soprano Erna Berger and tenor Julius Patzak were too expensive.[149] One may assume that ideology played a certain role in the attraction between Pfitzner and one or two of the famous artists, such as Ney, who was a fanatical Nazi believer, whereas Gieseking was more of an opportunist and Hoelscher had joined the Nazi Party, but probably no more. Yet it is also obvious that apart from politics, these musicians all genuinely liked Pfitzner's music and in daily dealings their chemistry with him was better than that of others.[150]

So among the singers Pfitzner was compelled to work with, whether he was accompanying them for Lieder recitals or they figured in one of his operas, names such as Gottlieb Zeithammer, the bass; Rosalind von Schirach, the soprano; Irmgard Pauly, the contralto; and Günter Baum, the baritone were merely run-of-the-mill, whereas contralto Lore Fischer had something of a reputation.[151] When at the beginning of the war Johanna Egli, another less accomplished contralto, started sulking because he was not using her as much as she would have liked, Pfitzner became extremely annoyed and gave her a dressing-down.[152] He had good reason, for Abendroth had taken him to task a few years earlier for having permitted the singer Maria Schäfer, known neither then nor now, to perform his songs in Berlin, to the piano accompaniment of Maria Greiser, whose husband was then deputy Gauleiter and senate president of Danzig. Not only had Nazi politician Greiser been beside himself, but so had all the critics, for "Frau Schäfer has a particularly 'small' voice, whose tonal substance is neither strong nor noble and resonates merely in a very limited range, namely only at the heights." To be sure, Pfitzner was not serving his reputation by choosing such interpreters for his works.[153] Musically therefore, he fared a lot better with the young soprano Schwarzkopf, whom he got to admire after her debut with him during "Posen Music Week" in September 1942. However, she disillusioned him from a human perspective when she cavalierly canceled a commitment she had made, to concertize with the master during the "Hans-Pfitzner-Tage des Meister-Eckehart-Werkes," in 1943 in Erfurt. "Schwarzkopf has sorely disappointed me," he complained to Morgenroth, for "no sooner had I learned my parts than she pulled out." And then he put his problem in a nutshell: "Only second-rate artists are dependable, for as soon as a little prima donna has some currency, she lets you down." Schwarzkopf, ambitiously moving to the top, obviously could not waste much time with someone who was clearly on his way out, despite the enchanting personal letters she sent to the composer.[154]

If Pfitzner suffered what was perhaps unavoidable friction with respectable German musicians, he experienced serious tension with two titans: Furtwängler, the conductor, and Strauss, the composer. In the case of Furtwängler, the difficulties stemmed from Pfitzner's recognition that as the first orchestra leader in the land, Furtwängler should unreservedly want to premiere any and all of Pfitzner's novel compositions, and on the composer's terms. Quite clearly, here too Pfitzner, the polymath, wished to teach the younger man some lessons in conducting, even back in the Weimar Republic. While accusing Furtwängler of being a prima donna who, nonetheless, still had not conquered his old habit of dragging the tempi, the documents show very clearly that in this case it was he, Pfitzner, who was being precious. In particular, Furtwängler must have resented constantly being compared to Pfitzner's friend Walter, but on the whole, he appreciated Pfitzner's traditional mode of composition that he himself was trying to emulate and thought *Palestrina* the master's "greatest work."[155]

Pfitzner's in essence never silent grouching and petty intrigues against Furtwängler, ruthlessly encouraged by the craven Abendroth, and the knowledge that a few respectable musicians like Ney preferred his own conducting, were interrupted shortly after Hitler's political takeover when the composer found it convenient to get Furtwängler on side in his bid for the intendantship of the Berlin municipal opera. Pfitzner well realized Furtwängler's indispensability as a go-between in communications about the matter with both Göring and Goebbels, to whom the conductor had direct access.[156] After this effort had failed, it was the pension affair in which Pfitzner needed Furtwängler's services next. Beyond that, Furtwängler tried to oblige the composer in various ways—for instance by assuming a decisive role in the refounding of the Pfitzner Society and asking Pfitzner repeatedly to conduct in Berlin. He also showed his goodwill by premiering new works such as the Cello Concerto in G major, opus 42, with the Berlin Philharmonic in Hamburg, in September 1935. But because the conductor—as he was doing in the case of Hindemith—promised much and delivered little, he was not able to speak with Goebbels or Göring as quickly and strategically as Pfitzner had wished him to, and so the composer's needling continued unabated. Then, at the founding festival of the new Pfitzner Society in Berlin on 2 February 1938, Pfitzner and Furtwängler, for all appearances in harmony, both conducted the composer's works.[157]

From then on, as it became obvious that Furtwängler, despite going through the motions, had had little or nothing to do with the final pension settlement in 1937, relations between the two musicians froze. As much as possible, Furtwängler tried to avoid musical commitments involving Pfitzner, especially as conductor of his works—even the cantata *Von deutscher Seele,* which he professed to love almost as much as *Palestrina.* At the same time, Pfitzner and Abendroth delighted in catching the conductor's every new weakness, whether it be musical or political. Furtwängler's own, wartime, pronouncements on Pfitzner reveal a man not sure of his own judgment. In 1940, he noted derogatorily that Pfitzner peddled his genius "from door to door." This was tempered one year later when he remarked somewhat muddled that Pfitzner's work, "however weak and fragile it may sometimes appear, has one thing at least: the intellect has regained its rightful place." In 1943—Pfitzner had until then all but dismissed the conductor—Furtwängler wrote charitably that "the old Pfitzner has the courage to make his music 'warts and all.' The importance of this only becomes clear if one considers that almost everyone else has lost this courage." It was one of several confessions by a man who throughout his life had tried in vain to compose music of the sort that Pfitzner was known for.[158]

Worse than Furtwängler, the presence of Richard Strauss for Hans Pfitzner was an unrelenting nightmare that haunted him throughout his entire professional life. During the careers of the two musicians, who were almost exactly five years apart in age, Strauss to the German-rooted Pfitzner remained an existential threat, while for the older, urbane Olympian Pfitzner was an occasional, albeit pernicious nuisance he could well have done without.[159]

At the core of this problematic relationship was the fact that Pfitzner and Strauss—admirers of Wagner both—were conductors *and* composers, and that it was apparent early that of the two, Strauss was the more elegant conductor and the more imaginative composer, as was reflected by acclamatory audiences and enthusiastic critics anywhere, whereas Pfitzner had to struggle for recognition every step of the way.

However, Pfitzner and Strauss were not fated to be enemies, for actually, apart from their common love of Wagner—both being signally influenced by *Tristan und Isolde*—they held quite a few things in common.[160] In the Empire, they shared its political and social values, although Pfitzner's station was not nearly the same as Strauss's. They were then both qualified anti-Semites. Their contempt for the Weimar Republic united them briefly and notoriously in an anti–Thomas Mann campaign at the dawn of the Third Reich, when the Nobel laureate, by that time a supporter of Weimar and a foe of the Nazis, launched a carefully qualified public critique of Hitler's idol Wagner. Aesthetically, as traditionalist post-Romantics essentially suspicious of the modernists, Pfitzner and Strauss were in agreement. From the bottom of their hearts they despised allegedly contrived, newfangled opera of the French or Italian style (loathing, in particular, Puccini), cheap operetta, and what they considered the modish aberration called jazz.[161]

Yet apart from their upbringing, social standing, and inherited wealth, all of which divided them significantly, there were other differences, often tied to temperament, but also deriving from the peculiar mode in which they practiced their art. One important differentiation lay in the music itself: Whereas Pfitzner's was dark, brooding, and serious in a specifically Teutonic mold, that of Strauss, who loved Mozart and Berlioz in a way Pfitzner could not understand, often was light, colorful, and cheery, playfully ironic and uplifting, as in *Till Eulenspiegel* or *Capriccio*. Very telling was both composers' treatment of Eros in their libretti and musical themes: the sensuousness of Herod's daughter in *Salome* or the teasing sexuality of the conductor's wife Christine in *Intermezzo* contrasted sharply with Pfitzner's motifs, whose ponderous German seriousness tolerated only expressions of pure if tragic love, as he demonstrated in *Die Rose vom Liebesgarten* and *Das Herz*. In their choice of musical and textual materials the two composers were also dissimilar, with Strauss contracting brilliant librettists for his works, such as Hofmannsthal, Zweig, and, not least, Clemens Krauss and himself, and Pfitzner having to make do with poor copies of those authors such as James Grun and Mahner-Mons (the one positive exception being himself as the inventive librettist for *Palestrina*). In accordance with their national and especially international rankings, Strauss always had choice singers for his opera premieres—employing the prima donna of her day, Lotte Lehmann, in no less than three debuts in the 1920s alone.[162] Pfitzner, on the other hand, had to be content with second- to third-rate artists, happening upon the already stellar Schwarzkopf late in his career only because it was early in hers.

The chronicle of the unfortunate relationship between Pfitzner and Strauss is so long as to warrant a separate study. It began in March 1900 when in a Berlin concert the first act of Pfitzner's *Die Rose vom Liebesgarten* was disadvantageously wedged between Strauss's *Tod und Verklärung* and *Ein Heldenleben*. The audience's reaction amounted to a triumph for Strauss and a humiliation for his younger peer.[163] Until 1917, while Strauss's universal success was fueled by impassioned reactions to his *Salome* (1905) and *Der Rosenkavalier* (1911), Pfitzner struggled along on the basis mostly of *Die Rose vom Liebesgarten* and *Der arme Heinrich,* until the triumph of *Palestrina* in 1917 under Walter buoyed him.[164] But 1917 also marked the year when Strauss refused to sign an anti-French declaration inspired by the hypernationalism of Pfitzner and some of his more famous contemporaries, including, at that time, Gerhart Hauptmann and Thomas Mann, a denial over which Pfitzner seethed.[165]

The beginning of the republic institutionalized Strauss's artistic success to the same degree that it provided roots for Pfitzner's world pessimism and personal bitterness. In 1919 he remarked that although his operas would probably strain, it was different with Strauss, "who constantly has several works in the repertories."[166] Pfitzner's later documented grudge against Dresden appears to have been cemented in 1927 when he felt resentment over the fact that, as he saw it, *Der arme Heinrich* had been overlooked in favor of a "Strauss Week."[167] Even before the Third Reich, the Nazi Walter Abendroth poured oil into the fires of discontent between the two composers in public pronouncements and private comments to his mentor, a malicious practice he continued well into World War II and could have gotten him a libel suit, had Strauss set his mind to it. Here, too, Abendroth played the Mephistopheles to Pfitzner's Faust.[168]

In 1933–34, tension between the two composers was exacerbated because of Pfitzner's perceived rejection by the Nazi state on the one hand and Strauss's exaltation as president of the RMK on the other. The situation was further compounded by Pfitzner's knowledge that Strauss was big enough to defy the Nazis' ban against the 1933 Salzburg Festival attendance, whereas he had been cowed into submission, and by Clemens Krauss's appointment to the Berlin Staatsoper, which augured badly for any program of Pfitzner works.[169] Although Pfitzner was made a member of the presidial council of the RMK, along with Furtwängler, Hindemith, and others, he resented serving in that agency as long as it was headed by Strauss.[170]

However, things hardly improved after Strauss's fall from power in July 1935. For in the highest echelons, Strauss's music, if not his personal pres-

ence, continued to be preferred, and in greater Munich, where both composers were at home, conductor Krauss, after 1936, saw to it that Strauss
remained dominant. Pfitzner's complaints about this unavoidable state of
affairs for him became an obsession, his favorite slur being that Strauss's
"dubious Jewish things" were being favored.[171] Those charges, of course,
were grounded in fact. Although Pfitzner was constantly being performed
throughout the Reich, Strauss beat him handily in places where it counted:
5 Pfitzner concert performances by the Berlin Philharmonic in the 1938–39
season versus 30 by Strauss; 61 Pfitzner opera stagings in Munich from
January 1933 to October 1943 as opposed to 317 by the master from
Garmisch.[172] Toward the end of the Third Reich, although Strauss himself
had personally fared very badly in his relationship with the highest leaders,
Pfitzner's self-esteem vis-à-vis Strauss was so low that he compared himself
to "scum," the way Beethoven had been scum opposite Rossini, Schumann
opposite Mendelssohn, and Wagner opposite Meyerbeer—all truly German
victims of foreigner or Jews by Pfitzner's standards.[173] These twisted musings came from a man who had had the bad fortune, apart from composing
less convincingly than Strauss, to be born in the same season, only one
month apart, as his nemesis, with that fatal five-year difference calling for
Strauss festivals at the same time there should have been Pfitzner celebrations, and that inasmuch as there were, these were doomed to be the lesser
causes célèbres.[174]

Apart from professional matters, Pfitzner's personal life also consisted of a
string of misfortunes. It almost seems as if, in his Schopenhauerian mood, he
had willed that this be so from the beginning of adulthood—a self-fulfilling
prophecy that certainly came to fit his own conception of Palestrina, the eternally anguished, infallible master.

As a child, Hans had had disagreements with his musician father who
had granted piano lessons to his older and less gifted brother, Heinrich,
with the siblings remaining estranged forever after. His relationship with
Maria (Mimi) Kwast, the daughter of his Frankfurt teacher, was complex
from the beginning. Before he married her in Canterbury in 1899 after an
abduction from Germany that had the police chasing after them, she had
been deeply in love with the Australian composer Percy Grainger. Pfitzner, a
favorite of the racy Alma Mahler in Vienna in 1905, had an affair with Ilse
von Stach, the librettist of his Christmas play *Das Christelflein,* later in
Berlin, causing Mimi to move in with a Düsseldorf actor. By 1912, the almost broken marriage was mended with Cossmann's help; Mimi died in
1926 of cancer, ostensively mourned by her husband, who would not find
his second wife, the divorcee Amalie (Mali) Stoll, until 1939.[175]

One might assume that Pfitzner would have found consolation with his
children, but the opposite was the case. His first son, Paul, born in 1903,
contracted meningitis by 1919 and by 1921 was in a private sanatorium;
terminally ill, he died in hospital in 1936. His fourth child, Johannes, died
at birth in 1911.[176] But it was with Peter (b. 1906) and Agnes (b. 1908)
that he was to experience his greatest hardships. Both of them wanted to

become musicians, very much against the wishes of their father, who allegedly did not think them gifted enough for an artist's avocation but might just as well have been jealous. Had the composer's wife Mimi still been alive, she might have been able to mediate; instead, the headstrong children turned against their self-righteous father, who preferred intermittent concert-touring to nurturing a family at home. Agnes settled for a course of medical studies, financed by her father, and eventually became a physician. But increasingly alienated from the composer, she committed suicide shortly after his seventieth birthday in May 1939.[177]

Peter Pfitzner's case was even sadder, for with his father's encouragement he might well have become an excellent musician. Because of the composer's obstinacy, the son used funds paid to him by his father, ostensibly to study law, but in reality to take training with the Munich composer Hans Sachsse, and as an opera director in Stuttgart and Bayreuth. In the fall of 1937, the young Pfitzner had six of his songs premiered during a Munich "Music Week" featuring "young German composers"; whether his father was in attendance is doubtful, for the two at this time were embroiled in a lawsuit over money. It did not help that Peter Pfitzner had close friends like the modern (by Nazi standards) composer Werner Egk, whom the old man loathed, but by 1940 at least Peter had obtained a position as intendant. During the war he was hoping that Egk, now influential and a confidant of Tietjen, would help him win a prestigious post; the paternal colleague Furtwängler, too, was to do his share. But none of this transpired, for the young artist fell on the Eastern front in February 1944, with his wife, Dr. Ingeborg Pfitzner, totally ignored by her father-in-law.[178] Throughout the bitter relationships with these two children, the affluent Pfitzner kept wailing how much money they were costing him; already in 1937 he had integrated his offspring into the entire hostile cosmos. As he complained to the devoted Abendroth: "I must say, I will soon have enough. This, then, the harvest of my life. My daughter betrays me, my son defrauds and curses me and drags me into court, and what is known as 'the world' treats me exactly in the manner you have described to me."[179]

Poor Pfitzner. As if none of this had been his fault! Indeed, he, who had his charming and witty side, took care not to appear as an avaricious grouch to everybody, even late in his life, especially when younger women were involved. Pfitzner, about whom contemporaries have observed that he absolutely radiated in the presence of attractive ladies,[180] shortly before Hitler's rule afforded himself the luxury of an amorous relationship with a student who could have been his granddaughter. The fact that it, too, turned into a near disaster was as much the fault of this love-starved widower as his calculating young friend.

Pfitzner met Elisabeth (Lilo) Martin as her teacher in his composition class at the Munich Akademie der Tonkunst. At the beginning of January 1933, at the latest, he was on intimate terms with her, as a stack of love letters from his own hand proves; she seems to have written him next to nothing. Even by those days' standards he was thus clearly violating his professional code of ethics. Whether sexual favors were exchanged is not known (Pfitzner was then almost sixty-four); what is certain is that Martin used her professor's weakness self-servingly, while she remained as one of only two students in his master class.[181] Because she was in her early twenties, she probably had a regular boyfriend, possibly a fellow student, trying to keep her suitor at bay as much as possible, without hurting his feelings or her own professional prospects. Sensing this, Pfitzner frequently expressed his doubts and desperation, but he also tried to cajole her, weighing in with his formidable authority. "My beloved Lilo . . . are you there? And there for me?," he trembled in January 1933, later to declare that "you alone can assure my existence or cause me to fall."[182] Disillusioned, he threatened her with total banishment in April, knowing well that she was still dependent on his instruction. The original poem he mailed to her on that occasion is a testimonial of his abject fright as much as his potential evil; it bears the hallmarks of unrequited love.[183]

Whatever had happened, probably an act of infidelity on her part, the two had made up by the spring of 1934. At that time, Martin was accomplished enough to be especially featured as Pfitzner's master pupil in public Munich recitals; the composer also used his influence with the broadcast system to get it to play her—as yet unfinished—sonata on the air waves.[184] By the summer he was twisting the arm of Leipzig Gewandhaus conductor Hermann Abendroth, Walter's successor, to exert pressure on Breitkopf and Härtel to have her "opus 1" published—successfully, it seems.[185] The second step, in the fall, was to get his friend Gieseking to perform this opus, for Pfitzner thought her to have "tremendous talent as a composer," adding quickly that the Leipzig firm was about to publish the work. The pianist replied, ever so smoothly, that these days it was simply too cumbersome "to learn new pieces," unless, of course, they were by Pfitzner.[186] Martin evidently understood the scenario, for from now on her responses to the master grew colder.[187] By this time, too, Pfitzner had lost his position at the Munich academy (whether the inappropriate relationship had actually contributed to this has so far not been ascertained); his influence on Martin was reduced, not least, because he began new rounds of concert touring. "Will you write me a few lines?," he inquired of her in early 1935, supplying a hotel address in Berlin, and, collegially, "what are you working on now?"[188] But the budding composer had no more use for old Hans, for she was soon to be married to one Horand Röhmer.[189]

Hans Pfitzner, the man who thrived on feeling sorry for himself, was haunted in old age by sickness, isolation, and the ravages of war. Because of his constantly deteriorating eyesight, which only temporarily improved after an operation, he could not, like Strauss, continue composing, but, driven also by his obsession with money, chose instead to go on his often lonely concert tours, conducting his favorites mostly from memory. In August 1943 he was laid up in a Giessen orthopedic clinic for inflammation of the joints. The traveling (occasioning traffic accidents such as the one in Berlin 1936), bad hotel food, and sheer physical exhaustion connected with music making all contributed to wearing the already frail man down further.[190]

In addition, enemy bombardments disturbed him after 1939. At first he was nonchalant. Once in Cologne, he was in his hotel room when the concierge urged him to seek protection in the basement. Stoically, Pfitzner the German refused, and was lucky.[191] But at the end of August 1942, in a train near Nuremberg with his wife Mali, enemy fire destroyed almost all of the carriages, while the couple emerged, unhurt, from its sleeper car.[192] By the summer of 1943, when Munich was increasingly attacked by enemy planes, Hans and Mali Pfitzner sought evacuation from their expensive villa, perhaps to a small town in Saxony, deemed safer. But when this did not materialize, his house was, predictably, destroyed in a massive air raid just a few weeks later. The Pfitzners were fortunate to have escaped after seeking shelter in their cellar. They had lost almost everything save some books, correspondence, music, and, ironically, Pfitzner's cherished caches of wine and cognac stored in the cellar. What should he celebrate with them now?[193]

What followed was a series of humiliating makeshift stayovers and relocations, but it is significant that once again, intermediate regime echelons were trying their best to salvage what was left of their cultural icon. These efforts involved the RMK in Berlin, the Gauleiter of Munich and Silesia, and, of course, Ludwig Schrott, the ever loyal local party official who also served in the Pfitzner Society, still extant.[194] When Munich and its hinterland could not come up with anything suitable for the master, he found asylum in a primitive apartment in Rodaun, a suburb of Vienna, where he moved in April 1944. A few weeks before Germany's capitulation Pfitzner and his wife, in flight from the advancing Red Army, were reevacuated to a shabby refugee camp back in the old Reich. It happened to be in Garmisch, only a stone's throw from Richard Strauss's famous villa on Zoeppritzstrasse. By that time, contact between the two composers had long ceased.[195]

IV

After 1945, many members of the German music establishment were surprised to learn that Hans Pfitzner was scheduled to appear before a court of law to be denazified.[196] The reason for this procedure, which affected other musicians such as Furtwängler, Egk, Ney, and Strauss as well, and which in his case officially began in Munich in October 1947, was his nominal appointment, by Joseph Goebbels in 1936, to the post of Reichskultursenator, a position of such scant influence that the otherwise politic Pfitzner never used it.[197] Hence the very rationale on which the proceedings against him were based was wrong; as has been shown earlier, the extent to which he had actually been a follower of Hitler and the Third Reich was complex and extremely difficult to define, and it certainly eluded the judicial categories of the postwar era.

As in the case of most of Pfitzner's colleagues, the trial proved farcical beyond belief, manifested, from the beginning, by the fact that the jurists could not even get the date of his political appointment right.[198] At the end of March 1948, the hearings were suspended and Pfitzner was removed from the black list of the American OMGUS occupation authorities, which theoretically meant that the path was cleared for his return to public life in the American zone. Although this was as it should have been as early as the spring of 1945, the formal reasons for his technical acquittal adduced during court proceedings were the wrong ones, for his case was speciously argued throughout.[199]

The main argument of the defense, which then turned into the official tenor of the court, was, as Pfitzner's attorney Eugen Lehr instructed Hans Rosbaud, that the composer had been opposed to the Third Reich as a matter of principle and had never benefited from its existence. Rosbaud duly repeated this in writing for the court, singling out Pfitzner's "unequivocal opposition to National Socialist thoughts and methods" and the "slights he suffered especially at the hands of the National Socialists."[200] Witnesses for the defense, not all of whom were present in person, such as Wetzelsberger and Meissner portrayed Pfitzner as an antiauthoritarian, freedom-loving artist, a political naïf who had not realized the criminal nature of the Nazi regime until after January 1933, when it was too late, and hence became one of its first and most prominent victims. It was purposely ignored, as must have been known by many, that Pfitzner had got himself into a peculiar type of opposition to the regime because it would not play his tune.[201] And as for the political naivity, several contemporaries had been aware that Pfitzner knew the terror machine of the regime well enough to urge its application against his own enemies when it suited him, the sufferings of his friend Cossmann and others notwithstanding.[202] Undoubtedly also, certain of Pfitzner's colleagues were informed that at least on one occasion, he had called himself a National Socialist in the Führer's mold, in a written indictment against Rode that he had widely circulated.[203]

Tied to this premise was the legend, perpetrated at length by his defenders, that his entire oeuvre or at least parts of it had been suppressed by various Reich agencies, especially Gauleiter Mutschmann in Saxony, who had instigated a "blanket prohibition." With reference to Pfitzner's operas *Das Christelflein* and *Palestrina,* much was made of the alleged fact that it was because of the Christian element in these works and, by dint of authorship, Pfitzner's own catechism of beliefs as a Christian that he had been persecuted.[204] Although this line of defense made Pfitzner look almost like a victim of the infamous Church Struggle, it totally ignored the fact that any opposition to the two operas mentioned on *Christian* weltanschauung grounds, insofar as it had occurred, had been misplaced, because Pfitzner's Palestrina bore Germanic characteristics, and *Christelflein* had been written as a, commercially viable, concession to convention—as, indeed, it was to have replaced Engelbert Humperdinck's celebrated play *Hänsel und Gretel* (1893). Besides, everyone who really knew Pfitzner was fully conversant with his status as a practicing non-Christian.

It fitted this construed pattern of victimization that, as many of his colleagues knew, Pfitzner had had an altercation with Göring, which now was said to have occurred over the principle of artistic and personal freedom, whereas it really had had to do with Pfitzner's complaint over pension money and his perceived neglect at Göring's Staatsoper. Much was made of the fact that Göring had threatened the composer with the concentration camp; hence what "personal courage" the composer must have possessed. That this version has so far only been verified as a recollection by Pfitzner himself (he had certainly made sure to spread this around) was no issue in 1947. In connection with the Göring episode, the old canard of Pfitzner's "forced retirement" in Munich in the summer of 1934, of which he himself had informed the Americans immediately in 1946, was revived as well; one witness even had it that Pfitzner had been dismissed from Munich *and* Berlin, there by Reich Education Minister Bernhard Rust.[205]

Pfitzner's relationship to Jews also was turned into a charade in that Munich courtroom, when almost everyone there attested to his philosemitism, parading, without qualification, the examples mostly of Walter and the anti-Semitic Cossmann. One version read that his first wife Mimi had been half Jewish, a variation of this a full Jew by Nazi standards; how, then, could such a man have been an enemy of the Jews? As if all his anti-Jewish diatribes during the Weimar Republic had never been published. There were some gaffes and indiscretions: the non-Jewish (and quite anti-Semitic) Alma Mahler-Werfel was counted among Pfitzner's close Jewish friends, as was Mahler himself, who had never especially got along with the young composer, staging his *Die Rose vom Liebesgarten* in 1905 only at his wife's insistence. Pfitzner's meeting with Hitler in 1923 had failed, claimed the attorney Leer, because the composer had "sharply" defended the Jews. Schoenberg's genuine impulse to help out his colleague in distress by professing that he had always known Pfitzner as a German nationalist in the tradition of Wagner, "hence slightly tainted by anti-Semitism," but otherwise as someone who would never have made concessions to the regime, rang hollow from a confessing Jew who, in the 1930s, had devised grand schemes of revenge against all would-be destroyers of Jewry. Possibly, Schoenberg's action was now motivated, as Hans Heinz Stuckenschmidt has reported, by his empathy with Pfitzner's theory of intuition in musical invention.[206]

Other half-baked stories, inconsistencies, and lies rounded out this spectacle of a formal rehabilitation for a man who would not have suffered any kind of reconstruction, anywhere, anytime. It was said, for instance, that Pfitzner had received no official assistance after having been bombed out in 1943, whereas in fact authorities at various levels had strained to provide him with a new home.[207] Pfitzner's compromising relations with Greiser and Frank were played down in trying to whitewash the composer.[208] Some of the witnesses actually were duplicitous, redundant, or otherwise out of order, as was Mahler-Werfel, who inveighed against Pfitzner's detractors with a wholly implausible statement.[209] Werner Egk was more forthright when he admitted that he had really nothing to say about Pfitzner in all those years—possibly his friendship with the fallen son, Peter, motivated such inaction.[210] Pfitzner's problematic alter ego Furtwängler perfunctorily entered a positive plea for this, in his words, representative of Beethoven's Germany, at the same time that he privately condemned Pfitzner's "particular style of wanting forcibly to impose an intellectual picture on the external world! There is something 'National Socialist' in the very tendency."[211] The gruffy Knappertsbusch, once even more bellicose than Furtwängler and a convinced Nazi at heart, feigned indignation, when he barked that "we were, everyone in his own fashion, resistance fighters, who through some miracle never got caught."[212]

Certainly in full awareness of this trial, but actually too ill to appear at it in person, Pfitzner tried to justify his thoughts and actions to himself and to the outside world.[213] With his superior intelligence, he knew he had done something wrong in other people's eyes and probably suffered from a bad conscience himself, if only he could sort things out for his own peace of mind and explain himself to the world. So he sat down to reflect on the reasons for the existence of Adolf Hitler and the Third Reich, his thoughts being triggered by the perhaps still puzzling personal experience with the Führer in 1923 but also by his own reminiscences about what he had considered to be the afflictions of the Weimar Republic. He now decided that although Hitler as a "proletarian" type personally was unacceptable, and, though not a born criminal, was evil through the terror he had wrought, an evil that could not be associated with the German people as a whole, his mission after 1918 had been a just one, because the Allies had humiliated Germany in World War I. World War II had been a *bellum iustum* and Hitler's waging of it a rectifying act, if only because he had exposed the hypocrisy of Germany's enemies, most of all the uncultured United States, although in other respects Hitler may have remained vile (not least, by implication, for not having supported him, the elite composer).

Regarding Hitler and the Jews, Pfitzner arrived at a surprisingly frightening corollary, as he averred that "World Jewry" was a problem, indeed a "racial problem," but also an "ideological problem." Genocide was nothing new; the Americans had practiced it before on their native Indians and never were punished for it: Hence Hitler had had himself covered by international precedent. *How* he extinguished the Jews may have been a different matter, and any excesses certainly were subject to condemnation, but only insofar as they were truly verified, and not just hearsay (in the manner of the Allies having wrongfully accused the Germans of heinous cruelty in Belgium during World War I). After all, atrocities such as those that may have transpired in concentration camps were known to occur during every major revolution, at the hands of individual brutes who had always existed everywhere, if least of all among Germans. In sum: Why did Hitler engage Germany in World War II? "With respect to this question I still believe in Hitler's honesty and goodwill. He wanted to rejuvenate and liberate his fatherland and, beyond that, render a great service to *Europe* by driving out the Jews—if necessary, eliminate them by radical means. For in *World*

Jewry he realized the singular danger for the fortunes of all peoples, and the one reason for all the malignancy in the world, in fact for just about everything."[214]

What one finds here is not only a rationalization of doubts Pfitzner may have harbored about the Third Reich, Hitler, and his own relationship to him but a scarcely altered restatement of his chauvinistic and misanthropic utterances once signally published in his three-volume invective of the 1920s.[215] However, in one particular respect these postwar musings strike the reader as much more disturbing. For they show that Pfitzner, like his erstwhile idol Hitler, had taken initial reasonings about the unworthiness of Jews to their most extreme conclusion, physical extinction, thus paralleling Hitler's physical implementation of the Holocaust with his own, mental, complement of *post festum* moral approval.

Pfitzner's recalcitrance was fostered by his unshaken conviction that he continued to be, singularly, Germany's, if not the world's, most important composer, whom the uncultured Americans had no right to place on their black list to prevent performances of his music in 1946.[216] Not the least of his problems was that he now had to defend himself to former friends, among them some who had long been adversaries, who saw in him the collaborator of an evil empire. His admirer of decades ago, Thomas Mann, had publicly made known his views about the responsibility of the entire German people for the Nazi crimes. Pfitzner was enraged; there ensued a brief exchange between him and their mutual friend, Walter, in which the conductor accused Pfitzner of minimizing the Nazis' infamy and guilt and the composer repeated his thoughts about Germany's historic rights and greatness, in particular repudiating Mann. For the time being, both Pfitzner and Walter had to agree that they were in opposite, irreconcilable camps, and there was no further correspondence; after being solicited by Leer, Walter wrote merely a general character reference for Pfitzner, too noncommittal to be effectively used at trial. Pfitzner, on the other hand, could not forgive Walter for having shown his own key letter to him of 5 October 1946 to Mann, who had made it into the cornerstone for an article he published, in honor of Hermann Hesse's seventieth birthday, in *Neue Zeitung* on 30 June 1947. In this article Pfitzner was dismissed as just a senile crank who throughout his lifetime had spoken "much militant nonsense." The incensed composer typed yet another reply filled with the same old, tired arguments—an open letter which at the time remained unpublished. It signified Pfitzner's spiritual bankruptcy, not that of Mann or Walter.[217]

There were only few, infrequent public performances of Pfitzner's works after 1945.[218] His *Werkverzeichnis* was not even complete, for his publishers had left out of it *Krakauer Begrüssung*, that special piece Pfitzner had composed for Hans Frank in 1944.[219] Of his old followers and students, three stood out in some effort to assist him. Klemperer, on his way to Budapest, visited Pfitzner in the old people's home at Ramersdorf near Munich, where he was then staying. Klemperer later apologized for not being able to help him convincingly at his trial (because he had not seen Pfitzner for years) but thought he might conduct his Symphony in C major, opus 46.[220] Gerhard Frommel of Frankfurt kept in touch with Pfitzner for a while, expressing interest in Pfitzner's newest compositions.[221] Rosbaud tried to do more than anyone. During 1946–47, he visited Pfitzner off and on, encouraging him to compose a symphonic work for choir, for the Goethe Year of 1949—a mandate Pfitzner had received from his old friend, conductor Hermann Abendroth, now in Russian-occupied Weimar. Rosbaud prevailed upon the city of Munich to do everything possible to keep Pfitzner there, lest he be lost to the Soviet zone (apparently, Vienna was also interested). Pfitzner's new composition should be commissioned for a Goethe Festival in Munich, and the composer should be treated accordingly. What he and his wife especially needed was a decent flat of their own.[222] The inertia of city authorities at the time paralleled their failure to keep Rosbaud as their Philharmonic's Generalmusikdirektor.[223]

After a life filled with stress, much of it brought on by his restless energy, Hans Pfitzner was, at the end of his career, sick, old, and a broken man. After several hospital stays in Garmisch, for his eyes and for a fractured arm, he had been moved to the Ramersdorf nursing home some time in 1946. "Another final resting place the world was not able to offer me, something I would truly hold against my fatherland, if I still possessed one," lamented Pfitzner, the German, in October 1947. By early 1948 he was suffering from speech paralysis, the result of an arteriosclerotic disorder. He sustained his first stroke in October, then, after a successful evacuation to Salzburg in January 1949, a second one in March. Again he was in and out of hospital. On 22 May he died, just having turned eighty. Among his last possessions were 2,000 books and volumes of music, several bookshelves and tableware, some old carpets, folders filled with massive correspondence, a bust of Arthur Schopenhauer, and one of Hans Erich Pfitzner.[224]

7

Arnold Schoenberg

Musician of Contrasts

I

Of several inconsistencies in the extant biographies of Arnold Schoenberg, one stands out. Many years ago Hans Heinz Stuckenschmidt wrote that Schoenberg "had learned early to do without success," because he came to be satisfied with the kind of praise that "all creative work finds in itself."[1] This view is contrasted with a later one that in 1912 Schoenberg refused to return to Vienna from Berlin because "he could not overcome his resentment for the rejection of his music before he had left Vienna."[2] Indeed, divergent interpretations of Schoenberg's personal life and career appear to symbolize contradictions between biographical facts that defy manipulation and transcend assessment.

The ambiguities regarding Schoenberg's nationality are a case in point. Was he an Austrian, a German, an American, or a Jew? Whereas the *New Grove Dictionary of Music and Musicians* has called him an "Austro-Hungarian," this is merely a technical designation and only partially correct. In fact, it is unclear during various phases of his life how Schoenberg himself would have defined his nationality, although especially as far as music was concerned, he always saw himself as part of the German-Austrian cultural tradition.[3] He was born in Vienna, on 13 September 1874, in the fin-de-siècle Habsburg Empire, the son of a Jewish father hailing from Hungarian Szécsény and a Jewish mother born in Bohemian Prague. The parents had come to Vienna from Pressburg (Bratislava), the capital of Slovakia, which until World War I was under the suzerainty of the Hungarian Crown. Hence, Schoenberg initially possessed Hungarian citizenship. However, when the Habsburg Empire was subdivided after the Treaty of Saint Germain (1919), he was not recognized as a citizen of the new Austrian Republic but of the Czechoslovak Republic (CSR), of which Bratislava was now the southernmost hub. Hence, as his mother would have been had she remained in Prague, he became a Czech. There is an irony in this, for the mechanics of this succession remind us of the passage of religiocultural identity from mother to child in Jewish practice, which would occupy Schoenberg so much during the last decades of his life. Having failed to obtain Austrian or German citizenship during his Vienna and Berlin years, Schoenberg immigrated to the United States as a Czech and was actually stateless when he became a U.S. citizen in April 1941, after the CSR had ceased to exist in March 1939. Yet although Schoenberg was Hungarian, Czech, and American, successively, hardly any musician has become as closely identified with the modernism of Weimar Germany as he was. To compound this complexity, his music also became known as that of the leader of the Second Viennese School, with the gravity of that circle in Vienna through Schoenberg's earlier years, and the permanent position there of his two most famous students, Alban Berg and Anton Webern.[4]

Since 1925 a professor of composition at the Preussische Akademie der Künste in Berlin, Schoenberg became restless during the final years of the Weimar Republic. His existence there seems to have been marked by inconsistencies resulting from the irreconcilability of extremes: On the one hand he was an artist already widely recognized as the father of modern music; on the other a man being haunted by the consequences of ideological, economic, and political instability. He was enjoying his musical triumphs, as in the companionship with Spanish cellist Pablo Casals and progressive Radio Frankfurt conductor Hans Rosbaud, who provided him with the opportunity to broadcast his views on music and actually performed his works to his greatest satisfaction. Casals, whose native Spain Schoenberg cherished as clement vacation territory, was prepared to support and premiere the composer's newest work around the time of the origins of the Third Reich, his Cello Concerto after Georg Matthias Monn.[5]

This was in sharp contrast to the strong reactionary currents in cultural life already during the last years of the Weimar Republic, which, in the words of Stuckenschmidt, "preceded the anti-modernistic retrograde aesthetic of the National Socialist mass taste."[6] Stuckenschmidt's adjoining observation that Schoenberg would have become the immediate target of Nazi persecution in the event of Hitler's takeover, then always imminent, even if he had not been Jewish, is certainly correct.[7] Already in September 1930, immediately after the stupendous Reichstag victory of the NSDAP, Schoenberg's friend and colleague Franz Schreker had warned him of "Hitler-Berlin" and a possible dismissal from the academy.[8] At the end of 1931, because of Chancellor Heinrich Brüning's restrictive decrees affecting civil servant salaries, Schoenberg was complaining about excessive income taxes.[9] Only half in jest did he write from Barcelona to Joseph Asch, an influential New York Jew, whether it was not possible that some rich American Jews finance his, Schoenberg's, modestly comfortable life in Spain, lest he had to return "to the swastika men and pogromists in Berlin."[10]

After Hitler's entrenchment, Schoenberg's dismissal from the academy predictably occurred at the hands of its president, composer Max von Schillings, in several legalistic steps, starting in early March 1933 and being completed only in September. Schoenberg was present at the 1 March council meeting when Schillings announced that "the Jewish influence at the Academy must be eliminated."[11] Schoenberg, his second wife, Gertrud, and their baby daughter, Nuria, were in Paris on 17 May, ostensibly by way of a vacation which at that time still seemed extendable to the Riviera or to Spain, the country of Casals.[12] But not least because he had been forewarned by his Berlin colleague Otto Klemperer, it soon became clear to Schoenberg that Paris represented exile rather than the usual holiday excursion.[13]

Schoenberg was plagued in Paris, and later in Arcachon in the Gironde, by economic woes and uncertainty over his future. He was expecting monies the Germans still owed him from Berlin, and to that end he enlisted the help of Wilhelm Furtwängler, who, he knew, had influence with the Nazi authorities. This relationship with the famous conductor highlighted another oddity in the composer's life at that time. Although Furtwängler admittedly was no friend of avant-garde music, he had premiered Schoenberg's serial *Variationen für Orchester,* opus 31 (1926/1928), in Berlin in December 1928, in an effort to portray himself as a master even of the most modern genre. This effort had turned into a disaster, with Schoenberg remarking to Furtwängler later that he, too, would have to accept his share of the blame. To the added chagrin of the composer, thereafter Furtwängler had never tried to perform the piece again.[14] The relationship between the two men had remained frosty, with Furtwängler as skeptical as ever of the music of the Second Viennese School.[15] Notwithstanding all that, in early summer of 1933 Schoenberg seized the initiative when, by telegram, he asked the venal conductor for help.[16] If this move may have been mercenary, Furtwängler's intervention with Prussian Culture Minister Bernhard Rust turned out to be ambivalent at best, when he gratuitously characterized the composer as the leading exponent of music in "international left-wing press circles" as well as the "Jewish International" and emphasized that one should not turn him into a martyr.[17] These barbs and the otherwise condescending tone of Furtwängler's missives, which were unknown to Schoenberg, were symptomatic of a strained relationship between conductor and composer, and Schoenberg's own, insistent, letters to the conductor did not help.[18] The affair ended with Furtwängler having effected no changes yet fancying himself in Schoenberg's good graces nonetheless.[19] Until after World War II, neither had anything good to say about the other; they had been strange bedfellows from the very beginning.[20]

From France, Schoenberg's anticipated move to Spain, if only temporarily but with Casals's help, did not materialize.[21] In Schoenberg's opinion, an unconscionably low contract offer from Oxford University Press, in return for much-needed cash, wrecked a possibility of publishing his more recent compositions with the British firm.[22] Schoenberg, who had a small family, was intermittently sick, had little to live on, nothing of substance to do (not even some guest conducting), and other family members, who had been left behind, to console.[23] At this rather desperate point the private if inconspicuous Malkin Conservatory in Boston offered Schoenberg the opportunity to teach some courses, hence providing him with the opportunity to emigrate to the United States.[24]

Although he was now safer politically, Schoenberg's personal and financial fortunes did not immediately improve after his arrival in America in November 1933. Teaching the few and unexceptional students at the Malkin Conservatory turned out to be arduous, the more so because he also had to teach some students in New York. Schoenberg could not stand the icy winters and the humid summers of the East Coast, and again he had to contend with various ailments. Additional work in cities such as New York and Baltimore in the spring of 1934 got him more money but was more onerous—what with having to give public lectures about his method of composition in English, a language he still did not speak well, let alone write it. Although Princeton was host to him and New York's Juilliard School of Music offered him a position after his unattractive Boston contract expired in March 1934, Schoenberg decided not to linger on the East Coast and to try, instead, the sunnier shores of California, where he could nurse a chronic heart condition complicated by asthma and engage more easily in his beloved game of tennis.[25] He would, in fact, altogether have preferred to return to Europe, perhaps England for guest-conducting contracts, or Italy, which appealed to him not just for its temperate climate.[26] "This produce here: everything is spoiled; everything stinks; not just the produce. It almost seems that something springs to life here only when it stinks," he wrote, profoundly disillusioned, to Webern in the spring.[27] These were his private sentiments. But in public, he was full of praise, especially about music and musicians in the United States: yet another inconsistency in this composer's biography.[28]

Schoenberg was drawn to Hollywood by the expectation that his name as that of a composer of note would attract many American film-score writers, whom he would teach for generous fees. The fact that only some of them came to take "a few lessons in discords" he tended to blame on the economic circumstances, the vagaries of the film industry, and, mostly, on the failure of Americans to recognize his own historic importance.[29] The gap between anticipation and reality which this particular experience represented became symptomatic for the range of various career encounters in Schoenberg's American phase, perceived mostly negatively, from the subjective perspective of the composer, even if, at the other end of the spectrum, the historian today can also detect happy and positive developments.[30]

But in Schoenberg's fatalistic interpretation of this sequence, one misfortune ineluctably led to another. To be sure, he rejoiced at the Californian environment, his modest but comfortable new Brentwood house,[31] valuable new personal relationships, painting, and frequent games of tennis, as well as his soon growing new family. But also, he was often quite sick, with old and new diseases badgering him. "I had a few things, for instance, diabetes, severe stomach pains, heart disorders," he informed his daughter Trudi sardonically in June 1945, "breathing difficulties, dizzy spells, swollen legs and feet, rashes on my legs—nothing else, I think."[32]

Schoenberg's continual feeling of neglect was to a large extent fueled by his economic situation, which, from May 1933 on, remained tenuous at best. In the summer of 1935 he was appointed to the University of Southern California (USC) in Los Angeles to teach composition for a year, at a salary of $3,000, far from the $12,000 he had imagined in Paris. The workload turned out to be relatively heavy, up to four classes per week, plus extra lectures for which he received little more money. Schoenberg was unhappy at USC from the start, because of the teaching chores, the failure of the university to publicize his courses properly, and the relatively cumbersome commuting from Brentwood to south central Los Angeles. For the coming academic year, Schoenberg was to be reappointed but at no increase in salary. Declining the offer, Schoenberg chose a new position instead, professor of music at the larger and more prestigious University of California at Los Angeles (UCLA), on a campus much closer to his home. From July 1936 to June 1937 his new salary was fixed at $4,800 a year.[33]

By 1938 Schoenberg was earning $5,100 per year from UCLA, in addition to approximately $2,000, most of which came from teaching private pupils. His house was then valued at $17,500, on which he still owed $11,500. At that time, he considered himself having less to live on than the year before, because of higher expenses. One to two years later he felt that he was getting by reasonably comfortably, but only after hard work, much of it private teaching, with no funds left over for unexpected expenditures such as dentures.[34]

In October 1941 Schoenberg complained to his university administrators that his salary had not been increased for the last three years. Robert Sproul, the president, replied that this circumstance was "a reflection, in large part, of the distressing financial condition of the University during that period," and that with a larger budget, Schoenberg would have benefited commensurate with his stature.[35] Today one cannot help but think that this was a lame excuse on the part of UCLA authorities for continuously exploiting the famous composer. A year later, as Schoenberg found paying off the mortgage on his house an increasing burden, the John Simon Guggenheim Memorial Foundation rejected his bid for a fellowship, which he wanted toward the completion of his *Jakobsleiter* and *Moses and Aron*. This was another misjudgment, for Aaron Copland had received one in 1925–26, Roger Sessions in 1926–27, Roy Harris in 1927–28, and Walter Piston in 1935; Schoenberg's student John Cage would receive one in 1949, and his eventual successor at UCLA, Lukas Foss, in 1945.[36]

In 1942 the university warned the professor that in two years' time he would have to retire, at the age of seventy. Schoenberg was then making $5,400 a year. It was on this salary and his years of service at UCLA that his retirement pension would be based. That turned out to be little enough—only $29.60 a month after he had become an emeritus in the spring of 1944.[37] Incensed at getting so paltry an annuity, one that had to be supplemented heavily with private students' fees for the Schoenbergs to make ends meet, the composer rescinded an earlier agreement to have his private papers donated to the UCLA archives. (They went, instead, to USC.) Financial strictures of one sort or another may in fact have motivated him to consider moving to New Zealand in 1944, where the U.S. dollar would go farther, or back to Germany, where his old, devoted friend Hans Rosbaud was trying to entice him in the late 1940s.[38] But if New Zealand was too impractical and exotic as a refuge, the German scheme was fraught with far too many difficulties resulting from a lack of guarantees for adequate housing and support from Rosbaud's new employer, Südwestfunk of Baden-Baden. There, rather than a friend of Schoenberg, music section chief Heinrich Strobel was known to be an age-old supporter of Hindemith and Stravinsky.[39] Schoenberg died in Brentwood on 13 July 1951, never having set foot on European soil again.

Schoenberg's economic insecurity was always compounded by feelings of artistic and professional neglect. In fact, his opinion that he should be remunerated generously was based on the quite logical assumption, for him, that as one of the leading composers of the twentieth century he deserved it. The trouble was that as a university or private teacher he was not being paid enough for his lessons, and as a composer he was not sufficiently celebrated in the United States, at least not in a manner that would ensure him substantial material rewards.

Hence his complaints were endless. Already in 1934 he noticed that his works were not as well-known on the West Coast as he would have liked: "I never thought there is a city of that importance as San Francisco and Los Angeles, which have not played any of my works during twenty-five years."[40] A few years later he viewed this lacuna within the context of overall American proficiency when he observed that in the United States "there exist perhaps ten good orchestras and a few second- and third-rate ones. Most conductors, however, are definitely third-rate, at best. It is very sad."[41] He also thought that U.S. society at large did not care much about his art and made insufficient efforts to integrate it into the cultural life of the nation.[42] This sentiment may have paralleled Schoenberg's disappointment in Viennese and late Weimar society, but he was aware, of course, that in Europe a major composer occupied pride of place as a matter of principle. One year before his death, Schoenberg was unwilling to participate in a Hollywood Bowl ceremony, for, as he noted, his music had not been performed there for fifteen years.[43] When in 1945 Schoenberg declined to accept the honor of Doctor of Laws from UCLA and four years later refused to join its department of music's Composers' Council, he was expressing the bitterness of a man for whom the American honors, however ample they may objectively have been, fell short of satisfying the standards of a more universal recognition.[44]

II

As had been the case already back in Europe, in the Western hemisphere, too, Schoenberg the teacher was having more success after 1933 than Schoenberg the composer. This was unusual for a man who thought of himself as the greatest composer of his day, and, like Pfitzner, kept a bust of himself in his own house, but it had its roots as much in contemporary confusion about his compositional output as in the manner in which he regarded any teaching activity: nothing less than an avocation.[45] It was also quite in contrast to Stravinsky's attitude.[46]

Again in contrast with his later high self-esteem as a composer, it was with a pronounced sense of humility that he wrote in the preface of his *Harmonielehre* in 1911 that he had "learned this book from my students." Far from being disingenuous, Schoenberg continued to say that he wished to demonstrate any principle from the ground up, without applying rigid rules, in a process committing the pupils as much as their teacher. If a pupil found a better device, he should use it, meaning that a teacher should possess the courage to lose face, for he was not infallible.[47] At about the same time Schoenberg assured the Vienna Academy of Music, credibly, that "I believe myself suited to communicate to the young what would otherwise not be communicated to them."[48]

His superb reputation as a teacher preceded him even in these early times. He wanted to study with Schoenberg, wrote Kurt Weill in June 1919, for "he understands his pupils instantly, makes them aware of the smallest mistakes, opens up totally new perspectives and does not subject his students to his own interpretations, as is known about Pfitzner and many others."[49] The composer's didactic philosophy eventually became legend. Already during his European phase Stuckenschmidt remarked of Schoenberg that he was "extraordinarily mobile and always ready for discussion." He did not press his teaching content into a system but remained flexible, adapting himself to each individual pupil. When he showed them what was wrong, he was rather more like a colleague than a teacher.[50] As a result, elaborated his American student Dika Newlin later, he was looked upon by his pupils as a father figure: "They were overawed by him."[51] His occasional student David Raksin, a Hollywood film composer and himself reputed for his song "Laura," destined to be a jazz classic, was impressed by Schoenberg as a "warm-hearted, even charming man, who went out of his way to convey his criticism in a friendly fashion."[52]

Following Schoenberg's teaching career in exile leads one to the depths and heights of this man's musicianship and the inconsistencies in interpersonal relations for which he has already become sufficiently known. Although excelling as a teacher, Schoenberg did not suffer fools gladly; there is a marked correlation between the circumstances in which he was allowed to teach, the quality of students he was assigned or had to accept privately for money's sake, and his overall happiness. Often his feelings were ambivalent. Throughout the Boston-New York ordeal in 1933–34, which, on

the whole, devastated him because of the inadequacy of the setting and ineptitude of his pupils, among the latter he found "two really talented ones
and a few with some talent." Hence: "The actual teaching experience I enjoyed."[53] In early 1935, Schoenberg became infuriated when the lawyer of
a private student came after him because the student felt poorly served.[54]
Later on that year, USC disappointed him because of the small size of its
classes and, initially, an amateurish clientele, but typically, Schoenberg
knew what to make of that and ingeniously designed courses for university
students *and* "the general public." Now, to teach laymen composition was
something no one in Europe had thought Schoenberg, the arcane inventor
of twelve-tone music, to be capable of doing! Admittedly, at the end of his
USC term Schoenberg still felt "like Einstein, forced to teach arithmetic in a
public school."[55]

Schoenberg's tenure at UCLA, from 1936 to 1944, turned out to be only
a small improvement over tenure at USC, for he continued to be faced with
a disproportionately large group of undertalented students, as he ruefully
reflected after retirement.[56] His initial ambition had been to build up a program that would allow for gradual increments in difficulty, challenging students from the lowest to the doctoral level, with him, eventually, teaching
only the master classes. Although UCLA President Sproul, after several
months of hesitation, acceded to these wishes in principle and allowed for
Schoenberg's assistant, Gerald Strang, to assume an intermediate teaching
role, nothing much changed, so that by May 1938 Schoenberg was complaining that the earlier promise to him, "to erect a large music program,"
had not yet been kept.[57] Although shortly thereafter a more variegated system of music instruction was put in place, with Strang assuming a stronger
role, Schoenberg remained disenchanted with UCLA's music department,
especially as a graduate program, as he had conceived of it, was never fully
realized.[58]

It appears that Schoenberg vented his anger over those less than ideal
conditions on the more backward of his pupils. Newlin has recounted how
the master, an acerbic wit, played many a trick on unsuspecting and, presumably, dull, classroom denizens. But sometimes even the best ones, including herself, the future musicology professor, could not escape his
wrath.[59] More significant, however, was Schoenberg's admission, to students, colleagues, and friends that some of these American pupils possessed
true intelligence and a few even had real talent.[60] In 1939 he proudly wrote
to Webern of "very nice pedagogic successes," and Newlin thought him to
be "a very inspiring teacher" all along.[61]

If Schoenberg, in all of this, did not force his method of serial composition on his students but taught conventional harmony, it reflected not
so much his suspicion of American capabilities as his strong belief in the
roots of Occidental music, for he had adhered to a similar didactic method-
ology back in Europe.[62] These roots he recognized in Bach's, Mozart's,
Beethoven's, and Brahms's writings. It was only in advanced classes that
atonal techniques could be studied, and only at the express wishes of indi-

vidual students. This reticence on the part of the master irked some of the more ambitious pupils like Newlin, but on one hand Schoenberg wanted to avoid potential abuse of his system purely for the sake of "interesting tricks," of the kind that newfangled movie composers might employ. On the other hand, in his role as a teacher as much as composer, Schoenberg was, first and foremost, a craftsman, as he had demonstrated in his *Harmonielehre* of 1911. "Should I be able to instruct a pupil in the basics of the craft that supports our art, in the manner of a carpenter, then I will be satisfied," he had stated then.[63] Referring to the group of laymen he had taught at the beginning of his Los Angeles career, Schoenberg remarked in 1943, in yet another text for neophytes, that back then he had devised a syllabus for beginners, to help his students to the point where "even those with little creative ability and musicianship could write a small minuet or even a scherzo that was not quite impossible."[64] Surely these were the reminiscences of a teacher of both overpowering musicianship and great humility.

As a composer, too, Schoenberg rejected labels that would stereotype him as the inventor of the atonal school, and still in Paris in June 1933, before the Americans were to rain confusion upon him, he was uncomfortable with the epithet of Schoenberg, "the father of modern music."[65] As the master himself said and as has repeatedly been emphasized in more recent times, his modernism was a consequence of systematic evolution in stages over decades, not a sudden break with tradition.[66] In his pre-1900 works, the composer had already taken "the first steps in the development of chromaticism that was to lead him to abandon triadic harmony and tonality itself."[67] In Schoenberg's own view, one important way station to further experimentation had been his First String Quartet in D minor of 1905, with its complicated contrapuntal style, whose performance had caused scandals in Vienna and Dresden.[68] Schoenberg's Three Piano Pieces, opus 11, of 1909, a key year, have been described as "among the first masterpieces of free atonality."[69] In Alexander Ringer's characterization, the first of these Piano Pieces "eschewed the harmonically crucial relationships between consonance and dissonance in favour of chordal formations employed for purposes of accentuation and punctuation in a largely rhetorical context."[70] This was still only part of the way to "atonality." In his *Harmonielehre* of 1911 Schoenberg wrote very little about "atonality and other forbidden themes" but rather a lot about "the technique and harmonics of our predecessors."[71] One year later *Pierrot lunaire* followed, with its revolutionary *Sprechstimme* and the "tremendous intensity of its musical language"—a showcase example of German expressionism.[72]

This led to the works of the 1920s, with Schoenberg's new method of composition, employing "twelve tones related only to one another."[73] It would give rise to new generalizations and misunderstandings. Schoenberg later always resisted typecasting as an "atonal" composer.[74] He was not teaching his students "twelve-tone composition," he insisted, but "composition in the sense of musical logic."[75] The entire sequence of changes,

Schoenberg explained again in 1937, never had anything to do with revolution but was an orderly process; it represented "ascendance to a higher and better order."[76]

After his move to the United States, so it has been averred by some, Schoenberg made concessions to a more conventionally adjusted music audience by at times retracting the serial style of composition in favor of traditionally tonal constructions.[77] It is true that many, if not most, Americans found twelve-tone music difficult to comprehend. But there were those who were listening attentively, expecting him to maintain his integrity as the modernist he had become. When Schoenberg's new Suite for String Orchestra in G major was performed in New York by the Philharmonic Symphonic Orchestra under Klemperer in the summer of 1935, apparently marking a return to tonality, the sophisticated *New York Times* critic Olin Downes was dismayed, finding it "thickly and muddily written," in an "affectation of the old sturdy manner, and thereafter mordant counterpoint." For him it was "Ersatz music, music on and of paper."[78] Yet all this Suite was doing was marking the beginning of a phase in which Schoenberg took the liberty of switching between serialism and tonality (by which he may have intended to show that he still was master of the universal art of composition; he himself said later that he had given in to a long-standing desire "to return to the old styles").[79] Altogether it was, as Stuckenschmidt has rightly pointed out, no question of "turning back."[80]

In the American period, then, Schoenberg alternated between the old and the new style. Before coming to Boston in 1933, Schoenberg had been working on a Concerto for String Quartet and Orchestra after a Concerto Grosso by Handel, not an atonal work.[81] Next came the Suite for String Orchestra of 1934, again in a tonal mold, perhaps to please himself but also to be playable by U.S. youth orchestras.[82] For Schoenberg's following, serial compositions proved to be extremely difficult to play, pushing instrumentalists to the limits of their capacity. This was exemplified by the next work, the Violin Concerto, opus 36, written between 1934 and 1936. Dedicated to Webern, it was first performed by violinist Louis Krasner, with the Philadelphia Orchestra under Leopold Stokowski on 6 December 1940.[83]

Elizabeth Sprague Coolidge, that vaunted patron of contemporary music, commissioned another twelve-tone work, the String Quartet No. 4, opus 37, in 1936; the Kolisch Quartet, the composer's favorite chamber ensemble, performed it at UCLA in the following year, with Schoenberg's friend George Gershwin attending.[84] The Second Chamber Symphony had been written, by 1940, for his friend Fritz Stiedry in New York, the conductor of the New Friends of Music Orchestra. The work continued a score Schoenberg had abandoned in 1906; he now expanded it in the extended tonal style in which he had begun it. Stiedry performed it in 1941.[85] Several months later Schoenberg scored a special version of it for two pianos, to be performed by a UCLA fraternity; the composer himself thought it "a very brilliant piece."[86]

Thereafter the D minor *Variations on a Recitative,* opus 40, for solo organ, and composed in the fall of 1941, despite its "serial feature" was another of the "tonally-based works of this period."[87] A serial work "with quasi-tonal leanings" was the Piano Concerto, opus 42, composed in 1942 and first performed by Schoenberg's long-standing pianist friend, Eduard Steuermann, with the NBC Symphony Orchestra under Stokowski in New York, on 6 February 1944.[88] As was discovered in the early 1980s, Schoenberg wanted to express in it the hatred of humankind, and the Jews in particular, against the evil Nazi empire. Reportedly, Stokowski thought the concerto "very difficult even partially to grasp without study" but "one of the landmarks of musical history." Despite his admiration for Steuermann, Downes again disliked the work, finding it "disagreeable and unconvincing."[89]

After the largely serial *Ode to Napoleon* with reciter in 1942, Schoenberg's *Theme and Variations,* opus 43a for band, of July 1943, was composed in G major and constituted his second, expressly tonal, work since coming to the United States; it was also arranged for orchestra (opus 43b). Serge Koussevitzky featured it with the Boston Symphony Orchestra in October 1944.[90] Schoenberg's third American tonal work, in 1948, was a new setting of three folk songs for a mixed a cappella chorus of four voices, which he had already arranged in 1929. They have been described as "modal counterpoint with Romantic-sounding harmonies added to the simple, diatonic folk tunes," based on late-medieval German melodies.[91] Also in 1948, the cantata *A Survivor from Warsaw,* a tribute to Holocaust victims, like his *Kol nidre* of 1938, contained Jewish liturgical elements.[92] In August–September 1946 Schoenberg wrote the String Trio, opus 45, one of the most important of his last compositions. "He divided the score into three 'parts' separated by two 'episodes' of different serial construction."[93] The twelve-tone Fantasy for Violin with Piano Accompaniment, opus 47 of 1949, a one-movement piece, was to be Schoenberg's final instrumental work.[94] Already at that time, recurrent ailments were preventing him from extending his productivity much further. After a few more, serial, choral compositions, he occupied himself again with his oratorio *Die Jakobsleiter,* which he had begun in 1917, but it was to remain unfinished.[95]

If Schoenberg—moving, as he was, between a complicated tonality and an even more complicated serialism—throughout his stay in the United States pronounced that he desired nothing more than that ordinary people would know and whistle his melodies, he was certainly deceiving himself. Judged by his output, he did not possess this Weillian gift of instant popularity and merrymaking, yet neither could he always reliably entice even the most academic of conductors, in Los Angeles or in New York, to play his arcane music.[96]

In the United States, Schoenberg had two major complaints regarding the performance of his oeuvre. The first was that not enough of it was being played, the second that of the little that was, it stemmed from his early, post-Romantic period. In particular, he heaped scorn on the Americans' predilection for *Verklärte Nacht.* New music hardly anyone dared to present, criticized Schoenberg as late as 1945, six years after he had been hoping against hope that "there must come soon a time when all the American orchestras will have to perform my works as regularly as they perform today already Debussy, Sibelius and Ravel. I am the next to whom the younger generation will turn, as soon as they get the places now occupied by older uncles and aunts. All depends on the right propaganda."[97]

Schoenberg blamed the U.S. musical establishment for these oversights and imbalances, singling out three well-situated conductors who could have supported him but chose not to. "Thanks to the attitude of most American conductors and under the leadership of Toscanini, Koussevitzky, and of Walter, suppression of my works soon began with the effect that the number of my performances sunk to an extremely low point," he lamented in 1949.[98]

At various times, Schoenberg had unflattering things to say about every one of these three. In late 1934 he accused Koussevitzky of having been an itinerant bassist who could not even read a score and who, since being moored in Boston for the last ten years, had not performed a single work of his. Such a low opinion of the conductor did not prevent Schoenberg from offering newer compositions to him, for example, the Suite for String Orchestra, five years later. When, after another five years, in October 1944, Koussevitzky had performed Schoenberg's *Theme and Variations,* opus 43b (the concert version), the composer complained about the conductor's "disregard of my metronomical indications." The Suite as well as the Theme and Variations having been tonal rather than serial, Schoenberg upbraided Koussevitzky's inability to conduct his "more difficult" pieces and gratuitously ranted against the conductor's "general ignorance as a musician and as a man."[99]

Toscanini had long been known as an enemy of modern music, holding that he was able to conduct only what he could trace to song by the human voice and hence retain in his ear: That excluded atonal works.[100] But rather than understanding this and placing it in perspective, Schoenberg chose to take it personally when he remarked: "I have often wondered why Toscanini has never played one of my works. Though there are enough reasons in his limitations: his education is probably or rather ostensibly very low, that of a skillful orchestra musician: his taste is low, not only because it is that of a band leader, which he was during the first war." Schoenberg defined Toscanini as a "third-rate conductor" who, when playing German music, becomes ridiculous: "He has really no idea what this music is all about." In 1945 Schoenberg wished to offer Toscanini, for performance, his Second Chamber Symphony of 1940, which, although not serial, was anything but conventional in style. With his black sense of humor, he expected Toscanini to refuse it, but, quipped the master, "I would like to have it on paper."[101]

The relationship between Schoenberg and Bruno Walter, however, was rather more complicated. Schoenberg had been on amicable terms with him by the time the conductor, younger by two years, had moved from Vienna to Munich in 1913 and was planning rehearsals of the *Gurrelieder* for a performance with the Munich Philharmonic. This then had to be post-poned because of a conflict with Schreker's *Der ferne Klang;* professing his innocence, Walter had suggested a late fall 1914 date for the perfor-mance. But that did not come to pass either because of the outbreak of World War I.[102]

That could have been enough to annoy any composer. But to make mat-ters worse, after Schoenberg's "emancipation of the dissonance," the musi-cally conservative Walter had taken a dislike to the Second Viennese School, although at a personal level he admitted sympathies for Berg. Even for the earlier phase of this acquaintance, Walter conceded later that al-though he found Schoenberg "a pure and incorruptible idealist" as well as "a powerfully and uniquely intuitive musician," he felt "increasingly un-able to follow him on his way, because I considered it a devious way." Schoenberg and Walter were in touch with one another after the former's move to the United States, and at the end of 1934 the composer wrote to his friends that although he liked Walter as a conductor, he had his diffi-culties with the man somewhere else. As was his wont, Schoenberg did not mince any words: "As a private person, he has always been a repulsive pig, and I get ill just thinking of him; hence I try to avoid it as best I can." Such strong sentiments may in part be traced to Walter's sometimes fero-cious outbursts of anger, to which his favorite singer Lotte Lehmann has at-tested, but the deeper reason would have to be Walter's attitude to Schoen-berg's modern oeuvre, which, as Schoenberg correctly observed, Walter ignored completely. No wonder that Schoenberg continued to bear him a grudge.[103]

On his part, this did not keep Walter from highlighting Schoenberg's ear-lier, celebrated works, such as *Verklärte Nacht,* which he professed to love from days gone by, with the New York Philharmonic or NBC Symphony for broadcast, but he did this only sporadically, refusing to consider Schoenberg's bolder, more contemporary pieces, such as his Second Cham-ber Symphony. Walter, like Schoenberg, had adored Mahler; after Mahler's death, *Verklärte Nacht* was on the edge of what Walter could identify with. Nonetheless, in June 1948 Walter expressed his satisfaction over the fact that besides himself, "also Stokowski has a work by Schoenberg on his pro-gram and I think it very desirable to mention that the purpose of the Phil-harmonic Symphony Society is to commemorate in this way Schoenberg's 75th birthday."[104]

The reference to Leopold Stokowski as a conductor favorable to Schoen-berg's music provides yet another clue as to the veracity of the composer's recurrent claim that he was by and large ostracized in the United States. Stokowski, the most famous of the indigenous U.S. conductors, had already performed Schoenberg's *Fünf Orchesterstücke* (1909) in the early 1920s, as well as *Gurrelieder* and excerpts from *Die glückliche Hand* (1910/13) shortly before the composer's arrival in America (even though, characteris-tically, Schoenberg chided Stokowski for not having provided the composer with royalties). Stokowski's interest in Schoenberg was an abiding one, which he proved by intermittently featuring him and agreeing to the premiere of his new piano concerto. Already in 1940 Schoenberg commended Stokowski on his "brave stand toward my work and against illiterate snobs"—signs of approval which in the master's idiosyncratic language could not get any stronger. When, later, Stokowski recorded the *Gurrelieder* for RCA Victor, Schoenberg was critical of some aspects of the conductor's interpretation and the soloists, but admitted that "the orchestra plays very fine."[105]

But there were other conductors who staked their reputation on Schoenberg, established ones, such as Dimitri Mitropoulos, or ones not as well-known, such as Nicholas Slonimsky, Harold Byrns, Ingolf Dahl, and Robert Craft. Slonimsky, in fact, had had his eight-week Hollywood Bowl contract canceled in 1933 for shocking his audience with works by Schoenberg and other moderns, such as Edgar Varèse and Charles Ives. Schoenberg himself was invited to conduct his oeuvre, not often but at irregular intervals. He conducted *Pelleas und Melisande* with the Chicago Symphony as early as February 1934 and *Verklärte Nacht* with the Boston Symphony in March. Shortly after, the influential New York League of Composers invited him to conduct chamber works, thereafter staging "a very large reception, at which 2,000 people were reported to be present, and of whom I must have shaken 500 hands, and the sponsors' committee apparently contained everybody from New York who is in any way interested in art. Soon after there was a second, similarly big-time reception, but I cannot remember who organized it." Right at the beginning of his U.S. career, these were not the words of a man neglected, but at that time he was, of course, something of a novelty.[106]

There were other signs of recognition by the American establishment, even though this may not have manifested itself as much as Schoenberg would have liked, for example, in monetary terms. In December 1935, a special concert and dinner, sponsored by the Trojan chapter of Phi Mu Alpha, a prestigious music fraternity, featured Schoenberg's works and himself as conductor. More than a 1,000 guests had been invited to the event, and the vice president of the California Symphony Association was quoted in the press as saying that "Southern California has considered itself most fortunate to have had Arnold Schoenberg as a resident here," welcoming this occasion, for the people of Los Angeles, "to honor this great musician."[107] The Kolisch String Quartet was at hand to play his works, for instance, all his quartets at UCLA in 1936, while Steuermann stood by as Schoenberg's favorite pianist. In October 1939 the master was invited to be the guest of honor and main speaker at the annual convention of the nation's largest and most important organization of music educators, the Music Teachers National Association, in Kansas City, Missouri. Schoenberg accepted and was enthusiastically welcomed.[108] Two years later the University of California asked Schoenberg to be the Annual Faculty Research Lecturer, requesting him to speak about his serial method of composition. This was the first time, since 1925, that a composer had been esteemed in this way.[109] In the spring of 1945 the university scheduled a special Schoenberg music festival, which included separate concerts on three days, featuring a cross-section of his music, from the songs for male voice, opus 1 (before 1900) to his *Variations on a Recitative* for organ, opus 40 (1941). Manuscripts from his hand were shown in an adjacent, special exhibition.[110] In May 1947, Schoenberg received a prize of $1,000 from the American Academy of Arts and Letters "for outstanding achievements."[111] And a year later the Los Angeles chamber concert series "Evenings on the Roof," organized since 1938 by the Schoenberg admirers Frances Mullen and Peter Yates, put on an all-Schoenberg program, celebrating the tenth anniversary of the highly prestigious run. Altogether from 1939 to 1954, the Roof series mounted nine all-Schoenberg programs—more than for any other composer.[112]

But if everything is tallied up, Schoenberg was right to feel neglected. Much of this feeling was reflected in his relations with collaborators, and it became exemplarily manifest throughout his tortured friendship with Otto Klemperer. Matters of significance for the two men were perennially complicated by the fact that Schoenberg was always prone to exaggerate the problems with his contemporaries, to the same extent that he emphasized his own importance and, concomitantly, neglect. But they were further compounded by Klemperer's long-standing illness as a severe manic depressive, additional ailments, and all manner of difficulties arising therefrom—in the area of financial stability and interpersonal relations generally.[113]

Of course, Gustav Mahler also was Klemperer's idol. The two Mahler disciples, Schoenberg and Klemperer, first met in Munich in 1911, when a composition by Klemperer was performed there, something Schoenberg clearly did not appreciate. In 1912 Schoenberg conducted *Pierrot lunaire* in Hamburg (next to the premiere in Berlin), and Generalmusikdirektor Klemperer was impressed. But he himself was reluctant to try his hand at Schoenberg's *Fünf Orchesterstücke,* written in 1909, after the composer had made a significant break with tonality. Schoenberg registered but chose to ignore it.[114] However, this seems to have sowed the seeds of distrust between the two musicians, with Klemperer retaining what Peter Heyworth has called "an element of ambivalence" to contemporary music—something of a paradox because Klemperer was to make his reputation in the Weimar Republic on the interpretation of what were considered the modernist works, as well as on a bold reading of the classics.[115]

In the 1920s, Klemperer conducted *Verklärte Nacht* and *Pelleas und Melisande,* both of course written before 1909. The distrust surfaced again in Berlin when, in 1928, after Klemperer had been appointed to the Kroll-Oper, Schoenberg thought him and Walter part of an intrigue to prevent his assumption of the directorship at the Hochschule für Musik. Then, at the Kroll in July 1930, Klemperer conducted Schoenberg's *Glückliche Hand,* with Alexander von Zemlinsky conducting *Erwartung.* Although Schoenberg agreed with the musical renditions of the two one-act operas, he disliked the stage designs. Moreover, Klemperer neglected other opportunities to present Schoenberg's works while at the Kroll, so that the composer nursed a grudge against him until December 1932, when he refused to attend a banquet in Klemperer's honor, to which, among others, Furtwängler and Walter had been invited.[116]

The distrust between the two musicians was transplanted to the United States, although they felt strangely dependent on one another. Klemperer was already conductor of the Los Angeles Philharmonic when Schoenberg arrived in the city. Over the extended period of their American exile, another paradox materialized in Schoenberg's life: Although Klemperer was not to conduct any of Schoenberg's more advanced, serial, works, in total he undertook more of Schoenberg's compositions than did his successors at the Philharmonic.[117]

Even though Klemperer had welcomed Schoenberg to American shores in February 1934, the composer immediately identified the conductor as one of the wire pullers behind the scene who allegedly tried to restrict his performances. Hence in November Schoenberg repeated the affront of Berlin by not showing up for a banquet in Klemperer's honor, ignoring the fact that Klemperer had just scheduled a performance of *Verklärte Nacht,* which occurred on 13 December.[118] However, as Heyworth has observed for that occasion: "Schoenberg's belief that his music had been 'suppressed' bordered on the grotesque: even to musical Los Angeles he was in 1934 scarcely more than a name."[119]

Until 1940 the two men endured an on-and-off relationship yet never lost touch. Schoenberg's anger against Klemperer over the issue of his modernist works did not go away, although Klemperer was doing his best to accommodate the master's wish list, including transcriptions of older works, such as those by Monn and Handel. Doubtless Klemperer was partly guided by the dictates of his employers and the average taste of the Los Angeles audience. He himself was not in principle opposed to the serial technique, he said later, for used "in the right way," the system could express the composer's intentions, even if "Schoenberg sometimes went a little far, as in his ban on repeating notes."[120]

In 1936, the two émigrés' relationship reached another climax of paradoxy. On the one hand, Klemperer antagonized Schoenberg by refusing his invitation to talk things over, for Schoenberg regretted "not being able to have regular contact with the only decent musician in this region." Yet on the other, Schoenberg accepted Klemperer shortly thereafter as a private pupil. And whereas Schoenberg assumed a professorship at UCLA after Klemperer's recommendation for the post, Klemperer was recommended by the master as musical adviser to Hollywood director William Dieterle for a proposed Beethoven film. At the end of the year Klemperer even appeared willing to conduct Schoenberg's new Violin Concerto, opus 36, even though it was serial, had it not been for Sprague Coolidge, who in this case would not grant supporting funds.[121]

In 1940 Klemperer's medical condition had worsened, which led to another crisis. By the summer Schoenberg had learned that Klemperer planned to conduct *Pierrot lunaire* and his new violin concerto in New York, whereas the composer wished to record the first work in Los Angeles and then perform it in New York himself. Although Schoenberg thought he had to show compassion for a man so seriously ill by now, he also smarted over Klemperer's remark that his music had become "alien" to him. Hence he was wondering in September "how the broken (artistic) bridge would ever work again." Matters went on from there. Klemperer insisted that he had not been invited to a party given in Schoenberg's honor by his New York publisher G. Schirmer in late November; he had seen an invitation in Franz Werfel's room. Klemperer now furiously proceeded to remind Schoenberg of the service he had rendered for him at UCLA, of having sent his daughter Lotte to Schoenberg for lessons, and of having lent him, without being paid back, the sum of $200. To counter the composer's constant squabbling, he added a list of all of Schoenberg's works he had ever performed, starting with *Verklärte Nacht* and *Pelleas und Melisande* 1920 in Cologne. The letter finished with the strongest words yet exchanged between the two: "All my personal relations with you are broken and I shall never see you again."[122]

The two musicians, each in his own way lost in the United States, had made up again by the end of the year, and during the following months there were no incidents. When Klemperer saw Schoenberg once more in 1942, he found him "milder."[123] Indeed, in 1943 the composer tried to get Klemperer appointed to a new opera division in the music department of UCLA; Sproul did not react, probably because he feared scandal on account of Klemperer's unpredictability.[124] But it was not on a note of personal friendship that they parted, when, after the end of World War II, Klemperer got set to spend much more time in Europe. To the day of his death, Schoenberg preferred to remember Klemperer as the conductor who had closed the concert halls of Los Angeles to his works and who had been a miserable private student in 1936; he refused to attend Los Angeles area functions with the conductor even when his own compositions were featured.[125] It was Klemperer who, in his deplorable physical and mental state, attempted to make amends in the final years, evidently getting nowhere. In his fragmented memoirs, he had mostly good things to say about the composer he had so admired and who, in his stern Old Testament way, ultimately proved so unrelenting.[126]

III

As the pattern of his relationship with conductors has already suggested, crusty old Schoenberg thrived on his enemies. His world, a New York acquaintance once wrote, was "populated by an awful lot of bad guys and by very few good guys."[127] Schoenberg's sense of self-worth, superiority, and despisement of others was based on the conviction that he was always right, especially on musical matters, where he would not flinch. Adversaries

were the best corroboration of his historic greatness, as he himself perceived it; he cut his teeth on them. "Should I make new enemies?" he cried
out in 1945, "I am entirely satisfied with my old ones. In fact, I am very
happy with them: everyone of them is a good illustration to my justification
of contempt for them. New enemies could not do better in this respect,
than my dear, dear old ones."[128] Clearly, a puckish Schoenberg relished
mischief. When interviewer José Rodriguez suggested that Schoenberg's
violin concerto (1934–36) was unplayable unless the violinist grew a new
fourth finger, Schoenberg crowed like a naughty child: "Yes, yes, that will
be fine. The Concerto is extremely difficult, just as much for the head as for
the hands. I am delighted to add another unplayable work to the repertoire.
I want the Concerto to be difficult and I want the little finger to become
longer. I can wait."[129]

As in the case of Kurt Weill and as a rule, Schoenberg got along worst
with fellow émigrés, certainly because in one or two cases he considered
them to be in the way, if not actually dangerous competitors, but also because he disliked them on personal grounds. This may have been so in the
case of Erich Wolfgang Korngold, a fellow Jew from Vienna, where his contempt might have been fueled by Korngold's success as a commercial film-
music composer.[130] Hollywood success was sometimes also the hallmark of
Ernst Toch, he too originally from Vienna, but there was more to that out-
of-joint relationship than mere envy or contempt. Schoenberg and Toch
had been on cordial terms when both were living in Germany before January 1933.[131] When, from Paris in the summer of 1933, Schoenberg tried to
enlist Toch's support toward a scheme to organize Jews against Nazism and
Toch did not react, the friendship began to cool. Although both soon were
neighbors on the California coast, they hardly saw each other. Toch was
not making such bad money in the Hollywood studios, and when his serious works were performed in public, Schoenberg tended to be conspicuously absent. They sparred nastily on the occasion of Schoenberg's seventy-
fifth birthday in the spring of 1949, when Toch expressed his astonishment
over that "unclarified silence" between them. This relationship remained
unresolved.[132]

Two non-Jews also were problematic acquaintances: Hindemith and
Stravinsky. Of Hindemith, about whom Schoenberg had said in 1932 that,
apart from his pupils and next to the "Aryans" Bartók, Hauer, and Krenek,
he found himself closest to, we have heard already; later they became rivals
for the favors of German post-1945 audiences.[133] As for Stravinsky, during
the 1930s and 1940s the cognoscenti were divided (as they are divided
today) over who was the greater of these two giants in the modern camp,
yet Schoenberg was acutely aware that the Russian émigré, whom he had
long ago called *der kleine Modernsky,* was far more affluent than himself
and blessed with U.S. establishment connections he could only dream of.
Both composers avoided each other carefully in public on the West Coast,
Schoenberg being sure to denigrate his rival's musical style in class whenever the opportunity arose, sometimes characterizing it as "rhubarb coun-

terpoint." Schoenberg's students were strictly forbidden to meet with Stravinsky whenever he was in Los Angeles.[134] This attitude seems to have changed toward the end of Schoenberg's life, when both slowly developed more interest for the other's work; after Schoenberg's death, Stravinsky is known to have been an admirer, himself adopting "twelve-tone and serialist techniques in his last years," inspired, not least, by Webern. Thus vanity, for the longest time, once again prevented two great minds from fertile congregation.[135]

Why was it that Schoenberg got along so well with Ernst Krenek, a fellow Viennese émigré though not a Jew? The answer cannot be simple, as Schoenberg was a self-contradictory man beyond the scrutiny even of the most psychologically skillful biographer. Perhaps the decisive factor was that Krenek, who, since 1930 and especially 1938, composed in the serial style, always acknowledged Schoenberg as his mentor, and Schoenberg cherished adoration. Already in 1932 Schoenberg had said that he liked Krenek. Krenek had just written several admiring essays about the master when he came face to face with him at Klemperer's house in December 1937. The two were a match after that. More than a year later Krenek audited Schoenberg's classes and came away admiring the older's didactic technique and recognizing in him the consummate teacher that he was. At the same time, he was delivering public lectures, nationwide, on the Second Viennese School. Later, as Krenek was readying himself for a teaching career in the United States, both men were exchanging views on the difference between American and European pedagogic approaches. Krenek became an acolyte, and he, the confirmed serialist also, loved Schoenberg's earlier works, which were on the cusp of serialism. He had heard *Pierrot lunaire* yesterday, Krenek wrote on 18 November 1940, "this is music as it should be." Schoenberg's Second Chamber Symphony was played on the radio, Krenek enthused in February 1942, "very clear and well laid out." Krenek was then in St. Paul, the orbit of Mitropoulos, who had been known to champion Schoenberg consistently, earning the master's firm respect.[136]

Schoenberg's relations with U.S. composers and representatives of the music and entertainment scene were mixed as well. A cordial friendship tied him to George Gershwin, cemented by their mutual love of tennis and serious painting, and if Schoenberg appreciated Gershwin's genius, he also could not fail to notice how much the younger man idolized him. There was never any doubt about who was the master. It is reported that once, after the performance of Schoenberg's complicated string quartets, Gershwin mentioned to his tennis partner that he too would like to write a quartet some day. "But it will be something simple, like Mozart." Immediately, Schoenberg shot back: "I'm not a simple man—and, anyway, Mozart was considered far from simple in his day." Schoenberg, who had just sat for a portrait by his colleague, deeply grieved over Gershwin's death from brain cancer in July 1937, broadcasting a eulogy for him, which was later published.[137]

His relationship with Aaron Copland, Jewish like Gershwin and the doyen of contemporary U.S. composers, characteristically was not so smooth. It was one of Schoenberg's many idées fixes that in 1949, on the brink of the Cold War, he thought Copland, in alliance with others like Nadia Boulanger, Bruno Walter, and Toscanini, bent on suppressing his music in the United States, for the sake of traditionalism. Less than pleased, Copland protested against the linking of his name with that of Joseph Stalin, averring, at the same time, that "I can't be listed as an apostle and propagandizer of the twelve-tone system; but since when is that a crime?" Copland demanded an apology from Schoenberg, for, "unlike Stalin, I have no desire to suppress his music!" Rather dishonestly, Schoenberg retorted that "it is very easy to live in peace with me," professing that he liked Copland's compositions and desired a harmonious relationship with him, which is evidently what transpired, until the master's death in 1951.[138]

As one of the reputed coconspirators planning to undo him, Schoenberg, in his letter to Copland, listed his own publisher G. Schirmer in New York.[139] Typical for Schoenberg, he was under the impression that after the death of his trusted friend and former president of Schirmer, the cultured Carl Engel, in 1944, his own music was systematically being neglected there. His widow, Gertrud, was to pick up that particular thread after his death.[140] Schoenberg also felt personally slighted by *New York Times* music critic Olin Downes when he disparagingly wrote about Mahler, whom Schoenberg worshipped.[141] The New York–based American Society of Composers, whose officers had actually been magnanimous to Schoenberg shortly after his arrival on U.S. shores, also fared unkindly at Schoenberg's hands, being classified by the composer as among his many detractors, when he informed the Society in April 1941: "No, certainly, it was not vanity and it was not hunger for publicity, when I now tell you: I wonder why my name is never mentioned in your publications."[142] Schoenberg was equally cross with RCA Victor for not recording enough of his music, for having allegedly violated his recording rights, and, not least, for withholding from him a complimentary gramophone, which he plainly thought was his due.[143]

Schoenberg had a most curious encounter with leaders of the U.S. film industry, several conflicting versions of which exist. According to fellow émigré and script writer Salka Viertel, Steuermann's sister, who knew absolutely everybody in Los Angeles at the time and brokered the meeting, the most credible account is this: An executive at Metro Goldwyn Mayer in 1935 had heard a New York concert performance of *Verklärte Nacht* and, truly transfigured, decided that Schoenberg must write the film music to Pearl S. Buck's *The Good Earth*. Schoenberg met with the executive and decided to put a price on his cooperation with the movie business, whose film scores he generally detested, even though he was always hoping to give private lessons to Hollywood composers. The final fee Schoenberg demanded was $50,000, and for his act of artistic prostitution (à la Toch and Korngold) he wished to reserve the right to keep the entire musical production under his control, as well as the actors' spoken words. When asked in the studio what he meant by that, Schoenberg replied: "They would have to speak in the same pitch and key as I compose it in. It would be similar to 'Pierrot Lunaire' but, of course, less difficult." Thereupon the producer decided to resort to some Chinese folk songs, around which the studio's sound department head would write some lovely music. Whether Schoenberg was disappointed by this turn of events is hard to judge. To Alma Mahler-Werfel he made it sound as if he had purposely asked for such a high amount to make sure to be rejected by the film industry he so despised. But he also admitted to her that as a composer he needed such monies to free himself from university teaching. Indeed, he might just have been able to persuade the studio bosses to allow him to use serial music and *Sprechstimme,* but in the event of such a Hollywood victory, his contempt for composers such as Korngold notwithstanding, his bruised ego would have been pampered and he would have become nationally well-known and also wealthy.[144]

If such relations were ambigious, so was his friendship with pupils and admirers of yore, at least periodically. In the United States, Schoenberg missed his champion students, Alban Berg and Anton Webern, terribly. He missed Berg so much that he wished to create for him, who was financially always insecure—especially after being shunned by the antimodernist Austrofascist establishment—a situation in the New World that he and his wife Helene could build on for the future. Was this the better to control the younger composer's emotions? For in the early years of Nazi rule Schoenberg was afraid that Berg would succumb to the spell of German Nazism— then intermittently illegal in Austria, if only to be able to have his works performed in the Reich. (This trade-off was not unrealistic, because Erich Kleiber did conduct Berg's *Fünf symphonische Stücke aus Lulu für den Konzertgebrauch* in Berlin, having secured express permission from Göring, in November 1934, after Berg had sufficiently touted his "Aryan" lineage to the Germans.) In late 1933, Berg was able to lay Schoenberg's fears at rest—for the time being. A year later, Schoenberg wanted Berg to be part of an antifascist "Defensive Cultural Alliance," also to include Webern and Krenek. After Berg's death in December 1935, which much disturbed his teacher, Schoenberg became a possible candidate for completing Berg's unfinished opera *Lulu.* But the master refused, because he had found certain anti-Semitic allusions in Berg's *Particell* and libretto. Whereas he was able to ascribe Berg's indiscretion to the Austrian's political and ideological immaturity and was ready to forgive him personally, he felt that the very process of forgiving precluded his formal participation in the completion of *Lulu.*[145]

Regarding Webern and National Socialism, Schoenberg was no less suspicious. To be sure, the Austrian was incensed about his teacher's treatment by the Nazis in early 1933 and wrote to him emotionally in early summer. But Schoenberg's anxiety at the turn of 1933 affected Webern as much as Berg, because for months they had both been silent: "Since, after all, we Jews have experienced it a hundred times in these days that the unbelievable has happened, that people had suddenly become Nazis who yesterday were still friends." In January 1934, Webern quickly allayed Schoenberg's fears with an impassioned condemnation of the Berlin regime, but how could he realistically convince its victim? As if to reassert a claim on him, Schoenberg replied that "Europe has lost every meaning for me if I do not have my faithful friends there, you above all." In June 1937, Schoenberg again had reason to believe that Webern had succumbed to the Nazi spell, even though Austria was still autonomous. He had dedicated his violin concerto to his pupil, but how could he now be sure? Once more Webern placated him, although by this time he was already flirting with the Nazi movement, thinking, like Berg before him, that this would improve his commercial prospects. Impecunious, he asked Goebbels's RMK for a handout in 1940, after he had already become an admiring reader of Hitler's *Mein Kampf* and was beginning to trace the Führer's victories in the West with enthusiasm. Schoenberg did not know, but he might have had a sixth sense when he conveyed, in October 1939, the cryptic message to his publisher Schirmer: "Please reduce—for the time being—the dedication to Mr. Webern on my Concerto for Violin to: TO ANTON WEBERN. I realize it might be dangerous to say more than that." (It would have been unless Schoenberg, the Jew, tried to avoid compromising Webern, the "Aryan.") Perhaps later one could say: "To my dear friend Anton von Webern in gratitude for his unsurpassed loyalty." Well, one could not. Loyal to Schoenberg Webern had remained, right through the first years of war, when, on Schoenberg's birthday in 1941, he tried to relay to the master a message of undying affection. But Webern's immediate family now included active National Socialists.[146]

The third European friend Schoenberg came to mistrust was Hermann Scherchen. The conductor had been a staunch supporter of the composer long before World War I.[147] But in August 1950—the Cold War was now on—Schoenberg suddenly believed he had heard that Scherchen had turned into a card-carrying Communist. Point blank, and as only Arnold Schoenberg could, he asked Scherchen whether that was true. Earlier, such beliefs would not have disturbed an artistic relationship, Schoenberg explained. But in the recently changed circumstances, he felt honor-bound to view every Communist as an enemy and could not "even continue a purely artistic communion with him."[148] "As the true socialist form of society," retorted Scherchen, who, it was no secret, had always resided in Social Democracy's left field, "every convinced socialist knows only the Communist one." No, he was not a member of a political party, nor had he ever been. Communism as an ideology was to change mankind for the better, not to erect a power structure for certain social strata. And besides, art was above politics. Nevertheless, Scherchen would respect Schoenberg's decision to break off relations but continue to esteem him unabated.[149] Unfazed, Schoenberg replied that he wanted to discuss the possibility of a continued professional relationship with his legal adviser. "Communism forces us to strike back, since it aggressively threatens us."[150] In November Schoenberg communicated to Scherchen the embarrassing message that his lawyer had given him the green light, because Scherchen's name was on no U.S. black list. "Hence there is nothing to be said against a continuation of our artistic and publishing relationship," as long as Scherchen had nothing else on his mind than conducting and publishing the composer's works. Still, Schoenberg asked Scherchen for a final, binding declaration.[151]

In retrospect, Schoenberg's treatment of Scherchen, one of his most loyal supporters over decades, appears cruel. But when it came to politics, the right-wing Schoenberg stood only on principle. Yet Scherchen, himself no Good Samaritan, knew how to take this, and apart from that, Schoenberg also had his nice and charming side, showing it in the company of a few personal friends such as Gershwin but, most important, in the close circle of his family and in his attempt to assist colleagues who were trapped in Nazi-dominated Europe.

If Schoenberg really was an artist with a tough veneer and a soft core, his ties with members of his immediate family prove this beyond a doubt. He had ongoing problems with his son Georg ("Görgi," b. 1906) from his first marriage with Mathilde von Zemlinsky, dating back to before 1933. He thought Görgi a lazy good-for-nothing and for years had to support him financially when he himself did not earn much. The composer sought, for the longest time, to bring Görgi over to the United States. Görgi seemed capable of copying music but little else, and, a full Jew by Nazi standards, he ultimately survived the Holocaust in Vienna (after uncomplicated stays in Germany and France) because he was married to a non-Jew and thus allowed to enlist for heavy work in the food industry.[152]

There also was occasional friction between Schoenberg and his other grown-up child, daughter Gertrud ("Trudi," b. 1902), who was married to his pupil Felix Greissle, soon to work for Schirmer in New York, after Schoenberg had been successful in persuading the two to emigrate in 1938. Yet on the whole, his bonds with these children were strong.[153] In his old age, however, nothing would match the love for his second wife, Gertrud, née Kolisch, and their three young children: Nuria, Ronald, and Lawrence. According to Newlin, who saw them often, they could do no wrong. When Ronnie became teenage tennis champion of Los Angeles, his father was beside himself with pride. The Schoenbergs also lovingly adopted their perpetual house guest, the teenager Lotte Klemperer, then greatly suffering from the absence of her father. Lotte was frequently present when the Schoenbergs entertained colleagues and friends, which they did generously and with humor and warmth, belying the patriarch's stern exterior.[154]

Schoenberg's brother-in-law, his former pupil, Rudolf Kolisch, and Kolisch's wife also came over. Already renowned in Europe, Kolisch now served as the principal violinist of the U.S.-based celebrated string quartet of the same name. It goes without saying that they played much of Schoenberg's work.[155] That the composer worried greatly about his brother Heinrich and his cousin Hans Nachod, neither of whom he would ever see in California, is documented.[156] He tried his best to help endangered colleagues to extricate themselves from Nazi fangs and find their way to the United States, but with little success. Yet his genuine concern in these critical matters is touching, and his letters lay bare the soul of a man who cared about his fellow human beings, some of whom, like Prague opera director Karl Rankl, were not even Jewish.[157]

Neither was Alma Mahler-Werfel, the former femme fatale of Vienna and, just then, condescending anti-Semite that she was, married to the second of her "little Jews," Franz Werfel.[158] "Almschi," this awesomely gifted woman and superb manipulator of men, increasingly addicted to Benedictine liquor, had remained in touch with her old friend Arnold, who asked her in 1936, when she was still living in Vienna, to help in the transaction of some of his Austrian assets to the United States. After the Anschluss, Alma and Werfel were in France, he hesitating to leave his beloved Europe, and she restless, with little money, and dreaming of a new life in the United States. When in early 1939 Werfel was invited to New York, which gave the couple a chance to emigrate, Alma got her hopes up and informed Schoenberg that in the course of the transfer she was going to rely "*much* on your help." In April Schoenberg showed himself pleased, writing that their eventual arrival in California would be "a great relief and joy to us." In August he mentioned that Thomas Mann might help Werfel in the arrangement of a U.S. lecture tour. The Werfels joined the Central European circle of intellectuals and artists in California, after a perilous flight from France, in December 1940.[159]

It was Mahler-Werfel, whom Katia Mann has characterized in her memoirs as "by nature fairly evil," who committed an indiscretion that would cause what Stuckenschmidt later termed a "rare and utterly regrettable discord" between Schoenberg and Thomas Mann. Some time in the mid-1940s she insinuated to the composer that the poet was using central musical ideas of his in the conceptualization of a new novel, without at all acknowledging him.[160] This novel was *Doktor Faustus: Das Leben des deutschen Tonsetzers Adrian Leverkühn erzählt von einem Freunde.*[161]

The friendship between Schoenberg and Mann had always been tenuous at best, but it had been a mutually respected relationship. Mann, brought up on and aesthetically molded by Beethoven, Pfitzner, and especially Wagner, with singular preferences, such as the conducting art of Bruno Walter, and precious aversions, as the music of Richard Strauss, had once wanted to become a musician and now had a professional musician for a son—his youngest, Michael, a violist with the San Francisco Symphony. Apart from Walter, he also had several exiled musician friends, among them Lotte Lehmann, Krenek, Hanns Eisler, Toch, and, grating on Schoenberg, the composer's foil Stravinsky, whose charm beguiled the novelist.[162]

Katia Mann did not particularly like Schoenberg, whom she thought tyrannical, because in his presence one could not smoke, which made her chain-smoking daughter Erika suffer. And she thought his two darling boys, Ronnie and Larry, spoiled and extremely naughty.[163] Schoenberg and Mann had been in polite correspondence before 1933, but in California they almost became neighbors.[164] They would meet in their homes, at novelist Vicki Baum's or Salka Viertel's, perhaps even the Walters'.[165] Their relationship was tested in 1938–39 when Schoenberg tried some of his radical political ideas on Mann, concerning his new, militant, Jewish consciousness and skepticism toward democracy. Calling himself a "progressist conservative," he asked Mann for help in placing an article he had written for publication. The exchange about this left Mann clearly vexed; he replied politely that he was disturbed by Schoenberg's "violent attitude," no less than by his "spiritual disposition," which altogether he identified as being close to the fascistic. The poet laureate disapproved of a "certain proclivity to terrorism," which he found in contradistinction to the spiritual qualities of Judaism that Schoenberg so justly highlighted. Had Schoenberg not been Schoenberg, he might have had reason to feel embarrassed, but at the time, the incident did not affect the two men's relationship.[166]

In the fall of 1943 Schoenberg sent over to Mann the manuscript of his older and only partly finished composition, *Die Jakobsleiter,* along with a copy of his much earlier *Harmonielehre,* an unspecified edition. The writer found the former's religious poetry "half-baked" but took great interest in the textbook, not returning it to the composer for years.[167] At that time Mann was already well into the writing of his latest novel, *Doktor Faustus,* whose hero "finally now is going to be a *musician* (composer)."[168] Schoenberg did not know it, but already since the spring of that year Mann had been in the habit of sounding him (and other musicians) out about musical specificities.[169] And while Mann listened to Stravinsky, Krenek, or Walter explain things, he is alleged to have read Schoenberg's *Harmonielehre* in the winter of 1943–44. By the fall of 1944 he was bragging to an acquaintance how the novel's hero, the composer Adrian Leverkühn, "without knowing anything about the Viennese, invents the 12-tone technique, all by himself." In March 1945, Mann was ready to admit to Walter that "the 'new,' the 'radical' music, even the Schoenberg system," figured importantly in his new book.[170] Although the preserial *Harmonielehre* could have had little if anything to do with this, Mann was soon suffering from a bad conscience; "Schoenberg will quit his friendship," he brooded in September 1944.[171]

When the book was finally published in Stockholm in 1947, it looked as if the novelist had at least thought of Schoenberg, for between its covers, Adrian Leverkühn virtually recreated that master's serial method of composing. To conclude from this, however, that Leverkühn was in any way supposed to represent Schoenberg, would be erroneous;[172] Mann denied this instantly, and as Hans Vaget has recently reemphasized, although the novelist admittedly saw parts of his own persona in the fictitious composer, beyond that Leverkühn's character was a composite of several of his acquaintances, as were other characters in the book.[173] Besides, one has reason to believe that because of his pangs of guilt Mann would have taken care not to make the resemblance between Schoenberg and Leverkühn too obvious.

In any event, to try some fence mending, Mann had sent the book to Schoenberg with but a cryptic dedication, inscribed with his own hand: "To the Actual One"; yet he was under no illusion as to what the composer's eventual reaction would be.[174] When the whole extent of the insult had become clear to Schoenberg, he was understandably hurt. Several exchanges between the two aesthetes followed, some of them in the print media. Essentially Schoenberg demanded of Mann that he publicly admit to intellectual "robbery" and publish a full apology. Rather than going to such lengths, however, Mann decided to include an afterword with all subsequent editions of the novel in any language, stating that the "style of composition described in the 22nd chapter, twelve-tone or serial technique, in reality is the intellectual property of a contemporary composer and theoretician, Arnold Schoenberg."[175] To call the inventor of historic serialism "*a* contemporary composer" was yet another slight to Schoenberg, and in November 1948 he complained about it bitterly.[176] Throughout 1949 Mann, somewhat disingenuously, insisted that if Schoenberg wanted to make an enemy of him, he would not succeed.[177] In January 1950 Schoenberg wrote to Mann that he wished to "bury the hatchet"; Mann agreed this would be a good thing, but the acrimony remained, and the two men never saw each other again.[178] It was after Schoenberg's death in July 1951 that Mann wrote to Stuckenschmidt that as far as he was concerned, it had always been Schoenberg who had carried a grudge, again not admitting even in a word that it had been he, the novelist, who had violated the composer's integrity in the first instance. Stuckenschmidt later published that letter in his first biography of the master, conveying the impression that the two men had totally reconciled.[179]

Matters might not have deteriorated so much had Theodor Wiesengrund Adorno not become involved. The former German music critic belonged to the circle of experts Mann was starting to consult on a regular basis in the summer of 1943. Apart from a work about Beethoven's late period he was showing Mann the manuscript of his new book, *Philosophie der neuen Musik* (to be published in 1949), which contained some unpleasantries toward Schoenberg, later characteristically exaggerated by the composer.[180]

His father a Jew, the thirty-five-year-old Adorno had come to the United States, via Oxford, in 1938. Once a student of Bernhard Sekles, he had studied composition with Berg in Vienna in 1925, and from 1928 to 1931 had edited the progressive journal *Musikblätter des Anbruch*. Thereafter, until his emigration in 1934, he was working as a music critic and untenured university lecturer (*Privatdozent*) in Frankfurt.[181] He had some compositions to his name, enough at least for Schoenberg to count him as a member of his school, "without his having been my pupil."[182] In those days, Adorno was a true admirer of the founder of serialism; Schoenberg gave him his Frankfurt broadcast texts to read and considered collaborating with him on a "dictionary of musical (aesthetics or) theory."[183]

In 1934, himself an expert on the twelve-tone method, Adorno conveyed doubts about the entire concept to Krenek (fearing that the serialists would lapse into formalism), doubts which, reified, were imparted to Mann during their frequent meetings after July 1943. Although Adorno's criticism, as Mann himself observed, may have been of the sort advanced students are entitled to toward their teacher, it is possible that in the process of listening to Adorno, Mann was pushing Schoenberg the composer into the background and embracing Adorno as his musical mentor, which he would consistently acknowledge from 1943 to 1946: "The description of serial music and its criticism, reduced to dialogue, as is offered in the 22nd chapter of *Faustus,* is totally based on Adorno's analyses."[184] Adorno's influence was formally recognized when the novelist mentioned one half of his complicated surname, "Wie-sengrund," in chapter 8 of *Doktor Faustus.*[185]

By 1948 a reflective Mann began to distance himself from the music critic, deploring in October 1951 that Adorno was trying to create the impression that it had been he who "actually wrote the *Faustus.*"[186] Indeed, experts such as Vaget warn today that nothing could have been farther from the truth.[187] In October 1951 Schoenberg was no more. But in 1947 he had already been on to Adorno when he insisted that "Thomas Mann's Adrian Leverkühn does not know the essentials of composing with twelve tones. All he knows has been told him by Mr. Adorno who knows only the little I was able to tell my pupils."[188] Later still he grumbled that "this repulsive Wiesengrund-Adorno" might attack him with impunity (in *Philosophie der neuen Musik*), yet perhaps one could still "push his snout in."[189]

In the end, Schoenberg threw legitimate doubts on Thomas Mann's ability to understand serialism at all, when he once more elaborated that "Leverkühn is one of these amateurs who believe that composing with twelve notes means nothing else than the continuous application of the basic set and its inversions."[190] The Nobel laureate might have concurred. For in his 1951 letter to Stuckenschmidt he ultimately admitted that he understood the new music "only very theoretically. Though I know something of it, I cannot really enjoy and love it. I have after all publicly explained that the triad-world of the 'Ring' is basically my musical home."[191] Thus wrote Thomas Mann, who, despite several musical metamorphoses, had essentially remained a Wagnerian.[192] In matters concerning his own art, Schoenberg had left him behind.

Thomas Mann returned to Europe and, after his death in 1955, was buried there. The funeral for Schoenberg, the other exiled European, took place in California, with his national identity ultimately unresolved. After his disappointment with UCLA and after his surviving manuscripts, papers, and artifacts went to USC, that university, in 1974, established an Arnold Schoenberg Institute for the study of the life and work of the composer and facilities for music recital. But this foundation for Schoenberg's personal and artistic legacy proved to be merely a temporary one. By the 1990s, serious differences between the composer's heirs and USC administrators had developed; there was talk about the institute's dissolution or its move somewhere else: Besides such unlikely places as the University of Arizona, The Hague, Berlin, Vienna, and New York were mentioned. Then, by the spring of 1998, Vienna had been chosen (Berlin having missed out by a hair's breadth); a shipment from Los Angeles deemed to be worth tens of millions of dollars, including the master's piano and 160 original paintings, arrived in a new Arnold Schönberg Center in the Palais Fanto on Schwarzenberg-platz.[193] The opening ceremonies on 15 March 1998 featured the String Quartet No. 2 in F-sharp minor, opus 10 (1907/8), only partly tonal, and the String Quartet No. 3 (1927), with that ten-year interval essentially marking the transformation from expanded tonality to serialism.[194] It seemed that at least in spirit Arnold Schoenberg, the musician of contrasts, had been repatriated.

8

Richard Strauss

Jupiter Compromised

I

Of all the composers before him, Richard Strauss adored Mozart. He was especially fond of the "godly Mozart's" *Jupiter* symphony, which he loved to conduct and reflect about as a perfect work of art.[1] At the end of his long life, fond as he was of classical mythology, Strauss himself composed an opera around Jupiter—the god who had loved four mortal queens and sought the affection of the mortal Danae.[2] At the August 1944 Salzburg dress rehearsal, the composer's favorite baritone, Hans Hotter, performed in the male lead of *Die Liebe der Danae* to Strauss's exquisite satisfaction: "a real Jupiter of godly proportions."[3] The magnificent Hotter-Jupiter later gave his daughter Gabriele's hand in marriage to Strauss's grandson, Richard Jr., an act of serene, poetic justice. Hotter's Jupiter was the foil for Strauss's own. For Strauss himself was Jupiter.

During his lifetime Strauss, the acclaimed Jupiter of several composer generations, who had been called the successor to Wagner and Brahms before he was twenty-one,[4] in various ways touched the careers of the seven composers portrayed in the foregoing chapters, all arguably more mortal than Strauss himself. As we have seen in the case of Pfitzner, these encounters were not always pleasant. Pfitzner, of whom Strauss said in 1927 that he was cheap, a man who had habitually betrayed his wife Mimi with young conservatory students, apparently wanted Hugo von Hofmannsthal, Strauss's ingenious librettist and friend, to write an opera text for him also, which elicited sarcasm from both the composer and the author of *Der Rosenkavalier*.[5] By 1935 Strauss had had enough of Pfitzner's many needle pricks over the decades, complaining to a Nazi official that "this man constantly behaves most maliciously against me."[6] Whereas Kurt Weill as a young man was sufficiently impressed by Strauss to acknowledge him as one of the major influences (and Bertolt Brecht once maligned Weill as a "fake Richard Strauss"), Arnold Schoenberg proactively sought out the master's opinion on music he had written, if later having to endure Strauss's slight that he, Schoenberg, would have been better off shoveling snow.[7] Although in 1923 Strauss had rudely asked the young Hindemith why, with his talent, he would not compose decent music rather than that atonal stuff, two years earlier he had already informed his Vienna opera codirector Franz Schalk that in Donaueschingen he had heard "a very naughty, crazy, but rather promising quartet by Hindemith," whose skills as a performer he admired to the point of wanting to lure him to the Austrian capital as concert master. As already suggested, Hindemith would touch Strauss's own career rather significantly in the turbulence of the Third Reich.[8] To Werner Egk, in alliance with whom Strauss would face Joseph Goebbels over serious-music rights in 1941, Strauss reportedly said in his best Bavarian dialect around that time, with reference to Egk's *Columbus:* "So you are the new Meyerbeer. But without melody."[9]

Other colleagues were not stung by Strauss's sharp tongue. In 1942, fellow Bavarian Carl Orff was comforted that his *Carmina Burana* had been much enjoyed and that he was on the right track to good music theater, yet Strauss was impish when he suggested that Orff consult with Joseph Gregor for more fitting libretti—Gregor was currently the author suffering Strauss's daily contemptuous criticism.[10] Strauss may not have taken much notice of fellow Bavarian Karl Amadeus Hartmann, but after the catastrophe of 1945 it could not have escaped him to what exalted position that Munich composer had risen, one of whose first musical impressions had been *Salome*. Indeed, Hartmann confirmed that he would fully support the city's belated plans for celebrating Strauss's eighty-fifth birthday through a "Strauss Week" in 1949, although a few months later the master was dead. Yet it is also true that in Hartmann's own, later, programs of the Musica Viva, Strauss's compositions did not figure, because they predated the modern works now preferred by Hartmann and his circle.[11]

Strauss signed his letter to Orff with "Dr. Richard Strauss," as he would all his letters after receiving his first honorary doctorate from Heidelberg in 1903 (his second would come from Oxford in 1914).[12] Why would a man of his artistic standing consistently use such a token of bourgeois respectability, in Germany fitting a Gymnasium teacher or a barrister, but not a genius, Jupiter? The answer lies in Strauss's uncertainty about his own social origins and, consequently, an ongoing, compulsive need to assert and reassert himself vis-à-vis his peers and, especially, as Pamela Potter has observed, temporal authority, whatever and whenever that might be.[13]

Although Strauss's lineage on his mother's side was unquestionably of the wealthy Bavarian *haute bourgeoisie,* he himself maintained that his father Franz Joseph, the renowned hornist and music professor, had been the son of a tower keeper, since the Middle Ages a perfectly respectable position in Germany.[14] In reality, however, this father had been the illegitimate son of a lowly provincial court clerk, who had moved to his uncle, a small-town tower keeper in the Upper Palatinate near Bohemia, only later.[15] This knowledge must have filled the young Strauss with a profound sense of social insecurity, as it later did another young man born near Bohemia, destined to be Germany's Reich Chancellor, whose father, Alois Schicklgruber, was also illegitimate.[16]

Richard Georg Strauss was born on 11 June 1864 into a comfortable Munich home; his wealthy uncle on his mother's side, Georg Pschorr of the beer brewer dynasty, provided more than a minimum guarantee of material security. Indeed, in the early 1890s Onkel Georg financed a trip to Greece and Egypt for the young artist, for the sake of strengthening his health.[17] Eventually, the upwardly mobile Strauss family assimilated easily with Bavaria's social establishment, Richard's aunt Amalie Pschorr having married into a knighted family and his younger sister, Johanna, marrying a Lieutenant Otto Rauchenberger, who, as a general, was later ennobled. It fit this picture when Richard himself, in 1894, wed singer Pauline de Ahna, the daughter of a general serving in the Bavarian war ministry; Pauline Strauss was and always considered herself an "aristocrat."[18] Franz Strauss's final position was as a professor at the Royal Music School, which later became the Bayerische Akademie der Tonkunst.

Having served as a conductor under the rulers of the Kingdom of Bavaria, Dukedom of Saxe-Meiningen, and the Kingdom of Prussia until the end of World War I, Richard came to be in close contact with members of the higher aristocracy, to say nothing of dozens of lesser nobility. His respect for his employers, the princes, princesses, and their noble administrators, never wavered, although at times he could become impatient with some of the least artistically gifted, a Lieder-composing Weimar princess, for example, and even Kaiser Wilhelm II, who seemed to grasp nothing of what he was trying to do.[19] When on an extended, parentally financed visit to Berlin in 1883–84, Strauss enjoyed the company of young Prussian officers, whom he thought exemplarily well behaved.[20] Later, on a country estate near Naples, he basked in the benevolence of Italian Count Biagio Gravina and his wife, Blandine, the daughter of Cosima Wagner, herself born a countess.[21] Strauss liked the prospect of receiving a Meiningen ducal decoration for his work, and when he was so honored, he was beside himself with joy.[22] It was characteristic of this model subject that when the opportunity for dedicating a composition to his immediate superior, in this case Intendant Graf Georg von Hülsen-Haeseler (Berlin), presented itself, he seized it, although he had plenty of reasons to criticize the count in matters of cultural policy, affecting his own creativity.[23] Strauss was well settled in the feudal order of the outgoing nineteenth century when the Great War broke out, and when at its end in 1918–19 Bavarian Bolsheviks threatened revolution in his home ground of Munich and Garmisch, he was confident that loyal government troops would quash the anarchy to his satisfaction, as indeed they did.[24]

Predictably, during World War I Strauss was patriotic, as were equally prolific contemporaries, even those who would later extol the republic, for example, the sociologist Max Weber and the writer Thomas Mann. Especially at the beginning of the conflict, Strauss shared the general exuberance regarding the assumed superiority of the German cause and even, seen from the growing pseudo-scientific point of view, the superiority of the German race. "It is uplifting to realize," he observed to von Hofmannsthal in August 1914, "that this country and people are only at the beginning of a great development and must and shall obtain hegemony in Europe without question."[25] He admired the early victories of the imperial army and more than ever was convinced of "these Germans," whom he tought to be "a wonderful, strong people, still not touched much by culture, yet nonetheless strong and heroic."[26] Even toward the end of the war, when his enthusiasm had waned considerably, he implored his Parisian friend Romain Rolland to ensure that the French cease what had been imparted to him as "the bad treatment inflicted on poor German prisoners, who are suffering terrible inflictions, insults, and even torture, at the hands of your compatriots."[27]

Strauss's view of an unshakable, time-honored political and social order was but a larger dimension of the image he had of his personal situation and family life. For an artist of renown whose own father had risen from oblivion, it was essential that he keep his affairs respectable and under control. Hence Franz Strauss's admonishing letters to his son Richard, whom he suspected of living loosely in Berlin in the early 1880s, were quite unnecessary; the tall, handsome Richard, elegant and fluent in conversation, was not a rogue.[28] Having almost married into the then socially and economically imperiled Wagner family of Bayreuth (he had successfully avoided Cosima's promptings to wed her daughter Eva),[29] he married the talented and personable Pauline de Ahna, herself a model of beauty and respectability, if always with an uncommon temper. Because of this temper, Strauss was adamant that his critical parents, once and for all, accept his new wife unconditionally, so that he could continue what he needed: a harmonious family life.[30] He greeted the birth of his only child, Franz Alexander, in 1897 with enthusiasm; Franz would stick with him through the troubled National Socialist times as a sort of personal aide, even when the two of them had shouting matches because of Franz's predilection for some planks in the Nazi platform.[31] It was for the sake of personal and familial stability also that Strauss early on sought to make himself economically independent; while earning enough in his various positions as Hofkapellmeister, he truly came to riches after performances of his operas *Salome* (1905), *Elektra* (1909), and *Der Rosenkavalier* (1911). Having deposited what appear to have been millions of marks, the fruits of thirty years of work, with the London financier Sir Edgar Speyer just before World War I, he lost all of this when the British confiscated the money in August 1914, never to return it as part of Allied war reparations.[32] Undaunted, Strauss began anew, successfully securing his villa in Garmisch and the economic well-being of his small family, though it meant having to accept engagements overseas and to toil in positions of dependence until 1924, when he finally could do what he had wanted all along: retire to the Vienna home and his country house in Garmisch and compose, interrupted only by occasional conducting tours.[33]

Still, Strauss's prewar trust in British banks reveals yet another character trait that makes one doubt the one-sided portrait of a German chauvinist which has entered many post-1945 biographies.[34] Because of his urbane upbringing, which entailed recreational journeys to exotic places and concert tours in countries such as Brazil, something few other, older, German conductors could even dream of at that time, but also because of a keen intelligence that kept his mind open to international influences, Strauss, whatever he may have been as a citizen of Germany and Bavaria, also grew into a cosmopolitan, the likes of whom were rare in Germany before as well as after World War I.

He was "developing a taste for the English," the twenty-nine-year-old Strauss wrote home from Florence in 1893. He had met a young British girl on a ship from Naples, with whom he communicated poorly in four languages, including French, which he had learned passably in school.[35] Notwithstanding his patriotism, in September 1914 he went on record for refusing to sign a manifesto, authored by other German artists and intellectuals such as Gerhart Hauptmann and Thomas Mann, claiming that the German war was a fight of "Kultur" against Western money bags.[36] Toward the end of the war he welcomed the presence of French and Russians attending concerts in Switzerland—a neutral country.[37] By 1924—French troops had just withdrawn from an agonizing occupation of the German Ruhr Valley—Strauss was able to call Romain Rolland, the pacifist and humanitarian writer and Nobel Prize winner of 1916, his "best friend."[38]

Although Strauss seems to have harbored a lifelong suspicion of "republics," regarded newer overseas countries such as Brazil (whose audiences always cheered him wildly) as "colonies," and had a deep distrust of "Negroes," constituting one seed for his unmitigated dislike of jazz, he, unlike Pfitzner, accommodated himself well enough to postwar republican regimes.[39] For reasons not having anything to do with the establishment of the Weimar Republic, he left Germany in early 1919 for Austria for a five-year stretch, just as it came under a republican government of its own. Apart from inbred beliefs and hallowed traditions, Strauss seems to have judged political parties and regimes by the yardstick of how they treated culture, the way he understood it. Hence as early as 1890 he had alerted a no doubt shocked Cosima Wagner to the possibility of a Social Democratic government in Germany, or that party's majority in the Reichstag, for which one could hold out hope, as "all other political parties have sufficiently proved their 'culture phobia.'"[40] When it became clear that Germany had lost the war, he quickly adopted the truism that "historical facts just have to be accepted" and immediately entered into talks with republican bureaucrats regarding the administration of culture. One minister in Berlin, he wrote home to Pauline, was eager to deal with musician associations, and over such happy prospects it was worthwhile "forgetting about the entire stupid revolution."[41] After the end of his duties in Vienna in 1924 he still, derogatorily, called the First of May the "workers' holiday"— he, who had never even seen a proletarian's home from the inside.[42] To Strauss, ever suspicious of the United States and France, the German republic remained tolerable as long as it upheld (his) minimal cultural standard; when this became too difficult during the Depression because of financial cutbacks, Strauss came to compare it to the cultural level of "soccer and boxer-indulging England."[43] Nevertheless, Harry Graf Kessler's observation of June 1928 that Strauss advocated the necessity of a dictatorship at this time must be taken with a grain of salt, because Kessler himself discounted the sincerity of that remark, possibly made sarcastically, over a casual breakfast, in his own diary.[44] There is certainly no evidence that Strauss, out of temperament or political persuasion, welcomed the rise of the Nazi movement in the 1920s or early 1930s, before January 1933, let alone was close to its leaders, in the manner of Winifred Wagner. Quite the contrary. In 1930, after a friend had informed Strauss of his meeting with Alfred Rosenberg, who at that time was shoring up support for his racist cultural ideals among the German educated elite, including the Wagner heiress, Strauss described the Nazi Party philosopher as a "twenty-six-year-old adolescent, who did not have a clue."[45] January 1933, of course, represented the watershed. Significantly, Strauss was now of the opinion that Hitler was anything but a man who did not have a clue. To Munich Nazi Party official Paul Ehlers he said, a few months after the power change, that God could be thanked if finally Germany had a Reich Chancellor who was interested in the arts.[46] How its politicians handled art, especially music, and especially the works of Richard Strauss, was and would remain in the composer's opinion the foremost criterion of a German government's worth, above and beyond the ideas he himself had grown up with and largely abided by.

Strauss's appointment by Goebbels as president of the Reich Music Chamber in November 1933 was the logical consequence of a lifetime of efforts spent on behalf of the professional interests of German musicians in general and composers in particular. In this consistent endeavor, Strauss's eminent position as a nationally renowned artist had, early on and naturally enough, placed him in the front ranks of his musician colleagues. His initial taking charge of musicopolitical matters matched the pioneering role he was filling as composer and conductor in the two decades before World War I; he was a champion in both fields.

Since the late 1890s, Strauss's activities in the musicopolitical realm were predicated on personal aesthetic convictions that appear immutable from his formative years to the end of his life. As a conservatively inclined German conscious of the cultural roots of the *Bildungsbürgertum,* he preferred

German music over any foreign type, with few exceptions, and in particular he rejected what he considered to be a brand of light or even cheap French and Italian music, especially the compositions of Charles Gounod and Giacomo Puccini.[47] This, however, did not prevent him from appreciating non-German orchestras, whenever their qualities convinced him, as did that of Charles Lamoureux in Paris at the turn of the century.[48] Conversely, not all of the more current German works pleased him; most operas by Pfitzner and all by Siegfried, the son of Richard Wagner, to him were conceptually anathema.[49] To the same extent that he adored Richard Wagner's music, which, in his day, had been on the modernist edge, he detested the modernist experiments of contemporary progressives such as Schoenberg, Hindemith, and Alban Berg.[50] But apart from jazz, which was not even worthy of discussion, the bane of his musical existence was operetta, especially that by Franz Lehár.[51]

Under any regime, and the more powerful and influential he became himself, in his heart of hearts he wanted the abhorred musical genres censored so as not to endanger the serious works of his peers, and especially his own. Having himself reached the zenith of modernity with *Elektra* (the first joint creation, perhaps not coincidentally, with Hofmannsthal), just before World War I, Strauss was thereafter possessed of a sense of *sacro egoismo*. This he was the last to deny, as composer or conductor (in which field he considered as his equals only Arturo Toscanini and Arthur Nikisch, exempting not even Furtwängler).[52] In 1918 von Hofmannsthal once took him to task for this aloof attitude, fearing, with some justification, as events were to show, that if Strauss were to assume the codirectorship of the Vienna opera, he would then subordinate any of that opera's legitimate concerns to his own oeuvre. Significantly, Strauss contradicted his partner only mildly.[53] More mundanely, prima donna Lotte Lehmann, who adored Strauss, has called him "egocentric in the extreme."[54] Toward the end of his career, Strauss was convinced that he represented the *finale* of Occidental music, after Bach, Mozart, Beethoven, and Wagner. He rationalized his uniqueness thus: "I am the last mountain of a large mountain range. After me come the flatlands."[55] In a strictly traditionalist sense, he was of course correct.

The goals Strauss set himself in a sort of broad reform of the German music scene along aesthetic and organizational lines were practical and, to him, eminently reasonable ones. He wanted to implement available educational resources to elevate popular familiarity with music to the highest level possible. He wished to cut back qualitatively inferior and therefore bad municipal orchestras and operatic stages, regardless of a community's size. In 1913, for instance, he thought that the fair city of Nuremberg had a terrible orchestra, whereas smaller towns such as Quedlinburg or Krefeld had decent ones. Sufficient money should be expended to hire only the best musicians or singers, and for the sake of optimal quality he was not against the star system. He pleaded with the republic's foreign minister Gustav Stresemann to grant more official German honors to worthy foreign artists, commensurate with their reputation, so that foreign governments would treat visiting German artists like himself equally respectfully.[56]

Strauss's objectives for composers, whose situation he knew best, included better copyright protection of their works vis-à-vis publishers, preferred treatment for serious-music composers, and an extension of a creator's personal royalty margin for his estate from the present thirty to at least fifty years. These goals could best be achieved through a centralized organization of musicians as in a recognized interest lobby or union, and his and his associates' eventual plan of a central chamber as an effective administrative tool on behalf of all German musicians was in keeping with other such professional ideals of the post-World War I era, for instance, those of physicians and lawyers, matching the corporativist trend of the time.[57]

In conjunction with colleagues such as Max von Schillings, Friedrich Rösch, and Siegmund von Hausegger, Strauss began his activity on behalf of composers in the summer of 1898, when he tried to organize 160 colleagues in an association against publishers, theater managers, and concert presenters. With more than 100 behind him within a few weeks, he sought to reform the copyright law of 1870, which favored publishers over composers, by a legal extension of the thirty royalty years that had to be granted by parliament. A new copyright law was passed by the Reichstag in 1901, affording a broader basis of protection for literary and musical works but not yet extending the thirty-year limit. To push ahead with this and related goals (such as composers' control over reprints), Strauss, in that year, assumed the leadership of the Allgemeiner Deutscher Musikverein (ADMV), founded in 1859 by Franz Liszt. Two years later a more official alliance representing composers, the Genossenschaft deutscher Tonsetzer (GDT), was in place, soon incorporating over 200 members and whose presidium he also acquired. In 1915, after some composers had split from the GDT, another performing rights society, parallel and largely contradictory to Strauss's efforts, had come into existence, the Gesellschaft für musikalische Aufführungs- und mechanische Vervielfältigungsrechte (GEMA); it also included publishers. There were ugly court battles over jurisdiction, augmenting the confusion and legal limbo of composers. By 1930, GEMA and the GDT under Strauss had reached a mutual understanding with a view to fusion; at this point Strauss was worried once again over the strengthened predominance of music publishers and, among composers in a period of strong popular-culture growth, the preponderance of light-music and potentially wealthier composers over the serious-music ones.[58]

Because he had not achieved his musicopolitical aims in the past and thought that Hitler would be more sympathetic to the arts than any royal or republican cabinet had been, but also because, a conservative and social elitist by nature—I would prefer to call him an aesthetocrat—he put certain stock in authoritative decision making that would by-pass parliament, Strauss welcomed the coming of the Third Reich, hoping that it would help him on his way. Although he may have known better, he made light of its violent side. To his friend, the eminent publisher Anton Kippenberg, he wrote at the end of March 1933: "I have returned with great impressions from Berlin and am full of hope for the future of German art, once the first storms of revolution have subsided."[59] With the help of two assistants from the 1920's experience in the GDT—Julius Kopsch, a musician and lawyer, and Hugo Rasch, a composer and music critic—he managed to forge important working contacts with bureaucrats in Goebbels's new Reich propaganda ministry, within whose competence the attainment of his reform plans, especially regarding the composers' rights, rested. Toward that end, Strauss also continued to work for an amalgamation of his GDT with the old GEMA, which was directed by Leo Ritter, another lawyer, whom he was in the process of winning over. What aided Strauss here was that such a merger was wholly in the interest of the Nazi leaders, who championed centralization of any kind, as long as they had their stooges in the system.[60]

During the Bayreuth Festival in July, at which he conducted, Strauss was able to meet Minister Goebbels for the first time. Goebbels was suitably impressed by "this great musician" and duly made a note of the master's professional worries. A few days later he wrote to Strauss encouragingly, informing him that his ministry had already come a long way in consideration of the composers' concerns and that collaboration with the Reich justice ministry, for the sake of a definitive draft for a law to be promulgated, was now being enacted. At the end of the month Strauss was hopeful that his discourse with "the very art-inspired and sensitive Dr. Goebbels" was going to bear fruit.[61]

But a few days into August Strauss became aware that the Reich justice ministry's draft for a new composers' royalty law, which Goebbels had allegedly inspired, was not to his liking, for it was too longwinded and not yet squarely in the interest of his flock. Strauss thought that a Hitler cabinet should be able to issue something more forceful and direct, to a point where confusing "interpretations by lawyers" would not any more be necessary. Strauss was borrowing National Socialist jargon when he wrote that "meanwhile, new dynamics of the state have materialized through the National Socialist revolution, whose purpose is to lend a new content as well as new form to the entire public cultural life."[62] In the following weeks Strauss could not help but feel that Goebbels was stalling, and, mobilizing his Berlin assistants Kopsch and Rasch, he was eagerly looking forward to more talks with the minister.[63] Moreover, Strauss still had to work on Ritter to get Ritter and his GEMA fully over to his side.[64]

Goebbels clearly was playing for time, holding out promises of reform according to Strauss's guidelines in return for the master's clear commitment to serve the wider cultural policies of the new Reich, not merely the narrow interests of composers. A deal between the two men seems to have been struck during a personal meeting in the fall, when Strauss had come to realize that at the helm of some larger, Nazi-created organization he might be the internationally renowned figurehead the regime wanted, whereas at the same time he could implement all his manifold reforms, especially those concerning his nearest colleagues, if need be by fiat. This, then, was the immediate background to an understanding between Strauss and Goebbels that the composer act as head of a new corporativist professional chamber according to the fascist model now also successfully tried by dictators such as music-loving Mussolini (whom Strauss admired in any case), and that in return, and within that organizational framework, Strauss could service his detailed music-specific interests, those dear to his heart for decades. The pending consummation of the pact was symbolized in the second half of October, when Strauss's new opera *Arabella* was performed in Berlin, several times to a full house. Green with envy, Pfitzner's trusted mole Walter Abendroth reported to his mentor that during one evening the Führer and "half of the government" had been present. Hans Hinkel, Göring and Goebbels's special deputy for culture in Berlin, had applauded most excitedly.[65]

In his quest to control the politics of musicians in the Third Reich, Strauss was beset by a number of problems, more at the personal-relations rather than the administrative level. All things considered, because of the representation of these problems, then as now, they did more lasting damage to Strauss's image than he actually deserved. But he was by no means innocent.

Signally the most important of them was the so-called Walter affair. As far as can be reconstructed on an incomplete and conflicting source base, this is what happened. The Jewish Bruno Walter, permanent guest conductor of the Berlin Philharmonic, traveled from Leipzig, where he had been prevented by Saxon authorities from honoring one of his regular conducting engagements at the Gewandhaus, to the capital, to conduct there on 20 March, 1933. But on the day before, in the office of the prominent Jewish concert agency of Wolff and Sachs, he was told that the new Nazi propaganda ministry, represented here by State Secretary Walther Funk, had put pressure both on him and on agency proprietor Louise Wolff to desist from conducting, for otherwise order during the concert could not be guaranteed, meaning that the Nazis planned to disrupt it. On the other hand, the ministry appears to have insisted that the concert not be canceled, so that a substitute conductor became necessary. Louise Wolff and her daughter Edith asked Strauss, who happened to be in the capital, to step in for Walter. Upon Strauss's adamant refusal, an unknown conductor from Bremen was hastily contracted. However, Louise Wolff, whose deceased husband Hermann had known Strauss well since the 1880s, then implored Strauss to change his mind for a number of reasons, the most obvious being that the Bremen conductor would not draw any crowds. In these unsettling times she was in need of earnings and of a secured future for her agency; moreover, the Berlin Philharmonic, already deeply in debt, would stand to lose RM3,500 To make her arguments more persuasive, Wolff employed Strauss's well-known Berlin-based collaborators Kopsch and Rasch as go-betweens; Strauss was also told that before leaving Berlin for Vienna, Walter himself had recommended Strauss to Wolff. Convinced primarily by the plight of the orchestra, with which he had had a professional relationship for nearly fifty years, Strauss finally consented to conduct on the condition that his fee of RM1,500 go to the musicians, and the evening of 20 March was saved.[66]

By his various detractors, Strauss was promptly accused of self-interest, and as late as 1987 Gerhard Splitt has charged him with an "anti-Semitic act."[67] Unbeknownst to Strauss, the Nazis themselves lent substance to that charge by immediately claiming that Strauss had not allowed himself to be scared off by "threatening letters from Jewish-inflamed America."[68] To be sure, much of the opposition to the composer originated in the United States, where there was already a strong core of anti-Hitler musicians led by Toscanini.[69] Without knowing any of the background, Thomas Mann, Strauss's old adversary, registered his displeasure with Strauss one day after the event, calling him a "lackey."[70] Mann's children, Erika and Klaus, went farther, after a personal survey of the U.S. cultural and émigré scene. They accused Strauss of having replaced Walter, a few days before the Berlin affair, at the Leipzig Gewandhaus concert, even though Strauss had had nothing at all to do with the event.[71] Some years later, an equally deliberate and harmful distortion of the situation poured out of the United States from the pen of Friedelind Wagner, Winifred's defiant daughter, when she wrote that "scarcely was the ink dry on the newspaper announcing that Walter had been forced to resign, when Richard Strauss offered himself by wire as replacement for his old friend and colleague."[72] Seeing this interpretation right after the war, Strauss's longtime Swiss friend Willi Schuh, neither a Nazi sympathizer nor afraid to criticize the composer, made the truth known to the prospective German-Swiss publishers of Wagner's memoirs and thus, under the threat of a libel suit, had the incriminating paragraph changed.[73] Because Splitt's claim that Kopsch and Rasch had been sent by the Nazi regime to secure Strauss's cooperation, although unproved, has never been refuted, Strauss has been reproached for "opportunism" even in most recent times.[74]

There can be no argument that Strauss had been imprudent in agreeing to stand in for Walter after all, for he must have realized that charges of opportunism and anti-Semitism would be raised in the anti-Nazi camp, whether or not true. It may even be held that although Strauss, technically, was not opportunistic in accepting the conductor's date, because this was anything but a premeditated act, he also knew it would not hurt the copyright reforms he was trying to push through at government level, especially with Rasch and Kopsch involved. Yet although a case for Strauss as an anti-Semite can and will be made in a qualified fashion later, anti-Semitism had nothing to do with his initial decision not to relieve Walter, nor did it influence him in changing his mind several hours later. The instrumental factor was something else. As Michael Kennedy has stated unequivocally, Strauss "did not like Walter, nor did Walter like him."[75]

Their relationship went back to the late 1890s, and it was largely unpleasant. Walter, born 1876, had first heard Strauss in Berlin, when his *Tod und*

Verklärung was newly performed there. Walter's impression was mixed; he was "excited and disturbed, rather than deeply moved and uplifted."[76] In late 1898 Walter, who was then a young conductor in Riga, already envied Strauss for his court conductor's position in Berlin; a few months later he sarcastically remarked that Strauss's "mediocrity" was just right for Berlin and haughtily added that his, Walter's, brand of dynamic conducting was "actually quite superfluous."[77] In 1901, when Walter was briefly a Kapellmeister under Strauss in Berlin, he tended to compare the experienced maestro unfavorably with his idol Gustav Mahler.[78] But this did not keep him, two years later, from using Strauss for the premiere of a symphonic fantasy he had written; he himself thought it to be "original in its invention and strong in its feeling," as he tried to impress Strauss, asking for a hearing in Vienna. Evidently Strauss, the chairman of the ADMV, so far had looked favorably on Walter's efforts, and not least because of this the work was performed at the next music festival in Frankfurt in 1904.[79] But the incident had not brought Walter any closer to Strauss; on the contrary, in 1907 he talked to his new friend Pfitzner about all the negative aspects of the Vienna music scene, "all this dirt" (as opposed to Pfitzner's music), including the blossoming of *Salome,* "meaning the whole Strauss."[80]

Between 1911 and 1913 Walter discussed a senior conductor's job in Munich with the Royal Bavarian theater administration—Walter wanted to leave Vienna—which Strauss once again supported.[81] But as soon as Walter was appointed to the prestigious post, in January 1913, Strauss, still in Berlin at the time, felt neglected. Walter's first Strauss opera, *Ariadne auf Naxos,* was presented in January, not at all to the satisfaction of its creator. The two had a heated exchange about their differences in March.[82] Yet this was only the beginning: From then on Strauss never stopped complaining about the paucity of his works in the Munich seasonal repertoire. Strauss came to believe that Walter would go out of his way to conduct operas other than his own, for instance the lesser-known *Der Barbier von Bagdad* by Peter Cornelius (1824–74), a follower of Liszt and friend of Wagner. Strauss's agitation about this belief to his friend Hofmannsthal and his threat never to set foot on that Munich stage again got so bad that the poet had difficulty calming the composer down.[83] To be fair to Strauss, he had a point. It was Walter himself who admitted to Pfitzner in early 1921 that since August 1920, nine works of his had been staged, as opposed to only five of Strauss's.[84] To add insult to injury, Walter then attempted to coopt Strauss as an influential member in the founding of a Pfitzner Society, explaining disingenuously that "a Richard Strauss Society today would be senseless—today your name and oeuvre rule the musical world."[85]

However, over the years Bruno Walter became very secure in his conductor's shoes and, like Strauss, began acquiring world renown, and the tension seems to have eased. At the beginning of the 1930s Walter was conducting Strauss operas not only all over Europe but also in New York, where he had become a regular guest.[86] In the spring of 1933 therefore, though the earlier unpleasantries could not have been forgotten, Strauss hardly harbored a grudge against Walter, despite the fact that, incensed about all the adverse publicity affecting him after the March event and using his coarse Bavarian argot, in June 1935 he wrote to his new librettist Stefan Zweig of Walter as a *schmieriger Lauselumpe,* a "mean and lousy scoundrel."[87] Although Walter himself did his share to obfuscate the facts surrounding the unfortunate incident, never admitting, for instance, that he himself had asked Louise Wolff, through his wife, to second Strauss (as her daughter has testified he did), Strauss profited from him in the performance halls.[88] In the United States, Walter insisted on conducting Strauss's compositions before and during the war, for concert performances and radio transmissions, even though his close friend Erika Mann was adamantly opposed to this. Walter also differed with Otto Klemperer on this matter, who for his part was determined not to conduct Strauss for "as long as I possibly can."[89] Moreover, in 1947, when Strauss was the accused in a denazification trial, Walter defended the composer against Dutch charges that his *Metamorphosen* (1945) had been dedicated to Hitler.[90]

For Strauss, Thomas Mann played a negative key role throughout most of his life, and it was he and his aesthetic and political ideals that caused the maestro to stumble once again, in what has become known as the Mann Protest. This was an action by prominent conservative Munich citizens, most of them influential in the local art scene; its initiator was Walter's successor as Munich Generalmusikdirektor, Hans Knappertsbusch, who wanted to strike out as much against Mann as against Mann's friend and ally Walter. After a critical Wagner lecture by the Wagner disciple Mann, held at Munich University in February 1933 and then in a number of European cities, Mann was attacked, in an article published in the *Münchener Neueste Nachrichten* on 16 April for having belittled Wagner. The article was based on a Berlin newspaper report about Mann's speech in Amsterdam. Mann himself was reviled as an antinationalist, for his "cosmopolitan-democratic views." Apart from Knappertsbusch, Pfitzner (the former friend of Mann and increasingly alienated from Walter), Intendant Baron von Franckenstein, Professor of Fine Arts Olaf Gulbransson, Professor of Composition Siegmund von Hausegger, and Strauss were among the signatories.[91]

There has been speculation about why Strauss would have lent his name to what was essentially a cowardly action, for Mann was already in Switzerland at that time and could not properly defend himself in a Nazi state, which had endorsed the Protest through some politicians' signatures. Whatever else his motives, as in the case of Walter, sheer dislike of his adversary in this particular case would surely have been one. The relationship between Strauss, the most famous musician, and Mann, the most famous man of letters, however tenuous, may be traced to the end of the nineteenth century. In March 1884, Strauss, through his various connections in Berlin, got to know the Pringsheims, Mann's future parents-in-law, who invited Strauss to visit them in Munich, where Professor Pringsheim, a Wagnerian, taught mathematics at the university.[92] Strauss followed up on this, and by 1898 he had met Katia and her twin brother, Klaus, a budding musician, some of whose Lieder he later performed.[93] It appears certain that Strauss did not face Mann personally until January 1920, at the Walters' house for tea, long after Mann had married Katia in 1905.[94] Still, of those early years Katia Mann remembered later: "We knew Strauss quite well. I had already met him in my parents' home, and as a very young musician my twin brother revered him."[95]

Whereas Strauss does not seem to have taken notice of Mann's early writings, Mann himself was affected by Strauss's compositions at least by 1895, probably the just-premiered *Till Eulenspiegels Lustige Streiche*.[96] Mann's interest in Strauss's oeuvre grew with the premiere of *Salome,* which he attended in Dresden in 1905. Mann, who had just authored *Wälsungenblut,* a piece with incest at its core, was obviously fascinated by a work that was then considered the apex of decadence in opera.[97] But this endorsement changed after the premiere of *Elektra* in 1909, whose musical modernism Mann could not identify with, especially as he regarded Strauss's "progress" as "drivel," epigonal in the extreme after *Parsifal,* created by Mann's (and Strauss's) idol Wagner.[98] From then on Mann's appreciation of Strauss's works vacillated; he found *Der Rosenkavalier* stylistically awful, tried to drive a wedge between his friend, the poet Hofmannsthal, and Strauss, and turned, instead, to the austere Pfitzner.[99] *Die Frau ohne Schatten,* performed under Walter's baton in Munich in 1920, touched him with its "beauty of sound" but also with "triviality and ennui."[100]

Until today, and not unlike the case of Bruno Walter, speculation centers on two issues: Who had persuaded Strauss to join the signatories, and why, in the end, did he agree to sign? The questions are related, for whoever asked Strauss would have informed him of the vituperative purpose of the anti-Mann declaration. Mann himself records that a mutual friend told him in 1934 of Strauss's own version of the event, namely, that his old Munich colleague von Hausegger had pressured him to sign; independently of this record, it was alleged that Strauss had not even read Mann's disquisition. Yet Strauss reportedly defended himself by insisting that, after all, Mann had uttered unacceptable things about Wagner.[101] As for Strauss's responsibility, it is inconsequential whether or not he had seen Mann's piece or even the declaration before or after their publication. Strauss is known not to have informed himself of certain other documents issued in his name, which proved harmful to him in the end.[102]

As for the instigator, Hausegger's role is unlikely. At least two other persons could have led Strauss on: his good friend Gulbransson, who loved to draw the artist's remarkably beautiful hands, and Knappertsbusch, yet another musician whose conducting Strauss approved of and who served as one of Strauss's more regular Skat partners.[103] As for the Norwegian Gulbransson, he was not known to be excessively political and in addition was a very old and loyal friend of Katia Mann.[104] This leaves Knappertsbusch, and indeed he is the most plausible candidate for several good reasons. Stridently nationalistic and fundamentally in agreement with the Nazis, he had been the originator of the anti-Mann diatribe, because of Mann's close friendship with Knappertsbusch's rival Walter. It was he who had the largest stake in collecting as many signatures as possible.[105] Moreover, in a letter of 21 April now housed in the Strauss family archive, which I have found only recently, Strauss directed a strong request to the conductor that he meet with him, one day after a short sequel to the primary newspaper attack was published. The wording is significant: Strauss had to approach Knappertsbusch "in an urgent matter (regarding Thomas Mann)."[106] Strauss wanted to take Knappertsbusch to task for something, because he felt embarrassed.

What had happened here? That this entire action was out of character with Strauss's earlier attitude toward collective defamations of any kind is suggested by his refusal to sign anti-Allied statements during World War I. He was reminded of this when, on 19 April, Peter Suhrkamp, of the S. Fischer firm, Mann's publisher, sent a letter to him. In this document, heretofore also unknown, Suhrkamp did not mince any words. He wrote that he was surprised to find Strauss's name among those of the cosignatories and, knowing Strauss, at first thought this a mistake. Evidently Strauss had not seen Mann's text before he agreed to sign. Had Strauss compared the Protest with Mann's actual speech? For clearly, neither bore any resemblance to the other. Was it not clear that, contrary to the accusations, Mann was a devotee of Wagner? Anyone who knew Mann's style would be able to interpret the meaning underneath correctly. "I know full well that this protest was not directed against Thomas Mann's essay on Wagner, but against his political stance, and that, toward that end, the Wagner essay was merely being used. You of all people, revered Doctor, could never agree to a method that defames the work of an artist because of his political conviction." And with that Suhrkamp included a copy of Mann's Wagner essay, which had just appeared in the *Neue Rundschau*, expressing his hope that Strauss could redress the damage.[107] It stands to reason that the composer then read Mann's speech for the first time and was able to compare it with the hate piece. Unfortunately, his urgent call to Knappertsbusch, on receipt of Suhrkamp's letter, remained in vain.

It is still not crystal-clear why Strauss so disliked Thomas Mann; the records are silent on this point. Was it because Mann early on appreciated Pfitzner's music but found fault with Jupiter's? Was it because Mann came to embrace the Weimar Republic, whereas Strauss remained, at best, impervious? Was it that Strauss's sense of Eros disagreed with Mann's own? Or was it, as Hans Vaget has eloquently suggested, in rivalry, albeit with dissimilar means, for the mantle of Richard Wagner?[108]

Strauss became embroiled in two lesser incidents that, rightly or wrongly, laid him open to criticism even by contemporaries. One involved the wrongful dismissal by Saxon Nazis of Dresden Generalmusikdirektor Fritz Busch shortly before the Walter affair. On 7 March 1933, Busch was placed on a permanent leave of absence, which then turned out to be irreversible, because he appeared to the Saxon Gauleiter Martin Mutschmann and his cronies, even with Berlin disagreeing, as an enemy of the regime.[109] Strauss was immediately compromised, for he had planned the premiere of his new opera *Arabella*, "to a lissome musical setting in the waltzingly tuneful manner of *Der Rosenkavalier*," for 1 July within the projected Dresden Festival (the Saxon capital was his favorite venue for premieres). Moreover, the work was dedicated to Busch and the Dresden Intendant Alfred Reucker, who had now also been fired.[110]

Promptly, Strauss and the new Nazi-imposed Intendant Paul Adolph found themselves in a quandary. As far as Adolph was concerned, he insisted on honoring the contracts by having the opera staged as planned, under the conductorship of a new maestro not yet appointed. As the successor to Reucker, Adolph wished to profit from that artist's reputation, but he also needed to bow to the regime leaders, for his wife was Jewish. In one hard letter to Strauss, Adolph mentioned the possibility of litigation, not so much to target the composer, whom he preferred to compel morally, as to harm his publisher Otto Fürstner.[111]

Strauss's attitude was much more differentiated. He valued the loyalty of Busch and wanted to reward him for it, provided his "leave" was really just a leave; besides, he knew that the experienced conductor would guarantee a splendid performance. Hence, at first he considered moving the premiere to another stage, if necessary, under a conductor congenial to his works, and postponing the date of 1 July. He thought at first of Erich Kleiber, who was, in fact, an early candidate as Busch's successor in Dresden. Strauss's position was fairly strong, for he had the unqualified backing of his old influential friend Heinz Tietjen in Berlin, as well as that of many of the Dresden musicians. When Kleiber's cooperation became unrealistic (although Tietjen would have released him from his Berlin contract early), Strauss and Tietjen considered the possibility of asking Clemens Krauss in Vienna, who already had demonstrated a special affinity with Strauss's works.[112]

By June 1933 matters had developed to the point where it was certain that Karl Böhm would soon become Fritz Busch's replacement as Generalmusikdirektor of the Sächsische Staatstheater but in the meantime Krauss would premiere *Arabella* on 1 July, as planned.[113] And so it happened. One influential critic commended work and performance without being enthusiastic.[114] But that was not the end of it for Strauss.

As in the case of Walter, he was now maligned for having violated the interests of a man who was, by enemies of the Nazi regime, generally viewed as one of its victims. One of these was Fritz Busch's younger brother Adolf, the violinist, an uncompromising foe of the Nazis and living in Switzerland, where he befriended and influenced Thomas Mann.[115] Fritz Busch himself and his wife, Grete, were furious with Strauss, controlling sentiment against him from their various abodes of exile, although Busch much later conceded that Strauss had done nothing more than to honor his contracts. But by February 1937 Strauss had broken off all relations with Busch, noting that "he is deadly opposed to me."[116]

The irony here is twofold. First, Strauss had really tried, through very skillful maneuvering in the beginning to save the opera for Busch, and in the spring of 1934 he even attempted to get his friend Reucker rehabilitated, through personal intercession with Mutschmann and his henchman Manfred von Killinger, as well as with Tietjen, if to no avail.[117] Second, Fritz and Grete Busch were not bona fide refugees from the Nazi regime. Although they had been wronged by the Saxon administration, the conductor had always had Göring on his side, through whose good offices he had been hoping to land a position as Staatsoper director in Berlin—a solution Hitler himself would have approved. But when this came to naught, the Buschs were sent on a semiofficial culture and propaganda mission to Argentina, which Hinkel had prepared and chaperoned from afar, and only thereafter, still feeling unrewarded by the regime, did the stubborn Busch take his final leave from Germany.[118]

The last episode played in Bayreuth. If it is difficult to fault Strauss for his handling of the Dresden crisis, the same cannot be said in the case of the Wagner festival in the summer of 1933. Part of Toscanini's April protest, in the wake of the Walter affair, had been a letter to Hitler refusing his already promised participation in the July Bayreuth events. No one, including Winifred Wagner, could persuade the maestro to change his mind.[119] Thereupon Frau Wagner and Tietjen prevailed on Strauss to take Toscanini's place and conduct *Parsifal* in Bayreuth. Strauss complied, again without taking a fee; *Parsifal* was a success.[120]

Strauss was once more attacked for this act, by, among others, his current librettist, Stefan Zweig.[121] But in a letter Strauss penned for Winifred Wagner in September we may at least find the beginnings of an explanation, if by no means an excuse. He characterized his festival role as "my modest help for Bayreuth," by way of repaying a great debt he owed to the master of masters, Wagner.[122] Subjectively, this feeling of debt might be acknowledged. A special significance was attached to Strauss's choice of *Parsifal,* because it was long considered by the Bayreuth clan to be the quintessential Wagner oeuvre, willed by Wagner himself to Bayreuth alone. Strauss had promised Cosima Wagner in 1899 to preserve this monopoly for Bayreuth, if, as he was hoping, his copyright reforms were successful. They were not, a "Lex Parsifal" or "Lex Cosima" was never passed by the Reichstag, and consequently the opera was in the public domain from 1913, thirty years after its composer's death. During the stewardship of Winifred Wagner after World War I, she and Strauss became closely allied over the question of extending the thirty-year protection period in general and establishing a special Bayreuth privilege for *Parsifal* in particular; Frau Wagner, in fact, was able to bank on an October 1923 promise by her house guest, Hitler, that as soon as he was the head of the German government, that privilege would be written in stone. Strauss acted in the interest of the Wagner family when he asked Hitler, during the festival, for a 1 percent royalty levy on all Wagner performances in Germany, for the benefit of Bayreuth. At the time, Hitler refused; despite his Bayreuth meeting with Goebbels, Strauss himself had not yet finalized his reform of the copyright system.[123]

Strauss's presence in Bayreuth hence was the result of artistic loyalties, the function of a tactical alliance in matters of copyright reform with the present mistress of the Green Hill, and, without question, the maestro's own vanity, tempered by an overall sense of moral and political indifference which, tactical and calculated, bordered on the unconscionable. Tactlessness is the least of the misdemeanors one could charge Strauss with here. To accept any of the aforementioned explanations as excuses is illegitimate, for doing so would open the floodgates to apologists.[124]

II

To claim, as both his detractors and defenders have done, that Strauss as president of the Reich Music Chamber (RMK) was naive, not really functioning, or duped, because he was fundamentally an "apolitical" artist, amounts to the simplification and even misrepresentation of some very complex issues.[125] Strauss himself gave rise to this widespread misunderstanding when he insisted, in his now famous Gestapo-intercepted letter to Stefan Zweig of 17 June 1935, that he had only "mimicked" the president.[126] But as new archival evidence shows, and despite Strauss's own self-depiction as apolitical, nothing could have been further from the truth.[127] In keeping with his pre-November 1933 objectives, Strauss was a sincere and dedicated RMK president, and he thought of himself as a consummate politician, as, indeed, he had been as leader of the ADMV and GDT. The reasons for his failure by the spring of 1935 have to do rather with his idiosyncratic administrative style, his reluctance to identify himself with the totalitarianism of the Nazi regime, and, not least, with his personal vanity and huge professional self-interest.[128]

Part of the conventional interpretation is that Strauss became president of the RMK on 15 November 1933 without even having been asked.[129] This is a myth. As a logical consequence of the bilateral dealings between Goebbels and the composer since the spring, Strauss received a telegram on 10 November 1933 from Ministerial Counselor Hans Rüdiger of the Promi, asking him whether he wished to accept the position and participate in the opening festivities on 15 November.[130] Although we do not have Strauss's answer in writing, we must assume that he went through the formal motions of agreeing. Strauss was present at the opening of the overarching Reich Culture Chamber (RKK) in Berlin, where he conducted his own *Festliches Präludium*.[131] Goebbels then decided, as president of this RKK, to grant Strauss a dual appointment, both as RMK president as well as "Leader of Professional Composers," a corporativist office which Strauss had occupied for some time and Goebbels thought just right for inclusion in the new music chamber. (There were parallel departments for musicians, headed by violinist Gustav Havemann, and eventually for choirs, headed by theologian and church musician Fritz Stein.)[132] In the following months, Strauss, as RMK president, promulgated impressive enactments. Some of these were the attempt to centralize all musicians by a decree of 15 December 1933; summoning all German composers to appear at a Composers' Festival in Berlin on 18 February 1934; Strauss's elaboration, on that occasion, of the broader aims of future German music policy, largely along corporativist lines; and the prohibition of particularist lobbies acting locally and without authorization from the Berlin-based RMK.[133] For Strauss, these directives were exercises in authoritarian decision making, of the kind he may have wished for in republican times, but they did not amount to totalitarian arbitrariness.

In keeping with his "sharply delineated conception of art," Strauss had both a more narrow and a broader agenda, the first of which marked a direct continuation of his pre-RMK policy and in which, characteristically, he was most successful, and the latter of which he pursued less vigorously, with correspondingly disappointing results.[134] On the top of his list was, of course, the redoubled pursuit of copyright protection for composers. A new organization, the staatlich genehmigte Gesellschaft zur Verwertung musikalischer Urheberrechte (Stagma), was created by the late spring of 1934, with the help of Goebbels's State Secretary Funk, rendering all precursors on the publishers' or composers' side obsolescent or extinct. Located within the RMK, Strauss was the head of Stagma, and Leo Ritter, once on the other side, his loyal subordinate as its managing director.[135]

The attempt to extend the copyright period for composers from thirty to, ideally, seventy years took Strauss somewhat longer, and to reach a qualified success by the end of 1934, he had to solicit the help of music lover Hans Frank, Bavarian minister of justice and extraordinary justice commissioner in Berlin. When Goebbels finally consented to Germany's adherence to what was the international Berne Convention, he conceded only fifty years' protection, which had to dissatisfy Strauss's ally Winifred Wagner, whose father-in-law had been dead for over fifty years, and thus his master creation *Parsifal* would remain unrepatriated to Bayreuth. But Strauss and Wagner considered this solution merely provisional, hoping for a seventy-year term sometime in the future, through Hitler himself, whom Wagner knew well and to whom Strauss was talking frequently these days.[136]

Yet another area in which Strauss scored creditably on behalf of the RMK was that of international composers' cooperation. Strauss had some vested interests in this cooperation because the international body from which Germany seceded in the spring of 1934, the International Society for Contemporary Music (ISCM) on which Karl Amadeus Hartmann depended, promoted what Strauss and the Nazis regarded as atonal music. Thus in February 1934, at the German Composers' Convention in Berlin, Strauss sought to assemble congenial (meaning traditionalist-oriented) composers from countries neutral or friendly to Nazi Germany, on the model of the ADMV, now presided over by his friend von Hausegger. The Counseil Permanent pour la Coopération Internationale des Compositeurs was founded on 6 June 1934 in Wiesbaden to compensate for Germany's abandonment of the ISCM, but also to insist on the composers' royalty rights (hence aiding Strauss's other ongoing battle). Initially thirteen nations were involved, but soon the number grew to about twenty. Here Germany secured its hegemonial claim by having Strauss appointed president. As in the case of Strauss's earlier communication with Stresemann, it was clear that, from his point of view, the more that agreeable (i.e., nonoffensive) foreign composers could be performed in Germany, the more his own works, and those of his acceptable German colleagues, would be played abroad. Among the foreign composers Strauss favored most were the Frenchman Paul Dukas (1865–1935) and the Italian Adriano Lualdi (1885–1971), but he also favored Gian Francesco Malipiero and Ottorino Resphigi, again from Italy, Ernst von Dohnányi, from Hungary, and Edward Elgar, from Britain. As Fred K. Prieberg has rightly observed, they were all decidedly of the second rank and hence no competition to Jupiter. When, in December 1934, Carol-Bérard, the French delegate to the Conseil, planned the first French "non-atonal, international music festival" for the summer of 1935 in Vichy—after an initial German meeting at the Hamburg Tonkünstlerfest earlier that year—Strauss thought this extremely important, as a chance for "those of our German composers, who up till now have not been featured abroad." Clearly Strauss was flattered in the role of champion for his lesser national peers.[137]

As for the rest of his agenda, the quality of music to be enjoyed by Germans was important to Strauss. Naturally, he was mainly concerned with opera. Again he expanded on ideas he had held for decades; now he thought the time had come for their realization. Operettas, especially those by Lehár, should be banned, perhaps to the circus; Offenbach's *Orpheus in the Underworld,* Johann Strauss's *Die Fledermaus,* and his *Zigeunerbaron* might be regarded as exceptions. Strauss hated potpourris, snippets of operas, especially by Wagner and himself, played, in the worst of cases, by light-entertainment orchestras at resorts. In line with his quest for German composers' copyright protection, he wished to reduce operas by Frenchmen and Italians, such as Verdi and Puccini, whose works were already in the public domain and thus cheaply performed, in favor of contempory German or Austrian works. In any concert or opera situation Strauss wanted to have no more than one third of foreign music included. Not surprisingly, his overall judgment was highly subjective; in a wish list of operas to be favored or reintroduced to German stages he mentioned *Ingwelde* by his friend Max von Schillings, *Der faule Hans* and *Wem die Krone* by his long-forgotten mentor Alexander Ritter, and—bowing to Bayreuth—even *An allem ist Hütchen schuld* and *Sonnenflammen* by the long-ignored Siegfried Wagner. After a national survey had been done, he must have noted to his satisfaction that all his significant operas were being performed and most of Richard Wagner's, and also that the despised Cornelius was absent. Whereas he did not think that Pfitzner's *Das Herz* was worthy of consideration, he insisted that Beethoven's little-known incidental music *Die Ruinen von Athen* (1811) be offered—an arrangement by himself. On no account did he accept Gounod's *Faust,* Rossini's *Guillaume Tell,* and Verdi's *Macbeth,* because in his experience they always came out mangled.[138]

To ensure that quality opera would survive in Germany, Strauss, at another level of his reform attempt and in consultation with Tietjen, wished to redefine the performance parameters. This called for some organizational changes, but here, too, he was quite sure of himself. Because in his opinion too much mediocrity was spread over too many operatic venues, he wished to consolidate the stages, weed out incompetent artists, and increase incentives for the superior ones. Strauss always valued the leading singers of their day and, not without using his rustic charm, was willing to go to great lengths to secure them. In July 1919 he wanted to have famous soprano Lotte Lehmann put in a "suitcase" and delivered to him in person, so she could not elude the role of the dyer's wife for the premiere of *Die Frau ohne Schatten* in Vienna later in the fall.[139] On that occasion, Lehmann received the highest possible fee permitted by the Austrian ministry of finance.[140]

According to Strauss, some smaller opera houses, such as the one in Eisenach, should be closed altogether, because, understaffed, they performed "caricatures" of serious works, whereas others, like Gera's and Stuttgart's, should be enlarged and enriched. In constant touch with Tietjen, he wrote to Göring in January 1934 that he could salvage the national opera situation with an additional budget of RM10 million, including higher fees for better singers. Truly able musicians might be kept on beyond their regular retirement age. He was not happy with intendants such as Wilhelm Rode at Goebbels's own Deutsches Opernhaus in Berlin. The propaganda minister wanted the Deutsches Opernhaus to compete with Göring's prestigious Staatsoper, but Strauss thought it hopelessly inferior. He preferred to see it reduced to a sort of pops opera to start familiarizing the masses with high culture.[141]

Indeed, Strauss was concerned about proper musical education as well, especially that of young singers, the better to profit for his own purposes. He wanted private music instruction in the home revivified and toward that end encouraged the production of thousands more upright pianos and the graduation of legions of music teachers. Since January 1933 he had become worried about pubescent youths spoiling their voices, because of the constant demand for singing in the streets by various paramilitary formations, above all the Hitler Youth. The general level of musical sophistication should be raised by teaching pupils harmony, counterpoint, and analysis in postelementary schools in order to have more knowledgeable audiences for the operas. Alas, both Professor Stein, the RMK's supervisor of choirs, and Professor Karl Straube, director of Leipzig's famous Thomaner boys' choir, issued warnings. Stein thought Strauss's demands unrealistic, because secondary-school students "could not even read music," and Straube explained that his Thomaner were not interested in becoming professional musicians and hence did not need to be that highly qualified.[142]

Strauss's failure to implement most of his music reforms was predicated on his style of administration and his personal or institutional relationships with regime leaders. As RMK president he enacted policy in two mutually conflicting ways, eventually resulting in a state resembling bureaucratic chaos. The first group of Berlin subordinates with whom he dealt were handpicked men from the preregime days, whom, he thought, he could trust; the second group consisted of representatives of the RKK or the Promi, chosen by Goebbels or Hinkel, or, out of necessity, by Strauss himself, who were much too prominent and self-assertive for the composer to like. These groups were infiltrated by moles, beholden to one or two Nazi potentates with their own vested agendas, notably Bavarian Minister of Culture Hans Schemm, Deputy Führer Rudolf Hess, and, especially, Nazi Party ideologue Alfred Rosenberg. To all intents and purposes Strauss, mostly in Garmisch and hence an absentee president, delegated authority to the first group, which he then expected to act according to his wishes, but then he counterbalanced such power-of-attorney by arbitrarily weighing in with his own direct orders, making for anarchic leadership in the end.

Usually, the first-mentioned group of Strauss loyalists could accept this mixed regime style of trust and dictatorship without being thrown too much out of kilter, but they were a remarkably weak and craven lot. Not coincidentally—and this was an aspect of Strauss's initially keen sense of politics—most had solid regime connections. The lawyer, Julius Kopsch, was a member of the Nazi Party and Rosenberg's Kampfbund für deutsche Kultur, since the days before 1933, when educated Nazis such as Winifred Wagner tended to be attracted to it. Composer Hugo Rasch, who had fought with Strauss against excrescences such as jazz since the 1920s, was a leader in the Stormtroopers (SA), a party member, and chief music critic at Rosenberg's influential daily, the *Völkischer Beobachter*. Leo Ritter, soon Strauss's exclusive creature, joined Rasch's SA unit, later also becoming one of its leaders. Strauss hired two other cronies along the way, first Gerd Kärnbach as manager of the composers' section on 15 November 1933, then Hermann Stange, who eventually was appointed RMK deputy president. Strauss practiced favoritism here: Stange had featured his works as Generalmusikdirektor in Sofia, Bulgaria, before the political changeover, and in April 1934 found himself looking for a job in Germany, with Strauss honoring the principle of quid pro quo.[143]

The second, not exclusively Strauss-appointed, group of men consisted of Heinz Ihlert, a small businesman, occasional piano player, and Nazi Party member whom the Promi had installed as general manager of the RMK; Ihlert's protector Professor Gustav Havemann, the musicians' section chief and once a prolific but now fading solo violinist with a questionable Marxist past (all the more loyal he would prove to Goebbels); and Furtwängler, picked by Strauss so that he could contain him and charged with the responsibilities of a vice president.[144] These three men, along with some others like Hausegger and Hans Pfitzner (who predictably remained invisible) were invited to the presidial council meetings, held at regular intervals in

Berlin, most of which Strauss missed. Others again, like Stein, joined later. Ihlert was always present, often in a presiding function—surely important, for it was here that larger and smaller issues of policy were aired and recommended for adoption. But because Ihlert was also at the immediate end of Strauss's direct command line from Garmisch to Berlin, he turned out to be the one person who was in the know and held all the strings.[145]

What followed after 15 November 1933 was a carousel of intrigues, wire pulling, and internecine battles, with Strauss often not knowing what was going on, or oblivious to it, but being, of course, the object of much of this and held responsible in the end. In early 1934 Havemann began these rounds by using the absence of the master from Berlin as a pretext to assert greater powers for the presidial council.[146] For his part, Ihlert, certainly in cahoots with Havemann, sought to increase his own influence in the council, especially in the absence of Furtwängler.[147] But no sooner had Strauss dressed down Havemann than he had to suffer his first real blow, when it turned out that his helper Kopsch was revealed as having a shady past, including sexual harassment of office secretaries and financial irregularities. Nazi authority investigations into Kopsch's past took months and detracted from Strauss's authority; Kopsch was finally dismissed from the RMK in October 1934, but a few months later won a lawsuit against the chamber, with financial penalties, which hurt Strauss even more.[148] During those months of 1934, Gerd Kärnbach, Strauss's other assistant, was found wanting and also was let go in the fall.[149]

Some time early in 1934, Furtwängler was beginning to make trouble. He complained to Strauss that he was not being apprised sufficiently about matters concerning the RMK, and he insisted on his authority. Strauss's sarcastic reaction from Garmisch was that as vice president it was certainly legitimate for Furtwängler to convene the presidial council to keep himself abreast of things, so why did he not do it? Indeed, until April or so, the rivaling conductor presided over several Berlin meetings, but by summer he was already too busy. Although Strauss had appointed Furtwängler himself for tactical reasons, the whole man was anathema to him, one reason being Furtwängler's systematic neglect of Strauss's operas at the Staatsoper. Therefore by November 1934 Strauss had concluded that "the harmful Furtwängler must be booted from the presidial council." Without Strauss's own doing, this was to transpire at the beginning of December, with the onset of the Hindemith scandal, implicating Furtwängler.[150]

In the final analysis, this series of frictions was reduced to a confrontation between Strauss and the Promi-appointed Ihlert; it was Ihlert who began to tie the noose for Strauss. In April 1934 he complained to the RMK president that "in most cases, there was no proper bookkeeping" in the chamber; this was a pretext for him to become more active.[151] Predictably, Strauss charged Ihlert a few weeks later with setting up his own "side government."[152] In August, Strauss stated flatly that at the Berlin RMK everybody was constantly conjuring up the "leadership principle." But when the so-called leader issues directives, said Strauss, "those are not being followed by most of my associates, instead they are sabotaged."[153] Around that time strawmen around Hess and Rosenberg were conspiring against Strauss, malevolently citing his almost total dependency on Ihlert.[154] By October Strauss had decided that none of the meetings in Berlin were sensible; nonetheless, he once again tried to strengthen his rule by emphasizing the powers he had delegated to Rasch.[155] In mid-November, against the background of those troubles, Strauss was thinking of throwing in the towel. But his two reasons for staying on thereafter were the unfinished business surrounding his precious copyright reform and the unfolding demise of Furtwängler—any resignation at that time could have been misinterpreted as Strauss's solidarity with the conductor.[156] Matters were exacerbated in early 1935, when, after Furtwängler's dismissal, Ihlert himself, with Havemann's help, aspired to the position of RMK vice president, a post that Strauss defiantly handed to his ally Stange. It was Stange who now bore the brunt of further attacks, with Strauss himself simply staying put in Garmisch.[157] At the end of June his prestige suffered further when Friedrich Mahling, long an advocate of musicians' concerns and now the publisher of a RMK-internal music journal, was dismissed, allegedly because he had employed a non-"Aryan" as his assistant.[158]

Whatever the extent of Strauss's failure as a politician within Goebbels's cultural empire, there is no question that his role there was political, and that the failure—apart from his absenteeism and tactical mistakes—was based, to a large extent, on a policy not dictatorial enough. Strauss was a right-wing conservative who liked the glitter of the dictatorial tools he saw in action after January 1933, but he was too much steeped in a traditional bourgeois world with its broad political spectrum, rather than a one-dimensional, revolutionary-totalitarian one, to understand the real makeup of the Nazis and to use those tools efficaciously himself.

This is why Strauss talked a lot about "censorship" and "proscription" but never managed to implement them. To him it was unfathomable to prohibit a Mahler symphony, ever, and he welcomed the presence of a "foreigner" such as Toscanini at the Salzburg Festival in 1934 even after the scandal of Bayreuth in 1933.[159] In spite of his personal opposition to atonal music, Strauss had enough influence in the presidial council to rule out the censorship of atonal compositions by the RMK.[160] The attempt by the Nazis to replace Mendelssohn's immortal incidental music to *A Midsummer Night's Dream* with house-made "Aryan" compositions in 1935 made him cynical, and to Karl Böhm he joked that his own Egyptian *Helena* was not of "Teutonic origins."[161]

Although, as will be explained later, Strauss could never fully rid himself of the vestiges of an early brand of anti-Semitism from his youth, his policy in the RMK was for the Jews, not against them. For the RMK, Strauss had not endorsed Article 10 of the first implementation decree of 1 November 1933, subsequent to the law establishing the overarching RKK, providing the "legal" means for the exclusion of Jewish musicians. In fact, in December 1933 he had drawn up RMK statutes of his own that never mentioned

Jews, though this was unheeded in Berlin.[162] In 1934 he hinted to Göring that with the progress of anti-Semitic policy in the Reich, the disallowance of Jewish audiences in "Aryan" concerts was not conducive to the financial state of the already suffering orchestras.[163] Under his headship, the RMK presidial council decided not to press for the dismissal of the non-"Aryan" conductor of the music society "Concordia."[164] When, as he frequently did, at the turn of 1934 Goebbels once again called for a quicker solution of the "Jewish Question" in the music chamber, Strauss considered that an "embarrassment," declaring that he wished to have "no active part in it."[165] Later he said that such anti-Jewish measures were a violation of "all established rules of decency."[166] Finally, in May 1935, Ihlert used Strauss's refusal to cooperate in these matters as a special weapon in his cabal to unseat him.[167]

Strauss proved tolerance and human decency in two remarkable cases, both of which had the potential to contribute to his downfall. In the first he defended the renowned music critic Hans Heinz Stuckenschmidt, that staunch champion of atonality, from the vicious attacks of Nazi music writer Fritz Stege, first a favorite of Rosenberg and then of Goebbels.[168] In early December 1934 Strauss objected to the fact that Stege—and others like him—polemicized against Stuckenschmidt, as if he had to be singled out. Stuckenschmidt was a much better writer and showed "a lot more wit and understanding" as a music critic than did Stege, who, Strauss was afraid, might replace his friend Rasch as music chief of the *Völkischer Beobachter*. Rasch had been fired from this post after having praised certain aspects of Berg's *Lulu,* excerpts from which had just been conducted by Kleiber in Berlin. Strauss thought that Rasch had received just retribution for approving of a piece like *Lulu,* but trading him for a Stege was quite another matter.[169]

In April 1934, Strauss had compared Stuckenschmidt favorably to the majority of German music critics, because, in his opinion, Stuckenschmidt had not lowered himself to the level of others who would write such nonsense as likening "the German master" Paul Hindemith to Bach and Handel: "This really makes you vomit!"[170] Strauss's outburst was characteristic of his hatred for the moderns, but it did not reflect his true relationship with the composer of *Mathis der Maler.*

Commensurate with Strauss's knowledge of Hindemith's Weimar experiments, the older composer regarded the younger one with suspicion. But it could not have escaped him—as indeed it had not escaped the equally traditionalist Furtwängler—that just at the end of the republic Hindemith had been starting to change and that his *Mathis* essays were in a safely tonal style. Besides, even during Hindemith's earlier, wilder phase, Strauss had grudgingly acknowledged that superb musician's talents. And so, Strauss being Strauss and personal tastes and dislikes notwithstanding, he had called Hindemith into the presidial council during the founding phase of the RMK.[171] During the first German Composers' Festival in Berlin on 18 February 1934, Strauss had Hindemith's *Konzertmusik für Streicher und*

Blechbläser performed.[172] But already during the summer of that year Hindemith's publisher Willy Strecker wrongly thought that Strauss was waging an internal RMK campaign against the younger man, an interpretation that was later uncritically repeated by some of Hindemith's biographers.[173]

By these and other biographers, this was made into the springboard for another attack by Strauss on Hindemith, when Goebbels had condemned the young man, in so many words, after that damaging Furtwängler article, in his Sportpalast speech of 6 December.[174] The attack was in the form of a telegram which Strauss allegedly sent to Goebbels, congratulating the minister on "weeding out undesirable elements."[175] The *Times* of London translated the gist of this on 12 December, and Thomas Mann expressed his profound dissatisfaction with it two days later.[176] Postwar critics of Strauss have claimed that Strauss had sent the telegram just in time for Goebbels to read it immediately after his speech, and knowledge of this incensed the anti-Nazi composer Gottfried von Einem to the point where he, who was on the board of directors of the Salzburg Festival after 1945, expressed his determination to have none of Strauss's works performed there for three years.[177]

Yet the conventional view does not represent even half of the truth. What happened was that in his speech of 6 December, Goebbels unmistakably referred to Hindemith, his "youthful works" and "naked women in the most obscene and kitschy, banal situations in a bath on stage," without even once mentioning the composer's name.[178] But he also spoke out against atonal music, contrasting it negatively with the works of Richard Wagner, for whom "being German was a matter in its own right."[179] It was these combined references to his beloved Wagner and the hated atonal composers that moved Strauss on 10 December, four days after he had returned from a triumphal concert tour to Holland highly lauded by the German authorities, to have a telegram sent from Garmisch, with the following text: "I am sending hearty congratulations and enthusiastic agreement with the great cultural speech. Reverently Yours, Heil Hitler, Richard Strauss."[180]

A number of factors are important here. First, it had not been Strauss himself who sent the telegram but his son Franz, who had thought this a good idea in view of the difficulties Strauss had recently been having in the RMK. According to music copyright lawyer Franz Strauss after the war, he and his father had been impressed by Goebbels's invectives against atonality, which they had come across in a partial newspaper reprint of Goebbels's speech. It had been Franz's idea to draft the telegram, his father had approved of this, and it was sent.[181] Franz's action does not excuse Strauss, even if it is possible that Strauss never read the telegram, for it was dispatched in his name and with his knowledge. But his motivation, not against Hindemith but against the terrible atonal composers, is clear. At that very time Strauss was incensed about the Berlin performance of excerpts from Berg's *Lulu* and saddened by the realization that because of this, his trusted aide, Hugo Rasch, would lose his post at the *Völkischer Beobachter* and, presumably, much needed influence for Strauss with the regime's upper echelons.[182] Moreover, on 14 December, the same day that Strauss chided Rasch for having committed his folly, Strauss sent Rasch another letter regarding RMK matters, in which he clearly wrote: "In matters of Hindemith you had better ask the state secretary! As far as I am concerned, he may stay!"[183] What Strauss referred to here was Hindemith's continued presence as a member of the RMK presidial council—sufficient proof that he had never intrigued against him or meant any harm to him when sending the telegram to Goebbels, although, in typically Straussian fashion, he once again had not foreseen the variety of possible interpretations to the contrary.

Strauss's actions in the aftermath of the Hindemith affair bore out his goodwill toward the younger composer. At a presidial council meeting in mid-March 1935, attended by both himself and his son, it was agreed that Strauss should speak to Goebbels about the case and should stress two points. First, Hindemith should be reinstated as professor at the Hochschule für Musik in Berlin. Second, the presidial council had raised no objections against Hindemith's oeuvre on the grounds of atonality insofar as a special advertisement for this musical style had not been discernible. A special program committee of the RMK (to be established later) should guarantee this status quo. (Because of developments in the RMK, but probably also because Strauss really did not care about policing, such a committee was never founded.)[184] According to Hindemith himself, Strauss did what he had promised and reported about it during another presidial meeting on 30 March. Strauss also told Hindemith that unless the Promi could not manage to defeat its scruples, Hindemith, who had not yet formally resigned from the Hochschule, should expect to be teaching again shortly. Moreover, the RMK would stand behind any Kapellmeister's efforts to have Hindemith's works performed.[185] In early April, Strauss was prepared to take Hindemith's *Mathis* libretto to Goebbels, as proof of his fellow composer's positive attitude.[186]

By that time, Goebbels could not have been much impressed any more, because, after all, Strauss was championing an artist whom he, the minister, had nationally chastised. And as much as Goebbels was aware of the international publicity value Strauss was still generating for the Third Reich—what with Germany's most famous composer being the head of the Nazi Music Chamber and giving stunning concerts abroad—he was also aware that Strauss was using his RMK position to further his own ends. For politicians such as Goebbels, who had some overview, it was clear that instead of avoiding what were obvious conflicts of interest, Strauss was always keen to have his oeuvre elevated by exploiting the authority of his office.

Strauss's Berlin performance of his *Festliches Präludium* on 15 November 1933 was only the first of such incidents. Then, for the composers' festival concert in Berlin in mid-February 1934, not only were Strauss's *Till Eulenspiegels lustige Streiche* and *Arabella* featured at the Staatsoper, but Tietjen also conspired with Ihlert to have 400 free tickets for *Arabella* made available through the Prussian ministry of culture.[187] Tietjen then saw to it, even before the arrival of Clemens Krauss in early 1935, that the works of his composer friend were not neglected in Berlin, coincidentally also the seat of the RMK: Strauss's birthday (his seventieth was in June 1934) was the ideal occasion, hence *Intermezzo, Die ägyptische Helena,* and *Ariadne auf Naxos* were scheduled.[188] Goebbels may have sneered when in July 1934, as Strauss was presenting one of his plans for opera reform, he read that the small town of Gera might be downsized, because the Weimar stage could easily manage "the great works by Wagner, the more important Verdi compositions, and my main oeuvre in dignified fashion."[189] Later that year Strauss complained to the minister that the national broadcast network performed not even 40 of his 160 songs.[190] When Hermann Stange had become RMK vice president, it was his turn to grant a favor. So on 23 April 1935 he duly directed a "Richard Strauss Evening" in Berlin, conducting Strauss's symphonic fantasy *Aus Italien,* among other compositions, and Strauss used his position to recommend to him Charlotte Dahmen, a singer his father had still known from Vienna. As if he had no other worries at that time, Strauss also lectured Stange on the ideal qualities of an opera Kapellmeister, among them a feeling for the "dramatic line of a Wagnerian and Straussian opera act."[191] Next to Richard Wagner, Jupiter's *sacro egoismo* was the standard.

Increasingly controversial from several vantage points, Strauss's role in the RMK after several months in office gave rise to more and more friction between himself and his superiors. However, he tried to maintain his composure as a servant of the state who was used to respecting authority in all the forms he had encountered it throughout his entire career, but also as an artist with aesthetic principles who for the longest time found it difficult to doubt the sincerity of regime leaders such as Göring, Goebbels, and especially Hitler. In December 1933 he had composed a song, *Das Bächlein,* which, out of gratitude over his RMK appointment, he dedicated to Goebbels and whose closing lines contained a tasteless paean to Hitler: "He who has called me from the stone, will, I think, be my Führer, my Führer, my Führer!"[192] The honeymoon continued into early 1934. During his speech for the opening of the first RMK workshop in Berlin on 13 February Strauss asserted that after Hitler's ascension to power much had already changed in Germany, not only in the political but also in the cultural arena. He expressed special gratitude to Goebbels for having created the culture chamber legislation.[193] After amiable exchanges with Göring as head of the Berlin Staatsoper, Strauss wrote home to Pauline: "I am settling a thousand things here in person with the greatest success and absolute authority." Then he prided himself on rubbing shoulders privately with Goebbels and Hitler, and on Göring's extraordinary kindness. "I am optimally stationed here and may accomplish whatever I want."[194] In March 1934 Strauss again praised Hitler publicly, this time in Munich, on having united Germany, and a few days later he wrote to Karl Böhm from France that every once in a while he would explain to inquisitive journalists "that Hitler actually exists and is no figure of legend, and that the Germans really do not intend to march into Paris within the next eight days."[195]

The mood started to change in April 1934 when some of Strauss's ideas regarding operatic reform at Goebbels's Deutsches Opernhaus had filtered through and were beginning to be resisted by prominent members of that institution, notably the singer Gerhard Hüsch and his mistress, soprano Rosalind von Schirach.[196] Goebbels himself expressed his displeasure in May, entering in his diary that *Intermezzo* (at the rivaling Staatsoper) had been "banal, blasé and without taste."[197] Although the minister sent a perfunctory letter congratulating Strauss on his seventieth birthday in June, the regime prevented the master from attending the Salzburg Festival, as he had planned to do (and had done with impunity in 1933), ostensibly for political reasons; Strauss was merely permitted to put in a brief personal appearance at Krauss's staging of *Elektra*.[198] In August Goebbels himself expressed strong reservations about Strauss's opera reforms and in particular singled out the Deutsches Opernhaus, which he did not wish to see diluted in quality. Exactly two months later Goebbels's counselor von Keudell criticized Strauss's administrative and financial laxities, as they had come to light in the newly constituted Stagma.[199] This led directly to Strauss's frustrated letter to Tietjen of November, in which he threatened that if Goebbels did not agree with his long-term plans for retirement from the RMK, "then I can still resign *momentarily.*"[200]

Toward year's end and into 1935, Strauss may have thought that his rival Furtwängler's dismissal from most of his posts and what he may have regarded as a politic communication in the form of a telegram to Goebbels would improve his situation. For political reasons and because he still believed in Hitler as the presumptive savior of German art he dined with the Führer and a visiting British politician on 26 March 1935, and two days later he personally demonstrated to Hitler his newly composed *Olympische Hymne*. That day he committed to his notebook that Hitler had accepted the piano score he had given him, with the words: "It will be a precious memento."[201] On 17 April, Strauss met with the Führer again, to wish him a happy birthday and to discuss the old idea of the 1 percent royalty level (now to be extended beyond Bayreuth). In a letter from Garmisch the next day Strauss expressed his "warmest thanks for the precious, scintillating hour" and his hope for Hitler's prolonged health, for the continued protection of "German art."[202]

Yet not only did Hitler reject the proposal of the "culture tithe" unconditionally, but his government now began to place restrictions on Strauss's hitherto unencumbered private transfer by automobile across the German-Austrian border, a mere ten miles behind Strauss's Garmisch villa, hindering travel to his second residence in Vienna or to the long-favored spas in South Tyrol and Switzerland.[203] By the middle of June 1935, Strauss was fuming. "The good minister is always talking propaganda," he wrote to Goebbels's aide von Niessen, "but he has no time to receive you and me, to discuss and implement the most important reforms."[204] On 20 June Strauss cynically remarked to Stange that as far as he was concerned, the RMK presidial council might have 100 members, yet even they would not be able to cope with all the work.[205] In early July, Strauss had reason to confide to his notebook that one must be living in sad times if it was necessary that an artist of his rank had to ask the permission of Goebbels, a mere lad of a minister, what to compose and perform.[206] By this time the problem Strauss had been having with his new opera, *Die schweigsame Frau,* and its librettist Stefan Zweig had superseded all his other troubles and was about to get the better of him and his family.

Contrary to received wisdom, Strauss's difficulties with Stefan Zweig were not the solitary reason, and not even the main reason of his permanent fall from grace in the Nazi Reich; they were merely contributory to the complex combination of motives already mentioned. They highlighted a number of Strauss's weaknesses as well as his strengths, and they were as much cause of his future predicament as they were a symptom of his often troubled personal relationships.

Disconsolate over the death of his longtime friend and author Hugo von Hofmannsthal in 1929, Strauss did not know where to turn for a writer of similar renown. Then in the late summer of 1931 Anton Kippenberg, the founder of the Insel Verlag who was supplying the composer with many good books on a regular basis, mentioned one of his authors, Stefan Zweig, born in Vienna in 1881.[207] Strauss and the reputed Zweig met in November in Munich, and they immediately began talking about a libretto for *Die schweigsame Frau.*[208] By October 1932 Zweig was reading to Kippenberg the first act of the new opera; Kippenberg felt "entranced."[209] Strauss himself could not believe his luck, for he had thought the "unforgettable Hugo" irreplacable.[210]

Throughout 1933, Strauss and Zweig continued to work on the opera, with the plot based on a text created by the English writer Ben Jonson, a contemporary of Shakespeare, "Epicene, or The Silent Woman." Strauss had to tread carefully, for if by the definition of the new Nazi rulers Hofmannsthal had been half Jewish, Zweig was a full Jew. Whereas Strauss was running the risk of being compromised, especially at a time in which he wanted to accomplish so much politically, Zweig, albeit not living in Nazi Germany, was beginning to suffer a whole series of indignities. In a first incident in April 1933 Goebbels, during a radio talk, quoted what Zweig believed to be "an infamous passage" from his namesake, Arnold Zweig, a lesser writer who, born in Silesia, was already in Palestine. Strauss, quite depressed about this confusion, immediately promised to intercede, through Rasch and with Rosenberg, to effect a correction.[211] Stefan Zweig later joined Thomas Mann and other anti-Nazi intellectuals in a protest against the Berlin regime, thus endangering Strauss.[212] But to defuse tension, Strauss spoke to Zweig about the "goodwill of the new German government" with regard to cultural renewal, and by early 1934 the opera libretto was completed, Strauss being well along with the composition of the music and hoping to interest Zweig in a continuation of their relationship.[213]

In the spring of 1934 Strauss's enemies within Nazi Party circles, chief among them Rosenberg, hectored Goebbels again about the composer and the "Arnold Zweig" business.[214] After being notified by State Secretary Funk, Franz Strauss hastened to assure the ministry that the Austrian Stefan Zweig had nothing to do with nor was he related to "the nasty namesake Arnold."[215] Telling Zweig about this event in May, the composer reassured the writer of his support, adding that Goebbels had no "political objections" against him. Yet Strauss must have humiliated Zweig by his statement that "all efforts to relax the stipulation against Jews here are frustrated by the answer: impossible as long as the outside world continues its lying propaganda against Hitler."[216] In early August Strauss further embarrassed Zweig by writing that while he had been shadowed by Nazi agents in London, his "magnificent conduct" had been found "'correct and politically beyond reproach.'"[217]

Later that month Rosenberg, obviously not having listened to his music expert Rasch, put even more pressure on Goebbels, and the minister confronted Rosenberg with Franz Strauss's arguments.[218] To assuage Strauss, Goebbels told him on 1 September 1935 that Hitler had personally permitted the premiere of *Die schweigsame Frau* and asked the composer what time and operatic venue he desired. The minister would then inform the press and enlighten it as to the grounds on which this exception had been made.[219]

Dresden, Strauss's preferred stage for premieres, was chosen, and a time for the summer of 1935 was set.[220] Yet at the end of September Strauss— approaching that first nadir of his discontent with the Promi and the RMK in November—was becoming wary.[221] Strauss now was quite aware of Zweig's growing embarrassment, that he had been shadowed, and had been approached about the whole matter by British journalists in July, and that, despite his assurances to the contrary, he was worried about the fate of the entire venture. Strauss was loath to lose Zweig as his librettist. And so, short of giving Goebbels a flat denial, he answered him on 20 September that there were worse things than ordinary theater scandals (as Goebbels had implied could happen, perhaps on the pattern of the Walter affair), which might even generate some welcome propaganda, as they had done for *Salome*. "Worse is an audience attending a performance out of curiosity, but which then withholds applause out of coldness, creating the sort of icy atmosphere in which even a good work will freeze, or a press, which, aptly trained in this technique, knows how to praise a piece in a way that no one, after such a 'clean bill of health,' will be moved to buy a ticket for the next performance. And empty houses are the death of every play." All things considered, Strauss preferred to wait with the premiere.[222]

In this letter to Goebbels, Strauss had correctly identified the essence of Nazi-style totalitarian pressure and, one might assume, he was beginning to disabuse himself of the notion that dictatorial controls or, in fact, the Third Reich, were meant for a man like him. To Zweig he wrote that no final decision had been made and a meeting with the minister was imminent in November—a meeting which, according to the records, never took place and hence reinforced his desire to resign.[223]

As he decided not to do so at this time, and as in fact he had completed the score for *Die schweigsame Frau* at the end of October, he went along with the Dresden plans to have the opera premiered there under Böhm, late in June 1935.[224] In vain did Zweig implore him, in February of that year, to hold back the work; for this time Strauss had decided to give his alliance with the regime leaders yet another chance: "Fate must take its course."[225] Then, on 23 February, Zweig made the firm decision to withdraw from his partnership with Strauss definitively, because after those compromising events he could only work for him in secret, and that, surely, would be beneath Strauss. Strauss replied that he was saddened and did not wish "an anti-Semitic government" to interfere between them. Why, therefore, not conceive "a second Zweig opera"? He would talk to Goebbels about it. Obviously buoyed for the moment, Strauss went to see both Goebbels and Funk in late March and was, foreseeably, turned down. Yet Strauss continued to implore Zweig to continue working with him in secret, suggesting that Goebbels might accept that if it was kept well hidden.[226]

The following weeks were occupied with Strauss's energetic attempts to hold on to Zweig as librettist, who offered informal advice if needed, and suggested as his replacement the Viennese theater historian Joseph Gregor. But beyond that Zweig continued to insist that he himself would stay away. These weeks were also filled with preparations for the premiere under Böhm and Intendant Adolph at the Dresden Staatsoper, set for 24 June, with Hitler and Goebbels to be in attendance.[227]

On 15 June 1935 Zweig sent off another letter from Vienna to Strauss, reiterating his arguments why further collaboration was impossible and emphasizing his solidarity with fellow Jewish artists persecuted by the Nazis. He expressed misgivings about Strauss's part in *Die schweigsame Frau,* an opera by the chief of the Nazi music chamber. And, although this letter has not yet been found, he evidently mentioned the Walter and Toscanini affairs.[228]

Strauss received the letter in Dresden, where he was attending the rehearsals for the premiere. It made him so furious that he produced the now notorious letter of 17 June, trying to defend himself against most of Zweig's charges and maintaining a play-acting role as RMK president.[229] This letter was intercepted by the Gestapo already in Dresden and kept in Gauleiter Mutschmann's office for several days. One of its first consequences appears to have been that Mutschmann, on his own authority and without Hitler's and Goebbels's knowledge (as before in the Busch affair), now put pressure on Adolph, who with a Jewish wife was vulnerable in any case, to strike Zweig's name from the program. Strauss noticed the modified program on 22 June and threatened to leave Dresden on the same night, unless Zweig's name was restored. This was done, and thereafter Adolph lost his post.[230] The premiere of *Die schweigsame Frau* commenced as planned, on 24 June, with the talented, attractive Maria Cebotari in the title role. Four days later Strauss, now back in Garmisch, wrote to Zweig that the performances in Dresden had been wonderful and that in fact he had reason to hope for a rapprochement with Goebbels, to complete the lagging reform work.[231]

Contrary to Strauss's expectations, Hitler and Goebbels could not attend the premiere because bad weather prevented their plane from reaching Dresden. The common explanation that the two politicians remained in Berlin because of Strauss's treasonous letter is invalid, for Mutschmann did not send a copy of it to the Reich Chancellery until 1 July.[232]

After that date Strauss's fate was sealed, at least as far as Joseph Goebbels was concerned. By 5 July the minister had decided that "Strauss finally must go."[233] Thereupon Goebbels's representative von Keudell visited Strauss, who at the time was in consultation with his new librettist Joseph Gregor in Berchtestgaden and compelled him to resign. Strauss sent a letter to Goebbels on 6 July, asking to be released for "health reasons." The minister granted him leave three days later.[234] Those reasons were then published in the German press.[235] As for *Die schweigsame Frau,* it was prohibited, never again to be performed in the Third Reich.[236]

In September 1935, after Strauss had been ostracized, an official in Hinkel's office remarked that the composer, in the completion of his *Die schweigsame Frau,* had sought the collaboration of four Jews: Zweig as librettist, Otto Fürstner as music publisher, Ben Jonson as the original text author, and the musician who had arranged the piano score.[237] By contrast, in his letter of 17 June 1935, Strauss had accused Zweig of "Jewish obstinacy," and in an earlier one he had disrespectfully referred to the "pleading of a Jewish lawyer."[238] How do these sets of circumstances fit together: Strauss being accused as a friend of the Jews *and* for making anti-Semitic remarks? The truth is that Strauss, as an adolescent and a young man, was an anti-Semite in the mold of the cultured German upper bourgeoisie toward the end of the nineteenth century. It was unfortunate that this anti-Semitism (to which Thomas and Heinrich Mann also fell victim) assumed a virulent quality through the superimposition of pseudo-scientific arguments on the old religious, economic, and aesthetic reasons, arguments fostered, ironically, by the rise of the natural sciences and positivism, particularly in Germany. A small anti-Semitic party sent representatives to the German Reichstag for the first time. This happened in the 1880s, when Strauss was in his formative years and not protected from prejudices pervading his environment.[239]

Four persons in particular influenced him in this direction: his father, Franz Strauss; his mentor, Hans von Bülow; the minor composer Alexander Ritter; and Cosima Wagner. After World War I Franz Schalk, his codirector in Vienna, may have added venom of his own, but by then Strauss's world view had long been set and, as an anti-Semite, he was actually beginning to mellow.

Franz Strauss worked under Kapellmeister Hermann Levi in Munich, Wagner's old conductor-associate, and he hated him. Levi, accused by the older Strauss of inconsistent tempi, was the negative role model when during recitals at home the father would shout at his son (who accompanied the hornist at the piano): "You are hurrying like a Jew!"[240] The aversion to Levi, whom at the beginning Richard Strauss had actually liked, was exacerbated when, in 1889, the year of Hitler's birth, Franz Strauss was abruptly pensioned, with Levi's complicity. Strauss during that summer was in Bayreuth and saw Levi on a daily basis but tried to avoid him. In the fall of 1893 the ailing Levi wished to hire the talented Strauss as his associate in Munich, which caused no small embarrassment to the upwardly mobile young genius; he hesitated, but by 1894 he had moved to Munich for the second time.[241] Not surprisingly, and in keeping with the pattern of anti-Semitic development both as an individual vexation and a sociopolitical movement, Strauss generalized on the basis of particularities and in the 1880s and 1890s spouted slogans about "terribly many Jews" in Frankfurt or "reprehensible Jew commotions in Berlin," where one could easily fall into the "garlic-scented hands" of "scoundrels."[242]

In the summer of 1885 Strauss was hired as assistant conductor by Hofkapellmeister Hans von Bülow in Meiningen, and he succeeded him at the ducal court already in the fall—until 1886, when he went to Munich for the first time as Dritter Kapellmeister under Levi. He remained a devoted friend of Bülow until his death in 1894. Bülow was not only an unreconstructed Wagnerian (despite his later love of Brahms) but, according to Nike Wagner, also "difficult, unbalanced, a depressive and choleric character," and a dyed-in-the-wool anti-Semite.[243] Over the years Strauss and Bülow exchanged invectives against Jews, often centering on Levi; by 1890 Strauss thought that Bülow's growing personal idiosyncrasies resulted from the evil influence of his Jewish entourage in Berlin and Hamburg.[244]

Alexander Ritter, born in 1833, was a violinist and composer whose mother had been a close friend of Wagner and who ended up marrying Wagner's niece Franziska, the daughter of Richard's brother Carl Albert. He became an acolyte of Liszt and, eventually, a friend of Bülow, through whom he met Strauss during the Meiningen period. When Strauss left for Munich in 1886, Ritter also moved there.[245] Strauss's abiding reverence for this man remains a mystery, for Ritter was a failure as a composer, making some of his living as a musician and music salesman, and much older than Strauss. Perhaps Ritter's family relationship with Wagner had something to do with the friendship. Moreover, already tuned in by Bülow, Strauss relied especially on Ritter's well-anchored Jew hatred in his own anti-Levi stance at Munich. Here, too, the impressionable Strauss followed the stereotype when he put stock in his father's opinion that Ritter had "once been harmed by a Jew."[246]

During the summer of 1889 in Bayreuth, Strauss's relationship with Cosima Wagner was amicable; in August 1894 he conducted the Festival's *Tannhäuser*. Intermittently, they kept in touch, Frau Wagner advising the young man in his dealings with Levi, whom she knew well.[247] Her own anti-Jewish views reinforced Strauss's anti-Semitism. Was it to ingratiate himself that he reported to her in January 1890 about Frankfurt's "prima donna and Jewish pursuits"?[248] In fact, Strauss's anti-Semitic remarks to the Bayreuth matriarch until 1894 are among the most wicked things he ever uttered about Jews.[249]

But, with the constant and singular exception of Hermann Levi, they were also nonspecific and rather more like the stereotypes reflecting the anti-Semitic *Zeitgeist,* because almost everybody did it. The young Strauss was a conformist to society, and these were some of its tendencies at the time—distasteful, but nothing like the collective killer instinct Daniel Jonah Goldhagen has ascribed to pre-Hitlerian Germans.[250] The more mature and urbane Strauss became, and the more he got to thinking on his own, away from the psychotic Bülows and Ritters, the less frequent these outbursts were. In his letters to Schalk from 1918 to 1923, the anti-Semitic remarks are already far more dispersed if not yet toned down; in communications to the partly Jewish Hofmannsthal, there is the occasional aside, albeit not against him.[251]

As far as is known, Strauss has not put himself on record as an anti-Semite for the remainder of the 1920s and early 1930s, with one significant, deplorable, exception. When in 1932, with Nazism poised to take over, Otto Klemperer visited the Strausses in Garmisch, they talked about politics over tea. To Strauss's musings about what might happen if all Jewish conductors were to leave Germany, Klemperer replied that this probably would not paralyze the music scene. Hereupon Pauline Strauss, in her inimitably clumsy manner, invited Klemperer to see her "if they want to harm you." Strauss countered: "That would be just the right moment to stick up for a Jew!" Although Klemperer claimed this had been such a naive remark that one could not even fault Strauss for it, he never forgave the composer, especially as Strauss did not inquire how he was faring when they met again at the Salzburg Festival in the summer of 1933. Klemperer boycotted Strauss's works until 1936.[252]

During the Third Reich, the remainder of Strauss's anti-Semitism continued in this offhand vain and was never ad hominem. Yet although it was not calculated either, there is no question that it was tasteless. Not having purged himself of his tendency to generalize, Strauss preferred to call the hated operetta genre "Jewish," because he knew that Paul Abraham, Leo Fall, and Emmerich Kálmán were Jews and he probably thought Lehár to be one, although he was not. And, Strauss wrote to Zweig, there were such people as "Jewish lawyers" and such attitudes as "Jewish obstinacy."[253]

But even in this early phase, for every Levi whom Strauss may have disliked as a Jew, there must have been three other Jews he admired, irrespective of their religious or ethnocultural background. While in Berlin in 1883–84, he met rich, cultured Jews who patronized him, such as Bismarck's confidant Gerson von Bleichröder, one of whose daughters enchanted him. Such encounters were repeated during his Hofkapellmeister years in the capital in the early 1900s, when he knew the influential Willi Levin, also a champion of Pfitzner, and the "fundamentally kindhearted Baroness Cohn-Oppenheimer."[254] One of his favorite musicians, always, was Mendelssohn, and while in Berlin he was awe-struck by Brahms's associate, the Jewish master violinist Joseph Joachim.[255] He had ties of friendship to Gustav Mahler, although that composer's complex personality may have precluded a deeper relationship, and Strauss seems to have been somewhat intimidated by the slightly older man. Still, Mahler confessed in 1894 that "among all the gods," Strauss was his only friend.[256] Conductor Leo Blech adored Strauss after hearing *Tod und Verklärung* in 1893, and thereafter Strauss entrusted Blech with the Berlin premiere of operas such as *Elektra* and *Ariadne auf Naxos,* well into the 1920s.[257]

Strauss continued to befriend and support Blech into the Third Reich.[258] Indeed, his general policy of trying to prevent anti-Semitic regulations as RMK president was in keeping with the fealty and friendship he now owed to many prominent Jewish artists, including Max Reinhardt, for whom he personally intervened in Goebbels's office—without success.[259] In late 1933 Strauss also tried to mediate on behalf of Professor Jani Szanto, dismissed from the Bayerische Akademie der Tonkunst, again to no avail.[260] When in early 1935 Strauss was informed that Paul Dukas, one of the French composers to be favored by the new German-dominated Counseil Permanent, was a Jew, the president of the RMK took no action.[261] Strauss was in full sympathy with his Jewish publisher Otto Fürstner, whom he had known as a young boy and who had to emigrate to England in 1935. Contrary to charges made against him after 1945, Strauss did not enrich himself, after the transferral of the business from Fürstner to the "Aryan" Johannes Oertel by even a penny, and Fürstner safeguarded all of Strauss's foreign rights.[262] And far from harboring resentment against him, soprano Rose Pauly, whom Strauss always valued highly, along with other singers such as Lotte Lehmann, the wife of a Jew who had to emigrate to the United States, sent him cordial letters from New York in 1941, and he replied in kind, asking Pauly to convey greetings to all the mutual friends.[263] As late as March 1942 Strauss remarked cryptically to Clemens Krauss that he hoped that the author of the poems, settings of which his wife Viorica Ursuleac was about to perform in Spain, was not "unknown" there as in Germany (he was referring to Heinrich Heine).[264]

This, then, is neither the profile of a Nazi anti-Semite nor that of a typical German preregime Jew hater. It may be ironic, but there were occasions when fanatical Nazis accused Strauss of proximity to Jewish persons and Jewish culture—not just in the case of Hofmannsthal and Zweig. In 1927 a Viennese scholar was taken to task for opposing the bestowal of an honorary degree on Strauss because of the composer's well-known collaboration with "the Jew" Hofmannsthal.[265] After 1933, several of Strauss's stage works—chiefly *Salome, Josephslegende,* and *Die ägyptische Helena*—were criticized and even regionally indicted for their allegedly Jewish contents.[266] The regime kept a file on Strauss, including in it a document stating that the composer had made an arrangement of Mozart's *Idomeneo* based on the text by the Viennese Jew Lothar Wallerstein, for whom Strauss wrote a letter of reference when Wallerstein had to flee Europe in 1938. Other regime leaders held it against him that he acknowledged Hermann Levi's classic translation into German of the text of Mozart's *Così fan tutte.*[267]

But the most wicked Nazi anti-Semitic attacks against Strauss occurred as early as 1934, above all because of his *personal* association with Jews:

There were Hofmannsthal and Zweig. There were his rounds of Skat with Jews. There was the fact "that his son has a Jewess as a wife" and that, most damning perhaps, "Dr. Richard Strauss allows himself to be photographed with his Jewish grandchildren."[268]

III

It has been said that after the Zweig-letter affair Richard Strauss continued his artistic career as before, within a framework of improved relations with the Nazi regime, because he now was rid of the burden of "all musicopolitical offices."[269] This judgment is wrong from at least three perspectives. First, Strauss's artistic career did suffer, because certain of his works could not be performed as before, and under an increased emotional strain and after the loss of his valued librettist he found it more difficult to produce. Second, even after July 1935 he did not take leave from all his offices and duties, as some of them had been beyond the RMK. And third, relations with the regime did not improve but, on the contrary, deteriorated, to the point where he was treated as a pariah by 1944. More than ever before July 1935, Strauss found himself on a slippery slope.

Although he had been planning to resign from the unrewarding post of RMK president since the fall of 1934, Strauss had planned to do it on his own terms. Therefore, he was surprised to see himself tossed out by the propaganda minister, even though, it is true, he had never been on consistently friendly terms with him. Strauss had all the more reason to think that Hitler himself was of a different mind, because he had been the Führer's honored guest on official occasions, had performed for him at private audiences, and thus might have received the impression that Hitler actually liked his music, especially his Lieder.[270] Hence Strauss's first order of business in mid-July 1935 was damage control, via a direct application to the Führer, with whom he was eager to clarify the immediate cause of his dismissal, without touching on the deeper and more long-standing problems. On 13 July he wrote Hitler a letter in which he distanced himself from the charges of having made light of his RMK position and not comprehending anti-Semitism. The recent dispatch to Zweig, he wrote, "does not represent my view of the world nor my true conviction." Politically, he tried to defuse the situation by stressing his apolitical posture. Praising Hitler as "the great architect of German social life," he then concluded: "Confident of your high sense of justice, I beg you, my Führer, most humbly to receive me for a personal discussion, to give me the opportunity to justify myself in person."[271]

In private conversation in 1993, Strauss's grandson Richard Strauss Jr. characterized this letter to me as the saddest document his grandfather had ever written. Strauss's biographer George Marek has referred to it hyperbolically as representing "the nadir of Strauss's morality."[272] Whatever the interpretation, there is no question that it reflected badly on Strauss, especially as he never received an answer to it from Berlin.[273] At that time, in his still frantic search for rehabilitation, Strauss sent a demure note to Rasch in October stating that should he ever in his life meet Goebbels again in person, he wished to present him with a medal in recognition of his work toward Stagma and the composers' copyright cause. And he hinted that he would be in Berlin at the beginning of November.[274] Obviously, Goebbels was in no hurry to see him, so Strauss next turned to his old friend Tietjen, beseeching him to intervene with both Goebbels and Hitler and asking his advice as to how to behave at future official functions in Berlin. Tietjen cautioned restraint.[275] This was in December. February 1936 found Strauss rather despondent. During the Winter Olympics in Garmisch he complained to Winifred Wagner that neither Hitler nor Goebbels had come to see him. After he had had a chance to speak with Frau Magda Goebbels briefly in the Munich Vier Jahreszeiten hotel, an adjutant had called him at home to report crisply that the minister refused to meet with him. Would Frau Wagner speak to the gentlemen again? Yet the Bayreuth heiress had already warned the master that during those busy weeks of the Olympics she had better not approach the politicians lest she stir up too much of a tempest.[276]

Strauss was in fact afraid that he would never be able to conduct the Olympic Hymn officially in person. He had not composed the hymn on order of the Third Reich but on order of the International Olympic Committee, yet he depended on the regime leaders for approval; thus he even repeated to Frau Wagner what Hitler had told him personally in March 1935, after having received the piano score as a gift, that it would be a "precious memento."[277] On the other hand, the Olympic Hymn was also a pawn in Strauss's hands to ensure that he would continue to play some role in the Third Reich, even without the RMK office, the unfortunate Zweig-letter affair, and his current reputation as a philosemite.

The hymn was rehearsed in Berlin in June; Goebbels came to listen and found it "wonderful."[278] On 1 August, at the opening of the Summer Games, it was duly premiered under the composer's direction; an Electrola record was appropriately marketed in the fall.[279] Goebbels was in fact quick to realize that Strauss on a leash could still be as useful to Germany's prestige as he had always been, which explains why in the coming years he was allowed to continue reaping international accolades, in London, Paris, and Rome. From Buenos Aires, Kleiber wrote Strauss in late 1936 that the composer of *Salome* was still venerated there "like a god."[280] As Walter Abendroth correctly observed to Pfitzner (who would have given his left arm to play this particular part), "in the long run Strauss is indispensable to this Reich as an international publicity factor."[281] Strauss himself, not yet fully aware of the other, vindictive side of the minister, who from now on would distinguish carefully between the composer as a heaven-inspired genius and the person as an unsavory individual, ecstatically wrote to his wife in March 1936, after a triumphant tour to Belgium, of the success he had secured for the sake of German prestige merely through his oeuvre: "I would like to see another German artist do this, during this time, in those hostile foreign lands. For this feat I am actually entitled to the most golden medal of the propaganda ministry."[282] And in January 1937 he noted: "Well, it's going ahead again."[283]

One part of his career was going ahead not least because Strauss was still needed as advertisement for Nazi Germany's continued efforts on behalf of the international composers' union, which it sought to control. In September 1935, the festival of the Counseil Permanent pour la Coopération Internationale des Compositeurs actually took place, as planned, in Vichy, with Strauss acting as president. During the business meeting, condolences were expressed to Madame Dukas on the recent passing of her Jewish husband, Paul. Among the featured works were those of Dukas and, of course, Strauss.[284] After a follow-up festival in Stockholm in February 1936, during which, among others, the ballet *Le train bleu* (1924) by the French Jew Darius Milhaud was performed, there was a meeting in Dresden in May 1937, which, in President Strauss's presence, played music by the half-Jewish Bulgarian Pantcho Vladigerov.[285] When in June 1942, at the Counseil's gathering in Berlin, Strauss was reelected as its president for another five years, Goebbels showed himself pleased.[286]

At a circumscribed functional level, then, a new, mutually calculated relationship existed between Strauss and the Third Reich, beginning with the summer of 1936 and lasting into 1944. It required of Strauss to show off his regime-marketable qualities and a continuation of the subservient, sometimes groveling, attitude that had first manifested itself in that self-demeaning letter to Hitler in July 1935. Of the regime leaders it required a minimum of concessions that cost them nothing—such as nationally observing his birthdays, especially his seventy-fifth, giving him pride of place on occasions of high culture, and awarding him prizes. In these situations, the regime ratcheted up large publicity profits as long as they were needed, whereas Strauss swallowed his patrician pride and exploited chances to flatter his ego.

After the Olympics and more role playing at the requisite Counseil Permanent gatherings, the next prominent event at which Strauss could make a statement was the Reich Music Festival of May 1938 in Düsseldorf, which, without his doing, was tied to the infamous Exhibition of Degenerate Music. Cunningly, Goebbels decided as early as January 1938 that Strauss should be used here; Strauss took the bait and in April wrote to his publisher excitedly that "on the personal invitation of Herr Doktor Goebbels I am going to conduct *Arabella* and *Festliches Präludium* at the Reich Theater Week in Düsseldorf on 26 and 27 May!!" And so it came to pass.[287]

The next incident, with Strauss displaying humility and reaping benefits from it, involved a number of sequences. For lack of a better man, Strauss had acquired a new librettist whom he deemed far inferior to Hofmannsthal or Zweig (who had recommended him), the aforementioned theater scholar Joseph Gregor (1888–1960). Variously denounced to the

Promi as a politically active Catholic and a Jew, the "Aryan" Gregor came under political pressure after the Anschluss in March 1938. In June, Strauss feared that this pressure would jeopardize his collaboration with the scholar, and so he beseeched his new ally in the Promi, head of the music section Heinz Drewes, to extend his protection. Strauss and Gregor's first joint production, *Der Friedenstag,* was duly premiered in Munich at the end of July; their second, the opera *Daphne,* in Dresden under Böhm in October, after Strauss's old patron, Walther Funk, now minister of economics, had been to tea in Garmisch in August. To safeguard this cooperation for the future (Gregor was about to write the libretto for *Die Liebe der Danae*), Strauss sent another of his devout letters to Hitler in June 1939, including with it the scholar's latest book, a biography of Strauss. Hitler conveyed polite thanks.[288]

Der Friedenstag was performed in Vienna in June 1939, as part of the seventy-fifth birthday festivities nationwide, with, in this case, Hitler himself attending and Goebbels hosting a reception in the Imperial hotel.[289] Other such celebrations took place in Berlin, under Strauss's friend Tietjen, as well as in smaller cities, such as Frankfurt and Münster.[290] Göring sent him a telegram.[291] For the occasion, Goebbels endowed a new, annual, "National Composer's Prize" in the amount of RM15,000.[292] Even Strauss's seventy-sixth birthday was celebrated in 1940 by such centers as Munich and Berlin, with Goebbels's sophisticated tabloid *Reich* reporting.[293] During the same year Strauss's *Festmusik zur Feier des 2600jährigen Bestehens des Kaiserreichs Japan,* which he had composed against the background of time-honored veneration by Japanese musicians, was premiered in Axis-allied Tokyo. Characteristically, in the spirit of their tacit understanding, Goebbels sent Strauss a telegram applauding that "German art has achieved a glorious triumph in the Far East."[294]

Within this qualified framework, the following years brought forth additional tokens of, as well as rewards for, regime loyalty. Strauss participated as juror in a Munich prize competition, which was won by the dedicated young Nazi composer Cesar Bresgen.[295] He officiated again, along with Furtwängler and others, at a composition contest for the Vienna Männer-Gesangverein.[296] He himself received a cash award of RM6,000—the highest prize category for composers established by the RMK—in 1942.[297] He was invited to be the subject of a documentary film, showing him conducting the Berlin Philharmonic, for a special Promi "celebrity" collection ordered by Goebbels.[298] In December 1941 the minister and the composer met in Berlin and talked for the better part of an evening. "He has totally gotten over my earlier confrontation with him and once again is toeing the line," noted Goebbels in his diary, adding that one should try to retain a good relationship with him, as, after all, "he is our greatest and most valuable, most representative musician."[299] Not quite a year later Goebbels sponsored the premiere of *Capriccio* under Clemens Krauss in Munich.[300] As late as May 1944 he decided that Strauss should receive that RM6,000 prize again, and as sponsor he confirmed the premiere of *Die Liebe der Danae* for the Salzburg Festival that summer.[301]

However, even in his more official dealings with the regime during this period, when the piper played for the party and the party paid the piper, things did not always go smoothly, and those crises were a symptom of what really went on underneath between Strauss and the higher echelons. A most telling example is that pertaining to his continuing function as an advocate of composers' rights. After Strauss had secured, through Stagma in 1934–35, a composer copyright for fifty years, it became clear that because of the rise of the entertainment industry in the 1920s the creators of *U-Musik* were contributing a much larger share to the national royalty total than those of *E-Musik,* which was enjoyed by the elite few. To ensure that serious-music composers would not starve, Goebbels had decided on a so-called *Ernstes Drittel,* a "serious one third," meaning that one third of all the profit intake nationwide should be reserved for these classical composers. Although this was, in absolute terms, less than the money generated by light-music composers, the "one third" favored classical composers disproportionately to their actual production. This came to be resented by *U-Musik* composers, and by 1940 they had lobbied Goebbels to make a decision in their favor. Goebbels tended to agree with a change amounting to the handout of more money to the manfacturers of lighter fare, because by the time the war was on he was convinced of the relatively greater value of Paul Lincke's or Eduard Künneke's operettas or Herms Niel's pop tunes for the average consumer taste possessed by the soldiers at the front, over that of Bach or Beethoven, sure to please only a few officers. Hence by the fall of 1940 Goebbels had made up his mind to do away with the one-to-two ratio (considered a minimum "right" by the serious composers) and instead wished to make up part or all of the expected loss to *E-Musiker* by giving them, arbitrarily as it seemed, special allotments—mere handouts as far as Strauss was concerned.[302]

When a group of Munich composers heard about this, they were disturbed and called on Strauss for help. Although his position in Stagma as well as in the RMK had officially ceased, they as well as Goebbels knew that as the architect of the original scheme he could not be overlooked as their natural spokesman. There was a meeting in November in the Vier Jahreszeiten hotel attended by Strauss, Hausegger, Joseph Haas, and even Pfitzner. A document was drawn up, "Thoughts on The New Distribution Scheme by Stagma," which conjured up the original pro-Stagma intentions and assumed goodwill on Goebbels's part. Reportedly, Strauss then sent this document to Stagma manager Leo Ritter along with a letter indicating that in accordance with the approved statutes "we ourselves are making the decisions regarding distributions. Doktor Goebbels has no business interfering."[303] If not the final, this serves as one of the most persuasive proofs that Strauss never understood the workings of totalitarianism.

Until March 1941 there were a number of conferences involving Goebbels, Ritter, Paul Graener (Strauss's successor in the RMK composers' section), and Werner Egk, soon to succeed the colorless Graener. Goebbels increased his *E-Musik* allotment, but the *E-Musiker* were not yet satisfied. On 28 February, came the showdown. It is not clear whether Strauss was summoned by the ministry or decided on his own to come, but according to Egk, who is not entirely reliable, they were all kept waiting in an anteroom so Goebbels could have it out with Strauss. "Your father had a repulsive collision with Mr. Goebbels," Kopsch later wrote to Franz Strauss. If we can believe eyewitness Egk, after their private meeting Goebbels ordered the rest of the group to step in so they could watch his continuing humiliation of the composer. Ritter had to recite the incriminating sentence from Strauss's letter. After acknowledging his authorship, Strauss was screamed at by Goebbels: "Be quiet, and take note that you have no idea of who you are and who I am!" Then Goebbels ranted against the composer for having run down Lehár: "Lehár has the masses, you don't! Stop babbling about the significance of *Ernste Musik*! This will not revalue your stock! Tomorrow's culture is different from that of yesterday! You, Mr. Strauss, are of yesterday!"[304]

Furthermore, 1941, the year in which Strauss met with Goebbels in Berlin, was to bring to the fore the composer's own personal problems with his Jewish relatives, because it was then that he asked the new Gauleiter of Vienna, Baldur von Schirach, for help against the regime's anti-Semitic course threatening his family. Schirach, on the other hand, was increasingly at odds with Goebbels over cultural policy.

In Vienna in January 1925, Franz Strauss had married Alice von Grab, the twenty-year-old daughter of wealthy industrialists from Prague, and they started to live in Strauss's newly built Viennese villa at Jacquingasse, situated in the luxuriant Kammergarten. A few weeks later Hofmannsthal met Alice; he found her as personally charming as she was bright.[305] Strauss, who himself had treasured his tight-knit family when he had been growing up, immediately became very fond of her and, subsequently, of his two grandchildren, Richard Jr., born in 1927, and Christian, born 1932. This, incidentally, is one of the factors underlying what looked like never-ending greed to outsiders: Because Strauss acknowledged total obligations to his family, he felt honor-bound to provide for all its members with the rewards from his oeuvre. During the war he once reminded Böhm that unlike tenured civil servants who just had to get through an eight-hour day, he was constantly dependent on royalties from seventeen stage works. "They constitute the daily bread for my family, which is more insecure than the state-guaranteed monthly salary of these gentlemen, complete with pension!"[306]

In the summer of 1938, after Strauss had served in his two important functions of Olympia Hymn composer-conductor and showcase musician at the first Reich Music Festival (which also had its significant anti-Semitic side), Goebbels, in collusion with the SS under Himmler and Heydrich, was stepping up anti-Jewish policy as a prelude to the November pogrom, for which he would later have to assume historical responsibility.[307] Hence in July 1938 Heydrich's underlings in the SS Reich Security Office were reminding SS leaders placed as liaison in the Promi of much unfinished business, for instance, that Strauss, who had written that critical letter to his Jewish librettist Zweig, maintained "relations with Jewish circles at home and abroad, probably because of his Jewish daughter-in-law."[308] And so Goebbels was tipped off for certain precipitous action to be taken against Alice Strauss, by way of harassment, during the ensuing *Kristallnacht* of 9–10 November. That the action was harassment, without ideological undertones, harassment ultimately aimed at Strauss, is proved by the fact that as a Jewish woman married to an "Aryan," Alice Strauss normally would not have been subject to the raid that followed; moreover, these activities were usually initiated against males, not females. Moreover, as the daughter-in-law of Germany's most illustrious composer, Frau Strauss normally would have been left alone, as was the Jewish wife of Strauss's "Aryan" nemesis Franz Lehár, Hitler's favorite living musician, or the Jewish wife of a less famous man, journalist Jochen Klepper, who freelanced for German Radio.[309]

On 9 November Alice Strauss and her husband Franz were with Munich friends in Grossweil, some twenty miles north of Garmisch, to hunt chamois—one of their pastimes. They were suddenly alerted by a hunter nearby to go home immediately, as "Jews were being persecuted in Garmisch." Once home they learned that early in the morning, eleven-year-old Richard had been stopped on the way to school by a Stormtrooper with a revolver, who asked briskly: "Where is your Jew mother?" The trembling child divulged the Grossweil venue and then was led to the market square, where he witnessed Jews from the region being corraled and manhandled. Six-year-old Christian was also fetched and forced to spit on the Jews, and the children themselves were spat upon. Meanwhile two other Stormtroopers came to the Strauss villa on Zoeppritzstrasse close to the Western mountain range hoping to find Alice Strauss there. They turned the property upside down, finding only the gardener. The next morning Alice and her two sons drove to Munich to hide out in a hotel for a few days. Back in Garmisch, the regional administrator, Landrat Wiesend, came to ask her to leave town immediately. Alice had the presence of mind to say that her absent parents-in-law had entrusted her with the care of the estate and that therefore she could not leave. She was then told not to step out into the spacious garden, to avoid being harmed by the unpredictable anger of the citizens. When she replied that only the night before neighboring farmers had visited to offer their apologies, Wiesend shut up but prescribed house arrest for fourteen days, confiscating all of Alice's Austrian papers indefinitely. Alice Strauss promptly succumbed to a gall-bladder inflammation.[310] In light of these traceable facts, it is unfathomable that as well-respected a writer as Fred K. Prieberg, and as late as 1991, the year Alice died, in a particularly savage portrait of Strauss saw fit to legitimize the Nazi slander by pointing out that Frau Strauss had been seen, haughty, arrogant, and "high on a horse," in town, demonstrating her privileges among the common people. For one thing, Prieberg supplies no evidence.[311] For another, Frau Strauss assuredly did not even know how to sit on a horse, nor had the Strauss family ever had anything to do with horses.[312]

Upon his return home, Strauss was shocked. Incensed at the November pogrom, he immediately took the position that his daughter-in-law and her children had to be treated exactly like himself.[313] The first man he trustingly turned to was Tietjen, but the opera wizard, then and in the months to follow, only alluded to talks with Göring, Goebbels, and Hitler, doing nothing, lest he himself get burned; therefore Strauss's later dedication of *Die Liebe der Danae* to him signified nothing.[314] In Vienna on the occasion of his birthday festivities in June, when Strauss had demonstratively taken his "half-Jewish" grandson Richard with him to have him play, on stage, a few measures of the *Rosenkavalier-Duett* on his flute, he had been able to talk to Goebbels, apparently with scant results.[315] Therefore on 20 June Strauss sat down to write a letter to Drewes, now Goebbels's right-hand man in matters of music policy and known to be sympathetic. Still fully aware of his market value, Strauss drew up a no uncertain wish list. He wanted *German* documents for his daughter-in-law (especially passport and driver's license to chauffeur him and the boys as necessary) and that again she be allowed to accompany him in public. For his grandchildren, Richard and Christian, he wished to have a guarantee that their school and university education not be encumbered, that they could follow regular careers and wed brides like full "Aryans." They were also to benefit from an inheritance accruing to them from their rich Jewish relatives in Bohemia. Neither should his son Franz suffer any setbacks. Strauss ended by saying that worries such as the current ones were not conducive to his creativity, hinting broadly that both the minister and the Führer would know what he meant.[316]

In the following months, because Strauss could not be sure about Goebbels, he composed his *Festmusik* for the Japanese government, not to fulfill an official German commission, as has wrongly been alleged, but at the request of Tokyo and free of charge, in the hope of Japanese intervention in his case—a hope that again proved futile.[317] In the spring of 1941 Goebbels appears to have heeded one part of Strauss's request by getting Hitler to extend limited "Aryan" privileges to his grandsons concerning their formal education.[318] But because no guarantees were given regarding Alice and Franz and there was more Nazi Party chicanery targeting the couple's hunting privileges, the Strauss family remained at risk.[319]

It was at this point that Baldur von Schirach as Gauleiter of Vienna stepped in. Having been in office for about a year, he was eager to conduct his own cultural politics and, in music, to favor more modern composers such as Carl Orff and Rudolf Wagner-Régeny, but to add luster to his administration he also wished to tie the famous Strauss more permanently to Vienna. (Schirach and Franz Strauss had examined stamp collections as children when Strauss was working in the Weimar-Meiningen area and

Carl von Schirach, Baldur's father, had been the Intendant of the Weimar stage.)[320] In the summer Schirach sent his plenipotentiary in cultural matters, Walter Thomas, to Garmisch to sound out the master. Strauss immediately sensed new chances and agreed to come, on the condition that Schirach would protect him. The Gauleiter was hesitant because he was already beginning to annoy Goebbels and Hitler and he knew that the Führer was unrelenting insofar as the "Jewish Question" was concerned. But in the end he extended vague promises to Strauss, without wanting to be quoted.[321] Strauss and his family moved to the Jacquingasse in December 1941, with the composer commuting between Vienna and Garmisch, as demands dictated.

By this time a drama in Strauss's extended family had begun to unfold which was to end tragically and augured badly for the future. Alice had relatives: her mother, Marie von Grab, already safe in Lucerne; an aunt Gertrud, married to a neurologist in Prague; and also in Prague, her grandmother, Paula Neumann, who had been born in 1861 and thus was three years older than Strauss. In 1924 Paula's husband, Richard Neumann, the industrialist then living in Reichenberg (Bohemia, CSR), had willed a fortune to his wife and his four daughters: Marie, Gertrud, Hilda, and Hanna. By the fall of 1941, the Strauss family was helping to get the ailing Paula Neumann out of Prague, and perhaps some of the other Jewish relatives; they were also attempting to salvage for Richard and Christian the Reichenberg real estate which was on the point of confiscation, as Jewish property, by the German authorities. With the help of Richard Strauss and her daughter in Lucerne, Paula Neumann managed to secure a Swiss entry visa, but she could not receive the proper authorization from the German occupiers to leave the Nazi Protectorate of Bohemia and Moravia. She was beholden to the Jewish congregation (forced to act as agents of the Gestapo), to whom she had already ceded all but her barest possessions.[322]

Franz and Alice Strauss and Aunt Gertrud Kramer in Prague attempted in January 1942 to move Paula Neumann to Vienna, but the attempt seems to have hinged on special permission to be given by one SS-Obersturmbannführer Dr. Günther of the Prague Gestapo. The Strauss family believed they still had a chance because the Swiss visa was extended to 1 September at the end of July. On 11 August Strauss himself wrote a moving letter to Günther—from one Herr Doktor to another—appealing to a "human kindness" that never existed in the first place. Strauss reminded Günther that during the past winter Schirach had already written to the Reichsprotektor for Bohemia (and chief of SD and Gestapo) Reinhard Heydrich, now "prematurely deceased" (Heydrich had been assassinated by Czech patriots in May). The answer from Heydrich's office had been unsatisfactory. Because the physician Kramer and his wife Gertrud had since been deported to the concentration camp of Theresienstadt, "the old woman is without help, and I am urgently asking you to assist me in getting her to the Swiss border." But the letter was written to the wind, and Paula Neumann was carted off to Theresienstadt as well. Strauss made one more attempt, riding in his large car right up to the Theresienstadt gates, announcing, "I am the composer, Richard Strauss," only to be turned back by dumbfounded SS guards. And so Frau Neumann died, reportedly of spotted fever. Other Jewish relatives of Alice Strauss were also murdered, twenty-six in all, in the Nazis' Eastern camps.[323]

It clearly did not look good for Strauss's children, as Schirach, too, appeared impotent.[324] Hence Strauss was casting about for other allies. In June 1943, Hans Frank, the General-Governor of Occupied Poland and jurist, who had helped Strauss years ago with Stagma problems, revered his music, and for months had wanted him to conduct in Cracow, invited Strauss, Franz, and Alice to his luxurious Kressendorf Castle so that the composer could "breathe like a human" for a change.[325] Luckily, Strauss did not take him up on that. And while he was getting nowhere with letters to Himmler and Reich Commissar Arthur Seyss-Inquart of Occupied Holland in the matter of his grandsons' inheritance, Goebbels conspired with the Gestapo to harass Alice Strauss further in Vienna.[326] Later that year during winter—while their parents were in Garmisch—the younger Strausses were on a social visit to friends in Vienna, where they played a card game. Suddenly eight Gestapo officers stormed into the drawing room, pointed out that the hostess, a Frau Painsipp, was half Jewish, and asked Franz Strauss in the presence of his wife why he did not divorce her. This evening ended without further incident. But a few days later, two Gestapo men in their long leather coats came to the Jacquingasse at 3:00 AM, taking Franz and Alice with them, while the children were sleeping. They were driven to SS headquarters and Gestapo jail and held in separate cells for several days and nights. Repeatedly interrogated, Alice Strauss was asked if she knew Schuschnigg (which she denied), and why she "hadn't yet taken off for Israel." She answered that she had two teenage children and was serving as Richard Strauss's secretary. Franz Strauss was assaulted with different questions, but he suffered less from those than from the eczema that plagued him throughout the war.[327]

In 1943 and 1944, the Nazi regime stepped up its various restrictions against the Strauss family. Back in Garmisch, the composer's house was to be partially occupied by bombed-out civilians as a war measure. Strauss, with a sick wife and himself in failing health, worked for months to avoid it, but in the end he was told to give up the detached servants' house.[328] Only the general confusion at the very end of the war obviated the measure. This after Hitler had wanted to give Wilhelm Furtwängler, for his various services to the state, a new villa on a Bavarian lake or at least to build him an elaborate bunker, to shield him from air attacks.[329] Strauss vainly tried to solicit Schirach's help with the problem, and during one of the regional Kreisleiter's threatening visits, in January 1944, General-Governor Frank happened to drive up Zoeppritzstrasse, to pay a social call. His presence ameliorated the situation momentarily, and the grateful composer sent Frank a card with four lines of verse comparing the General-Governor to Lohengrin—a tasteless act, but understandable from the perspective of a frightened old man.[330] Indeed, there were new Gestapo orders to arrest Alice Strauss and place her in a forced-labor camp, but sympathetic gendarmes ignored them.[331] No additional privileges were extended to the grandsons; on the contrary, in June 1944 Goebbels was firm that they should never be able to assume "officer's rank in the German Wehrmacht." By 1 November young Richard was working in a subordinate position in the Viennese brewery of a close family friend, who shielded him from being drafted into forced labor set up everywhere by the dreaded Organisation Todt.[332] Franz Strauss's hunting privileges were once again called into question (Frau Alice's had already been rescinded) because a local Nazi chieftain envied the Strausses their rented shoot near Grossweil and complained to Himmler. The SS Chief and Heydrich's successor SS-Obergruppenführer Ernst Kaltenbrunner decided not to extend Franz Strauss's hunting license and earmarked him for conscription in the war industry. In early 1945 Franz ended up helping out in a nearby military hospital.[333] He, who in the first years of the Nazi regime had been sympathetic to some of its ideology, had been cured after the pogroms of 1938.[334]

On balance, despite noted highlights, Richard Strauss's life and career after July 1935 were overshadowed by the consequences of his failure as RMK president, the Stefan Zweig affair, and close family ties. There can be no talk about a "comfortable life among the Nazis," as Bernard Holland found as late as 1991.[335]

Strauss increasingly suffered from adversities which today might strike us as trivial but to him meant a deprivation of physical comforts to which he thought he was entitled as conducive to his art, and signifying, moreover, a decrease in national prestige. These difficulties, about which he conducted a large correspondence with what friends in high places he still had, included the threatened loss of his gardener and chauffeur to the draft, a constant need for gasoline to operate his automobile and heating materials for the houses as well as warm textiles for the winter. He also wished foreign currency to take him to his spa or special Strauss events in Switzerland and permission to cross the German border (which, unlike Furtwängler, was denied him by early 1944).[336] To these ends he usually approached Schirach, Tietjen, Reich Economics Minister Funk, and Hans Frank, who ever and again proffered his assistance to lure the composer to Cracow, which Strauss, unlike Pfitzner, continued to resist, for reasons not yet clear.[337]

In the professional realm, where Strauss was needed by the Reich and could hold his own throughout most of the war, he was seriously beginning to lose favor at the beginning of 1944, when the Nazi leaders started to realize that cultural propaganda had to be subordinated to Total War, proclaimed by Goebbels earlier. Coterminously, Strauss had become too much of a nuisance, mostly to the minister, and because of his close ties with the upstart Schirach. Because of the immediate ban on *Die schweigsame Frau* for the Reich, opera stages, such as Munich's, which had planned to have it performed later in 1935 and beyond, quickly had to change their repertory.[338] Munich's Walleck even found excuses to cancel *Salome* and *Elek-*

tra, two of Strauss's more controversial operas in orthodox Nazi eyes, scheduled for the end of the year.[339] However, in 1941–42, when the first winds of the storm had blown over, Strauss was, still or again, the most frequently performed living opera composer in Germany.[340] His popularity was buoyed after 1942, in no small degree because of Schirach and the Vienna stage, so that even Orff—also favored by that Gauleiter—became quite jealous. Strauss was awarded a special silver medal and the Beethoven Prize Schirach had a hand in granting—some compensation, Strauss must have felt, for the proliferation in Vienna of the modern music (Orff, Wagner-Régeny, Egk).[341] The qualitatively superior performances in Vienna became a straw for Strauss to hold on to, especially when the empathetic Böhm arrived on the scene in early 1943, despite Goebbels's strong potential for sabotage.[342] In Berlin even Tietjen did what he could, planning Strauss operas as late as January 1944. Indeed, by then Hitler himself had decreed—altogether less menacingly than Goebbels—that although Strauss was not to associate with regime leaders any more, his music should not be banned.[343]

Certainly Strauss did not care about the loss of personal ties to the higher echelons in that final year of war, as his own few party friends could not be deterred. What he did care about and what almost broke his heart was the manner in which his 1944 birthday celebrations were conducted and the cancellation of the Salzburg Festival in late summer, which was to premiere one of his last operas, the one about Jupiter.

It was his eightieth birthday, which should have been observed in June throughout the Reich. Whereas music experts in the Rosenberg camp had already decided to all but ignore the event, Schirach in Vienna wanted impressive festivities, on the model of earlier years. And so, of course, did Frank in Cracow. Hitler was ambivalent, leaning toward Goebbels, who wished to forbid all formalities. At this point—a rare turn in his attitude to Strauss, which so far had been vituperative—Furtwängler intervened and prevailed upon Goebbels not to demoralize the composer completely. Goebbels relented; after discussions with Hitler it was decided that although all local celebrations already planned had to be canceled, Vienna should be allowed to go ahead with one solitary major event, a new production of *Ariadne auf Naxos,* at which Schirach himself was permitted to be present. Goebbels and Hitler sent congratulatory telegrams which were sufficiently bland; Goebbels also made a pointedly meaningless gift of a bust of Christoph Willibald Gluck (to whom Strauss had never related), rather than the Mercedes complete with ample gasoline stamps which Drewes would have preferred to give. In a letter in June 1944, Strauss expressed lip-service gratitude over the artifact, but he was clearly disappointed, especially as, once again, permission to travel to Switzerland had been denied. He expressed his hope for the upcoming Salzburg Festival on 1 August, as whose protector the minister functioned, and looked forward to the premiere of *Die Liebe der Danae.*[344]

Indeed, in one of his better moods at the height of the war, Goebbels apparently had asked for this opera to be first performed at Salzburg.[345] However, because of the havoc wrought by war, the original premiere date of 1 July had had to be postponed to 15 August, with a dress rehearsal two days earlier.[346] On 6 August Strauss still had reason to believe that both the dress rehearsal and the premiere would occur, and that he might even see Goebbels at the latter (a possible change for the better?).[347] However, on 15 August the festival fell victim to Goebbels's blanket cancellation of cultural events. Still, a dress rehearsal took place in Salzburg on the next day, under Krauss's direction. Richard Strauss was present, following the conductor's every move. He was extremely serious. At the end of the rehearsal Krauss spoke a few moving words. Then Strauss came to the fore, greeted the musicians by lifting his hands, and, fighting back his tears, said: "Perhaps we shall meet again in a better world."[348] As Strauss wrote later to Wieland Wagner, Jupiter had taken his final leave from this beautiful world.[349]

This time the god had failed, albeit only on the Salzburg stage. Strauss's remaining weeks, until the end of the war, were bitter ones: He was in ill health, his wife was even worse off, and the rest of his family was insecure at best. Strauss fell further as the end of the Third Reich drew near; he was hurting increasingly from *Weltschmerz*. It was an all-pervading pain caused as much by the knowledge that his own oeuvre had irreparably suffered as by the certainty that, universally, Germany's culture, as he had known it, was finished. On 17 November he let Böhm know: "It is difficult if one has worked for almost 70 years for nothing and sees one's life work turn into dust, together with all that dear music of the Germans!"[350] A week later, this time to Tietjen: "My life's work is destroyed."[351] And in January 1945 he again wrote to Böhm: "It is a terrible life, just vegetating toward the inevitable."[352]

IV

When U.S. troops entered Garmisch on 30 April 1945, they were able to take the town without a struggle. Richard Strauss, though mentally broken and physically ill, was relieved that the tyranny was over. The next day, several jeeps drove up the sumptuous driveway from Zoeppritzstrasse. Not knowing who lived in the villa, the Americans wanted to occupy it. A U.S. major announced to Franz and young Richard Strauss that the house had to be evacuated within the next twenty minutes. Alarmed by his grandson but unfazed, Strauss reached for some pieces of paper in his desk drawer, stepped outside, and met the officers. Calmly and with great dignity, the tall man stood upright before them and said in his best English: "My name is Richard Strauss. I am the composer." He then showed the documents around. They were parts of the original scores of *Der Rosenkavalier* and *Salome,* as well as certificates of honorary citizenship from U.S. cities. "Here, you may look at them if you want." Respectfully, the Americans took three steps back. A few days later, Strauss and his family invited several officers for supper, prepared with the resources still in the house, including wine from the cellar. Reciprocating with dinner invitations of their own, the U.S. officers remained Strauss's best friends.[353]

After a while the composer learned that the villa in Vienna, whence grandson Richard had earlier made his way by bicycle, had been pillaged by Russian troops; an original letter by Mozart had been lost; and at the Salzburg Festival site, 1,500 piano scores and 100 full scores of *Die Liebe der Danae* were destroyed. But no member of the Strauss family had perished or been seriously hurt; Strauss's own health improved over the summer months, and so did Pauline's, who last had been suffering from pneumonia.[354] The couple wanted to get away from Garmisch to a warmer climate for the fall and winter, perhaps their beloved Switzerland, perhaps Lugano, but they did not receive official permission from the Americans to leave until 11 October, because by then, of course, the Americans had learned that Strauss had been president of the Nazi RMK. After Richard and Pauline Strauss departed, it turned out that Strauss would have to stay longer than at first expected because of further complications with his health, including appendicitis.[355]

Immediately, and until the formal conclusion of a denazification trial, many rumors floated around, in Germany as well as abroad, concerning Strauss's current and past situation. In Switzerland reporters from the yellow press hunted him. There was much talk about his Nazi record (his tasteless poem for Frank was published there), and it was quite impossible to have any of his works performed there.[356] In Germany, people in the street talked about Strauss having crossed the border illegally; then it was said he had assumed Austrian citizenship to escape all reponsibility in Germany and that he was living in Bohemia or Vienna. (Indeed, on 31 January 1947 the new Austrian government offered Strauss Austrian citizenship *honoris causa,* which he accepted, not least to safeguard the future of the Jacquingasse estate.) By early 1947 more rumors abounded about his past role in the Third Reich, and the German tabloids wondered whether Strauss, after a formal court trial, might be classified as a Nazi activist. Even four years after his death there was hearsay that he had written a special hymn for General-Governor Hans Frank.[357]

In Garmisch and Munich the German denazification trial against Strauss got under way in early 1947, after it had been ascertained that he had never been a member of any of the obvious Nazi Party organizations but had served as RMK president in the propaganda ministry, from 1934 to 1935 (as was falsely claimed), and that he had voluntarily resigned, "in order to forestall the threatened expulsion."[358] There were other allegations: that, like Furtwängler, he had been a Preussischer Staatsrat; that he had had a hand in the "Aryanization" of the Jewish Fürstner publishing company; that he had cultivated connections to the highest regime leaders; that he had conducted for Bruno Walter in Berlin and Hans Knappertsbusch in Munich.[359] German media, such as Hamburg's daily *Die Welt,* went further, saying that having used his political connections to shield his Jewish daughter-in-law was irregular and that, indeed, Strauss had secured privileges for her after composing the *Festmusik* for the Japanese government.[360]

This assortment of charges shows how ill prepared and uninformed the court was generally, as would be the case in so many of those denazification trials, but as in Carl Orff's case it also points up the occupiers' misconceptions about cultural life in the Third Reich at the time, and specifically about Richard Strauss. Strauss had never been a Prussian State Counselor (as he had never been in Göring's employ). The Fürstner "Aryanization" had not been right, but it was a comparatively orderly business; any part Strauss had played in it had been toward helping Fürstner, on his way to London, as much as possible, and leaving him all the foreign rights. The Walter replacement story of 1933 was once again distorted, and the court falsely assumed that Knappertsbusch, for whom Strauss was supposed to have stood in in 1935, had been released from his post for "political reasons."[361] Here nothing could have been further from the truth, for Knappertsbusch had been a Nazi relieved of his position by Hitler, who happened not to like him, and it was not Strauss but Clemens Krauss (an obvious but inexcusable confusion of names) who eventually conducted in Munich in his stead—after 1936.[362] As for the newspaper accusation regarding Alice Strauss, it was juridically not even tenable; in 1947–48 nobody seems to have known the true background of the genesis of *Festmusik,* including the fact that the Japanese either did not want or were unable to stop the chicanery against the Jewish woman.

Because of his health, Strauss himself was allowed to wait out the result of the trial in Switzerland. There was much bumbling on the side of the prosecution as well as of the defense, not least in the handling of the evidence presented by witnesses. One such well-meaning person, for instance, wanted to vouch for the fact that Strauss had always been a "democrat of the purest type" and hence could not have approved of the Nazis.[363] Strauss may have been many things, but never in his life was he a "democrat." Simplifying an entirely complex issue, his lawyer Karl Roesen used as his main defense strategy that by June–July 1935 Strauss had served his RMK role and had become a nuisance to the Nazi regime. Then, after Strauss had "thoroughly organized everything" and wanted to realize his own ideas, Goebbels had to let him go.[364] In any event, several months into the proceedings obvious falsehoods and misrepresentations could be cleared up and it was found that Strauss did not fit any of the Nazi categories; hence the proceedings were stopped. On 7 June 1948, Strauss was formally vindicated as "not incriminated" by the applicable criteria of Nazi political involvement.[365] Attorney Roesen explained to him that day that matters had taken so long because any existing formalities had to be painstakingly observed; any formal errors might have given the press, which all the while had just been drooling, an excuse to start sensationalizing and, to boot, Strauss, like Furtwängler in Berlin, might have had to be called to testify in person. Roesen congratulated Strauss on having obtained this positive verdict just short of his eighty-fourth birthday.[366]

Richard and Pauline Strauss returned to Garmisch on 10 May 1949, to get on with their lives. On his eighty-fifth birthday on 11 June Strauss was honored by the State of Bavaria and the City of Munich, there was to be a Strauss Foundation, and he received an honorary doctorate in law from the university.[367] If only his hometown had treated him like this from the beginning. His relationship with old friends and colleagues had stabilizied, normalized, even before his return. Strauss even had a warm exchange with Fritz Busch.[368] Winifred Wagner sent commiserating letters to the family, if self-pitying for what the Allies were about to do to her and the Bayreuth Festival, but the composer and Alice Strauss were in touch with her oldest son Wieland, who was credited by them with good intentions.[369]

A few communications were reminiscent of uglier times or in no way conducive to good feeling in the present or the future. Former Reich Minister of Economics Walther Funk sent his greetings from a U.S. internment camp in late 1945. "You well know how I always suffered with you and attempted to help. But I have become the victim of such errors, having played down everything much too much, so that now I have to atone for it."[370] Strauss had another problematic encounter with Thomas Mann, vicariously, through Mann's oldest son, Klaus. As early as May 1945 Klaus Mann, in the American uniform of a war reporter for *Stars and Stripes,* appeared at the Garmisch villa together with another uniformed correspondent, the Jewish émigré Curt Riess, in the disguise of a "Mr. Brown." Unrecognized, Mann teased stories out of Strauss which then he could, perfidiously, publish in the U.S. Army newspaper in what would amount to an attempt at character assassination. According to Mann, Strauss said that the Nazis were criminals because they had prevented the performance of his operas, especially *Die Liebe der Danae* at the end; they had dared to impose on his family strangers to be quartered in his villa; they had caused the destruction of eighty opera houses, so now his works could not be played. There were some exceptions, said Strauss, Governor Hans Frank for instance, a man with "delicate artistic taste." Hitler himself appreciated good music, "music by Richard Strauss," for instance. And Mann cited Strauss as saying, of the Zweig affair: "Naturally, after this experience, my relations with the Government remained a little cool for some time. But in the course of years, both the gentlemen in Berlin and I forgot about the unpleasant affair. In general, I have been treated very decently ever since." Mann published his "interview" in *Stars and Stripes* on 29 May 1945 and gloated to his father about it.[371] When Strauss found out about the trickery, he was incensed and sat down to write a letter to his old adversary in California, but in the end he decided not to send it.[372] As for Thomas Mann, he had scarcely been able to conceal his disgust of Strauss as a "Hitlerian" composer while still being compelled to listen to his works during the Nazi period—either as conducted by his friend Walter or on radio.[373]

Toward the end of the war Mann had excoriated *Salome* as a work of decadence by associating its heroine at the Graz premiere on 16 May 1906 with the second visit of composer Adrian Leverkühn to the alluring but syphilitic harlot Esmeralda, who would then infect him—in the novel *Doktor Faustus,* published in 1947.[374] It may be doubted whether Strauss ever read this book before his death, but after the Klaus Mann visit, he felt insulted when U.S. officers in Munich asked him why he had not emigrated, as had Thomas Mann.[375]

Richard Strauss composed surprisingly much between the end of the Third Reich and his death in 1949, and there were plenty of Strauss performances, nationally as well as internationally. It is moot at this point to list these accomplishments, but some highlights may be mentioned.[376] In June 1946 Strauss proudly wrote to Schirach's erstwhile adjutant, Walter Thomas, from Lausanne that after having recuperated he had recently composed "some superfluous absolute music, two small sonatas for 16 winds, a string piece, *Metamorphosen,* an oboe concerto."[377] The *Metamorphosen* (1945) were later held to be a lament about the destruction of German culture, physically by Allied bombing and spiritually by the Nazis. Yet to interpret the *Eroica* quotation at the end as Strauss's "disappointment in his Führer equivalent to Beethoven's Napoleon transformation from savior to tyrant" would be placing unjustified credence in Strauss as a former disciple of Adolf Hitler.[378] His *Vier letzte Lieder* (1948), performed only after his death, were Strauss's outstanding achievements in old age.[379]

Strauss received accolades from the United States and an invitation by his old admirer Sir Thomas Beecham to London, where, albeit a frail man now, he conducted his works in October 1947. Asked by a journalist what his next plans were, he answered with his characteristic sense of humor: "Well, to die, of course!"[380] Straus died in his Garmisch home from heart failure on 8 September 1949.[381] It was the end of an era, not only musically speaking. Whereas Jupiter's legend had been damaged during his lifetime, his Garmisch villa was declared a historic site by the State of Bavaria on 30 September 1949, exactly one week after the founding of the Federal Republic of Germany.[382]

Conclusion

Composers in the Postwar Era
Until the 1960s

This book represents the last in a trilogy on the interrelationship between sociopolitical forces on the one side, and music and musicians in the Third Reich, on the other. The first of these dealt with jazz and jazz musicians and their fans in the context of German fascism and was published in 1992.[1] The second dealt with composers and practitioners mostly of serious music and was published five years later.[2] The current volume has attempted to concentrate on eight of the composers already mentioned in the second volume; their choice was dictated by their relative and absolute importance but also by the existence of a modicum of primary documents, from which biographical and musical data could be culled.

The perhaps strange sequence of these books was not intended, but, rather, the consequence of my private inclinations and tastes. I began to work in the historiography and musicology of jazz because of a very active personal interest in that art form, not least as a modern-jazz performer for several years; as a historian of the Third Reich, the question of how—presumably anti-Nazi—jazz musicians and aficionados got along with Nazis ultimately intrigued me. When I was finished with that puzzle, I was surprised to find that some jazz-indulging men and women were Nazis, and that the Nazi regime itself used the officially condemned genre for its devious political purposes. Hence the preconceived notion of jazz as a natural vehicle of resistance to fascism had been jettisoned. Thereafter, I was plagued by a guilty conscience for having preferred a study on jazz to a study on serious music (which genre, after all, came first!) but was also interested in a comparison of "legit" musicians (as jazz lingo would have it) with other professions, such as physicians, teachers, and lawyers, some of whom I had previously analyzed.[3] Therefore I then embarked on the *Twisted Muse* project, my second volume in this series. During its completion it occurred to me that several composers as creators of possibly contentious music mentioned in that book, Jews and non-Jews alike, deserved a closer look within the framework of my earlier studies; hence the present volume.

After the publication of *The Twisted Muse*, during the academic review process, I was taken to task by an esteemed colleague for having authored a useful treatise which, unfortunately, was lacking a conclusion.[4] I plead guilty as charged. My explanation, though it cannot serve as an excuse, is that I was overwhelmed by the often seemingly contradictory patchwork-quilt evidence I had found and, as with the jazz project, by a posteriori insights I originally had not expected. Although historians should refrain from moral judgments in any case, I was finding it difficult to describe any of the human situations I encountered as typical or to pronounce any one of my characters save a precious few as either fully guilty (or, if you will, responsible), or fully innocent (or noninvolved): "One and all—musicians and singers, composers and conductors, all of whom had to make a living as artists in the Third Reich—emerged in May 1945 severely tainted, with their professional ethos violated and their music often compromised: gray people against a landscape of gray."[5]

At the time of publication I thought that this sentence represented a conclusion of sorts, but instead of making it the point of departure for a true conclusive chapter at the end, I had used it and preceding sentences, not very strategically, as the last statement of my introduction, which, as happens so often, was written when the manuscript had been done. All three books completed, perhaps it is now appropriate to offer insights on a few themes or principles they all share, however obvious those might be. The first would be that politics and the arts do not good bedfellows make, even in a democratic society, and that their mutual relationship gets worse in a fascist polity such as the Third Reich. The second would come as a result of specific reflection on the structure of this totalitarian Reich, which showed so little homogeneity as to allow for exceptions and contradictions in the arts and in artists' behavior. The surprising persistence of jazz, jazz musicians, and jazz fans from 1933 to 1945 is a case in point here, as is the formal lack of control the regime ultimately exerted over classical-music content. A third general observation concerns the corruptibility of artists when placed in other than ordinary circumstances: Jazz musicians who, in a tolerant democracy, would never ever have politics, but wine, women, and song, on their minds sold their skills to the propaganda ministry to enhance the war effort against Great Britain (regaling Wehrmacht soldiers and trying to lure British prisoners-of-war); serious-music composers like Hindemith who waited till the last possible moment to emigrate or who, like Orff, dismissed the thought of emigration outright and came to serve the rulers in some questionable capacity; conductors such as Furtwängler who paraded their vanity under dictatorial auspices but simultaneously on the pretense of serving a different, true, and pre-Hitlerian fatherland. In the pages of all three volumes, a uniform portrait appears only for the certified victims, foremost the Jews, who were not offered an opportunity by that criminal regime to compromise their art and morality, as did their "Aryan" colleagues. This is what set apart the Weintraub Syncopators jazz ensemble, Germany's best in 1932, who were dispersed in all directions, from Fritz Brocksieper and his "Charlie's Orchestra," so eager to serve Goebbels (and with Brocksieper being a quarter Jewish). This is what distinguished Kurt Weill from the quarter-Jewish Carl Orff, who saw nothing wrong with replacing the fully Jewish Felix Mendelssohn's incidental music to *A Midsummer Night's Dream* with his own creation in 1938–39, and Arnold Schoenberg from Richard Strauss, who, Jupiter that the latter was, never even considered emigration as a device to escape the immorality of his tactical commitment to the Nazis.

By way of concluding the current project on composers, specific reflections are called for, with some of them, to be sure, going back to themes that were touched on in the two preceding volumes. The first category would concern what I conceive as the comparability of the principals involved. Roughly, what did they have in common, and what separated them? The second category fastens on some of the historic ironies encountered in writing up and analyzing the eight biographies. Such ironies could be serendipitous, but they could also be the logical consequence of acts consciously, purposefully, committed by our heroes. Although neither type is provable, ironies are still important because they link characters together, shedding additional light on them, if only behind the foreground dramas of history. And third and last, what about the problem of continuity beyond the decisive break marked by 8 May 1945, when Nazi Germany surrendered to the Allies: Was there a Zero Hour, and was there one for culture, and, in particular, for the musical culture of the nation? What, if anything, did the eight composers have to do with a return to well-honed pre-1933 traditions, an acceptance or rejection of Nazi-tried values and practices, or the invention, or reinvention, of new musical genres, including some specific only to themselves?

Social historians with interdisciplinary interests tend to work comparatively, so the question of how the eight composers were similar to or different from one another was a natural one for this study. From a purely technical point of view, comparisons among all composers would probably have been feasible. Two or three such opportunities came my way, with no place to elucidate in the main body of the book, but probably as material for this conclusion. For example, it might have been possible to compare more closely Orff and Egk, not only as would-be moderns in the Third Reich, but also their peculiar tactics as opportunists.

However, some of these comparisons would be more of the musicological, if not the anecdotal, kind, and for that reason alone hardly called for.

In sociopolitical terms, they are risky because certain circumstances pertaining to any one of the composers could have been specific only to him, impacting on and reflecting only his particular fate, so that other composers in these circumstances would deserve different judgments. This is why even the comparison of the survival strategies of Orff and Egk is precarious, to say nothing of those used by these two composers on the one hand, and Richard Strauss on the other.

Then again, it is possible to organize the composers into subgroups, to see what distinguished each category and how it would have differed from others. One could imagine several such groupings: Jews versus non-Jews; traditionalists versus modernists; Nazi fellow travelers versus resisters versus the indifferent; the German-rooted versus the emigrants, and so on. But although an organization of these categories would seem sensible, difficulties are lurking here as well. Some men may have belonged to several categories, depending on what phases of their lives we are examining: Orff, for instance, was anything but a "fellow traveler" before the premiere of *Carmina Burana* in June 1937 yet increasingly became one thereafter. With all his attachment to the cause of music in the Third Reich after 1941 and his subsequent functions in the Reich Music Chamber, Werner Egk may have harbored a certain anti-Nazi animus, for the details about the tragic fate of his anti-Nazi son, Titus, are credible, and till Titus's violent death Egk had a strong hand in his socialization. Weill would go out of his way to declare himself a bona fide American after 1935, but the latest research about him makes us doubt that he was so thoroughly uprooted and alienated from all things German, including the German arts, as he himself and others would have us believe. Hans Pfitzner professed to be an anti-Semite, yet, with all the applicable caveats, why then should two of his closest friends, Bruno Walter and Paul Nikolaus Cossmann, have been Jews? Will it ever be known whether Strauss was politically indifferent, enthusiastically for the Nazis, or, despite his groveling letters to them, a hater of Hitler and Goebbels, and hence of the Third Reich, of the highest order? Probably he was all and none of these, depending on the point in time.

Instead, I would like to explore yet another question, to help clarify why the eight composers reacted to the allures and pressures of their times in characteristically distinctive ways. This question relates to the putative *German* quality of music (in Germany), and how the composers behaved in its perceived presence or absence.

Only recently, younger musicologists have identified "The German" as a criterion of music, and consequently as something that shaped the careers of musicians—especially composers—in Germany, from Beethoven to Orff.[6] Applied to our portraits, this element crosses political party lines, ethnocultural or artificial racial divisions, and even aesthetic and sometimes geographic borders. By implication—if phenomena be viewed as antinomal—it includes the alternative, namely "The Non-German," clearing the path for xenophobia.

Certainly until 1945, the Germans as a people, not only in the Hitlerian *völkisch* sense, defined themselves and their history decisively through *Kultur*—they said they always had it, and nobody else did. In their collective view, this is what set them apart from materialistic British money-bags, degenerate French hedonists, insensitive American pragmatists, work-shirking Italian fools, and the alcoholized denizens of a half-Asiatic Russian empire. Moreover, nothing in the German mind has defined *Kultur* so quintessentially as its music—German music. It has been suggested that this was so because of the key function music fulfilled in shaping a German identity through the nineteenth century.[7] Ever since that time there was a "collective assumption of the superiority of the German . . . in music," writes Riethmüller.[8] By extension, then, German music was a yardstick with which to measure the German national character, to gauge the depth of the German soul. To uphold German music was divine duty, to neglect it was high crime.

This concept is key for an explanation of several phenomena encountered between the covers of this book, not least the continued acceptance of Strauss by the Nazi leaders, for they never disagreed among themselves that he always wrote very German music, a taboo for the Jewish-getto Kulturbund.[9] The Nazis showed great nervousness when this quality was put in doubt, as with Strauss's "Jewish" opera *Salome* or the ballet *Josephslegende*. Werner Egk risked censure in 1938, when his opera *Peer Gynt* featured the Nordic protagonist in a Latin American bar, beguiled by exotic women and the sounds of a jazzy tango.

It is clear how non-German or merely half-German composers fit into this scheme of things. The partly Italian, partly German composer Ferruccio Busoni, who retreated to Switzerland during World War I because he did not wish to offend either his mother country or his fatherland, since 1915 in opposite camps, was well aware of the danger posed by "German chauvinism in matters musical." Already in 1919, having returned to Berlin, he labeled the German music establishment "the German music police atmosphere."[10] The most terrifying exponent of genuine music as exclusively German was Hans Pfitzner, who throughout the 1920s sharply polemicized against all the enemies "of our national art, especially music."[11] Once in power, through their various propaganda speeches, the Nazi leaders made very sure that they understood well Richard Wagner's original dictum, that "the German has the exclusive right to be called 'musician.'" Germany was "the first music nation in the world," insisted Reich Propaganda Minister Goebbels.[12]

The corollary was an axiom about the enemy. For cultural and political nationalists like Pfitzner, music existed that was merely forgettable, and music that was the completely destructive opposite of the German character. To Pfitzner, the xenophobe, this was American jazz (as it was observed invading Germany in the 1920s) and "aharmony," which was his term for what the Nazis later vilified as "atonality," chiefly the music of the Second Viennese School. "To base absolute music on the principle of cacophony, in and of itself senseless sounds," wrote Pfitzner in 1926, "even to declare that which harmonically makes sense more or less, or totally, off limits—which cannot even happen without the expenditure of hard work—is the same for aesthetics as insanity is for the spirit, or torture for the body."[13] And to Pfitzner as for the Nazis later, the people who propelled both jazz and "aharmony" were, of course, the Jews.[14] By the logic that music was the ultimate criterion of national identity, "Jewish" jazz and atonal music could serve, for the Nazis, as a potential weapon in an attack on the Germans' sovereignty, hence, as an existential question, assume eminently political functions—notwithstanding the fact that neither Pfitzner, nor the Nazis knew what the true definition of German music, even in a metaphysical or metaphorial sense, actually was.[15] And as for Busoni, once the object of Pfitzner's scorn, he was perplexed: "I wish I knew what German depth in music is. I feel quite helpless! In Beethoven I can hear a great humanity, liberty, and originality, in Mozart the joy of life and beauty of form (really Italian characteristics), in Bach feeling, worship, greatness, and perfection. German, pronouncedly German ways, as they are border-transcending in Beethoven, Mozart, and Bach, actually constitute reduction, provincialization. The following are German: Lohengrin, Freischütz, male choirs, and our celebrated contemporary Max Reger. Schumann, too. But where is the depth here that Dante and Michelangelo would not have?"[16]

Besides Pfitzner, the only other composer in our group who came close to sharing the German proprietary view was Strauss. And, if the anti-Semitic element is extracted, there was more than a trace of this belief in Schoenberg: Witness Schoenberg's absurd judgment regarding Toscanini and his noncomprehension of German music. In the case of Strauss, too, the anti-Semitic consideration was negligible, even in his early career (consider the documented respect for his peer, Gustav Mahler), but what made him partially xenophobic was his distrust of jazz and his dislike of many French and Italian composers, especially Puccini. And, like Pfitzner, Strauss thought atonality or serialism an un-German aberration. Strauss's position makes for an interesting comparison and contrast with Weill, who was for many years an acolyte of the master from Garmisch and appreciated the significance of Mozart and his *Jupiter* symphony for Strauss well, thinking that only Strauss, as conductor, could bring to life the mysterious forces inherent in that particular work.[17] At the same time, and for us quite understandably, Weill cherished not only jazz but good operetta, which Strauss loathed, and in opera, Puccini was for him a genius, because he "reflected the modern conception of psychology in human relationships."[18]

Whereas Weill, Hartmann, and Hindemith would not have subscribed to the view about the uniqueness of German music in the universe, Orff and Egk were in a somewhat different position. They were pushed in that direction. Although their artistic pedigree was sufficiently cosmopolitan—what with Stravinsky looming large there—they were impelled by the Nazi regime to conduct themselves as specifically modern "German" composers.[19] Like Strauss's, their new music was officially represented at the German-hosted Olympic Games in Berlin; they took part, actively or passively, in Nazi RMK prize competitions; and both received state commissions (Egk in Düsseldorf; and Orff in Frankfurt and Vienna). Both were Bavarians, with Orff insisting more strongly on his *alt-bairische* roots than Egk, and in fact using them in his excuse not to emigrate. Egk, on the other hand, thought nothing of accepting an important role in the Nazi RMK, while being attracted to Paris during wartime, which might have emphasized his international side—but it was a Paris whose cultural life was, after all, dominated by German purveyors of culture.[20] Our analysis must stop short of a discussion of possibly "German" characteristics of Orff and Egk's compositions, even in the case of *Carmina Burana*, the most obvious candidate, because it would have to fail for the same reason that the Nazis were not able to arrive at a binding definition of such Germanness in music.[21]

That Weill should have admired Strauss yet not have known about his phobia against Puccini and operetta is surely ironic. In the mid-1920s Weill also applauded Pfitzner for his works *Palestrina* and *Von deutscher Seele*, appreciating in particular that Pfitzner had agreed to adapt his opera *Der arme Heinrich* for radio and planned to direct it himself. This could have established a link, albeit a curious one, between one of the most modern and one of the most reactionary composers of twentieth-century Germany. Yet Weill and his kind, of course, were attacked by Pfitzner at that time when he wrote that "the anti-German, in whatever shape it appears, as atonality, internationalism, Americanism, German pacifism, is accosting our existence, our culture, from all sides." Himself not expressing any malice, Weill nevertheless regretted that "Pfitzner has lost many sympathies through his political posture and his vituperative stance against the new art."[22]

Other ironies tied together other composers. Why should Strauss have been trying, in early 1935, to rehabilitate Hindemith the modernist within the RMK at the same time he congratulated Goebbels for having taken a stance against all modernists in the Reich? Why should Egk be chosen, by the propaganda ministry, as some kind of patron saint of a specifically Nazi new-music modernity when in fact he had already proven (through *Peer Gynt*) that his modernism was potentially beyond Nazi comprehension? And is it not ironic that Egk, who was supported in his role as composer section leader in the RMK, after the summer of 1941, by Orff, was left alone by his former friend and teacher when trying to shake off his Nazi past after May 1945? Apart from the same young woman for whom both Orff and Egk may have been lusting, a central figure in this play could have been the U.S. culture officer Newell Jenkins, whom Orff appears to have monopolized for his own purposes: Jenkins, too, weaves historic irony into the tapestry of this chronicle by first becoming Orff's student in 1938 and then meeting him again in 1945, quite accidentally but just in time to throw the composer a life line. One of the most outrageous ironies lies in the fact that Otto von Pasetti—the notorious gambler and philanderer who early on in the Nazi regime had wiled away his time with Lotte Lenya and then embezzled the proceeds from the sale of the Berlin estate of both Lenya and Kurt Weill, hence anything but an exemplar of morality—should be in Jenkins's position in Austria in 1945. Now, as a freshly anointed U.S. screening official, he was writing important reports about artists such as Furtwängler and Strauss.[23]

In one of these papers Pasetti pointed to crass inadequacies in any denazification-of-culture attempt, as indeed, again ironically, Pasetti himself, with his imperfect knowledge of English, served as a prime example of this failure. The denazification of German society by the four victorious Allies was a priority on their agenda right from the first day of the country's occupation in May 1945, and it was to be accomplished, to a large extent, through the use of culture, including music. Grave difficulties had to be overcome. At the risk of generalization, they were, in the main, technical ones for the victors and conceptual ones for the vanquished. Early on the Germans created the catch word "Zero Hour," an imaginary hiatus in time, to mark a new beginning. But because resurrection out of a void was impossible, questions arose such as what viable pre-Nazi traditions to revive, or how to define a new "modernity" with which one wanted to be identified. Again, this applied to the realm of politics as well as culture in the broadest sense, because culture, in so many ways, could always reflect the politics of the day, if not influence it.[24]

The difficulties arising from 8 May 1945, marking Zero Hour, to the mid-1960s, when both West and East Germany had been stabilized sufficiently to render their political and cultural systems workable, were enormous and today almost defy analysis.[25] For the purpose of this conclusion, which is seeking some final perspective on the eight composers, several questions suggest themselves. Ultimately, they all exist in some thematic relationship to what seems to be the multifaceted, elusive, phenomenon of Zero Hour. For example, what was the nature of denazification and the attendant political reformation, in particular as it involved culture? What role did music have in this resurrected culture? And in the new music scene, did our eight composers attain significance, and of what sort?

The problems are complex because they are contained within grids that are superimposed upon and partially interlocked with one another to make the final dilemma multidimensional. In political terms, denazification eventually gave way to German regional self-government and then to national sovereignty. But this happened across three different Western Allied occupation zones, and an Eastern one, which became opposed to the combined Western ones as a block. Eventually, then, there were two Germanys. The degrees to which culture was used in or affected by the political processes varied over time, according to occupational zone, or—especially after the beginning of the Cold War at the turn of the 1940s—depending on the ideologically determined blocks. The concept of Zero Hour posited fundamental questions concerning continuity versus discontinuity: If starting fresh from a void was impossible, what pre-1933 traditions were to be reinstated, harking back how far? Was everything the Republic of Weimar had produced worthy of emulation? Apart from democratic precepts in the realm of culture, one can think of "modernism" as the defining force in Weimar culture,[26] but in music would this mean the dictatorship, say, of a resuscitated Second Viennese School over all other approaches? Was anything from Wilhelmian days salvageable, perhaps the highest forms of Romanticism or post-Romanticism, as exemplified by Mendelssohn and Brahms and, continued through the Weimar era, by Strauss? Circumventing the reprehensible Third Reich, or floating above or underneath it, as it were, was there an absolute, indestructible German cultural legacy, assumed to be positive, that had been invisible but now could be resumed? (This is what Furtwängler liked to suggest after 1945.) Not least, were there impulses from the Third Reich that were positive and capable of invigorating a new beginning? These were, and still are, formidable issues, to the extent that as recently as 1996 and with particular reference to culture, one German historian has stated that "discontinuity and continuity were contradictory elements of the same structure, often hardly to be separated from the other."[27]

Although in long-winded and convoluted processes German society was formally denazified and its politics redemocratized, the experience was as tortuous for the Western Allies, especially the Americans, as it was traumatic for the Germans. Denazification, including that of compromised artists, was at first conducted by the occupying forces and then left to the Germans, who pursued the Frankfurt Auschwitz Trial of the early 1960s; underlying this was the paradoxical assumption that denazified artists would aid in the construction of a freedom-loving, democratic society. By and large, the incongruities and partial injustices in these proceedings caught and then nominally whitewashed only the little people but allowed the bigwigs to go free. These difficulties were compounded by differences of conception as to the nature and degree of German guilt and requisite remedies—among the Americans (who tended to be the toughest), French, and British, the Western "block" on the one hand, and the Russian on the other.[28] The Russians attempted to make the most decisive break with the past, but any resocialization, so it became clear, was subjected to the greater goal of locking in Communism, and this extended to the arts as well.[29] For dedicated denazifiers, it must have proved frustrating that the dangers of Communism from the East at the end of the 1940s, in the words of cultural historian Richard Pells, "aborted the de-Nazification crusade before it accomplished its mission."[30] And as Germany herself was concerned, Gerhard A. Ritter has correctly observed that the Western two-thirds of the country may have successfully introduced democracy along with its cultural accoutrements by the 1950s and 1960s, but at the same time there was a formal resurgence of Nazism in the shape of several, albeit minuscule, neo-Nazi parties, such as the Sozialistische Reichspartei (SRP), which had to be outlawed by the new Bonn government in 1952. Yet neo-Nazism raised its ugly head again in the 1960s.[31] At the core here was a lingering problem: Because of the perceived completion of a formalized cleansing process, a German sense of collective guilt (or, as Federal President Theodor Heuss put it so much better, a sense of collective shame) was abandoned.[32] Although in itself sensible, this abandonment was etched in stone by hypernationalist pamphleteers and patriotic politicans such as Chancellor Adenauer, who kept reminding all and sundry that every Wehrmacht soldier had fought gallantly.[33] That feeling led to the entrenchment of a "draw-the-line mentality," permitting the abuse of the artificial construct of Zero Hour as a self-exculpatory mechanism.[34] Behind this screen old fascist dangers would only hide, not disappear, and new threats could constitute and reproduce themselves. What resulted was no "renazification" of German society, but a situation in which former Nazis infiltrated most facets of the newly created nation, except for political-party governance: the justice system and the economy, the bureaucracy at large and education.[35] Did they also infiltrate culture?

Culture in Germany was by no means prostrate after the surrender. The Germans needed it habitually, by self-definition, and the occupying Allied forces supported its immediate revival within their respective repoliticization programs, hence with vested interests. By late summer 1945 Berlin, otherwise a giant rubble field, again had a "vital and dynamic cultural scene."[36] In Munich, Hartmann had started what was to become, by September, his Musica Viva series, and though the city's unharmed Prinzregententheater was too small, it was usable, and Stuttgart was eager to recruit an Intendant, because it was the only city in Germany with a major stage still standing.[37] In the Soviet occupation zone, incredibly knowledgeable Russian officers immediately put into service everything that touched on the German Classics; Goethe and Schiller were icons, and the town of Weimar was a shrine.[38]

All the arts—the graphic arts, literature, theater, and film—represented a curious mixture of modernism and reaction.[39] But in none of them was reaction more predominant than in music. This was not obvious at first because there were several manifestations of a new beginning. The Americans, for example, saw to it that the Bayreuth Festival would not continue as in the past. They took away Winifred Wagner's control of it and eventually handed it to her sons, Wieland and Wolfgang Wagner. In July 1951 the two brothers started on a new note.[40] In Baden-Baden by the turn of the 1940s the French had helped in the founding of Südwestfunk, a progressive station that acquired Hans Rosbaud, then from Munich, as its modernist conductor and Heinrich Strobel of 1920s *Melos* fame as section chief for music. Other new radio stations such as Cologne's, Berlin's, and Hamburg's tried to follow Baden-Baden. Südwestfunk reestablished the Donaueschingen modern-music festival. *Melos* itself was revived as an avant-garde platform. In addition to Hartmann's Musica Viva series in Munich, the Internal Summer Courses for New Music were founded at Darmstadt in 1946. Both Strobel and Hans Heinz Stuckenschmidt played a prominent role in these ventures. For all who wanted to see and hear, xenophobia was gradually being replaced by the welcome extended to foreign or emigrant modern-music artists, such as Stravinsky, Hindemith and Schoenberg, Olivier Messiaen, Luigi Dallapiccola, Luigi Nono, Bruno Maderna, Pierre Boulez, Rolf Liebermann, and John Cage. Serial music and then electronic music dominated the Darmstadt events.[41] Also in Darmstadt, the German branch of the ISCM was recreated, with the first postwar festival taking place in Frankfurt in 1951.[42]

Modern German or Austrian musicians who came to the fore included Hartmann, Boris Blacher, and Gottfried von Einem, whose opera *Dantons Tod* was premiered at a reopened Salzburg Festival in 1947.[43] But the two postwar composers who attained world renown, and who had been in kneepants during most of Hitler's regime, were Hans Werner Henze and Karlheinz Stockhausen. Henze was born in 1926; during the war he was socialized as an antiauthoritarian, not least while playing chamber music "in an atmosphere of imminent peril in the partially Jewish household of a friendly neighbour." Drafted into the Wehrmacht in 1944, he was eventually assigned to a propaganda-film unit. By 1946 he was studying with Wolfgang Fortner in Heidelberg, who taught him harmony, counterpoint, and the art of the fugue. At Darmstadt, he learned serial techniques from Webern's student René Leibowitz, a French-Polish Jew; by 1948 in Paris, Henze was Leibowitz's private pupil. Other influences on Henze were those of Stravinsky and, especially, Schoenberg. Yet in 1953 Henze left for Italy, out of an ineradicable hostility for his home country, one of whose most famous postwar sons he became. Henze composed operas, ballets, chamber music, and choral and solo vocal works as well as symphonies; politically, he moved decidedly to the left. He was a composer whose artistic development occurred in conscious reaction to the fascist experiences of his youth.[44]

Stockhausen was born in 1928 and became known as a pioneer of electronic music. His fate was also shaped by the pernicious forces of National Socialism. He had lost both parents; his mother was killed by the "euthanasia" scheme against "life not worthy of life" in 1941. Until 1951, his formal studies were at Cologne's Hochschule für Musik and the city's university. His main influences there were Stravinsky, Bartók, and Schoenberg, but as he visited Darmstadt in the summer of 1951, he was impressed by Webern and the music of a new generation of serial composers. Back in Cologne, he began to work with Herbert Eimert, who had founded the Studio for Electronic Music at Cologne Radio. January 1952 found Stockhausen in Paris, where he was taking lessons from Messiaen, whom he had previously met at Darmstadt. In Paris, he began what would turn out to be his long friendship with Boulez. Along with Luigi Nono and others, Boulez and Stockhausen were at this time developing a form of serialism that extended the Schoenbergian twelve-tone doctrine, one in which serial principles were also applied to aspects of sound such as duration, dynamics, and tempo ("total serialism"). This extreme tendency toward abstraction led him to electronic composition as music's most rational expression. Stockhausen's renewed interest in instrumental music by the late 1950s was revolutionary as well; his *Klavierstück XI* of 1956 gave the performer radically new freedom to determine the form of the work in any given performance: "19 'groups' are laid out on a single sheet of paper, and the pianist, starting with any one of them, is to play them spontaneously in a random order." By 1960, electronic and instrumental music were combined. Because Stockhausen remained in Germany, commencing a teaching career at the Cologne Hochschule für Musik in the mid-1960s, he became the most important German composer of the postwar era. As recently as 1996, the Free University of Berlin awarded him an honorary doctorate. "Rapid mechanization toward the end of the present century now has, for the first time, affected music and fully involved compositional techniques," read the laudation. Stockhausen was acclaimed as a composer "who did not close himself to these developments from the beginning, but helped them along through his compositional know-how."[45]

In their careers, both Henze and Stockhausen were touched by jazz in some important way.[46] Indeed, for a number of years after May 1945 jazz came to flourish in Germany. It was being held over from the Nazi period, when for a small but knowing elite it had served as a symbol of freedom and opposition against tyranny. Jazz clubs—often the cavernous basements of old buildings—sprang up all over Germany, particularly in university towns. Several German professional players, who had either been active in the Third Reich, like trombonist Walter Dobschinski, or belonged to the rebellious urban Swing youth groups, like saxophonist Emil Mangelsdorff in Frankfurt and pianist Jutta Hipp in Leipzig, connected easily to the outgoing Swing à la Benny Goodman and incoming Bebop idioms. The progressive Südwestfunk assumed a key role in Baden-Baden; its impresario Joachim Ernst Berendt, whose father was murdered in Dachau, actively embarked on jazz programming and the founding of jazz festivals, such as the unique Berliner Jazztage. In the U.S. occupation zone, much aid was lent by soldiers, who employed German musicians in their clubs and brought them together with visiting soloists from the United States. Soon there was a new generation of impressive German jazz musicians: Klaus Doldinger, the saxophonist, Michael Naura, the pianist, Wolfgang Schlüter, the vibraphonist, and Heinz von Moissi, the drummer.[47]

But in terms of a lasting entrenchment of progressive forces, there were problems with all these developments. Instead of staying in Germany and serving as an example, Henze left for Italy, whereas Stockhausen became too specialized as an esoteric postserialist. Wieland Wagner, the new senior boss of the Bayreuth Festival, had been Adolf Hitler's favorite Wagner; he had been exempted from military service and instead been granted an SS rank.[48] In Baden-Baden, Strobel's integrity as a modern appeared in doubt, because he had made concessions to the Nazis while staying in Paris during the time of occupation. Generalmusikdirektor Rosbaud, although never a member of the Nazi Party, had been in Strasbourg during the war, and hence, at least nominally, a servant of Nazi cultural imperialism directed against the French.[49] Hartmann's Musica Viva remained confined to Munich; it did not have a lasting influence on similar movements elsewhere in Germany. And Darmstadt as well as Donaueschingen became much too monopolized by Strobel and Stuckenschmidt, whose worship of the avant-garde turned elitist and intolerant: Henze accused them (and Stockhausen) later of leaving the concert hall whenever they heard tonal music.[50] Not least, the new modernist Meccas failed to attract, permanently, Nazi Germany's most prominent expatriates: Schoenberg, Weill, and Hindemith—if for different reasons. The avant-garde in Germany remained isolated and unable to fertilize the broader musical spectrum.[51]

Moreover jazz, very much like serial or electronic music, only reached a tiny fraction of aficionados in the clubs and listeners to radio and recordings.[52] Even the Allies were not consistent in their support of it; in the British zone, jazz was consigned to the popular-music or light-entertainment category and bereft of institutional or financial backing.[53] In the Eastern zone, at first it survived, camouflaged as dance music played by radio dance orchestras, but then fell prey to defamation as just another manifestation of American capitalism.[54] In German society, old prejudices against jazz as the product of "niggers" were continued and actually endorsed from on high by theorists of Theodor W. Adorno's ilk, who saw fit to polemicize against it, as he had done before and after 1933, as merely a form of "popular music" with unjustifiably high pretenses.[55] Hans Schnoor, one of the most entrenched Nazi music critics and now a member of the Old Guard, in 1962 called jazz "primitive musical narcotics"; his colleague Walter Abendroth spoke of it as a hotbed for the "most brutal" stimuli.[56] With the exception of Berendt's station and perhaps two or three more (Frankfurt and Cologne being among them), radio held back, especially in stodgy Munich. Over and beyond the time of the fall of the Berlin Wall in 1989, jazz programming notoriously was tucked into the late-late-night shows, as part of un-German music.[57]

After May 1945, there was hardly a Zero Hour in German music, because no new musical genre was created and the musical practitioners remained the same, despite the few exceptions. In post–World War II Germany, the serious-music tradition was by and large the same as it had been, autonomously in the Weimar Republic and captured in the Third Reich.[58]

Composers and performers were not really denazified, at least not effectively; Jenkins remembers that they had trouble understanding what that was all about.[59] As Goebbels had needed them, musicians, like other artists, were again needed in all the occupation zones (which vied with each other for their services); the musicians took advantage of this situation.[60] The most famous German musicians were not laid off from work too long. Furtwängler, for instance, who had compromised himself severely until 1945, though never a party member, made the best of his resistance legend before a denazification court in Berlin in December 1946 and was soon back on the podium.[61] Party members Herbert von Karajan and Elisabeth Schwarzkopf, both denazified in Austria by concealing their Nazi pasts, joined Furtwängler in the concert rounds. The same happened to pianist

Walter Gieseking, who had committed several questionable political acts and after a short pause performed again (in Mainz) as early as 1945, as did violinist Wolfgang Schneiderhan, a former Nazi Party member.[62] Nazi-compromised conductor Clemens Krauss, Strauss's old favorite, had to teach in Salzburg and Vienna before he was allowed to conduct the Vienna State Opera again, but that happened already in 1950—and not a trace of his 1920s modernism could be found in him.[63]

Furtwängler became once more the major exponent of a nationalist conservative musical agenda, which suffered no avant-garde. As he had done in the Third Reich, he preferred to perform the paragons of the Classical, Romantic, and post-Romantic eras.[64] In the concert halls and on opera stages, this music also predominated: Mozart, Schubert, Wagner, and Reger; only now it was not owned by the Nazis any more.[65] In Protestant church music, too, Ernst Pepping and Johann Nepomuk David, whose neo-Baroque works had been played after 1933 with Nazi blessings, prevailed. Church organist and party member Hugo Distler, whose music was equally as popular, had already committed suicide because he could not bear the conflict.[66]

These musicians were assisted by conservative music journalists and publicists, some of whom were tied to (formerly Nazi) music-publishing firms such as Bärenreiter in Kassel, which now produced the reactionary journal *Musica*. Andreas Liess, Fred Hamel, and Walter Abendroth, apart from presenting monographs of their own, used *Musica* as a convenient anti-modern platform against everything that was not a "synthesis of polyphony and melody." It seemed to bother nobody that Abendroth, Pfitzner's old friend and a former Nazi and pronounced anti-Semite, after 1947 found his way into the newly constituted liberal weekly *Die Zeit* as chief of its culture desk. Hamel, too, an old friend of Carl Orff, had been a well-established critic during the Third Reich, and so had Karl Holl: all of them now active on the restoration front. Karl Laux placed his skeleton in the closet to safely reside in the Soviet occupation zone, whence he served to stifle every form of modernism after the reactionary Zhdanov rulings in early 1947.[67] Composers who had worked for the Nazis in one role or another and now became prominent again, not least as teachers, included Wolfgang Fortner, Karl Marx, Cesar Bresgen, and Armin Knab.[68] They guarded the sanctum sanctorum of German Music.

Among the keepers of this sanctum there also ranked, once again in influential positions at institutions of higher learning, formerly Nazi musicologists and music instructors. Chief among them was Joseph Maria Müller-Blattau, who in 1940 had published a devout biography of his former teacher Hans Pfitzner, which, saturated with anti-Semitism, praised the composer as the champion of "German musicians." A new, cleansed, edition was then printed after 1945.[69] Having issued a book on "Germanic musical heritage," simultaneously in a series of Himmler's SS-Ahnenerbe and one of the Hitler Youth, and a member of the SA, Müller-Blattau, when still a professor at Freiburg, had been observed strutting about in a

Nazi Party uniform.[70] In 1941 Müller–Blattau went to conquered Alsace to join the new Reichsuniversität Strassburg, an SS-sponsored institution like the one in Posen, a fact that both the German handbook *Das Grosse Lexikon der Musik* and the standard *New Grove Dictionary of Music and Musicians* have suppressed or euphemized as "war service."[71] After having served as a lecturer, Müller-Blattau was in 1958 once again appointed full professor at the newly founded University of Saarbrücken, where he commenced to instruct a new generation of music scholars in German Music. One of them edited the second *Festschrift* for his teacher on the occasion of his seventieth birthday (there had been one for his sixty-fifth already); a professor of musicology himself, he was the son of a former official of the RMK who had gone against the grain and been dismissed.[72] "As a scholar and author," exulted Christoph-Hellmut Mahling in his introduction, "you have traversed manifold regions of music"—surely not just of music. Among the well-wishers were such dyed-in-the-wool Nazi musicologists as Wilhelm Ehmann, Gotthold Frotscher, and Alfred Quellmalz, but others who affixed their stamp of approval included Erich Doflein, Strobel, Adorno, and Carl Dahlhaus, the latter two contributing papers. Predictably, the book was published by Bärenreiter. A noted German musicologist recently was shocked to find that the text of one of Müller-Blattau's Nazi works, which he had bought in a used-book store, had been blacked out by the small-town music school which had used it for its pupils after 1945. What shocked him were not the parts that had been deleted but those that had been left intact.[73]

Other reinstated academics were Bruno Stürmer, who had served the music needs of the Hitler Youth and already in the 1940s joined the Hessische Landesmusikschule in Darmstadt.[74] Wolfgang Stumme, the chief of the youth music section under Baldur von Schirach's command, became a lecturer at the renowned Folkwang Hochschule for the arts in Essen. As justification for having joined the Hitler Youth in a leading position Stumme said in 1968 that he had been able to work there "freely and objectively," glossing over his wartime pamphleteering against jazz, his edition of war songs in the honor of the Führer, and his exhortation in song to all young men to shed their heroes' blood at the fronts.[75] Further defending himself, Stumme maintained that it had not been he who had sought another teaching position after his return from Russian captivity in 1949, but that he had been asked to join by the Essen Hochschule.[76]

Moreover, in this context one must mention Wolfgang Boetticher and Friedrich Blume, the latter an active National Socialist music scholar until 1945 and, after Zero Hour, continuing on as a full professor in Kiel. In 1939 Blume had subscribed to the aims of "musical work in the Hitler Youth."[77] He was "profoundly German," wrote the nationalistic Munich music librarian Alfons Ott in the 1980 *New Grove* volume, as Blume made his postwar mark as editor of West Germany's most important music encyclopedia, *Musik in Geschichte und Gegenwart*.[78] Those seventeen volumes, with the first published in 1949 and the last in 1986 (after Blume's death in 1975), were not replaced until the late 1990s. As they were standard handbooks for every German music student, even a cursory examination revealed a blatant neglect of twentieth-century music and a systematic blanking out of any biographed German musician's Nazi past.[79] In the Third Reich Blume published more politic things, such as thoughts about the immutable differences between "Nordic" and "Jewish" music, yet to be fully corroborated by German science.[80]

Wolfgang Boetticher, finally, was discovered in the late 1990s as actively having aided Alfred Rosenberg's wartime pillage of music artifacts in occupied countries, especially France, while he was a young musicologist and a member of the SS. In 1942 he had edited Schumann's letters and essays in a volume sponsored by Rosenberg's anti-Semitic Hohe Schule; the introduction stylized Schumann, like Wagner, as a German hero, contrasting him positively with his Jewish contemporaries Mendelssohn and Meyerbeer. Boetticher retired as professor of musicology from the University of Göttingen according to plan and was still teaching courses in 1998, when the university was forced, by public pressure, to take him out of circulation.[81]

Why did these academics find their survival beyond the cutoff point of 1945 so easy? It was a function of the sham denazification that most incriminated professors in any academic discipline who had initially been suspended from German universities because of their Nazi past found their way back to the halls of learning relatively quickly.[82] Scholars who had upheld the ideal of German Music in the Weimar Republic, as they had in the Third Reich, were all the more easily readmissable as they were upholding the idea of German culture in the way most educated Germans were able to understand it.

After 1945 and into the 1960s, the cross-current of opinion, agitated discourse, and sometimes violent dispute, depending on the ideological or aesthetic perspectives, had their effect on the reception of the eight composers from Pfitzner to Schoenberg. This reception or its lack of it concerned their music, past and present, but sometimes also their personae.

As the most conspicuously conservative composer, Hans Pfitzner, who died in 1949, pleased the members of the Old Guard. He pleased Schnoor so much that Schnoor called the composer "arch-German" and "Praeceptor Germaniae" in a current music history, *Harmonie und Chaos*, separating the wheat from the chaff, and in its polemical style reminiscent of Pfitzner's own published diatribes of the 1920s.[83] Yet the problem was that Pfitzner's popularity had been waning toward the end of the Weimar Republic and had had to be artificially propped up with Nazi Party help. Although the Allies did not expressly forbid his repertoire, except in the U.S. zone for over a year after July 1946, he was heard much more seldom after 1945 than before, especially since his cultist following had been diminished.[84] But his oeuvre maintained the distinction of quintessentially German Music for a long time, and he remained the leading hero of the conservatives, nationalists, and restorationists, including those who bewailed the passing of Pfitzner's alter ego, Adolf Hitler.

About Strauss, also dead in 1949, there could be no argument, from the left or from the right, and from whatever aesthetic vantage point. His historic greatness had been established long before the Nazi reign; like Pfitzner, he was "denazified" in a court of law; his music was never on any Allied index and was played profusely in German concert halls and on all the stages.[85] Non-German bans such as the Israeli one notwithstanding, his place in history and the definable quality of his music as post-Romantic made it as naturally a part of German Music as it kept him out of the post-1945 arguments of the conservatives, if not of modernists and post-serialists (those who looked up to Stockhausen). All but current avant-garde musicologists and critics continued to subscribe to the view that Strauss had had his high moment of modernism in 1909, with the premiere of *Elektra*, and if some thought that his post-World War I works were somewhat inferior to his earlier ones, it really did not detract from his popularity in most camps.

The case of Hindemith was more complex. He had his early Weimar avant-garde side, and this, combined with his expatriate status, brought his works to the Darmstadt new-music festivals and made him popular there for a while. Heinrich Strobel, who had recreated the avant-garde journal *Melos*, and Hindemith's loyal publisher Willy Strecker of Schott's Söhne had much to do with that. In the Soviet sector, Hindemith too fell victim to the anti-"formalism" campaign waged against Schoenberg and others. But already the German premiere of his opera *Mathis der Maler* in Stuttgart in December 1946 was an anachronism for a once avant-garde composer. His neo-Classicism was deemed incrementally out of date at Darmstadt, until he had to make room for Schoenberg around 1949. Thus Hindemith himself became embittered, to the point where the systematic refutation of the serialism of the Second Viennese School became a major theme of his last ten years. So although he had the ear of the followers of modernism for some time, he was perceived as sufficiently conservative, especially in memory of the *Mathis der Maler* symphony of 1934, to please the members of the Old Guard—to the same degree that he was criticized by such Young Turks as Henze. Writers such as Schnoor and Abendroth tolerated Hindemith but took obvious pleasure in classifying the former "Bad Boy of Music" (to paraphrase the American composer George Antheil) as being of middle ground. In 1962 Schnoor applauded Hindemith for never having given in to the serialists, but how tragic was it for an artist to find himself in a place "which cannot even be vaguely compared with the positions of his great precursors Strauss, Pfitzner, Reger!"[86]

By birth, Carl Orff was Hindemith's exact contemporary, but he lived twenty years longer—until 1982. In terms of his musical style, Orff continued to play the chameleon-like role he had already honed, in other ways, until 1945. In line with his charismatic temperament, he managed to create around himself a cultist following, similar to the one Pfitzner had enjoyed in his halcyon years, and really a continuation of that early, specifically Orffian and self-serving, aura. "There is an Orff cult around Munich with 'oh's' and 'ah's' about its hero at the drop of a hat," noted the U.S. music officer John Evarts in 1947, who disliked him for his "self-proclaimed Bavarianness."[87] Those disciples, often bordering on the syco-phantic, in addition to admiring Orff's original *Schulwerk* efforts (which now proceeded to the global stage), thought of him either as a modernist or a traditionalist, praising him in both capacities.

Strictly speaking, Orff remained a traditionalist within the safe confines of the tried-and-true tonal order, displaying, rather, a new preference for invoking on the contemporary stage themes from Classical antiquity in his operas. He did not turn to serialism as did Fortner now, or Hartmann, and as had Krenek. Works such as *Carmina Burana, Die Kluge,* and the new *Die Bernauerin* were repeatedly scheduled; on their basis Orff was simply able to continue the success and national prominence he had reached in the Third Reich until 1945. As they did Hindemith, conservatives patronized this artist who carefully cultivated his "Bavarian" roots and soon knew how to sidle up to the ruling arch-Catholic Christian Socialist Party, for not composing in the twelve-tone style. In addition, they may have appreciated his pronounced dislike of jazz.[88] But some of them called his music "banal"; they recognized his cult-craving airs and condemned them. Schnoor referred to the "conviction of an egocentric favored by fortune" and divined that this was in the hallowed tradition neither of the German nor of the entire Occidental music culture. Other critics have remarked, merely a few years after his death, that Orff smarted from the implicit accu-sation that he was not like the "real" moderns, and that he therefore con-strued more modern-sounding works such as *Antigonae* (requiring a choir, percussion, and six pianos), which he had begun while on the payroll of Gauleiter Baldur von Schirach in Vienna and which was premiered at the Salzburg Festival in 1949. One measure of whether there was truth to this might have been the fact that the East Germans included it on their antifor-malist index at the turn of the 1940s. However, like most other composers, Orff was soon back in vogue in the German Democratic Republic (DDR), as evinced by the performance of his trademark work *Carmina Burana* in Wittenberg in 1960, albeit only with piano accompaniment.[89] Modern or not, there is no evidence that former Nazis would have acknowledged Orff's post-1945 oeuvre as a continuation of any real or imagined Nazi style of composition, perhaps by way of a misinterpretation of his most fa-mous work, as indeed it was not. What his adversaries would make of this later is quite another matter.

In those first two postwar decades, writes Jost Hermand, Carl Orff as much as Egk increasingly took recourse to "'avant-gardistic' style devices, in order to be at all taken seriously in the camp of their modernist col-leagues."[90] If this judgment were to have applied to Orff, it certainly would have to be applied to his friend, rival, and colleague Werner Egk. Actually, Egk was remarkably similar to Orff in that whatever modernism he dis-played stopped well short of serialism. But, unlike Orff, Egk associated himself with Strobel's efforts at Südwestfunk Baden-Baden (conducting works by Henze, among others) and put in at least one appearance at Darmstadt. That gave him a cultist, elitist, air, different but no less precious than Orff's own. Egk also enjoyed a fair postwar popularity which, unlike the one based on Orff's *Carmina Burana*, was not to spread wings abroad. But in the immediate postwar decades, it had a great deal to do with Egk's remarkable circumspection as a music establishment figure who had survived, in typical fashion, a denazification trial (whereas Orff had craftily avoided it) and knew well how to blow his own horn. However, if in the 1990s Orff's name was generally known around the world, Egk's was known only to the cognoscenti.[91]

Egk's post-1945 modernism musically stopped at the same limit at which it had been before the Nazi catastrophe: patterned after Stravinsky. In that sense, there was no change. For example, this was obvious in the ballet *Abraxas,* which in many ways reminded the audience of Egk's earlier opera *Peer Gynt*. Egk's modernism progressed in this work's sexually charged story line. In typically Egkian fashion and after a script by his own hand, after Heinrich Heine, Faust, the hero, entered into erotically daring liaisons, with Archisposa, the Devil's consort, and Bellastriga, the lascivious seductress. The work was prohibited by the Catholic-bigoted Bavarian culture ministry in 1948. And now the old Nazi collaborator Egk found it convenient to insinuate that he had become the victim of censure, as bad as or worse than under the Nazis. Yet generally, and always the opportunist, Egk kept himself sufficiently to the left of the fashion spectrum to sustain a favorable comparison with Stravinsky, while right-positioned enough to salute the antimodernists' campaign and become an object of commendation for the neo-fascist Schnoor and his compatriot Alois Melichar. Egk's neither-fowl-nor-fish situation served him well as a champion of the postwar German music establishment till his death in 1983.[92]

Karl Amadeus Hartmann died on 5 December 1963, three weeks before Hindemith and twenty years before Egk. Although as an anti-Nazi he had denied himself to the German music establishment and his musical allusions to the Second Viennese School were sufficiently pronounced, he remained conspicuously absent as an object of discussion among members of the Old Guard. Yet his Musica Viva series, favoring, in particular, modern composers, could hardly have escaped them. That series, of course, more than anything, marks his place in the history of modern music in Germany, tied intimately to the circumstance that he profoundly influenced younger rising stars like Henze (who was correspondingly disappointed by Hindemith and charmed for a while by Egk). But if the truth be told, Hartmann's music, apart from Munich, the venue he controlled, was not performed much in the new occupied zones: with one periodic exception, that being the Soviet zone, later the DDR.[93] This undoubtedly had much to do with Hartmann's own ideological leanings and his friendship with Communist scientist Robert Havemann (as, earlier, his sympathies with poet Johannes R. Becher). With his music, which was fully exposed to the public only after 1945, Hartmann showed himself on the cusp of traditionalism and the avant-garde, in a more convincing manner than both Orff and Egk, but it too was a position that left him unclaimable by either camp, rendering him neither controversial nor trend setting. Hartmann, the man or his music, was not even an issue for the Old Guard (except that it dispatched him quickly as a "Scherchen crony"); his Musica Viva had been a catalyst for the moderns to be resuscitated after 1945, but it fell into oblivion after his death in 1963.[94]

This leaves the two Jewish refugees in our musical cohort, Weill and Schoenberg. They are, in fact, the only true refugees, for Hindemith must be discounted. As Jews, neither one returned to Germany, not even for a visit, although Weill had actually been planning one before his death in 1950 and Schoenberg was tempted to get himself repatriated by Rosbaud. Would they have known or been interested in the fact that in April 1946, 8 percent of all Germans in the American zone thought that "the music of Jewish composers is no good," that eight months later only 22 percent felt émigré Jews should return to Germany unconditionally, and that in October 1951 about the same proportion held the Jews partially responsible for what happened to them under the Nazi regime?[95] As late as 1961, 73 percent of all Germans still thought that Jews were a "different race."[96] And well into the 1960s the German bureaucracy, through its actions and wittingly or not, contributed to a revival of anti-Semitism, which had been suppressed only momentarily and insufficiently.[97]

Although members of the Old Guard could not say so openly after 1945, they dismissed Weill and Schoenberg not least because they were Jews. For appearance's sake, in his polemic against Schoenberg, Melichar deplored the "bad" kind of anti-Semitism because it discredited the "justified" kind.[98] In the case of Schnoor we can infer the dislike of Jews from his unreserved admiration of Pfitzner's polemics of the 1920s, which had had a strong anti-Semitic underpinning. Schnoor's tirades against Weill's conception of what Schnoor took to be pseudo-culture are in fact indistinguishable from Pfitzner's own. Patronisingly, Schnoor called Weill a once modest young man who had committed the sacrilege of comparing his early songs with Wagner's *Wesendonk-Lieder*. Wagner, the Guardian of German Music! Weill's earlier association with the Communist Brecht was another reason why his music was rarely performed in postwar Germany. Decisive for the high-culture crowd, however, was that irrespective of Jews and Brecht, Weill was accused of having sold his soul to the commercialism of America.[99] This did not prevent Norbert Schultze, a conniving German who had composed "Lili Marleen" and the reprehensible "Engellandlied" for the Nazis with good profit, to ingratiate himself with Weill in a sugar-sweet letter in November 1945, assuring Weill how much he had thought of him during the war and asking Weill to please open doors to him in the United States.[100]

Schoenberg constituted a more serious issue. For a few years he was the patron saint of the Darmstadt Festival, and a favorite for Musica Viva, Südwestfunk, and in several concert and opera venues. As such, he was seminally influential in the development of both new heralds of the West German music scene, albeit just vicariously: Henze and Stockhausen. But the unchallenged priority of his music was established a mere two years before his death in 1951, and by 1955 Anton Webern had taken Schoenberg's place in the new-music scene, just as Schoenberg had taken Hindemith's by 1949. During the 1950s, Schoenberg also was consistently condemned by the antiformalists in the DDR.[101]

However, for all the members of the right wing in postwar German culture, whether former Nazis or merely fortified traditionalists, Schoenberg was the main target. Consequential opposition to him and his music was an article of faith. His twelve-tone technique declared a "trick," he was proclaimed anathema to genius. He was likened to the Jewish Sigmund Freud, who had lost his currency in Germany even in the 1920s. Former Nazi musicologists like Friedrich Blume, who were once again teaching at German universities, were cited as evidence in those postwar harangues. Adherents to "twelve-tone fascism" were vilified as would-be revolutionaries: would-be only by dint of their presumed impotence. "Atonality" was identified with "anatural" phenomena, by way of a sexual insinuation; this identification paralleled Pfitzner's concept of "aharmony" in the 1920s. Biology was conjured up in the manner of the Nazis, when they had claimed that the blood of the Jews could be made visible as such in a test tube: Schoenberg's music was called "biologically inferior."[102]

The campaign against Schoenberg and the Second Viennese School reached its apex as it was extended to the electronic experiments of Stockhausen, Eimert, and others.[103] As German Music reentrenched itself by the 1950s and 1960s, it seemed as if new developments in this art would be blocked forever, and a critical retrospective would be prevented. Bach, Beethoven, Wagner, and Strauss reigned unchallenged. Indeed, well into the 1990s, young untenured German musicologists have been generally afraid to examine the recent history of their country's music critically, out of fear for their livelihood.[104] Even non-German scholars are not exempt. Ever since I published details regarding Carl Orff's "White Rose" resistance-in-the-Third-Reich mendacity in 1995, pressure has been applied to me, through phone and telefax, by the director of the Munich Carl-Orff-Zentrum, behind which stands the reactionary Orff Foundation, to make me change my Orff portrait for the current book. This included a threat to discredit me among my German colleagues and ad hominem attacks during a specially organized Munich press conference in February 1999.[105] If the muses suffered in the resurrection of the German nation after 1945, that of music, the "magical language of emotion,"[106] surely suffered the most.

Notes

CHAPTER 1: EGK

1. I.e. Elisabeth née Karl.

2. The biographical details to ca. 1934 are according to Werner Egk, *Die Zeit wartet nicht* (Percha, 1973), 5-204, 286; Ludwig Lade, "Werner Egk," *Melos* 13 (1934), 10–13; Ernst Krause, *Werner Egk: Oper und Ballett* (Wilhelmshaven, 1971), 17–25.

3. Preannouncement for May 1931 in handbill, "Vereinigung für Zeitgen. Musik," SM, Kulturamt/143; Scherchen to Egk, 24 May, 16 June, 5 July, and 10 Aug. 1933, BS, Ana/410; Egk, *Zeit*, 185–99; Hermann Scherchen, *Alles hörbar machen: Briefe eines Dirigenten, 1920 bis 1939,* ed. Eberhardt Klemm (Berlin, 1976), 145, 165–68, 173, 191, 195.

4. Otto Oster, "Der Musiker Werner Egk," *Kölnische Zeitung,* 5 July 1939; Orff in *Carl Orff und sein Werk: Dokumentation,* 8 vols. (Tutzing, 1975–83), 2:121–22 (quote); Egk, *Zeit,* 65–69.

5. Preannouncement for May 1931 in handbill, "Vereinigung für Zeitgen. Musik," SM, Kulturamt/143; Orff to Reusch, 2 May 1932, CM, Allg. Korr.; enclosure with letter Hörburger to Egk, 26 Oct. 1933, SM, Kulturamt/276.

6. Orff to Doflein, 25 Sept. 1933, CM, Allg. Korr.; Jemnitz to Hartmann, 3 Jan. 1934, BS, Ana/407; Werner Egk, "Schulmusik," *Völkische Kultur* 2 (1934), 85–86. On *Schulwerk* and HJ, see Michael H. Kater, *The Twisted Muse: Musicians and Their Music in the Third Reich* (New York, 1997), 192.

7. Werner Egk, "Wege der Harmonik," *Völkische Kultur* 2 (1934), 139–41. On Lorenz, see BAB Lorenz; Michael H. Kater, "The Revenge of the Fathers: The Demise of Modern Music at the End of the Weimar Republic," *German Studies Re-*

view 15 (1992), 299; Stephen McClatchie, "Alfred Lorenz as Theorist and Analyst," PhD dissertation, University of Western Ontario, 1994, esp. 31–47. I am indebted to Dr. McClatchie for making this work available to me.

8. Krause, *Egk,* 10. Similarly: Ludwig F. Schiedermair, *Musiker Schicksale: Aus dem Leben grosser Komponisten* (Berlin, 1990), 236.

9. *VB,* 23 May 1931 and 22 Jan. 1932.

10. See Ludwig Lade, "Unsichtbare Oper," *Melos* 12 (1933), 303–6; Kater, *The Twisted Muse,* 182–83; Joan Evans, "Die Rezeption der Musik Igor Strawinskys in Hitlerdeutschland," *Archiv für Musikwissenschaft* 55 (1998), 91–109.

11. Corr. (1933) SM, Kulturamt/249; corr. (1934) SM, Kulturamt/276; Doflein to Orff, 8 Dec. 1933, CM, Allg. Korr.; *Melos* 12 (1933), 350; reviews of *Columbus* in *VB,* 8 Apr. 1934; *München-Augsburger Abendzeitung,* 9 Apr. 1934; *Bayerischer Kurier,* 10 Apr. 1934.

12. Ludwig Schrott, "'Nicht so dreist, nicht so stolz . . .': Eine notwendige Richtigstellung," *DM* 27 (1935), 353–55.

13. See the interpretation by Fred K. Prieberg, *Musik im NS-Staat* (Frankfurt am Main, 1982), 318–19.

14. Sutermeister to Orff, 23 Dec. [1936], CM, Allg. Korr.

15. Egk to Schuh, 26 Mar. 1936, BS, Ana/410.

16. *Neueste Zeitung,* Frankfurt am Main, 23 May 1935; *Mittag,* Düsseldorf, 23 May 1935; Werner Oehlmann, "Die Oper Werner Egks," *ZM* 108 (1941), 639–40.

17. Stege in *Artist* (23 July 1936), 843; and in *Unterhaltungsmusik* (10 Feb. 1938), 157 (the function Stege exemplarily referred to here was one of the many Nazi-sponsored "Strength-through-Joy" events). Also idem, "Werner Egk und der dramatische Kunsttanz: Zur Uraufführung seines 'Joan von Zarissa,'" *ZM* 107 (1940), 144.

18. Egk to Dressel, 10 Nov. 1936; Egk to Vondenhoff, 31 May 1936; Egk to Schuh, 14 Mar. 1938, BS, Ana/410; opera schedule for Coburg, 1935/36, BH, Reichsstatthalter/669/7; Egk, *Zeit,* 238; Hermann Stoffels, "Das Musiktheater in Krefeld von 1870–1945," in Ernst Klusen et al., *Das Musikleben der Stadt Krefeld, 1870–1945,* 2 vols. (Cologne, 1979/80), 2:176, 217.

19. Paul to Gertrud Hindemith, [June 1935], PF, Paul und Gertrud Hindemith-Korr. Hindemith's original term is *"Schuhplattelmelodik."*

20. Strecker to Hindemith, 9 Apr. 1936, PF, Schott Korr. (quote); Bergese to Orff, 8 Apr. 1936, CM, Allg. Korr.; Egk, *Zeit,* 255.

21. Egk, *Zeit,* 257–58.

22. *TG* 2:624 (quote); *AMZ* 63 (1936), 281, 347; Prieberg, *NS-Staat,* 273–74; Nicolas Slonimsky, *Music Since 1900,* 4th ed. (New York, 1971), 630.

23. Electrola EH 982. See *Skizzen* (Oct. 1936), 15.

24. *AMZ* 63 (1936), 281.

25. *Skizzen* (Nov. 1936), 9.

26. Richard Ohlekopf in *Signale,* Aug. 1936.

27. Rudolf Stephan, "Zur Musik der Dreissigerjahre," in Christoph-Hellmut Mahling and Sigrid Wiesmann, eds., *Bericht über den Internationalen Musikwissenschaftlichen Kongress Bayreuth 1981* (Kassel, 1984), 148.

28. Albrecht Riethmüller, "Komposition im Deutschen Reich um 1936," *Archiv für Musikwissenschaft* 38 (1981), 266.

29. Egk, *Zeit,* 238–53.

30. Gottfried von Einem, recorded interview, Vienna, 30 Nov. 1994, APA.

31. Oehlmann, "Oper," 642; Julius Kapp, *Geschichte der Staatsoper Berlin* (Berlin, n.d.), 235.

32. Werner Egk, "Musik als Ausdruck ihrer Zeit," in Alfred Morgenroth, ed., *Von deutscher Tonkunst: Festschrift zu Peter Raabes 70. Geburtstag* (Leipzig, 1942), 205–9; idem, *Zeit,* 301–2; Petschull to Strecker, 17 Apr. 1939, PF, Schott Korr.; Ehrenberg report, 27 May 1939, SM, Kulturamt/396; Karl Holl in *Frankfurter Zeitung,* 3 Dec. 1940; Walter Dirks in *Neueste Zeitung,* Frankfurt am Main, 6 Dec. 1940; Paul Zoll in *ZM* 107 (1940), 364; Oehlmann, "Oper," 642; Kapp, *Geschichte,* 235. Critically: Michael Walter, *Hitler in der Oper: Deutsches Musikleben, 1919–1945* (Stuttgart, 1995), 178–80, 198–200.

33. See Hans Bergese to author, Berlin, 19 Oct. 1995, APA.

34. Gottfried von Einem, recorded interview, Vienna, 30 Nov. 1994, APA (last quote). Einem's version, not contained in Egks's memoirs, today is generally accepted. See Slonimsky, *Music,* 681; Prieberg, *NS-Staat,* 320. Also see Egk, *Zeit,* 311–13; *TG* 3:567 (1st two quotes); *Angriff,* 17 Feb. 1936 and 8 Dec. 1937. Hitler took Eckart and his translation of Ibsen's *Peer Gynt* very seriously. See his remarks of 19/20 Feb. 1942 recorded in Werner Jochmann, ed., *Adolf Hitler: Monologe im Führerhauptquartier, 1941–1944: Die Aufzeichnungen Heinrich Heims* (Hamburg, 1980), 284. Two years previous to that, and only one year after having attended the Egk performance, Hitler complained to Goebbels about Egk's tendency to "write such outlandish librettos": *TG* 4: 51.

35. Egk, *Zeit,* 313.

36. *Düsseldorfer Nachrichten,* 7 May 1939 (quote). See also *DAZ,* Berlin, 20 May 1939. The only other opera chosen was Alfred Irmler's *Die Nachtigall.*

37. *Berliner Börsenzeitung,* 6 May 1939.

38. "Reichsmusiktage 1939 Düsseldorf, 14.–21. Mai: Unter der Schirmherrschaft des Herrn Reichsministers für Volksaufklärung und Propaganda Dr. Goebbels," BS, Ana/410; *VB,* 22 May 1939 (1st quote). For the second quote and the degenerate-music exhibition see Kater, *The Twisted Muse,* 78–79.

39. Egk, *Zeit,* 318.

40. Karl Holl in *Frankfurter Zeitung,* 4 July 1940; Karl Laux in *JdM 1943,* 122. See section III of this chapter.

41. Krause, *Egk,* 193–94; Stege, "Werner Egk," 143–46; Oehlmann, "Oper," 642.

42. Bauer to Orff, 16 May 1941, CM, Allg. Korr.; *ZM* 108 (1941), 420. Also see Otto Oster, "Der Musiker Werner Egk," *Kölnische Zeitung,* 5 July 1939; Friedrich Welter, *Musikgeschichte im Umriss: Vom Urbeginn bis zur Gegenwart* (Leipzig, n.d.), 335–36; Eugen Schmitz, "Oper im Aufbau," *ZM* 106 (1939), 382.

43. *ZM* 110 (1943), 62, 64.

44. Orff to Strecker, 13 Apr. 1935 (1st quote); Willms to Orff, 16 May 1935 (2nd quote), CM, Schott. Korr.; Orff to Hofmann, 11 June 1935, in Frohmut Dangel-Hofmann, ed., *Carl Orff—Michel Hofmann: Briefe zur Entstehung der Carmina Burana* (Tutzing, 1990), 103 (3rd quote); Orff to Willms, 6 June 1935, CM, Schott Korr. (last quote).

45. Egk, *Zeit,* 257; Michael H. Kater, "Carl Orff im Dritten Reich," *Vierteljahrshefte für Zeitgeschichte* 43 (1995), 15; Orff to Walter, 10 Oct. 1935 (1st quote); Knab to Orff, 29 June 1936 (2nd quote), CM, Allg. Korr.

46. Gail to Orff, postal stamp 10 [month ?] 1938; von der Müll to Orff, [Jan. 1938]; Ruppel to Orff, 3 June 1941; Schuh to Orff, 15 June 1941, CM, Allg. Korr.;

Hans Wagner, *200 Jahre Münchner Theaterchronik, 1750–1950* (Munich, 1958), 156; Kater, "Orff," 9–11.

47. Willms to Orff, 8 Aug. 1938; Orff to Willms, 10 Aug. 1938, CM, Schott Korr.; Orff to Sutermeister, 8 Dec. 1938, CM, Allg. Korr. (quote).

48. "Statistik um die Arbeit des Orchesters," [Berlin Philharmonic, 1938/39], BA, R55/197.

49. The figures appear to be for net amounts. See "Military Government of Germany: Fragebogen," sign. Werner Egk, 16 Oct. 1945; Beisler to Kläger, 23 Sep. 1946, AM, Egk; Kater, "Orff," 30.

50. See "Gertrud Orffs Tagebuch," beginning June 1939, CM; Kater, "Orff," 30, n. 176.

51. Sutermeister to Orff, 5 June and 1 Dec. 1935, 17 Mar., 16 Apr., [summer] and 23 Dec 1936, 7 Oct. 1938, 7 Sept. 1940, CM, Allg. Korr.; *GLM* 8:48–49. The relationship between Sutermeister and Orff is sketched in Jürg Stenzl, "Im Reich der Musik: Heinrich Sutermeister und Carl Orff zwischen 1935 und 1945," paper, International Colloquium, "Zur Situation der Musik in Deutschland in den dreissiger und vierziger Jahren," CM, 23 Nov. 1994.

52. Bergese to Orff, 16 Mar. 1938, CM, Allg. Korr. (quote); Hans Bergese to author, Berlin, 19 Oct. 1995, APA.

53. *AMZ* 63 (1936), 281; Peter Muck, *Einhundert Jahre Berliner Philharmonisches Orchester: Darstellung in Dokumenten,* 3 vols. (Tutzing, 1982), 2:140; Norbert Schultze, "Lieber Berufskamerad," Nov. 1940; "Mitteilungen der Fachschaft Komponisten der Reichsmusikkammer," Nov. 1940, OW, 40.

54. Entry for 28 Feb. 1941 in Egk's pocket calendar, BS, Ana/410 (1st quote); *TG* 4:521 (2nd quote); Kopsch to Richard Strauss, 24 Jan. 1941; Kopsch to Franz Strauss, 21 July 1946, RG; Egk, *Zeit,* 341-44. See also Kopsch to Egk, 11 Apr. 1943; Kopsch to Richard Strauss, 1 May 1943, RG.

55. Kater, *The Twisted Muse,* 24–27, 188.

56. Entries in Egk's pocket calendars for 4–11 May, 7 June, 10 July 1941 (BS, Ana/410); *TG* 4:653; *AMR,* 15 July 1941, BA, RD33/2-2; Egk, *Zeit,* 345.

57. Egk, *Zeit,* 345; Orff to Bergese, 15 July 1941, CM, Allg. Korr. Also see Oscar Fritz Schuh, *So war es—war es so? Notizen und Erinnerungen eines Theatermannes* (Berlin, 1980), 58.

58. Prieberg, *NS-Staat,* 322 (1st quote); *Unterhaltungsmusik* (4 July 1941), 618. Egk's interpretation of his job as that of an attorney of his colleagues was immediately made public and then repeated during his denazification trial. See *ZM* 108 (1941), 637; *Münchner Neueste Nachrichten,* 12 July 1941; *12 Uhr Blatt,* Berlin, 29 July 1941; Egk, "Eidesstattliche Erklärung," 10 Mar. 1946, AM, Egk; and section III below.

59. Mackeben to Graener (quote) and to Hinkel, 14 Apr 1941, BAB Theo Mackeben. Also see *AMR,* 15 July 1941, BA, RD33/2–2; Michael H. Kater, *Different Drummers: Jazz in the Culture of Nazi Germany* (New York, 1992), 94.

60. *DAZ,* Berlin, 11 July 1941; *VB,* 11 July 1941; *Münchner Neueste Nachrichten,* 12 July 1941; *12 Uhr Blatt,* Berlin, 29 July 1941.

61. Corr. BAB Egk; Egk's pocket calendars, passim (BS, Ana/410).

62. The composer most consistently and, in terms of the amounts, most highly favored here was Richard Strauss. Expressly excluded from the competition of 1942 was "quarter Jew" Boris Blacher, actually in Egk's circle of closer acquaintances. Orff was included, because his partial Jewishness was not known to anyone. Prieberg's communication that Egk awarded himself a prize of RM4000 in the

1942 competition is based on a misreading of the documentary evidence, which clearly shows that he got none (as he had originally proposed that he should not), despite the insistence of his RMK cojurors. See corr. BAB Egk; Prieberg, *NS-Staat,* 267; and now, wrongly, Walter, *Hitler,* 273, n. 26.

63. *ZM* 109 (1942), 372; entries in Egk's pocket calendars for: 2 May 1941, 27 Mar., 16 and 26 May, 15 June, 4 and 5 July 1942 (BS, Ana/410); Prieberg, *NS-Staat,* 26–27.

64. This was the Ständiger Rat für die internationale Zusammenarbeit der Komponisten, of which, from Germany's side, Richard Strauss and Emil Nikolaus von Reznicek, were also members. See *ZM* 109 (1942), 331; *JdM 1943,* 16; Egk, *Zeit,* 281–82. See chapter 8, e.g. at n. 137.

65. Werner Egk, "Hugo Rasch, ein Siebziger!" *Mitteilungen der Fachschaft Komponisten in der Reichsmusikkammer,* Apr. 1943; *MK* 1 (1943), 19; Eckhard John, *Musikbolschewismus: Die Politisierung der Musik in Deutschland, 1918–1938* (Stuttgart, 1994), 293, n. 82.

66. *Podium der Unterhaltungsmusik* (10 Sept. 1942), 269.

67. See Kater, *The Twisted Muse,* 164–72. Egk had ridiculed this school as a "restoration of old men" as early as 1934, but later conceded that it was necessary at a transient stage, on the way to a new German music. See his remarks in *Melos* 13 (1934), 233; Egk, "Musik," 26; *VB,* 14 Feb. 1943.

68. *ZM* 108 (1941), 637; *Deutsche Zeitung Norwegen,* 19 July 1941; *Leipziger Neuste Nachrichten,* 23 July 1941; *12 Uhr Blatt,* Berlin, 29 July 1941.

69. See Kater, *The Twisted Muse,* 190–95, 226–32.

70. Egk [to Goebbels], "Vorschläge Oper," [Oct. 1941], BAB Egk; Hanns Meseke, "'Uraufführungserfolge': Der neue 'Vater der Komponisten' an die Kameraden der Kunstbetrachtung," *Deutsche Presse* (13 Sept. 1941), 183–84; Fritz Stege, "Kreuz und quer durch die Musik," *Unterhaltungsmusik* (15 Aug. 1941), 705–6. On Goebbels's cultural aims see Kater, *The Twisted Muse,* 177–79.

71. Karl Holl, "Werner Egk, ein Musiker unserer Zeit: I," *Frankfurter Zeitung,* 4 July 1940.

72. Idem, "Werner Egk, ein Musiker unserer Zeit: II," ibid., 5 July 1940.

73. Egk as quoted by Anton Würz in *ZM* 108 (1941), 725.

74. Egk, "Musik," 25 (quote). On p. 26 Egk talks about "photographed poor copy of the most banal everyday events," a clear reference to Weill's *Der Zar lässt sich photographieren.*

75. Werner Egk, "Worum es ging und worum es geht," *VB,* 14 Feb. 1943.

76. On the annihilative force of Nazi language, see Victor Klemperer, *"LTI": Die unbewältigte Sprache: Aus dem Notizbuch eines Philologen* (Munich, 1969); Cornelia Berning, *Vom "Abstammungsnachweis" zum "Zuchtwart": Vokabular des Nationalsozialismus* (Berlin, 1964).

77. Egk, *Zeit,* 336.

78. *ZM* 108 (1941), 683, 688; ibid. 109 (1942), 138, 273, 282; *MK* 2 (1944), 61–62; Friedrich Stichtenoth in *Generalanzeiger,* Frankfurt, 14 Jan. 1942; Karl Holl in *Frankfurter Zeitung,* 15 Jan. 1942; Werner Oehlmann in *Reich,* 21 June 1942; Egk's pocket calendars, 1941–44, BS, Ana/410.

79. Kratzi (Bremen) in *ZM* 109 (1942), 326. The original German phrase is "*arteigene Musik*".

80. Von Schirach to Egk, 30 Oct. 1941, BAB Egk; Kupfer to Orff, 10 Mar. 1942; Jarosch to Orff, 14 Mar. 1942, CM, Allg. Korr.; Junk to Pfitzner, 18 Mar. 1942, SMM, 9; Junk to Pfitzner, 6 May 1942, in Elisabeth Wamlek-Junk, ed., *Hans*

Pfitzner und Wien: Sein Briefwechsel mit Victor Junk und andere Dokumente (Tutzing, 1986), 139–40; Victor Junk, "Die 'Woche zeitgenössischer Musik in Wien,'" *ZM* 109 (1942), 241–47; Junk in *ZM* 109 (1942), 117. Also see Oliver Rathkolb, *Führertreu und gottbegnadet: Künstlereliten im Dritten Reich* (Vienna, 1991), 68–76.

81. Minutes of broadcast meeting, 7 Jan. 1942, BA, R55/695; Leiter Rundfunk to [Goebbels], 25 Apr. 1944, BA, R55/559; Rudolf Schulz-Dornburg, "Wo stehen die deutschen Komponisten unserer Zeit? Bemerkungen über eine neue Sendereihe," *Reichsrundfunk* (28 Sept. 1941), 266; entry for 26 Feb. 1942, Egk's pocket calendar, BS, Ana/410.

82. Entries in Egk's pocket calendars for 1–6 Mar., 9–12 June 1941 (BS, Ana/410); *MK* 1 (1943), 109. For the Oct. 1941 letter, see text in this chapter near n. 70.

83. Entry for 7–27 Mar. 1943 in Egk's pocket calendar, BS, Ana/410; Drewes to Graener, 26 Mar. 1943, BS, Fasc. germ. (Drewes) (quote).

84. Egk, *Zeit,* 349; entries in Egk's pocket calendars for 3–10 June, 24 June–2 July, 5–22 July 1942 (BS, Ana/410).

85. Hans Borgelt, "Diskussion um 'Peer Gynt': Werner Egks Oper im Urteil der französischen Kritik," *MK* 1 (1943/44), 179–81; entries for 21 Sept.–13 Oct. 1943 in Egk's pocket calendar, BS, Ana/410.

86. *TG* 3:317 (quote). See also Prieberg, *NS-Staat,* 315.

87. Entry for 16 June 1942 in Egk's pocket calendar, BS, Ana/410.

88. Krauss to Strauss, 2 Mar. 1942, in Götz Klaus Kende, *Richard Strauss und Clemens Krauss: Eine Künstlerfreundschaft und ihre Zusammenarbeit an "Capriccio"* (Munich, 1960), 231. That venture was stalled, apparently because of technical difficulties, but Krauss did tour Vichy France (Kater, *The Twisted Muse,* 55).

89. Weill to UE-Direktion, 26 Feb. 1933, WC, Weill/UE corr.

90. Egk to Lang, 18 Jan. 1944; Egk to Strobel, 22 Jan. 1944; Egk to Piersig, 1 Mar. 1944; Egk to Götze, 8 Mar. 1944; Egk to Lehmann, 8 Mar. 1944 and 30 June 1944, BS, Ana/410; Prieberg, *NS-Staat,* 310–17.

91. Karl Böhm, *Ich erinnere mich ganz genau: Autobiographie* (Zurich, 1968), 85–86.

92. Kater, *The Twisted Muse,* 201.

93. Annemay Schlusnus in Eckart von Naso, *Heinrich Schlusnus: Mensch und Sänger* (Hamburg, 1957), 180–81.

94. Erna Berger, *Auf Flügeln des Gesanges: Erinnerungen einer Sängerin,* 2nd ed. (Zurich, 1989), 59.

95. "Military Government of Germany: Fragebogen," sign. Werner Egk, 16 Oct. 1945; Beisler to Kläger, 23 Sept. 1946, AM, Egk.

96. Rathkolb, *Führertreu,* 176; *TGII* 13:333.

97. BAB Ney; BAB Egk. See Kater, *The Twisted Muse,* 30–33, 69–70.

98. Kater, "Orff," 20–23.

99. Von Holthoff to Orff, 8 Jan. 1942; Meissner to Orff, 28 Feb. 1942; Tietjen to Orff, 28 Mar. 1942, CM, Allg. Korr.; *ZM* 108 (1941), 53; Werner Oehlmann, "Orff—Egk—Zandonai: Moderne Oper in Berlin/Anmerkungen zu Konzerten," *Reich,* 28 Dec. 1941; *MK* 2 (1944), 26.

100. Orff to Ruppel, 23 Feb. 1942; Jarosch to Orff, 14 Mar. 1942, CM, Allg. Korr.; Victor Junk in *ZM* 109 (1942), 117–18; Junk, "'Woche,'" 246; "Staatsoper Wien," 17 Feb. 1942, facsimile in Andrea Seebohm, "Unbewältigte musikalische Vergangenheit: Ein Kapitel österreichischer Musikgeschichte, das bis heute

ungeschrieben ist," in Liesbeth Waechter-Böhm, ed., *Wien 1945: Davor/danach* (Vienna, 1985), 146.

101. Leiter Rundfunk to [Goebbels], 25 Apr. 1944, BA, R55/559; Schulz-Dornburg, "Komponisten," 266; *ZM* 109 (1942), 91.

102. Maler to Orff, 12 Feb. 1942; Reusch to Orff, 14 Feb. 1942; Aulich to Orff, 22 Mar. 1943; *Koralle* to Orff, 30 Mar. 1943, CM, Allg. Korr.; NSDAP-Partei-Kanzlei to Gauleitung München-Oberbayern, 27 June 1942, BAB Orff; Otto Eckstein-Ehrenegg, "Die tieferen Ursachen der Opernkrise und der Weg zu ihrer Überwindung," *ZM* 109 (1942), 63; *AMZ* 69 (1942), 26; Werner Oehlmann, "Lebendige Musik," *Reich,* 21 June 1942; Fritz Chlodwig Lange in *JdM 1943,* 92–93.

103. Strecker to Orff, 26 Jan. 1943, CM, Schott Korr.

104. See the statistics in Gotthold Frotscher, "Die Oper in der Gegenwart," in Wolfgang Stumme, ed., *Musik im Volk: Gegenwartsfragen der deutschen Musik* (Berlin-Lichterfelde, 1944), 261; table regarding opera stagings in Munich, 1 Jan. 1933–2 Oct. 1943, in Petra Maria Valentin, "Die Bayerische Staatsoper im Dritten Reich," MA thesis, Munich, 1985.

105. Kater, *The Twisted Muse,* 195, 227–28. See also Thomas Eickhoff, *Politische Dimensionen einer Komponisten-Biographie im 20. Jahrhundert—Gottfried von Einem* (Stuttgart, 1998), 17–86.

106. Ruppel to Orff, 9 July 1941; Bergese to Orff, 25 Nov. 1941; Orff to Blacher, 4 Apr. 1942; Kurzbach to Orff, 12 Mar. and 5 May 1943; Gorvin to Orff, 8 Nov. 1943; David to Orff, 14 Nov. 1944, CM, Allg. Korr. Several meetings between Egk and von Einem, fewer with Wagner-Régeny, are documented in Egk's pocket calendars (1942–44), BS, Ana/410. See also Kater, *The Twisted Muse,* 188.

107. On Blacher and von Einem, see Kater, *The Twisted Muse,* 226–32; Eickhoff, *Dimensionen,* 39–86.

108. See Egk to Hinkel, 2 Sept. 1941, BDC Egk; Schüler to Egk, 31 Dec. 1946, AM, Egk; Hans Bergese to author, Berlin, 11 Mar. 1996, APA.

109. Declaration under oath by Fritz Schulte, 4 Mar. 1946, and Erna Eckstein in "Protokoll der öffentlichen Sitzung," 17 Oct. 1947; Ruppel deposition, 11 Oct. 1947, AM, Egk; author's interview with Gertrud Orff, Munich, 5 Aug. 1992, APA; Brigitte Bergese to author, Leukerbad, 4 Oct. 1995, and Hans Bergese to author, Berlin, 19 Oct. 1995, APA.

110. Egk's deposition in "Anlagen zum Fragebogen," [1947], AM, Egk; Egk cited in Berndt W. Wessling, "Werner Egk setzt sich zur Wehr: Gespräch mit dem Komponisten zu den Vorwürfen wegen seiner Tätigkeit im Dritten Reich," *Weser-Kurier,* Bremen, 19 June 1969.

111. Entries for 28 June, 5 Nov., 24–25 Nov., 29–30 Dec. 1942, 14 Jan. 1943, 23 and 28 Apr., 5–13 May 1943, in Egk's pocket calendars, BS, Ana/410.

112. Hinkel to Voigt, 4 May 1943; Voigt to Hinkel, 8 May 1943; Framm to Egk, 2 July 1943, BAB Egk.

113. In a camp near Werner Egk's birthplace. See Egk to Strobel, 22 Jan. 1944, BS, Ana/410.

114. Egk's pocket calendar, BS, Ana/410 (quote); Egk cited in Wessling, "Werner Egk setzt sich zur Wehr"; Brigitte Bergese to author, Leukerbad, 4 Oct. 1995, and Hans Bergese to author, Berlin, 19 Oct. 1995, APA. Also see Gottfried von Einem, recorded interview, Vienna, 30 Nov. 1994, APA; Egk, *Zeit,* 369.

115. Gottfried von Einem, recorded interview, Vienna, 30 Nov. 1994, APA; Boris Blacher in Josef Müller-Marein and Hannes Reinhardt, eds., *Das musikalische*

Selbstportrait von Komponisten, Dirigenten, Instrumentalisten, Sängerinnen und Sängern unserer Zeit (Hamburg, 1965), 412.

116. The first quote represents the verdict of Italian composer Goffredo Petrassi, as printed in Harvey Sachs, *Music in Fascist Italy* (London, 1987), 142; the second is Boehmer as quoted in Fred K. Prieberg, "Der Fall Werner Egk: Ein trauriges Beispiel für eine traurig kompromittierte Generation," *Zeit*, 29 Apr. 1969. Also see Prieberg, *NS-Staat*, 24–25; and the judgment of Munich music critic Helmut Mauró, in *Süddeutsche Zeitung*, Munich, 19 June 1995.

117. Prieberg, "Der Fall Werner Egk."

118. Dietmar Polaczek, "Richard Strauss—Thema und Metamorphosen," in Karl Corino, ed., *Intellektuelle im Bann des Nationalsozialismus* (Hamburg, 1980), 73.

119. Seebohm, "Vergangenheit," 151.

120. Frederic Spotts, "And the Bands Played On: Musicians in the Third Reich," *Opera News* (July 1995), 25.

121. See Lt. Hugoboom to Kimental, 14 Nov. 1945; Stenzel to Öffentlicher Kläger, 27 June 1946; Egk to Weidinger, 29 Mar. 1947, AM, Egk; Egk to Schroer, 21 Sept. 1946, BS, Ana/410. Background in: Hajo Holborn, *American Military Government: Its Organization and Policies* (Washington, D.C., 1947), esp. 53–73; Lutz Niethammer, *Entnazifizierung in Bayern: Säuberung und Rehabilitierung unter amerikanischer Besatzung* (Frankfurt am Main, 1972); Harold Zink, *American Government in Germany* (New York, 1947).

122. Brigitte Bergese to Orff, 12 Sept. 1943, CM, Allg. Korr. (quote); various entries for 1945 in "Gertrud Orffs Tagebuch" CM; Gertrud Orff interview, Munich, 5 Aug. 1992, APA; Brigitte Bergese to author, Leukerbad, 4 Oct. 1995, and Berlin, 7 Mar. 1996; and Hans Bergese to author, Berlin, 19 Oct. 1995, APA.

123. That this had indeed been Egk's intention is clear from letter Mayer to Orff, 10 Sept. 1948, CM, Allg. Korr.

124. Brigitte Bergese's exclamation to Orff, according to her letter to me of 4 Oct. 1995. Also her letter to me of 7 Mar. 1996, APA. Jenkins's meeting at the Orffs that day is confirmed by entry for 24 Dec. 1945 in "Gertrud Orffs Tagebuch" CM; and Newell Jenkins, recorded interview, Hillsdale, N.Y., 20 Mar. 1993, APA.

125. Newell Jenkins, recorded interview, Hillsdale, N.Y., 20 Mar. 1993, APA (1st quote); Jenkins to Orff, 7 Jan. 1946, CM, Allg. Korr. (2nd quote).

126. Heinz Trojan and Kurt Hinze, *Beschäftigungsverbot, Vermögenssperre und Sühnemassnahmen nach dem Gesetz zur Befreiung von Nationalsozialismus und Militarismus vom 5. März 1946: Kommentar für die Praxis* (Wiesbaden, 1947).

127. Egk application for clearance, Lochham, 10 Mar. 1946, AM, Egk; Egk, *Zeit*, 370.

128. Beisler to Kassationshof München, 18 Aug. 1947; Stenzel assessment, 12 May 1947 (quote); Herf to Spruchkammer München-Land, 7 July 1947; minutes of public proceedings, Spruchkammer München-Land, 17 Oct. 1947, AM, Egk; *Melos* 14 (1947), 350.

129. Orff's statement cited in "Ermittlungsbericht zu Werner Egk," 7 Nov. 1946, AM, Egk. For Gertrud Orff, see text below at n. 156.

130. Gottfried von Einem, recorded interview, Vienna, 30 Nov. 1994, APA.

131. See Heinrich Strobel, "Orffische Zwiesprach: Zur Uraufführung der 'Bernauerin,'" *Melos* 14 (1947), 297–99; Orff to Schuh, 7 Nov. 1947; Orff to Sutermeister, 25 Dec. 1947, CM, Allg. Korr.; Brigitte Bergese to author, Leukerbad, 4 Oct. 1995, and Hans Bergese to author, Berlin, 19 Oct. 1995, APA.

132. Orff to Schuh, 17 Dec. 1947, CM, Allg. Korr. To von Einem Orff wrote: "Egk is alright again, but it was a nasty business. More about this in person" (22 Dec. 1947, CM, Allg. Korr.).

133. Egk to Hanka, 27 Oct. 1947, BS, Ana/410. Similarly Egk to Schuh, 27 Oct. 1947, ibid.

134. Entry for 27 Dec. 1947 in "Gertrud Orffs Tagebuch" CM.

135. Minutes of proceedings, Kommission für Kulturschaffende, 21 Mar. 1946, AM, Egk (quote); Prieberg, "Der Fall Werner Egk"; Karl Schumann, *Werner Egk: Werkverzeichnis* (Mainz, 1976), 7–15; Klaus Kreimeier, *The Ufa Story: A History of Germany's Greatest Film Company, 1918–1945* (New York, 1996), 211, 312; Gerd Albrecht, *Nationalsozialistische Filmpolitik: Eine soziologische Untersuchung über die Spielfilme des Dritten Reichs* (Stuttgart, 1969), 550; Pierre Cadars and Francis Coutarde, *Le cinéma nazi* ([Paris, 1972]), 337. In his memoirs, Egk does not mention the first two works and tries to downplay the political importance of the HJ commission (*Zeit*, 333–34).

136. Minutes of proceedings, as in n. 135. See n. 32.

137. Typical example ibid.

138. A charge Prieberg leveled in blanket fashion in 1969: See his "Der Fall Werner Egk."

139. Minutes of public proceedings, Spruchkammer München-Land, 17 Oct. 1947; Holl to Beisler, 16 Sept. 1947 (quote), AM, Egk. On Kloss see Kater, *The Twisted Muse*, 34.

140. Egk to Schüler, 10 Dec. 1946, BS, Ana/410. Italics in original. The result is Schüler's letter to Egk, dated 31 Dec. 1946 (AM, Egk), more or less delivering what Egk had asked for, on offical stationery, but not in the form of a deposition under oath.

141. Tietjen telegram to Amtsgericht München, 15 Oct. 1947, AM, Egk. Also see Tietjen to Egk, 28 June 1946, BS, Ana/410.

142. Von Tiedemann to Stenzel, 27 June 1946; von Einem, Hanka, Schuh, Schneider, Moralt certification, 11 Sept. 1947; Rutz certification, 11 Sept. 1947; Strobel memorandum, 12 Sept. 1947; Brust deposition under oath, 14 Sept. 1947; Reindl deposition under oath, 28 Sept. 1947; Stuckenschmidt deposition under oath, 29 Sept. 1947; Harth opinion, 29 Sept. 1947; Ruppel declaration, 11 Oct. 1947; minutes of public proceedings, Spruchkammer München-Land, 17 Oct. 1947, AM, Egk.

143. Egk to Hinkel, 8 Nov. 1941; Hinkel to [Goebbels], 21 Aug. 1941; Hinkel to Egk, 28 Aug. 1941, BAB Egk; Egk to Schüler, 10 Dec. 1946, BS, Ana/410; Egk to von Tiedemann, 12 Aug. 1941; Egk deposition under oath, 10 Mar. 1946; von Tiedemann to Stenzel, 27 June 1946; Wetzelsberger to Spruchkammer München-Land, 30 July 1946; Egk to Spruchkammer München-Land, 5 Aug. 1946; von Prittwitz-Gaffron to Egk, 17 Feb. 1947; Beisler to Kassationshof München, 18 Aug. 1947; von Tiedemann declaration under oath, 15 Oct. 1947; Hartmann declaration under oath, 9 Sept. 1947; Harth opinion, 29 Sept. 1947; minutes of public proceedings, Spruchkammer München-Land, 17 Oct. 1947; "Anlagen zum Fragebogen," [1947], AM, Egk.

144. Hinkel to Egk, 1 Nov. 1944; Egk to Hinkel, 25 Jan. 1945, BAB Egk; Egk to Schüler, 27 Jan. 1946, BS, Ana/410; Seeger certification, 7 Apr. 1946; Piersig to Egk, 27 Jun. 1946; von Tiedemann to Stenzel, 27 June 1946; Schonger certification, 1 July 1946; Wetzelsberger to Spruchkammer München-Land, 30 July 1946; Schüler to Egk, 31 Dec. 1946; Beisler to Kassationshof München, 18 Aug. 1947; von

Einem, Hanka, Schuh, Schneider, Moralt certification, 11 Sept. 1947; Rutz certification, 11 Sept. 1949; Stuckenschmidt deposition under oath, 29 Sept. 1947; Furtwängler certification, 15 Oct. 1947; minutes of public proceedings, Spruchkammer München-Land, 17 Oct. 1947, AM, Egk; Egk, *Zeit,* 326–27, 347–48, 363–65.

145. For the time in question (1943), neither in Egk's pocket calendars nor in any of Wagner-Régeny's documents on the period, nor in any statement Wagner-Régeny could have made (and significantly did not make) at Egk's trial. See Rudolf Wagner-Régeny, *Begegnungen: Biographische Aufzeichnungen, Tagebücher, und sein Briefwechsel mit Caspar Neher* (Berlin, 1968); idem, *An den Ufern der Zeit: Schriften, Briefe, Tagebücher,* ed. Max Becker (Leipzig, 1989); Dieter Härtwig, *Rudolf Wagner-Régeny: Der Opernkomponist* (Berlin, 1965); Kater, *The Twisted Muse,* 194–95.

146. Gottfried von Einem, recorded interview, Vienna, 30 Nov 1994, APA; Kater, *The Twisted Muse,* 195.

147. Egk application for clearance, Lochham, 10 Mar. 1946; "Meldebogen auf Grund des Gesetzes zur Befreiung vom Nationalsozialismus und Militarismus vom 5. März 1946," sign. Egk, 4 May 1946; Egk to Spruchkammer München-Land, 5 Aug. 1946, AM, Egk.

148. Von Einem statement, 3 July 1945, AM, Egk (quote); Gottfried von Einem, recorded interview, Vienna, 30 Nov. 1994, APA; author's telephone conversation with von Einem, Munich-Vienna, 12 Oct. 1994.

149. Eickhoff, *Dimensionen,* 103, 107.

150. Von Einem to Egk, 19 May 1946 and 3 July 1947, BS, Ana/410; Egk to Schuh, 27 Oct. 1947, BS, Ana/410; von Einem to Orff, 13 Sept. 1947, CM, Allg. Korr.; Norcross to [Austrian] Federal Chancellor, 17 Sept. 1946; Figl to Alliierte Kommission für Österreich, 4 Nov. 1946, OSW, BKA/Entnazifizierung 1399/46-Pr; Hansjakob Kröber, *Herbert von Karajan: Der Magier mit dem Taktstock* (Munich, 1986), 105. *Circe* was renamed *Siebzehn Tage und vier Minuten* in 1966 (Schumann, *Egk,* 8; *GLM* 2:409); Eickhoff, *Dimensionen,* 102–7.

151. Von Einem to Egk, 4 Jan. and 26 Nov. 1947 (quote), BS, Ana/410.

152. Strobel in minutes of public proceedings, Spruchkammer München-Land, 17 Oct. 1947, AM, Egk.

153. Egk to Spruchkammer München-Land, 5 Aug. 1946 (quote); Gsovsky deposition under oath, 10 July 1946; von Borresholm to Kommission für Kulturschaffende, 12 July 1946; Egk in "Anlagen zum Fragebogen," [1947], AM, Egk; Egk to Schüler, 27 Jan. 1946, BS, Ana/410.

154. Elisabeth Hartmann, recorded interview, Munich, 13 Dec. 1994, APA.

155. Ibid. (quote); Hartmann deposition under oath, 11 Mar. 1946; Hartmann to Spruchkammer München-Land, 5 Sept. 1947, AM, Egk. See also Hartmann's totally noncommittal letters, to the Danish composer Knudåge Riisager, who inquired about Egk, 30 Dec. 1946, and to Egk's and Hartmann's old patron Scherchen, 28 Jan. 1948, BS, Ana/407; Kater, *The Twisted Muse,* 238.

156. See Gertrud Orff and Klaus Eckstein depositions under oath, both 4 Mar. 1946, AM, Egk (as samples for several others, all identical); Egk's own description of the scheme in minutes of public proceedings, Spruchkammer München-Land, 17 Oct. 1947, AM, Egk; Gertrud Orff interview, Munich, 5 Aug. 1992 (quote). "Gertrud Orffs Tagebuch" (CM) has no entries for Mar./Apr. 1945 which could substantiate such activities.

157. Keilhold et al. judgment, Spruchkammer München-Land, 17 Oct. 1947; Herf to Berufungskammer München, 30 Apr. 1948, AM, Egk.

158. Entry for 7 Sept. in 1945 "Gertrud Orffs Tagebuch" CM; Egk to Schüler, 27 Jan. 1946; Egk to Rennert, 6 May 1947, BS, Ana/410; Vondenhoff to Spruchkammer München-Land, 22 Mar. 1947; Beckmann to Berufungskammer München, 16 Feb. 1948, AM, Egk; *Melos* 14 (1947), 306; Egk, *Zeit,* 373; Schumann, *Egk,* 8; *GLM* 2:409.

159. Otte to Spruchkammer München-Land, 28 Sept. 1947, AM, Egk.

160. Some of these shortcomings are addressed by Clemens Vollnhals in his "Entnazifizierung: Politische Säuberung unter alliierter Herrschaft," in Hans-Erich Volkmann, ed., *Ende des Dritten Reiches—Ende des Zweiten Weltkriegs: Eine perspektivische Rückschau* (Munich, 1995), 369–92.

161. See *Melos* 14 (1946), 53; ibid. 14 (1947), 126.

162. Beisler to Kassationshof München, 18 Aug. 1947, AM, Egk.

163. See *Melos* 14 (1947), 229, 262–63, 307, 352, 393; ibid. 15 (1948), 60.

164. *GLM* 2:408; Egk, *Zeit,* 418–39; Krause, *Egk,* 30–31.

165. Schumann, *Egk,* 7–15.

166. On their Nazi careers, see Kater, *The Twisted Muse,* 55–65.

167. Quotation is Prieberg's in "Der Fall Werner Egk" (see n. 116). Also see Egk's tortuous self-defense in Wessling, "Werner Egk setzt sich zur Wehr" (n. 110).

CHAPTER 2: HINDEMITH

1. *Münchener Neueste Nachrichten,* 22 [?] Sept. 1929; Fred K. Prieberg, *Lexikon der Neuen Musik* (Freiburg im Breisgau, 1958), 191–92; Berndt W. Wessling, *Furtwängler: Eine kritische Biographie* (Stuttgart, 1985), 286; Eva Hanau, *Musikinstitutionen in Frankfurt am Main, 1933 bis 1939* (Cologne, 1994), 20; Jürgen Mainka, "Hindemith und die Weimarer Republik," *Hindemith-Jahrbuch* 17 (1988), 168–69. On the Weimar cultural context, see John Willett, *Art and Politics in the Weimar Period: The New Sobriety, 1917–1933* (New York, 1978), 67–167; *NG* 8:575–81.

2. Mainka, "Hindemith," 168.

3. Andres Briner et al., *Paul Hindemith: Leben und Werk in Bild und Text* (Mainz, 1988), 113, 115.

4. Hindemith-Pfitzner corr. (1925–26), OW, 80 and 453. On the Pfitzner-Hindemith relationship in general see also Pfitzner to Abendroth, 16 Nov. 1941, OW, 288/177; Ludwig Schrott, *Die Persönlichkeit Hans Pfitzners* (Zurich, 1959), 130–31.

5. Paul Hindemith, "Wilhelm Furtwängler," in Martin Müller and Wolfgang Mertz, eds., *Diener der Musik* (Tübingen, 1965), 184.

6. Weill to Curjel, 22 June and 2 Aug. 1929 (quote), WC, Curjel corr. In public and disingenuously, Weill denied there was a conflict: Kurt Weill, *Musik und Theater: Gesammelte Schriften,* ed. Stephen Hinton and Jürgen Schebera (Berlin, 1990), 303–4. On the *Lindberghflug* see Kim H. Kowalke, *Kurt Weill in Europe* (Ann Arbor, Mich., 1979), 73, 343, n. 121. Also see Lys Symonette and Kim Kowalke, eds., *Speak Low (When You Speak Love): The Letters of Kurt Weill and Lotte Lenya* (Berkeley, 1996), 59–60.

7. According to Strecker to Hindemith, 25 Feb. 1931, PF, Schott Korr. On Fortner's pre-1933 modernism, see *NG* 6:723; *MGG* 4:580–82.

8. Orff to Reusch, 24 Jan. 1932, CM, Allg. Korr. See also handbill, "Vereinigung für zeitgen. Musik," [Spring 1931], SM, Kulturamt/143.

9. Hindemith to Strecker, 8 Sept. 1931, PF, Schott Korr.

10. Hindemith to Strecker, 16 July 1932, PF, Schott Korr.

11. James E. Paulding, "Mathis der Maler—The Politics of Music," *Hindemith-Jahrbuch* 5 (1976), 121.

12. Briner et al., *Hindemith,* 131.

13. Quoted in Luther Noss, *Paul Hindemith in the United States* (Urbana, Ill., 1989), 69.

14. On the genesis, see Hindemith to Strecker, 17 June 1933, PF, Schott Korr.; Claudia Maurer Zenck, "Zwischen Boykott und Anpassung an den Charakter der Zeit: Über die Schwierigkeiten eines deutschen Komponisten mit dem Dritten Reich," *Hindemith-Jahrbuch* 9 (1980), 69–70; Andres Briner, *Paul Hindemith* (Zurich, 1971), 100; Briner et al., *Hindemith,* 140.

15. Paulding, "Mathis der Maler," 121. A corroborating analysis is in Hermann Danuser, *Die Musik des 20. Jahrhunderts* (Regensburg, 1984), 227–28, 241–42.

16. See the contemporary press reports reprinted in *Melos* 13 (1934), 125–26; Peter Muck, *Einhundert Jahre Berliner Philharmonisches Orchester: Darstellung in Dokumenten,* 3 vols. (Tutzing, 1982), 2:111; Briner et al., *Hindemith,* 146; and Ludwig Strecker to Hindemith, 14 Mar. 1934, PF, Schott Korr.; Giselher Schubert, *Hindemith: Mit Selbstzeugnissen und Bilddokumenten* (Reinbek, 1990), 85.

17. Heinrich Strobel, "Hindemiths 'Symphonie Mathis der Maler,'" *Melos* 13 (1934), 96–97; idem, "Hindemiths neue Sinfonie," ibid., 127-31; Strecker to Hindemith, 4 Aug. 1933, PF, Schott. Korr.; Wessling, *Furtwängler,* 179; Michael H. Kater, *The Twisted Muse: Musicians and Their Music in the Third Reich* (New York, 1997), 179.

18. Strobel, "Hindemiths 'Symphonie Mathis der Maler,'" 96.

19. Maurer Zenck, "Boykott," 119.

20. Wilhelm Pinder, *Die deutsche Kunst der Dürerzeit: Text,* 2nd ed. (Cologne, 1953; 1st ed. 1943), 253–75; *Führer durch die Ausstellung Entartete Kunst* [Munich, 1937], 9; Stephanie Barron et al., *"Degenerate Art": The Fate of the Avant-Garde in Nazi Germany* (Los Angeles, 1991), 315–24; Peter Selz, *German Expressionist Painting* (Berkeley, 1974); Michael H. Kater, "Anti-Fascist Intellectuals in the Third Reich," *Canadian Journal of History* 16 (1981), 275–76. Specifically on Nolde, see Selz, *Emil Nolde* (Garden City, N.Y., 1963), 70–71; Robert Pois, *Emil Nolde* (Washington, D.C., 1982), 187–203; William S. Bradley, *Emil Nolde and German Expressionism: A Prophet in His Own Land* (Ann Arbor, Mich., 1986), 73–75, 114–16. On Benn, see Jürgen Schröder, "Benn in den dreissiger Jahren," in Karl Corino, ed., *Intellektuelle im Bann des Nationalsozialismus* (Hamburg, 1980), 48–60.

21. Geoffrey Skelton, *Paul Hindemith: The Man Behind the Music: A Biography* (London, 1975), 112; Briner et al., *Hindemith,* 140.

22. Maurer Zenck adroitly takes umbrage at earlier postwar versions of Hindemith's "inner emigration." See her "Boykott," 69–70, 117, 120, 125, 127; and Heinrich Strobel, "Mathis der Maler," *Melos* 14 (1947), 65–68; Briner, *Hindemith,* 108.

23. *VB,* 27 Apr. 1932.

24. Briner et al., *Hindemith,* 132. Also see Edgar Rabsch, "Das Ende war der 'Plöner Musiktag': Bericht über einen Modellfall musikalischer Bildung," in Carl Dahlhaus and Walter Wiora, eds., *Musikerziehung in Schleswig-Holstein: Dokumente der Vergangenheit, Aspekte der Gegenwart* (Kassel, 1965), 127–28.

25. According to Franz Reizenstein, Hindemith's Jewish pupil in those years,

"Some Aspersions Answered," *Composer,* no. 15 (Spring 1965), 8; Skelton, *Hindemith,* 108.

26. Strecker to Hindemith, 5 Apr. 1933, PF, Schott Korr. (quote); Karl Grunsky, *Der Kampf um deutsche Musik* (Stuttgart, 1933), 30, 62; *DKW,* no. 22 (1933), 11; Skelton, *Hindemith,* 108; Briner et al., *Hindemith,* 137.

27. Von Hoesslin declaration, 27 Apr. 1933, BAB Franz von Hoesslin.

28. Friedrich Welter as quoted in Schubert, *Hindemith,* 84; Jensen in *DM* 26 (1933), 150 (2nd quote).

29. Hinkel to Hamburger Volkshochschule, 11 Oct. 1933, PF, Musikhochschule Berlin.

30. Claus Neumann, "Moderne Musik—Ein 'Ja' oder 'Nein'?" *ZM* 100 (1933), 546; in the same vein see Walter Berten, "Paul Hindemith und die deutsche Musik," ibid. 536–44; Kater, *The Twisted Muse,* 179.

31. See Furtwängler's revealing comments about Plön in "Der Fall Hindemith," *DAZ,* 25 Nov. 1934; Briner, *Hindemith,* 104; Hans Heinz Stuckenschmidt, *Zum Hören geboren: Ein Leben mit der Musik unserer Zeit* (Munich, 1979), 130; Maurer Zenck, "Boykott," 118.

32. Hanau, *Musikinstitutionen,* 73.

33. Hindemith to Strecker, 9 Feb. 1934; almost identical: Hindemith to Strecker, 5 Feb. 1934, PF, Schott Korr. The spirit of these letters is prefigured by Alban Berg's remark to his wife already on 16 May 1933: "[I hear that] the German government is about to give a mandate to Hindemith for the reorganization of the entire musical life" (in Alban Berg, *Briefe an seine Frau,* ed. Helene Berg [Munich, 1965], 627). Also see Hindemith to Strecker, 15 Apr. 1933; Strecker to Hindemith, 8 Feb. 1934, PF, Schott Korr.; Skelton, *Hindemith,* 115; Maurer Zenck, "Boykott," 71–72.

34. See Willy to Ludwig Strecker, 4 Aug. 1933, PF, Schott Korr.; Reinhart to von Freyhold, 16 Aug. 1933, in Peter Sulzer, *Zehn Komponisten um Werner Reinhart: Ein Ausschnitt aus dem Wirkungskreis des Musikkollegiums Winterthur, 1920–1950,* 3 vols. (Winterthur, 1979–83), 3:221; Schubert, *Hindemith,* 79; Briner et al., *Hindemith,* 138.

35. Professors Fritz Stein and Gustav Havemann. See Maurer Zenck, "Boykott"; Havemann to Hess, 21 Dec. 1933, BAB Havemann; and corr. in PF, Musikhochschule Berlin.

36. Benn's letter to Gertrud Hindemith of 21 Oct. 1933 in Schröder, "Benn," 55; Hindemith to Toch, 23 Sept. 1933, ETA, 36 (1st quote); Hindemith to Strecker brothers, 5 Sept. 1933, PF, Schott Korr. (last quote). The rumors were published nationwide in the local German press, according to *Melos* 12 (1933), 307; and *Artist,* 22 Sept. 1933.

37. Weidemann to Ihlert, 21 Feb. 1934; minutes of 7th RMK presidial council meeting, 3 Mar. 1934, RG; *Melos* 13 (1934), 112; Maurer Zenck, "Boykott," 73; Wessling, *Furtwängler,* 279–80; Muck, *Jahre,* 2:110; Briner et al., *Hindemith,* 143.

38. Both themes are invoked in the article "Der Fall Hindemith," in *Mitteldeutsche National-Zeitung,* Halle, 6 Nov. 1934. Quote ibid.

39. Strecker to Hindemith, 29 Mar. [falsely referring to Conrad as Hermann] and 12 June 1934, PF, Schott Korr.; Willms to Orff, 12 June 1934, CM, Schott Korr.; *Melos* 13 (1934), 155, 207, 253; Jonathan Petropoulos, *Art as Politics in the Third Reich* (Chapel Hill, N.C., 1996), 201.

40. Strauss to Kopsch, 2 Apr. 1934, RG (quote); Strecker to Hindemith, 12 July 1934, PF, Schott Korr.; Wilhelm Altmann, "Kritische Opernstatistik," *DM* 26

(1934), 903; Skelton, *Hindemith*, 117; Maurer Zenck, "Boykott," 75; Joan Evans, *Hans Rosbaud: A Bio-Bibliography* (New York, 1992), 28.

41. Preussner to Orff, 4 Oct. 1934, CM, Allg. Korr.; Briner et al., *Hindemith*, 143. E.g. see *DM* 27 (1935), 246–47.

42. Corr. of Oct.–Dec. 1934, BA, R55/1182; Karrasch to [Goebbels], 16 Oct. 1934, BA, R55/1184.

43. Strecker to Hindemith, 30 Oct. 1934; Hindemith to Strecker, 15 Nov. 1934, PF, Schott Korr.; Stenger to Schulte-Strathaus, 24 Nov. 1934, BAB Havemann; *Skizzen* (Nov. 1934), 18; *Frankfurter Zeitung*, 16 Nov. 1934; Fritz Stege, "Komponisten, die man nicht aufführt," *Westen*, Berlin, 18 Nov. 1934; Maurer Zenck, "Boykott," 77–78.

44. Gertrud Hindemith to Strecker brothers, 5 Oct. 1934; Hindemith to Strecker, 28 Oct. and 11, 15, 18 Nov. 1934; Strecker to Hindemith, 14 Nov. 1934, PF, Schott Korr.

45. Wilhelm Furtwängler, "Der Fall Hindemith," *Deutsche Allgemeine Zeitung*, Berlin, 25 Nov. 1934.

46. Details in Kater, *The Twisted Muse*, 181, 199.

47. Hindemith to [Stein], 5 Dec. 1934, PF, Musikhochschule Berlin; Thomas Mann, *Tagebücher, 1933–1934*, ed. Peter de Mendelssohn (Frankfurt am Main, 1977), 585; *GLM* 4:95.

48. Furtwängler, "Denkschrift," Jan.–May 1935, ZNF (quote); Wilhelm Furtwängler, *Notebooks, 1924–1954*, ed. Michael Tanner (London, 1989), 85-86, 129, 141, 145, 147.

49. Kater, *The Twisted Muse*, 195–203.

50. *DM* 27 (1935), 246–47; Friedrich W. Herzog, "Der Fall Hindemith—Furtwängler," ibid., 241–45; *VB*, 2 Dec. 1934; Kater, *The Twisted Muse*, 181–82.

51. On Strauss's approval, his son Franz sent an applauding telegram to Goebbels, the content of which his father was familiar with. See chapter 8 at n. 181; Strauss to [Rasch], 14 Dec. 1934, RG (quote).

52. Karla Höcker, ed., *Wilhelm Furtwängler: Dokumente—Berichte und Bilder—Aufzeichnungen* (Berlin, 1968), 85. But see Furtwängler's hypocritical letter to Gertrud Hindemith, [Feb.] 1935, PF, Furtwängler Korr.

53. For the hurt, see Hindemith to Havemann, 3 Feb. 1935, PF, Schott Korr.

54. Briner, *Hindemith*, 108 (quote). I am following the much earlier, and pioneering, interpretation by Claudia Maurer Zenck, "Boykott," 117.

55. Hindemith to Strecker, 23 Jan. 1935, PF, Schott Korr.; Hanau, *Musikinstitutionen*, 128–29.

56. Gertrud Hindemith to Strecker, 29 Jan. [1935], PF, Schott Korr.; Maurer Zenck, "Boykott," 89.

57. Hindemith to Strecker, 13 Feb. 1935, Schott Korr. (quote). On Turkey as an anti-Hitler émigré haven, see Fritz Neumark, *Zuflucht am Bosporus: Deutsche Gelehrte, Politiker und Künstler in der Emigration, 1933–1953* (Frankfurt am Main, 1980).

58. Minutes of 13th meeting of RMK presidial council meeting, 26 Feb. 1935, and 14th meeting, 16 Mar. 1935 (quote), RG; Hindemith to Strecker, 31 Mar. 1935, PF, Schott Korr.; Stein to Strecker, 6 Apr. 1935, PF, Musikhochschule Berlin; Maurer Zenck, "Boykott," 91.

59. Details are in Cornelia Zimmermann-Kalyoncu, "Paul Hindemiths Türkei-Jahre—oder: Wie organisiert man Atatürks Musikreformen?" *Hindemith-Jahrbuch* 15 (1986), 28–38; idem, *Deutsche Musiker in der Türkei im 20. Jahrhundert* (Frankfurt am Main, 1985); Briner et al., *Hindemith*, 148–49.

60. Hindemith to Stein, 21 Feb. 1935, PF, Musikhochschule Berlin.

61. Hindemith report, enclosed with letter Havemann to Führer et al., 18 June 1935, BAB Hindemith. Also see Hindemith to [Stein], Easter 1935, PF, Musikhochschule Berlin.

62. Strecker to Hindemith, 9 May 1935, PF, Schott Korr.

63. Paul to Gertrud Hindemith, 29 May 1935, PF, Paul and Gertrud Hindemith Korr.

64. Ansgar Diller, *Rundfunkpolitik im Dritten Reich* (Munich, 1980), 132.

65. Skelton, *Hindemith*, 129; Maurer Zenck, "Boykott," 93.

66. Maurer Zenck, "Boykott," 94; facsimile [ca. 10 July 1935] in Albrecht Dümling and Peter Girth, eds., *Entartete Musik: Zur Düsseldorfer Ausstellung von 1938: Eine kommentierte Rekonstruktion* (Düsseldorf, [1988]), 167.

67. Gertrud Hindemith to Strecker brothers, 12 July [1935]; Strecker to Gertrud Hindemith, 18 Sept. 1935, PF, Schott Korr.; Stein to Hinkel, 22 July 1935; Hinkel to [Goebbels], 29 Aug. 1935, PF, Musikhochschule Berlin.

68. Strecker to Hindemith, 20 Aug. 1935, PF, Schott Korr.

69. Furtwängler to Hindemith, 30 Sept. 1935, PF, Furtwängler Korr.; Gertrud Hindemith to Strecker, 8 Oct. 1935; Paul to Gertrud Hindemith, Dec. and [Christmas] 1935, PF, Paul and Gertrud Hindemith Korr.; Briner et al., *Hindemith*, 138; Hanau, *Musikinstitutionen*, 131.

70. Hindemith declaration under oath, 17 Jan. 1936, PF, Musikhochschule Berlin. Hindemith's old friend, conductor Hans Rosbaud, for instance, swore an identical oath upon the assumption of his duties as Generalmusikdirektor in Münster in 1937 (Rosbaud, "Betr. Treuegelöbnis und Verpflichtung," [1937], LP, 423/1/2).

71. Hindemith to Strecker, 23 Jan. 1936, in Dieter Rexroth, ed., *Paul Hindemith: Briefe* (Frankfurt am Main, 1982), 159–60 (quote); Skelton, *Hindemith*, 130; Maurer Zenck, "Boykott," 98.

72. Havemann to Hinkel, 27 Jan. 1936, PF, Musikhochschule Berlin; Strecker to Hindemith, 20 Apr. 1936, and to Furtwängler, 13 June 1936, PF, Schott Korr.; Skelton, *Hindemith*, 131, 133; Rudolf Stephan, "Zur Musik der Dreissigerjahre," in Christoph-Hellmut Mahling and Sigrid Wiesmann, eds., *Bericht über den Internationalen Musikwissenschaftlichen Kongress Bayreuth 1981* (Kassel, 1984), 144; Briner et al., *Hindemith*, 138, 148.

73. Quote *TG* 2:676; also Maurer Zenck, "Boykott," 101–2; Strecker to Hindemith couple, 1 July 1936; Strecker to Hindemith, 28 Sept. 1936; Petschull to Strecker, 11 Oct. 1936, PF, Schott Korr.; Skelton, *Hindemith*, 134; Briner et al., *Hindemith*, 157; Schubert, *Hindemith*, 86.

74. Wolfgang Fortner in Josef Müller-Marein and Hannes Reinhardt, eds., *Das musikalische Selbstportrait von Komponisten, Dirigenten, Instrumentalisten, Sängerinnen und Sängern unserer Zeit* (Hamburg, 1965), 393; Ulrich Günther, *Die Schulmusikerziehung von der Kestenberg-Reform bis zum Ende des Dritten Reiches: Ein Beitrag zur Dokumentation und Zeitgeschichte der Schulmusikerziehung mit Anregungen zu ihrer Neugestaltung* (Neuwied, 1967), 192; Danuser, *Musik*, 209.

75. *TG* 2:701, 753; Gertrud Hindemith to Strecker brothers, 23 Oct. 1936, and to Willy Strecker, 28 Oct. 1936; Strecker to Hindemith, 31 Oct. 1936, PF, Schott Korr.; Stein to Furtwängler, 22 Mar. 1937, PF, Musikhochschule Berlin; Hindemith to [Stein], 22 Mar. 1937, facsimile in Dümling and Girth, *Entartete Musik*, 168; Zimmermann-Kalyoncu, *Musiker*, 58.

76. Gertrud to Paul Hindemith, 13 and 18 Apr. [1937], PF, 3.144.12–21;

Gertrud Hindemith to Strecker, 19 Apr. 1937, PF, Schott Korr.; Furtwängler to Gertrud Hindemith, 20 Apr. 1937, and to Stein, 18 Aug. 1937 (quote), PF, Furtwängler Korr.

77. Gertrud Hindemith to Reinhart, 19 Apr. [1937], in Sulzer, *Komponisten,* 3:225; Hindemith to Strecker, 21 Sept. 1938, in Rexroth, *Briefe,* 181 (quote); Hans Severus Ziegler, *Entartete Musik: Eine Abrechnung* (Düsseldorf, [1938]), 31–32; Briner, *Hindemith,* 121; Maurer Zenck, "Boykott," 107; Zimmermann-Kalyoncu, *Musiker,* 60; Schubert, *Hindemith,* 94.

78. See Maurer Zenck, "Boykott," 110; Noss, *Hindemith,* 57.

79. Strecker to Hindemith, 9 June and 1 Oct. 1931, PF, Schott Korr.; Leo Schrade, "Hindemith in der Neuen Welt," *Melos* 22 (1955), 315; Prieberg, *Lexikon,* 194; Noss, *Hindemith,* 7–10; Dorothy Lamb Crawford, *Evenings on and off the Roof: Pioneering Concerts in Los Angeles, 1939–1971* (Berkeley, 1995), 15–16.

80. Strecker to Hindemith, 27 Apr. and 22 Oct. 1934, PF, Schott Korr.

81. Strecker to Hindemith, 5 Feb. 1935; Hindemith to Strecker, 13 Feb. 1935 (quote), PF, Schott Korr.

82. Strecker to Hindemith, 5 Feb. 1935, PF, Schott Korr.

83. Noss, *Hindemith,* 16–17.

84. Gertrud Hindemith to Strecker, 14 Mar. 1937, PF, Schott Korr.

85. See, in particular, Luther Noss, "Hindemith's Concert Tours in the United States: 1937, 1938, 1939," *Hindemith-Jahrbuch* 7 (1978), 121–42; idem, *Hindemith.*

86. Gertrud Hindemith to Strecker, 19 Apr. 1937; Voigt to Strecker, 23 Apr. 1937, PF, Schott Korr.; Noss, "Concert Tours"; idem, *Hindemith,* 21–25, 29–30, 34, 38–39; Schubert, *Hindemith,* 87–88.

87. Noss, *Hindemith,* 32 (Hindemith's 1st quote), 34, 38–39; idem, "Concert Tours," 131–37 (Hindemith's 2nd quote 133); Schubert, *Hindemith,* 92.

88. Paul to Gertrud Hindemith, 28 Jan. 1939, in Rexroth, *Briefe,* 187 (1st two quotes); Hindemith to Strecker, 18 Oct. 1939, PF, Schott Korr. (last quote).

89. On the latter, see Noss, *Hindemith,* 44.

90. See Hindemith's letters, reproduced in Rexroth, *Briefe,* 184–323; Noss, "Concert Tours," 137–41; Noss, *Hindemith,* 42–58.

91. Paul to Gertrud Hindemith, 26 Feb. 1939 and 27 Mar. 1939 (quote), in Rexroth, *Briefe,* 202, 224.

92. Strecker to Emil [Preetorius], 15 May 1939; Hindemith to Strecker, 9 and 15 July 1939; Strecker to Hindemith, 11 and 20 July 1939, PF, Schott Korr.

93. Strecker to Reinhart, 13 Jan. 1940, in Sulzer, *Komponisten,* 3:228–29; Skelton, *Hindemith,* 169–70; Luther Noss, "Hindemith's First Eight Months as A Resident of the U.S.A.," *Hindemith-Jahrbuch* 11 (1982), 127; Briner, *Hindemith,* 141; Noss, *Hindemith,* 59; Schubert, *Hindemith,* 101.

94. Paul to Gertrud Hindemith, 14 Feb. 1940, partially cited in Noss, "First Eight Months," 126.

95. Hindemith to Hugo Strecker, 9 Nov. 1940, PF, Schott Korr.; Noss, "First Eight Months," 128–37; Noss, *Hindemith,* 80–81, 87 (quote); Schubert, *Hindemith,* 105.

96. See [Gertrud Hindemith] to Reinhart, 4 Oct. [1941], in Sulzer, *Komponisten,* 233; Nicolas Slonimsky, *Music Since 1900,* 4th ed. (New York, 1971), 728, 743, 781, 788; Noss, "First Eight Months," 141–45.

97. Noss, "First Eight Months," 138–40; idem, *Hindemith,* 65–66, 70, 74–75, 94–97; Newell Jenkins, recorded interview, Hillsdale, N.Y., 20 Mar. 1993, APA (1st quote); Schubert, *Hindemith,* 106; Briner, *Hindemith,* 144–45 (2nd quote 145); Slonimsky, *Music,* 717; Briner et al., *Hindemith,* 169.

98. Joan Evans to author, Toronto, 22 Aug. 1998, APA.

99. The interpretation of "fiasco" by Briner has been tempered by Noss's more informed and up-to-date analysis of the events. See Briner, *Hindemith*, 146–47; Noss, *Hindemith*, 84–86 (Noss's quote); Hindemith to Strecker, 30 May 1941, PF, Schott Korr. (Hindemith's quote). See also Luther Noss, *A History of the Yale School of Music, 1855–1970* (New Haven, Conn., 1984), 143–46.

100. Hindemith to Straumann, [Nov. 1949], in Rexroth, *Briefe*, 246–47; Noss, *Hindemith*, 89–92; Briner et al., *Hindemith*, 222–34.

101. Ulrich Dibelius, *Moderne Musik, 1945–1965: Voraussetzungen, Verlauf, Material* (Munich, 1966), 26.

102. Skelton, *Hindemith*, 241.

103. Friedrich Welter, *Musikgeschichte im Umriss: Vom Urbeginn bis zur Gegenwart* (Leipzig, n.d.), 297.

104. Ludwig Schiedermair, *Die deutsche Oper: Grundzüge ihres Werdens und Wesens* (Bonn, 1940).

105. Walter Trienes, *Musik in Gefahr: Selbstzeugnisse aus der Verfallszeit* (Regensburg, 1940), 107–10.

106. Example is letter Strecker to Orff, 2 Apr. 1942, CM, Schott Korr. Also see *Melos* 14 (1947), 255; Stephan, "Musik," 144.

107. Rösch to "sehr geehrte Herren," 29 Jan. 1943, PF, Schott Korr.; *Melos* 14 (1947), 187; Cesar Bresgen, *Mittersill 1945—Ein Weg zu Anton Webern* (Vienna, 1983), 76; Gernot Gruber, "Zur Hindemith-Rezeption in Österreich seit 1943," *Hindemith-Jahrbuch* 13 (1984), 144–46; Rudolf Wagner-Régeny, *Begegnungen: Biographische Aufzeichnungen, Tagebücher, und sein Briefwechsel mit Caspar Neher* (Berlin, 1968), 107.

108. Kabasta to Reinhart, 19 Feb. 1940, SM, Kulturamt/177; "Vortrag Dr. Fritz von Borries anlässlich eines Hindemith-Konzerts im März 1941"; Kinzel to Hindemith, 19 Aug. 1943; Brandt to Schott's Söhne, 31 July 1944, PF, Schott Korr. Also see Maurer Zenck, "Boykott," 109–10.

109. See the articles in Gabriele Clemens, ed., *Kulturpolitik im besetzten Deutschland, 1945–1949* (Stuttgart, 1994); Hermann Glaser, "Der Weg nach innen: Kultur der Stunde Null, die keine war," in Hans-Erich Volkmann, ed., *Ende des Dritten Reiches—Ende des Zweiten Weltkriegs: Eine perspektivische Rückschau* (Munich, 1995), 771–94.

110. Peter Heyworth, *Otto Klemperer: His Life and Times*, 2 vols. (Cambridge, 1983, 1996), 2:158.

111. Schott's Söhne to [Hartmann], 5 June 1946, BS, Ana/407.

112. *Melos* 14 (1946), 15.

113. Ibid. 14 (1947), 269, 392, 395. The German original title was *Unterweisung im Tonsatz*.

114. Ibid., 264, 349–50; ibid. 15 (1948), 56 (quote).

115. Briner et al., *Hindemith*, 192.

116. Joan Evans to author, Toronto, 22 Aug. 1998, APA.

117. Schott's Söhne to [Hartmann], 5 June 1946, BS, Ana/407; *Melos* 14 (1946), 20, 22, 24–27, 52, 56–57; *Melos* 14 (1947), 90–91, 118–19, 125, 223–24, 229–30, 265–67, 308, 353, 355, 394, 425; *Melos* 15 (1948), 19, 57, 59–61, 147–48; Muck, *Jahre*, 3:318.

118. "Einladung! Neue Musik Donaueschingen 1947"; Orff to Rennert, 7 Jan. 1947, CM, Allg. Korr.; *Melos* 14 (1947), 154, 228, 263; Skelton, *Hindemith*, 224.

119. Hindemith to Strecker brothers, 29 Aug. 1945, PF, Schott Korr. (quote);

Hindemith's letter to Strecker of 26 Dec. 1945, partially cited in Briner et al., *Hindemith,* 190–92, and Schubert, *Hindemith,* 107–8.

120. Hartmann to Hindemith, 4 Feb. 1946; Hindemith to Hartmann, 5 Mar. 1946, BS, Ana/407.

121. Hindemith to Strecker, 15 July 1946, in Rexroth, *Briefe,* 240 (quote); Heinrich Strobel, "Melos 1946," *Melos* 14 (1946), 2, 4; Strobel, "Mathis der Maler," *Melos* 14 (1947), 65–68; Norbert J. Schneider, "Phasen der Hindemith-Rezeption, 1945–1955," *Hindemith-Jahrbuch* 13 (1984), 125–26.

122. Joan Evans to author, Toronto, 22 Aug. 1998, APA. See Heinrich Strobel, *Paul Hindemith* (Mainz, 1928).

123. This is what Joan Evans suggests in her letter to author, Toronto, 22 Aug. 1998, APA.

124. Amar to Rosbaud, 18 May (1st quote), 29 Aug. and 10 Dec. 1946; 17 Feb. 1947, LP, 423/1/12; Hindemith to Strecker, [beginning of 1947], in Rexroth, *Briefe,* 244 (2nd quote). Eventually Amar moved from Turkey to Freiburg. See Neumark, *Zuflucht,* 122, 227–28.

125. *Melos* 14 (1947), 254–55, 263–64; Skelton, *Hindemith,* 231–45 (Hindemith's letter to Strecker partially quoted 234; 2nd quote 237); Briner et al., *Hindemith,* 202–3.

126. NG 8:576; David Neumeyer and Giselher Schubert, "Arnold Schoenberg und Paul Hindemith," *Journal of the Arnold Schoenberg Institute* 13 (1990), 4–5.

127. Schoenberg memorandum, Nov. 1923, AI, Text Manuscript: Strauss.

128. Schoenberg to Scherchen, 12 Aug. 1924, in Erwin Stein, ed., *Arnold Schoenberg: Letters* (New York, 1965), 111.

129. Reizenstein, "Aspersions," 7.

130. Schoenberg memorandum, 5 Oct. 1932, AI, gen. corr.

131. Schoenberg to Berg, 2 Jan. 1935, printed in Juliane Brand et al., eds., *The Berg-Schoenberg Correspondence: Selected Letters* (New York, 1987), 460–61.

132. Strecker's phrase according to Skelton, *Hindemith,* 127. Also see Maurer Zenck, "Boykott," 90.

133. Noss, "Concert Tours," 140; Paul to Gertrud Hindemith, 27 Mar. 1939, in Rexroth, *Briefe,* 223 (quote).

134. Entry for 26 May 1939 in Dika Newlin, *Schoenberg Remembered: Diaries and Recollections (1938–76)* (New York, 1980), 77–78.

135. Otto Klemperer, *Meine Erinnerungen an Gustav Mahler und andere autobiographische Skizzen* (Freiburg im Breisgau, 1960), 27.

136. Schoenberg to [Rufer], 18 Jan. 1949 and 10 Feb. 1950, AI, gen. corr.

137. Schoenberg to Zillig, 3 Mar. 1951, AI, gen. corr.

138. With the exception of the Hindemith/Brecht *Lehrstück* (1929). See *Melos* 14 (1946), 50 (quote), 51, 85; Danuser, *Musik,* 291; Schneider, "Phasen," 123–24.

139. Munich "Musica Viva" program for 1947–48, BH, Staatstheater/14395; *Melos* 14 (1947), 120, 154, 188, 260, 307, 349, 352, 393; Schneider, "Phasen," 125–27.

140. Schneider, "Phasen," 127–29. Quotation by Wolfram Gerbracht ibid., 129.

141. Ibid., 129–33 (Hindemith's phrase 131). Albrecht Riethmüller, "Versuch über Hindemith," *Hindemith-Jahrbuch* 26 (1997), 32; Joan Evans to author, Toronto, 22 Aug. 1998, APA. On Leibowitz, see *GLM* 5:87.

142. Schneider, "Phasen," 133–35.

CHAPTER 3: WEILL

1. Jerome Barry, "Kurt Weill: 'Von Berlin zum Broadway': Lecture-Recital," in Otto Kolleritsch, ed., *Die Wiener Schule und das Hakenkreuz: Das Schicksal der Moderne im gesellschaftspolitischen Kontext des 20. Jahrhunderts* (Vienna, 1990), 157; David Farneth, "Chronology of Weill's Life and Work," in Kim H. Kowalke, ed., *A New Orpheus: Essays on Kurt Weill* (New Haven, Conn., 1986), 343–44.

2. Kim H. Kowalke, *Kurt Weill in Europe* (Ann Arbor, Mich., 1979), 32–33; Ronald Taylor, *Kurt Weill: Composer in a Divided World* (Boston, 1992), 40–41.

3. Weill to parents, 30 Aug. 1924, WC, Hans/Rita Weill coll.; see also *NG* 20:300–1.

4. Kowalke, *Weill in Europe*, 52. See also *NG* 20:309.

5. Weill to "Meine Lieben," 1 Apr. 1926, WC, Hans/Rita Weill coll. See also *NG* 20:301.

6. *NG* 20:301 (quote), 309; Kowalke, *Weill in Europe*, 67.

7. *NG* 20:309; Hans W. Heinsheimer, *Best Regards to Aida: The Defeats and Victories of a Music Man on Two Continents* (New York, 1968), 132–33; Taylor, *Weill*, 164–65.

8. Weill to UE-Direktion, 14, 20, 25 Mar. and 4 May 1930, WC, Weill/UE corr.; Kowalke, *Weill in Europe*, 62.

9. Weill to UE-Direktion, 25 Oct. 1930 (quote), and 27 Oct. 1930, WC, Weill/UE corr.

10. On the general background of this, see Michael H. Kater, "The Revenge of the Fathers: The Demise of Modern Music at the End of the Weimar Republic," *German Studies Review* 15 (1992), 300–7.

11. Weill to UE-Direktion, 3 Jan. 1931, WC, Weill/UE corr.

12. Weill to UE-Direktion, 5 Mar. and 15 July 1931; and to Heinsheimer, 15 July 1931, WC, Weill/UE corr.

13. Heinsheimer to Weill, 16 Sep. 1931 and 20 May 1932, WC, Weill/UE corr.; Jürgen Schebera, *Kurt Weill: Leben und Werk* (Königstein, 1984), 150; Taylor, *Weill*, 183–84.

14. Weill to UE-Direktion, 29 May 1932; Weill to Generalintendant [Tietjen], 16 May 1932 (quote), WC, Weill/UE corr.

15. Weill to Heinsheimer, 15 Aug. 1932; Weill to UE-Direktion, 7 and 20 Sept. 1932, WC, Weill/UE corr.

16. Weill to UE-Direktion, 26 Dec. 1932; Weill to Heinsheimer, 19 Jan. 1933 (quote), WC, Weill/UE corr.; Schebera, *Weill*, 169; Stephen Hinton, "'Matters of Intellectual Property': The Sources and Genesis of 'Die Dreigroschenoper,'" in Hinton, ed., *Kurt Weill: The Threepenny Opera* (Cambridge, 1990), 42–46; Taylor, *Weill*, 172.

17. Weill to UE-Direktion, 6 Feb. 1933, WC, Weill/UE corr. (quote). See also Albrecht Dümling, *Lasst euch nicht verführen: Brecht und die Musik* (Munich, 1985), 365–66.

18. See n. 17; *NG* 20:305 (quote); David Drew, ed., *Über Kurt Weill* (Frankfurt am Main, 1975), 109–14; Schebera, *Weill*, 153–59; Kowalke, *Weill in Europe*, 83–84; Ian Kemp, "Music as Metaphor: Aspects of *Der Silbersee*," in Kowalke, *New Orpheus*, 131–46. On Gottschalk, see *TGII* 2:247, 253; Annedore Leber, ed., *Das Gewissen steht auf: 64 Lebensbilder aus dem deutschen Widerstand, 1933–1945* (Berlin, 1960), 72–75.

19. Weill to UE-Direktion, 26 Feb. 1933, WC, Weill/UE corr.

20. Ibid.; Weill to UE-Direktion, 6 Feb. 1933, WC, Weill/UE corr.

21. Hans Curjel, "Erinnerungen um Kurt Weill," *Melos* 37 (1970), 83–84; Kowalke, *Weill in Europe,* 84; Taylor, *Weill,* 195–97.

22. Weill-UE corr. (Mar.–Oct. 1933), WC, Weill/UE corr.

23. Weill to Heinsheimer, 3 Apr. 1933, WC, Weill/UE corr.; Weill to "Meine Lieben," 23 July 1933, WC, Hans/Rita Weill coll.; *NG* 20:301, 309; Harry Graf Kessler, *Tagebücher, 1918–1937,* ed. Wolfgang Pfeiffer-Belli (Frankfurt am Main, 1982), 768.

24. See Kessler, *Tagebücher,* 773; Schebera, *Weill,* 175.

25. Weill to Lind, 17 Apr. 1934, WC, Lind corr.; Weill to Curjel, 19 Apr. 1934, WC, Curjel corr.; Walter to Weill, 23 Aug. 1934, WC, 50/71; Weill to UE-Direktion, 5 May and 11 Sept. 1934, 8 Apr. 1935, WC, Weill/UE corr.; Weill to Lenya, 21 Aug. 1934 and 10 Feb. 1935, in Lys Symonette and Kim H. Kowalke, eds., *Speak Low (When You Speak Love): The Letters of Kurt Weill and Lotte Lenya* (Berkeley, 1996), 138, 160; *NG* 20:301, 305–6, 309; Arno Huth in Drew, *Über Kurt Weill,* 122; David Drew, *Kurt Weill: A Handbook* (Berkeley, 1987), 60; Farneth, "Chronology," 352; Stephen Hinton, "Grossbritannien als Exilland: Der Fall Weill," in Horst Weber, ed., *Musik in der Emigration, 1933–1945: Verfolgung, Vertreibung, Rückwirkung* (Stuttgart, 1994), 213–27.

26. Michael H. Kater, *The Twisted Muse: Musicians and Their Music in the Third Reich* (New York, 1997), 92.

27. Ibid., 106–7.

28. Ibid., 105, 107–8, 120; Peter Jelavich, *Berlin Cabaret* (Cambridge, Mass., 1993), 275–77, 280–82; Michael H. Kater, *Different Drummers: Jazz in the Culture of Nazi Germany* (New York, 1992), 177–79, 181.

29. Weill to UE-Direktion, 15 July 1931, 11 June and 26 Dec. 1932; Hertzka to Weill, 17 July 1931, UE-Direktion to Weill, 29 Mar. 1933; Weill to Heinsheimer, 3 Apr. 1933, WC, Weill/UE corr.; Schebera, *Weill,* 183; Symonette and Kowalke, *Speak Low,* 77.

30. See Weill's corr. with Lenya (Mar.–May 1934), in Symonette and Kowalke, *Speak Low,* 115–27.

31. Kurt to Ruth [Weill], 28 Jan. 1920, WC, Eve Hammerstein coll. (1st quote); Weill to Jolles, 27 May 1949, WC, Weill/Jolles corr. (2nd quote); Taylor, *Weill,* 216–17, 247.

32. Schebera, *Weill,* 184; Drew, *Weill: A Handbook,* 61.

33. *NG* 20:305–6 (1st quote); Weill to Lenya, 13 Feb. 1937, in Symonette and Kowalke, *Speak Low,* 206 (2nd quote); Weill to Motty, 6 Feb. 1937, WC, 47/3; Weill to Alma Mahler-Werfel, 1 Mar. 1937, WC, 47/15; Pinto corr. (Jan.–Mar. 1937), WC, 49/57; Kurt to Hanns [Weill], 31 May 1937, WC, Hans/Rita Weill coll.; Drew, *Weill: A Handbook,* 61–62; Donald Spoto, *Lenya: A Life* (Boston, 1989), 124; Taylor, *Weill,* 226–27.

34. Weill to Lenya, 3 May 1936 and 28 Jan. 1937 (quote), in Symonette and Kowalke, *Speak Low,* 193, 196; *NG* 20:302, 306; Farneth, "Chronology," 353.

35. Weill to Lenya, 3, 13, 17 Mar. (quote), and 11 Apr. 1937, in Symonette and Kowalke, *Speak Low,* 211–12, 216–17, 219–20, 230; Farneth, "Chronology," 353.

36. Lenya to Weill, 4 May 1938, in Symonette and Kowalke, *Speak Low,* 260–61.

37. Matthew Scott, "Weill in America: The Problem of Revival," in Kowalke, *New Orpheus,* 287–92 (quote 292); Drew, *Weill: A Handbook,* 63–64; Spoto,

Lenya, 145; Taylor, *Weill,* 245, 258 (Taylor falsely gives 1942 as the starting year of *Lady in the Dark*).

38. This is the important question Albrecht Riethmüller poses in his Berlin letter to the author of 27 Oct. 1997, APA, which, nonetheless, must remain unanswered in this context.

39. Weill to Ira Gershwin, 11 Apr. 1941, WC, 47/5; Weill to Arthur [Lyons], 16 June 1941, WC, 47/10; Lyons to Weill, 21 June 1941, WC, 48/45; Farneth, "Chronology," 355.

40. Weill to Dietrich, 24 July and 11 Aug. 1942, WC, 47/3; Dietrich to Weill, 27 July and 5 [?] Aug. 1942, WC, 48/29; Weill to Lenya, 26 Sept. and 1 Oct. 1942, in Symonette and Kowalke, *Speak Low,* 364, 367; Weill to parents, 14 Aug. 1943, WC, Weill/Parents corr.; Donald Spoto, *Blue Angel: The Life of Marlene Dietrich* (New York, 1992), 176–80.

41. Farneth, "Chronology," 356; Drew, *Weill: A Handbook,* 65; Taylor, *Weill,* 282.

42. Weill to Eddie [Wolpin], 30 Nov. 1943, WC, 47/15; Weill to Dreyfus, 31 Dec. 1943, WC, 47/3; "List of Broadcasts on Speak Low for Week of Dec. 4th to 12th Inclusive," [Dec. 1943], WC, 48/24; Kapp to Weill, 4 Jan. 1944, WC, 48/28; Weill to Cheryl [Crawford], 30 Jan. 1944, WC, 48/26; Weill to parents, 18 Jan. 1944 (1st quote) and 30 Apr. 1944 (2nd quote), WC, Weill/Parents corr.; Farneth, "Chronology," 356; Drew, *Weill: A Handbook,* 65.

43. Weill to parents, 30 Apr 1945, WC, Weill/Parents corr.

44. Weill to Brown, 31 Aug. 1945, WC, 47/2; Weill to Life Magazine, 21 Feb. 1947, WC, Weill/Life Magazine corr.; *Melos* 14 (1946), 50; *Melos* 14 (1947), 307, 351.

45. Farneth, "Chronology," 357; Symonette and Kowalke, *Speak Low,* 464.

46. Generally, and treating the United States as a haven of refuge, see Anthony Heilbut, *Exiled in Paradise: German Refugee Artists and Intellectuals in America, from the 1930s to the Present* (Boston, 1984), even though this book is not documented and contains several errors of fact and judgment. With a view to musicians (mostly Jewish) and treating many countries of refuge, see Hanns-Werner Heister et al., eds., *Musik im Exil: Folgen des Nazismus für die internationale Musikkultur* (Frankfurt am Main, 1993).

47. Heister et al., *Musik.* Time and circumstances according to illustration no. 22 in Taylor, *Weill.*

48. Symonette and Kowalke, *Speak Low.*

49. On this last aspect, see Maurice Abravanel as quoted in Spoto, *Lenya,* 121–22.

50. Taylor, *Weill,* 274.

51. Weill to Lenya, 20 Feb. 1937, in Symonette and Kowalke, *Speak Low,* 209.

52. Weill to Arthur [Lyons], 16 June 1941, WC, 47/10; Lyons to Weill, 21 June 1941, WC, 48/45.

53. Weill to Meyer [Weisgal], 12 Aug. 1936, WC, 47/15 (quote); Meyer Weisgal, *So Far: An Autobiography* (New York, 1971), 122–40.

54. Taylor, *Weill,* 261; Weill to Lenya, 1, 12, 20, 26 July 1944, 4, 7, 21 Aug. 1944, in Symonette and Kowalke, *Speak Low,* 376, 388, 396, 402, 411, 413, 427.

55. Weill to Lenya, 3 [?] July 1943, in Symonette and Kowalke, *Speak Low,* 369.

56. Weill to Lenya, 11 Aug. 1935, ibid., 187.

57. Weill to Lenya, 26 Aug. 1935 (2nd quote) and 13 Feb. 1937 (3rd quote), ibid., 189, 206; Weill to UE-Direktion, 15 June 1932, WC, Weill/UE-Direktion corr. (1st quote); Weill to Reinhardt, 27 Nov. 1935, WC, 47/13.

58. Peter Heyworth, *Otto Klemperer: His Life and Times,* 2 vols. (Cambridge, 1983, 1996), 2:28; Weill to Lenya, 20 Feb. 1937 and 30 Apr. 1942 (quotes), in Symonette and Kowalke, *Speak Low,* 209, 343.

59. Weill to Lenya, 5, 8 and 10 Apr. 1942 (quote), in Symonette and Kowalke, *Speak Low,* 318, 320, 322.

60. I am borrowing Peter Gay's phrase. See his *Weimar Culture: The Outsider as Insider* (New York, 1968).

61. Alan Kendall, *George Gershwin: A Biography* (London, 1987), 84; Kowalke, *Weill in Europe,* 151.

62. Weill to Lenya, 17 May 1934, in Symonette and Kowalke, *Speak Low,* 127.

63. Taylor, *Weill,* 218.

64. Weill to Lenya, 13 Feb., 31 Mar., 14 and 29 May 1937 (quote), in Symonette and Kowalke, *Speak Low,* 206–7, 226, 240, 243; Ronald Sanders, *The Days Grow Short: The Life and Music of Kurt Weill* (New York, 1980), 218–19; Spoto, *Lenya,* 124, 126.

65. Heilbut, *Exiled,* 149.

66. Kurt to Hanns [Weill], 6 Feb 1919, WC, Hans/Rita Weill coll. The original German of the last phrase is *"gewollt modern."*

67. Kurt to Hanns [Weill], 20 June 1919, WC, Hans/Rita Weill coll.

68. Kurt to Hanns [Weill], 27 June 1919, WC, Hans/Rita Weill coll.

69. Alan Chapman, "Crossing the Cusp: The Schoenberg Connection," in Kowalke, *New Orpheus,* 105; Kurt Weill, *Musik und Theater: Gesammelte Schriften,* ed. Stephen Hinton and Jürgen Schebera (Berlin, 1990), 21, 27, 204 (quote), 205. Also see Kowalke, *Weill in Europe,* 156, 462; Alexander L. Ringer, *Arnold Schoenberg: The Composer as Jew* (Oxford, 1990), 86–87; Guy Rickards's liner notes for the 1967 recording of Weill's First Symphony, reissued 1996 on *EMI Classics* compact disk no. 7243 5 65869 2 5.

70. Chapman, "Crossing," 105; Drew, *Weill: A Handbook,* 44.

71. Chapman, "Crossing," 105–6 (1st quote 106); Kowalke, *Weill in Europe,* 156–57 (2nd quote is a phrase attributed to Schoenberg's student Marc Blitzstein, cited 360, n. 151).

72. Weill to UE-Direktion, 11 Sept. 1934, WC, Weill/UE corr.

73. Weill as quoted in Taylor, *Weill,* 251; see also Drew, *Weill: A Handbook,* 45.

74. Symonette and Kowalke, *Speak Low,* 464.

75. Weill to UE-Direktion, 15 June 1932, 6 Feb. and 14 Mar. 1933, WC, Weill/UE corr.; Brecht to Weigel, [May 1933], in John Willett, ed., *Bertolt Brecht: Letters, 1913–1956* (London, 1990), 135; Heinsheimer, *Regards,* 139–40 (Brecht quoted 140); Bruce Cook, *Brecht in Exile* (New York, 1983), 131–32; Kowalke, *Weill in Europe,* 62, 81; John Fuegi, "Most Unpleasant Things with *The Three-penny Opera*: Weill, Brecht, and Money," in Kowalke, *New Orpheus,* 162–71. The left-leaning author Albrecht Dümling has taken a pro-Brechtian stance in his interpretation of the Paris Weill-Brecht collaboration (*Lasst,* 366–70), whereas Jürgen Schebera who, having had to toe the party line as a writer in the Communist German Democratic Republic in 1984, has totally ignored the differences (*Weill,* 171). Brecht's idiosyncratic pre-1933 relationship to music, with special reference to Weill, has been analyzed by Kim H. Kowalke in his "Singing Brecht versus Brecht Singing: Performance in Theory and Practice," in Bryan Gilliam, ed., *Music and Performance During the Weimar Republic* (New York, 1994), 74–93.

76. Schebera, *Weill,* 185; Fuegi, "Things," 175; James K. Lyon, *Bertolt Brecht in America* (Princeton, 1980), 7–13.

77. Weill to Brecht, 9 Feb. 1939; Brecht to Weill, 23 Mar. and 4 June 1939, WC, Weill/Brecht corr.; Fuegi, "Things," 173–75.

78. Hauptmann to Weill, 14 Mar. 1941, WC, 48/37; Salka Viertel, *Kindness of Strangers* (New York, 1969), 258; Taylor, *Weill,* 256–57. Actor Fritz Kortner's daughter Marianne quoted in Matthias Matussek, "Tortenschlacht um Brecht," *Spiegel* (7 Apr. 1997), 184.

79. Symonette and Kowalke, *Speak Low,* 306.

80. Weill to Brecht, 9 Mar. 1942, WC, Weill/Brecht corr.

81. Weill to Muse, 31 Mar. 1942, WC, 47/11.

82. Wiesengrund Adorno to Weill, 31 Mar. 1942, WC, 48/18. See Kater, *Different Drummers,* 28, 33.

83. See Weill to Brecht, 7 Apr. 1942, WC, Weill/Brecht corr.; Michael H. Kater, "Weill und Brecht: Kontroversen einer Künstlerfreundschaft auf zwei Kontinenten" (in press).

84. Weill to Lenya, 8 Apr. 1942, in Symonette and Kowalke, *Speak Low,* 320.

85. Brecht to Weill, [Apr. 1942], WC, 48/22.

86. Weill to Lenya, 16 Apr. 1942; Lenya to Weill, 19 Apr. 1942, in Symonette and Kowalke, *Speak Low,* 328–29, 332–33.

87. Marton to Weill, 15 Apr. 1942, WC, 48/46; Weill telegram to Marton, 20 Apr. 1942, WC, 47/11; Weill to Brecht, 20 Apr. 1942, WC, Weill/Brecht corr.; Weill to Lenya, 19 Apr. 1942, in Symonette and Kowalke, *Speak Low,* 331 (quote).

88. Marton to Weill, 21 Apr. 1942, WC, 48/46.

89. Weill to [Eslanda] Robeson, 11 June 1942, WC, 47/13.

90. Weill to Lenya, 1 Oct. 1942, in Symonette and Kowalke, *Speak Low,* 367; Heilbut, *Exiled,* 189–90; Schebera, *Weill,* 214–15; Drew, *Weill: A Handbook,* 64–65; Taylor, *Weill,* 279–80; Lyon, *Brecht in America,* 274.

91. Aufricht to Weill, 24 Dec. 1943, WC, 48/19; Speiser to Weill, 10 Jan. and 7 Feb. 1944, WC, 50/67; Weill to Maurice [Speiser], 30 Jan. 1944, WC, 47/14; Drew, *Weill: A Handbook,* 65; Taylor, *Weill,* 271; Willett, *Brecht: Letters,* 354–65, 367–68, 371, 376, 381–82, 385.

92. Weill to Maurice [Speiser], 22 Jan. 1944, WC, 47/14.

93. Weill to Lenya, 18 May 1945, in Symonette and Kowalke, *Speak Low,* 459 (quote); Viertel, *Kindness,* 283–85.

94. Weill to Erika Neher, 2 July 1946, WC, Weill/Erika Neher corr.

95. Drew, *Weill: A Handbook,* 67.

96. Fuegi, "Things," 177–81.

97. Drew, *Weill: A Handbook,* 68.

98. John Simon, "Faithful in Their Fashion," *New York Times Book Review* (23 June 1996), 17, 20.

99. Lenya's testimony in Symonette and Kowalke, *Speak Low,* 12–23; Spoto suggests an early amorous relationship with Révy (*Lenya,* 34); also communication to author by Kim H. Kowalke, President of the Kurt Weill Foundation for Music, New York, 16 Mar. 1997; Lenya quoted in Spoto, 67); Taylor, *Weill,* 65.

100. Kurt to Hanns [Weill], 15 May 1919, WC, Hans/Rita Weill coll.; Kurt to Ruth [Weill], [1920], WC, Eve Hammerstein coll.

101. Quote according to Symonette and Kowalke, *Speak Low,* 51. See also Spoto, *Lenya,* 67–69.

102. In an interview with radio jazz host Katie Malloch in Montreal, broadcast on CBC-FM (Canadian national network) on 8 May 1993: "Even your wife and family comes secondary to your music."

103. Maurice Abravanel as quoted in Symonette and Kowalke, *Speak Low,* 51. See also Spoto, *Lenya,* 68.

104. Spoto's biography of Lenya and Taylor's of Weill (with the latter being based, often uncritically, on the former) tend to overemphasize the mutual-tolerance and arrangement aspect. It is one of the many merits of Symonette and Kowalke's edition of the couple's correspondence that, not least through their painstaking annotations, the human suffering of both marriage partners becomes transparent.

105. Felix Joachimson (later Jackson) as quoted in Symonette and Kowalke, *Speak Low,* 51.

106. Spoto, *Lenya,* 101; Taylor, *Weill,* 178.

107. Some historians have intimated that this infidelity took the form of homosexual exploits, to have dated from the birth of Neher's son in 1924; hard evidence to that effect has so far not surfaced (David Farneth, Director, WC, to author, New York, 13 June 1996, APA). It is maintained that Neher's (new) sexual preference "was virtually common knowledge for his associates." In the Weill couple's correspondence, no reference is made to it because "Weill and Lenya take it for granted" (Kowalke to author, Rochester, N.Y., 3 July 1996, APA). An opposite view is held by Hans Jörg Jans, the director of the Carl-Orff-Zentrum in Munich, who interviewed actress Maria Wimmer in Vienna before her death in 1996. Reportedly, Wimmer, who began a liaison with Neher in 1934, broke into "raucous laughter" when Jans mentioned the suspicion of homosexuality to her (Jans's personal communication to author in Munich, 21 Aug. 1996. Also see John Willett, *Caspar Neher: Brecht's Designer* [London and New York, 1986], 117–32; Vana Greisenegger-Georgila and Hans Jörg Jans, eds., *Was ist die Antike wert? Griechen und Römer auf der Bühne von Caspar Neher* [Vienna, 1995]).

108. Taylor, *Weill,* 178, 195, 234.

109. Weill to Erika Neher, 29 Jan. 1933, in Symonette and Kowalke, *Speak Low,* 76.

110. Weill to Erika Neher, [May 1933], ibid., 80.

111. Weill to Erika Neher, 2 May 1936, WC, Weill/Erika Neher corr. Also see letter of 4 May 1933, ibid.

112. Weill to Erika Neher, [1936], WC, Weill/Erika Neher corr.

113. Weill to Erika Neher, 29 May 1936, WC, Weill/Erika Neher corr.

114. Spoto, *Lenya,* 114.

115. Lenya's remark as paraphrased by Hans Heinsheimer and quoted ibid., 105; also see Symonette and Kowalke, *Speak Low,* 66.

116. Spoto, *Lenya,* 108, 111–17; Symonette and Kowalke, *Speak Low,* 71, 80. On *Mahagonny Songspiel* see NG 20:301, 303, 309; Kowalke, *Weill in Europe,* passim. Regarding Pasetti, Lenya much later conceded that he was "a crook, who sold the house and stole the money. . . . He was nothing, he was just shit" (in interview with Gottfried Wagner, quoted in Symonette and Kowalke, 154, n. 3).

117. Symonette and Kowalke, *Speak Low,* 163; Weill to Lenya, 11, 19, and 26 Feb., 20 Mar. 1935, ibid., 164, 168–69, 172, 176; Spoto, *Lenya,* 117–19.

118. Taylor, *Weill,* 227.

119. Weill to Lenya, 3 May 1936, in Symonette and Kowalke, *Speak Low,* 193; Spoto, *Lenya,* 128–30.

120. Symonette and Kowalke, *Speak Low,* 242.

121. Ibid., 285; Spoto, *Lenya,* 156, 173.

122. Symonette and Kowalke, *Speak Low,* 294, 367; Spoto, *Lenya,* 167, 170.

123. See e.g. Spoto, *Lenya,* 131–32, 166; Taylor, *Weill,* 227.

124. "Contended" in the original. Weill to Jolles, 27 May 1949, WC, Weill/Jolles corr.

125. Spoto, *Lenya,* 131, 136–37; Taylor, *Weill,* 227.

126. Spoto, *Lenya,* 152–60; Symonette and Kowalke, *Speak Low,* 249–361.

127. See Weill to Lenya, 1 Aug. 1944, in Symonette and Kowalke, *Speak Low,* 408–9.

128. Spoto, *Lenya,* 131–32, 136–37, 162.

129. Weill to Lenya, 8 Mar. 1935, in Symonette and Kowalke, *Speak Low,* 174.

130. Ibid., 521.

131. Lenya to Weill, 26 June 1944, ibid., 372.

132. Weill to Lenya, 28 June, 1, 3, 5, 10, 17, 20, 23 July 1944; Lenya to Weill, 2 and 18 July 1944, ibid., 376, 378–80, 385, 392, 395–96, 399.

133. Previous, playful, corr. makes it clear that she was actually referring to Kurt's genitals. Lenya to Weill, 7 July 1944, ibid., 382.

134. Weill to Lenya, 28 July 1944, ibid., 404. Weill and Lenya both often wrote "Joe" instead of "Jo."

135. Weill to Lenya, 1, 7, 9 Aug. 1944; Lenya to Weill, 4 and 16 Aug. 1944, ibid., 408–9, 413, 415, 422.

136. See the photograph of Jo and Thomas Révy (ca. 1944) ibid., no. 66.

137. Weill to Lenya, 18 Aug. 1944, ibid., 426.

138. Lenya to Rita Weill, 28 Sept. 1944; Weill to Lenya, 11 Apr. 1945 (quote), ibid., 446, 448.

139. Ibid., 483.

140. According to Spoto, *Lenya,* 178.

141. Symonette and Kowalke, *Speak Low,* 483. The quotes are from an interview with Maurice Abravanel in the WC.

142. See Kater, *The Twisted Muse,* 76–78.

143. See the misleading interpretations in Schebera, *Weill,* 193 (1st quote); and Taylor, *Weill,* 7 (2nd quote).

144. See Gay, *Weimar Culture.*

145. See text at n. 1.

146. Kurt to Hanns [Weill], 2 May and 4 Sept. 1918, WC, Hans/Rita Weill coll.

147. Weill to Mamuschka [mother], 31 Dec. 1924, WC, Hans/Rita Weill coll.

148. Weill to UE-Direktion, 15 June 1932, WC, Weill/UE corr.

149. Guy Stern, "Der literarisch-kulturelle Horizont des jungen Weill: Eine Analyse seiner ungedruckten frühen Briefe," in Kim H. Kowalke and Horst Edler, eds., *A Stranger Here Myself: Kurt Weill-Studien* (Hildesheim, 1993), 80–83.

150. See Kurt to Hanns [Weill], 3 July 1919, WC, Hans/Rita Weill coll.; Kurt to Ruth [Weill], [1920], WC, Eve Hammerstein coll.; Weill to Curjel, 13 June 1929, WC, Weill/Curjel corr. On Jewish anti-Semitism, see Sander L. Gilman, *Jewish Self-Hatred: Anti-Semitism and the Hidden Language of the Jews* (Baltimore, 1986).

151. Kurt to Hanns [Weill], 2 May 1918, WC, Hans/Rita Weill coll.

152. Kurt to Hanns [Weill], 9 May 1918, WC, Hans/Rita Weill coll.

153. Kurt to Hanns [Weill], 15 Nov. 1918, WC, Hans/Rita Weill coll.

154. Kurt to Hanns [Weill], 27 June 1919, WC, Hans/Rita Weill coll.

155. The quote is from Drew, *Weill: A Handbook,* 60.

156. Weisgal, *So Far,* 120–21.

157. Weill to Reinhardt, 6 Oct. 1934, WC, 47/13 (quote); Paul Bekker (1937) reprinted in Drew, *Über Kurt Weill,* 127; Schebera, *Weill,* 193; Taylor, *Weill,* 212.

158. Schebera, *Weill,* 179.

159. As quoted in Niza to Weill, 20 Apr. 1937, WC, 49/56.

160. Bekker reprinted in Drew, *Über Kurt Weill,* 126; Gottfried Reinhardt, *The Genius: A Memoir of Max Reinhardt* (New York, 1979), 247. Also see Taylor, *Weill,* 213.

161. See Cook, *Brecht,* 131–32; Kowalke, "Formerly German: Kurt Weill in America," in Kowalke and Edler, *Stranger,* 53.

162. Weill to Lenya, 17 May 1934; 13 Feb. 1937; 17 Mar. 1937; 24 Apr. 1937; 11 Mar. 1942; 21 Aug. 1944 (quote); 30 Aug. 1944, in Symonette and Kowalke, *Speak Low,* 127, 207, 219, 234, 308, 427, 436. On Jewish movie moguls see Otto Friedrich, *City of Nets: A Portrait of Hollywood in the 1940s* (New York, 1986).

163. Weill to Lenya, 3 Mar. 1937 (1st quote); 30 Jan. 1937 (2nd quote); 17 July 1944 (3rd quote); 4 June 1947 (4th quote), in Symonette and Kowalke, *Speak Low,* 212–13, 198, 392, 473.

164. Weill to Lenya, 17 Apr. 1942, ibid., 330 (1st quote); Weill quoted ibid., 191.

165. See Walter Laqueur, *The Terrible Secret: Suppression of the Truth About Hitler's "Final Solution"* (Harmondsworth, 1983).

166. Ben Hecht, *A Child of the Century* (New York, 1954), 550–57, 574 (quote 553).

167. Weill to parents, 5 Feb. 1943 and 17 Apr. 1943 (quote), WC, Weill/Parents corr.; Taylor, *Weill,* 278.

168. Putterman to Weill, 13 May 1946, WC, 49/55; Kowalke, *Weill in Europe,* 18.

169. Quotation from *NG* 20:308.

170. Kowalke's phrase encapsulates the various charges of Weill's critics, with whom Kowalke himself disagrees. See his *Weill in Europe,* 156.

171. Quoted ibid., 87. Taylor as late as 1991 criticized it, rather differently, as a piece of "entertainment value which gives it the character of a symphonietta rather than a symphony" (*Weill,* 202).

172. Symonette and Kowalke, *Speak Low,* 485; Heinrich Strobel, "Erinnerung an Kurt Weill," *Melos* 17 (1950), 136 (quote).

173. Hans Heinz Stuckenschmidt, *Twentieth-Century Composers: Germany and Central Europe* (London, 1970), 145; Curjel, "Erinnerungen," 84; Peter Heyworth, ed., *Conversations with Klemperer* (London, 1985), 78–79; Kowalke, "Formerly German," 37; Stephen Hinton, "Fragwürdiges in der deutschen Weill-Rezeption," in Kowalke and Edler, *Stranger,* 31. I owe my insight into the Jarnach-Weill relationship to Albrecht Riethmüller (letter to author, Berlin, 27 Oct. 1997, APA).

174. Quoted in Barry, "Weill," 163.

175. Hellmut Kotschenreuther, *Kurt Weill* (Berlin-Halensee, 1962), 79 (1st quote); also see Schebera, *Weill,* 189–91; Barry, "Weill," 163 (2nd quote).

176. See Schebera, *Weill,* 171, 189–91, 203; idem, *Kurt Weill: An Illustrated Life* (New Haven, Conn., 1995), esp. 239–337. For a criticism of Schebera's prejudice as expressed in this latest volume see Robert Fulford's comments in *Globe and Mail,* Toronto, 3 Jan. 1996.

177. Taylor, *Weill,* xi–xii, 213, 224, 253, 258 (also see n. 170); Simon, "Faithful in Their Fashion," *New York Times Book Review* (23 June 1996), 17.

178. See Stephen Hinton's review of Taylor, *Weill,* in *Kurt Weill Newsletter* 10, no. 2 (Fall 1992), 17. On the traditional cultural establishment's contempt for jazz, see Neil Leonard, *Jazz and the White Americans: The Acceptance of a New Art Form* (Chicago, 1962); Kater, *Different Drummers,* 21–22. Also see the conclusion of this book.

179. Kowalke and Edler, *Stranger,* 9.

180. Strobel, "Erinnerung," 136; Ernst Krenek, "Amerikas Einfluss auf einge-wanderte Komponisten," in Habakuk Traber and Elmar Weingarten, eds., *Verdrängte Musik: Berliner Komponisten im Exil* (Berlin, 1987), 104. Also see Joachim Lucchesi, "'Fremd bin ich eingezogen'? Anmerkungen zu einer geteilten Biographie," in Kowalke and Edler, *Stranger,* 61.

181. See the contemporary remarks by Marc Blitzstein, George Maynard, and Paul Bekker reproduced in Drew, *Über Kurt Weill,* 127–32.

182. Weill as quoted in Kowalke, *Weill in Europe,* 156.

183. Weill quoted in Kowalke, "Formerly German," 43.

184. Klemperer in Heyworth, *Conversations,* 78 (1st quote); Weill to UE–Direktion, 1 June 1934, WC, Weill/UE corr. (2nd quote). I have translated Weill's original term *Moritat* as "ballads."

185. Weill to UE-Direktion, 1 June 1934, WC, Weill/UE corr.

186. Weill as quoted in Heinsheimer, *Regards,* 140; Weill, *Musik und Theater,* 110.

187. Kurt Weill, "The Future of Opera in America," *Modern Music* 14 (1937), 183–88. See also Weill to Lenya, 28 Sept. 1942, in Symonette and Kowalke, *Speak Low,* 366; Lucchesi, "'Fremd bin ich eingezogen'?," 65.

188. Weill to Kalmus, 28 July 1937, WC, Weill/UE corr.; Weill to Jolles, 27 May 1949, WC, Weill/Jolles corr. (1st quote); Weill to Lyons, 12 Feb. 1941, WC, 47/10 (2nd quote).

189. On "opera," see Weill to Lenya, 7 Feb. 1942, 3 July 1944 and 11 May 1945, in Symonette and Kowalke, *Speak Low,* 288–89, 378, 458; Weill to parents, 30 Apr. 1945, WC, Weill/Parents corr.; Weill to parents, 11 July 1949, quoted in Kowalke, "Formerly German," 51, n. 46.

CHAPTER 4: HARTMANN

1. Karl Amadeus Hartmann, *Kleine Schriften,* ed. Ernst Thomas (Mainz, 1965), 9–11; Andrew McCredie, "Die Jahre der schöpferischen Reifung (1927–1935) und die postum veröffentlichten Kompositionen der Kriegszeit (1939–1945)," in *Karl Amadeus Hartmann und die Musica Viva: Essays, bisher unveröffentlichte Briefe an Hartmann, Katalog* (Munich, 1980), 46; Guy Rickards, *Hindemith, Hartmann, and Henze* (London, 1995), 23, 40, 55.

2. Elisabeth Hartmann, recorded interview, Munich, 13 Dec. 1994, APA; Hartmann, *Schriften,* 11; Rickards, *Hindemith,* 105.

3. Hartmann, *Schriften,* 11–12; McCredie, "Jahre," 48; Habakuk Traber and Elmar Weingarten, eds., *Verdrängte Musik: Berliner Komponisten im Exil* (Berlin, 1987), 165–66.

4. Elisabeth Hartmann, recorded interview, Munich, 13 Dec. 1994, APA; McCredie, "Jahre," 48–50; *Hartmann,* 230, 232.

5. *Melos* 11 (1932), 29; Hartmann, *Schriften,* 12 (quote); Andrew McCredie, "Karl Amadeus Hartmann (1905–1963): New Documents and Sources in a Decennial Perspective," *Miscellanea Musicologica: Adelaide Studies in Musicology* 7 (1974), 153; McCredie, "Jahre," 50–55; Traber and Weingarten, *Verdrängte Musik,* 167; Hanns-Werner Heister's liner notes (1991) for compact disk, *Karl Amadeus Hartmann: Klavierwerke/Piano Works,* Virgin Classics Digital VC 7 91170-2 (London, 1991). On the uses of *Kunstjazz* by German avant-garde com-

posers of the 1920s, see J. Bradford Robinson, "Jazz Reception in Weimar Germany: In Search of a Shimmy Figure," in Bryan Gilliam, ed., *Music and Performance During the Weimar Republic* (Cambridge, 1994), 107–34. My critique of this on the whole stimulating article is in my article "Music: Performance and Politics in Twentieth-Century Germany," *Central European History* 29 (1996), 95–97.

6. McCredie, "Jahre," 59. See also Max See, "Erinnerungen an Karl Amadeus Hartmann," *Neue Zeitschrift für Musik* 125 (1964), 99–101.

7. Hartmann, *Schriften,* 12.

8. Niemeyer to Hartmann, 24 Mar. 1933, BS, Ana/407.

9. Schott's Söhne to Hartmann, 23 Aug. 1933, BS, Ana/407.

10. See *Melos* 12 (1933), 307.

11. Hartmann to Hindemith, 4 Feb. 1946, and to Galimir, 1 Feb. 1948, and to Krenek, 20 Mar. 1948, BS, Ana/407; Hartmann, *Schriften,* 70–71, 74–75.

12. Elisabeth Hartmann, recorded interview, Munich, 13 Dec. 1994, APA.

13. Ibid.; Andrew McCredie, *Karl Amadeus Hartmann: Sein Leben und Werk* (Wilhelmshaven, 1980), 34, 44–45; Hanns-Werner Heister, "Zur musikalischen Sprache des Widerstands: K.A. Hartmanns 'Concerto funebre für Solo-Violine und Streichorchester,'" in Christoph-Hellmut Mahling and Sigrid Wiesmann, eds., *Bericht über den Internationalen Musikwissenschaftlichen Kongress Bayreuth 1981* (Kassel, 1984), 488–89; Karl H. Wörner, "Die Musik von Karl Amadeus Hartmann," *Schweizerische Musikzeitung* 92 (1952), 352; Andreas Jaschinski, *Karl Amadeus Hartmann—Symphonische Tradition und ihre Auflösung* (Munich, 1982), 12; Albrecht Dümling in Dümling and Peter Girth, eds., *Entartete Musik: Zur Düsseldorfer Ausstellung von 1938: Eine kommentierte Rekonstruktion* (Düsseldorf, [1988]), 172.

14. Joan Evans to author, Toronto, 22 Aug. 1998, APA.

15. McCredie, *Hartmann,* 35–37; idem, "Documents," 157; Wörner, "Musik," 349.

16. *Unterhaltungsmusik* (30 Mar. 1938), 404; McCredie, *Hartmann,* 38; Fred K. Prieberg, *Musik im NS-Staat* (Frankfurt am Main, 1982), 275.

17. Belgisch Nationaal Instituut voor Radio-Omroep to Hartmann, 14 Mar. and 15 Apr. 1940, BS, Ana/407; McCredie, *Hartmann,* 55.

18. McCredie, *Hartmann,* 37, 40–41 (1st two quotes); Hartmann to Escher, 14 Nov. 1935, BS, Ana/407 (3rd quote); Luigi Dallapiccola, "Meine Erinnerungen an Karl Amadeus Hartmann," *Melos* 37 (1970), 333 (4th quote); Brod cited in *Hartmann,* 236; *Frankfurter Zeitung* cited in McCredie, *Hartmann,* 42.

19. McCredie, *Hartmann,* 51.

20. Hartmann to Jemnitz, 7 May 1936, BS, Ana/407.

21. *Hartmann,* 240; Karl Heinz Ruppel, "Karl Amadeus Hartmann: Versuch eines Portraits," ibid., 30 (quote); Hartmann, *Schriften,* 53; McCredie, *Hartmann,* 55.

22. Collaer to Hartmann, 22 Oct. 1940 and 9 Jan. 1941, BS, Ana/407; *Hartmann,* 358; McCredie, *Hartmann,* 56.

23. Hartmann to Schlee, 22 Dec. 1942, BS, Ana/407; McCredie, *Hartmann,* 61.

24. Hartmann to Havemann, 4 Feb. 1946, BS, Ana/407 (quote); McCredie, *Hartmann,* 62–63.

25. *Hartmann,* 242 (quote); McCredie, *Hartmann,* 63; Rickards, *Hindemith,* 115–16. On the Dachau death march, see Otto-Ernst Holthaus, ed., *Der Todesmarsch der Häftlinge des Konzentrationslagers Dachau im April 1945: Eine Dokumentation mit dem Bericht über die Einweihung eines Mahnmals am 22. November*

1992 *in Grünwald* (Grünwald, 1993). On the liberation of Dachau, see Nerin E. Gun, *The Day of the Americans* (New York, 1966).

26. Stagma to Hartmann, 2 Jan. 1941, BS, Ana/407. See also Stagma to Hartmann, 21 Dec. 1939 and 6 Apr. 1940, BS, Ana/407; Michael H. Kater, *The Twisted Muse: Musicians and Their Music in the Third Reich* (New York, 1997), 204.

27. McCredie, *Hartmann,* 39.

28. Kater, *The Twisted Muse,* 17, 80–81.

29. The personnel files of the RMK in the BAB contain many different references to musicians who at any given time had not yet supplied the required information.

30. Elisabeth Hartmann, recorded interview, Munich, 13 Dec. 1994, APA (1st quote); RMK to Hartmann, 4 Dec. 1935; Wachenfeld to Hartmann, 22 Jan. 1936, BS, Ana/407; Hartmann RMK file card, 11 July 1941, BAB Hartmann (2nd quote).

31. Elisabeth Hartmann, recorded interview, Munich, 13 Dec. 1994, APA.

32. As Fred K. Prieberg has correctly noted: *Musik und Macht* (Frankfurt am Main, 1991), 210.

33. Von Feldmann to RMK, 5 May 1934, RG.

34. Ständiger Rat für Internationale die Zusammenarbeit der Komponisten. Prieberg, *NS-Staat,* 208–9. See chapter 1, n. 64.

35. McCredie, *Hartmann,* 39.

36. Elisabeth Hartmann, recorded interview, Munich, 13 Dec. 1994, APA; McCredie, *Hartmann,* 40; Traber and Weingarten, *Verdrängte Musik,* 169; Gabriele E. Meyer, "Münchener Philharmoniker," SM, Av.Bibl./23933 (17); Rickards, *Hindemith,* 92.

37. Ihlert to Hartmann, 21 Sept. and 9 Oct. 1935, BS, Ana/407.

38. Hartmann to Hába, 14 Nov. 1935; Hartmann to Frau Scherchen, 1 Jan. 1936; Hartmann to [Collaer], [beginning of 1938], BS, Ana/407.

39. Elisabeth Hartmann, recorded interview, Munich, 13 Dec. 1994, APA.

40. Prieberg, *Macht,* 210.

41. Without a shred of proof. See Rudolf Lukowsky, "Bekenntnis zur Humanität: Karl Amadeus Hartmann—ein bedeutender bürgerlicher Musiker," *Musik und Gesellschaft* 20 (1970), 383; Rickards, *Hindemith,* 80, 92.

42. Hartmann RMK file card, 11 July 1941, BAB Hartmann.

43. "Ausführliches Gesamturteil" by Meyer, Ortsgruppenleiter Siegestor, 23 Dec. 1941, BAB Hartmann.

44. Ibid.

45. Hartmann to Hindemith, 4 Feb. 1946; and to Riisager, 30 Dec. 1946, BS, Ana/407.

46. Elisabeth Hartmann, recorded interview, Munich, 13 Dec. 1994, APA.

47. Hartmann to Schlee, 15 Jan. 1946, BS, Ana/407.

48. Elisabeth Hartmann, recorded interview, Munich, 13 Dec. 1994, APA.

49. Ibid.

50. Ibid.; Schott's Söhne to Hartmann, 23 Aug. 1933; Jemnitz to Hartmann, 16 Dec. 1933 and 3 Jan. 1934, BS, Ana/407; Hartmann to Frau Scherchen, 1 Jan. 1936, BS, Ana/407; Ruppel, "Hartmann," 32; Kater, *The Twisted Muse,* 138, 140, 149, 171.

51. *Hartmann,* 85.

52. Kater, *The Twisted Muse,* 72–74.

53. Hans Moldenhauer and Rosaleen Moldenhauer, *Anton von Webern: A Chronicle of His Life and Work* (New York, 1979), 540–41. Hartmann's letter to his wife quoted ibid.

54. Facsimile of telegram in *Hartmann,* 250.

55. Elisabeth Hartmann quoted in Gabriele E. Meyer, "Münchener Philharmoniker," n.d., SM, Av.Bibl./23933 (18).

56. Hartmann to USFRT Paris, 20 Apr. 1946, BS, Ana/407 (all quotes); Elisabeth Hartmann, recorded interview, Munich, 13 Dec. 1994, APA; Andreas Jaschinski, "Anmerkungen zu Karl Amadeus Hartmann: Musik als Widerstand," *Fono-Forum* (Nov. 1981), 29; Rickards, *Hindemith,* 104–7.

57. Hartmann to Scherchen, 9 Feb. and 22 May 1937; Gibson to Hartmann, 1 Feb. 1939, BS, Ana/407; Elisabeth Hartmann, recorded interview, Munich, 13 Dec. 1994, APA; *Hartmann,* 233–34, 299 (quote); Traber and Weingarten, *Verdrängte Musik,* 168–69; Rickards, *Hindemith, 95.*

58. More convincing in his withdrawal was the religiously motivated Protestant journalist Jochen Klepper, who in December 1942 took his own life over the pending deportation of his Jewish stepdaughter. See his published diary, *Unter dem Schatten deiner Flügel: Aus den Tagebüchern, 1932–1942* (Munich, 1976).

59. Riisager to Hartmann, 11 May 1933 (quote) and 15 Nov. 1934, BS, Ana/407.

60. Galimir to Hartmann, 30 Dec. 1934, BS, Ana/407.

61. Palotai to Hartmann, 13 Mar. 1936, BS, Ana/407.

62. McCredie, *Hartmann,* 38.

63. This was later incorporated into his Fifth Symphony. Radio Svizzera Italiana to Hartmann, 15 Apr. 1939, BS, Ana/407; *NG* 8:268.

64. Hartmann to Scherchen, 27 Dec. 1936, BS, Ana/407; Dragotin Cvetko, "Aus H. Scherchens and K. A. Hartmanns Korrespondenz an S. Osterc," in Heinrich Hüschen, ed., *Musicae Scientiae Collectanea: Festschrift Karl Gustav Fellerer am 7. Juli 1972* (Cologne, 1973), 73–75; *Hartmann,* 272.

65. Fiorillo to Hartmann, 27 Apr. 1937 (1st quote), and 27 May 1938 (2nd quote), BS, Ana/407. On Fiorillo, see *The New Grove Dictionary of American Music,* 4 vols., ed. H. Wiley Hitchcock and Stanley Sadie (London, 1986), 2:129.

66. Sacher to Hartmann, 5 Jun. 1939, BA, Ana/407.

67. Hartmann to Scherchen, 27 Dec. 1936 and 5 Jan. 1937, BS, Ana/407; Cvetko, "Korrespondenz," 73–75 (quote Hartmann to Osterc, 9 July 1936, partially reprinted 73). The collusion between Hartmann and Scherchen in this matter is obvious from Hartmann's letter to Osterc, 15 Oct. 1936 (BS, Ana/407), which was written at Scherchen's residence in Winterthur during the composer's visit there, and on which Scherchen penned the following remark to Osterc: "You have to do *everything* possible to ensure the acceptance of Hartmann's piece." Undoubtedly Hartmann saw this before the letter was mailed.

68. Sacher to Hartmann, 30 Jun. 1938, BS, Ana/407.

69. Hartmann to Sacher, 20 Aug. 1938, BS, Ana/407.

70. Sacher to Hartmann, 31 May 1939, BS, Ana/407.

71. Hartmann to Sacher, 4 June 1939 (1st quote); Sacher to Hartmann, 5 June 1939 (2nd quote), BS, Ana/407.

72. McCredie, *Hartmann,* 45–46; *Hartmann,* 238.

73. Memorandum, "Emil Hertzka-Gedächtnis-Stiftung Wien," [1937]; Scheu to Hartmann, 21 May 1937, BS, Ana/407; McCredie, *Hartmann,* 47; *Hartmann,* 298–99.

74. McCredie, *Hartmann,* 50; idem, "Jahre," 58; *Hartmann,* 235–38; Dallapiccola, "Erinnerungen," 333; Windham to Hartmann, 1 Jan. 1938; Kutscher to Hartmann, 2 Aug. 1938, BS, Ana/407.

75. Skulsky to Hartmann, 3 Nov. 1938; Hartmann to Onnou, 24 May 1939; Belgisch Nationaal Instituut voor Radio-Omroep to Hartmann, 14 Mar. 1940; Collaer to Hartmann, 9 Jan. 1941; Hartmann to Collaer, 6 Oct. 1941, BS, Ana/407; McCredie, *Hartmann,* 51–52, 56.

76. Kater, *The Twisted Muse,* 127–29.

77. Guido von Kaulla, *"Und verbrenn' in seinem Herzen":* Die Schauspielerin *Carola Neher und Klabund* (Freiburg im Breisgau, 1984), 126.

78. Hartmann, *Schriften,* 12.

79. Elisabeth Hartmann, recorded interview, Munich, 13 Dec. 1994, APA.

80. Michael H. Kater, "Carl Orff im Dritten Reich," *Vierteljahrshefte für Zeitgeschichte* 43 (1995), 5–6; McCredie, "Jahre," 49; McCredie, *Hartmann,* 30–31; chapter 1 at n. 2.

81. Hartmann, *Schriften,* 12 (quote); Elisabeth Hartmann, recorded interview, Munich, 13 Dec. 1994, APA.

82. Elisabeth Hartmann, recorded interview, Munich, 13 Dec. 1994, APA.

83. Ulrich Dibelius, "Karl Amadeus Hartmann ist tot," *Melos* 31 (1964), 9.

84. See Karl Dietrich Bracher et al., *Die nationalsozialistische Machtergreifung: Studien zur Errichtung des totalitären Herrschaftssystems in Deutschland, 1933/34,* 2nd ed. (Cologne, 1962); Ian Kershaw, *The Nazi Dictatorship: Problems and Perspectives of Interpretation,* 2nd ed. (London, 1989); Thomas Childers and Jane Caplan, eds., *Reevaluating the Third Reich* (New York, 1993).

85. *Hartmann,* 358, 360; McCredie, *Hartmann,* 32.

86. *Hartmann,* 361; McCredie, *Hartmann,* 32.

87. Elisabeth Hartmann, recorded interview, Munich, 13 Dec. 1994, APA; E. Hartmann as quoted in Gabriele E. Meyer, "Münchener Philharmoniker," n.d., SM, Av.Bibl./23933.

88. Scherchen to Egk, 16 and 28 June, 5 July, and 10 Aug. 1933, BS, Ana/410.

89. Röntgen to Hartmann, 20 Feb. 1934 and 22 Sept. 1935, BS, Ana/407.

90. Hartmann to Scherchen, 16 Nov. 1935, BS, Ana/407. See also Hartmann to [Auguste] Scherchen, 1 Jan. 1936, BS, Ana/407.

91. *Hartmann,* 236–37; Elias Canetti, *The Play of the Eyes* (New York, 1986), 42–50.

92. Hartmann, *Schriften,* 14; McCredie, *Hartmann,* 34, 43.

93. Hartmann to Scherchen, 16 Nov. 1935, 22 May 1937, 17 Jan. 1938, 2 Dec. 1938 (quote), BS, Ana/407; Hartmann to [Auguste] Scherchen, 1 Jan. 1936, BS, Ana/407; Scherchen to Hartmann, 3 Jan., 11 May and 19 June 1937, 2 Feb., 19 May and 14 Nov. 1938, BS, Ana/407; Scherchen to Auguste Jansen-Scherchen, 18 Oct. 1935, in Hermann Scherchen, *Alles hörbar machen: Briefe eines Dirigenten, 1920 bis 1939,* ed. Eberhardt Klemm (Berlin, 1976), 257.

94. Scherchen to Hartmann, 4 Dec. 1935; Hartmann to Scherchen, 16 Jan. 1936, BS, Ana/407.

95. Dallapiccola, "Meine Erinnerungen," 334.

96. Alexander Jemnitz, "Artikel aus der Budapester Zeitung 'Népszava' 5. April 1936"; Hartmann to Jemnitz, 29 June 1936, BS, Ana/407.

97. See n. 67 above.

98. Hartmann to Scherchen, 5 Jan. and 9 Feb. 1937, BS, Ana/407.

99. Scherchen to Hartmann, 11 May 1937, BS, Ana/407. Hartmann's remark, ibid., is undated.

100. Hartmann to Scherchen, 22 May 1937, BS, Ana/407.

101. Rózsavölgyi & Co. to Hartmann, 20 Nov. 1937, BS, Ana/407.

102. See Scherchen to Hartmann, 2 Feb. and 19 May 1938; Hartmann to Scherchen, 8 May 1938, BS, Ana/407.

103. Elisabeth Hartmann recalls that Scherchen made snide remarks about the pretty pair of shoes she was wearing, insinuating, on that basis, pro-Nazi sympathies on her part and, at the same time, his own intention to seduce her (recorded interview, Munich, 13 Dec. 1994, APA).

104. Hartmann to Scherchen, 20 Aug. and 2 Dec. 1938; Scherchen to Hartmann, 14 Nov. 1938, BS, Ana/407.

105. Jemnitz to Hartmann, 24 Nov. 1938, BS, Ana/407.

106. Scherchen to Hartmann, 17 Jan. and 21 May 1939; Hartmann to Scherchen, 20 July 1939; Reinhart to Hartmann, 22 July 1939, BS, Ana/407; *Hartmann,* 358.

107. Scherchen to Karl [Amadeus Hartmann], 17 July and 30 Nov. 1940, 22 Nov. 1941, BS, Ana/407.

108. Scherchen to Hartmann, 30 Nov. 1940; Haug to Hartmann, 27 July 1942; Hartmann to Haug, 15 Aug. and 1 Oct. 1942, BS, Ana/407.

109. Scherchen to Karl [Amadeus Hartmann], 6 Oct. 1940, 22 Nov. 1941, and 9 Nov. 1942, BS, Ana/407; Scherchen to Hartmann, [1940], in *Hartmann,* 246.

110. Scherchen to Karl [Amadeus Hartmann], 4 Nov. 1940 and 28 Jan. 1942, BS, Ana/407.

111. K. A. Hartmann to Elisabeth Hartmann, Nov. 1942, in Moldenhauer, *Webern,* 542; Webern to Hartmann, 14 Dec. 1942, in *Hartmann,* 86; Jemnitz to Hartmann, 8 Mar. 1944, BS, Ana/407 (quote).

112. McCredie, *Hartmann,* 66.

113. Elisabeth Hartmann, recorded interview, Munich, 13 Dec. 1994, APA; McCredie, *Hartmann,* 67.

114. Elisabeth Hartmann, recorded interview, Munich, 13 Dec. 1994, APA; McCredie, *Hartmann,* 69.

115. McCredie, *Hartmann,* 69.

116. Hartmann to Sacher, 23 Dec. 1945; Hartmann to Scherchen, 28 Jan. 1947, BS, Ana/407 (quote); McCredie, *Hartmann,* 68; Rickards, *Hindemith,* 124.

117. Hartmann to Schlee, 15 Jan. 1946, BS, Ana/407; McCredie, *Hartmann,* 69.

118. Hartmann to Sacher, 23 Dec. 1945, and to Riisager, 30 Dec. 1946, BS, Ana/407; *Melos* 14 (1947), 90, 125, 266, 352. On Fortner's Nazi past, see Kater, *The Twisted Muse,* 170–71.

119. Hartmann to Hindemith, 4 Feb. 1946; Hindemith to Hartmann, 5 Mar. 1946, BS, Ana/407; text at n. 118 in chapter 2.

120. Hartmann to Hindemith, 4 Feb. 1946, BS, Ana/407.

121. Elisabeth Hartmann, recorded interview, Munich, 13 Dec. 1994, APA.

122. Scherchen to Hartmann, 3 May 1946; Hartmann to Scherchen, 23 May and 10 July 1946 (quote), BS, Ana/407.

123. Hartmann to Scherchen, 28 Jan. 1947, BS, Ana/407.

124. Hartmann to Krenek, 20 May 1948, BS, Ana/407.

125. Elisabeth Hartmann, recorded interview, Munich, 13 Dec. 1994, APA; *Melos* 14 (1947), 181. On Graener and Trapp, see Kater, *The Twisted Muse,* 24–28.

126. Hartmann to Schlee, 15 Jan. 1946, BS, Ana/407; Hartmann (1962) quoted in Hartmann, *Schriften,* 76. For the historical background, see Michael H. Kater, "Problems of Political Reeducation in West Germany, 1945–1960," *Simon Wiesenthal Center Annual* 4 (1987), 99–123.

127. Ulrich Dibelius, "Karl Amadeus Hartmann ist tot," *Melos* 31 (1964), 10.

128. McCredie, *Hartmann*, 67–69.

129. Elisabeth Hartmann, recorded interview, Munich, 13 Dec. 1994, APA; "Abdruck für die Spielzeit 1947/48 . . . ," BH, Staatstheater/14395; *Melos* 14 (1947), 308; Karl Heinz Ruppel, "Komponist, Vorkämpfer und Organisator: Karl Amadeus Hartmann," *Melos* 22 (1955), 252; Ruppel, "Musica Viva, 1945–1958," in idem, ed., *Musica Viva* (Munich, 1959), 16; Ekkehart Kroher, "Musik als Gleichnis für Mensch und Zeit: Zur Erinnerung an den Komponisten Karl Amadeus Hartmann," *Musik und Medizin* 8 (1981), 153; Hartmann as interviewed by Wolf-Eberhard von Lewinski in *Melos* 31 (1964), 14–15; McCredie, "Documents," 172; *LI,* 899; Rickards, *Hindemith,* 150, 153.

130. "Abdruck für die Spielzeit 1947/48 . . . ," BH, Staatstheater/14395; *Melos* 31 (1964), 14; Hans Werner Henze, "Laudatio," in *Hartmann,* 11–19; Henze in Hartmann, *Schriften,* 89; Karl-Robert Danler, *Musik in München: Neubeginn 1945—Olympische Spiele 1972—eine musikgeschichtliche Wegstrecke* (Munich, 1971), 30; Rickards, *Hindemith,* 150.

131. Elisabeth Hartmann, recorded interview, Munich, 13 Dec. 1994, APA; Scherchen to Hartmann, 26 Oct 1948, BS, Ana/407; *Hartmann,* 243–46; Ruppel, "Musica Viva," 40.

132. Elisabeth Hartmann, recorded interview, Munich, 13 Dec. 1994, APA; Orff to Sutermeister, 25 Dec. 1947, CM, Allg. Korr.; *Hartmann,* 321, 328, 332, 334; Ruppel, "Musica Viva," 32; Ruppel, "Komponist," 252.

133. Elisabeth Hartmann, recorded interview, Munich, 13 Dec. 1994, APA (1st quote); "Eidesstattliche Erklärung" by Hartmann, Munich, 11 Mar. 1946 (2nd and 3rd quotes); Hartmann to Spruchkammer München-Land, 5 Sept. 1947 (4th quote), AM, Egk; *Hartmann,* 318, 321, 328, 334–35, 350, 353; Ruppel, "Musica Viva," 31–32; Ruppel, "Komponist," 252.

134. Hartmann to Pinter, 1 July 1946, BS, Ana/407; Hartmann, *Schriften,* 12, 16 (quote); *Hartmann,* 357–63; Joachim Herrmann, "Form und Fantasie: Zum Schaffen Karl Amadeus Hartmanns," *Musica* 9 (1955), 421; Kroher, "Musik," 50; Jaschinski, "Anmerkungen," 29; Rickards, *Hindemith,* 128–29.

135. "Abdruck für die Spielzeit 1947/48 . . . ," BH, Staatstheater/14395; *Melos* 14 (1947), 261, 341, 425; *Melos* 15 (1948), 184; *Hartmann,* 251, 258, 360; Hans Werner Henze in Hartmann, *Schriften,* 89; *NG* 8:267; Ruppel, "Komponist," 250; Rickards, *Hindemith,* 154–57.

136. *Hartmann,* 241, 278; Rickards, *Hindemith,* 149–50.

137. Hartmann to Havemann, 4 Feb. 1946; Havemann to Hartmann, 4 Mar. 1946 (quote), BS, Ana/407; Traber and Weingarten, *Verdrängte Musik,* 179–80; Rickards, *Hindemith,* 130; Lukowsky, "Bekenntnis," 381–88. On Schoenberg and his circle in the DDR, see Fred K. Prieberg, *Musik im anderen Deutschland* (Cologne, 1968), 41, 74–75, 83, 281, 299–300; Ernst Hermann Meyer, in Wes Blomster, "The Reception of Arnold Schoenberg in the German Democratic Republic," *Perspectives of New Music* 21 (1982/83), 114–37; Frank Schneider, "Von gestern auf heute: Die Wiener Schule im Schatten von Komponisten der DDR," in Rudolf Stephan and Sigrid Wiesmann, eds., *Bericht über den 2. Kongress der Internationalen Schönberg-Gesellschaft: "Die Wiener Schule in der Musikgeschichte des 20. Jahrhunderts"* (Vienna, 1986), 124–25; Ulrich Dibelius and Frank Schneider, eds., *Neue Musik im geteilten Deutschland: Dokumente aus den fünfziger Jahren* (Berlin, 1993), 112–17. On Becher, see Günter Albrecht et al., *Lexikon deutschsprachiger Schriftsteller von den Anfängen bis zur Gegenwart,* 2 vols. (Leipzig, 1972), 1:52.

CHAPTER 5: ORFF

1. Karl Heinz Ruppel's preface in Andreas Liess, *Carl Orff: Idee und Werk* (Zurich, 1955), n.p.

2. Jens Malte Fischer, "Vergangenheit, die nicht vergehen will: Carl Orff und das Dritte Reich," *Süddeutsche Zeitung,* Munich, 14 Mar. 1995.

3. Hans Maier, *Carl Orff in seiner Zeit: Rede anlässlich Carl Orffs 100. Geburtstag, München, Prinzregententheater, 7. Juli 1995* (Mainz, 1995), 4.

4. Orff to Pietzsch, 28 Apr. 1946, CM, Allg. Korr.; Wolfgang Seifert, "'. . . auf den Geist kommt es an': Carl Orff zum 75. Geburtstag—Kommentar und Gespräch," *Neue Zeitschrift für Musik* 131 (1970), 376; Orff cited in *Neue Musikzeitung* (Apr./May 1975), 3 (quote), and in Fred K. Prieberg, *Musik im NS-Staat* (Frankfurt am Main, 1982), 324.

5. Signed transcript of interview with Gertrud Orff, Munich, 5 Aug. 1992, APA.

6. Hans Heinz Stuckenschmidt, "Braune Klänge," *Melos* 14 (1946), 11; similarly idem, "Die Musen und die Macht: Musik im Dritten Reich," *Frankfurter Allgemeine Zeitung,* 6 Dec. 1980.

7. Ernst Krause, *Werner Egk: Oper und Ballett* (Wilhelmshaven, 1971), 9; Carl Dahlhaus, "Den Notlügen auf der Spur: Fred K. Priebergs Chronik der Musik im NS-Staat," *Frankfurter Allgemeine Zeitung,* 13 Feb. 1982.

8. Rudolf Wagner-Régeny, *An den Ufern der Zeit: Schriften, Briefe, Tagebücher,* ed. Max Becker (Leipzig, 1989), 107.

9. Ludwig F. Schiedermair, *Musiker Schicksale: Aus dem Leben grosser Komponisten* (Berlin, 1990), 236.

10. Franz Willnauer, "Vorwort des Herausgebers," in idem, ed., *Carmina Burana von Carl Orff: Entstehung—Wirkung—Text* (Mainz, 1995), 9 (quote); Reiner Pommerin, "Some Remarks on the Cultural History of the Federal Republic of Germany," in Pommerin, ed., *Culture in the Federal Republic of Germany, 1945–1995* (Oxford, 1996), 9.

11. Karl Laux, *Musik und Musiker der Gegenwart* (Essen, 1949), 181–91.

12. "Carl Orff Remembered . . . Courtesy: Carl Orff und sein Werk, Dokumentation. Verlag Hans Schneider, Tutzing," [Fall/Winter 1995], PA Tamara Bernstein; Bernstein quoted in *Globe and Mail,* Toronto, 30 Dec. 1995.

13. Hannelore Gassner, "Chronologie," in Hans Jörg Jans and Wolfgang Till, eds., *Welttheater: Carl Orff und sein Bühnenwerk: Eine inszenierte Ausstellung im Münchner Stadtmuseum in Zusammenarbeit mit dem Orff-Zentrum München vom 6. September bis 3. November 1996* [Munich, 1996]; "Tafel 11 Ein Sommernachtstraum," ibid. A similar lacuna already is in Gassner's "Werkverzeichnis," in Godela Orff, *Mein Vater und ich: Erinnerungen an Carl Orff* (Munich, 1992), 119.

14. Andrea Seebohm, "Unbewältigte musikalische Vergangenheit: Ein Kapitel österreichischer Musikgeschichte, das bis heute ungeschrieben ist," in Liesbeth Waechter-Böhm, ed., *Wien 1945: Davor/danach* (Vienna, 1985), 151; Harvey Sachs, *Music in Fascist Italy* (London, 1987), 198.

15. Quoted in Fred K. Prieberg, *Musik und Macht* (Frankfurt am Main, 1991), 277.

16. Jörg Bremer, "Heimat haben sie nicht mehr gefunden: Die Nöte der 'Jeckes': Deutsche Juden in Israel," *Frankfurter Allgemeine Zeitung,* 6 June 1992; Eleanore Büning, "Die Musik ist schuld," *Zeit,* Hamburg, 7 July 1995.

17. Matthew Gurewitsch, "Cosmic Chants," *Atlantic Monthly* (Aug. 1995), 93.

18. Cited in Kim H. Kowalke, "The Brecht Connection," *Stagebill* (Mar. 1997), 10.

19. Text for Exhibit 299, "Assault on the Arts: Culture and Politics in Nazi Germany," Exhibition, New York Public Library, 27 Feb. to 28 May, 1993.

20. Alex Ross, "In Music, Though, There Were No Victories," *New York Times,* 20 Aug. 1995.

21. George Steiner quoted in *Kulturchronik,* no. 6 (1998), 24 (translated from his original statement in *Süddeutsche Zeitung* [Munich]); Nicolas Slonimsky, *Music Since 1900,* 4th ed. (New York, 1971), 674 (2nd quote. This text did not yet appear in the 2nd ed. of 1938).

22. Reported on the Internet (amslist@ucdavis.edu) by Craig De Wilde, Senior Lecturer, Monash University, Clayton, Australia, on 30 Apr. 1996 (printout APA).

23. Donald W. Ellis, "Music in the Third Reich: National Socialist Aesthetic Theory as Government Policy," PhD dissertation, University of Kansas, 1970, 133 (1st quote); *Frankfurter Allgemeine Zeitung,* 13 May 1994 (2nd quote); *Komponierende Frauen im Dritten Reich: Eine Veranstaltung im Rahmen der Reihe "1933—Zerstörung der Demokratie, Machtübergabe und Widerstand"* (Berlin, 1983), 5.

24. *Globe and Mail,* Toronto, 28 Sept. 1996.

25. Paraphrased in letter von Einem to Orff, 25 Aug. 1946, CM, Allg. Korr.

26. Gerald Abraham, *The Concise Oxford Dictionary of Music* (Oxford, 1986), 840.

27. Dagmar Kraemer and Manfred Stassen, "'Berlin Cabaret,'" *Kulturchronik,* no. 4 (1992), 45.

28. Berthold Goldschmidt quoted in *Spiegel* (5 Sept. 1994), 208.

29. Godela Orff, *Vater,* 14, 21; Lilo Gersdorf, *Carl Orff: Mit Selbstzeugnissen und Bilddokumenten* (Reinbek, 1981), 17–24; Liess, *Orff,* 8–10.

30. Gersdorf, *Orff,* 25–46; Liess, *Orff,* 14; Karl Marx in Horst Leuchtmann, ed., *Carl Orff: Ein Gedenkbuch* (Tutzing, 1985), 98–101; Orff in *Carl Orff und sein Werk,* 8 vols. (Tutzing, 1975–83), 1:65–67; Werner Thomas, *Das Rad der Fortuna: Ausgewählte Aufsätze zu Werk und Wirkung Carl Orffs* (Mainz, 1990), 136–37.

31. Orff to Laaff, 20 Jan. 1932, CM, Allg. Korr.; Gunild Keetmann in Leuchtmann, *Orff,* 65; Orff in *Carl Orff und sein Werk,* 1:67–68; 2:15, 21; 3:10–15, 115; NG 13:708–9; Wilhelm Twittenhoff, *Orff-Schulwerk: Einführung in Grundlagen und Aufbau* (Mainz, 1935), 28; Thomas, *Rad,* 149–66.

32. Programs, "1. Neue Musikwoche München 1929" (quote); "Woche Neuer Musik 2.–11. Oktober 1930"; "Festwoche Neuer Musik München 15.–22. Mai 1931"; excerpt from *Münchener Neueste Nachrichten,* Sept. 1929, SM, Kulturamt/143; Orff in *Carl Orff und sein Werk,* 2:141–42, 196–97; Karl Marx in Leuchtmann, *Orff,* 104; Gudrun Straub et al., *Karl Marx* (Tutzing, 1983), 26–28.

33. [Memorandum, n.d.], "Als der Münchner Bachverein . . . ," SM, Kulturamt/265; Orff in *Carl Orff und sein Werk,* 2:143, 145, 176; Liess, *Orff,* 23–25; Karl Marx in Leuchtmann, *Orff,* 108.

34. Orff in *Carl Orff und sein Werk,* 2:152; Heinrich Strobel cited ibid., 176; Orff to Salomon, 14 Feb. 1932 and 18 July 1947; Orff to Reusch, 2 May 1932; Orff to Reinhard, 11 May 1932; Kestenberg to Orff, 31 Dec. 1932, CM, Allg. Korr.

35. Fritz Neumeyer, "Alte Musik in unserer Zeit," *DKW,* no. 31 (1933), 2–3; Reinhold Conrad Muschler, "Hingabe an die Kunst; Wege zu Bach," ibid., no. 34 (1933), 10–11; Harald Busch, "Lanze für den Barock!," ibid., no. 38 (1933), 9–10; Muschler, "Alte Musik im Rahmen ihrer Zeit," ibid., 16.

36. Orff, *Vater,* passim.

37. Gersdorf, *Orff,* 16, 24.

38. Orff to Schilling, 9 Feb. 1932, CM, Allg. Korr.

39. Karl Marx in Leuchtmann, *Orff,* 102, 105.

40. Orff to Reusch, 24 Jan. 1932, CM, Allg. Korr.

41. Quotes ibid. and Orff to Preussner, 16 Dec. 1932, CM, Allg. Korr.

42. Herbert Rosenberg, "Neue Chormusik," *Melos* 11 (1932), 143 (1st quote); Orff to Strobel, 20 Oct. 1932; Orff to Doflein, 27 Dec. 1932 (2nd quote), CM, Allg. Korr.

43. Schulz-Dornburg to Orff, 17 Dec. 1932; Preussner to Orff, 21 Dec. 1932; Orff to Schulz-Dornburg, 28 Dec. 1932, CM, Allg. Korr.

44. Orff to Salomon, 23 Jan. 1933, CM, Allg. Korr.

45. Brosig to Orff, [1932], CM, Allg. Korr.; Carl Orff, *The Schulwerk* (New York, 1976), 114; Inge Lammel, "Die beiden Berliner 'Scherchen-Chöre,'" in Horst Seeger and Wolfgang Goldhan, eds., *Studien zur Berliner Musikgeschichte: Eine Bestandsaufnahme* (Berlin, 1988), 36.

46. Orff to Doflein, 6 Mar. 1931, CM, Allg. Korr.

47. Orff, *Vater,* 35.

48. Jöde to Orff, 26 Jan. 1932; Orff to Jöde, 19 May 1932; Orff to Reusch, 6 July 1932; Rosendorff to Orff, 21 Sept. 1932; Orff to Preussner, 28 Dec. 1932; Kestenberg to Orff, 31 Dec. 1932, CM, Allg. Korr. See also Leo Kestenberg, *Bewegte Zeiten: Musisch-Musikantische Lebenserinnerungen* (Wolfenbüttel, 1961), 57–58.

49. Orff to Reusch, 2 May and 6 July 1932; Reusch to Orff, 20 June and 5 July 1932; Orff to Goetsch, 4 Oct. 1932; Kelbetz to Orff, 10 Sept. 1932, CM, Allg. Korr.; Georg Götsch and Ludwig Kelbetz, *Männerchor oder singende Mannschaft: Männerchor in der Entscheidung* (Hamburg, 1934). Also see Ulrich Günther, *Die Schulmusikerziehung von der Kestenberg-Reform bis zum Ende des Dritten Reiches: Ein Beitrag zur Dokumentation und Zeitgeschichte der Schulmusikerziehung mit Anregungen zu ihrer Neugestaltung* (Neuwied, 1967), esp. 40; Michael H. Kater, "Carl Orff im Dritten Reich," *Vierteljahrshefte für Zeitgeschichte* 43 (1995), 16–17; Kater, *The Twisted Muse: Musicians and Their Music in the Third Reich* (New York, 1997), 138, 147.

50. Reusch to Orff, 20 June 1932, CM, Allg. Korr.

51. On Katz, see *IBD,* 600; *NG* 9:828; Theo Stengel and Herbert Gerigk, *Lexikon der Juden in der Musik: Mit einem Titelverzeichnis jüdischer Werke* (Berlin, 1941), 132; Kater, *The Twisted Muse,* 103. On Doflein, see *GLM* 2:331. Doflein's wife was the sister of the by Nazi standards not fully "Aryan" keyboard artist Edith Axenfels (later known as Edith Picht-Axenfels).

52. Orff to Salomon, 21 Jan., 14 Feb. 1932, and 18 July 1947; Orff to Sinzheimer, 27 July 1932; Katz to Orff, 18 Aug. [1932]; Seiber to Orff, 12 Oct. 1932; [Günther] to Seiber, 21 Oct. 1932, CM, Allg. Korr; *Carl Orff und sein Werk,* 3:201. Also see *GLM,* 7:194, 325–26; Stengel and Gerigk, *Lexikon,* 236, 260; Michael H. Kater, *Different Drummers: Jazz in the Culture of Nazi Germany* (New York, 1992), 17.

53. Alan E. Steinweis, "Weimar Culture and the Rise of National Socialism: The *Kampfbund für deutsche Kultur,*" *Central European History* 24 (1991), 402–23; Kater, *The Twisted Muse,* passim; Kater, "Carl Orff im Dritten Reich," 6–8.

54. Kupfer to Orff, 21 Dec. 1933, CM, Allg. Korr. (1st and 2nd quotes); Orff to Hofmann, 1 Aug. [1933], in Frohmut Dangel-Hofmann, ed., *Carl Orff—Michel Hofmann: Briefe zur Entstehung der Carmina Burana* (Tutzing, 1990), 13 (3rd quote).

55. Paul Ehlers, "Die Musik und Adolf Hitler," *ZM* 106 (1939), 356.

56. Laaff to Orff, 22 Jan. 1933; Ruppel to Orff, 2 June 1933; Doflein to Orff, 16 June 1933, CM, Allg. Korr.; Orff to Strecker, 15 May 1933, CM, Schott Korr.; Orff to Döbereiner, 29 Jan. 1934, BS, Ana/344/I/B/Orff. Also see Alan E. Steinweis, *Art, Ideology, and Economics in Nazi Germany: The Reich Chambers of Music, Theater, and the Visual Arts* (Chapel Hill, N.C., 1993), 32–38.

57. Orff to Doflein, 25 Sept. and 3 Dec. 1933; Orff to Schmidt, 22 Oct. 1933, CM, Allg. Korr.; Ehlers to Fiehler, 6 Dec. 1933; "Münchner Bach-Verein e.V.: Schütz-Händel-Fest der Stadt München," [for 31 Oct. 1934]; Steidle to Kulturamt, 9 Feb. 1943, SM, Kulturamt/265; "Münchner Bach-Verein e.V. im Kampfbund für Deutsche Kultur," program for 1934–35, SM, Kulturamt/275; Ehrenberg memorandum, 30 Oct. 1935, SM, Kulturamt/319; BAB Büchtger; Max Neuhaus, "Johann-Sebastian-Bach-Feier," *VB*, 13 Apr. 1934.

58. Orff to Strecker, 15 May 1933, CM, Schott Korr.; Günther, "Erklärung über meinen Eintritt in den Kampfbund für deutsche Kultur," [Spring 1947], CM, Allg. Korr.

59. Dorothee Günther, "Wiedergeburt des deutschen Tanzes," in Rudolf von Laban et al., eds., *Die tänzerische Situation unserer Zeit: Ein Querschnitt* (Dresden, 1936), 13–21; Prieberg, *NS-Staat*, 325; Kater, "Carl Orff im Dritten Reich," 14–15.

60. Kater, "Carl Orff im Dritten Reich," 30.

61. Idem, "Das Problem der musikalischen Moderne im NS-Staat," in Albrecht Riethmüller, ed., *Bruckner-Probleme: Internationales Kolloquium, 7.–9. Oktober 1996 in Berlin* (Stuttgart, 1999), 169–84.

62. Idem, "Carl Orff im Dritten Reich," 5; *NG* 13:708–9.

63. Orff to Strecker, 15 May, 19 May (1st quote), and 30 Aug. 1933 (2nd quote); Orff to Willms, 25 Mar. 1934, CM, Schott Korr.; Orff to Döbereiner, 29 Jan. 1934, BS, Ana/344/I/B/Orff.

64. Hans Fleischer, "Quertreiber an der Arbeit," *DKW*, no. 22 (1933), 11; Orff to Fleischer, 21 Sept. 1933, CM, Allg. Korr. (quote); Orff to Willms, 22 Sept. 1933, CM, Schott Korr. On Nazi-sanctioned *Hausmusik* see Kater, *The Twisted Muse*, 130–34; on the Nazi blacklisting of jazz until 1939, see Kater, *Different Drummers*, 29–56.

65. Orff to Willms, 7 Feb. 1934, CM, Schott Korr. On *Volkslied* and National Socialism, see Kater, *The Twisted Muse*, 135–67.

66. Orff to Willms, 7 Mar. 1934, CM, Schott Korr.

67. Willms to Orff, 29 Mar. 1934, CM, Schott Korr.

68. [Schott Verlag], "Orientierung über Carl Orff," [May 1941], CM, Schott Korr.

69. Wolfgang Stumme, "Gemeinsamkeit musikerzieherischer Aufgaben," in idem, ed., *Musik im Volk: Grundfragen der Musikerziehung* (Berlin, 1939), 15; Ludwig Kelbetz, *Aufbau einer Musikschule* (Wolfenbüttel, 1939), 16; Prieberg, *NS-Staat*, 325; Kater, "Carl Orff im Dritten Reich," 17–18. Orff's post-1945 statement regarding his victimization by the Nazis because of their alleged proscription of his *Schulwerk* is in *Carl Orff und sein Werk*, 3:203, and Prieberg, *NS-Staat*, 324.

70. Orff to Strecker, 12 Feb. 1934, CM, Schott Korr.; Schulz-Dornburg to Orff, 7 Sept. 1935; Orff to Reusch, 18 Nov. 1935; Orff to Rapp, 16 Mar. 1936, CM, Allg. Korr.; Günther, "Wiedergeburt," 18.

71. Payr, Reichsstelle zur Förderung des deutschen Schrifttums, "Gutachten für Verleger," 10 Apr. 1937, CM, Schott K. (1st quote); Orff to Georgiades, 12 Dec. 1935, CM, Allg. Korr. (2nd quote).

72. Orff in *Carl Orff und sein Werk*, 3:131.

73. Orff to Willms, 23 Apr. 1934, CM, Schott Korr.

74. Wilhelm Twittenhof [sic], "Jugend und moderne Musik," *Musik in Jugend*

und Volk 1 (1937/38), 370 (quote); idem, "Die Lehrgänge für Volks- und Jugend-musikleiter in Berlin und Weimar" (1938), reprinted in Dorothea Hemming, ed., *Dokumente zur Geschichte der Musikhochschule (1902–1976)* (Regensburg, 1977), 122–24; idem, "Rhythmische Erziehung," in Stumme, *Musik im Volk,* 193–205; Twittenhoff to Orff, 29 Oct. 1937, CM, Allg. Korr.

75. Reusch to Orff, 22 Aug. 1935; Twittenhoff to Orff, 29 Nov. 1936, CM, Allg. Korr.; Orff to Petschull, 12 June 1936, CM, Schott Korr.

76. Wilhelm Twittenhoff, *Orff-Schulwerk: Eine Einführung in Grundlagen und Aufbau* (Mainz, 1935); Rudolf Sonner, "Musik aus Bewegung," *DM* 29 (1937), 762–65; Twittenhoff to Orff, 23 Aug. 1937, CM, Allg. Korr.; Petschull to Orff, 19 Aug. 1937; Twittenhoff to Petschull, 11 Sept. [1937], CM, Schott Korr.

77. Reusch to Bergese, 5 Nov. 1933, and to Orff, 22 Aug. 1935, CM, Allg. Korr.; Fritz Reusch, *Musik und Musikerziehung im Dienste der Volksgemeinschaft* (Osterwieck, 1938); Reusch, "Die Musikerziehung an den Hochschulen für Lehrerbildung im Aufbau der Mannschaftserziehung," in Stumme, *Musik im Volk,* 72–82; Ulrich Günther, *Schulmusikerziehung,* 39–41, 94, 186–87, 189.

78. Orff to Kelbetz, 31 Oct. 1933, and to von Tiedemann, 29 July 1938, and to Bresgen, 23 Mar. 1939, CM, Allg. Korr.; Strecker to Orff, 15 Sept. 1937, CM, Schott Korr.; *Musik der Hitler-Jugend* (Wolfenbüttel, 1941), 31; Kater, *The Twisted Muse,* 138, 140, 142–46, 149.

79. Twittenhoff to Orff, 26 Apr. 1937, CM, Allg. Korr. On Stumme see Kater, *The Twisted Muse,* Chapter 4, passim.

80. Quotation Orff in *Carl Orff und sein Werk,* 4:43. See also Liess, *Orff,* 38–39, 44, 50; Ulrich Dibelius, *Moderne Musik, 1945–1965: Voraussetzungen, Verlauf, Material* (Munich, 1966), 80–81; Thomas, *Rad,* 33–51; Hermann Danuser, *Die Musik des 20. Jahrhunderts* (Regensburg, 1984), 214.

81. Skulsky to Hartmann, 16 Dec. 1939, BS, Ana/407.

82. Joan Evans, "Die Rezeption der Musik Igor Strawinskys in Hitlerdeutschland," *Archiv für Musikwissenschaft* 55 (1998), 91–109.

83. Willms to Orff, 29 Mar. 1935, CM, Schott Korr.; Orff to Hofmann, 12 June 1936, in Dangel-Hofmann, *Orff-Hofmann,* 113; Orff to Bergese, 22 May 1936, PA Bergese; Albert Richard Mohr, *Die Frankfurter Oper, 1924–1944: Ein Beitrag zur Theatergeschichte mit zeitgenössischen Berichten und Bildern* (Frankfurt am Main, 1971), 256.

84. Barthe to Meyer-Rogge, 9 Feb. 1938, CM, Allg. Korr.; Strecker to Orff, 15 Sept. 1937 and 9 Sept. 1938; Willms to Orff, 7 Sept. 1938; Menge to Orff, 17 Apr. 1941, CM, Schott Korr.

85. Herbert Gerigk, "Problematisches Opernwerk auf dem Tonkünstlerfest: 'Carmina Burana' von Carl Orff," *VB,* 16 June 1937; idem, "Carl Orffs 'Carmina burana,'" *DM* 29 (1937), 701–2.

86. See section II in chapter 2.

87. Gail to Orff, 25 Aug. 1937 and [?] Dec. 1938; Strecker to Orff, 6 Apr. 1938, CM, Allg. Korr.; Strecker to Orff, 6 Mar. 1937, 9 June and 13 July 1938; Orff to Strecker, 18 Feb. and 24 Mar. 1938, CM, Schott Korr.

88. On censorship and Rosenberg's diminishing politicocultural influence see Kater, *The Twisted Muse,* passim.

89. Prieberg, *NS-Staat,* 275; Kater, "Carl Orff im Dritten Reich," 9.

90. Eva Hanau, "Carl Orff in Frankfurt am Main: Zur kulturpolitischen Situation der Stadt in den Jahren 1933–1939" (in press for *Musikwissenschaftliches Archiv*).

91. Ibid.; *Das Deutsche Führerlexikon, 1934/35* (Berlin, n.d.), 255–56.

92. Krebs to Orff, 24 June 1937, CM, Allg. Korr.

93. For Frankfurt, see Friedrich Stichtenoth in *Generalanzeiger,* Frankfurt, 9 June 1937, and Walter Dirks in *Frankfurter Zeitung,* 10 June 1937. Quotation Orff to Strecker, 18 June 1937, CM, Schott Korr.

94. Orff to Hofmann, 26 June 1947, in Dangel-Hofmann, *Orff-Hofmann,* 139; Kupfer to Orff, 24 June 1937, CM, Allg. Korr.

95. Von der Nüll to Orff, 4 Oct. [1937] and [Jan. 1938], CM, Allg. Korr. See also Kater, *The Twisted Muse,* 59. On Rode, who once planned to dress his opera musicians in drag to humor Ernst Röhm, the homosexual chief of the Stormtroopers, see ibid., 29.

96. Matthes paraphrased in Strecker to Orff, 18 June 1938 (quote); Orff to Strecker, 8 Mar. 1939, CM, Schott Korr.

97. Orff to Strecker, 8 Mar. 1939, CM, Schott Korr.

98. Orff to Schmidt, 21 Oct. 1937, CM, Allg. Korr.

99. Orff to Schulz-Dornburg, 25 Jan. 1938; Städtische Bühnen Frankfurt am Main, "Woche der Lebenden" vom 19. bis 26. März 1939," CM, Allg. Korr.; Orff to Willms, 1 Apr. 1939, CM, Schott Korr.

100. Eigendorff to Professor [Pfitzner], 19 Mar. 1938, OW, 74.

101. Orff to Strecker, 8 Nov. 1938, CM, Schott Korr.; Orff to Sutermeister, 27 Oct. 1938, and to Sacher, 8 Dec. 1938, CM, Allg. Korr.

102. Orff in *Carl Orff und sein Werk,* 4:64, 71 (quote); Pietzsch to Orff, 16 June 1946, CM, Allg. Korr. Repetitions and variations on the theme are in Schiedermair, *Schicksale,* 241–42; Werner Thomas, "'Trionfo' oder Konsum? Werkidee und Rezeptionspraxis von Carl Orffs 'Carmina Burana,'" in *International Journal of Musicology* 1 (1992), 254–56; also see nn. 4 and 5, above.

103. See below, near n. 194.

104. Albrecht Riethmüller, "Die Erneuerung der Kirchenmusik im Dritten Reich—Eine Legende?" *Der Kirchenmusiker* 40 (1989), 166.

105. Meissner to Orff, 25 Mar. and 2 Apr. 1938 (quote), CM, Allg. Korr.

106. Prieberg, *NS-Staat,* 156–59; Kater, *The Twisted Muse,* 195.

107. Krebs quoted in Hanau, "Carl Orff."

108. Meissner to Orff, 31 May 1938; Orff to Meissner, 29 Mar., and to Wälterlin, 8 Dec. 1939, CM, Allg. Korr.; Orff to Strecker, 8 Nov. and 8 Dec. 1938, CM, Schott Korr.

109. *Führerlexikon,* 256.

110. This point is well argued by Hanau, "Carl Orff."

111. Willms to Orff, 12 Apr. 1938, CM, Schott Korr.

112. Strecker to Orff, 14 Dec. 1938, CM, Schott Korr.

113. Orff to Strecker, 16 Dec. 1938, CM, Schott Korr.

114. Orff to Strecker, 14 and 19 Feb. 1939, CM, Schott Korr.

115. Entry for 17 Aug. 1939 in "Gertrud Orffs Tagebuch," CM; Hanau, "Carl Orff."

116. Strecker to Orff, 26 Oct. 1939, CM, Schott Korr.

117. Orff to Beierle (quote) and to Lenssen, 20 Oct. 1939, CM, Allg. Korr.

118. Hanau, "Orff"; Reinhard Bollmus, *Das Amt Rosenberg und seine Gegner: Studien zum Machtkampf im nationalsozialistischen Herrschaftssystem* (Stuttgart, 1970), 122; Michael H. Kater, *Das "Ahnenerbe" der SS, 1935–1945: Ein Beitrag zur Kulturpolitik des Dritten Reiches,* 2nd ed. (Munich, 1997), 210.

119. Krebs to Orff, 1 Mar. 1943, CM, Allg. Korr. Also see entry for 20 Feb. 1943 in "Gertrud Orffs Tagebuch," CM.

120. *Carl Orff und sein Werk,* 8:360–63.

121. Ruppel to Orff, 3 June 1941, CM, Allg. Korr.

122. Kater, "Carl Orff im Dritten Reich," 20; entry for 17 Mar. 1944 in "Gertrud Orffs Tagebuch," CM.

123. Maier, *Carl Orff*, 9.

124. Jochen Peter Vogel, *Hans Pfitzner: Mit Selbstzeugnissen und Bilddokumenten* (Reinbek, 1986), 109; Strauss to von Niessen, 1 May 1935 (quote) and 11 June 1935, RG.

125. Orff to von Einem, 6 Dec. 1946 (1st quote); von Einem to Orff, 15 Oct. 1947 (2nd quote), CM, Allg. Korr.

126. Orff to von Einem, 22 Dec. 1947, CM, Allg. Korr.

127. Orff in *Carl Orff und sein Werk,* 5:219–33; ibid., 8:360–65; Prieberg, *NS-Staat,* 160; Hanau, "Carl Orff."

128. Orff in *Carl Orff und sein Werk,* 4:71, 195; Strecker to Hindemith, 12 Oct. 1940, PF, Schott Korr.; Orff to Hintze, 10 Nov. 1940, CM, Allg. Korr. Complicating the tangle of legends further, Hans-Günther Klein writes wrongly as late as 1984, that the Dresden staging was the first one after the Frankfurt premiere ("Viel Konformität und wenig Verweigerung: Zur Komposition neuer Opern, 1933–1944," in Hanns-Werner Heister and Klein, eds., *Musik und Musikpolitik im faschistischen Deutschland* [Frankfurt am Main, 1984], 155).

129. Orff to Lenssen, 9 Oct. 1940, CM, Allg. Korr.; Strecker to Orff, 9–10 Oct. 1940, CM, Schott Korr.; Ernst Krause's review in *ZM* 107 (1940), 722.

130. Orff to List, 11 Feb. 1941; Rosbaud to Orff, 15 June 1941; Rosenbusch to Orff, 14 July 1942; Bitter to Orff, 15 Aug. 1944, CM, Allg. Korr.; Strecker to Orff, 2 Nov. 1940 and 4 May 1943, CM, Schott Korr.; *ZM* 107 (1940), 802; *ZM* 108 (1941), 488; *ZM* 109 (1942), 161; *MK* 1 (1943), 107; *MK* 2 (1944), 105; Joan Evans, *Hans Rosbaud: A Bio-Bibliography* (New York, 1992), 36.

131. "Spielplan der Staatstheater," 31 Jan.–6 Feb., 7–13 Feb., 14–20 Feb., 28 Feb.–5 Mar. 1944, BH, Staatstheater/14395; *MK* 2 (1944), 63; Hans Wagner, *200 Jahre Münchner Theaterchronik, 1750–1950* (Munich, 1958), 161; Rudolf Hartmann, *Das geliebte Haus: Mein Leben mit der Oper* (Munich, 1975), 174.

132. Von Holthoff to Orff, 8 Jan. 1942; Orff to Pitz, 10 Jan. 1942; Tietjen to Orff, 28 Mar. 1942, CM, Allg. Korr.; Orff to Strecker, 24 Sept. 1942, CM, Schott Korr. (quote); Stege in *ZM* 109 (1942), 64.

133. See Kater, "Carl Orff im Dritten Reich," 32–33. Cf. the well-justified warning in Jens Malte Fischer, "Vergangenheit, die nicht vergehen will: Carl Orff und das Dritte Reich," *Süddeutsche Zeitung,* Munich, 14 Mar. 1995.

134. "I have absolutely no problem with calling *Carmina Burana* Nazi music" (Albrecht Riethmüller to author, 15 May 1997, APA); "aesthetics or not, *Carmina Burana* to me is fascist music" (Richard Taruskin in panel discussion at symposium, "The Politics of Music: Orff, Weill, and Brecht," coproduced by New York City Opera and Works and Process at the Guggenheim Museum, New York, 16 Mar. 1997).

135. Luise Rinser, *Saturn auf der Sonne* (Frankfurt am Main, 1994), 94.

136. Kater, *The Twisted Muse,* 177–239; idem, "Das Problem der musikalischen Moderne im NS-Staat."

137. Carl Niessen, ed., *Die deutsche Oper der Gegenwart* (Regensburg, 1944), 86.

138. Schuh to Orff, [14 Aug. 1941], CM, Allg. Korr.

139. Strecker to Orff, 1 Sept. 1943, CM, Schott Korr.

140. Baldur von Schirach, *Ich glaubte an Hitler* (Hamburg, 1967), 214; idem, "Die Sendung der Wiener Staatsoper," in *Das Programm der Staatsoper Wien,* no. 1 (1940–41), 1–3; Victor Junk, "Die 'Woche zeitgenössischer Musik in Wien,'" *ZM* 109 (1942), 241–47; Oscar Fritz Schuh, *So war es—war es so? Notizen und Erinnerungen eines Theatermannes* (Berlin, 1980), 64–65; Prieberg, *NS-Staat,* 333; Oliver Rathkolb, *Führertreu und gottbegnadet: Künstlereliten im Dritten Reich* (Vienna, 1991), 68–76; W. Th. Anderman [Walter Thomas], *Bis der Vorhang fiel: Berichtet nach Aufzeichnungen aus den Jahren 1940 bis 1945* (Dortmund, 1947), 151; Jonathan Petropoulos, *Art as Politics in the Third Reich* (Chapel Hill, N.C., 1996), 221–26; Hans Jörg Jans, "Von freundschaftlicher Zusammenarbeit in schwieriger Zeit: Exkurse," in Vana Greisenegger-Georgila and Jans, eds., *Was ist die Antike wert? Griechen und Römer auf der Bühne von Caspar Neher* (Vienna, 1995), 107 (quote); Kater, *The Twisted Muse,* 192–94.

141. Entries for 2 Apr., 2 July, 2 and 12–17 (quote) Oct. 1941 in "Gertrud Orffs Tagebuch," CM; Orff to Bergese, 18 Oct. 1941; Schuh to Orff, 19 Nov. 1941, CM, Allg. Korr.; Kater, *The Twisted Muse,* 193.

142. Orff to Tietjen, 14 Jan. 1942, CM, Allg. Korr.; Thomas, *Rad,* 210–11. This modifies my earlier version of events, in which I had written that Orff "accepted, as his first commission, the opera *Antigonae*" (Kater, "Carl Orff im Dritten Reich," 23). To avoid misunderstandings: The point is that Orff, not the Viennese, proposed the opera.

143. Der Reichsstatthalter in Wien, "Verträge mit den Komponisten Carl Orff und Rudolf Wagner-Régeny zur Förderung ihres künstlerischen Schaffens," sign. Orff and Thomas, Vienna, 27 Mar. 1942, OSW, OBlhV/1200a. I owe my knowledge of this doc. to the director of the CM.

144. Signed transcript of interview with Gertrud Orff, Munich, 5 Aug. 1992, APA; *MK* 2 (1944), 116. *Antigonae* was directed by Schuh at the Wiener Staatsoper in 1949 (Schuh, *So war es,* 108).

145. Signed transcript of interview with Gertrud Orff, Munich, 5 Aug. 1992, APA.

146. Orff to Bergese, 23 May 1942, PA Bergese (quote); entries for 5 Feb., 3 Mar. 1942, 2–11 Apr. 1943 in "Gertrud Orffs Tagebuch," CM; Gertrud Orff to author, Munich, 22 June 1994, APA; Orff to Ludwig, 10 Feb. 1942, and to [Ruppel?], and to Sutermeister, both 8 Mar. 1942; Strauss to Orff, [Spring 1942]; Würth to Orff, 9 Mar. 1943, CM, Allg. Korr.; Orff to Strauss, 10 Feb. 1942, RG; Strecker to Orff, 12 Feb. 1942; Orff to Strecker, 23 Apr. 1943, CM, Schott Korr.; program of Staatsoper Wien for 17 Feb. 1942, facsimile in Seebohm, "Vergangenheit," 146; Victor Junk's review in *ZM* 109 (1942), 117–18.

147. Strecker to Orff, 23 Sept., 23 Oct., and 3 Dec. 1943, CM, Schott Korr.; *MK* 1 (1944), 198.

148. Orff to Sutermeister, 16 Oct. 1938, and Lenssen, 29 Oct. 1939, and Liebeneiner, 14 Aug. 1941, and Schuh, 28 Aug. 1941; Krauss to Menge, 4 June 1938; Kraus to Orff, 18 May 1940; Hoffmann to Orff, 15 Nov. 1940; Ruppel to Orff, 9 July 1941; Dollinger to Orff, 5 Mar. 1944, CM, Allg. Korr.; Orff to Willms, 7 Feb. 1939, CM, Schott Korr.; *ZM* 107 (1940), 796.

149. *MK* 2 (1944), 226 (quote). See also Wiek to Orff, 16 July 1944, CM, Allg. Korr.; Willy Werner Götting in *ZM* 110 (1943), 136–37; *MK* 1 (1944), 188; Paul Hirth in *MK* 2 (1944), 25; W. M. Luther in *MK* 2 (1944), 153; entry for 20 Feb. 1943 in "Gertrud Orffs Tagebuch," CM; Slonimsky, *Music,* 766; Mohr, *Frankfurter Oper,* 394–95.

150. "Betr.: Verwendung des Staatszuschusses zur Verteilung an Komponisten ernster Musik," Berlin, 4 July 1942, BAB Werner Egk. On the Nazi qualifications of Knab and Fortner see Kater, *The Twisted Muse,* 140, 160, 163, 167–71, 173–74, 183, 239.

151. NSDAP, Ortsgruppe München-Marsplatz, "Ausführliches Gesamturteil," 30 June 1942, BAB Carl Orff.

152. Ellis, "Music," 133.

153. Orff to Strecker, 22 May 1941, CM, Schott Korr.; Pietzsch to Orff, 31 May 1941, CM, Allg. Korr. (quote).

154. ["To Whom It May Concern"], sign. Raabe, Berlin, 20 Feb. 1942, CM, Allg. Korr.

155. Orff to Strecker, 26 May 1943, CM, Schott Korr.

156. Aulich to Orff, 23 July and 23 Oct. 1943, CM, Allg. Korr.; Scherping to Reichsminister [Goebbels], 25 Apr. 1944, BA, R55/559.

157. As told by Orff to composer von Einem (Gottfried von Einem, recorded interview, Vienna, 30 Nov. 1994, APA).

158. Deutsche Wochenschau G.m.b.H. to Orff, 7 June 1944; Theater am Nollendorfplatz to Orff, 17 July 1944, CM, Allg. Korr. On Goebbels's interest in the production of newsreels see Michael H. Kater, "Film as an Object of Reflection in The Goebbels Diaries: Series II," to be published in *Central European History.*

159. Entry for 26 Aug. 1944 in *TGII* 13:333; entry for 30 Aug. 1944 in "Gertrud Orffs Tagebuch," CM; Rathkolb, *Führertreu,* 176.

160. Entry for 12 Sept. 1944 in *TGII,* 13:466.

161. Hinkel to Orff, 15 Nov. 1944, CM, Allg. Korr.

162. Enclosure with Orff to Hinkel, Dec. 1944, CM, Allg. Korr.

163. Entry for 10 May 1943 in *TGII* 8:264, 12 Nov. and 2 Dec. 1944 in *TGII* 14:206, 331–32, and 4 Jan. 1945 in *TGII* 15:65; see Orff to Strecker, 21 June 1938, CM, Schott Korr. On Gründgens, see Curt Riess, *Gustaf Gründgens: Eine Biographie* (Hamburg, 1965), 228–38.

164. Diehm to Orff, 21 Nov. 1945, CM, Allg. Korr.

165. Heinz Trojan and Kurt Hinze, *Beschäftigungsverbot, Vermögenssperre und Sühnemassnahmen nach dem Gesetz zur Befreiung von Nationalsozialismus und Militarismus vom 5. März 1946: Kommentar für die Praxis* (Wiesbaden, 1947); Hajo Holborn, *American Military Government: Its Organization and Politics* (Washington, D.C., 1947), 53–73; Harold Zink, *American Military Government in Germany* (New York, 1947), 92; Lutz Niethammer, *Entnazifizierung in Bayern: Säuberung und Rehabilitierung unter amerikanischer Besatzung* (Frankfurt am Main, 1972), 150–259.

166. Rischner to Orff, 2 Dec. 1945; Goetz to Orff, 3 Dec. 1945; Orff to Wilm, 7 Dec. 1945, to Jochum, 7 Dec. 1945, to Rischner, 9 Dec. 1945, and to Goetz, 28 Dec. 1945, CM, Allg. Korr.

167. Newell Jenkins, recorded interview, Hillsdale, N.Y., 20 Mar. 1993, APA; Orff to Dubs, 10 June 1938; Jenkins to Orff, 11 Sept. 1939 (quote), and 4 Nov. 1939, CM, Allg. Korr. Also see *Who's Who in American Music: Classical* (New York, 1985), 290; Nicolas Slonimsky, ed., *Baker's Biographical Dictionary of Music and Musicians,* 8th ed. (New York, 1992), 849–50; NG 9:598.

168. Newell Jenkins, recorded interview, Hillsdale, N.Y., 20 Mar. 1993, APA; Ulrich M. Bausch, *Die Kulturpolitik der US-amerikanischen Information Control Division in Württemberg-Baden von 1945 bis 1949: Zwischen militärischem Funktionalismus und schwäbischem Obrigkeitsdenken* (Stuttgart, 1992), 118–38; less re-

liably: Thomas Steiert, "Zur Musik- und Theaterpolitik in Stuttgart während der amerikanischen Besatzungszeit," in Gabriele Clemens, ed., *Kulturpolitik im besetzten Deutschland, 1945–1949* (Stuttgart, 1994), 55–59.

169. Newell Jenkins, recorded interview, Hillsdale, N.Y., 20 Mar. 1993, APA; entry for 24 Dec. 1945 in "Gertrud Orffs Tagebuch," CM; signed transcript of interview with Gertrud Orff, Munich, 5 Aug. 1992, APA; Brigitte Bergese to author, Leukerbad, 4 Oct. 1995, APA.

170. Jenkins to Orff, 7 Jan. 1946, CM, Allg. Korr.

171. Non-recorded interviews with Liselotte Orff, Diessen am Ammersee, 18 June 1992, and Werner Thomas (Heidelberg), Munich, 22 July 1992.

172. Newell Jenkins, recorded interview, Hillsdale, N.Y., 20 Mar. 1993, APA. This was corroborated in a recorded interview Professor David Monod of Wilfrid Laurier University (Waterloo, Canada) conducted with Jenkins in Hillsdale, N.Y., on 6 July 1996. I am grateful to David Monod for making the complete transcript of this interview available to me.

173. Werner Thomas, "Ein anderer 'Carl Orff im Dritten Reich': Eine Replik auf Michael H. Katers Studie 'Carl Orff im Dritten Reich,'" paper, International Colloquium, "Zur Situation der Musik in Nazi-Deutschland in den dreissiger und vierziger Jahren," at Carl-Orff-Zentrum, Munich, 23 Nov. 1994. This had followed my paper, "Selbstgleichschaltung oder Widerstand: Carl Orff im Dritten Reich," a slightly modified version of which was later published as "Carl Orff im Dritten Reich."

174. Sutermeister to Orff, 15 Dec. 1946, CM, Allg. Korr.

175. Renatus Wilms in *Frankfurter Allgemeine Zeitung,* 15 July 1995.

176. Confidential, Information Control Division, ICD Screening Center, Det.H-86, 2nd Mi.Govt.Bn. (Sep), APO 633, U.S. Army, to Chief, Intelligence Section, Office of Director of Information Control, Military Government for Germany (U.S. Zone), APO 742, US ARMY, 1 Apr. 1946, David M. Levy Papers, Department of Psychiatry, Cornell University, Medical College, New York. A transcribed copy of the report is deposited in CM and has been made available to me by its director.

177. Oliver Rathkolb, "Carl Orff und die Bernauerin: Zeithistorischer Rahmen zur Entstehungsgeschichte, 1942–1947," in program guide, "Volksoper Wien, Saison 1997/98," ed. Klaus Bachler (Vienna, Dec. 1997), 20–21.

178. Jenkins in interview with Monod, 6 July 1996, see n. 172. Similarly in Newell Jenkins, recorded interview, Hillsdale, N.Y., 20 Mar. 1993, APA.

179. As in n. 176.

180. Jenkins in interview with Monod, 6 July 1996, see n. 172.

181. Newell Jenkins, recorded interview, Hillsdale, N.Y., 20 Mar. 1993, APA; entry for 19 Jan. and 5 Mar. 1946 in "Gertrud Orffs Tagebuch," CM; Isenstead to Orff, 28 Feb. 1946; Jenkins to Orff, 26 Mar. and 26 Nov. 1946; Preussner to Orff, 26 July 1946; Ley to Orff, 13 May 1947, CM, Allg. Korr.; Evarts to Bauckner, 16 July 1946, BH, Staatstheater/14395; Orff in *Carl Orff und sein Werk,* 8:363; Slonimsky, *Music,* 837.

182. Maier's phrase encapsulates the white-washing efforts of Orff defenders after World War II, especially of the CM and the Orff Foundation, through denial and obfuscation (*Carl Orff,* 11).

183. Orff in *Carl Orff und sein Werk,* 2:126, 207; Karl Marx in Leuchtmann, *Orff,* 101.

184. Orff to Georgiades, 12 Dec. 1935; Bergese to Orff, 5 Dec. 1937 and 6 Apr. 1938, CM, Allg. Korr.; Bergese to Petschull, 5 Apr. 1938, CM, Schott Korr.; Maria

Bruckbauer, ". . . Und sei es gegen eine Welt von Feinden!" Kurt Hubers Volks-
liedsammlung und -pflege in Bayern (Munich, 1991), 86–87, 141.

185. Clara Huber to author, Munich, 30 Sept. 1993, APA.

186. Corr. for 1935–36 in SM, Kulturamt/480, quote from "Denkschrift zur
Neugründung und Angliederung der Deutschen Schule für Volksmusik und Tanz am
Trapp'schen Konservatorium der Musik," [1935].

187. Kurt Huber, "Der Aufbau deutscher Volksliedforschung und Volks-
liedpflege," in Deutsche Musikkultur 1 (1936), 65–73, quotes 66, 68–69. Also see
Bruckbauer, Welt, passim. On Huber's exploits in Nazi musicology, see Pamela M.
Potter, Most German of the Arts: Musicology and Society from the Weimar Republic to the End of Hitler's Reich (New Haven, Conn., 1998), passim.

188. Entries for 9 Feb., 13 Apr., 28 Aug., 18 Nov., 30 Dec. 1941; 1 and 16 Mar.,
24 Aug. 1942, in "Gertrud Orffs Tagebuch," CM; Bergese to Orff, 23 Dec. 1940
and 25 Feb. 1942; Orff to Jarosch, 22 Mar. 1942, CM, Allg. Korr.; Strecker to Orff,
10 Mar. and 7 Aug. 1941, CM, Schott Korr.; Bruckbauer, Welt, 204.

189. Entry for 24 Sept. 1942 in "Gertrud Orffs Tagebuch," CM; Christian Petry,
Studenten aufs Schafott: Die Weisse Rose und ihr Scheitern (Munich, 1968), esp.
92; Hans-Günter Richardi, "Kurt Huber und Alexander Schmorell vor dem
Henker," Süddeutsche Zeitung, Munich, 13 July 1993.

190. Gertrud Orff to author, Munich, 12 Nov. 1993, APA; Clara Huber to author, Munich, 30 Sept. 1993, APA.

191. Documentary film, "O Fortuna: Carl Orff," produced by Tony Palmer,
Bayerischer Rundfunk/Ladbroke Productions (1995).

192. Clara Huber ibid.; Orff as quoted in Bert Wassener, "Carl Orff: 'Jeder muss
seinen eigenen Weg gehen,'" Westfalenpost, 8 Oct. 1960; George J. Wittenstein's
quote from his letter to author, Santa Barbara, CA, 21 Oct. 1997, APA. See also
Petry, Studenten aufs Schafott, 42.

193. Gertrud Orff to author, Munich, 7 and 12 Nov. 1993, APA; signed transcript of interview with Gertrud Orff, Munich, 5 Aug. 1992, APA.

194. Footage in documentary film, "O Fortuna: Carl Orff," produced by Tony
Palmer, Bayerischer Rundfunk/Ladbroke Productions (1995).

195. Dibelius, Musik, 79; Hugo Wolfram Schmidt, Carl Orff: Sein Leben und
sein Werk in Wort, Bild und Noten (Cologne, 1971), 8; K. Langrock in GLM
6:135. For other variants and simplifications, see Werner Thomas in Wilibald
Gurlitt, ed., Riemann Musik Lexikon, 12th ed., 3 vols. (Mainz, 1959–67), 2:345;
Fred K. Prieberg, Lexikon der Neuen Musik (Freiburg im Breisgau, 1958), 322;
Gersdorf, Orff, 87; Martin Konz in Neue Musikzeitung, no. 2 (1975), 3.

196. Orff in Carl Orff und sein Werk, 4:66.

197. Ibid.

198. See "Gesamtchronologie der Werk- und Wirkungsgeschichte," in Carl Orff
und sein Werk, 8:360–66; and the following: Orff to Kurzbach, 20 Jan. 1940, and
to Lenssen, 9 Oct. 1940, and to Lehmann, 24 Oct. 1940; Böhm to Orff, 7 June
1939; Pietzsch to Orff, 16 Jan. 1940; Jochum to Orff, 6 June 1940 and 2 Apr. 1942,
CM, Allg. Korr.; Orff to Strecker, 18 Feb. 1938 and 24 Sept. 1942; Strecker to Orff,
31 Oct. and 19 Dec. 1939; Willms to Orff, 16 Mar. 1940, CM, Schott Korr.;
Strecker to Hindemith, 12 Oct. 1940, PF, Schott Korr.; "Städtische Philharmonische
Konzerte [München] 1941–2: Mozart-Reihe," SM, Kulturamt/177; ZM 107
(1940), 374, 721–22; ZM 108 (1941), 49, 123; ZM 109 (1942), 558; MK 1 (1943),
107, 117, 148; MK 2 (1944), 25; Frankfurter Zeitung, 22 Feb. 1943; Reich, 9 Mar.
1941; Carl Orff und sein Werk, 5:209.

199. *Melos* 14 (1947), 90, 266, 307, 350.

200. Rinser's statement in documentary film, "O Fortuna: Carl Orff," produced by Tony Palmer, Bayerischer Rundfunk/Ladbroke Productions (1995); Rinser, *Saturn*, 88–89 (Hartmann quoted 96); Godela Orff, *Vater*, 55, 84; Bergese to Orff, 9 May 1948, PA Bergese. In a letter to author, Berlin, 19 Oct. 1995, APA, Bergese wrote: "Orff usurped everyone, who, he felt, could be of use to him."

201. Orff according to Huber in documentary film, "O Fortuna: Carl Orff," produced by Tony Palmer, Bayerischer Rundfunk/Ladbroke Productions (1995); Bergese to author, Berlin, 19 Oct. 1995, APA; Godela Orff, *Vater*, 84.

202. Newell Jenkins, recorded interview, Hillsdale, N.Y., 20 Mar. 1993, APA; also see Orff to Strecker (2 Aug. 1938, CM, Schott Korr.): "Through my American friends and students I have made several connections 'over there.'"

203. Newell Jenkins, recorded interview, Hillsdale, N.Y., 20 Mar. 1993, APA. On the Bavarian quality of Orff's oeuvre, see Ruppel, "Carl Orff und das Theater," [1947], CM, Allg. Korr.; Liess, *Orff*, 79; Thomas, *Rad*, 167–77.

204. Orff to Mein Lieber [Jenkins], 4 May 1947, CM, Allg. Korr.

205. Orff to Lieber Freund, 17 June 1947, and to Meyer, 26 Sept. 1948, CM, Allg. Korr. Jenkins wrote to me on 14 Nov. 1993 (letter APA), that he could not recall the specifics of their disagreement, only that "there *was* a cloud over our relationship at the end."

206. Rinser, *Saturn*, 131.

207. *JdM 1944*, 129; Hartmann, *Haus*, 149–50.

208. Orff to Krauss, 6 Feb. 1939, CM, Schott Korr.; Orff to Strecker, 25 Jan. 1939 and to Willms, 7 Feb. 1939, CM, Schott Korr. Also see Carl Orff, "Erinnerung an Caspar Neher," in Greisenegger-Georgila and Jans, *Was ist die Antike wert?*, 85.

209. Orff to Strecker, 23 Sept. 1942, CM, Schott Korr.; [Frau] Hansi Meissner to Orff, 15 June and 16 July 1946; Meissner to Orff, 1 July 1947, CM, Allg. Korr.

210. Orff to Lieber Freund, 17 June 1946, CM, Allg. Korr.; Orff in *Carl Orff und sein Werk*, 6:170. See Godela Orff's interpretation in *Vater*, 67.

211. Orff to Bergese, 15 July 1941, CM, Allg. Korr.; Schott's Söhne to Bergese, 28 July 1941; Bergese to Orff, 9 May 1948, PA Bergese; *JdM 1943*, 48–49; Orff in *Carl Orff und sein Werk*, 2:126; Bergese to author, Berlin, 30 Aug. 1995 and 11 Mar. 1996, APA; Carl Orff and Kurt Huber, *Musik der Landschaft: Volksmusik in neuen Sätzen: Aus dem Bajuwarischen Raum: Lieder und Tänze für Klavier von Hans Bergese*, Schott Edition Nr. 3569 (Mainz, 1942); Orff and Huber, *Musik der Landschaft: Volksmusik in neuen Sätzen: Aus dem Bajuwarischen Raum: Zwiefache Tänze für Klavier von Hans Bergese*, Schott Edition Nr. 3570 (Mainz, 1942).

212. Godela Orff, *Vater*, 20–22; her testimony in documentary film, "O Fortuna: Carl Orff," produced by Tony Palmer, Bayerischer Rundfunk/Ladbroke Productions (1995).

213. Godela Orff, *Vater*, 62; quotation Orff to Weidner, 17 Nov. 1943, CM, Allg. Korr.

214. Godela Orff, *Vater*, 53, 59, 62, 67–70; Heinrich Strobel, "Orffische Zwiesprach: Zur Uraufführung der 'Bernauerin,'" *Melos* 14 (1947), 297–99; Orff in *Carl Orff und sein Werk*, 6:169–70.

215. Rinser, *Saturn*, 122–23.

216. Godela Orff's testimony in documentary film, "O Fortuna: Carl Orff," produced by Tony Palmer, Bayerischer Rundfunk/Ladbroke Productions (1995); idem,

Vater, 15, 29, 45. Also see Orff's salacious remarks about the girls in *Carl Orff und sein Werk,* 3:114.

217. Newell Jenkins, recorded interview, Hillsdale, N.Y., 20 Mar. 1993, APA.; Bergese to Orff, 6 May 1941, CM, Allg. Korr.

218. H.-G. Schnell, Rinser's first husband, fell in 1943 on the Eastern front as member of a punitive batallion. See Günther Albrecht et al., *Lexikon deutschsprachiger Schriftsteller von den Anfängen bis zur Gegenwart,* 2 vols. (Leipzig, 1974), 2:221. Also Luise Rinser, *Gefängnistagebuch* (Frankfurt am Main, 1973); Rinser, *Saturn,* 87–99; Brigitte Bergese to author, Leukerbad, 4 Oct. 1995, and Berlin, 7 Mar. 1996, APA; Hans Bergese to author, Berlin, 30 Aug. 1995, APA. The relationship is corroborated in Jenkins's interview by Monod, 6 July 1996, see n. 172.

219. Peter C. Whybrow, *A Mood Apart: Depression, Mania, and Other Afflictions of the Self* (New York, 1997); Ronald R. Fieve, *Moodswing: The Third Revolution in Psychiatry* (New York, 1976); George Winokur and Ming T. Tsuang, *The Natural History of Mania, Depression, and Schizophrenia* (Washington, D.C., 1996); Edward L. Shorter, *A History of Psychiatry: From the Era of the Asylum to the Age of Prozac* (New York, 1997).

220. Testimonies of Rinser, Godela Orff, and Liselotte Orff in documentary film, "O Fortuna: Carl Orff," produced by Tony Palmer, Bayerischer Rundfunk/Ladbroke Productions (1995); Rinser, *Saturn,* 86–131. For the Weimar Republic, see Godela Orff, *Vater,* 23.

221. Newell Jenkins, recorded interview, Hillsdale, N.Y., 20 Mar. 1993, APA; Orff to Katz, 2 Aug. 1933; Katz to Orff, 22 July 1933; Kohrs to Orff, [Fall 1938], CM, Allg. Korr.; *IBD,* 600; Eckhard John, *Musikbolschewismus: Die Politisierung der Musik in Deutschland, 1918–1938* (Stuttgart, 1994), 324–35.

222. Kater, "Carl Orff im Dritten Reich," 30–31. After Jan. 1933, Orff's corr. with two other former Jewish friends, Max Sinzheimer and Karl Salomon, is also either sparse or noncommittal (CM, Allg. Korr.).

223. Whybrow, *A Mood Apart,* 11.

224. Luise Rinser's testimony in documentary film, "O Fortuna: Carl Orff," produced by Tony Palmer, Bayerischer Rundfunk/Ladbroke Productions (1995).

225. [Ms.] Jaeger to Orff, 12 Sept. 1973; Orff to [the deceased] Katz, 25 Sept. 1973, CM, Allg. Korr.

226. Elisabeth Hartmann, recorded interview, Munich, 13 Dec. 1994, APA; letter by Orff of Dec. 1963 [to the deceased Hartmann] printed in *Karl Amadeus Hartmann und die Musica Viva: Essays, bisher unveröffentlichte Briefe an Hartmann, Katalog* (Munich, 1980), 94. Also see text near n. 132, chapter 4.

227. Carl Orff, "Brief an Kurt Huber," 19 Jan. 1946, CM, Allg. Korr. The letter has been published in Clara Huber, ed., *Kurt Huber zum Gedächtnis: Bildnis eines Menschen, Denkers und Forschers, dargestellt von seinen Freunden* (Regensburg, 1947), 166–68.

CHAPTER 6: PFITZNER

1. Albert Innaurato, "A Haunting Opera Made of Cranky Obsessions," *New York Times,* 20 July 1997.

2. Alex Ross, "The Devil's Disciple: A Composer who Embraced the Third Reich Gets a New Hearing," *New Yorker* (21 July 1997), 72.

3. Bernard Holland, "Palestrina's Polyphony: Beautiful as Well as Pious," *New York Times,* 24 July 1997.

4. James R. Oestreich, "Maestros Serving Other Masters," ibid., 20 July 1997 (1st quote); Paul Griffiths, "Gifted but Obtuse: Pfitzner's Odd Lot," ibid., 25 July 1997 (2nd quote).

5. Gerald Abraham, *The Concise Oxford History of Music* (Oxford, 1986), 794, 798.

6. Author's telephone conversation with Gottfried von Einem, Munich-Vienna, 30 Nov. 1994, and Hans Hotter, Munich, 14 Dec. 1994; Hans Hotter, *"Der Mai war mir gewogen . . .": Erinnerungen* (Munich, 1996), 56, also 84–89, 97; ZM 109 (1942), 182.

7. Ney to Hoogstraten, 7 July 1933, EB, 0.6.

8. Abendroth to Pfitzner, 18 Oct. 1940, OW, 288.

9. W. Th. Anderman [Walter Thomas], *Bis der Vorhang fiel: Berichtet nach Aufzeichnungen aus den Jahren 1940 bis 1945* (Dortmund, 1947), 244.

10. Johann Peter Vogel, *Hans Pfitzner: Mit Selbstzeugnissen und Bilddokumenten* (Reinbek, 1989), 86.

11. Ibid., 8–99; Pfitzner to Reichsminister [Goebbels], 11 Apr. 1938, OW, 300; NG 14:612; Joseph Maria Müller-Blattau, *Hans Pfitzner* (Potsdam, 1940), 87; John Williamson, *The Music of Hans Pfitzner* (Oxford, 1992), 6.

12. Vogel, *Pfitzner,* 39.

13. NG 14:612–14 (1st quote 613); Mann to Amann, 30 June 1917, in Thomas Mann, *Briefe, 1889–1936,* ed. Erika Mann (Frankfurt am Main, 1961), 139 (2nd and 3rd quotes); Pfitzner to Rode, 29 Aug. 1932, BAB Pfitzner (last quote); Matthes to Pfitzner, 23 Dec. 1932, OW, 299; Müller-Blattau, *Pfitzner,* 88; Max Strub in Elly Ney, *Erinnerungen und Betrachtungen: Mein Leben aus der Musik,* 4th ed. (Aschaffenburg, 1957), 165; Vogel, *Pfitzner,* 93; Williamson, *Music,* 7, 12, 18, 254–55, 281.

14. Pfitzner to Fürstner, 24 Oct. 1932, MMP.

15. Pfitzner to Lilo [Martin], 6 June 1935, SMM, 20.

16. Williamson, *Music,* 259 (quote), 277, 280.

17. Winfried Zillig, *Von Wagner bis Strauss: Wegbereiter der Neuen Musik* (Munich, 1966), 155–56; NG 14:614.

18. Karl Wörner, "Hans Pfitzners Sinfonie in cis," *Melos* 12 (1933), 134.

19. Alexander L. Ringer, *Arnold Schoenberg: The Composer as Jew* (Oxford, 1990), 19; Constantin Floros, "Die Wiener Schule und das Problem der 'deutschen Musik,'" in Otto Kolleritsch, ed., *Die Wiener Schule und das Hakenkreuz: Das Schicksal der Moderne im gesellschaftlichen Kontext des 20. Jahrhunderts* (Vienna, 1990), 42.

20. Pfitzner to Scherchen, 23 Nov. 1920, BS, Autograph Pfitzner.

21. Pfitzner to Abendroth, 16 Nov. 1941, OW, 288; Ludwig Schrott, *Die Persönlichkeit Hans Pfitzners* (Zurich, 1959), 130–31.

22. Hindemith to Pfitzner, 18 Aug., 9 and 25 Sept., 30 Dec. 1925 (quote), 12 Jan. 1926, OW, 80; Pfitzner to Hindemith, 12 Sept. and [28?] Dec. 1925, 2 Jan. 1926, OW, 453; Andres Briner et al., *Paul Hindemith: Leben und Werk in Bild und Text* (Mainz, 1988), 113.

23. "Mitgliederverzeichnis des Hans Pfitzner-Vereins für deutsche Tonkunst," [Munich, n.d.], MMP; Walter Abendroth, "Hans Pfitzner, der Deutsche," *DM* 26 (1934), 561–65 (quote); Friedrich W. Herzog, "Hans Pfitzner in unserer Zeit," *DM* 31 (1939), 505–9; Mann to Pringsheim, 6 Nov. 1917, in Mann, *Briefe 1889–1936,* 141; Müller-Blattau, *Pfitzner,* 65, 82–83; Vogel, *Pfitzner,* 77–79.

24. Graf Westarp to Pfitzner, 26 Feb. 1932, OW, 299; Müller-Blattau, *Pfitzner,* 88; Schrott, *Persönlichkeit,* 23; Bernhard Adamy, *Hans Pfitzner: Literatur, Philosophie und Zeitgeschehen in seinem Weltbild und Werk* (Tutzing, 1980), 276; Williamson, *Music,* 22. For the broader ideological and political background, see Kurt Sontheimer, *Antidemokratisches Denken in der Weimarer Republik: Die politischen Ideen des deutschen Nationalismus zwischen 1918 und 1933,* 4th ed. (Munich, 1964); George L. Mosse, *The Crisis of German Ideology: Intellectual Origins of the Third Reich* (New York, 1964).

25. Hans Pfitzner, *Gesammelte Schriften,* 3 vols. (Augsburg, 1926–29); Pfitzner to Brockhaus, 24 Apr. 1927, MMP; Matthes to Pfitzner, 19 Apr. 1932, OW, 299; Pfitzner to Klein, 30 Apr. 1932, BAB Wilhelm Matthes; Herzog, "Pfitzner," 510; Müller-Blattau, *Pfitzner,* 78–79; Otto Klemperer, *Meine Erinnerungen an Gustav Mahler und andere autobiographische Skizzen* (Freiburg im Breisgau, 1960), 38; Adamy, *Pfitzner,* 279–81, 298; Eckhard John, *Musikbolschewismus: Die Politisierung der Musik in Deutschland, 1918–1938* (Stuttgart, 1994), 58–64.

26. Mann to Pfitzner, 19 May 1917, in Mann, *Briefe, 1889–1936,* 136.

27. Pfitzner, *Schriften,* 2, esp. 107–11, 244–49 (quote 244); Abendroth, "Pfitzner," 562; Herzog, "Pfitzner," 506; Müller-Blattau, *Pfitzner,* 78–81; John, *Musikbolschewismus,* 58–64.

28. Hans Pfitzner, *Die neue Aesthetik der musikalischen Impotenz: Ein Verwesungssymptom?* (Munich, 1920); Paul Bekker, *Beethoven* (Berlin, 1912); "Mitgliederverzeichnis des Hans Pfitzner-Vereins für deutsche Tonkunst," [Munich, n.d.], MMP; Pfitzner to Klein, 30 Apr. 1932, BAB Wilhelm Matthes; Müller-Blattau, *Pfitzner,* 66; Michael Karbaum, *Studien zur Geschichte der Bayreuther Festspiele (1876–1976): Teil I: Textteil* (Regensburg, 1976), 71; Peter Heyworth, *Otto Klemperer: His Life and Times,* 2 vols. (Cambridge, 1983, 1996), 1:107–10.

29. Hans Pfitzner, *Futuristengefahr: Bei Gelegenheit von Busoni's Ästhetik* (Leipzig, 1917); Williamson, *Music,* 15–16; Vogel, *Pfitzner,* 79; Michael H. Kater, *The Twisted Muse: Musicians and Their Music in the Third Reich* (New York, 1997), 115, 213. On Jewish self-hatred, see Peter Loewenberg, "Antisemitismus und jüdischer Selbsthass: Eine sich wechselseitig verstärkende sozialpsychologische Doppelbeziehung," *Geschichte und Gesellschaft* 5 (1979), 455–75; Sander L. Gilman, *Jewish Self-Hatred: Anti-Semitism and the Hidden Language of the Jews* (Baltimore, 1986); in connection with Cossmann: Peter Gay, *Freud, Jews, and Other Germans: Masters and Victims in Modernist Culture* (Oxford, 1979), 156–57.

30. See Adamy, *Pfitzner,* 301.

31. See the biographies of Pfitzner by Abendroth, Adamy, Müller-Blattau, and Vogel mentioned above, as well as Pfitzner's profuse corr., 1900–33, OW.

32. The most authentic description of the meeting is that from Pfitzner's own hand: notebook, [1946–47], OW, 331 (quote). A watered-down version of this was supplied to the composer's friend Abendroth and used for his biography (*Pfitzner,* 252); Pfitzner to Abendroth, 1 Nov. 1933 and 11 Apr. 1934, OW, 289; Schrott, *Persönlichkeit,* 60–61. The part about the rabbi surfaced later, and probably never known to Pfitzner, but paraphrased by Rosenberg and members of his entourage. See Herzog to Grohe, 16 July 1947, AM, Pfitzner; Schrott, *Persönlichkeit,* 62. Also see Gay, *Freud,* 195–96; Gilman, *Jewish Self-Hatred,* 244–48, 293–94; Jacques Le Rider, *Der Fall Otto Weininger: Wurzeln des Antifeminismus und Antisemitismus* (Vienna, 1985); Chaudak Sengoopta, "The Unknown Weininger: Science, Philosophy, and Cultural Politics in Fin-de-Siècle Vienna," *Central European History* 29 (1996), 453–93.

33. Abendroth, *Pfitzner*, 252.

34. The original may be examined in BS, 8 L.impr.c.n.mss.229.

35. Pfitzner to Hitler, [1 Apr. 1924—not mailed], BS, Autograph Pfitzner; Adamy, *Pfitzner*, 301.

36. Michael H. Kater, "The Revenge of the Fathers: The Demise of Modern Music at the End of the Weimar Republic," *German Studies Review* 15 (1992), 295–315.

37. Pfitzner to Brockhaus, 26 Oct. 1922, 24 Nov. 1923, and 14 Aug. 1924, MMP; Pfitzner to Hartmann, 29 Apr. 1927, OW, 297; Pfitzner to Zwissler, 14 Jan. 1929, OW, 283; Mann to Pfitzner, 23 June 1925, OW, 80.

38. Pfitzner to Brockhaus, 24 Nov. 1923, and to Oertel, 21 Aug. 1926 and 2 Nov. 1927, MMP; Brockhaus to Pfitzner, 8 Feb. 1924; Braunfels to Pfitzner, 26 Oct. 1927, MMP. Also see Gerald D. Feldman, *The Great Disorder: Politics, Economics, and Society in the German Inflation, 1914–1924* (New York, 1997), 631–835.

39. Pfitzner to Reinhart, 1 Jan. 1933, in Peter Sulzer, *Zehn Komponisten um Werner Reinhart*, 3 vols. (Zurich, 1983), 3:301.

40. [Oertel memorandum], 23 Feb. 1929; Blech to Fürstner, 7 June 1929; Tietjen to Pfitzner, 15 July 1929; Hörth to Pfitzner, 15 July 1929; [Oertel minutes], 11 Sept. 1929; [Oertel minutes], 30 Oct. 1929, MMP; Pfitzner to Oertel, 18 May, 9 July, and 28 Aug. 1929, and to Fürstner, 15 and 18 July 1929, and to Blech, 2 July 1929, and to Holy, 10 July 1929, MMP.

41. Williamson, *Music*, 303.

42. Fürstner to Pfitzner, 27 Mar. 1930, 16 and 21 Nov. 1931, 3 and 18 June 1932, 4 Oct. 1932, MMP; Pfitzner to Fürstner, 21 Nov. 1930, 14 Feb. 1931, 6 and 17 June 1932, and to Oertel, 14 Dec. 1931, 11 Feb. 1932, MMP; *Münchener Neueste Nachrichten*, 28 Mar. 1931; Goldenberger to Staatliche Akademie der Tonkunst, 4 May 1929, in Gabriele Busch-Salmen and Günther Weiss, eds., *Hans Pfitzner: Münchner Dokumente/Bilder und Bildnisse* (Regensburg, 1990), 36; Williamson, *Music*, 317–18.

43. Pfitzner to Knappertsbusch, 3 June 1931, OW, 300; Pfitzner to Franckenstein, 3 Apr. 1932, OW, 282; Knappertsbusch to Pfitzner, 9 June 1931; Franckenstein to Pfitzner, 7 Feb. 1934, OW, 297; Pfitzner to Fürstner, 18 July 1929, MMP (quote); Pfitzner-Franckenstein corr., etc. (1932), BH, MK/44737; *NG* 14:614; Williamson, *Music*, 334; Kater, *The Twisted Muse*, 40–41.

44. This sentiment is articulated by his biographer Erich Valentin, *Hans Pfitzner: Werk und Gestalt eines Deutschen* (Regensburg, 1939), 65.

45. Walter Abendroth, "Gegen Pfitzner-Boykott," *DKW*, no. 7 (1933), 15–16; Reinhold Conrad Muschler, "Schöpferische deutsche Kunst: Zu Pfitzners 'Christelflein,'" ibid., no. 36 (1933), 7–8; KfdK Westmark to Pfitzner, 22 June 1933; KfdK Gera, program for Pfitzner concert, 2 Oct. [1933], OW, 64.

46. Pfitzner-Spiegel-Rosenberg corr. (Apr.–May 1933), OW, 64.

47. *Berliner Tageblatt*, 28 July 1933; Pfitzner to Hinkel, 26 July 1933; Hinkel to Pfitzner, 28 July 1933, BAB Pfitzner; Pfitzner to Fürstner, 31 July 1933; Geissmar to Meister [Pfitzner], 12 Aug. 1933, MMP; Fiehler to Pfitzner, 1 Aug. 1933; Pfitzner to Fiehler, 3 Aug. 1933; N.N. to Fiehler, [?] Aug. 1933, OW, 218; Junk to Pfitzner, 3 Aug. 1933, in Elisabeth Wamlek-Junk, ed., *Hans Pfitzner und Wien: Sein Briefwechsel mit Victor Junk und andere Dokumente* (Tutzing, 1986), 102–3; Kater, *The Twisted Muse*, 29.

48. Pfitzner-Knappertsbusch-Franckenstein corr. (Feb.–May 1933), OW, 282, and (Feb.–Mar. 1934), OW, 297; Franckenstein to Pfitzner, 11 Aug. 1933; Pfitzner

to Franckenstein, 15 Aug. 1933 and 9 Mar. 1934, BH, Staatstheater/Neue Abgabe Pfitzner.

49. *Berliner Nacht Ausgabe,* 13 July 1933 (quote); *ZM* 100 (1933), 839; Pfitzner to Fürstner, 27 July 1933, MMP; Junk to Pfitzner, 3 Aug. 1933, in Wamlek-Junk, *Pfitzner,* 103; Pfitzner to Walter, 13 July 1933 (AM, Pfitzner) and 1 Sept. 1936 (OW, 76); Williamson, *Music,* 322. Pfitzner apologists Adamy, *Pfitzner,* 319–20, and Schrott, *Persönlichkeit,* 48–49, write without proof and wrongly that Frank dictated the letter to Pfitzner. However, beyond exerting moral pressure, Nazi authorities could do little.

50. Pfitzner to Hinkel, 6 Sept. 1933, BAB Pfitzner.

51. Pfitzner to Ihlert, 24 Jan. 1934; Kärnbach to Pfitzner, 31 Jan. 1934; program, "Erster deutscher Komponistentag," 18 Feb. 1934, OW, 250; Pfitzner to Abendroth, 8 Mar. 1934, OW, 289; Peter Muck, *Einhundert Jahre Berliner Philharmonisches Orchester: Darstellung in Dokumenten,* 2 vols. (Tutzing, 1982), 2:110.

52. Pfitzner to Hinkel, 6 Feb. 1934; Hinkel to Pfitzner, 9 Feb. 1934, BAB Pfitzner; Pfitzner to Spring, 14 and 26 Mar. 1934; Spring to Pfitzner, 15 Mar. 1934, OW, 250; Krauss to Pfitzner, 17 Mar. 1934, OW, 297.

53. Abendroth, "Pfitzner"; Erich Valentin, "Hans Pfitzner, der Deutsche," *ZM* 101 (1934), 481–83; [Oertel] memorandum, 9 May 1934, MMP; Pfitzner to Bauckner, 12 May 1934, BH, MK/44737.

54. Pfitzner to Knappertsbusch, 16 May 1934, in Busch-Salmen and Weiss, *Pfitzner,* 80–81; also text ibid, 34–35; Pfitzner to Knappertsbusch, 14 May 1934; Knappertsbusch to Pfitzner, 15 May 1934, OW, 282; [Siebert] memorandum, 9 June 1934, BH, MA/107485; Siebert to Pfitzner, 12 June 1934; Knappertsbusch to culture ministry, 12 June 1934 (quote), BH, MK/44737; Pfitzner to Siebert, 13 June 1934, OW, 211.

55. Bayerische Treuhand to Göring, 21 June 1937, OW, 211; Pfitzner to Furtwängler, 14 July 1937, OW, 73; Busch-Salmen and Weiss, *Pfitzner,* 41–55; Kater, *The Twisted Muse,* 216. On physicians' (and other social elites') incomes in 1936–37, see Michael H. Kater, *Doctors Under Hitler* (Chapel Hill, N.C., 1989), 32, 242.

56. Pfitzner to Lilo [Martin], 19 June 1934, SMM, 20.

57. Walleck to Diemer, 8 Nov. 1934, BH, Staatstheater/Neue Abgabe Pfitzner; Pfitzner to Lilo [Martin], 30 Dec. 1934, SMM, 20; Pfitzner to Göring, 17 Dec. 1934, 30 Jan. 1935, 8 Feb. 1935, 26 Apr. 1935, OW, 211; Göring to Pfitzner, 8 Jan. and 12 Feb. 1935; Scheffels to Pfitzner, 9 Jan. 1935; [Göring] telegram to Pfitzner, 2 Feb. 1935; Pfitzner protocol, 9 Feb. 1935 (quotes); Laubinger to Pfitzner, 11 Feb. 1935; Wolter to Pfitzner, Dec. 1935; wedding announcement Göring for 12 Apr. 1935 for Pfitzner, OW, 211; Adamy, *Pfitzner,* 323. Partially distorting: Schrott, *Persönlichkeit,* 55–57.

58. Boepple to interior ministry, 10 Sept. 1936, BH, MK/44737.

59. Funk to culture ministry, 14 July 1934; von Keudell to education ministry, 16 Aug. 1934; Funk to Wagner, 3 Feb. 1937, BH, MK/44737.

60. There is no proof that Hitler at that time was a follower of Bruckner, as is documented for later years, and if in those years he *said* he liked Bruckner, it was posturing, solely because of the common link with Linz, in disregard of the music.

61. Pfitzner to Lilo [Martin], 23 Aug. 1934, SMM, 20.

62. Entry for 9 June 1943 in *TGII* 8:448.

63. Pfitzner to "hochverehrter Herr Reichskanzler," 15 Mar. 1933, and to Cologne Deputy König, 15 Mar. 1933 (enclosed), in Hans Pfitzner, *Briefe,* ed. Bern-

hard Adamy. 2 vols. (Tutzing, 1991), 1:621–23; Pfitzner to Lulu [Cossmann], 9 July 1933, OW, 160; Pfitzner to Victor [Junk], 7 Dec. 1933, in Wamlek-Junk, *Pfitzner,* 107.

64. Pfitzner to Abendroth, 1 Feb. 1934, OW, 289; Williamson, *Music,* 327.

65. Pfitzner quoted in *Tag,* Berlin, 15 Aug. 1934.

66. Sellschopp circular, 25 Aug. 1934, SM, Kulturamt/312/2.

67. Pfitzner to Göring, 17 Dec. 1943, OW, 211; Brockhaus to Mali Pfitzner, 4 July 1947; Wetzelsberger declaration, 11 Dec. 1947, AM, Pfitzner.

68. Entry for 24 June 1937 in *TGII* 3:183.

69. Pfitzner to Abendroth, 9 Oct. 1937, OW, 288.

70. Pfitzner memorandum, 23 Nov. 1938, OW, 179.

71. Kater, *The Twisted Muse,* 49–54.

72. Pfitzner to Wolfes, 26 June 1939, printed in Adamy, *Pfitzner,* 330; Meissner to Pfitzner, 15 June 1938, OW, 74; program for "Pfitzner-Ehrung" on 70th birthday, Munich, 8 Mar. 1939, BH, MA/107486; Reitter to Pfitzner, 24 Feb. 1940, OW, 259. Krauss's role is highlighted in Pfitzner to Abendroth, 19 Oct. 1938, OW, 288. For the apologists, see Morgenroth declaration, 23 July 1947, AM, Pfitzner; Müller-Blattau, *Pfitzner,* 109.

73. Abendroth to Pfitzner, 18 Apr. 1939, OW, 288.

74. Abendroth to Pfitzner, 16 June 1939, OW, 288. On anti-Hitler remarks, see the more or less credible Hussla declaration, 21 July 1947; Morgenroth declaration, 23 July 1947; Pfeuffer declaration, 28 Aug. 1947; Trinius declaration, 6 Jan. 1948, AM, Pfitzner.

75. Pfitzner to Riebe, 20 June 1939, OW, 300.

76. Morgenroth to Pfitzner, 8 Jan. and 12 Feb. 1942, OW, 459.

77. Entry for 9 June 1943 in *TGII* 8:448; Pfitzner to Hinkel, 15 Sept. 1944, printed in Adamy, *Pfitzner,* 333 (quote).

78. Pfitzner to "Sehr geehrter Herr," May 1930, OW, 300; Williamson, *Music,* 318–19.

79. Boepple to interior ministry, 10 Sept. 1936, BH, MK/44737.

80. Pfitzner to Abendroth, 8 Mar. 1933, OW, 289; Pfitzner to Göring, 8 Feb. 1935, OW, 211.

81. Pfitzner paraphrased in *VB,* 6 May 1936; Pfitzner to Emma, 22 Nov. 1938, OW, 280 (quote).

82. See Abendroth to Pfitzner, [Mar. 1935], OW, 289; Abendroth to Goebbels, 10 Nov. 1933, BA, R55/1141/3–4; Junk to Pfitzner, 3 Aug. 1933, in Wamlek-Junk, *Pfitzner,* 103; Walter Abendroth, "Opernideale der Rassen und Völker," *DM* 28 (1936), 424–25.

83. Schemm to Pfitzner, 24 May 1933, OW, 300; Pfitzner to Abendroth, 27 May 1933, OW, 289.

84. Schwieger to Professor [Pfitzner], 4 Aug. 1934; Pfitzner to Gauleiter [Meyer], 4 Sept. 1934; Bartels to Gaupersonalamt, 13 Sept. 1934; Beyer to Professor [Pfitzner], 18 Sept. 1934, OW, 297.

85. Pfitzner as quoted in Schrott, *Persönlichkeit,* 133; Vogel, *Pfitzner,* 109; Kater, *The Twisted Muse,* 192, 195.

86. Pfitzner to Abendroth, 29 Sept. 1938, OW, 288.

87. Walter to Pfitzner, 14 Aug. 1936, AM, Pfitzner; Pfitzner to Bruno [Walter], 1 Sept. 1936; Walter to Hans [Pfitzner], 22 Sept. and 12 Oct. 1936, and 9 June 1937, OW, 76; Pfitzner to Bertil [Wetzelsberger], 21 May 1937, OW, 74; Pfitzner to Victor [Junk], 24 Sept. 1937 (SMM, 9/115) and 13 May 1938 (SMM, 9/118); Walter to

Hans [Pfitzner], 26 Aug. 1935 and 12 Oct. 1937 (quote), in Lotte Walter Lindt, ed., *Bruno Walter: Briefe, 1894–1962* (Frankfurt am Main, 1969), 233, 239–40; Bruno Walter, *Theme and Variations: An Autobiography* (New York, 1966), 318–20; *NG* 14:614.

88. Pfitzner to Paul [Cossmann], 1 Sept. 1932, MMP; Vogel, *Pfitzner,* 114–15.

89. Pfitzner to Hindenburg, 13 Nov. 1933, in Adamy, *Pfitzner,* 310–11; Adamy's text ibid; Pfitzner to Lulu [Cossmann], 9 July 1933; Frank to Himmler, 13 July 1933; Gürtner to Professor [Pfitzner], 20 Nov. 1933, OW, 160; Pfitzner to Hess, 9 Nov. 1933, SMM, 20; Erwein von Aretin, *Krone und Ketten: Erinnerungen eines bayerischen Edelmannes,* ed. Karl Buchheim and Karl Otmar von Aretin (Munich, 1955), 200–362; Wolfram Selig, *Paul Nikolaus Cossmann und die Süddeutschen Monatshefte von 1914–1918: Ein Beitrag zur Geschichte der nationalen Publizistik im Ersten Weltkrieg* (Osnabrück, 1967), 74–75.

90. The undocumented article by John W. Klein supplies no clues in this regard: "Hans Pfitzner and the Two Heydrichs," *Music Review* 26 (1965), 308–17. Also see Hess Stabsleiter to Ernst, 23 Jan. 1934, OW, 160; Louise [Lulu] Cossmann declaration, 7 July 1947; Grohe declaration, 15 Dec. 1947, AM, Pfitzner; Schrott, *Persönlichkeit,* 54.

91. Pfitzner to Drahn, 25 Jan. 1934, OW, 160.

92. Selig, *Cossmann,* 77–78; Adamy, *Pfitzner,* 311; Vogel, *Pfitzner,* 115.

93. "Ausführliches Gesamturteil" by Reinstein, 20 Feb. 1940, BAB Pfitzner.

94. Vogel, *Pfitzner,* 111.

95. Kremer to Pfitzner, 23 May 1935, OW, 283; Schrott to Pfitzner, 4 Jan. 1940, OW, 259; Schaal to Pfitzner, 21 Dec. 1943, OW, 257; Kernich to Pfitzner, 21 Mar. 1944; Schulze-Berghof to Pfitzner, 3 May 1944, OW, 65; Schulze-Berghof to Reichskassenverwaltung, 13 Apr. 1944, BAB Pfitzner; *ZM* 102 (1935), 787; *MK* 1 (1943), 38; *MK* 2 (1944), 109; Ulrike Gruner, *Musikleben in der Provinz, 1933–45: Beispiel: Marburg: Eine Studie anhand der Musikberichterstattung in der Lokalpresse* (Marburg, 1990), 74–75, 139–41.

96. Schrott to Pfitzner, 6 Apr. 1935; "Pfitznerwoche der NS-Kulturgemeinde München, 3. bis 8. Mai 1935," OW, 283; Hartmann memorandum, 15 June 1935; Schrott to Pfitzner, 10 Aug. 1935, OW, 120; Abendroth to Pfitzner, 23 Dec. 1937, OW, 288; Gauobmann [Schrott] to culture ministry, 8 Feb. 1936, BH, MK/40975; NSKG to Furtwängler, 17 Apr. 1937; Furtwängler to Matthes, 20 Apr. 1937; Draussmann to Furtwängler, 14 July 1937, ZNF; *VB,* 10 May 1935 and 10 May 1937.

97. Gebhardt-Pfitzner corr. (1941), OW, 126.

98. Kater, *The Twisted Muse,* 120–22.

99. Büro des Reichsstatthalters [Mutschmann] to Pfitzner, 19 Nov. 1941; Pfitzner to Nieland, 28 Dec. 1941, OW, 261; Mutschmann to Pfitzner, 6 Oct. 1944, OW, 65; Abendroth to Pfitzner, 23 Nov. 1941, OW, 288; Walther Meyer-Giesow, *Taste, Taktstock, Tinte: Ein Leben für die Musik* (Frankfurt am Main, 1968), 145–46.

100. Robert-Schumann-Gesellschaft to Pfitzner, 17 Dec. 1942; Pfitzner to Robert-Schumann-Gesellschaft, 24 Dec. 1942; Barth to Pfitzner, 12 Jan. 1943; Pfitzner to Barth, 18 Jan. 1943; Dost to Pfitzner, 22 Jan. 1943; "Aufruf" by Meyer-Giesow, 16 Aug. 1943, OW, 65; Robert-Schumann-Gesellschaft to Pfitzner, 24 Feb. 1943; "Veranstaltungsplan für das Schumann-Pfitzner-Fest in Zwickau vom 7.–10. Juni 1944," OW, 459; *MK* 1 (1943), 47–48; *MK* 2 (1944), 96; Meyer-Giesow, *Taste,* 146.

101. Pfitzner-Morgenroth corr. (1937–41), OW, 261 and 459; Graener to Pfitzner, 28 Apr. 1938, OW, 267; "Mitteilungen der Fachschaft Komponisten in der Reichsmusikkammer, November 1940," OW, 40; Goebbels-Stiftung to Pfitzner, 15 Oct. 1943, OW, 304; "Betr.: Verwendung des Staatszuschusses zur Verteilung an Komponisten ernster Musik," Berlin, 4 July 1942, BAB Werner Egk; "Die Reichskulturkammer," 2 (1944), BA, RD33/1 (73–74); MK 2 (1944), 36; Alfred Morgenroth, ed., *Hört auf Pfitzner! Kernsätze deutscher Kunstgesinnung aus seinen Schriften und Reden* (Berlin, 1938).

102. Drewes to Meister [Pfitzner], 13 Apr. 1938 (OW, 267) and 2 May 1938 (OW, 124); Pfitzner to Goebbels, 15 Nov. 1938, OW, 179; Pfitzner to Hermann, 18 Nov. 1938, OW, 280; Pfitzner to Hinkel, 8 Aug. 1941, OW, 459; Pfitzner to RMK, 25 Oct. 1942, OW, 459; Pfitzner to National-Zeitung Essen, 20 Dec. 1942, AM, Pfitzner; entry for 13 Jan. 1944 in *TGII* 11:82; Albrecht Dümling and Peter Girth, eds., *Entartete Musik: Zur Düsseldorfer Ausstellung von 1938: Eine kommentierte Rekonstruktion* (Düsseldorf, [1988]), 108; Vogel, *Pfitzner,* 109. Frank's continual falling out of favor may be traced in: *TGII* 5:305, 350, 364, 377, 552, 566–67; 6:64; 7:508; 8:226; 11:367; 13:167, 220–21, 274, 367.

103. Reichspropagandaamt Baden to Pfitzner, 3 Oct. 1940 (quote); program, "Oberrheinische Kulturtage," 15 Nov. 1940, OW, 245; Walter Dirks, "Hans Pfitzner in Strassburg: Die Oberrheinischen Kulturtage," *Frankfurter Zeitung,* 17 Nov. 1940.

104. ZM 108 (1941), 518.

105. Koch to Pfitzner, 13 May 1942, OW, 61; ZM 108 (1941), 130.

106. "Posener Musikwoche" corr. (May–Sept. 1942) OW, 61; BAB Pfitzner; *Ostdeutscher Beobachter,* 7 Sept. 1942; ZM 109 (1942), 558–59; MK 1 (1943), 157.

107. Frank to Pfitzner, 27 Sept. 1941, OW, 220. Details of the Frank-Pfitzner relationship (1941–45) may be gleaned from the corr. in OW, 65 and 220.

108. ZM 109 (1942), 42; Alfred Lemke, "Deutsches Musikleben in Krakau," ibid., 396–98; AMZ 69 (1942), 41; entry for 25 Apr. 1942 in *TGII* 4:167; Jonathan Petropoulos, *Art as Politics in the Third Reich* (Chapel Hill, N.C., 1996), 226–29. Hindemith's formal appointment occurred on 23 Apr. 1942 (Werner Präg and Wolfgang Jacobmeyer, eds., *Das Diensttagebuch des deutschen Generalgouverneurs in Polen, 1939–1945* [Stuttgart, 1975], 493).

109. Präg and Jacobmeyer, *Diensttagebuch,* 572; ZM 110 (1943), 45.

110. Pfitzner to Frank, 18 Dec. 1943, OW, 65.

111. Präg and Jacobmeyer, *Diensttagebuch,* 840, 885, 887.

112. Entry for 10 Sept. 1944 in *TGII* 13:450.

113. Frank to Pfitzner, 28 and 29 Mar. 1945, OW, 417; Pfitzner quoted in Adamy, *Pfitzner,* 338; Adamy's text, ibid.; Erich Stockhorst, *Fünftausend Köpfe: Wer war was im Dritten Reich* (Velbert, 1967), 163.

114. See, e.g., Pfitzner to Graf, 17 Feb. 1933, OW, 297; Pfitzner to Mohr, 12 July 1934, OW, 74; and Hans Pfitzner, *Werk und Wiedergabe* (=*Gesammelte Schriften,* 3 [Augsburg, 1929]).

115. Arnold to Orff, 16 Oct. 1939, CM, Allg. Korr.

116. Meissner to Orff, 5 July 1941, CM, Allg. Korr.

117. Pfitzner to Kleyensteuber, 4 June 1943, OW, 220.

118. For representative samples of typical Pfitzner complaints see: Pfitzner to Tonger, 22 Feb. 1934, OW, 250; and to Meyer-Giesow, 15 Jan. 1939, OW, 29; and to Gless, 8 Feb. 1939, OW, 280; and to Heinz, 17 Oct. 1940, OW, 259; and to

Hauptmann, 22 Mar. 1941, OW, 261; and to Schüler, 15 Aug. 1941, OW, 261; and to Abendroth, 31 Mar. 1943, OW, 288; and to Oertel (enclosed with Pfitzner to Deschler, 29 July 1943); Pfitzner to Deschler, 4 Sept. 1943, BS, Cod. germ. 8251.

119. Heger to Pfitzner, 24 Apr. 1934, OW, 123; Reichssender Berlin to Pfitzner, 4 July 1939; Danziger Konzertgemeinde to Pfitzner, 17 Nov. 1939, OW, 259; *Skizzen* (May 1934), 14; *VB,* 25 May 1939; *ZM* 107 (1940), 572; *MK* 2 (1944), 99; *Reichskulturkammer,* no. 5 (1944), 82.

120. Valentin-Pfitzner corr. (Mar.–Apr. 1940), OW, 259; *AMZ* 62 (1935), 769; *VB,* 21 Dec. 1935; *ZM* 109 (1942), 137.

121. [Pfitzner,] "Dirigierverpflichtungen vom 16. Oktober bis 26. Januar 1935," OW, 211; Schüler to Pfitzner, 25 Aug. 1941, OW, 261; "10 Sinfonie-Konzerte des Städtischen Orchesters Bielefeld in der Spielzeit 1941/42," OW, 126; *ZM* 108 (1941), 317; *MK* 1 (1943–44), 187; *MK* 2 (1944), 57; Werner Oehlmann, "Bekenntnis zur Kammermusik: Die Berliner Kunstwochen 1941," *Reich,* 1 June 1941.

122. Pfitzner to Hauptmann, 22 Mar. 1941, OW, 261.

123. "Konzertverein München e.V. Wintersaison 1932/33," SM, Kulturamt/208; "4. Jubiläums-Konzert," 27 Feb. 1934, SM, Kulturamt/473; *Melos* 13 (1934), 254; *Münchener Zeitung,* 9–10 Feb. 1935.

124. Pfitzner to Walleck, 9 Dec. 1935, BH, Staatstheater/Neue Abgabe Pfitzner.

125. "Richard Wagner-Verband Deutscher Frauen, Ortsverband München," May 1939, SM, Kulturamt/264; Konzertverein München e.V. to Fiehler, 7 Mar. 1938, SM, Kulturamt/177; Pfitzner to von Benda, 2 July 1939, OW, 259 (quote).

126. Münchener Philharmoniker to Siebert, 3 Jan. 1940, BH, MA/107486; Pfitzner to Professor [Kabasta], 29 June 1940, OW, 67 (quote); "Bericht über das Konzertjahr 1939/40," SM, Kulturamt/177.

127. *ZM* 109 (1942), 116; ibid. 110 (1943), 20; Fiehler in Walter Abendroth, ed., *Hans Pfitzner: Ein Bild in Widmungen anlässlich seines 75. Geburtstages* (Leipzig, 1944), 18.

128. Pfitzner to Graf, 17 Feb. 1933, OW, 297; *Frankfurter Zeitung,* 29 Aug. 1934; Albert Richard Mohr, *Die Frankfurter Oper, 1924–1944: Ein Beitrag zur Theatergeschichte mit zeitgenössischen Berichten und Bildern* (Frankfurt am Main, 1971), 150, 158, 184.

129. Pfitzner to Rosbaud, and to Derpsch, 10 Apr. 1934, OW, 250; Pfitzner to Generalintendant [Meissner], 12 July 1934, OW, 74; Mohr, *Frankfurter Oper,* 183; Walter Dirks in *Generalanzeiger,* Frankfurt, 11 July 1934; Karl Holl in *Frankfurter Zeitung,* 12 July 1934.

130. Pfitzner to Wetzelsberger, 24 Mar. 1938, OW, 74 (quote); *Neueste Zeitung,* Frankfurt, 10 Nov. 1937; Mohr, *Frankfurter Oper,* 266–67.

131. Meissner to Pfitzner, 15 June 1938, OW, 74.

132. *Frankfurter Zeitung,* 4 Oct. 1938.

133. Mohr, *Frankfurter Oper,* 151 (Pfitzner quoted ibid.), 307–8.

134. Ibid., 311–12.

135. Walter Dirks in *Neueste Zeitung,* Frankfurt, 6 May 1939; Wolfgang Steinecke in *Generalanzeiger,* Frankfurt, 17 Nov. 1939; Karl Holl in *Frankfurter Zeitung,* 18 Nov. 1939; *ZM* 108 (1941), 401–2; Mohr, *Frankfurter Oper,* 323–24, 334, 364.

136. Abendroth to Pfitzner, 20 May 1940, OW, 288.

137. Meissner to Pfitzner, 16 Dec. 1943, OW, 65; Mohr, *Frankfurter Oper,* 377.

138. Pfitzner to Junk, 15 Mar. 1936, SMM, 9/113; Pfitzner to Kern, 31 Mar. 1940, OW, 958; Vogel, *Pfitzner,* 44.

139. Junk to Pfitzner, 11 May 1938, OW, 958.

140. Mutzenbecher to Pfitzner, 5 Apr. 1939, OW, 124; Pfitzner to Junk, 12 Mar. 1940, SMM, 9/122; Pfitzner to Schütz, 12 Mar. and 21 Aug. 1940; and to Kern, 31 Mar. 1940; and to Junk, 16 May 1940, OW, 958.

141. Schütz to Doktor [Pfitzner], 11 Feb. 1941, OW, 958.

142. Pfitzner to Victor [Junk], 31 Aug. 1941, SMM, 9/125; ZM 108 (1941), 408, 521.

143. Junk to Pfitzner, 22 Sept. 1941, 12 and 18 Mar. 1942, OW, 958.

144. Witt to Meister [Pfitzner], 23 Apr. 1942, OW, 958; MK 1 (1943), 34, 111.

145. "Die Reichskulturkammer," 1 (1944), BA, RD33/1 (11); Anderman [Thomas], *Vorhang*, 245–46.

146. MK 2 (1944), 112–13.

147. Telegram, Munich, 29 Dec. 1944, BH, Staatstheater/14480.

148. See Hörburger to Raabe, 16 Nov. 1938, SM, Kulturamt/213/1.

149. Pfitzner to Gieseking, 16 Oct. 1934, OW, 299 (quote); Balzer to Pfitzner, 7 May 1937, OW, 124; Pfitzner to von Benda, 17 June 1939, OW, 259.

150. Ney to Hoogstraten, 20 June and 6 July 1933 (EB, 0.6); Ney in Abendroth, *Pfitzner: Ein Bild*, 103; Strub to Pfitzner, 31 Oct. 1936 (OW, 272) and 28 Apr. 1938 (OW, 267); ZM 109 (1942), 22; BAB Ludwig Hoelscher; Kater, *The Twisted Muse*, 70.

151. "Hessisches Landestheater. Viertes Sinfonie-Konzert," 3 Dec. 1934, OW, 122; Danziger Konzertgemeinde to Pfitzner, 18 Sept. 1939, OW, 259; DAZ, 21 Feb. 1934; ZM 107 (1940), 717; GLM 3:106–7.

152. Heinz to Hans [Pfitzner], 4 Oct. 1940, OW, 259; Egli to Frau [Mali] Pfitzner, 17 Dec. 1940; Pfitzner to Egli, 24 Dec. 1940; Egli to Meister [Pfitzner], 3 Jan. 1941, OW, 67; Pfitzner to Reinhard, 23 Feb. 1944, OW, 65; ZM 108 (1941), 411, 747.

153. Abendroth to Pfitzner, 9 Mar. 1936, OW, 289.

154. Schwarzkopf to Pfitzner, 21 Sept. 1942 (OW, 61) and 23 Feb. 1943 (OW, 65); Ohlendorf to Pfitzner, 30 Mar. 1943; Pfitzner to Ohlendorf, 8 May 1943, OW, 65; Pfitzner to Morgenroth, 26 May 1943, OW, 459 (quote).

155. Pfitzner to Oertel, 9 Jan. 1927; and to Brockhaus, 24 Apr. 1930; and to Paul [Cossmann], 1 Sept. 1932; and to Fürstner, 8 Sept. and 19 Oct. 1932, MMP; Wilhelm Furtwängler, *Notebooks, 1924–1954*, ed. Michael Tanner (London, 1989), 55 (quote).

156. Pfitzner to Abendroth, 18 Feb. 1933; Abendroth to Pfitzner, 25 Feb. 1933, OW, 289; Ney to Hoogstraten, 20 June 1933, EB, 0.6; Geissmar to Pfitzner, 12 Aug. 1933; [Fürstner] memorandum, 14 Aug. 1933, MMP; *Berliner Börsen-Zeitung*, 4 Apr. 1933; *Berliner Morgenpost*, 26 Feb. 1934.

157. Pfitzner to Geissmar, 5 July 1934; Geissmar to Pfitzner, 9 Aug. [1934]; Pfitzner to Furtwängler, 30 Sept. 1934, OW, 123; [Oertel] memorandum, 21 Sept. 1934, MMP; Pfitzner to Gieseking, 16 Oct. 1934, OW, 299; Berlin Philharmonic to Funk, 19 Dec. 1934, BA, R55/1148; Pfitzner to Walleck, 18 Dec. 1935, BH, Staatstheater/Neue Abgabe Pfitzner; Abendroth to Meister [Pfitzner], 30 Dec. 1935; Pfitzner to Abendroth, 3 Jan. 1936, OW, 289; Pfitzner to Abendroth, 27 Jan. 1936; Abendroth to Pfitzner, 22 Apr. 1936 and 3 Nov. 1937, OW, 288; Furtwängler to Pfitzner, 7 Jan. 1937; Abendroth to Pfitzner, 11 Jan. 1937, OW, 211; DM 27 (1935), 957; Muck, *Jahre*, 2:142; 3:283.

158. Furtwängler to Matthes, 29 July 1938, ZNF; Abendroth to Pfitzner, 19 Sept. 1938, [Spring 1940], 24 July 1940, 6 Oct. 1940, 5 Aug. 1942, 4 Nov. 1941;

Pfitzner to Abendroth, 15 Oct. 1940, OW, 288; von Benda to Pfitzner, 29 June 1939; Pfitzner to von Westerman, 19 Sept. 1939, OW, 259; Furtwängler to Rendschmidt, 10 July 1940; Pfitzner to Morgenroth, 16 Aug. 1940, and to Rendschmidt, 13 Sept. 1940, OW, 459; Morgenroth to Pfitzner, 15 Aug. 1940, OW, 67; Furtwängler, *Notebooks,* 132 (1st quote), 134 (2nd quote), 142 (3rd quote).

159. Strauss's not always temperate reaction to Pfitzner's wiles is amply documented in: Strauss to Schalk, 7 Mar. 1919, in Günter Brosche, ed., *Richard Strauss—Franz Schalk: Ein Briefwechsel* (Tutzing, 1983), 103–4; Strauss to von Niessen, 11 May 1935; Strauss to Hadamovsky, 1 July 1935; Strauss to Böhm, 5 Jan. 1944, RG; Strauss to Schuh, 8 May 1943, in *Richard Strauss: Briefwechsel mit Willi Schuh* (Zurich, 1969), 38–39; Schrott, *Persönlichkeit,* 125; Walter Panofsky, *Richard Strauss: Partitur eines Lebens* (Munich, 1965), 148–49, 276; Walter Thomas, *Richard Strauss und seine Zeitgenossen* (Munich, 1964), 199; Otto Strasser, *Und dafür wird man noch bezahlt: Mein Leben mit den Wiener Philharmonikern* (Vienna, 1974), 181; Vogel, *Pfitzner,* 48. Also see chapter 8 at n. 5.

160. Thomas, *Strauss,* 208.

161. Ibid., 217; Pfitzner to anon., 13 June 1944, OW, 300; Paul Egon Hübinger, *Thomas Mann, die Universität Bonn und die Zeitgeschichte: Drei Kapitel deutscher Vergangenheit aus dem Leben des Dichters, 1905–1955* (Munich, 1974), 124–30; Hartmut Zelinsky, ed., *Richard Wagner—ein deutsches Thema: Eine Dokumentation zur Wirkungsgeschichte Richard Wagners, 1876–1976,* 3rd ed. (Berlin, 1983); Hans Rudolf Vaget, "The Rivalry for Wagner's Mantle: Strauss, Pfitzner, Mann," in Reinhold Grimm and Jost Hermand, eds., *Re-Reading Wagner* (Madison, Wis., 1993), 143–45; Kater, *The Twisted Muse,* 41–43, 219–20; Kater, *Different Drummers: Jazz in the Culture of Nazi Germany* (New York, 1992), 21. The relationship between Wagner and Hitler has now been characterized, if unjustifiedly monocausally and hyperbolically, in Joachim Köhler, *Wagners Hitler: Der Prophet und sein Vollstrecker* (Munich, 1997). See Rudolf Augstein, "Siegfried, Lohengrin, Parsifal—Hitler?," *Spiegel* (21 July 1997), 154–61.

162. Lehmann, in world premieres, sang the roles of the composer in *Ariadne auf Naxos* (2nd version, Vienna, 1916), the dyer's wife in *Die Frau ohne Schatten* (Vienna, 1919), and Christine in *Intermezzo* (Dresden, 1924) (John Coveney, "Lotte Lehmann Remembered," *High Fidelity and Musical America* [June 1977], 17; GLM 5:86). See also Thomas, *Strauss,* 197; Williamson, *Music,* 316; Kater, *The Twisted Muse,* 219. I owe my insight into the Strauss-Berlioz relationship to Albrecht Riethmüller.

163. Schrott, *Persönlichkeit,* 125; Panofsky, *Strauss,* 147; Vogel, *Pfitzner,* 46–47.

164. Panofsky, *Strauss,* 148.

165. Thomas, *Strauss,* 212.

166. Pfitzner to Brockhaus, 12 Feb. 1919, MMP.

167. Pfitzner to Oertel, 12 Sept. 1927, MMP.

168. Abendroth to Pfitzner, 12 Sept. and 19 Oct. 1933, 11 Mar. 1934, OW, 289; Abendroth to Pfitzner, 12 Dec. 1935, 9 Jan. and 29 Nov. 1936, 13 Aug. and 8 Nov. 1937, 27 Aug. 1938, 13 June 1940, OW, 288; Abendroth to Pfitzner, 26 Mar. 1937, OW, 25; Abendroth to Matthes, 2 Jan. 1936, OW, 288; Walter Abendroth, "Hans Pfitzner," *DKW,* no. 25 (1933), 5; Abendroth, *Pfitzner,* 18, 23–24, 27–29, 100, 114, 221, 246, 297, 314, 349, 378, 413 (n. 16); Panofsky, *Strauss,* 151.

169. Pfitzner to Abendroth, 13 Sept. 1933, OW, 289; Pfitzner to Victor [Junk], 5 Dec. 1933, SMM, 9/99; Scheffels to Professor [Pfitzner], 29 Dec. 1934; Pfitzner to Scheffels, 2 Jan. 1935, OW, 211; Tietjen to Strauss, 29 Dec. 1934, RG; Pfitzner

to Heger, 18 Apr. 1934; Pfitzner to Schlösser, 2 Jan. 1935, OW, 123; Pfitzner to Schrott, 9 Apr. 1935, OW, 283; Pfitzner to Lilo [Martin], 10 Apr. 1935, SMM, 20.

170. Rasch to Pfitzner, 11 Nov. 1933; "Arbeitstagung der Reichsmusikkammer," Berlin, 13–17 Feb. 1934, OW, 250; minutes of 4th RMK presidial council meeting, 20 Jan. 1934, RG; Pfitzner to Abendroth, 27 Feb. 1934, OW, 289; Pfitzner to Franckenstein, 13 Mar. 1934, OW, 297; Hindemith to Willy [Strecker], 15 Nov. 1934, PF, Schott Korr.

171. Schrott to Nippold, 29 Apr. 1935, OW, 283 (quote); Pfitzner to Sander, 10 Oct. 1937, and to Strub, 9 Apr. 1938, OW, 280; Pfitzner to Abendroth, 19 Oct. 1938, 14 June 1940, and 3 June 1942, OW, 288; Pfitzner to Schlösser, 15 Nov. 1941, and to Morgenroth, 21 Nov. 1941, OW, 261; Pfitzner to Valentin, 24 Oct. 1939, OW, 249; Pfitzner to Morgenroth, 15 Feb. 1942, OW, 459; Pfitzner to Kraus, 10 Sept. 1939, SMM, 24; Pfitzner to Deschler, 19 July 1943, BS, Cod. germ. 8251. The "Jewish things" were Strauss's *Salome* (1905), *Josephslegende* (1914), and *Die ägyptische Helena* (1928–33). Also see chapter 8 at n. 266.

172. Berlin Philharmonic, "Statistik . . . Geschäftsjahr 1938/39," BA, R55/197; table in Petra Maria Valentin, "Die Bayerische Staatsoper im Dritten Reich," master thesis, Munich, 1985, (n.p.).

173. Pfitzner to anon., 13 June 1944, OW, 300.

174. See Elmendorff to Deschler, 19 June 1943, BS, Cod. germ. 8251.

175. Schrott, *Persönlichkeit,* 19; Vogel, *Pfitzner,* 23–24, 42–44, 50, 113; Françoise Giroud, *Alma Mahler or the Art of Being Loved* (Oxford, 1991), 61.

176. Pfitzner to Lilo [Martin], 22 July 1936, SMM, 20; Pfitzner to Mimilein [Pfitzner], 27 June 1921, in Pfitzner, *Briefe,* 1:328; Schrott, *Persönlichkeit,* 19; Vogel, *Pfitzner,* 44.

177. Pfitzner to Abendroth, 12 July 1938, OW, 288; Pfitzner to Emma, 22 Nov. 1938, OW, 280; Schrott, *Persönlichkeit,* 21; Vogel, *Pfitzner,* 113.

178. Pfitzner to Abendroth, 15 Sept. and 29 Dec. 1937, OW, 288; Pfitzner to Emma, 22 Nov. 1938, OW, 280; Peter Pfitzner to Egk, 25 Sept. 1936 and 3 Nov. [1941?]; Ingeborg Pfitzner to Egk, [Feb. 1944], BS, Ana/410; Erich Valentin, "Junge deutsche Komponisten," VB, 18 Oct. 1937; ZM 107 (1940), 338; Schrott, *Persönlichkeit,* 20–21; Vogel, *Pfitzner,* 113.

179. Pfitzner to Lilo [Martin], 26 Oct. 1934, SMM, 20; Pfitzner to Fiehler, [Oct. 1937], OW, 120; Pfitzner to Abendroth, 9 Dec. 1937, OW, 288 (quote).

180. Meyer-Giesow, *Taste,* 146–47; Rudolf Hartmann, *Das geliebte Haus: Mein Leben mit der Oper* (Munich, 1975), 136; Hans Heinz Stuckenschmidt, *Zum Hören geboren: Ein Leben mit der Musik unserer Zeit* (Munich, 1979), 122.

181. Pfitzner-Martin corr. (1933–34), SMM, 20.

182. Pfitzner to Lilo [Martin], 1 Jan. 1933 (1st quote) and 13 Feb. 1933 (2nd quote), SMM, 20.

183. Pfitzner to Lilo [Martin], 3 Apr. 1933, SMM, 20.

184. Pfitzner to Lilo [Martin], 19 June 1934, SMM, 20; *Der Deutsche Sender,* no. 14 (1–7 Apr. 1934), 27; "XIII. Vortragsabend: Kompositionen von Studierenden der Akademie," Munich, 27 June 1934, SM, Kulturamt/475; Grohe declaration, 15 Dec. 1947, AM, Pfitzner.

185. Hermann Abendroth to Meister [Pfitzner], 8 Aug. 1934, OW, 297; Pfitzner to Doktor [von Hase], 30 Sept. and 6 Oct. 1934; von Hase to Pfitzner, 4 Oct. 1934, OW, 298 (quote).

186. Pfitzner to Gieseking, 6 Oct. 1934 (1st quote); Gieseking to Pfitzner, 11 Oct. 1934 (2nd quote), OW, 299.

187. See Pfitzner to Gieseking, 16 Oct. 1934, OW, 299; Pfitzner to Lilo [Martin], 8 Nov. 1934, SMM, 20.

188. Pfitzner to Lilo [Martin], 9 Jan. 1935, SMM, 20.

189. Vogel, *Pfitzner,* 137, n. 395.

190. Pfitzner to Lilo [Martin], 26 Oct. 1934, SMM, 20; notice about Pfitzner concert in Munich, 27 Jan. 1936, BH, Staatstheater/Neue Abgabe Pfitzner; Pfitzner to Junk, 13 May 1938, SMM, 9/118; Pfitzner to Ambrosius, 27 Dec. 1938, OW, 252; Pfitzner to Heinz, 19 Oct. 1940, OW, 259; Rietschler declaration, 3 Dec. 1947, AM, Pfitzner; Valentin, *Pfitzner,* 66.

191. Schrott, *Persönlichkeit,* 75.

192. Mali Pfitzner to Junk, 5 Sept. 1942, SMM, 9/135; Schrott, *Persönlichkeit,* 76.

193. Pfitzner to Deschler, 29 Aug. and 15 Dec. 1943, BS, Cod. germ. 8251; Helmut to Pfitzner, 9 Oct. 1943, OW, 304; Schrott, *Persönlichkeit,* 77–78.

194. See the extensive corr. for 1943–44 in OW, 65, 257, and 304.

195. Pfitzner to Pesz, 7 Feb. 1944, OW, 257; Schrott, *Persönlichkeit,* 79–80; Vogel, *Pfitzner,* 118.

196. See Heinrich Strobel in *Melos* 15 (1948), 18.

197. Adamy, *Pfitzner,* 342.

198. Leer, defense plea, Munich, 12 Jan. 1948; Spruchkammer IV, judgment, Munich, 31 Mar. 1948, AM, Pfitzner.

199. Stenzel, expert report, Munich, 19 Sept. 1947; Spruchkammer IV, judgment, Munich, 31 Mar. 1948; Kleitz to Liaison and Security Officer, OMGUS, 22 May 1947, AM, Pfitzner; Pfitzner to Leonhard, 31 July 1946, OW, 306; Pfitzner to Doctor [Leer?], 3 Nov. 1946, OW, 300.

200. Leer to Professor [Rosbaud], 25 Nov. 1947, LP, 423/8/127; Rosbaud declaration, 27 Dec. 1947, AM, Pfitzner (quotes).

201. Meissner declaration, 24 Sept. 1947; Hartmann declaration, 28 Nov. 1947; Wetzelsberger declaration, 11 Dec. 1947; Rietschel declaration, 3 Dec. 1947; Leer, defense plea, Munich, 12 Jan. 1948, AM, Pfitzner.

202. See Pfitzner to Schrott, 16 Feb. 1936, OW, 427; Pfitzner to Riebe, 31 Mar. 1940, OW, 958; Pfitzner to Oertel, 21 Jan. 1944, OW, 257; Knauer declaration, 3 Oct. 1947, AM, Pfitzner.

203. Pfitzner, "Deutsche Opernkunst in Berlin ausge-Rode-t," in this case appended to Pfitzner to Rosenberg, 23 Nov. 1938, OW, 179.

204. Kössel declaration, 6 July 1947; Morgenroth declaration, 23 July 1947 (quote); Grohe declaration, 15 Dec. 1947; Leer, defense plea, Munich, 12 Jan. 1948; Spruchkammer IV, judgment, Munich, 31 Mar. 1948, AM, Pfitzner.

205. Frank declaration, 6 Dec. 1947 (1st quote); Leer, defense plea, Munich, 12 Jan. 1948 (2nd quote); Pfitzner, "Beilage zum Meldebogen," 24 Apr. 1946; Morgenroth declaration, 23 July 1947; Rietschel declaration, 3 Dec. 1947; Grohe declaration, 15 Dec. 1947; Siegel declaration, 18 Dec. 1947; Rosbaud declaration, 27 Dec. 1947; Spruchkammer IV, judgment, Munich, 31 Mar. 1948, AM, Pfitzner.

206. Leer, defense plea, Munich, 12 Jan. 1948 (1st quote); Schoenberg declaration, 10 Sept. 1947 (2nd quote); Kössel declaration, 6 July 1947; Hartmann declaration, 28 Nov. 1947; Rietschel declaration, 3 Dec. 1947; Wetzelsberger declaration, 11 Dec. 1947; Spruchkammer IV, judgment, Munich, 31 Mar. 1948, AM, Pfitzner; Hans Heinz Stuckenschmidt, *Arnold Schoenberg* (London, 1964), 130; Giroud, *Alma Mahler,* 50, 60–61; Kater, *The Twisted Muse,* 112.

207. Wetzelsberger declaration, 11 Dec. 1947, AM, Pfitzner.

208. Grohe declaration, 15 Dec. 1947; Leer, defense plea, Munich, 12 Jan. 1948; Spruchkammer IV, judgment, Munich, 31 Mar. 1948, AM, Pfitzner.

209. Mahler-Werfel to Leer, 2 Sept. 1947, AM, Pfitzner.

210. Egk to Spruchkammer IV, 30 Apr. 1948, AM, Pfitzner.

211. Furtwängler declaration, 10 Dec. 1947, AM, Pfitzner; Furtwängler, *Notebooks*, 168 (quote).

212. Knappertsbusch to Herr Dr. [Leer], 28 Dec. 1947, AM, Pfitzner. See Kater, *The Twisted Muse*, 40–55.

213. Pöschel, medical affidavit, 18 Mar. 1948; Spruchkammer IV, judgment, Munich, 31 Mar. 1948, AM, Pfitzner.

214. Pfitzner, "Glosse zum zweiten Weltkrieg," [typed version, 1946–47], OW, 431. An almost identical version in Pfitzner's handwriting is in his notebook, [1946–47], OW, 331 (see n. 32).

215. Pfitzner, *Werke*, 3 vols.

216. Pfitzner to Leonhard, 31 July 1946, OW, 306; Pfitzner to Herr Dr. [Leer], 3 Nov. 1946, OW, 300.

217. Vogel, *Pfitzner*, 86; Mann's quote printed ibid.; Pfitzner to Walter, 5 Oct. 1946, BS, Autograph Pfitzner; Pfitzner, notebook, [1946–47], OW, 331; Pfitzner, "Antwort auf Thomas Mann's Anrempelung vom 30. Juni 1947," 12 July 1947, OW, 431; Walter to Leer, 2 Sept. 1947, AM, Pfitzner; Walter to Pfitzner, 16 Sept. and 4 Nov. 1946, in Walter Lindt, *Walter: Briefe*, 289–91.

218. *Melos* 14 (1947), 188, 229, 307, 352, 355; ibid. 15 (1948), 59; Ludwig F. Schiedermair, *Musiker Schicksale: Aus dem Leben grosser Komponisten* (Berlin, 1990), 192.

219. Kater, *The Twisted Muse*, 214; Gerald Levitch, "Hitler's Willing Minstrels," *Globe and Mail,* Toronto, 9 Aug. 1997.

220. Klemperer to Pfitzner, 23 Dec. 1947, OW, 423; Heyworth, *Klemperer,* 2:166–67.

221. Wolfgang Osthoff, ed., *Briefwechsel Hans Pfitzner—Gerhard Frommel* (Tutzing, 1990), 82–86.

222. Rosbaud to Oberbürgermeister [Scharnagl], 6 Oct. 1947, LP, 423/6/89.

223. Rosbaud to Schoenberg, 26 Aug. 1948, LP, 423/33/631; Joan Evans, *Hans Rosbaud: A Bio-Bibliography* (New York, 1992), 44.

224. Pfitzner to Victor [Junk], 6 Feb. 1947, in Wamlek-Junk, *Pfitzner,* 150–51; Pfitzner to Intendant, 1 Oct. 1947, BH, Staatstheater/Neue Abgabe Pfitzner (quote); Pöschel, medical affidavit, 18 Mar. 1948, AM, Pfitzner; Mali Pfitzner to Held, 14 Apr. 1949; list, "Eigentum von Prof. Dr. Hans Pfitzner," [Oct. 1949], BH, MK/44737; Vogel, *Pfitzner*, 122–24; Schiedermair, *Schicksale*, 191.

CHAPTER 7: SCHOENBERG

1. Hans Heinz Stuckenschmidt, *Arnold Schoenberg* (London, 1964), 50.

2. Egbert M. Ennulat, ed., *Arnold Schoenberg Correspondence: A Collection of Translated and Annotated Letters Exchanged with Guido Adler, Pablo Casals, Emanuel Feuermann, and Olin Downes* (Metuchen, N.J., 1991), 56.

3. See Michael Mäckelmann, *Arnold Schönberg und Judentum: Der Komponist und sein religiöses, nationales und politisches Selbstverständnis nach 1921* (Hamburg, 1984), 237.

4. NG 16:701; Schoenberg to Magistrat Stadt Wien, 25 Mar. 1933, AI, gen. corr.;

Ernst Hilmar, ed., *Arnold Schönberg: Gedenkausstellung 1974* (Vienna, 1974), 328; Nicolas Slonimsky, *Music Since 1900,* 4th ed. (New York, 1971), 732.

5. Schoenberg to Rosbaud, 14 Mar. and 15 Apr. 1931; and to Casals, 20 Feb. 1933; and to Gerhard, 18 Mar. 1933, AI, gen. corr.; Schoenberg to Rosbaud, 7 Jan. 1933, in Erwin Stein, ed., *Arnold Schoenberg: Letters* (New York, 1965), 169–70; Joan Evans, *Hans Rosbaud: A Bio-Bibliography* (New York, 1992), 18–25.

6. Stuckenschmidt, *Schoenberg,* 105.

7. Ibid., 108.

8. Schreker to Schoenberg, 18 Sept. 1930, in Friedrich C. Heller, ed., *Arnold Schönberg—Franz Schreker: Ein Briefwechsel* (Tutzing, 1974), 72.

9. Schoenberg to Trudi [Greissle], 15 Dec. 1931, AI, gen. corr.

10. Schoenberg to Asch, 24 May 1932, AI, gen. corr.

11. Stein, *Schoenberg Letters,* 116 (quote); Rust to Präsident [von Schillings], 17 May 1933; von Schillings to Schoenberg, 23 May 1933, facsimiles in Nuria Nono-Schoenberg, ed., *Arnold Schönberg, 1874–1951: Lebensgeschichte in Begegnungen* (Klagenfurt, 1992), 291, 295; Willi Reich, *Schoenberg: A Critical Biography* (London, 1971), 187–88; Hilmar, *Schönberg,* 326.

12. Schoenberg to Gerhard, 18 Mar. and 15 Apr. 1933; and to Freund, 15 May 1933, AI, gen. corr.; Schoenberg to Berg, [20 Apr. and 20 May 1933], in Juliane Brand et al., eds., *The Berg-Schoenberg Correspondence: Selected Letters* (New York, 1987), 443–44; Reich, *Schoenberg,* 188.

13. Peter Heyworth, *Otto Klemperer: His Life and Times,* 2 vols. (Cambridge, 1983, 1996), 2:4.

14. Schoenberg to Furtwängler, 4 June 1929, AI, gen. corr.; Stuckenschmidt, *Schoenberg,* 102; Berndt W. Wessling, *Furtwängler: Eine kritische Biographie* (Stuttgart, 1985), 172–74.

15. See Schoenberg to Furtwängler, 23 Sept. 1929, AI, gen. corr.; Wilhelm Furtwängler, *Notebooks, 1924–1954,* ed. Michael Tanner (London, 1989), 58; Alban to Helene Berg, 17 May 1933, in Alban Berg, *Briefe an seine Frau,* ed. Helene Berg (Munich, 1965), 628.

16. Schoenberg telegram to Furtwängler, [May 1933], AI, gen. corr.

17. Furtwängler memorandum, [June 1933], BA, R56I/140 (1st quote); Furtwängler to Rust, 4 June 1933, BAB Furtwängler (2nd quote).

18. Schoenberg to Furtwängler, 8 June, 17 July, and 7 Sept. 1933, AI, gen. corr.

19. Schoenberg to Furtwängler, 30 Oct. 1934; Furtwängler to Schoenberg, 28 Nov. 1934, AI, gen. corr.

20. Schoenberg, memorandum about Furtwängler, [n.d.], AI, gen. corr.; Furtwängler, *Notebooks,* 162.

21. Schoenberg to Webern, 18 June 1933, in Ernst Hilmar, "Schönberg an Webern: Eine Auswahl unbekannter Briefe," in Hilmar, *Schönberg,* 53.

22. Schoenberg to Oxford University Press, 22 June, 3 Aug., and 1 Sept. 1933, AI, gen. corr.; Schoenberg to Berg, 17 Sept. 1933, in Brand et al., *Berg-Schoenberg Correspondence,* 445.

23. Schoenberg to Stein, 28 June 1933; and to Kalmus, 11 July 1933; and to Görgi [Schönberg], 18 July, 3 Aug. and 25 Sept. 1933, AI, gen. corr.; Schoenberg to Berg, [?] Aug. 1933, in Brand et al., *Berg-Schoenberg Correspondence,* 444; Schoenberg to Webern, 16 Sept. 1933, in Hilmar, "Schönberg an Webern," 55.

24. Malkin telegram to Schoenberg, 3 Sept. 1933, facsimile in Nono-Schoenberg, *Schönberg,* 295; Malkin telegram to Schoenberg, 15 Sept. 1933, in Hilmar,

Schönberg, 330; Schoenberg to Webern, 16 Sept. 1933, in Hilmar, "Schönberg an Webern," 54; Schoenberg to Trudi [Greissle], 14 Oct. 1933, AI, gen. corr.

25. Downes to Schoenberg, 15 Jan. 1934; Schoenberg to Kalmus, 17 Jan. 1934; and to Goehr, 20 Jan. 1934; and to Engel, 9 Mar. 1934; and to Görgi [Schönberg], 2 and 16 July 1934, AI, gen. corr.; Schoenberg to Webern, 1 Jan. 1934, in Hilmar, "Schönberg an Webern," 58; Hilmar, *Schönberg,* 333; Reich, *Schoenberg,* 193.

26. Schoenberg to Trudi [Greissle], 4 and 8 May 1934; Schoenberg to Görgi [Schönberg], 10 June 1934, AI, gen. corr.

27. Schoenberg to Webern, 12 Apr. 1934, in Hilmar, "Schönberg an Webern," 59.

28. Arnold Schönberg, *Stil und Gedanke: Aufsätze zur Musik,* ed. Ivan Vojtech (Frankfurt am Main, 1976), 304.

29. Schoenberg to Herz, 2 Sept. 1934; and to Stiedry, 12 Sept. 1934; and to Görgi [Schönberg], 28 Oct. 1934 and 16 June 1935; and to Bach, 13 Mar. 1935; and to Greissle, 7 June 1938, AI, gen. corr.; Schönberg circular [to his friends], Nov. 1934, LBI, AR-7049/10; Leonard Stein, "Musiker im Exil in Südkalifornien: Die ersten Jahrzehnte," in Habakuk Traber and Elmar Weingarten, eds., *Verdrängte Musik: Berliner Komponisten im Exil* (Berlin, 1987), 123; George Antheil, *Bad Boy of Music* (New York, 1981), 314 (quote).

30. See the more general observations by Alan Lessem, "The Emigré Experience: Schoenberg in America," in Juliane Brand and Christopher Hailey, eds., *Constructive Dissonance: Arnold Schoenberg and the Transformation of Twentieth-Century Culture* (Berkeley, 1997), 58–68.

31. Schoenberg to Webern, 13 Nov. 1934, in Hilmar, "Schönberg an Webern," 60–61; Schoenberg to Kolisch, 8 Dec. 1934, AI, gen. corr.; Schoenberg circular [to his friends], Nov. 1934, LBI, AR-7049/10.

32. Schoenberg to Trudi [Greissle], 16/19 June 1945, AI, gen. corr.

33. USC to Schoenberg, 1 July 1935 and 23 Apr. 1936, facsimiles in Nono-Schoenberg, *Schönberg,* 322, 327; Schoenberg to Stein, 28 June 1933, AI, gen. corr.; Schoenberg to Webern, 15 Jan. and 27 Aug. 1936, in Hilmar, "Schönberg an Webern," 62–63; Hilmar, *Schönberg,* 337.

34. Schoenberg affidavit for Rudolf Goehr, [1938], in Nono-Schoenberg, *Schönberg,* 344; Schoenberg to Greissle, 8 Jan. and 7 June 1938; and to Heinrich Schoenberg, 4 July 1939; and to Zemlinsky, 9 Feb. 1940; and to Trudi [Greissle], 21 June and 9 July 1941, AI, gen. corr.

35. Sproul to Schoenberg, 30 Oct. 1941, AI, Gertrud Schoenberg coll.

36. Schoenberg to Trudi [Greissle], 17 May 1942, AI, gen. corr.; Hilmar, *Schönberg,* 345; Stein, "Musiker im Exil," 125; *Directory of Fellows, 1925–1974: John Simon Guggenheim Memorial Foundation* (New York, 1975), 58, 79, 125, 168, 308, 356.

37. Benedict to Schoenberg, 3 June 1942 and 11 Aug. 1945; Underhill to Schoenberg, 30 June 1942, AI, Gertrud Schoenberg coll.

38. Powell to Schoenberg, 22 Sept. and 27 Dec. 1944, AI, Gertrud Schoenberg coll.; Schoenberg to Uncle Richard [Hoffmann sen.], 17 Oct. 1944; and to Blumauer, 3 June 1946, AI, gen. corr.; Rosbaud to Schoenberg, 7 Feb. 1949; Schoenberg to Rosbaud, 15 Feb. 1949, LP, 423/33/631.

39. Joan Evans, "Hans Rosbaud and the Music of Arnold Schoenberg," paper presented at International Conference, "Austria, 996–1996: Music in a Changing Society," Ottawa, Ontario, Canada, 4 Jan. 1996.

40. Schoenberg to Behymer, 7 Nov. 1934, AI, gen. corr.

41. Schoenberg to Rankl, 9 Feb. 1939, AI, gen. corr.

42. Schoenberg to Fraenkel, 26 Nov. 1935, AI, gen. corr.; Schoenberg to Sprague Coolidge, 5 Feb. 1937, facsimile in Nono-Schoenberg, *Schönberg,* 334.

43. See relevant corr. of June 1950, AI, gen. corr.

44. Sproul to Schoenberg, 3 Mar. 1945; Vincent to Schoenberg, 4 Nov. 1949, AI, Gertrud Schoenberg coll.

45. Schoenberg once applied to himself the definition *"Lehrer aus Leidenschaft"* (teacher motivated by passion), quoted in Nono-Schoenberg, *Schönberg,* 396. On Schoenberg's claim, see, e.g., Schoenberg to Varèse, 23 May 1939, AI, gen. corr.; Jost Hermand, *Beredte Töne: Musik im historischen Prozess* (Frankfurt am Main, 1991), 197; Dika Newlin, *Schoenberg Remembered: Diaries and Recollections (1938–76)* (New York, 1980), 94; Peter Yates quoted in Dorothy Lamb Crawford, *Evenings on and off the Roof: Pioneering Concerts in Los Angeles, 1939–1971* (Berkeley, 1995), 115.

46. Claudia Maurer Zenck, "Challenges and Opportunities of Acculturation: Schoenberg, Krenek and Stravinsky in Exile," in Reinhold Brinkmann and Christoph Wolff, eds., *Driven into Paradise: The Musical Migration from Nazi Germany to the United States* (Berkeley, 1999), 172–93.

47. Arnold Schönberg, "Vorwort," in *Harmonielehre,* 3rd ed. (Vienna, 1922), n.p.

48. Schoenberg to Board, Vienna Academy of Music, [Spring 1910], in Stein, *Schoenberg Letters,* 29.

49. Kurt to Hanns [Weill], [20 June 1919], WC, Hans/Rita Weill coll.

50. Stuckenschmidt, *Schoenberg,* 76.

51. Dika Newlin, "Why Is Schoenberg's Biography So Difficult to Write?" *Perspectives of New Music* 12 (1973/74), 42.

52. David Raksin, "Schönberg als Lehrer in Los Angeles: Erinnerungen eines Schülers," in Traber and Weingarten, *Verdrängte Musik,* 130.

53. Schoenberg quoted in Reich, *Schoenberg,* 192.

54. Schoenberg to Feiler, 8 Jan. 1935, AI, gen. corr.

55. List of Schoenberg's fall 1935 semester courses, [Sept. 1935], facsimile in Nono-Schoenberg, *Schönberg,* 322 (1st quote); Schoenberg on 16 Mar. 1936 quoted ibid., 330; Reich, *Schoenberg,* 200–2.

56. Schoenberg in Nono-Schoenberg, [1944/45], *Schönberg,* 399.

57. Schoenberg to Sproul, 14 May 1936; and to Herz, 2 May 1938 (quote), AI, gen. corr.; Sproul to Schoenberg, 25 and 27 June 1937, AI, Gertrud Schoenberg coll.

58. Allen to Schoenberg, 4 June 1938, AI, gen. corr.; Schoenberg to Webern, 8 July 1939, in Hilmar, "Schönberg an Webern," 66; Schoenberg on 1 Dec. 1939, quoted in Nono-Schoenberg, *Schönberg,* 362; Hilmar, *Schönberg,* 344; Newlin, *Schoenberg Remembered,* 106.

59. See choice examples of this in Newlin, *Schoenberg Remembered,* 21, 33–34, 53, 322–23.

60. Schoenberg-Nono, *Schönberg,* 362; Schoenberg quoted ibid., 399.

61. Schoenberg to Webern, 8 July 1939, in Hilmar, "Schönberg an Webern," 66 (1st quote); Newlin, *Schoenberg Remembered,* 14 (2nd quote), 286.

62. See, e.g., Ulrich Kramer, *Alban Berg als Schüler Arnold Schönbergs: Quellenstudien und Analysen zum Frühwerk* (Vienna, 1996).

63. Schoenberg to Adler, 20 Aug. 1912, in Ennulat, *Schoenberg Correspondence,*

94; Josef Rufer, "Hommage à Schoenberg," ibid., 32 (1st quote), 36–37; Schönberg, *Harmonielehre*, 7 (2nd quote). Also see Schönberg, *Stil und Gedanke*, 322; Stuckenschmidt, *Schoenberg*, 76; Walter H. Rubsamen, "Schoenberg in America," *Musical Quarterly* 37 (1951), 473; Dika Newlin, "Schönberg in America, 1933–1948: Retrospect and Prospect—I," *Music-Survey* 1 (1949), 131; Reich, *Schoenberg*, 201.

64. Arnold Schoenberg, *Models for Beginners in Composition: Music Examples* (1st ed. 1942), 2nd ed. (New York, 1943), 3.

65. Schoenberg to Stein, 28 June 1933, AI, gen. corr.

66. Arnold Schoenberg, "Selbstanalyse (Reife)," in Albrecht Dümling, ed., *Verteidigung des musikalischen Fortschritts: Brahms und Schönberg* (Hamburg, 1990), 141; Ethan Haimo, "Schoenberg and the Origins of Atonality," in Brand and Hailey, *Constructive Dissonance*, 72; Hermann Danuser, "Schoenberg's Concept of Art in Twentieth-Century Music History," in Brand and Hailey, *Constructive Dissonance*, 183–84.

67. *NG* 16:702.

68. Schönberg, *Stil und Gedanke*, 348–50.

69. Paolo Petazzi in his liner notes for compact disk, Arnold Schoenberg, *The Piano Music*, Deutsche Grammophon, Stereo 423 249–2.

70. Alexander L. Ringer, *Arnold Schoenberg: The Composer as Jew* (Oxford, 1990), 198.

71. Schönberg, *Stil und Gedanke*, 355. See also idem, *Harmonielehre*, 5–6.

72. *NG* 16:713; Ringer, *Schoenberg*, 87 (quote).

73. Danuser, "Concept," 183.

74. Schönberg, *Stil und Gedanke*, 302 (quote); Ringer, *Schoenberg*, 70.

75. Schoenberg quoted in Ringer, *Schoenberg*, 69.

76. Schoenberg to Slonimsky, 3 June 1937, quoted in Nono-Schoenberg, *Schönberg*, 341.

77. Boris Schwarz, "The Music World in Migration," in Jarrell C. Jackman and Carla M. Borden, eds., *The Muses Flee Hitler: Cultural Transfer and Adaptation, 1930–1945* (Washington, D.C., 1983), 141; Ernst Krenek, "Amerikas Einfluss auf eingewanderte Komponisten," in Traber and Weingarten, *Verdrängte Musik*, 104.

78. Heyworth, *Klemperer*, 2:53; Olin Downes's critique in the *New York Times* of 18 Oct. 1935, quoted in Ennulat, *Schoenberg Correspondence*, 226.

79. Schoenberg quoted in Hilmar, *Schönberg*, 334.

80. Stuckenschmidt, *Schoenberg*, 113. See also Rubsamen, "Schoenberg in America," 470; Hermand, *Beredte Töne*, 198–99.

81. Schoenberg to Berg, [Aug. 1933] and 17 Sept. 1933, in Brand et al., *Berg-Schoenberg Correspondence*, 444–45; Schoenberg to Webern, 16 Sept. 1933, in Hilmar, "Schönberg an Webern," 54; *NG* 16:720.

82. Schoenberg quoted in Hilmar, *Schönberg*, 334.

83. Ibid., 340; Rubsamen, "Schoenberg in America," 473.

84. Schoenberg to Sprague Coolidge, 3 Aug. 1936, in Nono-Schoenberg, *Schönberg*, 331; Rubsamen, "Schoenberg in America," 474.

85. Schoenberg to Stiedry, 1 Dec. 1938, in Nono-Schoenberg, *Schönberg*, 361; Rubsamen, "Schoenberg in America," 477–78; *NG* 16:717–18, 720; *GLM* 7:272.

86. Schoenberg to Trudi [Greissle], 17 May 1942, AI, gen. corr; Rubsamen, "Schoenberg in America," 478.

87. Reich, *Schoenberg*, 210; *NG* 16:705, 718 (1st quote); Joan Evans to author, Toronto, 22 Aug. 1998, APA (2nd quote).

88. *NG* 16:718 (quote).

89. Stokowski as quoted by Downes: see Downes's critique in the *New York Times* of 7 Feb. 1944, facsimile in Nono-Schoenberg, *Schönberg,* 391. Also See Slonimsky, *Music,* 780; Rubsamen, "Schoenberg in America," 479; Reich, *Schoenberg,* 213; Hilmar, *Schönberg,* 347; Peter Petersen, "'A Grave Situation Was Created': Schönbergs Klavierkonzert von 1942," in Otto Kolleritsch, ed., *Die Wiener Schule und das Hakenkreuz: Das Schicksal der Moderne im gesellschaftlichen Kontext des 20. Jahrhunderts* (Vienna, 1990), 65–91.

90. *NG* 16:720; Slonimsky, *Music,* 789–90. On *Ode to Napoleon* see Nono-Schoenberg, *Schönberg,* 395; Slonimsky, *Music,* 792.

91. Rubsamen, "Schoenberg in America," 482 (quote); Reich, *Schoenberg,* 230; *GLM* 7:272.

92. *NG* 16:719; *GLM* 7:273–74.

93. *NG* 16:718.

94. Rubsamen, "Schoenberg in America," 484; Reich, *Schoenberg,* 224.

95. Schoenberg to Scherchen, 6 Oct. 1950, in Hansjörg Pauli and Dagmar Wünsche, eds., *Hermann Scherchen, 1891–1966* (Berlin, 1986), 65; Rubsamen, "Schoenberg in America," 487; Reich, *Schoenberg,* 230.

96. Schoenberg as quoted in Rufer, "Hommage à Schoenberg," 14; see also Schoenberg to Rosbaud, 12 May 1947, LP, 423/33/631. Kurt Weill is known to have said he would be happy if every taxi driver could whistle his melodies. See Hermand, *Beredte Töne,* 163; Joachim Lucchesi, "'Fremd bin ich eingezogen'? Anmerkungen zu einer geteilten Biographie," in Kim H. Kowalke and Horst Edler, eds., *A Stranger Here Myself: Kurt Weill-Studien* (Hildesheim, 1993), 61.

97. Schoenberg to Scherchen, 12 Nov. 1945, and to Voigt, 28 Feb. 1939 (quote), AI, gen. corr. Also see Schoenberg to Webern, 1 Jan 1934, in Hilmar, "Schönberg an Webern," 58; Schoenberg circular [to his friends], Nov. 1934, LBI, AR-7049/10; Rubsamen, "Schoenberg in America," 480, 486.

98. Schoenberg in broadcast (Olin Downes), 23 Aug. 1949, AI, Recorded Statements.

99. Schoenberg circular [to his friends], Nov. 1934, LBI, AR-7049/10 (1st quote); Schoenberg to Koussevitzky, 22 Apr. 1939; and to Reiner, 29 Oct. 1944 (remaining quotes), AI, gen. corr.

100. As Vienna Philharmonic musicians' foreman Hugo Burghauser heard Toscanini say (*Philharmonische Begegnungen: Erinnerungen eines Wiener Philharmonikers* [Zurich, 1979], 38).

101. Schoenberg to Greissle, 27 Nov. 1945, AI, gen. corr.

102. Schoenberg to Walter, 10 Nov. 1913; Walter to Schoenberg, 12 Dec. 1913, AI, gen. corr.; Reich, *Schoenberg Letters,* 40, n. 3; Bruno Walter, *Theme and Variations: An Autobiography* (New York, 1966), 169.

103. Walter's quotes from *Theme and Variations,* 170; also see 316; Walter's remarks to Schoenberg on letter Demuth to Schoenberg, 18 June 1934, AI, gen. corr.; Schoenberg circular [to his friends], Nov. 1934, LBI, AR-7049/10; Lehmann to Constance [Hope], 28 July 1937, UCSB Library, Lotte Lehmann coll.; Newlin, *Schoenberg Remembered,* 57.

104. Schoenberg to Greissle, 4 Sept. 1943; and to Walter, 23 Dec. 1943; Walter to Schoenberg, 18 Dec. 1943, 2 Jan. and 6 Feb. 1944, AI, gen. corr.; Walter to Zirato, 17 and 29 Aug. 1943, 8 June 1948 (quote); Zirato to Walter, 23 Aug. 1943; [Zirato] to Walter, 9 Sept. 1943, NYA, Walter coll.; Bruno Walter, *Of Music and Music Making* (New York, 1961), 205–6. I owe my insight into the Mahler-Schoenberg-Walter relationship to Albrecht Riethmüller (letter to author, Berlin, 16 Feb. 1998, APA).

105. Schoenberg to Stokowski, 14 Nov. 1933, 19 Oct. 1939, and 17 Dec. 1940 (1st quote); and to Arnold [Greissle], 15 Oct. 1943; and to Scherchen, 12 Nov. 1945; Stokowski to Schoenberg, [1932/33], AI, gen. corr.; Schoenberg to Hinrichsen, 29 Sept. 1922, and to Johnson, 24 July 1950, in Reich, *Schoenberg Letters,* 78, 281 (2nd quote). Hear the compact disk, Pearl 9066, of a live recording of *Gurrelieder,* with the Philadelphia Orchestra under Stokowski, Rose Bampton, soprano, Paul Althaus, tenor, 9 Apr. 1932 (cf. *Schwann Opus* [Fall 1997], 796).

106. Schoenberg circular [to his friends], Nov. 1934, LBI, AR-7049/10; Schoenberg to Scherchen, 12 Nov. 1945, AI, gen. corr.; Schoenberg to Cowell, 6 Nov. 1948, in Stein, *Schoenberg Letters,* 256; Otto Klemperer, *Meine Erinnerungen an Gustav Mahler und andere autobiographische Skizzen* (Freiburg im Breisgau, 1960), 26; Rubsamen, "Schoenberg in America," 480, 484; Slonimsky, *Music,* 583; Hans Moldenhauer and Rosaleen Moldenhauer, *Anton von Webern: A Chronicle of His Life and Work* (New York, 1979), 409; Stein, "Musiker im Exil," 124; Crawford, *Evenings,* 32, 34, 42, 66–67, 92, 97; Nono-Schoenberg, *Schönberg,* 337.

107. Clipping from *Southern California Daily Trojan,* 5 Dec. 1935, facsimile in Nono-Schoenberg, *Schönberg,* 323.

108. Nono-Schoenberg, *Schönberg,* 360.

109. Hilmar, *Schönberg,* 344.

110. Ibid., 349; *NG* 16:720–21.

111. Stuckenschmidt, *Schoenberg,* 140.

112. Crawford, *Evenings,* 114, 116–17.

113. On Klemperer from World War I to his death in 1973, see Heyworth, *Klemperer,* vols. 1 and 2.

114. *NG* 16:708, 711; Klemperer, *Erinnerungen,* 25.

115. Heyworth, *Klemperer,* 2:237.

116. Schoenberg to Kestenberg, 18 June 1928, in Stein, *Schoenberg Letters,* 132; Klemperer, *Erinnerungen,* 26; Stuckenschmidt, *Schoenberg,* 102; Heyworth, *Klemperer,* 1:398–99.

117. Stein, "Musiker im Exil," 123; Albrecht Dümling, "Zwischen Aussenseiterstatus und Integration: Musiker-Exil an der amerikanischen Westküste," in Hanns-Werner Heister et al., eds., *Musik im Exil: Folgen des Nazismus für die internationale Musikkultur* (Frankfurt am Main, 1993), 314.

118. Klemperer telegram to Schoenberg, 6 Feb. 1934; Schoenberg to Klemperer, 8 Nov. 1934, AI, gen. corr.; Schoenberg circular [to his friends], Nov. 1934, LBI, AR-7049/10; Heyworth, *Klemperer,* 2:42, 84.

119. Heyworth, *Klemperer,* 2:84.

120. Schoenberg to Webern, 15 Jan. 1936, quoted in Nono-Schoenberg, *Schönberg,* 325; Heyworth, *Klemperer,* 2:86 (Klemperer quoted).

121. Schoenberg to Klemperer, 18 Mar. 1936 (quote); and to Charlotte Dieterle, 30 July 1936, AI, gen. corr.; Heyworth, *Klemperer,* 2:86–89.

122. Schoenberg to Klemperer, 25 Sept. 1940 (1st two quotes) and 28 Nov. 1940; and to Stiedry, 2 Apr. 1940; Klemperer to Schoenberg, 29 Sept. and 24 Nov. 1940 (last quote), AI, gen. corr.; Newlin, *Schoenberg Remembered,* 191, 243, 276; Heyworth, *Klemperer,* 2:110–11.

123. Klemperer, *Erinnerungen,* 26.

124. Schoenberg to Sproul, 12 Nov. 1943, AI, gen. corr.; Heyworth, *Klemperer,* 2:138.

125. Schoenberg to Greissle, 22 July 1944; and to Usher, 4 Jan. 1945; and to

Trudi [Greissle], 3 Feb. 1945, AI, gen. corr.; Schoenberg to Lehner, 10 Feb. 1949, in Stein, *Schoenberg Letters,* 269; Heyworth, *Klemperer,* 2:89.

126. Klemperer to Schoenberg, 2 Dec. 1946; Klemperer telegram to Schoenberg, 1 July 1947, AI, gen. corr.; Klemperer, *Erinnerungen,* 27–28; Heyworth, *Klemperer,* 2:212, 220.

127. Hans W. Heinsheimer, *Best Regards to Aida: The Defeats and Victories of a Music Man on Two Continents* (New York, 1968), 207.

128. Schoenberg to anon., 27 Nov. 1945, AI, gen. corr.

129. Schoenberg quoted in Slonimsky, *Music,* 723.

130. *Österreichische Musikzeitschrift* 43 (1988), 182.

131. Schoenberg to Toch, 2 June and 10 Oct. 1931, ETA; Toch to Schoenberg, 5 July 1931, AI, gen. corr.

132. Schoenberg to Toch, [early Summer 1933], facsimile in Nono-Schoenberg, *Schönberg,* 292; Newlin, *Schoenberg Remembered,* 139–40; Toch to Schoenberg, 11 Sept. 1949; Schoenberg to Toch, 13 Sept. 1949, AI, gen. corr.; Charlotte E. Erwin, "Ernst Toch in America," in Traber and Weingarten, *Verdrängte Musik,* 111.

133. Schoenberg memorandum, 5 Oct. 1932, AI, gen. corr. Also see chapter 2, at n. 3.

134. Klemperer, *Erinnerungen,* 27; Salka Viertel, *Kindness of Strangers* (New York, 1969), 259; Schwarz, "Music World," 144; Newlin, *Schoenberg Remembered,* 56 (quote), 78, 334; Hans Heinz Stuckenschmidt, "Das Problem Schönberg," *Melos* 14 (1947), 162.

135. Rubsamen, "Schoenberg in America," 484–85; Christopher Hailey, "Introduction," in Brand and Hailey, *Constructive Dissonance,* xi; Crawford, *Evenings,* 100; Riethmüller to author, Berlin, 16 Feb. 1998, APA.

136. See n. 106; Schoenberg to Krenek, 1 and 12 Dec. 1939, in Stein, *Schoenberg Letters,* 210; Krenek to Schoenberg, 18 Nov. 1940 (1st quote), 10 Feb. 1941 (2nd quote), 12 Apr. 1945, AI, gen. corr.; John L. Stewart, *Ernst Krenek: The Man and His Music* (Berkeley, 1991), 206, 218; Claudia Maurer Zenck, *Ernst Krenek— ein Komponist im Exil* (Vienna, 1980), 119.

137. Charles Schwartz, *Gershwin: His Life and Music* (Indianapolis, 1973), 277 (quotes); 319–20, n. 27; Schoenberg to Speiser, 25 Sept. 1934, in Stein, *Schoenberg Letters,* 189–90; Reich, *Schoenberg,* 203; Hilmar, *Schönberg,* 341; Slonimsky, *Music,* 651.

138. Schoenberg to Zillig, 15 July 1949, AI, gen. corr.; Copland to Thomson, 11 Sept. 1949 (Copland's quotes); Copland to Schoenberg, 13 Feb. 1950; Schoenberg to Copland, 21 Feb. 1950 (Schoenberg's quote), in Ennulat, *Schoenberg Correspondence,* 262–63, 269–71. Also see Howard Pollack, *Aaron Copland: The Life and Work of an Uncommon Man* (New York, 1999), 64–65, 69, 188.

139. Schoenberg to Copland, 21 Feb. 1950, in Ennulat, *Schoenberg Correspondence,* 271.

140. On the relationship until Engel's death, see Heinsheimer, *Regards,* 206–21.

141. See corr. (1948) in Ennulat, *Schoenberg Correspondence,* 241–47.

142. Schoenberg to Buck, 10 Apr. 1941, AI, gen. corr. Also see Schoenberg circular [to his friends], Nov. 1934, LBI, AR-7049/10.

143. Schoenberg to RCA Victor, 8 and 28 Feb. 1939, AI, gen. corr.

144. Schoenberg circular [to his friends], Nov. 1934, LBI, AR-7049/10; Viertel, *Kindness,* 206–8; Nono-Schoenberg, *Schönberg,* 319. Cf. Rubsamen, "Schoenberg in America," 472; Rufer, "Hommage à Schoenberg," 32.

145. Schoenberg to Alban Berg, 21 Nov. 1933 and 2 Jan. 1935 (quote); Schoenberg to Helene Berg, 1 Jan. 1936, in Brand et al., *Berg-Schoenberg Correspondence*, 448, 460–61, 471–72; Schoenberg to Webern, 1 Jan. 1934, in Hilmar, "Schönberg an Webern," 56; Juliane Brand and Christopher Hailey, "Further Correspondence: The Twelve Lost Berg Letters," *Journal of the Arnold Schoenberg Institute* 12 (1989), 133–74; Moldenhauer, *Webern*, 395; Gerhard Scheit, "Das sinkende Rettungsboot: Musik im Exilland Österreich," in Heister et al., *Musik im Exil*, 220–21; Nono-Schoenberg, *Schönberg*, 324; George Perle, *The Operas of Alban Berg*, 2 vols. (Berkeley, 1980, 1985), 2:282–88; Michael H. Kater, *The Twisted Muse: Musicians and Their Music in the Third Reich* (New York, 1997), 124.

146. Moldenhauer, *Webern*, 391, 393, 410 (Schoenberg's 1st quote), 411, 412 (Schoenberg's 2nd quote), 414, 531, 592; Schoenberg to Webern, 20 June 1937, facsimile in Nono-Schoenberg, *Schönberg*, 339; Schoenberg to Reese, 11 Oct. 1939, AI, gen. corr. (3rd quote); Kater, *The Twisted Muse*, 73–74.

147. Kurt to Hanns [Weill], [20 June 1919], WC, Hans/Rita Weill coll.; Schoenberg to Scherchen, 12 Aug. 1924, in Stein, *Schoenberg Letters*, 111; GLM 7:239.

148. Schoenberg to Scherchen, 31 Aug. 1950, in Pauli and Wünsche, *Scherchen*, 62–63.

149. Scherchen to Schoenberg, 30 Sept. 1950, ibid., 63–64.

150. Schoenberg to Scherchen, 6 Oct. 1950, ibid., 64.

151. Schoenberg to Scherchen, [2] Nov. 1950, ibid., 65–66.

152. Schoenberg to Trudi [Greissle], 18 Feb. 1932; Schoenberg to Görgi [Schönberg], 3 Sept. 1937, 29 Oct. 1938, 16 Feb. 1941, AI, gen. corr.; UE-Direktion to Weill, 19 June 1934, WC, Weill/UE corr.; Nono-Schoenberg, *Schönberg*, 385.

153. Schoenberg to Greissle, 7 June 1938; and to Görgi [Schönberg], 10 June 1938, AI, gen. corr.; Schoenberg to Trudi [Greissle], 16 Mar. 1934, 31 Mar. 1939, 27 Oct. 1941, 16/19 June 1945, AI, gen. corr.; Schoenberg to Trudi, 21 Apr. 1936, facsimile in Nono-Schoenberg, *Schönberg*, 333.

154. Lotte Klemperer to Gertrud Schoenberg, 15 Apr. 1941, AI, gen. corr.; Newlin, *Schoenberg Remembered*, esp. 249–52, 266; Katia Mann, *Meine ungeschriebenen Memoiren*, ed. Elisabeth Plessen and Michael Mann (Frankfurt am Main, 1981), 134; Rufer, "Hommage à Schoenberg," 12; Rubsamen, "Schoenberg in America," 475.

155. GLM 4:388; Newlin, *Schoenberg Remembered*.

156. Nono-Schoenberg, *Schönberg*, 333, 342.

157. See Schoenberg to Herz, 2 May 1938; and to Mengelberg, 9 Feb. 1939; and to Brunswick, 28 Dec. 1940, AI, gen. corr.; Schoenberg to Webern, 8 July 1939, in Hilmar, "Schönberg an Webern," 66–67; Nono-Schoenberg, *Schönberg*, 343, 381.

158. Mahler-Werfel quoted in Françoise Giroud, *Alma Mahler or the Art of Being Loved* (Oxford, 1991), 138.

159. Schoenberg to Mahler-Werfel, 23 Jan. 1936; Mahler-Werfel to Schoenberg, 3 Oct. 1938 and 2 Apr. 1939 (1st quote); Schoenberg to Mahler-Werfel, 24 Apr. 1939 (2nd quote), and 9 Aug. 1939, AI, gen. corr.; Giroud, *Alma Mahler*, 146–50; Peter Stephan Jungk, *Franz Werfel: Eine Lebensgeschichte* (Frankfurt am Main, 1987), 253–88.

160. Katia Mann, *Memoiren*, 132 (1st quote); Stuckenschmidt, *Schoenberg*, 14 (2nd quote); Bernhold Schmid, "Neues zum 'Doktor Faustus'-Streit zwischen Arnold Schönberg und Thomas Mann," *Augsburger Jahrbuch zur Musikwissenschaft* 6 (1989), 155; Schmid, "Neues zum 'Doktor Faustus'-Streit zwischen Arnold Schönberg und Thomas Mann: Ein Nachtrag," *Augsburger Jahrbuch zur*

Musikwissenschaft 7 (1990), 184; Schoenberg to Saturday Review of Literature, 13 Nov. 1948, in Thomas Mann, *Essays,* 6 vols., ed. Hermann Kurzke and Stephan Stachorski (Frankfurt am Main, 1993–97), 6:99.

161. My edition Frankfurt am Main and Hamburg: S. Fischer, 1967.

162. Mann to Walter, 16, 25, and 27 Aug. 1944, in Thomas Mann, *Selbstkommentare: "Doktor Faustus" und "Die Entstehung des Doktor Faustus",* ed. Hans Wysling (Frankfurt am Main, 1992), 29–31; Mann to Adorno, 30 Dec. 1945, ibid., 73; Mann, *Die Entstehung des Doktor Faustus: Roman eines Romans* (Amsterdam, 1949), 93; Lehmann to Constance [Hope], [19 June 1941], UCSB Library, Lotte Lehmann coll.

163. Katia Mann, *Memoiren,* 133.

164. Schoenberg to Mann, 1 and 8 Nov. 1930, in Stein, *Schoenberg Letters,* 144–45.

165. Thomas Mann, *Tagebücher, 1937–1939,* ed. Peter de Mendelssohn (Frankfurt am Main, 1980), 204, 211; idem, *Tagebücher, 1940–1943,* ed. de Mendelssohn (Frankfurt am Main, 1982), 152–53, 309; Viertel, *Kindness,* 259–60.

166. Schoenberg to Mann, 28 Dec. 1938 and 15 Jan. 1939 (1st quote); Mann to Schoenberg, 9 Jan. 1939 (Mann's quotes), AI, gen. corr.

167. Mann, *Tagebücher, 1940–1943,* 628; idem, *Entstehung,* 49–50 (quote); idem, *Selbstkommentare,* 292.

168. Mann to Walter, 6 May 1943, in Mann, *Selbstkommentare,* 10.

169. Idem, *Tagebücher, 1940–1943,* 572–73, 607, 625, 661; idem, *Selbstkommentare,* 12, 14, 16–17, 26; Kurzke and Stachorski in Mann, *Essays,* 6:436.

170. Idem, *Tagebücher, 1940–1943,* 661–62; Mann to Meyer, 28 Sept. 1944 (1st quote); Mann to Walter, 1 Mar. 1945 (2nd quote), in idem, *Selbstkommentare,* 34, 54, commentary in Mann, *Essays,* 6:436.

171. Mann to Meyer, 28 Sept. 1944, in idem, *Selbstkommentare,* 34.

172. See, e.g., Ringer, *Composer,* 70; and, as corrective, Mann, *Selbstkommentare,* 231.

173. Mann, *Selbstkommentare,* 248, 303; Vaget to author, Northampton, Mass., 19 Oct. 1997, APA.

174. Thomas to Michael Mann, 31 Jan. 1948, in Mann, *Selbstkommentare,* 157 (quote); ibid, 158, 164.

175. Mann to Marck, 22 Feb. 1948, ibid., 171 (1st quote); ibid., 166–68, 178, 180, 182, 185, 189; idem, *Doktor Faustus,* 511 (2nd quote); Schoenberg to Rufer, 25 May 1948, in Stein, *Schoenberg Letters,* 255.

176. Schoenberg to Saturday Review of Literature, 13 Nov. 1948, in Mann, *Essays,* 6:100; Schoenberg quoted in Reich, *Schoenberg,* 225.

177. See Mann, *Selbstkommentare,* 274, 290, 293.

178. Schoenberg to Mann, 2 Jan. 1950, in Stein, *Schoenberg Letters,* 278; Mann, *Selbstkommentare,* 328, 347.

179. Mann, *Selbstkommentare,* 325–26; Stuckenschmidt, *Schoenberg,* 11–12.

180. Mann to Adorno, 5 Oct. 1943, in Mann, *Selbstkommentare,* 16–17; idem, *Entstehung,* 41–42; Rose Rosengard Subotnik, "Adorno's Diagnosis of Beethoven's Late Style: Early Symptom of a Fatal Condition," *Journal of the American Musicological Society* 29 (1976), 242–46; Hans Rudolf Vaget, "*Salome* and *Palestrina* als historische Chiffren: Zur musikalischen Codierung in Thomas Manns *Doktor Faustus,*" in Heinz Gockel et al., eds., *Wagner-Nietzsche-Thomas Mann: Festschrift für Eckhard Heftrich* (Frankfurt am Main, 1993), 75. See Theodor W. Adorno, *Philosophie der neuen Musik* (Tübingen, 1949). I used the translation, *Philosophy*

of New Music (New York, 1973), 45–46, 48, 60–62, 67–77, 107–10, 120–24. See note 185, below.

181. *GLM* 1:13; *NG* 1:112.

182. Schoenberg to Geis, [?] Nov. 1932, AI, gen. corr.

183. Schoenberg to Adorno, 6 Dec. 1930, in Stein, *Schoenberg Letters,* 145–46 (quote); Schoenberg to Rosbaud, 13 Feb. 1932, ibid., 161; Adorno quoted (July 1930) in Joan Evans, "New Light on the First Performances of Arnold Schoenberg's *Opera* 34 and 35," *Journal of the Arnold Schoenberg Institute* 11 (1988), 165–66.

184. Adorno to Krenek, 28 Oct. 1934, in Wolfgang Rogge, ed., *Theodor Adorno und Ernst Krenek: Briefwechsel* (Frankfurt am Main, 1974), 52–55; Mann, *Entstehung,* 44 (quote), 45–47, 93, 135–38, 193–95; Schmid, "Neues," 153; Schmid, "Neues: Nachtrag," 178–80.

185. Mann, *Doktor Faustus,* 56; idem, *Entstehung,* 46.

186. Idem, *Selbstkommentare,* 358, 369–71; Mann to Lesser, 15 Oct. 1951, ibid., 369–71 (quote).

187. Hans Vaget, "Fünfzig Jahre Leiden an Deutschland: Thomas Manns 'Doktor Faustus' im Lichte unserer Erfahrung," paper delivered at international conference, "Thomas Mann: 'Doktor Faustus' 1947–1997," Humboldt-Universität Berlin, 4–7 June 1997.

188. Schoenberg as quoted in Ringer, *Composer,* 71. Also see Schoenberg to Saturday Review of Literature, 13 Nov. 1948, in Mann, *Essays,* 6:98.

189. Schoenberg to Zillig, 5 Dec. 1949, AI, gen. corr. Also see Schoenberg to List, 10 Dec. 1949; and to Rufer, 10 Feb. 1950, AI, gen. corr. Also see Schmid, "Neues," 169–70.

190. Schoenberg as quoted in Rufer, "Hommage à Schoenberg," 47.

191. Mann to Stuckenschmidt, 19 Oct. 1951, in Mann, *Selbstkommentare,* 326. English translation as in Stuckenschmidt, *Schoenberg,* 12.

192. This important point is also made by Vaget, "Fünfzig Jahre Leiden" (see n. 187); idem, "*Salome* und *Palestrina,*" 69; idem, "Whose Legacy? Thomas Mann, Franz W. Beidler and Bayreuth," *Wagner* 18, no. 1 (Jan. 1997), 3–19; idem, "Im Schatten Wagners," in idem, ed., *Im Schatten Wagners: Thomas Mann über Richard Wagner: Texte und Zeugnisse, 1895–1955* (Frankfurt am Main, 1999), 303–35.

193. Internet information, www.spiegel.de/kultur/aktuell/schoenberg.html., printout APA.

194. Internet information, www.schoenberg.at/festival/t4.htm., printout APA.

CHAPTER 8: STRAUSS

1. Willi Schuh, ed., *Richard Strauss: Briefe an die Eltern, 1882–1906* (Zurich, 1954), 295; Richard Strauss, *Betrachtungen und Erinnerungen,* ed. Willi Schuh (Zurich, 1949), 58, 124, 132–33, 173 (quote); Hans Heinz Stuckenschmidt, *Zum Hören geboren: Ein Leben mit der Musik unserer Zeit* (Munich, 1979), 133.

2. Brigitte Regler-Bellinger et al., *Knaurs Grosser Opernführer: Mit 400 Abbildungen und Notenbeispielen* (Munich, 1983), 460–62.

3. *NG* 18:234; Strauss to Willi Schuh, 25 Sept. 1944, in: Strauss, *Betrachtungen und Erinnerungen,* 168 (quote).

4. *NG* 18:218.

5. Willi Schuh, ed., *Richard Strauss—Hugo von Hofmannsthal: Briefwechsel: Gesamtausgabe,* 4th ed. (Zurich, 1970), 573, 586, 589.

6. Strauss to Hadamovsky, 1 July 1935, RG.

7. Kurt to Hanns [Weill], 6 Feb. 1919, WC, Hans/Rita Weill coll.; Franz Grasberger, *Der Strom der Töne trug mich fort: Die Welt um Richard Strauss in Briefen* (Tutzing, 1967), 171; Walter Thomas, *Richard Strauss und seine Zeitgenossen* (Munich, 1964), 218. For the quote, see chapter 3 at n. 75.

8. Strauss to Schalk, 3 Aug. 1921, in Günter Brosche, ed., *Richard Strauss— Franz Schalk: Ein Briefwechsel* (Tutzing, 1983), 224; chapter 2, passim and at n. 127 (for 1923).

9. According to Orff to Bergese, 23 May 1942, APA (quote). See text below at n. 304.

10. Strauss to Orff, [early 1942], CM, Allg. Korr.; Roland Tenschert, ed., *Richard Strauss und Joseph Gregor: Briefwechsel 1934–1949* (Salzburg, 1955).

11. Hartmann to Bayerische Staatstheater-Verwaltung, 10 Feb. 1949, BH, Staatstheater/14395; Horst Leuchtmann, "Viva la musica viva!," in *Karl Amadeus Hartmann und die Musica Viva: Essays, bisher unveröffentlichte Briefe an Hartmann, Katalog* (Munich, 1980), 144. Also 224.

12. Schuh, *Strauss: Briefe an Eltern,* 278; Schuh, *Strauss—Hofmannsthal,* 261; NG 18:221.

13. Pamela M. Potter, "Strauss's Friedenstag: A Pacifist Attempt at Political Resistance," *Musical Quarterly* 69 (1983), 409.

14. Strauss, *Betrachtungen und Erinnerungen,* 194.

15. Willi Schuh, *Richard Strauss: Jugend und frühe Meisterjahre: Lebenschronik, 1864–1898* (Zurich, 1976), 20–21.

16. These circumstances are now authoritatively explained in Ian Kershaw, *Hitler, 1889–1936: Hubris* (New York, 1998), 3–13.

17. Walter Deppisch, *Richard Strauss: Mit Selbstzeugnissen und Bilddokumenten* (Reinbek, 1968), 49–50.

18. Harry Graf Kessler, *Tagebücher, 1918–1937,* ed. Wolfgang Pfeiffer-Belli (Frankfurt am Main, 1982), 472–73.

19. Gabriele Strauss, ed., *Lieber Collega! Richard Strauss im Briefwechsel mit zeitgenössischen Komponisten und Dirigenten* (Berlin, 1996), 32, 333; Schuh, *Strauss: Briefe an Eltern,* 224, 229–30; Franz Trenner, ed., *Cosima Wagner— Richard Strauss: Ein Briefwechsel* (Tutzing, 1978), 233; Schuh, *Strauss,* 388; Deppisch, *Strauss,* 90; Rollo Myers, ed., *Richard Strauss and Romain Rolland: A Correspondence* (London, 1968), 123–24.

20. Schuh, *Strauss: Briefe an Eltern,* 36.

21. Trenner, *Wagner—Strauss,* 159–61.

22. Schuh, *Strauss: Briefe an Eltern,* 81, 91; Gabriele Strauss, *Collega,* 35.

23. Schuh, *Strauss: Briefe an Eltern,* 280; Schuh, *Strauss—Hofmannsthal,* 290, 419–20.

24. Grasberger, *Strom der Töne,* 237–39.

25. Strauss to Hofmannsthal, 22 Aug. 1914, in Schuh, *Strauss—Hofmannsthal,* 288.

26. Strauss to Hofmannsthal, 16 Jan. 1915, ibid., 294, also 289, 298.

27. Strauss to Rolland, 12 Feb. 1917, in Myers, *Strauss and Rolland,* 97.

28. Schuh, *Strauss: Briefe an Eltern,* passim.

29. Nike Wagner, *Wagner Theater* (Frankfurt am Main, 1998), 278.

30. Schuh, *Strauss: Briefe an Eltern,* 201–3.

31. On the latter, see text below at n. 334.

32. Richard Strauss, *Betrachtungen und Erinnerungen,* 244; Rudolf Hartmann, *Das geliebte Haus: Mein Leben mit der Oper* (Munich, 1975), 213.

33. Deppisch, *Strauss,* 130; Michael H. Kater, *The Twisted Muse: Musicians and Their Music in the Third Reich* (New York, 1997), 205.

34. The worst offender here is Gerhard Splitt, *Richard Strauss, 1933–1935: Ästhetik und Musikpolitik zu Beginn der nationalsozialistischen Herrschaft* (Pfaffenweiler, 1987).

35. Strauss to parents, 10 June 1893, in Schuh, *Strauss: Briefe an Eltern,* 179.

36. Myers, *Strauss and Rolland,* 160–61; Potter, "Friedenstag," 414.

37. Schuh, *Strauss—Hofmannsthal,* 364.

38. Rolland memorandum, 12 May 1924, in Myers, *Strauss and Rolland,* 165.

39. Ibid., 146; Schuh, *Strauss—Hofmannsthal,* 460–62, 541; Grasberger, *Strom der Töne,* 252, 374; Michael H. Kater, *Different Drummers: Jazz in the Culture of Nazi Germany* (New York, 1992), 21.

40. Strauss to Cosima Wagner, 22 Mar. 1890, in Trenner, *Wagner—Strauss,* 36.

41. Richard to Pauline Strauss, 31 Oct. 1918 (1st quote) and 6 Mar. 1919 (2nd quote), in Grasberger, *Strom der Töne,* 231, 237; Brosche, *Strauss,* 53.

42. Strauss to Hofmannsthal, 4 May 1926, in Schuh, *Strauss—Hofmannsthal,* 557. Cf. Myers, *Strauss and Rolland,* 112, 130.

43. Strauss quoted in Walter Panofsky, *Richard Strauss: Partitur eines Lebens* (Munich, 1965), 275. Also see Myers, *Strauss and Rolland,* 146.

44. Kessler, *Tagebücher,* 594. In contrast, note the undue weight Gerhard Splitt attributes to the remark, out of context, in his *Strauss,* 50–51.

45. Richard to Franz Strauss, 25 Oct. 1930, in: Grasberger, *Strom der Töne,* 333.

46. Paul Ehlers, "Die Musik und Adolf Hitler," ZM 106 (1939), 361.

47. Schuh, *Strauss: Briefe an Eltern,* 94, 212; Schuh, *Strauss—Hofmannsthal,* 580; *A Confidential Matter: The Letters of Richard Strauss and Stefan Zweig, 1931–1935* (Berkeley, 1977), 102; Myers, *Strauss and Rolland,* 138–39, 142, 153.

48. Schuh, *Strauss: Briefe an Eltern,* 219–20, 271.

49. Ibid., 218–19; Myers, *Strauss and Rolland,* 133; Schuh, *Strauss—Hofmannsthal,* 580.

50. Schuh, *Strauss—Hofmannsthal,* 541; Strauss to Doktor [Kopsch], 31 Aug. 1929, RG; W. T. Anderman [Walter Thomas], *Bis der Vorhang fiel: Berichtet nach Aufzeichnungen aus den Jahren 1940 bis 1945* (Dortmund, 1947), 241.

51. Schuh, *Strauss—Hofmannsthal,* 662, 644, 650; *A Confidential Matter,* 102.

52. Brosche, *Strauss,* 206, 208; Schuh, *Strauss—Hofmannsthal,* 363; Leon Botstein, "The Enigmas of Richard Strauss: A Revisionist View," in: Bryan Gilliam, ed., *Richard Strauss and His World* (Princeton, 1992), 11; NG 18:229.

53. Schuh, *Strauss—Hofmannsthal,* 417, 419–21.

54. Lotte Lehmann, *My Many Lives* (New York, 1948), 199.

55. Strauss quoted in Anderman [Thomas], *Vorhang,* 241.

56. Gabriele Strauss, *Collega,* 125; Richard Strauss, *Betrachtungen und Erinnerungen,* 28–31, 39–40; Brosche, *Strauss,* 53; Schuh, *Strauss—Hofmannsthal,* 591, 600; Strauss to Stresemann, 11 Feb. 1926; Stresemann to Strauss, 19 June 1926, RG.

57. On that aspect, see Max Butting, *Musikgeschichte, die ich miterlebte* (Berlin, 1955), 204; deposition under oath by Kopsch, 1 Mar. 1947, AM, Strauss. For the broader background, see Konrad H. Jarausch, *The Unfree Professions: German*

Lawyers, Teachers, and Engineers, 1900–1950 (New York, 1990); Michael H. Kater, *Doctors Under Hitler* (Chapel Hill, N.C., 1989), 19–25.

58. Typescript of speech by Julius Kopsch, "Die Neugestaltung des Rechts im deutschen Musikleben," [Berlin], 15 Feb. 1934, RG; [Werner Egk], "Zur wirtschaftlichen Lage der deutschen zeitgenössischen Komponisten ernster Musik," n.d., BS, Ana/410; Butting, *Musikgeschichte*, 204–5; Schuh, *Strauss*, 504–10; Barbara A. Peterson, "*Die Händler und die Kunst:* Richard Strauss as Composers' Advocate," in: Bryan Gilliam, ed., *Richard Strauss: New Perspectives on the Composer and His Work* (Durham, N.C., 1992), 118–19.

59. Strauss to Kippenberg, 29 Mar. 1933, RG.

60. Strauss to von Keudell, 12 July 1933, and to Rasch, 12 July 1933, NWH, 975/13-14; Strauss to Kopsch, 23 July 1933, RG.

61. Entry for 24 July 1933 in *TG* 2:450 (1st quote); Goebbels to Strauss, 31 July 1933; Strauss to Rasch, 31 July 1933, RG (2nd quote).

62. Strauss to Goebbels, 6 Aug. 1933, NWH, 975/16–8.

63. Strauss to Rasch, 27 Aug. 1933; Franz Strauss to Rasch, 16 Sept. 1933; Strauss to Goebbels, 27 Aug. 1933, RG; Strauss to Fürstner, 9 and 12 Sept. 1933, BS, Ana/330/I/Fürstner; Strauss to Rasch, 14 and 16 Sept. 1933, BS, Ana/330/I/Rasch.

64. Strauss to Ritter, 12 Sept. 1933, NWH, 975/16–1.

65. Abendroth to Pfitzner, 19 Oct. 1933, OW, 289/244/1 (quote); Tietjen to Strauss, 28 Oct. 1933, RG. In late Sept. 1933 Funk wrote to Strauss that Goebbels would be prepared to meet with him on 2 Oct. (Funk to Strauss, 26 Sept. 1933, NWH, 975/19).

66. Schuh, *Strauss: Briefe an Eltern*, 33, 194; *Münchener Neueste Nachrichten*, 19 Mar. 1933; Strauss quoted in Ferdinand Beussel, "Im Zeichen der Wende," *DM* 25 (1933), 670; Schuh to Verlag Hallwag A.G., 22 Aug. 1946, RG; deposition under oath by Kopsch, 1 Mar. 1947, AM, Strauss; Edith Stargardt-Wolff, *Wegbereiter grosser Musiker* (Berlin, 1954), 276–79; Bruno Walter, *Theme and Variations: An Autobiography* (New York, 1966), 298–99; Pamela M. Potter, "The Nazi 'Seizure' of the Berlin Philharmonic, or the Decline of a Bourgeois Musical Institution," in Glenn R. Cuomo, ed., *National Socialist Cultural Policy* (New York, 1995), 41–58.

67. Splitt, *Strauss*, 58. See the critical comment by Pamela M. Potter, "Strauss and the National Socialists: The Debate and Its Relevance," in Gilliam, *Strauss: New Perspectives*, 103.

68. Fritz Stege, "Berliner Musik," *ZM* 100 (1933), 458.

69. Kater, *The Twisted Muse*, 79–80.

70. Entry for 21 Mar. 1933 in Thomas Mann, *Tagebücher, 1933–1934*, ed. Peter de Mendelssohn (Frankfurt am Main, 1977), 15.

71. Erika Mann and Klaus Mann, *Escape to Life: Deutsche Kultur im Exil*, 2nd ed. (Munich, 1991), 170. This untruth has been repeated by Frederic Spotts, *Bayreuth: A History of the Wagner Festival* (New Haven, 1994), 171.

72. Friedelind Wagner, *Heritage of Fire* (New York, 1945), 88.

73. Schuh to Verlag Hallwag A.G., with a copy to Attorney Dr. Fritz Voser, 22 Aug. 1946, RG; Friedelind Wagner, *Nacht über Bayreuth: Die Geschichte der Enkelin Richard Wagners* (Berne, 1946), 137. See *Richard Strauss: Briefwechsel mit Willi Schuh* (Zurich, 1969), 129–33, 160–62, 165–69.

74. Splitt, *Strauss*, 42–59; Erik Levi, "Bowing Before the Nazis," in *Great Conductors* (*BBC Music Magazine*, special issue, 1998), 18.

75. Michael Kennedy, *Richard Strauss,* 2nd ed. (Oxford, 1995), 89.

76. Walter, *Theme and Variations,* 50.

77. Lotte Walter Lindt, ed., *Bruno Walter: Briefe, 1894–1962* (Frankfurt am Main, 1969), 31; Walter to Fernbach, 16 Jan. 1899, ibid., 34 (quotes).

78. Ibid., 128; Schuh, *Strauss: Briefe an Eltern,* 244.

79. Walter to Strauss, 5 Dec. 1903, in Walter Lindt, *Walter: Briefe,* 67–69 (quotes 68); Walter, *Theme and Variations,* 168.

80. Walter to Pfitzner, 18 Mar. 1907, in Walter Lindt, *Walter: Briefe,* 91.

81. Walter Lindt, *Walter: Briefe,* 127–33; Grasberger, *Strom der Töne,* 200–1.

82. Walter Lindt, *Walter: Briefe,* 135–37, 141–44, 402; Schuh, *Strauss— Hofmannsthal,* 203, 223; Walter, *Theme and Variations,* 216.

83. Schuh, *Strauss—Hofmannsthal,* 230, 293, 316–23, 362; Regler-Bellinger et al., *Knaurs Grosser Opernführer,* 76–79.

84. Walter to Pfitzner, 24 Jan. 1921, OW, 76.

85. Walter Lindt, *Walter: Briefe,* 170–72 (quote 171).

86. Walter to Strauss, 8 July 1932, RG; Zirato to Walter, NYA, Walter coll.

87. Strauss to Zweig, 17 June 1935, BAB Richard Strauss. I am using Potter's translation ("Strauss," 103).

88. Stargardt-Wolff, *Wegbereiter,* 277.

89. [Zirato] to Walter, 18 Aug. 1933; Press Department, Philharmonic-Symphony Society of New York, "For Release Friday, December 15, 1933"; extract from letter Harry Harkness Flagler to Walter, 4 June 1934; Walter to Zirato, 17 Aug. 1943; [Zirato] to Walter, 23 Aug. 1943, NYA, Walter coll.; Nicolas Slonimsky, *Music Since 1900,* 4th ed. (New York, 1971), 775; Thomas Mann, *Tagebücher, 1940–1943,* ed. Peter de Mendelssohn (Frankfurt am Main, 1982), 40, 344, 391, 395, 404–5; Erika Mann and Klaus Mann, *Escape to Life,* 170; Klemperer quoted in Peter Heyworth, *Otto Klemperer: His Life and Times,* 2 vols. (1983, 1996), 2:22.

90. Walter Lindt, *Walter: Briefe,* 299.

91. *Münchener Neueste Nachrichten,* 16 Apr. 1933; Paul Egon Hübinger, *Thomas Mann, die Universität Bonn und die Zeitgeschichte: Drei Kapitel deutscher Vergangenheit aus dem Leben des Dichters, 1905–1955* (Munich, 1974), 124–31; Hans Vaget, "The Rivalry for Wagner's Mantle: Strauss, Pfitzner, Mann," in Reinhold Grimm and Jost Hermand, eds., *Re-Reading Wagner* (Madison, Wis., 1993), 136–58; Kater, *The Twisted Muse,* 41–43.

92. Schuh, *Strauss: Briefe an Eltern,* 52.

93. Schuh, *Strauss,* 389, 514.

94. Hans Vaget, "Thomas Mann und Richard Strauss: Zeitgenossenschaft ohne Brüderlichkeit," *Thomas Mann Jahrbuch* 3 (1990), 59, 64.

95. Katia Mann, *Meine ungeschriebenen Memoiren,* ed. Elisabeth Plessen and Michael Mann (Frankfurt am Main, 1981), 104.

96. Vaget, "Thomas Mann und Richard Strauss," 58–59.

97. Ibid., 59.

98. Thomas Mann to Opitz, 26 Aug. 1909, in Thomas Mann, *Briefe, 1889–1936,* ed. Erika Mann (Frankfurt am Main, 1961), 78 (quotes); Vaget, "Thomas Mann und Richard Strauss," 59–60.

99. Vaget, "Thomas Mann und Richard Strauss," 61–63.

100. Thomas Mann quoted ibid., 64.

101. Tomas Mann, *Tagebücher, 1933–1934,* 422; Vaget, "Thomas Mann und Richard Strauss," 67.

102. See, e.g., text below at n. 182.

103. See Gulbransson's sketch of 16 Feb. 1936, underwritten *"Wie gehts Dir und Deinen schönen Hände"* [sic], RG. Also Myers, *Strauss and Rolland,* 122, 129.

104. Golo Mann, *Erinnerungen und Gedanken: Eine Jugend in Deutschland* (Frankfurt am Main, 1986), 519.

105. Kater, *The Twisted Muse,* 40–43.

106. *Münchener Neueste Nachrichten,* 20 Apr. 1933; Strauss to Knappertsbusch, 21 Apr. 1933, RG (quote).

107. Suhrkamp to Strauss, 19 Apr. 1933, RG (quote); Vaget, "Thomas Mann und Richard Strauss," 67.

108. Vaget, "Thomas Mann und Richard Strauss," 53–54, 61–62, 84–85. Also see idem, "The Rivalry for Wagner's Mantle," 136–57.

109. Kater, *The Twisted Muse,* 120–21.

110. Schuh, *Strauss—Hofmannsthal,* 701; Slonimsky, *Music,* 570 (quote). A contemporary evaluation is in Heinz Joachim, "'Arabella' von Richard Strauss," *Melos* 12 (1933), 245–47.

111. Adolph to Strauss, 14 Mar. and 12 Apr. 1933, RG; Fred K. Prieberg, *Musik im NS-Staat* (Frankfurt am Main, 1982), 208.

112. Strauss to Fürstner, 11 and 28 Mar., 8 Apr. 1933, BS, Ana 330/I/Fürstner; Strauss to Adolph, 17 Mar. 1933; Bauer to Herr Doktor [Strauss], 27 Mar. 1933; Tietjen to Strauss, 1 Apr. 1933; telegram Tietjen to Strauss, [?] Apr. 1933; Strauss to Fanto, 7 Apr. 1933, RG.

113. Beussel, "Im Zeichen der Wende," 670.

114. Joachim, "'Arabella' von Richard Strauss," 245–47.

115. Grete Busch, *Fritz Busch: Dirigent* (Frankfurt am Main, 1970), 70–71; Thomas Mann, *Tagebücher, 1933–1934,* 209.

116. Strauss to Otto [Fürstner], 24 Feb. 1937, BS, Ana 330/I/Fürstner (quote); Grete Busch, *Busch,* 72–73; Fritz Busch, *Pages from a Musician's Life* (Westport, Conn., 1971), 210; Fritz Busch quoted in Berndt W. Wessling, *Furtwängler: Eine kritische Biographie* (Stuttgart, 1985), 153.

117. Schmidt-Leonhardt to Strauss, 18 May 1934; Tietjen to Strauss, 23 May 1934; Strauss to Rüdiger, 19 June 1934, RG.

118. Kater, *The Twisted Muse,* 121–23.

119. Toscanini to Excellency [Hitler], 29 Apr. 1933, facsimile in Hans Mayer, *Richard Wagner in Bayreuth, 1876–1976* (Stuttgart, 1976), 211; Kater, *The Twisted Muse,* 79–80.

120. Mayer, *Wagner,* 134; Hugo Rasch, "Bayreuth im Jahre der deutschen Revolution," in *DKW,* no. 21 (1933), 5–6. Again, note the malicious distortion in Friedelind Wagner, *Heritage of Fire,* 92, Willi Schuh's demand for a correction under threat of legal action (Schuh to Verlag Hallwag A.G., 22 Aug. 1946, RG), and Wagner's subsequent changes in *Nacht über Bayreuth,* 143.

121. *A Confidential Matter,* xxii–xxiii; Strauss to Zweig, 17 June 1935, BAB Richard Strauss.

122. Strauss to Winifred Wagner, 23 Sept. 1933, in Grasberger, *Strom der Töne,* 347.

123. Trenner, *Wagner—Strauss,* 232–33; Schuh, *Strauss,* 505; Mayer, *Wagner,* 136; Spotts, *Bayreuth,* 120, 133–34, 140; Kennedy, *Strauss,* 89; Nike Wagner, *Wagner Theater,* 221.

124. In this I concur in Vaget's sound judgment in "Thomas Mann und Richard Strauss," 70.

125. Quote from Potter, "Strauss," 97; and Botstein, "Enigmas," 7. For the de-

tractors, see George R. Marek, *Richard Strauss: The Life of a Non-Hero* (London, 1967), 270; Berta Geissmar, *Musik im Schatten der Politik,* 4th ed., ed. Fred K. Prieberg (Zurich, 1985), 194. For the defenders, see Strauss's denazification attorney Roesen to Öffentlicher Kläger, 17 Jan. 1948, AM, Strauss; Lehmann, *My Many Lives,* 200; Panofsky, *Strauss,* 296; Stuckenschmidt, *Hören,* 133; Deppisch, *Strauss,* 139; Kennedy, *Strauss,* 90. Strauss's grandson Richard Strauss Jr. told me in a Munich telephone conversation on 9 June 1996 that the composer had been "a thoroughly unpolitical person."

126. Strauss to Zweig, 17 June 1935, BAB Richard Strauss. English-language quote according to *A Confidential Matter,* 100. Also see the humorous, self-deprecating reference to his wife, 30 Apr. 1934, in Grasberger, *Strom der Töne,* 354.

127. Strauss to Fürstner, 10 Mar. 1933, BS, Ana 330/I/Fürstner; Strauss cited in Hartmann, *Haus,* 185.

128. In this connection it is interesting that Splitt deliberately confuses "totalitarian" with "authoritarian," so as to skew his case against Strauss (*Strauss,* 97). As his anti-Strauss argumententation progresses, Splitt even finds it convenient to define Strauss as a "fascist" (216).

129. E.g., see Panofsky, *Strauss,* 282; Potter, "Friedenstag," 410.

130. Rüdiger telegram to Strauss, 10 Nov. 1933, AM, Strauss.

131. Facsimile of program in Wessling, *Furtwängler,* 276.

132. Goebbels to Strauss, 29 Nov. 1933, RG. On the RMK as part of the RKK see Alan E. Steinweis, *Art, Ideology, and Economics in Nazi Germany: The Reich Chambers of Music, Theater, and the Visual Arts* (Chapel Hill, N.C., 1993), passim.

133. [Strauss] "Presseveröffentlichung," [early Jan. 1934]; Strauss, "Einladung zum Ersten Deutschen Komponistentag in Berlin," 1 Feb. 1934; Strauss to Staatssekretär [Funk], 9 Apr. 1934, RG; Strauss "Begrüssungsansprache," ZM 101 (1934), 288–90.

134. The quote is from Schuh, in *Richard Strauss: Briefwechsel Schuh,* 8.

135. Strauss to Ritter, 4 Nov. 1933, NWH, 975/16-2; Strauss to Kopsch, 15 Mar. 1934; Strauss's draft of letter to Goebbels, [Apr. 1934]; Kärnbach to Strauss, 9 Jan. 1934; Funk to Strauss, 22 Jan. 1934; Funk, "Verordnung zur Durchführung des Gesetzes über die Vermittlung von Musikaufführungsrechten," 15 Feb. 1934; von Keudell to Strauss, 16 Feb. 1934, RG.

136. Strauss to Doktor [Kopsch], 18 Oct. 1934; and to Tietjen, 13 Nov. 1934; and to Winifred Wagner, 16 Dec. 1934; Tietjen to Strauss, 20 Nov. 1934; Winifred Wagner to Strauss, 28 Dec. 1934, RG; Steinweis, *Art,* 51; Kennedy, *Strauss,* 90.

137. The German term was "Ständiger Rat für die internationale Zusammenarbeit der Komponisten." See Strauss to von Hausegger, 31 Dec. 1934, in Grasberger, *Strom der Töne,* 357 (quotes); ibid., 361; Strauss to Freund [Rasch], 17 Jan. and 9 Dec. 1934, BS, Ana/330/I/Rasch; von Feldmann to RMK, 5 May 1934; Strauss to Tietjen, 6 June 1934; "Protokoll: Sitzung des Ständigen Rates in Hamburg," 3 June 1935, RG; Strauss to Freund [Rasch], 31 Dec. 1934, NWH, 975/13-20; Strauss to Fürstner, 9 Dec. 1934, BS, Ana/330/I/Fürstner; deposition under oath by Kopsch, 1 Mar. 1934, AM, Strauss; Prieberg, *NS-Staat,* 208–9; Splitt, *Strauss,* 174–80.

138. Strauss to Göring, 9 Jan. 1934; and to Havemann, 23 Feb. 1934; and to Laubinger, 12 Dec. 1934; and to Goebbels, 18 May 1935, RG; Strauss's list of opera titles, [6 Apr. 1935], BS, Ana/330/I/Niessen; *Melos* 13 (1934), 255; Panofsky, *Strauss,* 316–17.

139. According to Karpàth to Lehmann, 25 July 1919, UCSB, Lotte Lehmann

coll. Also see Strauss to Lehmann, 22 July 1919, 22 Mar. 1924, 9 Apr. 1928, ibid.; Lotte Lehmann, *Singing with Richard Strauss* (London, 1964), 21–23; Lehmann, *My Many Lives,* 197–98, 200.

140. Schalk telegrams to Lehmann, [1919], UCSB, Lotte Lehmann coll.

141. Strauss to Göring, 9 Jan. 1934; and to Goebbels, 27 Apr. and 4 July 1934 (quote); and to Ihlert, 11 Dec. 1934, and to von Niessen, 11 Apr. 1935; and to College [Stange], 19 Apr. 1935; and to Leonhard, 21 May 1935; Tietjen to Strauss, 20 and 28 June 1934, RG; Strauss to von Niessen, 18 and 27 Apr., 21 May 1935, BS, Ana/330/I/Niessen.

142. Strauss to Seldte, 20 Jan. 1934; and to Stein, 28 Feb. 1934; and to Goebbels, 5 June 1934; Stein to Strauss, 19 May 1934 (quote); Straube to Strauss, 20 May 1934, RG.

143. ZM 101 (1934), 290; Strauss to Stange, 20 Apr. 1931; Stange to Strauss, 23 Apr. 1934; Ritter to Strauss, 25 Apr. 1942, RG; Werner Egk, "Hugo Rasch, ein Siebziger!," *Mitteilungen der Fachschaft Komponisten in der Reichsmusikkammer* (Apr. 1943), n.p.; Walter Berten, "Hugo Rasch: Zum 70. Geburtstag eines deutschen Kämpfers und Musikers," *MK* 1 (1943), 19; Hugo Rasch, "König Jazz," *AMZ* 57 (1930), 929–32; Butting, *Musikgeschichte,* 203–4; Steinweis, *Art,* 48.

144. Müller memorandum, [1934], BAB Gustav Havemann; Steinweis, *Art,* 48; Kater, *The Twisted Muse,* 17–18, 23–24.

145. ZM 101 (1934), 290; see, e.g., minutes of 7th RMK presidial council meeting, 3 Mar. 1934, RG.

146. Havemann to Strauss, 5 and 7 Jan., 27 Feb., and 11 May 1934; Strauss to Havemann, 7 Jan. 1934 and [May 1934] RG; Havemann to Reichsleitung der NSDAP, 24 Feb. 1934, BAB Gustav Havemann.

147. Ihlert to Strauss, 9 Jan. 1934; minutes of 4th RMK presidial council meeting, 20 Jan. 1934, RG.

148. Ihlert to Strauss, 27 Jan. 1934; Stein to Strauss, 31 Jan. 1934; Ihlert to Kopsch, 14 Mar. 1934; Kopsch to Ihlert, 15 Mar. 1934; Schmidt-Leonhardt to Strauss, 15 Mar. 1934; judgment by Arbeitsgericht Berlin, 14 Feb. 1935, RG; Bullerian and Hempel to Hess, 20 July 1934, BAB Gustav Havemann.

149. Schmidt-Leonhardt to Strauss, 15 Mar. 1934; Kärnbach to Strauss, 30 May 1935, RG; Strauss to Rasch, 11 Aug. 1934, BS, Ana/330/I/Rasch; *DM* 27 (1934), 211.

150. Strauss to Havemann, 7 Jan. 1934; Ihlert to Strauss, 13 Apr. 1934; minutes of 11th RMK presidial council meeting, 31 Oct. 1934; Strauss to Freund [Tietjen], 13 Nov. 1934; Strauss to Richter, 14 Dec. 1934; Ihlert to Strauss, 4 Dec. 1934; Ihlert to Hinkel, 22 May 1935, RG; Strauss to Rasch, 11 June 1935, NWH, 975/13–24; Backhaus memorandum, 28 Aug. 1934, BDC Gustav Havemann; Grasberger, *Strom der Töne,* 349.

151. Ihlert to Strauss, 13 Apr. 1934, RG.

152. According to Ihlert to Strauss, 19 May 1935, RG.

153. Strauss to Rasch, 11 Aug. 1934, RG.

154. Backhaus memorandum, 28 Aug. 1934, BAB Gustav Havemann.

155. Strauss to Doktor [Kopsch], 4 Oct. 1934, BAB Richard Strauss; Strauss [ordinance], 12 Oct. 1934, NWH, 975/13–18.

156. Strauss to Freund [Tietjen], 13 Nov. 1934; and to Frank, 10 Dec. 1934, RG.

157. Ihlert to Strauss, 4 Jan. 1935; Havemann to Strauss, 14 Jan. 1935; Stange to Strauss, 25 Apr., 15 and 25 May 1935; Ihlert to Hinkel, 22 May 1935; Strauss to

Ihlert, 27 May 1935, RG; Bechstein to Goebbels, 13 June 1935, BAB Gustav Havemann.

158. Stange to Strauss, 29 June 1935, RG; Steinweis, *Art,* 53.

159. Hanke to Strauss, 17 Nov. 1933, RG; Grasberger, *Strom der Töne,* 348–49.

160. Minutes of 8th RMK presidial council meeting, 26 Mar. 1934, RG.

161. Strauss to Böhm, 5 Apr. 1934 (quote); Strauss to von Niessen, 1 May 1935, RG.

162. Strauss, draft statute, Garmisch, 28 Dec. 1933, RG; Kater, *The Twisted Muse,* 80.

163. Strauss to Göring, 9 Jan. 1934, RG.

164. Minutes of 7th RMK presidial council meeting, 3 Mar. 1934, RG.

165. Strauss to Doktor [Kopsch], 4 Oct. 1934, BAB Richard Strauss.

166. Rasch to Strauss, 18 Jan. 1935, NWH, 975/15; Strauss to Rasch, 5 Mar. 1935, RG (quote).

167. Ihlert to Hinkel, 22 May 1935, RG.

168. Kater, *Different Drummers.*

169. Strauss to Freund [Rasch], 9 Dec. 1934, BS, Ana/330/I/Rasch; Strauss to Doktor [Kopsch], [Dec. 1934], RG (quote); Strauss to Präsidialrat [Richter], 14 Dec. 1934, NWH, 975/19–3; Stuckenschmidt, *Hören,* 133–34; Kater, *The Twisted Muse,* 124.

170. Strauss to Doktor [Kopsch], 2 Apr. 1934, RG.

171. ZM 101 (1934), 290; Wessling, *Furtwängler,* 279.

172. Program, "Berufsstand der deutschen Komponisten: Festkonzert," 18 Feb. 1934, OW, 298.

173. Strecker to Hindemith, 12 July 1934, PF, Schott Korr. See Geoffrey Skelton, *Paul Hindemith: The Man Behind the Music: A Biography* (London, 1975), 117; Claudia Maurer Zenck, "Zwischen Boykott und Anpassung an den Charakter der Zeit: Über die Schwierigkeiten eines deutschen Komponisten mit dem Dritten Reich," *Hindemith-Jahrbuch* 9 (1980), 74–75.

174. The text of that speech is reprinted in Curt Riess, *Furtwängler: Musik und Politik* (Berne, 1953), 186–89. Cf. text at n. 51 in chapter 2.

175. Thus the wording in Skelton, *Hindemith,* 123; Glenn Watkins, *Soundings: Music in the Twentieth Century* (New York, 1988), 343. Also see Riess, *Furtwängler,* 190; Marek, *Strauss,* 272.

176. *Times,* London, 12 Dec. 1934; Mann, *Tagebücher, 1933–1934,* 587.

177. Riess, *Furtwängler,* 190; Skelton, *Hindemith,* 123; Watkins, *Soundings,* 343; Gottfried von Einem, recorded interview, Vienna, 30 Nov. 1994, APA. Whether Einem actually realized his goal is still questionable. See Thomas Eickhoff, *Politische Dimensionen einer Komponisten-Biographie im 20. Jahrhundert—Gottfried von Einem* (Stuttgart, 1998), 110–11, esp. n. 115.

178. As printed in Riess, *Furtwängler,* 187–88.

179. Ibid., 188 (quote), 189.

180. Printed in *Neue Freie Presse,* Vienna, 11 Dec. 1934. The only author I have found who got both text and date right is Dietmar Polaczek, "Richard Strauss—Thema und Metamorphosen," in: Karl Corino, ed., *Intellektuelle im Bann des Nationalsozialismus* (Hamburg, 1980), 67. For Strauss's Amsterdam concerts, see Deutsche Gesandtschaft Den Haag to Auswärtiges Amt Berlin, 4 Dec. 1934, BA, R55/1182.

181. Declaration by Franz Strauss, 22 Jan. 1948; Der Öffentliche Kläger bei der Spruchkammer Garmisch-Partenkirchen, "Klageschrift . . . gegen Dr. Richard Strauss," 13 May 1948, AM, Strauss.

182. See n. 50, above.

183. Strauss to Freund [Rasch], 14 Dec. 1934, RG. The state secretary in question was Walther Funk.

184. Minutes of 14th RMK presidial council meeting, 16 Mar. 1934, RG.

185. Hindemith to Strecker, 31 Mar. 1935, PF, Schott Korr.

186. Stein to Strecker, 6 Apr. 1935, PF, Musikhochschule Berlin. Also see Maurer Zenck, "Boykott," 91.

187. Tietjen to Meister [Strauss], 12 Jan. 1934; Ihlert to Strauss, 25 Jan. 1934, RG; program, "Berufsstand der deutschen Komponisten: Festkonzert," 18 Feb. 1934, OW, 298; program, "Erster deutscher Komponistentag," [16–18 Feb. 1934], OW, 250.

188. Tietjen to Meister [Strauss], 23 Mar. 1934 and 21 Feb. 1935, RG.

189. Strauss to Goebbels, 4 July 1934, RG.

190. Strauss to Goebbels, 1 Nov. 1934, RG.

191. Strauss to College [Stange], 19 Apr. (quote) and 25 Apr. 1935, RG; Peter Muck, *Einhundert Jahre Berliner Philharmonisches Orchester: Darstellung in Dokumenten,* 3 vols. (Tutzing, 1982), 3:266.

192. See Norman Del Mar, *Richard Strauss: A Critical Commentary on His Life and Works,* 3 vols. (1972), 3:395–96 (quote); Potter's balanced judgment in "Strauss," 104–5. The "stone" may have been a rather inelegant reference to the mountains behind Strauss's Garmisch house.

193. The speech is reproduced in Albrecht Dümling and Peter Girth, eds., *Entartete Musik: Zur Düsseldorfer Ausstellung von 1938: Eine kommentierte Rekonstruktion* (Düsseldorf, [1988]), 56–57.

194. Göring to Strauss, 5 and 19 Jan. 1934, RG; Richard to Pauline Strauss, 10 Feb. 1934, in Grasberger, *Strom der Töne,* 351 (quotes).

195. *VB,* 7 Mar 1934; Strauss to Böhm, 27 Mar. 1934, RG (quote).

196. Rosalind von Schirach and Gerhard Hüsch to Strauss, 2 Apr. 1934, RG.

197. Goebbels to Strauss, 2 May 1934, RG; entry for 21 May 1934 in *TG* 2:472 (quote).

198. Goebbels to Strauss, 8 June 1934; Funk to Strauss, 25 May and 6 June 1934, RG; Del Mar, *Strauss,* 3:53; Goebbels to Rosenberg, 25 Aug. 1934, IfZ, MA 596/737–39. Goebbels mentions *Frau ohne Schatten.*

199. Goebbels to Strauss, 25 Aug. 1934, RG; von Keudell to Strauss, 23 Oct. 1934, BAB Richard Strauss.

200. Strauss to Freund [Tietjen], 13 Nov. 1934, RG.

201. Entries in Strauss's notebook for 26 and 28 Mar. 1935, RG.

202. Strauss to Herr Reichskanzler [Hitler], 18 Apr. 1935, BAB Richard Strauss.

203. Wiedemann to Goebbels, 5 June 1935, BAB Richard Strauss; Strauss to Rüdiger, 3 June 1935; Schlösser to Staatssekretär [Funk], 5 June 1935; Rüdiger to Strauss, 5 and 21 June 1935, RG.

204. Strauss to von Niessen, 11 June 1935, RG.

205. Strauss to Stange, 20 June 1935, RG.

206. Strauss's notebook entry for 3 July 1935 cited in Panofksy, *Strauss,* 293.

207. *IBD,* 1288; Kennedy, *Strauss,* 86.

208. Panofsky, *Strauss,* 279.

209. Kippenberg to Meister [Strauss], 20 Oct. 1932, in: "Richard Strauss und Anton Kippenberg: Briefwechsel," *Richard-Strauss-Jahrbuch* (1959/60), 118.

210. Strauss to Doktor [Kippenberg], 22 Oct. 1932, ibid.

211. Zweig to Doctor [Strauss], 3 Apr. 1933, in *A Confidential Matter,* 33

(quote); Strauss to Zweig, 4 Apr. 1933, ibid.; Strauss's reaction to the radio address is in Franz Strauss to Rasch, 19 Mar. 1934, RG. Also see Stefan Zweig, *Die Welt von Gestern: Erinnerungen eines Europäers* (Berlin, 1965), 338–40. On Arnold Zweig (1887–1968), see *IBD,* 1286–87.

212. *A Confidential Matter,* 37.

213. Strauss to Doctor [Zweig], 21 Jan. 1934, ibid., 38.

214. See, e.g., Lürman to Rasch, 23 May 1934, AM, Strauss.

215. Funk to Strauss, 15 Mar. 1934; Franz Strauss to Funk, 19 Mar. 1934 (quote), RG.

216. Strauss to Doctor [Zweig], 25 [recte: 24] May 1934, in *A Confidential Matter,* 45 (both quotes).

217. Qoted ibid., xxi.

218. Rosenberg to Goebbels, 20 Aug. 1934; Goebbels to Rosenberg, 25 Aug. 1934, IfZ, MA, 596/737-44.

219. Goebbels to Strauss, 1 Sept. 1934, RG.

220. See Adolph to Strauss, 19 Sept. 1934, RG.

221. *A Confidential Matter,* 48–57.

222. Strauss to Goebbels, 20 Sept. 1934, RG.

223. *A Confidential Matter,* 59.

224. Adolph to Strauss, 17/29 Dec. 1934 and 7 Feb. 1935, RG; *A Confidential Matter,* 116, n. 40.

225. *A Confidential Matter,* 64–65; Strauss to Zweig, 20 Feb. 1935, ibid., 67 (quote).

226. Ibid., 67–68; Strauss to Zweig, 26 Feb. 1935, ibid., 69 (quotes); ibid., 71.

227. Ibid., 72–99.

228. The contents of this letter have been extrapolated from Strauss's answer to Zweig two days later. See ibid., xxii–xxiv.

229. Strauss to Zweig, 17 June 1935, BAB Richard Strauss.

230. Facsimile, advertisement for "Uraufführung Die schweigsame Frau," 24 June 1935, in *A Confidential Matter,* [112]; Panofsky, *Strauss,* 291.

231. Friedrich von Schuch, *Richard Strauss, Ernst von Schuch und Dresdens Oper,* 2nd ed. (Leipzig, 1953), 134–35; *A Confidential Matter,* 101–3.

232. Two authors who got the reason for Hitler and Goebbels's stay in Berlin right are Panofsky, *Strauss,* 291; and Kennedy, *Strauss,* 93. Panofsky also records the correct date of 1 July (292). See [Franz Strauss], "Richtigstellung der Briefaffaire an Stefan Zweig," n.d., RG.

233. Entry for 5 July 1935 in *TG* 2:490.

234. Goebbels to Strauss, 9 July 1935, RG (quote); Kennedy, *Strauss,* 93; personal communication to me from Professor Bryan Gilliam of Duke University, Durham, N.C., 10 Mar. 1999. Gilliam saw the notes for Willi Schuh's never completed 2nd volume of his Strauss biography.

235. *Fränkischer Kurier,* 15 July 1935; *AMZ* 62 (1935), 485; *AMR,* 24 July 1935, BA, RD33/2-1 (61).

236. Entry for 13 July 1935 in *TG* 2:493.

237. Zeitschel to Hinkel, 24 Sept. 1935, BAB Richard Strauss. The originator of the piano score is not known. That Jonson should have been described as Jewish was just another fiendish touch by the Nazis to hurt Strauss: He was not.

238. Strauss to Zweig, 17 June 1935, BAB Richard Strauss; Strauss to Zweig, 22 May 1935, in *A Confidential Matter,* 94.

239. Peter Pulzer, *The Rise of Political Anti-Semitism in Germany and Austria*

(New York, 1964); George L. Mosse, *Toward the Final Solution: A History of European Racism* (New York, 1980), 77–168; Paul Weindling, *Health, Race and German Politics Between National Unification and Nazism, 1870–1945* (Cambridge, 1989), 11–280.

240. According to Strauss in Schuh, *Strauss: Briefe an Eltern,* 198. Also see Schuh, *Strauss,* 136.

241. Schuh, *Strauss: Briefe an Eltern,* 105, 107–12, 125–28, 167–70, 173, 175–76, 182–83, 187; NG 18:220.

242. Strauss to Thuille, 15 June 1885, in Franz Trenner, ed., *Richard Strauss—Ludwig Thuille: Ein Briefwechsel* (Tutzing, 1980), 84 (1st quote); Strauss to parents, 5 Feb. 1890, in Schuh, *Strauss: Briefe an Eltern,* 128 (2nd quote).

243. NG 18:218–20; Nike Wagner, *Wagner Theater,* 268.

244. Schuh, *Strauss: Briefe an Eltern,* 127–28, 150; Gabriele Strauss, *Collega,* 34, 38, 68, 73, 96, 100; Willi Schuh and Franz Trenner, eds., *Hans von Bülow and Richard Strauss: Corespondence* (Westport, Conn., 1979), 74–76; GLM 1:387.

245. See the uncritical biography by Ritter's son-in-law Siegmund von Hausegger, in a series edited by Richard Strauss, *Alexander Ritter: Ein Bild seines Charakters und Schaffens* (Berlin, [1907]); MGG 11:564–65; NG 16:60.

246. Franz to Richard Strauss, 16 Mar. 1893, in Schuh, *Strauss: Briefe an Eltern,* 168; Schuh, *Strauss,* 136–37, 170–71, 200, 206.

247. NG 18:219–20.

248. Strauss to Cosima Wagner, 19 Jan. 1890, in Trenner, *Wagner—Strauss,* 22.

249. Ibid., 95, 115, 136, 153, 197. In contrast, I find Sander L. Gilman's argument, that Strauss expressed anti-Semitism in his opera *Salome* (by purposely equating cacophony with the avant-garde and Jews, or high-pitched singing with Jews) erroneous. Apart from these implausible equations, it seems to have escaped Gilman that Strauss's true avant-garde statement came a few years later, with *Elektra,* which had no "Jewish" theme. See Gilman's article, "Strauss and the Pervert," in Arthur Groos and Roger Parker, eds., *Reading Opera* (Princeton, 1988), 317–27. I am indebted to Professor Pamela M. Potter of the University of Wisconsin at Madison, Wis., for pointing me in this direction.

250. Daniel Jonah Goldhagen, *Hitler's Willing Executioners: Ordinary Germans and the Holocaust* (New York, 1996).

251. Brosche, *Strauss,* 28–29, 84, 93, 172, 318–19, 360; Schuh, *Strauss—Hofmannsthal,* 161.

252. Otto Klemperer, *Meine Erinnerungen an Gustav Mahler und andere autobiographische Skizzen* (Freiburg im Breisgau, 1960), 39–40 (quotes); Heyworth, *Klemperer,* 2:15, 22, 27, 77.

253. Strauss to von Niessen, 11 May 1935; and to Goebbels, 11 May 1935, RG. See above at n. 229.

254. Schuh, *Strauss: Briefe an Eltern,* 38, 266 (quote), 272; Trenner, *Strauss—Thuille,* 81; Walter, *Theme and Variations,* 124.

255. Schuh, *Strauss: Briefe an Eltern,* 30; Trenner, *Strauss—Thuille,* 51, 74, 80; Dietrich Kämper, ed., *Richard Strauss und Franz Wüllner im Briefwechsel* (Cologne, 1963), 10.

256. Mahler as quoted in Herta Blaukopf, ed., *Gustav Mahler—Richard Strauss: Briefwechsel, 1888–1911* (Munich, 1980), 152. Also see Schuh, *Strauss: Briefe an Eltern,* 193; Gabriele Strauss, *Collega,* 66; Klemperer, *Erinnerungen,* 21.

257. Von Holthoff to Strauss, 3 June 1923, RG; Panofsky, *Strauss,* 273; Schuh, *Strauss,* 261.

258. Strauss telegram to Rasch, 3 Feb. 1934, NWH, 975/13-16; Tietjen to Meister [Strauss], 26 Oct. 1934, RG.

259. Luis Trenker declaration under oath, 21 Jan. 1948, RG; Luis Trenker, *Alles gut gegangen: Geschichten aus meinem Leben* (Munich, 1975), 323–24; Strauss, *Betrachtungen und Erinnerungen,* 234.

260. Fischer to Staatskanzlei, 26 Jan. 1934, BH, MA/107485; Donald W. Ellis, "Music in the Third Reich: National Socialist Aesthetic Theory as Governmental Policy," PhD dissertation, University of Kansas, 1970, 74–75.

261. Strohm to Strauss, 18 Feb. 1935, RG; and further Counseil corr., ibid.

262. Oertel declaration under oath, 21 Jan. 1947; Fürstner to Vorsitzender der Spruchkammer, 3 Mar. 1947; Roesen to Spruchkammer, 12 Mar. 1947; Mutzenbecher declaration, 10 Nov. 1947, AM, Strauss; Ursula Fürstner, "Richard Strauss und der Fürstner-Verlag," *Mitteilungen der Internationalen Richard-Strauss-Gesellschaft,* no. 50 (1966), 9–10.

263. Pauly to Strauss, 16 Sept. 1940 and 14 May 1941, RG. Also see Adolph to Strauss, 11 May 1933, RG.

264. Strauss to Freund [Krauss], 22 Mar. 1942, in: Götz Klaus Kende and Willi Schuh, eds., *Richard Strauss Clemens Krauss: Briefwechsel* (Munich, 1963), 236.

265. Pamela M. Potter, *Most German of the Arts: Musicology and Society from the Weimar Republic to the End of Hitler's Reich* (New Haven, Conn., 1998), 98.

266. Schrott to Nippold, 29 Apr. 1935, OW, 283; Schlösser to Strauss, 5 Dec. 1934; Walleck to Strauss, 7 Nov. 1935; Strauss to Böhm, 2 June 1938; Papesch to Strauss, 6 July 1939; Strauss to Moralt, 8 July 1939; Franz Strauss to Moralt, 29 July 1939, RG; Reinhold Conrad Muschler, "Richard Strauss," *DKW,* no. 28 (1933), 7–8; Strauss, *Betrachtungen und Erinnerungen,* 224–29.

267. Fabricius to Körner, 18 Oct. 1935; RKK memorandum, 19 Dec. 1941, BAB Richard Strauss; Wallerstein declaration, 3 Mar. 1947, AM, Strauss. On Wallerstein, see *IBD,* 1204–5.

268. Enclosure to letter Bullerian and Hempel to Hess, 20 July 1934, BAB, Richard Strauss.

269. Splitt, *Strauss,* 225. Splitt's phrases have been copied verbatim, and mindlessly, by Peter Reichel, *Der schöne Schein des Dritten Reiches: Faszination und Gewalt des Faschismus,* 2nd ed. (Munich, 1992), 348.

270. Ernst Hanfstaengl, *Zwischen Weissem und Braunem Haus: Memoiren eines politischen Aussenseiters* (Munich, 1970), 56; *TGII* 12:527; Hans Severus Ziegler, *Adolf Hitler aus dem Erleben dargestellt,* 3rd. ed. (Göttingen, 1965), 172.

271. The English-language wording has been taken from Marek, *Strauss,* 283. According to Richard Strauss Jr. the original is housed in the Munich municipal library and available for inspection only by his permission. In June 1993, Strauss wanted to show it to me there, but never got around to it. Under circumstances not known to me the German original was published as early as 1953 in Riess, *Furtwängler,* 191–92.

272. Marek, *Strauss,* 283.

273. Riess, *Furtwängler,* 192.

274. Strauss to Freund [Rasch], 13 Oct. 1935, RG.

275. Tietjen to Strauss, 13 Dec. 1935, RG.

276. Winifred Wagner to Strauss, 9 Feb. 1936; Strauss to Winifred Wagner, 17 Feb. 1936, RG. Strauss also asked the Munich Staatsoper Intendant Oskar Walleck to intercede with Goebbels (Walleck to Strauss, 27 Feb. 1936, RG). Also see Roesen to Öffentlicher Kläger, 17 Jan. 1948, AM, Strauss.

277. Strauss to Winifred Wagner, 17 Feb. 1936, RG. In light of the fact that Strauss had made a gift of the composition to the Olympic Committee, he declined to profit from any film rights that would have been his (Franz Strauss to Fürstner, 24 Dec. 1937, BS, Ana/330/I/Fürstner).

278. Entry for 20 June 1936 in *TG* 2:630.

279. Ibid., 653; Muck, *Jahre* 3:274; *Skizzen* (Oct. 1936), 15.

280. *VB*, 9 Nov. 1936; Strauss to von Niessen, 28 Jan. 1937, BS, Ana/330/I/Niessen; Kleiber to Strauss, 4 Oct. 1938, RG (quote).

281. Abendroth to Meister [Pfitzner], 29 Nov. 1936, OW, 288.

282. Richard to Pauline Strauss, 25 Mar. 1936, in Grasberger, *Strom der Töne,* 376.

283. Strauss to von Niessen, 28 Jan. 1937, BS, Ana/330/I/Niessen.

284. Minutes of Vichy meetings, 16 Sept. 1935, enclosed with letter von Reznicek to Hinkel, 25 Oct. 1935, BAB Emil von Reznicek. Dukas's Jewish ancestry is confirmed in Emanuel bin Gorion et al., eds., *Philo-Lexikon: Handbuch des jüdischen Wissens* (Berlin, 1935), 152.

285. "Internationales Musikfest," Stockholm, 22–27 Feb. 1936, BAB Emil von Reznicek; Slonimsky, *Music,* 645–46; *GLM* 8:375.

286. *ZM* 109 (1942), 331; *JdM 1943,* 16; *TGII* 4:545.

287. *TG* 3:419; Strauss to Fürstner, 16 Apr. 1938, BS, Ana/330/I/Fürstner; Dümling and Girth, *Entartete Musik,* 109.

288. Strauss to Drewes, 6 June 1938, BS, Fasc. germ. (Drewes); Strauss to Drewes, 19 June 1938; Strauss to Freund [Böhm], 13 Aug. 1938, RG; Strauss to Mein Führer, 21 June 1939; [Hitler adjutant] Albert Bormann to Strauss, 23 June 1939, BAB Richard Strauss; Panofsky, *Strauss,* 353; *GLM* 3:355; Oliver Rathkolb, *Führertreu und gottbegnadet: Künstlereliten im Dritten Reich* (Vienna, 1991), 187. See Joseph Gregor, *Richard Strauss: Der Meister der Oper* (Munich, 1939).

289. Strauss to Mein Führer, 21 June 1939, BAB Richard Strauss; *Unterhaltungsmusik* (15 July 1939), 821.

290. Tietjen to Strauss, 17 May 1938; Strauss to Doktor [Drewes], 3 Feb. 1939, RG; *ZM* 106 (1939), 1134; Albert Richard Mohr, *Die Frankfurter Oper, 1924–1944: Ein Beitrag zur Theatergeschichte mit zeitgenössischen Berichten und Bildern* (Frankfurt am Main, 1971), 675–76.

291. Göring telegram to Strauss, 12 June 1939, RG.

292. *Unterhaltungsmusik* (20 July 1939), 976.

293. *ZM* 107 (1940), 466; Werner Oehlmann, "Richard Strauss: Festwochen in der Berliner Staatsoper," *Reich* (16 June 1940), 18.

294. Goebbels telegram to Strauss, [1940], RG (quote); Grasberger, *Strom der Töne,* 355; *NG* 18:235.

295. Kater, *The Twisted Muse,* 146.

296. *ZM* 109 (1942), 89.

297. "Betr.: Verwendung des Staatszuschusses zur Verteilung an Komponisten ernster Musik," Berlin, 4 July 1942, BAB Werner Egk.

298. Strauss to Kopsch, 26 Mar. 1941; Rosen to Strauss, 21 May 1942, RG; Strauss, "Angebotsschreiben," 20 Mar. 1943; Tobis Filmkunst to Strauss, 6 Apr. 1943, BAB Richard Strauss.

299. Entry for 5 Dec. 1941 in *TGII* 2:436.

300. *ZM* 109 (1942), 560; Panofsky, *Strauss,* 353.

301. Ritter to Egk, 25 May 1944, BAB Richard Strauss; Strauss to Drewes, 6 Aug. 1944, BS, Fasc. germ. (Drewes).

302. Norbert Schultze, "Lieber Berufskamerad!," Berlin-Wannsee, im November 1940, OW, 40; von Keudell to Doktor [Strauss], 31 Dec. 1940, RG. On Goebbels's priority of light over high-brow entertainment during the war see Kater, *Different Drummers,* 111–211.

303. Strauss to Kopsch, 24 Oct. 1940, AM, Strauss; "Einspruch Münchner Musiker gegen die Schrift 'Gedanken zu einem neuen Verteilungsplan der Stagma,'" [Nov. 1940], OW, 76; Strauss to Ritter, 23 Dec. 1940; Ritter memorandum, 24 Dec. 1940; Strauss to Ritter, 25 Dec. 1940; Strauss to Kopsch, 27 Dec. 1940, RG; Grasberger, *Strom der Töne,* 406; Helmut Grohe, "Strauss und Pfitzner an einem Tisch: Bericht von einer Konspiration Münchner Musiker im 'Dritten Reich,'" *Mitteilungen der Hans-Pfitzner-Gesellschaft,* no. 12 (1964), 11–15; quote according to Werner Egk, *Die Zeit wartet nicht* (Percha, 1973), 342.

304. Kopsch to Strauss, 24 Jan. 1941; and to Franz Strauss, 21 July 1946 (1st quote), RG; Egk, *Zeit,* 342–43 (remaining quotes); Strauss to Kopsch, 27 Jan. 1941, AM, Strauss; *TG* 4:483, 521; Grasberger, *Strom der Töne,* 407.

305. Panofsky, *Strauss,* 246; Schuh, *Strauss—Hofmannsthal,* 55.

306. Strauss to Böhm, 30 June 1943, RG.

307. Uwe Dietrich Adam, *Judenpolitik im Dritten Reich* (Düsseldorf, 1979), 204–32; idem, "Wie spontan war der Pogrom?," in Walter H. Pehle, ed., *Der Judenpogrom von 1938: Von der "Reichskristallnacht" zum Völkermord* (Frankfurt am Main, 1988), 74–93; Hermann Graml, Antisemitism in the Third Reich (Oxford, 1992); Kater, *Different Drummers,* 50–51.

308. SS-Obersturmbannführer Six (SD), to SS-Obersturmbannführer Pruchtnow (Promi), 22 July 1938, RG.

309. Kater, *The Twisted Muse,* 83; Jochen Klepper, *Unter dem Schatten deiner Flügel: Aus den Tagebüchern, 1932–1942* (Munich, 1976), 674–79; Adam, *Judenpolitik,* 316–33.

310. [Alice Strauss], "Tatsachenbericht über die Vorgänge im November 1938," n.d., RG; Roesen to Öffentlicher Kläger, 28 Jan. 1948, AM, Strauss.

311. Fred K. Prieberg, *Musik und Macht* (Frankfurt am Main, 1991), 224. See n. 371, below.

312. Communication to me by Richard and Dr. Christian Strauss, Garmisch, 5 June 1993.

313. Lönne declaration under oath, 24 Jan. 1947, AM, Strauss.

314. Tietjen to Strauss, 6 Jan., 24 Feb., 11 June and 5 July 1939; and 26 Oct. 1944, RG.

315. Tietjen to Strauss, 5 July 1939, RG; *Unterhaltungsmusik* (15 June 1939), 821; Otto Strasser, *Und dafür wird man noch bezahlt: Mein Leben mit den Wiener Philharmonikern* (Vienna, 1974), 181.

316. Strauss to Drewes, 20 June 1939, BS, Fasc. germ. (Drewes).

317. The Japanese ambassador to Berlin, Prince Konoye, was a brother of the well-known Japanese conductor and Strauss admirer Count Konoye. On the fee waiver, see Rosen to Strauss, 19 Nov. 1940, RG. The right interpretation is in Panofsky, *Strauss,* 297; *Richard Strauss: Briefwechsel Schuh,* 29. For the wrong interpretation, see Slonimsky, *Music,* 720.

318. RMK entry for Franz Strauss, 11 June 1943, BAB Franz Strauss.

319. Strauss to Hess, 19 Apr. 1941; Griehnert to Bergoldt, 26 June 1941; K-Gaupersonalamtsleiter to Strauss, 3 July 1941, BAB Richard Strauss.

320. See n. 140 in chapter 5; Roesen to Öffentlicher Kläger, 17 Jan. 1948, AM, Strauss; Henriette von Schirach, *The Price of Glory* (London, 1960), 162.

321. Strauss to Herr [Thomas], 20 June 1941; von Schirach to Strauss, 14 Aug. 1941, RG; Anderman [Thomas], *Vorhang,* 233; declaration under oath by Thomas, 20 Jan. 1947, AM, Strauss.

322. Richard Neumann, "Mein letzter Wille," Reichenberg, 30 Apr. 1924; Paula Neumann to Swiss General Consulate Prague, 24 Oct. 1941; Paula Neumann, "Schenkungsvertrag," 30 Oct. 1941; Swiss Consulate General Prague to Paula Neumann, 8 Dec. 1941; Jüdische Kultusgemeinde in Prag to Paula Neumann, 30 Dec. 1941; Jüdische Kultusgemeinde, "Einbekenntnis zur Kultussteuer," 2 Jan. 1942; Steuerreferat, Jüdische Kultusgemeinde, [to Paula Neumann], 6 Jan. 1942, RG.

323. Trude [Gertrud Kramer] to Alice [Strauss], 10 Jan. [1942]; Franz [Strauss] to Grossmamma [Paula Neumann], 18 Jan. 1942; Franz Strauss [to Passstelle Prag], 18 Jan. 1942; Trude [Gertrud Kramer] to Alice [Strauss], 23 Jan. 1942; Swiss Consulate General Prague to Paula Neumann, 11 Aug. 1942; Jüdische Kultusgemeinde in Prag, "Bestätigung" for Paula Neumann, 23 June 1942; Richard Strauss to Günther, 11 Aug. 1942 (1st quotes); Paula Neumann to Zentralstelle für jüd. Auswanderung Prag-Strechowitz, 2 Sept. 1942; Maria von Grab, "Beglaubigung" for Richard Strauss, 21 Jan. 1947, RG; communication to me from Richard and Dr. Christian Strauss, Garmisch, 5 June 1993 (last quote); Franz Trenner, "Alice Strauss: 3. Juni 1904–23. Dezember 1991," *Richard Strauss-Blätter,* Neue Folge, no. 27 (June 1992), 6.

324. See Strauss to Thomas, 19 May 1942, RG.

325. Frank to Strauss, 11 June 1943, AM, Strauss.

326. Strauss to Himmler, 15 Nov. 1943; and to Seyss-Inquart, 15 Nov. 1943, RG; Richard Strauss to author, Grünwald, 26 June 1998, APA.

327. Richard Strauss to author, Grünwald, 25 June 1998, APA. A hint of this is in Anderman [Thomas], *Vorhang,* 263.

328. Strauss to Schirach, 21 Nov. 1943, BS, Ana/330/I/Schirach; Schiede to Strauss, 30 Oct. 1943; Strauss to Böhm, 5 Jan. 1944; Strauss to Thomas, 22 Feb. 1944, RG; Drewes to Strauss, 23 Dec. 1943; Martin Bormann, "Bekanntgabe 12/44," 14 Jan. 1944; [Schiede] to Strauss, 14 Jan. 1944; Strauss to Hitler, 16 Jan. 1944; Strauss to Reichsminister [Lammers], 17 Jan. 1944; Lammers to Strauss, 27 Jan. 1944; Lammers to Himmler, 27 Jan. 1944, BAB Richard Strauss; *TGII* 11:102.

329. Kater, *The Twisted Muse,* 202. Also see *TGII* 11:169.

330. Strauss to Thomas, 6 Nov. 1943; Strauss to Doktor [Drewes], 3 Feb. 1944; [von Schirach memorandum, post–1945], RG; Roesen to Öffentlicher Kläger, 17 Jan. 1948, AM, Strauss. The original text of the rather crude poem, by Strauss's own hand, is:

Wer tritt herein so fein und schlank,
Es ist der liebe Herr Minister Frank.
Wie Lohengrin sei er von uns bedankt,
Denn viel Übles hat er von uns gewandt.

It is contained in Pasetti, U.S. Forces in Austria, "Annex to report No 121," 11 Dec. 1945, NAW, USACA, Box 21, 1 SB Exec. office. I owe my knowledge of this document to Professor David Monod of Wilfrid Laurier University, Waterloo, Canada, to whom I am very grateful. Also see Piper and Heiss, "Spruch . . . Dr. Richard Strauss . . . Begründung," 26 May 1948, AM, Strauss.

331. Schlumprecht declaration, 22 Feb. 1946, RG; deposition under oath by Reiser, 9 July 1947, AM, Strauss.

332. Entry for 1 June 1944 in *TGII* 12:380; Richard Strauss to author, Grünwald, 25 June 1998, APA; *Richard Strauss: Briefwechsel Schuh,* 77.

333. Kraus to Himmler, 22 Mar. 1944; Himmler and Brandt to Kraus, 25 Apr. 1944; Kaltenbrunner to Himmler, 6 Sept. 1944; Brandt to [SS-] Obergruppenführer [Kaltenbrunner], 13 Sept. 1944, BAB Franz Strauss; Strauss to Thomas, 21 Feb. 1945, RG.

334. See the letter by Richard Strauss to Gerhart Hauptmann, 29 Aug. 1934, facsimile in Dagmar Wünsche, ed., "Gerhart Hauptmann—Richard Strauss: Briefwechsel," *Richard Strauss-Blätter,* Neue Folge, no. 9 (June 1983), 20–21. Also see Knör to Rechtsanwalt [Roesen], 26 Apr. 1947, RG; Richard Strauss to author, Grünwald, 26 June 1998, APA. Oliver Rathkolb's remark (*Führertreu und gottbegnadet,* 183), that the "Vienna press" was passing snide remarks about Franz Strauss showing up in SA uniform before the Anschluss (when the Nazi movement was intermittently driven under ground in Austria), is hardly believable, because as the husband of a Jew, Franz Strauss was prohibited from joining any of the Nazi organizations. Franz Strauss's formal Nazi nonalignment has been corroborated by Richard Strauss's letter to me of 26 June 1998, see above. Besides, the two Vienna tabloids Rathkolb cites as his evidence do not exist with the dates he indicates (Fernleihe, Österreichische Nationalbibliothek, to Inter-Library Loan Service, York University Toronto, Vienna, Aug. 1998, APA).

335. Bernard Holland, "Taking Richard Strauss on His Particular Terms," *New York Times,* 18 Aug. 1991.

336. Raabe to Strauss, 19 May 1936; Kaindl to Strauss, 26 May, 21 Aug. 1942, 4, 23 and 30 Sept. 1943; Thomas to Strauss, 1 June 1942, 11 Sept. and 8 Oct. 1943, 15 Apr. 1944; Strauss to Thomas, 24 May, 4 and 29 June, 1 July 1942, 13 and 29 Sept. 1943, 18 Apr. 1944; Jerger to Doktor [Strauss], 20 July 1942, RG; Roesen to Öffentlicher Kläger, 17 Jan. 1948, AM, Strauss; Kende and Schuh, *Richard Strauss Clemens Krauss,* 41. See Strauss's bitter, handwritten remark on the negative notification by Klaus (Promi) to him, 6 Sept. 1944, AM, Strauss: "14 days ago Furtwängler conducted in Lucerne."

337. Frank to Meister [Strauss], 21 May and 19 Nov. 1942, AM, Strauss; Reichsamtsleiter to Mühlmann, 1 Apr. 1940, and to Adami, 3 Apr. 1940; Adami to Eisenlohr, 18 Apr. 1940; Benatzky to Eisenlohr, 30 Apr. 1940; Rosen to Eisenlohr, 12 May 1940; Reichsamtsleiter to Amt Generalgouverneur, 14 May 1940; Oberreichsleiter to Strauss, 4 Sept. 1941, BAB Richard Strauss; Frank to Strauss, 5 Nov. 1936; Funk to Strauss, 15 Mar. 1938, 26 May 1939, 31 Mar., 18 Nov. and 2 Dec. 1943, 15 July 1944; Strauss to Funk, 25 Apr. 1944; Tietjen to Strauss, 30 Dec. 1938 and 25 Aug. 1942; Schirach to Strauss, 13 Aug. 1942; Swarowsky to Doktor [Strauss], 22 May 1944, RG.

338. Reinhard to Kultusministerium, 10 Sept. 1935; Walleck to Kultusministerium, 23 Sept. 1935, BH, MK/40990; Rathkolb, *Führertreu und gottbegnadet,* 186.

339. Walleck to Strauss, 5 Dec. 1935, AM, Strauss.

340. Gotthold Frotscher, "Die Oper in der Gegenwart," in: Wolfgang Stumme, ed., *Musik im Volk: Gegenwartsfragen der deutschen Musik,* 2nd ed. (Berlin-Lichterfelde, 1944), 261.

341. Schirach to Strauss, 31 Dec. 1941; Strauss to Böhm, 13 June 1943, RG; Orff to Strecker, 24 Jan. 1943, CM, Schott Korr.; *Podium der Unterhaltungsmusik* (30 Dec. 1942), 397; *ZM* 110 (1943), 43.

342. See Schirach to Strauss, 20 Feb. 1942; *TGII* 3:474; *TGII* 11: 102.

343. Tietjen to Meister [Strauss], 22 Jan. 1944, RG; Martin Bormann, "Bekanntgabe 16/44," 24 Jan. 1944, BAB Richard Strauss; *TGII* 11:169, 407.

344. Jerger to Strauss, 24 Apr. 1944; Strauss to Funk, 25 Apr. 1944; Swarowsky to Doktor [Strauss], 22 May 1944; Stampe to Strauss, 9 June 1944; Goebbels to Strauss, 11 June 1944; Strauss to Drewes, 17 June 1944, RG; *TGII* 12:238; Roesen to Öffentlicher Kläger, 17 Jan. 1948, AM, Strauss; Hinkel to Schrade et al., 28 June 1944, BAB Richard Strauss; Dümling and Girth, *Entartete Musik,* 14; Rathkolb, *Führertreu und gottbegnadet,* 190–93. For Furtwängler's anti-Strauss cabal with Goebbels till May 1944, see *TG* 2:646, 4:198; *TGII* 3:469. Also see Kater, *The Twisted Muse,* 196.

345. Kende and Schuh, *Richard Strauss Clemens Krauss,* 261–62.

346. Götze to Strauss, 24 July 1944, RG.

347. Strauss to Drewes, 6 Aug. 1944, BS, Fasc. germ. (Drewes).

348. Swarowsky report for Frank, 20 Aug. 1944; Rudolf Hartmann, "Erinnerungen an die Einstudierung von Richard Strauss' Oper 'Die Liebe der Danae' in Salzburg im Jahre 1944," *Schweizerische Musikzeitung* 92 (1952), 241–42 (quote 242).

349. Strauss to Wieland Wagner, 18 Jan. 1946, RG.

350. Strauss to Freund [Böhm], 17 Nov. 1944, RG.

351. Strauss to Freund [Tietjen], 25 Nov. 1944, RG.

352. Strauss to Freund [Böhm], 11 Jan. 1945, RG.

353. This story was told to me by witness Richard Strauss, Garmisch, 13 June 1992. Also see Franz Trenner, ed., *Richard Strauss: Dokumente seines Lebens und Schaffens* (Munich, 1954), 260; *Richard Strauss: Briefwechsel Schuh,* 78–79; Panofsky, *Strauss,* 331.

354. Strauss to Otto [Fürstner], 15 Aug. 1945, BS, Ana/330/I/Fürstner; Strauss to Kippenberg, 24 Sept. 1945, RG; *Richard Strauss: Briefwechsel Schuh,* 78–85; Panofsky, *Strauss,* 334.

355. Roesen to Spruchkammer Garmisch-Partenkirchen, 18 Aug. 1946, AM, Strauss; *Richard Strauss: Briefwechsel Schuh,* 82, 85.

356. Strauss to Böhm, 11 May 1946, RG. See Pasetti report of 11 Dec. 1945, n. 330, above.

357. Roesen to Öffentlicher Kläger, 12 Mar. and 10 June 1947, AM, Strauss; Alice Strauss to Naor, 27 June 1953, RG; *Hochlandbote,* 28 Jan. 1947; *Melos* 14 (1947), 219–20; *Richard Strauss: Briefwechsel Schuh,* 109, 153.

358. Richard Strauss, "Meldebogen auf Grund des Gesetzes zur Befreiung von Nationalsozialismus und Militarismus vom 5. März 1946," in Strauss's absence signed by Roesen and Franz Strauss, 9 May 1946, AM, Strauss.

359. Stenzel, "Gutachten," 8 Jan. 1947, AM, Strauss.

360. *Welt,* Hamburg, 27 Jan. 1948.

361. Stenzel, "Gutachten," 8 Jan. 1947, AM, Strauss (quote).

362. Kater, *The Twisted Muse,* 40–55.

363. Knör to Rechtsanwalt [Roesen], 26 Apr. 1947, RG.

364. Roesen to Öffentlicher Kläger, 17 Jan. 1948, AM, Strauss.

365. Piper and Heiss, "Spruch . . . Dr. Richard Strauss . . . Begründung," 26 May 1948 (effective 7 June 1948), AM, Strauss. Also see Roesen to Vorsitzender der Spruchkammer, 17 May 1947, AM, Strauss.

366. Roesen to Strauss, 7 June 1948, RG.

367. Panofsky, *Strauss,* 344.

368. Grasberger, *Strom der Töne,* 473.

369. Winifred Wagner to Alice Strauss, 17 Dec. 1945, 30 Jan. 1947, 15 July 1947, 24 Apr. 1948; Strauss to Wieland [Wagner], 18 June 1946; Alice Strauss

to [Wieland] Wagner, 26 June 1946; Wieland Wagner to Strauss, 25 June 1949, RG.

370. Funk to Strauss [on U.S. P.O.W. stationery], 29 Nov. 1945, RG.

371. Cpl. Klaus Mann, Staff Correspondent, "Strauss Still Unabashed About Ties With Nazis," *Stars and Stripes* (29 May 1945), 4. The letter to Thomas Mann, 16 May 1945, is published in Klaus Mann, *Der Wendepunkt: Ein Lebensbericht* (Munich, 1981), 561–64. Among the lies Klaus Mann told (here to his father) was the canard about Alice Strauss on horseback (see text at n. 311). Rathkolb, however, thinks that Klaus Mann, like Splitt, was a "critical Strauss expert" who had been wrongly condemned for calumny (*Führertreu und gottbegnadet,* 269). Grandson Richard was present during the meeting between Strauss and Klaus Mann (personal communication, Garmisch, 13 June 1992).

372. See Polaczek, "Strauss," 75; Panofsky, *Strauss,* 332. On 13 June 1992 I was told about the letter by Richard Strauss Jr. as part of the family archive, but was not shown it.

373. Entry for 1 Feb. 1941 in Mann, *Tagebücher, 1940–43,* 218 (quote); ibid., 5, 45, 182, 227, 379; idem, *Tagebücher, 1937–1939,* ed. Peter de Mendelssohn (Frankfurt am Main, 1980), 8, 92, 94, 237, 391, 424; idem, *Briefe, 1937–1947,* ed. Erika Mann (Frankfurt am Main, 1963), 181.

374. Thomas Mann, *Doktor Faustus* (Frankfurt am Main, 1967), 153–54. Also see Schuh, *Strauss—Hofmannsthal,* 18; Vaget, "Thomas Mann und Richard Strauss," 72–82; Vaget, "*Salome* and *Palestrina* als historische Chiffren: Zur musikalischen Codierung in Thomas Manns *Doktor Faustus,*" in Heinz Gockel et al., eds., *Wagner-Nietzsche-Thomas Mann: Festschrift für Eckhard Heftrich* (Frankfurt am Main, 1993), 70–74.

375. Vaget, "Thomas Mann und Richard Strauss," 82; Hartmann, *Haus,* 185.

376. Beyond those, see: Schmidtbloss to Strauss, 19 Feb. 1946, RG; Evarts to Bauckner, 16 July 1946, BH, Staatstheater/14395; Rosbaud to Stein, 10 Aug. 1947, LP, 423/1/12; *Melos* 14 (1946), 27; *Melos* 14 (1947), 86; Muck, *Jahre,* 3:317.

377. Strauss to Thomas, 25 July 1946, RG.

378. Allan Kozinn, "Seeking Perspectives on Strauss," *New York Times,* 25 Aug. 1992.

379. *NG* 18:234; Ernst Krause, liner notes for the Philips recording, Jessye Norman accompanied by the Gewandhaus Orchestra under Kurt Masur, Leipzig, Aug. 1982, compact disk 411 052-2.

380. Levinger to Strauss, 8 Jan. 1946, RG; *Melos* 14 (1947), 125; Panofsky, *Strauss,* 339 (quote).

381. *NG* 18:218, 223.

382. Ehard to Hundhammer, 14 Jan. 1949; Sattler, "Vormerkung," 21 Sept. 1949; Lill to Franz Strauss, 30 Sept. 1949, BH, MK/36840.

CONCLUSION

1. Michael H. Kater, *Different Drummers: Jazz in the Culture of Nazi Germany* (New York, 1992).

2. Idem, *The Twisted Muse: Musicians and Their Music in the Third Reich* (New York, 1997).

3. Idem, *Doctors Under Hitler* (Chapel Hill, N.C., 1989); idem, "Hitlerjugend und Schule im Dritten Reich," *Historische Zeitschrift* 228 (1979): 572–623; idem,

"Die deutsche Elternschaft im nationalsozialistischen Erziehungssystem: Ein Beitrag zur Sozialgeschichte der Familie," *Vierteljahrschrift für Sozial- und Wirtschaftsgeschichte* 67 (1980), 484–512; idem, *The Nazi Party: A Social Profile of Members and Leaders, 1919–1945* (Cambridge, Mass., 1983).

4. Vernon L. Lidtke's review of *The Twisted Muse* in *American Historical Review* 103 (1998), 921–22.

5. Kater, *The Twisted Muse,* 6.

6. I am singling out Pamela M. Potter (Madison) and, especially, Albrecht Riethmüller (Berlin), who has made this question a central theme of several lectures and publications in recent years.

7. Celia Applegate, "What Is German Music? Reflections on the Role of Art in the Creation of the German Nation," *German Studies Review,* Special Issue (Winter, 1992), 21–32. Also see David B. Dennis, *Beethoven in German Politics, 1870–1989* (New Haven, Conn., 1996), 1–85.

8. Albrecht Riethmüller, "Ferruccio Busoni und die Hegemonie der Deutschen Musik," in Helga de la Motte-Haber, ed., *Nationaler Stil und europäische Dimension in der Musik der Jahrhundertwende* (Darmstadt, 1991), 65. Also see Pamela M. Potter, *Most German of the Arts: Music, Scholarship, and Society in the Rise and Fall of Hitler's Reich* (New Haven, Conn., 1998); Michael Walter, *Hitler in der Oper: Deutsches Musikleben, 1941–1945* (Stuttgart, 1995), 1–41.

9. Kater, *The Twisted Muse,* 101.

10. Riethmüller, "Ferruccio Busoni," 65–66.

11. Quote is from Hans Pfitzner, *Gesammelte Schriften,* 3 vols. (Augsburg, 1926–29), 2:109.

12. Wagner as quoted in Johann Peter Vogel, *Hans Pfitzner: Mit Selbstzeugnisen und Bilddokumenten* (Reinbek, 1986), 77; *TGII* 1:321 (2nd quote).

13. Pfitzner, *Gesammelte Schriften,* 2:115–20, 123 (quote).

14. Ibid., 108–10, 244–47; Kater, *Different Drummers,* 38–46.

15. Albrecht Riethmüller, "Komposition im Deutschen Reich um 1936," *Archiv für Musikwissenschaft* 38 (1981), 256–57; idem, "Ferruccio Busoni," 74; idem, "Zur Politik der unpolitischen Musik," paper, international colloquium, "Zur Situation der Musik in Deutschland in den dreissiger und vierziger Jahren," at Carl-Orff-Zentrum, Munich, 23 Nov. 1994; Kater, *The Twisted Muse,* 76, 178–79.

16. Busoni quoted in Albrecht Riethmüller, *Die Walhalla und ihre Musiker* (Laaber, 1993), 27.

17. Kurt Weill, *Musik und Theater: Gesammelte Schriften,* ed. Stephen Hinton and Jürgen Schebera (Berlin, 1990), 180.

18. Ibid., 348 (quote), 349.

19. Kater, *The Twisted Muse,* 177–92.

20. Riethmüller, "Komposition im Deutschen Reich," 266–67.

21. See Michael H. Kater, "Carl Orff im Dritten Reich," *Vierteljahrshefte für Zeitgeschichte* 43 (1995), 32–35; Jens Malte Fischer, "Vergangenheit, die nicht vergehen will: Carl Orff und das Dritte Reich," *Süddeutsche Zeitung,* Munich, 14 Mar. 1995; Riethmüller, "Komposition im Deutschen Reich," 276.

22. Pfitzner, *Gesammelte Schriften,* 2:119 (1st quote); Weill, *Musik und Theater,* 211 (2nd quote), 212.

23. Pasetti, U.S. Forces in Austria, "Annex to report No. 121," 11 Dec. 1945, NAW, USACA, Box 21, 1 SB Exec. office. See n. 330 in chapter 8.

24. Gerhard A. Ritter, *Über Deutschland: Die Bundesrepublik in der deutschen Geschichte* (Munich, 1998), 15–17.

25. For the difficulties arising from the concept Zero Hour, see Hans Günter Hockerts, "Gab es eine Stunde Null? Die politische, gesellschaftliche und wirtschaftliche Situation in Deutschland nach der bedingungslosen Kapitulation," in Stefan Krimm and Wieland Zirbs, eds., *Nachkriegszeiten—Die Stunde Null als Realität und Mythos in der deutschen Geschichte* (Munich, 1996), 145–52.

26. See Peter Gay, *Weimar Culture: The Outsider as Insider* (New York, 1968).

27. Hermann Glaser, "1945—Cultural Beginnings: Continuity and Discontinuity," in Reiner Pommerin, ed., *Culture in the Federal Republic of Germany, 1945–1995* (Oxford, 1996), 19.

28. Clemens Vollnhals, ed., *Entnazifizierung: Politische Säuberung und Rehabilitierung in den vier Besatzungszonen, 1945–1949* (Munich, 1991); idem, "Entnazifizierung: Politische Säuberung unter alliierter Herrschaft," in Hans-Erich Volkmann, ed., *Ende des Dritten Reiches—Ende des Zweiten Weltkriegs: Eine perspektivische Rückschau* (Munich, 1995), 369–92; Ritter, *Über Deutschland*, 30–31, 125–27; Hermann Glaser, *The Rubble Years: The Cultural Roots of Postwar Germany, 1945–1948* (New York, 1986), esp. 14, 108, 124; Reiner Hudemann, "Kulturpolitik in der französischen Besatzungszone—Sicherheitspolitik oder Völkerverständigung? Notizen zu einer wissenschaftlichen Diskussion," in Gabriele Clemens, ed., *Kulturpolitik im besetzten Deutschland, 1945–1949* (Stuttgart, 1994), esp. 189, 199; Clemens, "Die britische Kulturpolitik in Deutschland: Musik, Theater, Film und Literatur," in Clemens, *Kulturpolitik*, 201–4; Claudia Rauh-Kühne, "Die Entnazifizierung und die deutsche Gesellschaft," *Archiv für Sozialgeschichte* 35 (1995), 39.

29. Gerd Dietrich, "'. . . wie eine kleine Oktoberrevolution . . .': Kulturpolitik der SMAD, 1945–1949," in Clemens, *Kulturpolitik*, 219–36; Brewster S. Chamberlin, *Kultur auf Trümmern: Berliner Berichte der amerikanischen Information Control Section, Juli-Dezember 1945* (Stuttgart, 1979), 20–23; Vollnhals, "Entnazifizierung," 383–86; Fred K. Prieberg, *Musik im anderen Deutschland* (Cologne, 1968), 144; Ritter, *Über Deutschland*, 132–35.

30. Richard Pells, *Not Like Us: How Europeans Have Loved, Hated, and Transformed American Culture Since World War II* (New York, 1997), 43.

31. Ritter, *Über Deutschland*, 74–75, 126.

32. This abandonment was then decried, in different contexts, by Alexander Mitscherlich and Margarete Mitscherlich, in *Die Unfähigkeit zu trauern: Grundlagen kollektiven Verhaltens* (Munich, 1967). For a very early statement, see Karl Jaspers, *Die Schuldfrage* (Heidelberg, 1946).

33. Glaser, *The Rubble Years*, 100.

34. The quote is from Ritter, *Über Deutschland*, 124.

35. I am following Rauh-Kühne, "Die Entnazifizierung," 64–69. Also see Norbert Frei, *Vergangenheitspolitik: Die Anfänge der Bundesrepublik und die NS-Vergangengeit* (Munich, 1996).

36. Chamberlin, *Kultur auf Trümmern*, 10.

37. Recorded interview by David Monod with Newell Jenkins in Hillsdale, N.Y., on 6 July 1996. See n. 172 of chapter 5.

38. Dietrich, "Oktoberrevolution," 222.

39. As an example of reactionary tendencies in the representational arts, see Hans Sedlmayr, *Verlust der Mitte: Die bildende Kunst des 19. und 20. Jahrhunderts als Symptom und Symbol der Zeit* (Salzburg, 1948).

40. Sabine Henze-Döhring, "Kulturelle Zentren in der amerikanischen Besatzungszone: Der Fall Bayreuth," in Clemens, *Kulturpolitik*, 39–54; Frederic

Spotts, *Bayreuth: A History of the Wagner Festival* (New Haven, Conn., 1994), 200–72; Nike Wagner, *Wagner Theater* (Frankfurt am Main, 1998), 320–432.

41. Siegfried Mauser, "Emigranten bei den Internationalen Ferienkursen für Neue Musik in Darmstadt (1946–1951)," in Horst Weber, ed., *Musik in der Emigration, 1933–1945: Verfolgung, Vertreibung, Rückwirkung* (Stuttgart, 1994), 241–48; Jost Hermand, *Kultur im Wiederaufbau: Die Bundesrepublik Deutschland, 1945–1965* (Munich, 1986), 128, 199, 201–6, 433–35, 451, 456–60.

42. Ulrich Dibelius, *Moderne Musik, 1945–1965: Voraussetzungen, Verlauf, Material* (Munich, 1966), 233.

43. *GLM* 2:411.

44. *NG* 8:489–96 (quote 490). See Henze's statement, "Gefahren in der neuen Musik," *Texte und Zeichen* 1 (1955), 213–15.

45. Hermann Danuser, *Die Musik des 20. Jahrhunderts* (Regensburg, 1984), 301, 309–26; Hermand, *Kultur,* 452–61; *NG* 18:151–59 (1st quote 152); Ulrich Dibelius, "Musik," in Wolfgang Benz, ed., *Die Geschichte der Bundesrepublik Deutschland,* 4 vols. (Frankfurt am Main, 1989), 4:141; Albrecht Riethmüller, "Pionier im Land der Töne: Laudatio zur Erteilung der Ehrendoktorwürde der Freien Universität Berlin an Karlheinz Stockhausen am 17. Juni 1996," *Musikforschung* 50 (1997), 329–34 (2nd quote 330); Jürg Stenzl, *Luigi Nono* (Reinbek, 1998), 7–36.

46. *NG* 8:491; *NG* 18:151.

47. Kater, *Different Drummers,* esp. 202–11; Joachim Ernst Berendt, *Ein Fenster aus Jazz: Essays, Portraits, Reflexionen* (Frankfurt am Main, 1987), 163–214; Michael Naura, "Im Untertagebau der Jazzkeller," in *That's Jazz: Der Sound des 20. Jahrhunderts* (Darmstadt, 1988), 405–9; Hermand, *Kultur,* 355.

48. Kater, *The Twisted Muse,* 38; Henze-Döhring, "Kulturelle Zentren," 46.

49. Kater, *The Twisted Muse,* 67–69; chapter 1 at n. 90.

50. See Hermand, *Kultur,* 194–95, 559; Dibelius, "Musik," 140.

51. Dibelius, "Music," 145–47.

52. Hermand, *Kultur,* 363.

53. Clemens, "Britische Kulturpolitik," 202.

54. Bert Noglik, "Vom Linden-Blues zum Zentralquartett: Fragmentarisches zur Entwicklung des Jazz in der DDR," in *That's Jazz,* 422; Kater, *Different Drummers,* 209.

55. Theodor W. Adorno, *Introduction to the Sociology of Music* (New York, 1976), 31, 33 (quote); idem, *Prisms* (London, 1967), 121–32; Glaser, *The Rubble Years,* 11, 71, 211–12; Steiert, "Musik- und Theaterpolitik," 63; Hockerts, "Gab es eine Stunde Null?," 139–40.

56. Hans Schnoor, *Harmonie und Chaos: Musik der Gegenwart* (Munich, 1962), 20 (1st quote); Walter Abendroth, *Selbstmord der Musik? Zur Theorie, Ideologie und Phraseologie des modernen Schaffens* (Berlin, 1963), 32 (2nd quote).

57. Glaser, *The Rubble Years,* 71.

58. Albrecht Riethmüller, "Die 'Stunde Null' als musikgeschichtliche Grösse," paper at Zentrum für Zeitgenössische Musik, Dresden, 7 Oct. 1998.

59. Recorded interview by David Monod with Newell Jenkins in Hillsdale, N.Y., on 6 July 1966 (see no. 37).

60. Gabriele Clemens, *Britische Kulturpolitik in Deutschland, 1945–1949: Literatur, Film, Musik und Theater* (Stuttgart, 1997), 250–52; Elke Gerberding, *Kultureller Wiederaufbau: Darmstädter Kulturpolitik in der Nachkriegszeit (1945–1949)* (Darmstadt, 1996), 28.

61. Glaser, *The Rubble Years,* 109–10.

62. Kater, *The Twisted Muse,* 55–63, 69–70; Uwe Baur, "Alte und neue Töne: Musik im Diskurs," in Franz-Josef Heyen and Anton M. Klein, eds., *Auf der Suche nach neuer Identität: Kultur in Rheinlandpfalz im Nachkriegsjahrzehnt* (Mainz, 1996), 288.

63. *LI,* 394.

64. See Alois Melichar, *Überwindung des Modernismus: Konkrete Antwort an einen abstrakten Kritiker,* 3rd ed. (Vienna, 1954), 122; idem, *Musik in der Zwangsjacke: Die deutsche Musik zwischen Orff und Schönberg* (Vienna, 1958), 109; Hermand, *Kultur,* 215.

65. Hermand, *Kultur,* 126–27; Glaser, *The Rubble Years,* 209; Dibelius, "Musik," 131–32; Baur, "Alte und neue Töne," 331, 336–37. See only the music announcements and advertisements in *Melos,* for the late 1940s and 1950s.

66. Hermand, *Kultur,* 175–76, 509.

67. Ibid., 216–17 (quote 216), 495–99, 506–10; Fred Hamel, "Vom wahren Wesen der Musik: Pamphlet wider die akustische Gemischtwarenhandlung," *Musica* (Dec. 1957), 689–92; Abendroth, *Selbstmord der Musik,* 5–38; Glaser, *The Rubble Years,* 200, 349, n. 254; Prieberg, *Musik im anderen Deutschland,* 43, 141–42; Mauser, "Emigranten," 244; Thomas Steiert, "Zur Musik- und Theaterpolitik in Stuttgart während der amerikanischen Besatzungszeit," in Clemens, *Kulturpolitik,* 67. Werner G. Hahn relativizes the nefarious influence of Zhdanov in *Postwar Soviet Politics: The Fall of Zhdanov and the Defeat of Moderation, 1946–1953* (Ithaca, N.Y., 1982), 9–113.

68. Kater, *The Twisted Muse,* passim. See also Wolfgang Fortner, *Eine Monographie: Werkanalysen, Aufsätze, Reden, offene Briefe, 1950–1959* (Rodenkirchen am Rhein, 1960); Gudrun Straub et al., *Karl Marx* (Tutzing, 1983); Rudolf Lück, *Cesar Bresgen* (Vienna, 1974); Oskar Lang, *Armin Knab: Ein Meister deutscher Liedkunst* (1937, rpt. Würzburg, 1981).

69. Joseph Maria Müller-Blattau, *Hans Pfitzner* (Potsdam, 1940), 92 (quote); idem, *Hans Pfitzner: Lebensweg und Schaffensernte* (Frankfurt am Main, 1969).

70. As in n. 37. See Joseph Maria Müller-Blattau, *Germanisches Erbe in deutscher Tonkunst* (Berlin-Lichterfelde, 1938); Potter, *Most German of the Arts,* 104, 135.

71. *GLM* 5:385 (quote); *NG* 12:774. But see Potter, *Most German of the Arts,* 252. Also see "Die Reichsuniversitäten Strassburg und Posen," *Deutscher Wochendienst,* 174/43, no. 7488, 4 Sept. 1942, BA; Lothar Kettenacker, *Nationalsozialistische Volkstumspolitik im Elsass* (Stuttgart, 1973), 91.

72. See chapter 8 at n. 158; *Festgabe für Joseph Müller-Blattau zum 65. Geburtstag* [*Annales Universitatis Saraviensis,* 9, no. 1 (1960)]; Christoph-Hellmut Mahling, ed., *Zum 70. Geburtstag von Joseph Müller-Blattau* (Kassel, 1966), 7 (quote), 9–11, 15–27, 46–58.

73. Riethmüller, "Die 'Stunde Null' als musikgeschichtliche Grösse" (as in n. 58).

74. Kater, *The Twisted Muse,* 71–72; Gerberding, *Kultureller Wiederaufbau,* 64.

75. Rolf Seeliger, ed., *Braune Universität: Deutsche Hochschullehrer gestern und heute: Dokumentation mit Stellungnahmen* (Munich, 1968), 98–110 (Stumme quoted 108); Kater, *The Twisted Muse,* 143.

76. Stumme in Seeliger, *Braune Universität,* 109.

77. Friedrich Blume, "Musikforschung und Musikpraxis," in Hans Hoffmann and Franz Rühlmann, eds., *Festschrift: Fritz Stein zum 60. Geburtstag* (Brunswick, 1939), 19.

78. *NG* 2:820–21 (quote); *GLM* 1:308–9. See Melichar, *Überwindung des Modernismus,* 123.

79. See Hermand, *Kultur,* 217, 488.

80. Friedrich Blume, *Das Rasseproblem in der Musik: Entwurf zu einer Methodologie musikwissenschaftlicher Rasseforschung* (Wolfenbüttel, 1939), 3, 82–83. Also see Potter, *Most German of the Arts,* passim.

81. Wolfgang Boetticher, "Einleitung," in idem, ed., *Robert Schumann in seinen Schriften und Briefen* (Berlin, 1942), viii–xvi; Willem de Vries, *Sonderstab Musik: Music confiscated by the Einsatzstab Reichsleiter Rosenberg under the Nazi Occupation of Western Europe* (Leiden, 1996), passim; Potter, *Most German of the Arts,* 150–51, 188, 197, 245, 257–58; *NG* 2:846; *Frankfurter Allgemeine Zeitung,* 11 Dec. 1998; Gerhard R. Koch, "Das Grauen ist graubraun: Musik im Würgegriff der Nazis," *Frankfurter Allgemeine Zeitung,* 6 Oct. 1998; Günter Nawe, "Die eroberte Muse: Musik und Komponisten im Dritten Reich," *Kölnische Rundschau,* 3 Dec. 1998; Christoph Schwandt, "Sonderstab Musikplünderung: Uni setzt Lehrveranstaltungen von Wolfgang Boetticher aus," *Frankfurter Rundschau,* 2 Dec. 1998; Wolfgang Goertz, "'Im Sinne des Führerbefehls sichergestellt': Ein neues Buch über die Kunstraubzüge der Nazis und das Ende einer deutschen Musikwissenschaftlerkarriere," *Zeit,* Hamburg, 16 Dec. 1998.

82. Ritter, *Über Deutschland,* 35.

83. Schnoor, *Harmonie und Chaos,* 140 (1st quote), 117 (2nd quote), and passim.

84. Clemens, *Britische Kulturpolitik,* 145; Baur, "Alte und neue Töne," 331.

85. Ibid. Also *Melos* from 1946.

86. Glaser, *The Rubble Years,* 205; Dibelius, "Musik," 133–34; Baur, "Alte und neue Töne," 334–35; Prieberg, *Musik im anderen Deutschland,* 106, 109; Hermand, *Kultur,* 97, 216, 496–97, 510; Andres Briner et al., *Paul Hindemith: Leben und Werk in Bild und Text* (Mainz, 1988), 205–7, 218–70; Schnoor, *Harmonie und Chaos,* 159, 160 (quote), 189, 231, 261–62; Abendroth, *Selbstmord der Musik,* 37.

87. Evarts as quoted in David Monod, "Internationalism, Regionalism, and National Culture: Music Control in Bavaria, 1945–48," ms. (Feb. 1999), APA. The 2nd quote is Monod's. I am grateful to Professor Monod for letting me see this paper before publication in *Central European History.*

88. See Melichar, *Überwindung des Modernismus,* 52–57; idem, *Musik in der Zwangsjacke,* 12–13.

89. Werner Thomas, *Das Rad der Fortuna: Ausgewählte Aufsätze zu Werk und Wirkung Carl Orffs* (Mainz, 1990), 209–19; Schnoor, *Harmonie und Chaos,* 92, 94 (1st quote), 95, 189; Hermand, *Kultur,* 216, 503 (2nd quote), 510–11; Baur, "Alte und neue Töne," 331; Prieberg, *Musik im anderen Deutschland,* 57–59, 114; Melichar, *Musik in der Zwangsjacke,* 17, 18 (3rd quote), 19–40.

90. Hermand, *Kultur,* 503.

91. *Melos* 14 (1947), 423, 426; ibid. 15 (1948), 57, 60–61; Strobel memorandum, "Werner Egk und die Kulturfassade des Dritten Reiches," Südwestfunk, Baden-Baden, 12 Sept. 1947, AM, Egk; Werner Egk, *Die Zeit wartet nicht* (Percha, 1973), 388; Baur, "Alte und neue Töne," 333.

92. Heinrich Strobel, "'Abraxas' von Werner Egk," *Melos* 15 (1948), 14–18; Egk, *Zeit,* 377–417; Glaser, *The Rubble Years,* 206–9; Schnoor, *Harmonie und Chaos,* 189, 262; Melichar, *Überwindung des Modernismus,* 12, 119, 122; Melichar, *Musik in der Zwangsjacke,* 50, 170; Hermand, *Kultur,* 206, 449–50, 497, 503, 510–11.

93. Baur, "Alte und neue Töne," 335; Prieberg, *Musik im anderen Deutschland,* 107, 109.

94. Schnoor, *Harmonie und Chaos,* 94 (quote); Hermand, *Kultur,* 129–31, 448–49.

95. Richard L. Merritt, *Democracy Imposed: U.S. Occupation Policy and the German Public, 1945–1949* (New Haven, Conn., 1995), 132 (quote), 134, 136.

96. Hartmut Berghoff, "Zwischen Verdrängung und Aufarbeitung: Die bundesdeutsche Gesellschaft und ihre nationalsozialistische Vergangenheit in den Fünfziger Jahren," *Geschichte in Wissenschaft und Unterricht* 49 (1998), 110.

97. Hans Georg Lehmann, "Rückkehr nach Deutschland? Motive, Hindernisse und Wege von Emigranten," in Klaus-Dieter Krohn and Patrick von zur Mühlen, eds., *Rückkehr und Aufbau nach 1945: Deutsche Remigranten im öffentlichen Leben Nachkriegsdeutschlands* (Marburg, 1997), 54–55.

98. See the hidden anti-Semitic polemic in Alois Melichar, *Schönberg und die Folgen: Eine notwendige kulturpolitische Auseinandersetzung* (n. pl., 1960), 6–46.

99. Schnoor, *Harmonie und Chaos,* 54, 150, 151 (quote), 162; Baur, "Alte und neue Töne," 327; Hermand, *Kultur,* 216. In contrast to the other modern composers treated in this book (and not counting Strauss and Pfitzner), Weill is seldom mentioned in Ulrich Dibelius and Frank Schneider, eds., *Neue Musik im geteilten Deutschland: Dokumente aus den fünfziger Jahren* (Berlin, 1993).

100. Schultze to Weill, 6 Nov. 1945, WC, Weill/UE Corr.

101. *NG* 8:491–92; *NG* 18:151; Hermand, *Kultur,* 204–6, 404–6, 433, 451.

102. Schnoor, *Harmonie und Chaos,* 166, 171–72, 161, 182 (1st quote), 190–91; Abendroth, *Selbstmord der Musik,* 12, 16–19, 27–28, 32; Alois Melichar, *Die unteilbare Musik: Betrachtungen zur Problematik des modernen Musiklebens* (Vienna, 1952), 108–26; Melichar, *Überwindung des Modernismus;* Melichar, *Musik in der Zwangsjacke,* 58–185, 191–93; Melichar, *Schönberg und die Folgen,* esp. 6 (2nd quote). For the medical analogy, see Michael H. Kater, "Das Böse in der Medizin: Nazi-Ärzte als Handlanger des Holocaust," *Jahrbuch 1998/99 zur Geschichte und Wirkung des Holocaust* (Frankfurt am Main, 1999), 226.

103. Schnoor, *Harmonie und Chaos,* 191–98, 261–62; Melichar, *Schönberg und die Folgen,* 63, 78, 139–40, 142–43, 152, 154, 159, 171, 176, 181, 210, 235–36; Melichar, *Musik in der Zwangsjacke,* 240–43; Abendroth, *Selbstmord der Musik,* 32–33.

104. This was expressed to me by several young German music scholars, who shall remain unnamed. Also see Manuel Baug, "Überall quietschten die Rädchen: Böhm, Karajan, Knappertsbusch und die anderen: Neue Misstöne aus der deutschen Musikgeschichte," *Welt,* Hamburg, 5 Dec. 1998.

105. Jans telefax to author, Munich, 14 Nov. 1998, APA. See Fischer, "Vergangenheit, die nicht vergehen will" (as in n. 21); Reinhard J. Brembeck, "Mitläufer oder Widerstandskämpfer?," *Süddeutsche Zeitung,* Munich, 8 Feb. 1999; Jans, "Zum Forschungsauftrag des Orff-Zentrum München an Univ.-Doz. Dr. Dr. Oliver Rathkolb und Ergebnisse aus der Verifikations- bzw. Falsifikations-Analyse der Orff-Akte des Screening-Centers Bad Homburg," [introduction to Munich press conference, 10 Feb. 1999], ms., APA; Brembeck telefax to author, Munich, 10 Feb. 1999, APA; Brembeck, "Von zu grosser Liebe und verletztem Stolz," *Süddeutsche Zeitung,* 11 Feb. 1999.

106. The definition is Johann Gottfried Herder's.

Index